Great American Judges

AN ENCYCLOPEDIA

Great American Judges

AN ENCYCLOPEDIA

VOLUME TWO L–Z

John R. Vile

Foreword by Kermit L. Hall

ABC CLIO
Santa Barbara, California Denver, Colorado Oxford, England

Library of Congress Cataloging-in-Publication Data
Great American judges : an encyclopedia / [edited by] John R. Vile.
p. cm.
Includes bibliographical references and index.
ISBN 1-57607-989-9 (hardcover : alk. paper) — ISBN 1-57607-990-2 (e-book)
1. Judges—United States—Biography—Encyclopedias. I. Vile, John. R.
KF8775.A68G64 2003
347.73' 14' 0922—dc21
2003004203

07 06 05 04 03 10 9 8 7 6 5 4 3 2 1

This book is also available on the World Wide Web as an e-book.
Visit abc-clio.com for details.

ABC-CLIO, Inc.
130 Cremona Drive, P.O. Box 1911
Santa Barbara, California 93116-1911
This book is printed on acid-free paper.

Manufactured in the United States of America

Dedicated to those individuals
throughout American history
who have used their positions
as judges and justices to
perpetuate constitutional government
and equal justice under the law

Contents

VOLUME TWO

Sidebars

Great American Judges

AN ENCYCLOPEDIA

LANDIS, KENESAW MOUNTAIN

(1866–1944)

KENESAW MOUNTAIN LANDIS
Underwood & Underwood/Corbis

ALTHOUGH KENESAW MOUNTAIN Landis is best known as the first commissioner of major league baseball, he also garnered nationwide attention as a federal jurist. Serving as U.S. district judge for the Northern District of Illinois from 1905 to 1922, Landis presided over high-profile cases involving parties such as Standard Oil of Indiana, American labor leader William D. Haywood, and socialist leader Victor Berger. The strict discipline Landis exhibited from the bench convinced baseball executives to name him as professional baseball's first commissioner in 1921. Landis did not disappoint; his actions as commissioner did much to restore public confidence in the game that had been mired in the controversy surrounding the 1920 "Black Sox" scandal.

Landis was born on 20 November 1866 in Millville, Ohio, to Dr. Abraham Hoch Landis and Mary Kumler Landis. He was the couple's sixth child and their fourth son. Dr. Landis had served as a surgeon in the Union Army during the Civil War. During the battle of Kennesaw Mountain in northwest Georgia, a portion of Sherman's larger campaign known as the March to the Sea, Dr. Landis established a surgical headquarters in the shadow of the mountain. While he was tending to the medical needs of a Union infantryman, a Confederate cannonball ricocheted off a tree and struck Landis in the leg. A fellow surgeon promptly amputated the shattered limb.

After the birth of the future judge, it took Dr. and Mrs. Landis some time to decide on his name. In fact, the delay in providing a name prompted both family and community members to suggest a deluge of different names. Mary Landis did not like the name Abraham, so when Dr. Landis suggested calling their son "Kenesaw," the name and alternate spelling stuck. Clearly, the site of the doctor's personal tragedy remained in his thoughts.

Early influences on young Landis were his mother's religious zeal (which he did not follow) and his father's interest in journalism and politics. Mary Landis's ancestors had held positions as church bishops and a college president. Her father was among the first three United Brethren missionaries to visit Africa. The combinative influences of evangelism, journalism, and staunch Republicanism (Dr. Landis had converted from the Whig party to become a lifelong Republican) provided physically small Kenesaw the tools he would later exhibit to cower most who appeared before his bench.

Kenesaw was not the only child of Dr. and Mrs. Landis to gain notoriety. Son Walter became a famous newspaper writer and was later named as the first postmaster of Puerto Rico by Pres. Theodore Roosevelt. John Landis followed his father's footsteps into the medical profession. As health commissioner of Cincinnati, Ohio, he successfully transformed many of the unsanitary conditions existing at that time in that city. Frederick Landis and Charles Landis both served Indiana as U.S. congressmen and were serving in that capacity during the years of the Theodore Roosevelt presidency when Kenesaw was appointed to the federal bench.

When the Landis family moved to Logansport, Indiana, Kenesaw helped meet family expenses by delivering newspapers. He also took an early interest in baseball. Gifted with seemingly limitless energy and considerable agility, Landis played many sports, but baseball and bicycle racing were his favorites. During the early 1880s, the five-foot six-inch Landis played first base for a semipro baseball team in Goosetown. He became the team's manager at the age of seventeen. Kenesaw was offered a professional contract, but he turned it down, stating that he simply preferred to play for sport and the enjoyment of the game.

American history was Landis's favorite academic subject, particularly anything concerning Abraham Lincoln. His penmanship was far from perfect, however, and algebra proved to be the cause of Landis's dropping out of school at age fifteen. His father would not learn of this until six months later.

Disappointed with his single-dollar-per-week wage for delivering newspapers, Landis began working for three dollars per week as a junior clerk in Logansport's principal grocery store. He soon left the store to work as an errand boy in the dispatcher's office at the Vandalia Railroad. Denied an opportunity to become a brakeman for the rail company, Landis went to work for his brother Charles at the *Logansport Journal*. His duties included covering proceedings at the Cass County Courthouse. There, Landis became interested in the new profession of shorthand court reporting. After completing a training class, Kenesaw became the circuit court reporter in Lake County, Indiana. He held this position from 1883 to 1886.

In 1886, the young man dubbed "Squire" by his siblings (due to his imperious air) became involved in Republican politics. His friend Charles F. Griffin won the post of Indiana secretary of state. Landis became Griffin's aide. While serving in that capacity, the future judge became a member of the Indiana bar. Two years later, he left the secretary of state's office to read law with the Marion, Indiana, law firm of Custer and Stevenson.

A lack of clients convinced Landis that he needed a formal legal education. He attended the Y.M.C.A. Law School in Cincinnati for one year, and then he transferred to the Union College of Law in Chicago (now a part of Northwestern University). He graduated, was admitted to the Illinois bar, and hung out his shingle in Chicago all in 1891.

In 1893 Dr. Abraham Landis's former commanding officer, Walter Q. Gresham, became Pres. Grover Cleveland's secretary of state. Gresham, in turn, named the twenty-six-year-old Kenesaw as his personal secretary. During his two years in Washington, Secretary Gresham became ill, and Landis began attending cabinet meetings in his place. So impressed with Landis was President Cleveland that he offered Gresham's aide the post of minister to Venezuela. That position did not appeal to Landis, and he declined. He left Washington upon Gresham's death.

The twenty-eight-year-old Landis returned to Chicago to practice law in 1895. That was also the year he married Winifred Reed. The couple would have three children: a son, Walter Reed (named in honor of Walter Gresham); a daughter, Susanne; and a third child, Winnifred, who died soon after birth in 1901.

Kenesaw formed a partnership with James Uhl (former ambassador to Germany) and Frank James (former assistant postmaster general). He also became a regular fixture at games of the Chicago Cubs. Landis's favorite Cub was pitcher Mordecai Peter Centennial "Three Finger" Brown. In fact, Landis once asked an opposing lawyer, "Can't we get a postponement of the case until tomorrow? Brownie is pitching against Matty [Christy Mathewson] and I just can't miss that" (Watson 2000, 120).

Although he had been employed by a Democratic administration, Landis became heavily involved in Illinois Republican politics. In 1904, he served as campaign manager for gubernatorial candidate Frank Lowden. Lowden did not win that election (though he would later serve two terms as governor of Illinois), but Landis's actions and progressive attitude attracted the attention of Pres. Theodore Roosevelt. So, in 1905 when a jurist was needed for the newly created seat in the United States District Court for the Northern District of Illinois (which included Chicago and surrounding areas), Roosevelt appointed Landis.

Landis's antics on the bench angered many, but no one could argue that his courtroom was boring. He was known to squinch his nose, as if smelling an odor, if he believed that an attorney's line of questioning was suspicious. He told one witness, "Now, let's stop fooling around and tell exactly what did happen, without reciting your life history" (Watson 2000, 121). Once, when an aged defendant complained that he would never live long enough to complete a five-year sentence, Landis scowled at him and said, "Well, you can try, can't you?" (121).

Landis gained fame from the 1907 case involving the indictment of John D. Rockefeller's Standard Oil on 1,462 counts of accepting rebates from the Chicago and Alton Railroad. The six-week case was highlighted by Landis's order compelling Rockefeller to come to Chicago and testify in the matter. Once Rockefeller was on the witness stand, the judge did not hesitate to prod him when the latter seemed hesitant to answer certain questions. Not only did Rockefeller lose the case, but Landis imposed a then-unprecedented $29.24 million fine against Standard Oil. Upon learning of the verdict, Rockefeller stated, "Judge Landis will be dead a long time before this fine is paid" (Watson 2000, 121). He was right, for the verdict was later overturned on appeal.

The "Ryan Baby" case also cast Landis into the media spotlight. Mrs. Dolly Matters, the widow of a prominent Chicago banker, brought the baby home to Chicago from a visit to Canada. She claimed the child was the banker's posthumous heir. A shop girl from Ontario, Margaret Ryan, claimed, however, that she was actually the child's mother. She also claimed that hospital workers in Canada told her that her child had died at birth. Since no blood or genetic tests existed at that time, Landis had only the witnesses' testimony on which to base his decision. He awarded the child to Ryan. Although the United States Supreme Court reversed the judge's decision, he was later vindicated by a Canadian court decision awarding the child to Miss Ryan.

As the United States entered World War I in 1917, Landis's son Reed enlisted in the military and later earned his pilot's wings. Reed served with Britain's Twenty-Fifth Zero Squadron in France, and he took part in several battles. Reed's air kills once ranked him third behind Eddie Rickenbacker and Elliot Spring among American flying aces. Proud Kenesaw even considered enlisting, but Secretary of War Newton Baker asked him to serve stateside as a civilian.

The judge's sense of patriotism was exhibited in 1917 when he heard his first major sedition case involving members of the International Workers of the World (IWW). William "Big Bill" Haywood, then the IWW secretary, and 103 other members were charged with obstructing the nation's war program. Haywood and 93 other defendants were found guilty. Landis promptly handed down sentences totaling more than 807 years and fines in excess of $2.3 million. When the verdict was sustained on appeal, Haywood fled to Russia.

Landis also presided over the trial of Victor Berger, who was an editor and Socialist congressman from Milwaukee, and six other Socialist leaders who were also charged with impeding the U.S. war effort. Judge Landis loudly condemned and sentenced each of the defendants to twenty years in Leavenworth. On appeal, however, the defendants were granted bail in exchange for their future silence on matters involving the government and the war effort. Berger and his associates agreed.

War veterans and civilians affected by war who came before Judge Landis often gained his sympathy. Fred Still, who had been a worker on a freighter torpedoed by a German submarine, wrote a threatening letter to a government official demanding twenty-four dollars in back pay. When Still appeared before Landis, the judge learned that exposure from the sinking had caused Still to contract tuberculosis. The indictment was immediately quashed, and Kenesaw had the defendant sent to the hospital. Further, he personally saw to it that Still received his back pay.

Judge Landis's temper and reputation as a maverick have been well documented. He once imposed the maximum sentence allowed by law on a wealthy cattleman who was convicted of selling diseased animals. Pres. Woodrow Wilson, thinking the punishment too severe, commuted the sentence a few months later. The day after Landis learned of the president's actions, six men were found guilty in Landis's court of stealing sugar from freight cars. In setting them free, the judge proclaimed, "Stealing sugar is no more deserving of a prison sentence than selling diseased cattle" (Spink 1947, 25). Outraged by Kenesaw's act, President Wilson briefly considered asking for his resignation.

Judge Kenesaw Landis was most criticized, however, for the leniency he showed to an eighteen-year-old messenger who, while he was employed at a Chicago brokerage house, had stolen $750,000 worth of Liberty bonds. The bonds were later recovered, and Landis dismissed the charges. Stirring a great deal of public outrage, he stated, "I am going to set this boy free. I wish I had the power to jail the men who sent him out with $750,000 in bonds" (Spink 1947, 26).

Professional baseball first appeared in Landis's court in 1915, when the Federal Baseball League brought an antitrust suit against the American and National Leagues. The Federal League was seeking recognition as baseball's

Samuel A. Weiss (1902–1977)

Kenesaw Mountain Landis was not the only individual to establish himself in careers both as a judge and in professional sports. Like Landis, Samuel A. Weiss must surely rank among America's most colorful judges. Born in 1902 in Krotowoez, Poland, Weiss was brought to Glassport, Pennsylvania, as an infant. After graduating from Glassport High School, the stocky five-foot four-inch Weiss attended the University of Pittsburgh. Rejected by the football team there, he subsequently served as captain of the football team at Duquesne University during his years in law school.

Weiss set up a local law office and won nine of his first ten cases, including a homicide defense case that was precipitated when he wrote a cease and desist order for a friend that resulted in a confrontation in which his friend defended himself (Kelly 1947, 20–21). The judge noted that "it looks to me like you caused and won your first murder case" (21).

Weiss was elected to two terms in the lower house of the Pennsylvania legislature, where he supported Democratic and Progressive causes, including generous workmen's compensation legislation, but was unsuccessful in getting reform of the fee system used by justices of the peace. Weiss ran for the U.S. House of Representatives in 1940 and served there until 1945. During those years, Weiss also served as a referee for the National Professional Football League and was known as "the Sports Congressman of the nation" (Kelly 1947, 53). Weiss worked vigorously to keep professional sports alive during World War II, and he lobbied for the "Ernie Pyle" bill that provided higher pay to members of the armed forces who were serving in combat zones. He later supported the GI Bill of Rights.

Because he was Jewish, Weiss was sometimes the object of invective, especially

(continues)

third professional league. Landis heard the case quickly, but then he took the matter under advisement for several months. The financially troubled Federal League was eventually forced to sell out. Not only were the major league owners ecstatic over the result, but many Americans were also of the opinion that baseball would have been thrown into chaos had Landis ruled that organized baseball was a trust that needed to be broken up.

The baseball owners' gratitude toward Judge Landis was not forgotten when, in 1920, the American public became aware of the 1919 World Series fix. Public confidence in organized baseball was badly shaken, and the owners realized that powerful leadership would be needed in order to restore Americans' faith in the game. Landis was a logical choice. On 12 November 1920, a representative group of baseball owners visited the judge's Chicago courtroom. Hearing the owners' voices at the rear of the courtroom, the judge's voice boomed, "There'll be less noise in this courtroom or

(continued)

from Rep. John E. Rankin of Mississippi. In answering false charges that Rankin brought to the House floor, Weiss uttered words that showed his own loyalty to the nation and his understanding of its ideals.

> I am an immigrant lad, but I love my country just as dearly as does the gentleman from Mississippi. I am a Jew and proud of my heritage, but nothing transcends my love for my country, the country that guarantees to all of us freedom of religion, to worship as we desire to meet the needs of our souls, freedom of the press, and freedom of speech. No individual or group in this country, including the gentleman from Mississippi, has any priorities on America or its priceless freedom. All of us trace our heritage to some foreign source, including the gentleman from Mississippi. (Kelly 1947, 84)

During his third term in Congress, Weiss was elected to the Court of Common Pleas in Pittsburgh, Pennsylvania, where he presided from 1946 to 1967. As a judge he also continued his officiating on the football field. In 1946, at a home-field game at Duquesne, Weiss refused to give in to demands from the visiting Tennessee football team that African American player Charles Cooper be benched. Deciding, "No Cooper, no game," Weiss announced that ticket moneys would instead be refunded to the 3,000 individuals in attendance. Weiss earned a reputation, in the legislature, on the football field, and in the courtroom for knowing when to blow his whistle (Kelly 1947, 140).

Weiss retired in 1967 and served in 1968 as president of the Pennsylvania State Judicial Administration. He died in 1977.

References:

Kelly, George E. 1947. *Sammy Blows His Whistle: A Biography of Judge Samuel A. Weiss*. Washington, D.C.: Progress Press.

Http://bioguide.congress.gov/scripts/biodisplay.pl?index=W0002557. Accessed 12 March 2002.

I will order it cleared" (Watson 2000, 121). After the docket was completed, Landis invited the group into his chambers, where he was offered the job as professional baseball's first commissioner. Kenesaw voiced his flattery, but he opined that he did not want to leave the important matters before him as a jurist. The owners told him that he could retain both positions, earning $7,500 as judge and $42,500 as commissioner. Landis agreed and served in both capacities until he resigned from the bench in 1922.

Although all eight indicted members of the "Black Sox" were acquitted, Commissioner Landis banished all eight men from professional baseball for life, stating, "Regardless of the verdict of juries, baseball is entirely competent to protect itself against crooks, both inside and outside the game" (Watson 2000, 121). Over the next four years, Landis blacklisted seven other players and suspended thirty-eight more, either for throwing games or, more often, for failing to disclose that they had been approached by gamblers. When Bing Crosby attempted to buy an interest in the Pittsburgh Pirates, Landis refused because Crosby owned racehorses.

Landis had demanded absolute authority, and the owners acquiesced. The commissioner's power was demonstrated when he ordered Babe Ruth not to play in lucrative postseason barnstorming games. Ruth refused a summons to Landis's office and proceeded to play in the games. The commissioner promptly fined Ruth an amount equal to his entire 1921 World Series bonus and suspended him for the first six weeks of the 1922 season. During spring training, Ruth asked Landis for a pardon, but he received a two-hour lecture instead.

Along with Ruth, Commissioner Landis restored the public's confidence in the game. Hard though he was, many players, owners, and fans greatly respected his love for and protection of the game. Landis clearly opposed most changes proposed to increase attendance, however. He opposed integration, night baseball, and the farm system.

Landis remained baseball's commissioner for twenty-three years, and he did not miss a single World Series until 1944, when he was admitted to the hospital after complaining of shortness of breath. At seventy-eight, he had battled respiratory problems and prostate cancer for many years. In November 1944, the owners renewed Landis's contract as commissioner, but he died a week later. Two weeks after his death, he was inducted into the Baseball Hall of Fame. His Cooperstown plaque reads: "His integrity and leadership established baseball in the respect, esteem and affection of the American people."

Christopher L. Whaley

References and Further Reading:

"Kenesaw Mountain Landis (1866–1944)." Available at <http://www.inficad.com/~ksup/landis.html>. Accessed 1 January 2003.

"Kenesaw Mountain Landis: Baseball's First Commissioner/Restored Baseball's Integrity by Banning the Black Sox." Available at http://www.enel.net/beisbol>. Accessed 1 January 2003.

Pietrusza, David. 1998. *Judge and Jury: The Life and Times of Judge Kenesaw Mountain Landis*. South Bend, Ind.: Diamond Communications.

Spink, J. G. Taylor. 1947. *Judge Landis and Twenty-Five Years of Baseball*. New York: Thomas Y. Crowell.

Voight, David Quentin. 1973. *Dictionary of American Biography*. Supplement 3: *1941–1945*. New York: American Council of Learned Societies (reproduced in *Biography Resource Center*. 2001. Farmington Hills, Mich.: The Gale Group). Available at <http://galenet.galegroup.com/servlet/BioRC>.

Watson, Bruce. 2000. "The Judge Who Ruled Baseball." *Smithsonian Magazine* 31, no. 7 (October), 120.

LEVENTHAL, HAROLD

(1915–1979)

HAROLD LEVENTHAL
Courtesy of Art & Visual Materials, Special Collections Department, Harvard Law School Library

THE EXPERTISE IN REGULATORY issues that Harold Leventhal developed during his tenure in the executive branch served him well as a judge on the Court of Appeals for the District of Columbia Circuit, a court whose docket features a heavy concentration of cases presenting questions of that nature. Political scientist Jeffrey Brandon Morris characterized Judge Leventhal as a "hard-nosed [jurist] . . . in whom practicality was joined with compassion, [who] . . . brought to the court a quick-witted, superbly analytical and cultivated mind and a ready pen" (2001, 198). Harold Leventhal was born to Broadway theater producer Jules Joseph Leventhal and the former Sadie Wolcher on 5 January 1915 in New York City. He earned the A.B. degree from Columbia University (Green prize) in 1934, graduating Phi Beta Kappa. In 1936 Leventhal graduated first in his class from Columbia School of Law, earning the LL.B. degree (Toppan and Odronaux prizes). He was also editor in chief of the *Columbia Law Review*. Leventhal was admitted to the New York State bar in 1936 and the District of Columbia bar in 1946.

Prior to his appointment to the federal bench in 1965, Harold Leventhal's diverse career spanned both government service and private practice. He served as a law clerk for United States Supreme Court justices Harlan

Fiske Stone (1937–1938) and Stanley Reed (1938). Upon completion of these clerkships, Leventhal took a position as an attorney in the Office of the Solicitor General of the United States, 1937–1938 and 1938–1939. Harold Leventhal then moved to the U.S. Department of the Interior, becoming chief of litigation in the Bituminous Coal Division from 1939 to 1940. He served as assistant general counsel in the U.S. Office of Price Administration from 1940 to 1943, resuming this position briefly in 1946. Leventhal also served his country as a U.S. Coast Guard Reserve lieutenant commander from 1943 to 1946. Near the end of World War II, Leventhal joined the staff of Justice Robert Jackson during the Nuremberg Trial proceedings from 1945 to 1946.

Harold Leventhal subsequently left full-time government service, practicing law in the firm Ginsburg and Leventhal from 1946 to 1965. During that period, however, he continued government service in a limited capacity. In 1948, Leventhal served as executive officer of the Hoover Commission Task Force on Independent Regulatory Commissions. He briefly returned to the U.S. Office of Price Administration from 1951 to 1952, serving as general counsel. Additionally, Leventhal served as chief counsel to the Democratic National Committee from 1952 to 1965.

Leventhal also lectured at several prestigious institutions. He was visiting lecturer on regulated industries at Yale Law School (1957–1962); Regents lecturer at the University of California, Los Angeles (1974); Mooers lecturer at The American University (1975); and Sulzbacher lecturer at Columbia University (1976). On 1 March 1965, Pres. Lyndon B. Johnson appointed Harold Leventhal to the Court of Appeals for the District of Columbia Circuit, filling the seat vacated by Wilbur K. Miller.

Judge Harold Leventhal died unexpectedly after suffering a heart attack on 20 November 1979, following a tennis match with one of his law clerks in Washington, D.C. By special dispensation from Pres. Jimmy Carter, Harold Leventhal was interred at Arlington National Cemetery.

Judge Leventhal was considered a member of the liberal bloc of the District of Columbia Circuit. He was neither an unabashed judicial activist nor an unyielding judicial restraintist. Leventhal acknowledged inherent limitations of judicial intervention, endorsing prudent judicial activism in appropriate circumstances. According to Judge Leventhal,

> The courts should not shrink from entering political thickets when necessary to correct injustice, and they will not. But they should not plunge ahead blindly. The biblical ram that got its horns caught in the thicket was sacrificed. That was a noble step forward for mankind, as the Old Testament taught the use of animals to replace human sacrifice. But today's thickets re-

quire no judicial sacrifice. How should courts proceed in political thickets? Carefully; pragmatically. (1977, 387)

He is uniformly remembered as a brilliant, incisive, articulate, inquisitive, compassionate jurist and a warm, generous mentor. Judge Leventhal wrote opinions in a wide variety of doctrinal areas including criminal procedure, immigration, libel, privacy, civil rights, free speech, and trusts and estates.

Judge Harold Leventhal's legacy remains most pronounced in the area of administrative law. One of his most notable opinions focused on the non-delegation doctrine. At issue in *Amalgamated Meat Cutters v. Connally* (337 F. Supp. 737 [D.D.C. 1971]) was whether Pres. Richard Nixon's 1971 order imposing a ninety-day price and wage freeze pursuant to the Economic Stabilization Act of 1970 constituted an impermissible delegation of legislative authority to the executive branch.

Writing for a three-judge panel, Leventhal struck a balance between the union's argument that the delegation of authority was substantial and unrestrained and the government's position that the scope of delegated authority was far greater than that exercised by the president. The court held that the president's action fell squarely within the broad authority expressly delegated to the executive branch by Congress. Delegation of authority itself was not necessarily problematic; the critical factor, the court reasoned, was accountability in exercising delegated authority. Judge Leventhal concluded that "a standard of fairness and equity" was implicit in both the statute and its legislative history (337 F. Supp. 757). Therefore, Congress had established confines, albeit generous ones, for appropriate executive action. The exercise of delegated authority, then, was not limitless and devoid of accountability. Moreover, judicial review of such agency action provided an additional safeguard against potential abuse of delegated authority.

Perhaps Leventhal's most significant contributions to administrative law were articulated in *Greater Boston Television Corp. v. Federal Communications Commission* (444 F.2d 841 [D.C. Cir. 1970]). The question presented in this case focused on the criteria and rules applied by the Federal Communications Commission (FCC) to applicants seeking or renewing broadcast licenses. Specifically, the court held that the FCC's decision that renewal applicants must meet the identical criteria required of new applicants was neither unreasonable nor arbitrary. In the majority opinion, Judge Leventhal identified three important considerations for conducting judicial review of agency decisionmaking. First, courts have an obligation to assure that agencies have engaged in reasoned decisionmaking. Agency decisions must be the product of a rational, deliberative process rather than whim.

Second, Leventhal noted that judicial intervention was appropriate "if the courts become aware . . . that the agency has not taken a 'hard look' at the salient problems, and has not genuinely engaged in reasoned decisionmaking" (444 F.2d 851). Essentially, application of the hard look doctrine required judges carefully to scrutinize the decisionmaking process an administrative agency employed and the information upon which it based its conclusion. Such judicial inquiry, Judge Leventhal explained, should be triggered by a number of "danger signals" attracting the courts' attention. Courts should focus, for example, on whether the agency adhered to established, conventional procedures and whether the agency's conclusions were based on facts and reason.

Although the hard look doctrine clearly provides a rationale for careful judicial scrutiny of agency decisionmaking, Judge Leventhal did not perceive it as a blunt instrument to be wielded by activist judges against administrative agencies. Rather, Leventhal viewed the hard look doctrine as a means of promoting the public interest. The characterization of the respective roles played by administrative agencies and the courts as a "partnership" to promote the public interest comprised Leventhal's third consideration. Judge Leventhal surmised: "The court is in a real sense part of the total administrative process, and not a hostile stranger [to agencies]. . . . This collaborative spirit does not undercut, it rather underlines the court's rigorous insistence on the need for conjunction of articulated standards and reflective findings, in furtherance of even-handed application of law, rather than impermissible whim, improper influence, or misplaced zeal" (444 F.2d 852).

A third Leventhal opinion in administrative law is noteworthy because, in concert with the opinion written by Chief Judge David Bazelon, it further clarified the nature of judicial review of agency decisionmaking. At issue in *Ethyl Corp. v. Environmental Protection Agency* (541 F.2d 1 [D.C. Cir. 1976]) was whether the Environmental Protection Agency (EPA) had acted properly by requiring annual reductions of lead content in gasoline pursuant to its authority under the Clean Air Act to regulate gasoline additives having emissions that constituted health hazards. The court held that the EPA's decision was neither arbitrary nor capricious and, therefore, did not constitute an abuse of discretion.

In concurring opinions, Leventhal and Bazelon exchanged their respective visions of the nature of the hard look doctrine. Bazelon argued that judicial inquiry should focus exclusively on process; courts should determine whether a sound decisionmaking procedure had been established by agencies and avoid inserting themselves into substantive aspects of agency decisions. Conversely, Leventhal insisted that courts necessarily must concern themselves with substantive elements of agency decisions as well as with process. Judicial attention to substance as well as procedure, critics surmised, provided a rationale for potentially intrusive judicial interference with agency decisionmaking. Responding to his critics' assertion, Judge Leventhal articulated a sophisticated conception of judicial review: He underscored the necessity of judicious application of careful scrutiny by the courts, endorsing judicial restraint while cautioning that restraint must not degenerate into judicial neglect.

A fourth opinion of significance in administrative law focused on hybrid rule making. At issue in *American Airlines, Inc. v. Civil Aeronautics Board* (359 F.2d 624 [D.C. Cir. 1966]) was whether an agency had exceeded its rule-making authority in promulgating a rule restricting the sale of space on flights at wholesale rates to cargo-only carriers, thus excluding passenger airlines ("combination-carriers") from this practice. Combination-carriers argued that the rule effectively modified their licenses in the absence of formal adjudication.

Judge Leventhal, writing the majority opinion for an *en banc* circuit, recognized the importance of agency rule making to the administrative process. He acknowledged the appropriateness of agency use of its rule-making authority to resolve disputes of a recurring nature, refusing to endorse the argument that agencies were required to adjudicate in instances where rule making modified existing licenses. Leventhal insisted that

> rule making is a vital part of the administrative process, particularly adapted to . . . sound evolution of policy in guiding the future development of industries subject to intensive administrative regulation in the public interest, and that such rule making is not to be shackled, in the absence of clear and specific Congressional requirement, by importation of formalities developed for the adjudicatory process and basically unsuited for policy rule making. (359 F.2d 629)

Judge Leventhal articulated a position that was characteristically nuanced. Despite the endorsement of a generous application of rule-making authority, administrative agencies did not enjoy unfettered exercise of this power. Exercise of agencies' rule-making authority as a substitution for formal adjudication was confined to congressionally established parameters and judicial standards that agency action be neither unreasonable nor arbitrary.

Harold Leventhal distinguished himself on the federal bench as a jurist whose intellectual prowess, life experience, and sophisticated understanding of the law as it relates to American society enabled him to render balanced, reasoned decisions that promoted the public interest. In summarizing Judge Leventhal's legacy in the area of administrative law, former law clerk Robert T. Haar observed that when you look at Judge Leventhal's contributions to administrative law . . . [it appears that they] flow[ed] . . . very naturally from his belief in public service and his optimism about Government. The Judge believed that when Government agencies strayed from their legislative mandate or otherwise engaged in conduct which was fairly characterized as arbitrary and capricious, it was seldom because of bad faith or incompetence. For the Judge, the problems arose because you were asking good people to do difficult things, often for the first time. So the Judge saw judicial review of agency action as a constructive dialogue. The way to ensure that good people did the right thing most of the time was to ask them what they were doing and why they were doing it. This seemingly simple idea revolutionized agency rulemaking in the 1970s. ("Presentation" 1991, 95)

Essentially, Judge Harold Leventhal strove to achieve "pragmatic justice" (Leventhal 1967, 239).

Melanie K. Morris

References and Further Reading:

Estreicher, Samuel. 1980. "Pragmatic Justice: The Contributions of Judge Harold Leventhal to Administrative Law." *Columbia Law Review* 80: 894.

Leventhal, Harold. 1947. "The Role of the Price Lawyer." In *Problems in Price Control: Legal Phases*. OPA Historical Reports on War Administration. Washington, D.C.: U.S. Government Printing Office, 49.

———. 1967. "Cues and Compasses for Administrative Lawyers." *Administrative Law Review* 20: 237.

———. 1974a. "Environmental Decisionmaking and the Role of the Courts." *University of Pennsylvania Law Review* 122: 509.

———. 1974b. "Principled Fairness and Regulatory Urgency." *Case Western Reserve Law Review* 25: 66.

———. 1977. "Courts and Political Thickets." *Columbia Law Review* 77: 345.

———. 1978. "The Courts and the Labor Agencies." *University of Dayton Law Review* 3: 327.

Morris, Jeffrey B. 1972. "The Second Most Important Court: The United States Court of Appeals for the District of Columbia Circuit." Ph.D. thesis, Columbia University.

———. 2001. *Calmly to Poise the Scales of Justice: A History of the Courts of the District of Columbia Circuit*. Durham, N.C.: Carolina Academic Press.

"Presentation of the Portrait of the Honorable Harold Leventhal: Proceedings." 1991. 958 F.2d 81–97.

LINDE, HANS A.

(1924–)

HANS A. LINDE
Courtesy of Hans A. Linde

HANS A. LINDE, LEGAL SCHOLAR and Oregon Supreme Court justice, championed the philosophy that state judges should seek guidance in their state constitutions before consulting the federal Constitution. The movement Linde sparked later evolved into "new judicial federalism." Linde was born on 15 April 1924, in Berlin, Germany, the son of Bruno and Luise Linde. With the rise of the Nazis, the Linde family left Germany in 1933, moving to Copenhagen, Denmark, and finally arriving in Portland, Oregon, when Hans was fifteen. After serving briefly in the United States Army (he was naturalized in 1943, while in basic training at Camp Roberts, California), he attended Reed College in Portland, graduating in 1947 at the top of his class. He married Helen Tucker in 1945; they had two children.

In 1950, Linde earned a law degree from the University of California, Berkeley, where he was editor of the law review. Shortly after graduation, he moved to Washington, D.C., to serve as a law clerk for United States Supreme Court justice William O. Douglas. At the end of his clerkship, Linde remained in Washington, D.C., to work in the Office of the Legal Adviser of the Department of State. He also served as an adviser to the U.S. delegation to the United Nations General Assembly. In 1953, the Lindes returned to Portland. While in private practice, he volunteered as an adviser to the U.S. Senate campaign of Richard Neuberger, a Democratic state legislator who successfully defeated the Republican incumbent in 1954. Linde moved back to Washington in 1955 to work as Neuberger's legislative assistant. In 1958, Linde was appointed to the faculty of the University of Oregon School of Law in Eugene. He was a professor there until his appointment to the Oregon Supreme Court in 1977 (Witt 1989).

As a law professor, Linde developed his theory of the primacy of state constitutions in a number of widely read law review articles. Under Chief Justice Earl Warren, the United States Supreme Court applied many federal constitutional protections to state actions, relegating state constitutions to "legal swamplands (necessary perhaps, but no reason to visit them)" (McIntosh and Cates 1997, 67). Writing in the *Oregon Law Review,* Professor Linde advocated the primacy of state law and "denounced the common practice of reading state Bill of Rights provisions to be identical to those found in the federal constitution" (68). To render a decision according to Linde's philosophy, a state judge should consult the state constitution first, giving only a secondary consideration to federal law (McIntosh and Cates 1997, 68). In his article, he chided the Oregon Supreme Court for ignoring the Oregon constitution in its rulings. Members of the Oregon Supreme Court heard Linde's message. McIntosh and Cates recorded that "on at least three occasions the justices made specific reference to his [Linde's] article in their published opinions, each time stating their disagreement" (68).

Linde had a close working knowledge of the Oregon constitution. In 1961 and 1962, he was a member of the Oregon Constitutional Revision Commission. As chairman of the drafting subcommittee, he drafted changes to the Bill of Rights (Article 1), Article 7 on the judiciary, and Article 5 on the executive (Summers 1984, xiii). Linde also did appellate work on briefs submitted to the Oregon Supreme Court. He wrote the *amicus* brief the Oregon Newspaper Publisher's Association submitted to the court in the case of *Deras v. Myers* (272 Ore. 47, P.2d 541 [1975]). Basing its decision on the Oregon constitution, the court struck down limits on political campaign spending, about a year before the United States Supreme Court issued a similar ruling in *Buckley v. Valeo* (424 U.S. 1 [1976]).

Linde coauthored a casebook, *Legislative and Administrative Processes*, that was published in 1976. In the book, he argued that the procedures of policy-making and implementation are as important as the policy itself. The procedures followed in designing the policy determine the effect of the policy. The book received positive reviews.

In 1976, Oregon governor Robert Straub, a Democrat, appointed Hans Linde to fill the vacancy in the Oregon Supreme Court caused by Chief Justice Kenneth O'Connell's retirement. Linde took his seat as an associate justice on the seven-member court in January 1977. He campaigned for election to a full term in 1978 and faced no opposition in the nonpartisan race. Judge Patricia Wald related that the Oregon justice was interviewed in 1979 for a spot on the United States Court of Appeals for the District of Columbia (1996, 216). Linde was not nominated. After a hard-fought reelection campaign in 1984, he was reelected to a second six-year term. Linde remained on the Oregon Supreme Court until he retired in January 1990.

As a member of his state's highest court, Linde had an opportunity to implement his legal theory of the primacy of state constitutions. The first case the court heard with its newest justice was *State v. Flores* (280 Ore. 273; 570 P.2d 965 [1977]), a civil liberties case in which a Hispanic defendant waived his Miranda rights during a four-hour police interrogation. The four-person majority decision followed the Fourth Amendment of the U.S. Constitution as applied by the United States Supreme Court. Linde and two colleagues dissented, stating that the Oregon constitution provided more guarantees of individual liberty and should be applied before invoking federal constitutional provisions (McIntosh and Cates 1997, 69).

Linde was able to apply his philosophy to other significant cases the court heard in his first year. In *State ex rel Johnson v. Woodrich* (279 Ore. 31; 566 P.2d 859 [1977]), he was in the majority. The case involved a criminal defendant who offered an insanity defense. Using provisions from the state and federal constitutions, the court determined that the defendant could not be compelled to answer questions regarding the criminal act during a pretrial psychiatric examination. Although voting with the majority, Linde wrote a concurring opinion in which he argued that the ruling should have been derived exclusively from the Oregon constitution. Linde wrote the majority opinion in a case in which the court ruled that a defendant accused of a minor traffic infraction was guaranteed the right to legal representation (*Brown v. Multnomah County District Court*, 280 Ore. 95; 556 P.2d 52 [1977]). According to McIntosh and Cates, "his opinion repeatedly refers to the Oregon Bill of Rights and only occasionally to the Fourteenth Amendment" (1997, 70).

Justice Linde was able to persuade a majority of his colleagues of the correctness of his philosophy. The Oregon Supreme Court adopted Linde's position in the majority opinion in *Sterling v. Cupp* (290 Ore. 611; 625 P.2d 123 [1981]). In this case, male inmates of the Oregon State Penitentiary sued to stop prison officials from assigning female correctional officers to duties that involved frisking male inmates or the observation of male inmates in showers or toilets. In the opinion, which limited searches of intimate body areas by members of the opposite sex in cases other than emergencies, Linde wrote, "The proper sequence is to analyze the state's law, including its constitutional law, before reading a federal constitutional claim" (290 Ore. 611; 625 P.2d 126).

Charles Z. Smith (1927-)

Charles Z. Smith was born to a Cuban father and an African American mother in Florida in 1927 and has been known for achieving a remarkable number of firsts in his life. He was the first nonwhite to serve as a judge in the state of Washington, the first to be a superior judge in Washington, the first ever to serve on the American Bar Association's Standing Committee on the Federal Judiciary, and the first and only to serve on the Washington Supreme Court (Washington 1994, 187, 201).

Smith's parents separated before he was grown, but he was already living with the family of Dr. William H. Gray Jr., who was then president of Florida A and M University. Smith served in the United States Marines, then graduated from Temple University and moved to Washington, where he graduated from the law school at the University of Washington and served as a law clerk to a Washington Supreme Court justice. From there he joined a prosecuting attorney's office and later worked with Attorney General Robert Kennedy investigating and prosecuting union corruption.

After returning to Seattle, Smith was appointed to the municipal court and later to the Superior Court of King County, where he served from 1966 to 1973 and gained a reputation for innovative alternatives to prison, including literacy classes and community service. In 1973, Smith became a law professor at the University of Washington, where he served for a time as an associate dean before being appointed in 1988 to the Washington Supreme Court.

Smith says that he never actually pursued a judicial career and that "I never wanted to be a first anything, except my wife's first husband" (Washington 1994, 193). He has attributed his firsts to "being at the right place at the right time," but he also has noted that as a retired Marine lieutenant colonel with good credentials, people often consider him to be "safe" (200). Smith noted that "being a person of color means that you have extraordinary stresses that persons not of color don't have" (193), and he detailed elaborate security measures he has taken as a result of threats that he has received as a judge.

As a member of the American Bar Association's Standing Committee on the Federal Judiciary, Smith encouraged the committee to look at the cultural awareness of individuals before deciding whether they were good appointees. Smith is convinced that a judge needs to be a person of absolute integrity. He commented: "If a person loses sight of his or her integrity and humanity that person will not be successful in any endeavor, particularly not the practice of law. The practice of law is an honorable profession where integrity is just as important as ability. The person who wishes to function effectively in the practice of law at any level must have integrity and sensitivity" (Washington 1994, 199).

Smith continues to battle for greater minority representation in the judiciary. Asked whether he was excited about being the first nonwhite appointed to the court, Smith responded negatively and explained: "I'll be excited when there are five [out of nine] women on this court. I'll be excited when my daughter—if my daughter who is a lawyer wants to be a judge—is appointed to the supreme court. I'll be excited when my granddaughter—if my granddaughter who is two years old becomes a lawyer and wants to become a judge—is appointed to the supreme court" (Washington 1994, 208).

Reference:

Washington, Linn, ed. 1994. *Black Judges on Justice*. New York: The New Press, 186–208.

Linde was presented with an opportunity more fully to apply his philosophy in the 1983 case *State v. Kennedy* (295 Ore. 260; 666 P.2d 1316). Kennedy had been convicted of theft in a second trial after the first trial ended in a mistrial because of the prosecutor's misconduct. The appeals court in Oregon reversed the conviction, citing a few United States Supreme Court opinions. After the Oregon Supreme Court denied review, the state appealed to the United States Supreme Court. The Supreme Court reversed the decision on the basis of double jeopardy and due process under the federal Constitution and remanded the case back to the Oregon appeals court. The appeals court upheld the conviction based on Oregon law. The defendant appealed to the Oregon Supreme Court for review. Writing for a unanimous court, Linde began his opinion by stating "the history of this case demonstrates the practical importance of the rule, often repeated in recent decisions, that all questions of state law be considered and disposed of before reaching a claim that this state's law falls short of a standard imposed by the federal constitution on all states" (295 Ore., 262).

The United States Supreme Court expanded constitutional protections under Chief Justice Earl Warren. The Court under his successor, Warren Burger, turned away from increasing constitutional protections; thus, by the 1980s, liberals and libertarians looked to the states for protection from government. Justice Linde, as a leader of the movement for increasing judicial reliance on state constitutional law, became a lightning rod for supporters of "law and order."

Linde decided to seek reelection to a second six-year term in 1984. The nonpartisan elections for the Oregon Supreme Court are usually quiet events in which the incumbent faces token opposition. The 1984 election was different. Linde faced two opponents: Albin Norblad III, a judge from Marion County; and David Nissman, a Lane County deputy assistant district attorney. Nissman, the more active candidate because Norblad was slowed by a heart condition, was endorsed by law enforcement groups and Mothers Against Drunk Driving. These groups saw Linde as soft on crime because of his rulings limiting police power to search suspects and the government's power to impose the death penalty. A member of the Multnomah County district attorney's office wrote a letter to the editor describing the incumbent justice as "Public enemy number one." Throughout the campaign, Dep. Asst. Dist. Atty. Nissman and his supporters regularly referred to Linde as "Professor" Linde, never Justice Linde.

One case cited by the Nissman campaign as evidence that Linde was soft on crime was *State v. Lowry* (295 Ore. 337; 667 P.2d 996 [1983]). Police, searching for weapons on a person suspected of driving while intoxicated, found a bottle containing what was later determined to be cocaine. Linde's opinion held that the Oregon constitution required the police to have a search warrant before they could analyze the bottle's content.

The Nissman campaign listed Linde's positions in a "Fellow Oregonian" letter. The Nissman for Justice Committee concluded its lengthy list by stating "the keystone of his [Linde's] judicial career has been his tinkering with the Oregon Constitution by inventing previously unknown rights for criminal defendants. Searches that are absolutely legal under our federal bill of rights now run afoul of mysterious new rules created by Linde" (Collins 1991, 759–760). Nissman also challenged Linde's productivity on the court, suggesting that the justice was too much of an academic to be allowed to interpret laws. As a sitting justice, Linde indicated that it was not proper for him to defend decisions in which he had participated.

With 45 percent, Justice Linde received the most votes in the May 1984 primary. Nissman received 25 percent of the vote, coming in third behind Judge Norblad (29 percent). Since Oregon election law specified that a runoff election must be held if no candidate received more than 50 percent of the vote, Linde faced Norblad in November 1984. Linde won the runoff election.

Most observers would agree that Linde contributed to the development of state constitutional law, but McIntosh and Cates reported that Linde considered his contributions to Oregon tort law more significant (1997, 73). He held a conservative position on the judiciary's role in tort law, arguing that judges should issue rulings based on legal authority and not public policy criteria. According to Forell, Linde's view "is that state court judges should neither let their personal values show nor base their decisions on their own policy judgments" (1991, 816). In short, judges should avoid making decisions based on weighing competing social demands because such decisions would be political decisions.

Linde outlined his philosophy on torts in his dissent in *Harrell v. Travelers Indemnity Company* (279 Ore. 199; 567 P.2d 1013 [1977]). The case involved an automobile accident for which the plaintiff had received compensatory and punitive damages after a jury trial. The defendant's insurance company paid the compensatory damages but refused to pay the punitive damages. The plaintiff then sued the company, and a jury found in favor of the insurance company because the driver's liability insurance made no mention of coverage for punitive damages. The majority decided in favor of the insurance company, arguing that allowing insurance companies to cover punitive damages would frustrate efforts to discourage reckless driving and driving while intoxicated. In his dissent, Linde advocated judicial self-restraint. He pointed out that there was no policy developed by the legislature limiting punitive damages and argued that in the absence of such legislation the companies should have to pay.

Justice Linde created a new tort through his majority opinion in *Nearing v. Weaver* (295 Ore. 702; 670 P.2d 137 [1983]). Henrietta Nearing filed suit against the city of St. Helens and two of its police officers. She claimed that she had suffered personal injury due to the officers' failure to enforce Oregon state law protecting women from spousal abuse. Nearing's estranged husband physically assaulted her male friend after the police had assured her that the husband would be arrested for violating a restraining order. In his decision, Linde argued that the law created statutory liability and that the officers were liable for injuries sustained because they did not follow the law. "Oregon is the only jurisdiction in the United States in which police officers have been held strictly liable for injuries caused by a third party" (McIntosh and Cates 1997, 77–78). Responding to Chief Justice Ed Peterson's dissent, Linde pointed out that he was not making new law, only applying public policy that had been enacted by the legislature.

By the late 1980s, Justice Linde was the senior member of the court. Traditionally, the court elects the senior justice as chief justice. When his turn came, Linde refused the position. He did not want the administrative responsibilities of chief justice.

Justice Hans Linde retired from the Oregon Supreme Court on 31 January 1990. "The intellectual godfather" of the state court revival returned to academia (Toobin 1985, 11). He taught as a visiting professor at numerous law schools. In 2002, he was the Distinguished Scholar in Residence at the Willamette University College of Law in Oregon. He also served on the Oregon Law Commission, a body created in 1997 by the state legislature to conduct a continuous program of law reform. Since leaving the Supreme Court, Linde's writings have included numerous stinging critiques of the initiative process (Linde 2001). Even after retiring from the bench, Linde has continued to work in the area of state constitutional development.

John David Rausch Jr.

References and Further Reading:

Collins, Ronald K. L. 1991. "Hans Linde and His 1984 Judicial Election: The Primary." *Oregon Law Review* 70: 747–813.

Forell, Caroline A. 1991. "Replacing Pragmatism and Policy with Analysis and Analogy: Justice Linde's Contribution to Oregon Tort Law." *Oregon Law Review* 70: 815–854.

Linde, Hans A. 1970. "Without 'Due Process'—Unconstitutional Law in Oregon." *Oregon Law Review* 49: 125–185.

———. 1994. "Courts and Torts: 'Public Policy' without Public Politics?" *Valparaiso University Law Review* 28: 821–855.

———. 2001. "State Courts and Republican Government." *Santa Clara Law Review* 41: 951–971.

Linde, Hans A., and George Bunn. 1976. *Legislative and Administrative Processes*. Mineola, N.Y.: Foundation Press.

McIntosh, Wayne V., and Cynthia L. Cates. 1997. *Judicial Entrepreneurship: The Role of the Judge in the Marketplace of Ideas*. Westport, Conn.: Greenwood Press.

Nagel, Robert F., ed. 1995. *Intellect and Craft: The Contributions of Justice Hans Linde to American Constitutionalism*. Boulder, Colo.: Westview Press.

Summers, Robert S. 1984. "Hans A. Linde as Seen by a Junior Colleague—A Personal Tribute." *Annual Survey of American Law* (vol. 1 of 2 for 1984): xii–xv.

Toobin, Jeffrey. 1985. "Better than Burger: States' Rights for Liberals." *The New Republic*, 4 March, 10–11.

Wald, Patricia M. 1996. "Hans Linde and the Elusive Art of Judging: Intellect and Craft Are Never Enough." *Texas Law Review* 75: 215–235.

Witt, Elder. 1989. "Hans A. Linde: The Unassuming Architect of an Emerging Role for State Constitutions." *Governing Magazine*, July, 56–60.

LIVINGSTON, ROBERT R., JR.

(1746–1813)

Robert R. Livingston Jr.
Library of Congress

Robert R. Livingston, first chancellor of the state of New York, forged one of the great legal and political careers of any American age. Dubbed "the American Cicero" for his oratory by no less than Benjamin Franklin, Livingston had a hand in many of the epochal moments of the founding generation. A patriot during the Revolution, Livingston sat on the committee to write the Declaration of Independence, served as the first American secretary for foreign affairs during the war, helped lead the New York State Convention to ratify the Constitution, negotiated the Louisiana purchase, and financed Robert Fulton's steamboat project. Perhaps most memorably, Livingston administered the oath of office to George Washington, swearing him in as the first president of the United States. Yet, for all that, he seems to have dropped into a historical oubliette, noted for having been on the scene but rarely acknowledged alongside his more famous peers as a shaper of events. Nothing exemplifies this state of affairs better than his judicial career, of which few records and no systematic scholarship survive.

Over several generations, the Livingston family became one of the most prominent in the colony of New York. Landowners and lawyers, the Livingstons showed talents for enterprise and political machination that greatly enlarged their estates in the century prior to the Revolution. Robert Robert Livingston Jr., son of New York Supreme Court justice Robert Robert Livingston Sr.—given the redundant middle name to distinguish him from his father, Robert, and the various other family Roberts—was born on 27 November 1746 in New York City and was the great-grandson of the original Robert Livingston, the first lord of the manor. With such a mad proliferation of namesakes, the family took to calling its members by their titles. Robert Robert, the father, was "the Judge"; Robert Robert Jr., the son, eventually became known as "the Chancellor."

Given his privileged upbringing, Robert R. Livingston Jr. exhibited the high ambitions and aristocratic temperament that one would expect from a feudal scion. But the clan had also embraced Whiggish politics. In the New York of the 1760s, family dominated partisan divisions, and the Livingstons competed against the DeLanceys for political preeminence in the colony. Despite their elitism, the Livingstons were often seen as the "popular" party: defenders of Presbyterianism, resistant to Parliament, suspicious of property taxation. Such positions came at a cost. When the DeLanceys ran on a campaign of "No lawyer, no Presbyterian!" in 1768, taking advantage of backlash against the Stamp Act riots, the judge lost his seat in the colonial Assembly. He was later banned outright when the DeLanceys imposed a rule preventing the election of Supreme Court judges to the legislative body, although he continued to win elections (Dangerfield 1960, 39–40). The judge's son, Robert R. Jr., experienced these events during his formative years, and they influenced the agrarian ideology he carried with him into the Revolutionary War.

The young Robert was raised in New York City but spent holidays at the family's country estate, Clermont. Despite their tendency toward Presbyterianism, he was baptized in the Church of England and then enrolled at King's College, an Anglican hotbed, at the age of fifteen. Robert received an education in the classics and showed an early gift for rhetoric. He also became a close friend to John Jay, later the first chief justice of the Supreme Court of the United States. At the time of their graduation in 1765, Livingston and Jay delivered commencement speeches on the themes of "liberty" and "peace," respectively. The *New York Gazette* offered particular praise to Livingston, opining that "many of the audience pleased themselves that the young orator may prove an able and zealous asserter, and defender, of the rights and liberties of his country, as well as an ornament to it" (quoted in Scott 1907, 440).

After graduation Livingston began his legal apprenticeship, first under the strict tutelage of William Livingston, his father's cousin, later under the much less structured supervision of William Smith Jr., who left his charges alone to sort out the complexities of Blackstone, Finch, and Coke. He was admitted to the bar and shortly thereafter formed a partnership called Messrs. Jay, Livingston and Co. Although the partnership lasted from 1768 until 1772, it was only active for two years. Livingston also joined an elite organization of lawyers known as the Moot who met in taverns to dine and debate complex legal issues, ultimately handing down mock decisions. From this, he and Jay hatched a plan to invent their own inferior court judicial positions and propose themselves to the governor for appointments. The scheme was snuffed out by the DeLanceys, but Governor Tryon offered Livingston a position as recorder for the state of New York to compensate (Dangerfield 1960, 47–49). The position was less than what he had hoped for, but it gave him his first opportunity to preside over criminal trials. By 1775 Livingston's opposition to royal policies deprived him of the job.

Although his judicial career momentarily stalled, Livingston's political career soared. He was elected to the Continental Congress in 1775 and served intermittently until 1785. One of the congress's most active members, Livingston played an especially important role in setting judicial policy: Through his committee work, he helped create a national court of appeals and drafted commissions and instructions for its judges. When he was offered a nomination to serve on this court, however, he declined. Livingston's best-known responsibility during these years was his appointment to the committee that authored the Declaration of Independence, alongside Thomas Jefferson, John Adams, Benjamin Franklin, and Roger Sherman. Livingston's selection was likely an effort to co-opt his colony at a time when its participation was in doubt. But events relegated him to a marginal role. In poor health, and representing a state that could not decide what it wanted—other than to bind the hands of its delegates—Livingston stayed silent as Jefferson wrote the document and Adams and Franklin made the revisions. Although Livingston supported independence, which he saw as inevitable, he pushed for delay, suggesting that Americans might attract more support from Spain and France after a few more military victories had been won. Called home, Livingston never signed the final declaration.

Back in New York, Livingston sought to create a stable system of state governance. He served in the state Congress, sat on its Council of Safety, consulted on its military policy, and joined the convention to craft a new state constitution. The resulting product, authored mainly by Jay, with Livingston and Gouvernor Morris as his primary advisers, was a model of conservative republicanism—designed to promote independence while securing the rights of the propertied classes. Grounded in freeholder suffrage, the new government enacted a variety of checks to keep its branches within constitutional limits. The judiciary figured prominently in this process, particularly through institutions in whose design Livingston had a strong hand. The Councils of Revision and Appointment played significant roles in checking legislative and executive power: The former, made up of governor, chancellor, and Supreme Court, could veto legislative acts absent a two-thirds override; the latter, consisting of governor and four senators, dispensed patronage. The state courts built upon a hierarchy inherited from the British. The Supreme Court was the high court of law, the Chancery Court presided over questions of equity, and both were reviewed by the Court for the Trial of Impeachments and Correction of Errors, consisting of the chancellor, the Senate, and the Supreme Court (Dangerfield 1960, 88–91).

Conveniently, the convention decided to make initial appointments themselves, selecting Jay as the chief justice of the Supreme Court and Livingston as chancellor, technically the second highest position in the state after the governor. The Chancery Court was a holdover from British rule, but it had always been an underdeveloped institution. Chancery courts had originally emerged in England as alternatives to the rigid formalism of the law proper, which dealt only with actual harms to land, slaves, or specie and which imposed procedural restraints on evidence. Petitioners who fell outside these strictures could go directly to the king, who often delegated the broad power to grant equity to a clergyman known as "chancellor." In theory, equity courts were meant to compensate for the deficiencies of legal positivism by providing a less-structured forum within which the principles of "natural justice" might find voice (Mitford 1816, 2–3).

New York's chancery was created by ordinance of the lords of trade in England in 1701 but was rarely used. The early court consisted of the governor and his council, hence combining executive and judicial power. Conflicts over judicial authority between royal governors and colonial assemblies left the court unpopular, promoting regular but unsuccessful attempts by the Assembly to kill the court. When prerevolutionary tensions began to build, such a court smacked more than ever of arbitrary power. Nonetheless, Livingston, Jay, and the other conservative revolutionaries came to see the court as a useful check on the popular legislature and as an avenue for personal advancement, thus justifying its ongoing existence. The New York constitution drawn up in 1777 provided that the chancellor would serve during good behavior until the age of sixty. Presumably, this exclusion of the barely aged would prevent a court based so heavily on the chancellor's sole discretion from degenerating too much with his advancing years. In any event, Livingston occupied his position as the state's first chancellor from 1777 until 1801, by which time he was only fifty-five. The position was imbued with symbolic grandeur. D. T. Blake, a master and solicitor during the state court's early history, described the institution as "a tribunal, almost of time immemorial, with jurisdiction and powers emanating from justice, connected with the guardianship of widows, orphans, and all persons under divine visitation—in short, a tribunal before which no species of grievance, remediless at common law, can make its appearance in vain" (Blake 1818, xii). It should be no surprise that Livingston, an aristocratic American Whig with a strong sense of noblesse oblige, should find so much resonance in being titled "the Chancellor."

Livingston's approach to the job was more social than scholarly. The Chancery met several times a year in New York and Albany, but Livingston increasingly held court at his Clermont estate—a long and difficult trip from the city (Dangerfield 1960, 277). The minimalism in court structure also extended to its recordkeeping. Not until 1814, with the appointment of James Kent as New York's third chancellor, did the legislature require the publication of court reports. As a result, the substance of Livingston's chancellorship is something of a mystery. On taking the job, Kent disparaged the tenure of his predecessors: "The office . . . had no charms. The person who left it was stupid, and it is a curious fact that for the nine years I was in that office there was not a single decision, opinion, or dictum of either of my two predecessors (Chancellor Livingston and Chancellor [John] Lansing) from 1777 to 1814, cited to me or even suggested. I took the court as if it had been a new institution and never before known in the United States" (quoted in Scott 1907, 452–453). Kent's contempt for Lansing—an antifederalist who defended democracy and laissez-faire—is understandable; his dismissal of Livingston, who had expedited Kent's own admission to practice before the Chancery Court, may be either an indication of his concerns for structure and precedent or a product of his vanity. Jefferson offered a more positive portrayal when he described Livingston as "in every sense of the word, a wise, good, and great man, one of the ablest of American lawyers and statesmen" (quoted 451). Politics may also play a role in these evaluations. After he was snubbed for a major appointment in Washington's first administration, Livingston defected from the Federalists to the Jeffersonians, a move that also exacerbated a growing rift with Jay, who was not similarly denied.

Despite the absence of any chancery records, there are extant indications of Livingston's judicial philosophy and informal records of cases in which he was involved. Records of the Council of Revision show that he opposed "the confiscation and alienation laws directed against the Loyalists, laws granting special powers to the magistracy (lest the freedom of the citizenry be endangered), special taxes, the paper money bill of 1786, and the bill of 1785 to abolish slavery in New York" (Hayes 2002, 3). He was less than consistent on the issue of the Loyalists. Although Livingston continued to reassure Jay and Alexander Hamilton that he opposed punitive treatment of former Tories, he later dabbled in populism upon realizing that he could profit from speculation in Loyalist properties. Hamilton, who as a nationalist was suspicious of any man who would leave a post as secretary of foreign affairs to return to a state chancellorship, saw Livingston's opportunism as a betrayal (McDonald 1979, 75).

Not surprisingly, Livingston and Hamilton interacted often within the narrow confines of New York state law and politics. Hamilton argued cases before the Chancery Court, including *Le Guen v. Gouverneur and Kemble*, where he and Aaron Burr were co-counsel, and *Schuyler v. Ten Eych*, where he and Burr were opposing attorneys. In the former case, Hamilton represented Louis Le Guen, a Frenchman involved in a complex dispute over a shipment of West Indian cotton and indigo being warehoused in New York while he searched for a buyer who could transport the goods for sale in Europe. The case, a series of suits and countersuits, bounced between the law and equity courts. In one critical turn, Livingston ruled that the New York brokers, Gouverneur and Kemble, could introduce fraud charges against Le Guen in Chancery Court even though that issue had not originally emerged in the law trial. On this, he was overturned by the full Court of Errors, including both Kent and Lansing. The effect of the reversal was to restrict the chancellor's power to intervene in cases with settled jurisdiction in other courts (Goebel 1969, 2:82–85).

Livingston and Hamilton were allies in one of their most significant encounters: At the New York convention for ratifying the constitution, they led the nationalist cause. But neither man trusted the other. Hamilton consulted with the chancellor's estranged cousin, Robert Livingston Jr., during a case of intrafamily land dispute. The chancellor had built a grist mill on the stream bordering the two estates, to which he claimed exclusive rights. Infuriated, the manor lord pledged either to take his cousin to court or hire a gang to tear the mill down. Hamilton counseled prudence, but the breach was too deep. The effect of these events was to convince Hamilton that the chancellor's principles stopped at his own purse. After the manor lord's death, the chancellor reached out to his son by delivering a partly favorable opinion from the bench as to the division of the estate and handling of creditors, resulting in an ultimate reconciliation (Dangerfield 1960, 280–281).

Late in his chancellorship, Livingston became consumed with private enthusiasms: a water company that would serve as a republican bank (a Burr scheme), the speculations of natural history and scientific farming, and the quest to revolutionize transportation with steam power. He secured a monopoly from the state to pursue steamboat navigation on the Hudson River, although his early experiments were failures. After resigning as chancellor to become Jefferson's minister to France, however, he met Robert Fulton, who had the practical sense to complete the project. Once it proved successful, the two men found themselves competing with unlicensed rivals despite a state law imposing a stiff fine and boat confiscation on offenders. In *Livingston v. Van Ingen*, Livingston and Fulton sought to shut down their competitors, including James Van Ingen. The former chancellor found little sympathy when the case went before the Chancery Court, now controlled by Lansing. Appealing to natural law and Justinian's *Institutes*, Lansing held that rivers, like the air and sea, were given by God to all mankind and that any restrictions would violate the "privileges" of other states' citizens under the U.S. Constitution. Livingston objected: All civil laws violate "nature," and such a principle would prevent a state from ever granting monopolies to foster internal improvements. At the Court of Errors, Chief Justice Kent overturned Lansing, ruling that he had misread the Constitution and that monopolies must be presumed legitimate (Dangerfield 1960, 418–421). Aside from the interest it holds for involving each of New York's first three chancellors, this case also set up the more famous *Gibbons v. Ogden*—after Livingston's death, Chief Justice John Marshall decided against his heirs in *Gibbons* on grounds of national commerce power.

The judicial career of Robert R. Livingston Jr. was long and varied. If at times he resembles a founding era Forrest Gump—always in the picture, never at its focus—this results from his historical misfortune of having been a near-great in an age of titans. Taken on their own terms, his accomplishments outweigh his reputation, an ironic fate for a New York aristocrat who sought so long for the honor of a public legacy.

Robb A. McDaniel

References and Further Reading:

Blake, D. T. 1818. *An Historical Treatise on the Practice of the Court of Chancery of the State of New York*. New York: J. T. Murden.

Brandt, Clare. 1986. *An American Aristocracy: The Livingstons*. Garden City, N.Y.: Doubleday.

Dangerfield, George. 1960. *Chancellor Robert R. Livingston of New York, 1746–1813*. New York: Harcourt, Brace.

Goebel, Julius, Jr. 1964, 1969. *The Law Practice of Alexander Hamilton: Documents and Commentary*. 2 vols. New York: Columbia University Press.

Hayes, Robert C. 1928–1936. "Robert R. Livingston." In *Dictionary of American Biography Base Set*. New York: American Council of Learned Societies (reproduced in *Biography Resource Center*. 2002. Farmington Hills, Mich.: The Gale Group).

Horton, John T. 1969. *James Kent: a Study in Conservatism, 1763–1847*. New York: D. Appleton-Century, 1939. Reprint, New York: Da Capo Press.

Kierner, Cynthia A. 1992. *Traders and Gentlefolk: The Livingstons of New York, 1675–1790*. Ithaca, N.Y.: Cornell University Press.

McDonald, Forrest. 1979. *Alexander Hamilton: A Biography*. New York: W. W. Norton.

Mitford, John. 1816. *A Treatise on the Pleadings in Suits of the Court of Chancery, by English Bill*. New York: R. M. Dermut and D. D Arden.

Scott, James Brown. 1907. "Robert R. Livingston." In *Great American Lawyers: A History of the Legal Profession in America*, vol. 1, edited by William Draper Lewis. Philadelphia: John C. Winston Company.

LUMPKIN, JOSEPH HENRY

(1799–1867)

JOSEPH HENRY LUMPKIN

Hulton Archive

JOSEPH HENRY LUMPKIN, Georgia's first chief justice, played an important role in establishing the state supreme court on a firm foundation. Under his leadership, the court overcame widespread opposition to centralized judicial authority, which had kept Georgia from establishing a high court until 1845, more than fifty years after it became a state. In one of his earliest opinions, *Choice v. Marshall*, 1 Ga. 97 (1846), Lumpkin made his judicial philosophy clear: "We are prepared, although in our *judicial infancy*, to advance to the front rank in this warfare of principle against precedent. Beyond that, we dare not go. Judges cannot alter a law. . . . Their business is to declare what the law is, and not what it ought to be" (106).

Lumpkin was born near Lexington in Oglethorpe County, Georgia, the ninth of eleven children of John and Lucy Hopson Lumpkin, who had moved there from Virginia in 1784. Although his older brother, Wilson, a two-term governor of Georgia and member of the U.S. Senate, did not attend college, Lumpkin started his undergraduate studies at the University of Georgia in 1816. When the university suspended classes following the death of its president, Lumpkin transferred to Princeton (then named the College of New Jersey), where he graduated with honors in 1819.

Following graduation, he returned to Lexington and studied law in the office of Thomas W. Cobb, whose career included service in the U.S. House and Senate and as a judge of the superior court. Lumpkin was admitted to the bar in 1820 and the following year married Callender Cunningham Grieve, a native of Scotland. His law practice flourished in an age of circuit-riding lawyers and judges as he established a reputation for hard work and effective advocacy.

He served one term (1824–1825) in the state legislature as an ally of Gov. George M. Troup, a staunch champion of states' rights in Georgia's long-running conflict with the federal government on a number of issues, but primarily over Creek Indian lands. Although Lumpkin never ran again for public office, he maintained an active interest in politics, changing his affiliation over time from the Troup faction at the state level to the regional State Rights party and then to the national Whig party. In a letter to one of his daughters in 1853, he described his political independence, writing that he generally voted the Whig ticket, "but if the Democratic candidate is the better man or my personal friend, I unhesitatingly vote for him, in preference to his Whig opponent" (Lumpkin, Joseph Henry. Papers).

Lumpkin's eloquence as a trial lawyer was noted by many of his contemporaries and, combined with his reputation for intellect and integrity, made him one of the most successful lawyers in the state at an early age. His expertise in criminal law led to his appointment, at age thirty-four, as one of three commissioners to draft a revision of the Georgia Penal Code, which was enacted in 1833. Because of the absence of a supreme court in Georgia prior to 1845, the superior court judges met periodically in convention to achieve greater uniformity among the judicial districts. The first report of their combined decisions was published in 1836 by G. M. Dudley, who included a commentary by Lumpkin, indicating the prominent position he had achieved in the legal profession by that time.

While he was building his legal practice, Lumpkin was also involved in various educational, religious, and reform activities. Throughout his life he promoted several ideas for state funding of public secondary schools, primarily aimed at developing qualified students for colleges and universities in the state, who could, in turn, become teachers. In 1820, he helped found a literary society at the University of Georgia and thereafter maintained an active interest in the university's affairs as a former student, parent, faculty member, and longtime member of the board of trustees.

Lumpkin was a devout evangelical Christian whose religious commitment began with his conversion experience at a Methodist camp meeting in the early 1820s. Although he was raised as a Baptist, he joined the Presbyterian Church in 1828 and was active throughout his life in many aspects of church governance. At the same time, he became deeply involved in the temperance movement at both the state and national levels. At the first National Temperance Convention at Philadelphia in 1833, he was named one of sixteen vice presidents, and he served as president of the state temperance society for ten years.

His early reformist views caused a good deal of controversy within Georgia on more than one occasion. In a speech he gave at Boston in 1833, which received substantial negative coverage in Georgia newspapers, he made a clear declaration of support for emancipation. Twenty years later, in *Cleland v. Waters*, 16 Ga. 496 (1854), however, he noted in hindsight that "the true character of the institution of slavery had not been fully understood and appreciated at the South; and that she looked to emancipation, in some undefined mode, in the uncertain future, as the only cure for the supposed evil" (514).

Even after he no longer supported emancipation, Lumpkin agreed in 1847 to become a vice president of the American Colonization Society, whose mission was to send freed blacks to Africa. In *American Colonization Society v. Gartrell*, 23 Ga. 448 (1857), however, he ruled against the society, stating that "I was once, in common with the great body of my fellow citizens of the South, the friend and patron of this enterprise. I now regard it as a failure, if not something worse" (464). By then, he had also become convinced that slavery was divinely sanctioned, claiming in his report on law reform to the Georgia legislature: "Being recognized and regulated by the Decalogue, it will, we have every reason to believe, be of perpetual duration" (*Southern Recorder*, 4 December 1849).

When Georgia's supreme court was finally created in 1845, Lumpkin was elected by the legislature to the longest term of the three original judges. He was from the outset, therefore, generally recognized as the presiding judge, although it was not until 1863 that he was officially made chief justice. There were many defects in the legislative design of the court, but the greatest burden facing Lumpkin and his fellow judges was a requirement that they hold sessions at least annually in nine different cities within the state's five judicial districts. Also, unlike appellate courts in some other states, where reviews were limited to points of law, the Georgia court had to examine all errors alleged in each bill of exceptions.

In its first full year (1846), the court reversed superior court decisions in forty-four of the seventy-two cases it reviewed. One of Lumpkin's opinions, *Nunn v. State*, 1 Ga. 243 (1846), has received considerable attention in recent years, because of his review of the constitutional right to bear arms and his conclusion that "the right of the whole people, old and young, men, women and boys, and not militia only, to keep and bear *arms* of every description, not *such* merely as are used by the militia, shall not be infringed" (251).

In a report submitted to the legislature in 1849, Lumpkin made a number of recommendations for legal reform in Georgia. He proposed a fusion of

Rufe McCombs
(1918–)

Born in Decatur, Georgia, in 1918, Rufe Dorsey Edwards decided that she wanted to become a lawyer when in 1924 she was inspired by watching attorney Schley Howard in court. On the same day, she felt unjustly treated when a judge, citing her age, refused to allow her to tell her own story about how a neighbor girl had hurled a stone that had hit her in the head and resulted in the loss of much of her vision in one eye.

Overcoming an additional problem with stammering in her youth, some of which was spent in Jacksonville, Florida, Rufe eventually won a speaking award as a high school senior and went to Duke University on scholarship but later transferred to the University of Georgia. There she met her future husband, Mac McCombs, and was accepted into the Lumpkin Law School, where she was a student editor of the *Georgia Bar Journal*. During her schooling there, she reported that a professor asked her not to attend classes during his discussion of the law related to rape (McCombs 1997, 82).

When Edwards graduated, she found firms were more interested in her secretarial abilities than in her legal skills, and as World War II began, she was able to go to Washington, D.C., where she worked with the U.S. Department of Agriculture and became a hearings examiner. During that period she and Mac McCombs were married by Peter Marshall, who served with such distinction as a U.S. Senate chaplain. Later they moved to Atlanta, Georgia. She was there diagnosed with tuberculosis and had to quit her job and undergo long and painful treatments. She subsequently devoted time to raising a daughter, Grace, who was born in 1958.

When McCombs thought of returning to the legal profession, it was still difficult for women to find legal work, but she secured a job heading the Georgia Legal Services Program in Columbus, Georgia. She worked there from 1969 to 1975, secured a fair amount of attention, and successfully battled colon cancer, which required major surgery.

In 1975, McCombs successfully ran for a position as a Municipal Court judge in Columbus. She later discovered that she was the first woman in Georgia to win election to a judicial seat to which she had not been previously appointed (McCombs 1997, 167). McCombs, however, opposes affirmative action on behalf of women and has said that "Never have I wanted or sought a position based upon my gender" (168). When someone said that it was the right time for a woman to be elected to such a post, she said, "I'd much rather feel I got elected because I was qualified" (169).

(continues)

law and equity, following the example of David Dudley Field, author of New York's 1848 Code of Civil Procedure. He also sided with such noted legal reformers as Justice Joseph Story and Timothy Walker in promoting codification of Georgia's laws and argued that "it is right that every man should be enabled to read and understand the law for himself—and for this

(continued)

In 1978 McCombs ran unopposed for a state court judgeship. Once faced with an immigrant from China who wanted to give a special oath that involved dismembering a chicken, McCombs instead persuaded him to give an oath "as grandfather to grandmother" (McCombs 1997, 178). On another occasion, she had a bailiff escort out a visitor who had come to her courtroom dressed in a shower cap, a terry cloth robe, and pink slippers by noting that, as judge, she was the only one in the court permitted to wear a robe. As a judge, McCombs was often publicly critical of higher federal judges who she believed had strayed from their jobs as jurists into that of legislators.

In 1982 McCombs successfully ran against Albert Thompson (the first African American appointee in the position in Georgia) to become a Superior Court judge, but she did not make race an issue and believes that Thompson was hurt by a controversial decision he had made invalidating the death sentence for a juvenile. She later recalled a divorce case when she was a Superior Court judge, in which an attorney was questioning a witness about her marital faithfulness. After first claiming to have been absolutely faithful to her spouse and denying any extramarital affairs, the woman then said, apparently much to her counselor's chagrin, "Well, no one besides *my own attorney*" (McCombs 1997, 193). Initially opposed to capital punishment, McCombs says that her service on the court persuaded her that this penalty was sometimes appropriate. Throughout her career, McCombs found that people were sometimes surprised to see a female in her position. On one occasion where she did not realize the mistake until they were on their way, McCombs allowed her husband to speak before a college audience that had invited "Mr." Judge McCombs to speak.

Georgia has a mandatory retirement age for judges at seventy-five, but since retiring from her position, McCombs has continued to hear cases as a senior Superior Court judge. McCombs believes that perfect justice can only be established by God; in the meantime, humans have to do the best they can. McCombs recalls walking as a girl in her mother's shadow and watching their silhouettes: "I believe Justice seeks out Truths—the shadow of God. Too often though, Justice fails to see anything but its own silhouette. In order to find Truths, Justice must arch its back and walk uprightly. Human justice is a puny reflection of absolute Truths, but until God reveals to us more than just His shadow, it is our best hope" (McCombs 1997, 218).

Reference:

McCombs, Rufe, with Karen Spears Zacharias. 1997. *Benched: The Memoirs of Judge Rufe McCombs*. Macon, Ga.: Mercer University Press.

purpose it should be divested of all technicality and intricacy, as far as possible" (*Southern Recorder*, 4 December 1849).

As the sectional conflicts over slavery grew more intense, Lumpkin became increasingly concerned about the need for economic reform in Georgia and elsewhere in the South in order to achieve greater self-sufficiency. In his speeches as well as his judicial opinions, he promoted reduction of the South's dependence on agriculture and development of a more balanced economy by encouraging business and banking. In *Young and Calhoun v. Harrison and Harrison*, 6 Ga. 130 (1849), he wrote: "Civilization must advance; the improvements of society, diffusing plenty and prosperity, knowledge and refinement and morality all around, must not, cannot be restrained" (149).

He took a pragmatic approach to balancing economic interests, a decisionmaking approach that has been termed "legal instrumentalism" in recent years. In *Hightower v. Thornton*, 8 Ga. 486 (1850), he cited corporations as "proof, and in no small degree the cause of unparalleled advancement of modern civilization" (505), yet he also recognized a need to protect the poor and uneducated from the abuses of corporate powers. In *Mims v. Lockett*, 20 Ga. 474 (1856), he called for a change in the harsh common law rules, which still favored the rights of creditors over debtors in Georgia. His Protestant ethic, however, made him a strong believer in the need for hard work and self-reliance. Upholding a conviction for vagrancy in *Waddel v. State*, 27 Ga. 262 (1859), Lumpkin wrote, "I am quite satisfied that a large portion of the population of our towns could be convicted on stronger proof than this. It is time to give them a scare" (263).

During his service on the Supreme Court (1845–1867), Lumpkin wrote roughly one-third of the nearly 3,800 opinions contained in volumes 1 through 35 of the *Georgia Reports*. He authored more than half of the approximately sixty cases that dealt with important issues affecting the legal status of slaves, however, indicating that he had a strong interest in shaping Georgia's law as well as its public policy on slavery issues. Lumpkin's slavery opinions have probably received more attention from legal scholars over the past thirty years than those of any other southern jurist, with the possible exception of Thomas Ruffin. There was no uniform law of slavery among the southern states. As Lumpkin noted in *Bryan v. Walton*, 14 Ga. 185 (1853): "The condition of the African race is different in every slave State" and, therefore, "we must have recourse to our own local laws . . . and to such principles as are dictated by the peculiar genius of our people, and policy of our institutions" (199).

Economic factors were important considerations in many of his slavery decisions, as in *Cleland v. Waters*, 19 Ga. 35 (1855), in which he noted that "slaves constitute a portion of the vested wealth and taxable property of the State; that without them, a large part of our most productive lands would be worthless" (43). A number of his opinions reveal his racist and paternalistic views of blacks, but in *Cleland* he affirmed his religious conviction that "true, slaves are property . . . still they are rational and intelligent beings. Christianity considers them such . . ." (41).

Lumpkin's dedication to leading the Supreme Court caused him to turn down an appointment by Pres. Franklin Pierce to the newly formed federal court of claims in 1855 and also to decline a position in 1860 as the first chancellor of the University of Georgia. Even after Georgia's secession, his commitment to his role as chief justice was a factor in his declining Gov. Joseph Brown's offer of one of Georgia's seats in the Confederate Senate. The one diversion he did make from his judicial duties was in founding the law school at the University of Georgia in 1859. Lumpkin, his son-in-law, Thomas R. R. Cobb, and William Hope Hull formed the original faculty of what was initially chartered as the Lumpkin Law School.

The Supreme Court continued to hold sessions throughout the Civil War, and in *Edmonson v. Union Bank of Tennessee*, 33 Ga. 91 (1861), Lumpkin observed that President Lincoln was waging an "unnatural and unconstitutional war upon a portion of the states" (93). Five of his sons fought for the Confederacy, and his son-in-law, Thomas R. R. Cobb, was killed at Fredericksburg shortly after his promotion to brigadier general. In *Armstrong v. Jones*, 34 Ga. 309 (1866), Lumpkin commented that at the end "the Confederacy itself was extinguished, as completely as if its last champion had perished when Stonewall Jackson fell. Submission to the victorious North was absolute . . ." (312). Although his health was deteriorating in 1866, he still managed to write more than his usual one-third of the opinions issued by the court that year. The court held its first session of the following year on 4 June 1867 without him, and he died the next day at his home in Athens, Georgia.

Lumpkin is widely recognized as the most influential judge in Georgia during the early years of the Supreme Court. His political independence and leadership skills guided the court toward the front rank and earned him the highest respect from his fellow Georgians. Although he was an orthodox conservative in his pro-slavery views, he was also a proponent of economic, social, and legal reforms that would benefit the South while preserving its culture.

Paul DeForest Hicks

References and Further Reading:

Note: A collection of Lumpkin's papers is held by the Hargrett Rare Books and Manuscript Library at the University of Georgia. These include letters, mainly between Lumpkin and his daughter, Callie Lumpkin King, that are on loan to Hargrett from the Alexander King Law Library at the University of Georgia School of Law. Lumpkin's judicial opinions can be found in the *Georgia Reports*, vols. 1–35; see also the memorial to Lumpkin in volume 36.

Brantly, W. T. 1867. "Life and Character of Joseph Henry Lumpkin." Oration delivered in Athens, Ga., before the Phi Kappa Society. 5 August.

Hicks, Paul DeForest. 2002. *Joseph Henry Lumpkin, Georgia's First Chief Justice*. Athens: University of Georgia.

Huebner, Timothy S. 1991. "Encouraging Economic Development: Joseph Henry Lumpkin and the Law of Contract, 1846–1860." *Georgia Journal of Southern Legal History* 2 (Fall/Winter): 357–375.

———. 1992. "Joseph Henry Lumpkin and Evangelical Reform in Georgia: Temperance, Education and Industrialization, 1830–1860." *Georgia Historical Quarterly* 75 (Summer): 254–274.

Lumpkin, Joseph Henry. Papers. Hargett Rare Books and Manuscript Library at the University of Georgia.

Reid, John Phillip. 1982. "Lessons of Lumpkin: A Review of Recent Literature on Law, Comity and the Impending Crisis." *William and Mary Law Review* 23: 571–624.

Stephenson, Mason D., and D. Grier Stephenson. 1976. "To Protect and Defend: Joseph Henry Lumpkin, the Supreme Court of Georgia and Slavery." *Emory Law Journal* 25: 579–608.

MARSHALL, JOHN

(1755–1835)

John Marshall
Library of Congress

John Marshall was the firstborn son of Thomas Marshall (1730–1802) and Mary Randolph Keith Marshall (1737–1809) and was related through his mother to his future political rival, Pres. Thomas Jefferson. He was born near Germantown in Fauquier County, Virginia, on 24 September 1755 and educated at home by his mother and tutors. Subsequently, he was tutored by the Reverend Archibald Campbell at the Campbelltown Academy, where James Monroe was a fellow student. The Reverend James Thomson, an Episcopal clergyman from Scotland, completed Marshall's classical training with further tutoring. Both Marshall and his father joined the specially trained Virginia militia units as war with Britain became imminent in 1774 and 1775. After commissioned service in the Culpeper Minutemen and the Virginia Continental Line (1775–1779), John Marshall attended about three months of law lectures delivered by George Wythe at the College of William and Mary in 1780. While pursuing his studies he met and began his courtship of Mary Willis Ambler (1766–1831), whom he married on 3 January 1783.

Admitted to practice by the county court of Fauquier County on 28 August 1780, Marshall soon became active in local politics. Elected to represent Fauquier County in the Virginia House of Delegates (May 1782), he resigned his seat on 30 November 1782 to take his place as a member of the

Council of State, where he served for seventeen months. After his move to Richmond in early 1783, Marshall was again elected a Fauquier delegate in May 1784, doubtless qualifying by land ownership in Fauquier rather than by residence. Thereafter, he represented the city of Richmond, or Henrico County, from 1785 through 1788, in 1789 through 1790, and in 1795. In the House of Delegates he was a strong voice for national unity and for fiscal integrity in international and interstate transactions. As a Henrico district delegate to the June 1788 Virginia Ratifying Convention, Marshall was chosen by his proratification colleagues to refute arguments against the proposed federal judiciary and to deliver two other speeches supporting ratification of the federal Constitution.

Marshall's only judicial experience prior to his appointment as chief justice of the United States Supreme Court was a two-and-a-half-year term as recorder of the Richmond City Hustings Court (1785–1788). As an elected member of the Richmond City Common Hall, he was automatically a member of the Hustings Court, which was the municipal equivalent of Virginia's county courts, exercising broad general jurisdiction in civil cases and minor criminal jurisdiction in misdemeanors and acting as an examining court in the case of felonies. In trials of accused slaves, however, the Hustings Court exercised felony jurisdiction, including the power to impose capital punishment. Traditionally, the recorder of the court was an attorney, who presided over Hustings Court proceedings and who also was charged with prosecution and defense of cases involving the city.

Following his 1783 relocation to Richmond, Marshall's practice shifted to the higher state courts—the General Court, the High Court of Chancery, and the Court of Appeals. He rapidly gained a reputation for skill and logic in oral argument and was an acknowledged leader of the Richmond bar by 1787. The practice was rich and varied, providing him with mercantile clients along the East Coast and opportunities to assist Revolutionary War veterans in disposing of pay certificates and utilizing land grants. Among his more famous clients was Robert Morris of Philadelphia (1734–1806), the "Financier of the Revolution," whose daughter would later marry Marshall's brother, James Markham Marshall. The extended litigation over the Fairfax proprietary between the Commonwealth of Virginia and the heirs of Thomas, Lord Fairfax (1693–1781), involved Marshall at first as attorney for the Fairfax interests and later as a purchaser of the manor lands set aside as the lord's private property. With the opening of the United States Circuit Court for Virginia in early 1790, Marshall's active state appellate practice was augmented by a large number of federal cases in which Marshall defended Virginia debtors against their pre-Revolutionary British creditors. This group of cases formed the basis for his only argument before the United States Supreme Court, *Ware v. Hylton* (3 Dallas 199 [1796]).

As an active and influential Virginia Federalist, Marshall was offered several federal appointments by President George Washington. The needs of his growing family, coupled with financial commitments to the purchase of Fairfax manor lands, forced him to devote his energies to law practice. Pres. John Adams persuaded Marshall to accept a diplomatic assignment as one of three special envoys to France in what would become famous as the XYZ Mission (1797–1798). The French Directory refused formally to receive the U.S. ministers, and French intermediaries suggested that a bribe was required before negotiations could began. Along with his colleagues, Charles Cotesworth Pinckney (1746–1823) and Elbridge Gerry (1744–1814), Marshall vehemently refused to offer a bribe, both as a matter of principle and because they considered that such an act would compromise U.S. neutrality between France and Britain. As spokesman for the group, Marshall became a hero in the United States when the text of his rejection letter was published by the Adams administration. His triumphal return to the United States marked a major step on his way to national political stature.

At George Washington's insistence, Marshall campaigned for and won a seat in the U.S. House of Representatives, where he served from 4 December 1799 to 8 May 1800, when he resigned to accept John Adams's appointment as secretary of state. While in the House, Marshall defended President Adams's decision to extradite Jonathan Robbins to Britain to stand trial for crimes committed on a British naval vessel. Marshall was also a member of the committee that drafted the short-lived Bankruptcy Act of 1800. As secretary of state he directed diplomatic negotiations with revolutionary France, which were finally stabilized by ratification of the Consular Convention of 1800. President Adams's frequent absences from the capital required that Secretary Marshall pass upon many official appointments and supervise the day-to-day operations of the federal government. When the chief justiceship fell vacant unexpectedly in late 1800 and prompt action was required by the circumstances, President Adams nominated Marshall for the position on 20 January 1801. Marshall's confirmation by the Senate a week later launched a thirty-five-year judicial career that markedly altered the course of U.S. constitutional history and reshaped both the administration and the public image of the United States Supreme Court.

As chief justice, John Marshall achieved three major goals: (1) He reshaped the institutional structure and decisionmaking process of the Supreme Court; (2) he exercised leadership both within the Court and in the political arena, emphasizing the Court's unanimity in the pronouncement of federal law; and (3) he established the foundations upon which the Court would become the most active and most respected propounder of U.S. constitutional law. All three aspects of his work became immediately apparent in the announcement of the Court's 1803 opinion in *Marbury v. Madison* (1 Cranch 137).

Marshall took his seat on the Supreme Court bench at a time when the Jeffersonian Republican party dominated both the legislative and executive branches. The Court was at perhaps the lowest level of prestige it ever reached in both professional stature and public support. Composed of relatively elderly justices, it delivered its opinions seriatim—that is, each justice speaking separately—and its time and energy were sapped by the statutory requirement that the justices ride circuit throughout the United States for the trial of cases at the United States circuit courts.

Marbury v. Madison, also known as the Mandamus Case, refused an invitation to issue a writ of mandamus to Secretary of State James Madison. The relief was requested by William Marbury, who had been commissioned a District of Columbia justice of the peace but whose commission had been withheld by the incoming secretary of state, James Madison. After upholding in principle Marbury's right to the commission, Marshall considered the Supreme Court's original jurisdiction in light of Article 3 of the federal Constitution. Since mandamus powers were not conferred upon the Supreme Court by the Constitution, Congress was incapable of so expanding the Court's authority by enacting the Judiciary Act of 1789. Pointing out that the Constitution was a superior body of law to which federal statutes were required to conform, Marshall held that it was the Court's duty to follow the Constitution and to hold the statute void. Since the lower federal courts had already utilized judicial review, as had several state courts, this concept was scarcely original to John Marshall. It did proclaim the Supreme Court's intention, however, judicially to review congressional statutes when appropriate cases were brought before it.

The *Marbury* opinion's promulgation early in Marshall's chief justiceship gave notice that the Supreme Court was entering a new era. The use of an "opinion of the Court" would become a characteristic not only of the Marshall Court but of most successive eras of the Court's history. Marshall's political astuteness and his persuasive talents among his colleagues have been standards against which future chief justices have been judged. Leadership qualities of the chief justices have been noted in terms of their achieving unanimity of opinions among their colleagues and also in regard to shaping and protecting the public image of the Supreme Court. In addition, the collegial atmosphere of the Marshall Court, shaped to a considerable degree by its social ostracism in Jeffersonian Washington, welded the justices into a self-protecting small group, willingly accepting the gentle but skillful efforts of Marshall toward "image building" and achieving consensus among differing judicial viewpoints. Finally, six days after the *Marbury* decision was announced, the Supreme Court, in an opinion delivered by Justice William

Paterson, upheld the Jefferson administration's constitutional power to require Supreme Court justices to ride circuit and try cases in the lower federal courts (*Stuart v. Laird,* 1 Cranch 299 [1803]). In *Stuart* the Court skillfully avoided a direct confrontation with the Republican-controlled Congress. By acquiescing in congressional authority to regulate the lower federal courts, it provided assurances that the Marshall Court would not use judicial review to inhibit legislative policymaking even in regard to the federal judiciary. Correspondence between the justices shows that Chief Justice Marshall was influential in gaining agreement concerning the Supreme Court's circuit-riding duties, even though he recused himself from participating in the decision because he decided the case below, in the United States Circuit Court for Virginia. This deference to congressional policymaking was also demonstrated by the Supreme Court's willingness to uphold the legality of Thomas Jefferson's 1807 embargo legislation.

Beginning with *Fletcher v. Peck* (6 Cranch 87 [1810]), Marshall began to expand the scope of the Constitution's contract clause (Article 1, section 10). Prohibiting state laws and actions that impaired the obligations of contract, the provision was doubtless intended by the framers to protect interstate and foreign commercial traders against state laws or court rules that inhibited the collection of debts. In *Fletcher* Marshall held that a state land grant obtained through bribery could not be revoked by a subsequently elected legislature if property rights had vested in innocent purchasers for value. Further extension of contract clause protection was sanctioned by Marshall's opinion for the Court in *Dartmouth College v. Woodward* (4 Wheaton 518 [1819]), which invalidated a New Hampshire state statute that purported to revoke the 1769 royal charter granted to Dartmouth College. Here the chief justice held that the state, by succession to the sovereign rights of the Crown, was precluded from destroying the educational institution whose charter had formed the basis upon which private donors contributed to its support. Both *Fletcher* and *Dartmouth College* found their origin in Marshall's belief that security of private property rights was essential to a stable and flourishing American economy. Although his primary reliance was upon enlarging the scope of the Constitution's contract clause, he also saw the sanctity of private property as one of the basic foundations of a republican polity. This broader basis upon which to protect property rights involved Marshall in what would be his first dissent in a constitutional law case. In *Sturgis v. Crowninshield* (4 Wheaton 122 [1819]), the Supreme Court, in an opinion delivered by Marshall, had invalidated a New York state insolvency law that altered rights of creditors that arose prior to the effective date of the statute. From the 1827 decision in *Ogden v. Saunders* (12 Wheaton 213), from which Marshall dissented, it becomes clear that *Sturges*'s narrowly focused opinion resulted from a compromise

Sir Edward Coke (1552–1634)

Although the U.S. Constitution led to some distinct differences, law in the United States continues to be shaped by the heritage of common, or judge-made, law, which was inherited from England (by contrast, judicial rulings in many European democracies are based on judicial application of the civil code, especially prominent in France and Spain). English judges undoubtedly shaped American expectations of what judges were supposed to do. Few, if any, British judges have been more important to either the history of England or that of the United States than Sir Edward Coke.

Born in Norfolk County, England, Coke attended Trinity College at Cambridge University, received his legal training at London's Inner Temple, and became a member of the bar in 1578. He rapidly rose in his profession and served in a number of high offices under Queen Elizabeth I, including that of solicitor-general, speaker of the House of Commons, and attorney general. Coke became particularly known for his ferocity as a prosecutor in the latter position as he took on Essex, Southampton, Raleigh, and the conspirators in the Gunpowder Plot aimed at blowing up Parliament.

James I, still known for his doctrine of the "divine right of kings," elevated Coke to chief justice of the common pleas and, later, to chief justice of the King's Bench, but in these positions Coke began to interpose the common law against increasingly broad claims of royal prerogative. Basically, James believed that he was accountable only to God, whereas Coke believed that the king was also under the common law. When James I claimed the right to preside over the Star Chamber, Coke objected that "the King cannot take any cause out of any courts and give judgment upon it himself" (Bowen 1957, 304). Coke's *Reports* continued with the story:

> Then the King said that he thought the Law was founded upon Reason, and That he and others had Reason as well as the Judges. To which it was answered by me, that true it was that God had endowed his Majesty with excellent science and great endowments of Nature. But his Majesty was not learned in the Laws of his Realm of England; and Causes which concern the life, or Inheritance, or Goods, or Fortunes of his Subjects are not to be decided by natural Reason but by the artificial Reason and Judgment of Law, which requires long Study and Experience before that a man can attain to the cognizance of it; and that the Law was a golden Metwand [metewand, or measuring rod] and Measure to try Causes of the Subjects, which protected his Majesty in safety and Peace: With which the King was greatly offended, and said that then he should be under the Law, which was treason to Affirm (as he said). To which I said that . . . the King should not be under man, but under God and the Laws. (304–305)

Many scholars regard *Bonham's Case* (1610) as a prelude to Chief Justice John Marshall's assertion of the power of judi-

(continues)

(continued)

cial review (to ascertain whether legislation adopted by Congress was constitutional) in *Marbury v. Madison* (1803). In *Bonham's Case*, involving the legitimacy of a fine imposed on an unlicensed doctor, Coke further extended judicial power over Parliament, declaring that "when an Act of Parliament is against common right and reason, the common law will control it and adjudge such Act to be void" (Bowen 1957, 315). Ironically, this idea survived better in America than in England, where the idea of parliamentary sovereignty was fairly firmly established by the time of the American Revolution and was, in fact, one of the primary bones of contention between the mother country and her colony.

Coke's primary conflict continued to be with the king rather than the Parliament. In one confrontation just before his dismissal from the chief justiceship of the King's Bench in 1616, all the justices except Coke agreed that they would stay the trial of a case involving the king's prerogative. Coke alone had responded "that when the case should be, he would do that [which] should be fit for a Judge to do" (Bowen 1957, 374).

Dismissed from his judicial post, Coke went on to lead parliamentary opposition to the king's assumption of prerogative powers—opposition that led the king to imprison Coke briefly in the Tower of London. Coke was also influential in the impeachment of Francis Bacon, his longtime nemesis. More than any other figure in England, Coke was responsible for utilizing the principles of the Magna Charta (1215) to defend the rights of Parliament and of the people. Coke increasingly became known as the "oracle" of the common law, and his influence persisted through a number of writings and reports, including his *Institutes*, the first volume of which (first published in 1628 and generally known as *Coke on Littleton*) continued to be a primary staple in the education of lawyers in early American history.

The last paragraph of Coke's *Institutes* indicated, in the language and spelling of his era, his understanding, rooted deep in common law, of the need for constant revision of the law:

> And for that we have broken the ice, and out of our owne industry and observation framed this high and honourable building of the jurisdiction of the courts, without the help or furtherance of any that had written of this argument before, I shall heartily desire the wide hearted and expert builders (justice being *architectonica virtus*) to amend both the method or uniformity, and the structure it selfe, wherein they shall finde either want of windowes, or sufficient lights, or other deficiency in the architecture whatsoever. And we will conclude with the aphroisme of the great lawyer [Edmund Plowden] and sage of the law (which we have heard him often say) *Blessed be the amending hand.* (Bowen 1957, 524)

References:

Bowen, Catharine Drinker. 1957. *The Lion and the Throne: The Life and Times of Sir Edward Coke*. Boston: Little, Brown.

Walker, David M. 1980. *The Oxford Companion to Law*. Oxford: Clarendon Press, 240–241.

among the justices engineered by the chief justice. In 1819 as in 1827, they were sharply divided over the contract clause's restrictions upon state legislation touching insolvency proceedings. By 1827 Marshall was forced into dissent to defend his minority position. Apparently he believed that by their agreement the parties were bound by their freely given consent reenforced by principles of natural law and that any state interference with contract rights violated the federal Constitution's contract clause.

The contract clause decisions underline Marshall's strong attachment to private property as the bedrock upon which a prosperous commercial economy and virtuous republic were based. To an extent this mirrored Lockean philosophy that relied upon individual initiative and sanctity of property to maximize the stability and prosperity of the entire community. In an age marked by the rise of the common man to the exercise of electoral power, Marshall's property-related decisions may seem in retrospect to have been constructed to form a legal foundation for the rise of capitalism. Yet Marshall did not consider private property rights to be absolute, and he readily upheld regulatory legislation when the exercise of governmental power was essential to protect the public welfare.

Similarly, Marshall's views of the federal union and the extent of the federal government's power cannot be simplified by classifying him a "nationalist," either in political or economic terms. In his view of the federal union there was a clear and precise acknowledgment that within the limited sphere of federal activity prescribed by the Constitution, there was an essential balance between the police powers reserved to the states and the broad grants of national authority contained in the Constitution's enumeration of federal authority. The classic expression of that tension occurs in the two classic commerce clause decisions: *Gibbons v. Ogden* (9 Wheaton 1 [1824]) and *Willson v. Black Bird Creek Marsh Company* (2 Peters 245 [1829]). *Gibbons* set forth a broad and comprehensive definition of the interstate commerce clause, providing a basis upon which virtually all economic activity might fall within federal regulatory power. Marshall took care, however, to recognize that in the execution of their constitutionally recognized police powers, the various states might legitimately touch upon matters already regulated by Congress, and in such situations state laws would not be unconstitutional. He expressly refused to hold that the commerce clause was vested exclusively in Congress, preferring to leave the extent of federal power delineation to future adjudication by the Supreme Court. Such an occasion arose in *Willson,* in which matters of public health and safety were arguably an adequate basis upon which the Court might overlook a technical state intrusion into Congress's right to control navigation upon tidal creeks. In a short opinion for the Court, the chief justice used a balancing approach to declare the state action constitutional.

A similar federal-state tension existed in regard to the exercise of federal power under the necessary and proper clause and the concurrent power of taxation as it existed in both federal and state governments. In what is probably Marshall's most forthright statement of federal supremacy, *M'Culloch v. Maryland* (4 Wheaton 316 [1819]), he held that the Bank of the United States was an instrumentality of the U.S. government, justified constitutionally under a doctrine of implied powers and by a broad construction of the necessary and proper clause (Constitution, Article 1, section 8). As such, the bank could not be subjected to an arbitrary and discriminatory Maryland tax upon its bank note issue. Since the bank drew its authority from the sovereign people of all the states, it was inimical to the principle of supremacy for such a federal instrumentality to be taxed by the sovereign people of only one state. On the other hand, the chief justice felt it necessary to point out that in areas where the state of Maryland might legitimately tax its own citizens, it might tax federal instrumentalities similarly situated, presumably limited to situations where the tax was not discriminatory.

Delineating Marshall's care and caution in setting forth principles of federal power should not detract from his substantial achievements both within the Supreme Court and in articulating judicial positions that enhanced the power of the federal government. To him is due the credit for regularizing conference procedure, opinion delivery, and decision delivery. These vastly strengthened the chief justice's control of the Court and provided an ostensible public image of unanimity among the justices. To him is due the politically wise and cautious consideration of cases on appeal and the use of jurisdictional technicalities to avoid confrontation with the coordinate branches of the federal government. Finally, to him is due the great achievement of his judicial generation—putting flesh and muscle upon the skeletal federal Constitution they had been given by the 1787 Philadelphia convention.

Herbert A. Johnson

REFERENCES AND FURTHER READING:

Beveridge, Albert J. 1916–1919. *The Life of John Marshall*. 4 vols. Boston: Houghton Mifflin.

Clinton, Robert L. 1989. *Marbury v. Madison and Judicial Review*. Lawrence: University Press of Kansas.

Currie, David P. 1985. *The Constitution in the Supreme Court: The First Hundred Years, 1789–1888*. Chicago: University of Chicago Press.

Faulkner, Robert K. 1968. *The Jurisprudence of John Marshall*. Princeton, N.J.: Princeton University Press.

Haskins, George L., and Herbert A. Johnson. 1981. *Foundations of Power, John Marshall, 1801–15*. Vol. 2 of *History of the Supreme Court of the United States*. New York: Macmillan.

Hobson, Charles F. 1996. *The Great Chief Justice: John Marshall and the Rule of Law*. Lawrence: University Press of Kansas.

Johnson, Herbert A. 1998. *The Chief Justiceship of John Marshall, 1801–1835*. Columbia: University of South Carolina Press.

Kahn, Paul W. 1997. *The Reign of Law: Marbury v. Madison and the Construction of America*. New Haven, Conn.: Yale University Press.

Marshall, John. 1974–. *The Papers of John Marshall*. 10 vols. to date. Edited by Charles F. Hobson et al. Chapel Hill: University of North Carolina Press.

Newmeyer, R. Kent. 2001. *John Marshall and the Heroic Age of the Supreme Court*. Baton Rouge: Louisiana State University Press.

Rhodes, Irwin S., ed. 1969. *The Papers of John Marshall: A Descriptive Calendar*. 2 vols. Norman: University of Oklahoma Press.

Robarge, David. 2000. *A Chief Justice's Progress: John Marshall from Revolutionary Virginia to the Supreme Court*. Westport, Conn.: Greenwood Press.

Smith, Jean Edward. 1996. *John Marshall: Definer of a Nation*. New York: Henry Holt and Co.

White, G. Edward. 1988. *History of the Supreme Court of the United States*. Vols. 3 and 4: *The Marshall Court and Cultural Change, 1815–1835*. New York: Macmillan.

MARSHALL, THOMAS ALEXANDER

(1794–1871)

THOMAS ALEXANDER MARSHALL
Courtesy of Sara Zeigler

THOMAS ALEXANDER MARSHALL, a member of a Kentucky family with extensive political connections, served as a justice on the Kentucky Court of Appeals (at the time, the state's highest court) from 1835 to 1856 and again from 1866 to 1867. During his service on the court, Marshall held the position of chief justice multiple times. Although relatively little is recorded about his private life, his distinguished career in public service during one of the most turbulent periods in U.S. history marks him as a jurist of significant influence.

Marshall was born on 15 January 1794 in Woodford County, best known for its production of the items necessary to the profitable Kentucky "sins" of drinking bourbon, betting on the horses, and using tobacco. He was the second son of Humphrey Marshall, who played a leadership role in the successful effort to separate the territory that became Kentucky from Virginia. Humphrey Marshall wed a well-connected woman who shared his surname. Mary Marshall, mother of Thomas Alexander, was the sister of United States Supreme Court chief justice John Marshall, who authored key opinions that consolidated and solidified the power of the U.S. judiciary. Thomas

Alexander thus received an early education in politics, both legislative and judicial. In addition to observing his uncle's career, he was witness to his father's national-level political activity. Humphrey Marshall was elected to the U.S. Senate several times and ran as a staunch Federalist. In 1809, Humphrey's disagreement with another famous Kentuckian, Henry Clay, resulted in a duel, in which Clay was wounded. The Kentucky oath of office, given to all public officials, now requires that officials eschew participation in duels.

Given the harsh feelings between the elder Marshall and Henry Clay, it is ironic that Thomas Alexander married Eliza Price, the niece of Henry Clay, in 1816. Miss Price was reputed to be one of the loveliest women in Kentucky at the time. Certainly, for a young man with political aspirations, a niece of Henry Clay was a good "catch."

Thomas Alexander Marshall began his legal practice in 1816, after graduating from Yale in 1815 and studying law in Kentucky for a year. His political career began with a speech denouncing debt relief acts passed by the state legislature in late 1825 and early 1826. The acts resolved the state's fiscal challenges by authorizing the production of new currency and declaring it legal tender for all debts—past, present, and future. Marshall was a firm opponent, viewing the acts as both irresponsible and ineffective. Shortly afterward, Marshall was elected to the state legislature, beginning his term in 1826. He also served as a legislator at the national level, winning a single term to the U.S. House of Representatives in 1831.

It took little time for Marshall to move from the legislature to the judiciary. Like most states in the early nineteenth century, Kentucky used gubernatorial appointment as its means of judicial selection. Marshall was appointed to the high court by Governor Morehead in 1835 and was its chief justice from 1846 to 1849 and from 1854 to 1856. In 1849, Kentucky convened a constitutional convention, which altered the method of judicial selection from appointment to election. Kentucky was divided into four districts, each of which would select a judge for the Court of Appeals. At that time, Marshall expressed reluctance to run. He feared that his long tenure on the court had left him isolated from his constituents and incapable of winning the solid electoral support needed to retain his seat. Friends and colleagues prevailed upon Marshall to run, and he consented. His judgment about his political influence was proven incorrect—Marshall won his district by a significant margin.

During Marshall's tenure on the Court of Appeals, he had the opportunity to write on issues both mundane and divisive. Although most of the court's work focused on the crucial, but routine, work of building a body of precedent in matters such as contracts, probate, and marriage, the question of slavery dominated a number of key cases. Marshall declined to air his personal views on the slavery questions, and his opinions show a careful deference to the actions of the legislature.

Marshall's decisions were characterized by a painstaking, almost mind-numbing attention to detail. A decision regarding a land patent (*Gossum v. Sharp's Heirs*, 37 KY 14) demonstrated a thorough knowledge of the particulars of the parties' arguments as well as the specific features of the parcel in dispute. Several paragraphs were devoted to the names given to two sinkholes on the property, lest there be confusion as to which sinkhole was to be improved by one of the parties. In this case, as in all of his opinions that I have reviewed, Marshall carefully analyzed each claim, identifying precedents to support the ruling. That said, Marshall was fully prepared to abandon those common law practices that, in the specific context, would produce absurd results. The law was to be useful, practical, and flexible. Marshall clearly articulated this position in the case of *Turman v. White's Heirs*, in refusing to follow a well-established common law rule "as it is confessedly an arbitrary rule, out of the reach of common men, and not accordant with their notions of the meaning and effect of language; as it was founded upon a state of things which has not existed for centuries in England, and never in this State, and as it was intended to advance a policy at war with our institutions, and of which there has never been a trace in our State" (14 Monroe 56, 1854).

Marshall showed no inclination to depart from tradition in his rulings on marriage law. His opinions on marital disputes were consistently conservative and directed toward the preservation of the union, happy or unhappy, regardless of the preferences of the parties involved. One biographer attributed Marshall's position to the happiness of his own marriage, which endured for over half a century (Wolf 1908). Endurance, of course, did not necessarily represent a blissful union in a state that strictly limited divorce. The Marshalls' marriage was widely regarded as a successful union, however, and may have influenced Marshall's views. In denying relief to a wife who attempted to sue her husband for violating the terms of a privately drafted separation agreement, Marshall offered a rare glimpse into his personal opinion on the centrality of the marital institution to the moral integrity of a well-ordered state.

> The principle involved, however, is of deeper consequence than the mere adherence to the doctrine of the common law in relation to the disability of the husband and wife to contract with each other. The disability is itself founded in the wisest policy, and is an essential muniment *[sic]* to the inviolability of the nuptial contract, and to the maintenance of the institution of marriage.

> The well-being of society, as well as the policy of the law and the objects and duties of the marital contract require, that those who are united in marriage should live together. The law, indeed, furnishes, and can furnish, no coercive remedy for enforcing this duty. But, in addition to the inducements which are held out by the law of nature and the customs of society, in this very disability to contract with each other, in the utter incapacity, by their own mere will, to absolve each other from the reciprocal rights and duties which the law of their contract has imposed upon them, in the consequent dependence of the wife upon the husband, and the continued liability of the husband to support the wife, the law furnishes powerful motives, which operate most strongly upon those who might be least moved by other considerations, to the promotion of harmony and peaceful cohabitation in married life. (*Simpson v. Simpson*, 34 KY 141–142, 1836)

The most contentious political problem of Marshall's day was slavery, and there is no shortage of Court of Appeals cases on that issue in Kentucky. Although Kentuckians were more ambivalent about the "peculiar institution" than their neighbors farther to the south, Kentucky remained a slave state until the adoption of the Thirteenth Amendment in 1865. The fact that it bordered the North (and thus was on the route to freedom for fugitive slaves) complicated matters for Kentucky legislators and judges. Marshall's own views on slavery (unlike his clearly articulated perspective on marriage) were not clear. He was known as a strong proponent of states' rights but also as a staunch supporter of his uncle-by-marriage and noted abolitionist Henry Clay. There is no evidence that Marshall himself owned slaves.

In his judicial opinions, Marshall steered a safe course between the claims of the two competing factions, upholding pro-slavery laws without lauding them. In *Graves v. Allan* (52 KY 190, 1852), a case involving the will of a "free man of color" that granted bequests to his enslaved relations, Marshall ruled slaves could not hold bequeathed property because, like married women, they did not enjoy property rights. Yet Marshall also denied the slaveowners' claim to the same property, claiming that a bequest to their slaves was not the legal equivalent of a bequest to the owners. In short, Marshall declared the will to be utterly unenforceable, despite his affirmation of the testator's right to make bequests generally. The case maintained a delicate balance, recognizing the full legal rights of the freeman as well as the validity of laws denying those same rights to slaves.

Marshall also demonstrated a willingness to uphold antislavery statutes, holding constitutional an 1833 law prohibiting the importation of slaves into Kentucky (*Commonwealth v. Griffin*, 42 KY 208, 1842). Marshall's most famous opinion, the holding in *Strader v. Graham* (39 KY 350, 1840), again shows his unwillingness to take a political stand on slavery and his adeptness at balancing competing claims. This was a case of some historical import, as it was appealed to the United States Supreme Court and affirmed by that body. In the case, a testator and slaveholder, Charles Wilkins, emancipated his slave, David, in Wilkins's will. The executors of the estate, however, deeded David to one Mr. Snead, a creditor of Wilkins, upon determining that the resources remaining to the estate were insufficient to meet Wilkins's obligations to his creditors. Carefully analyzing the relevant (and conflicting) statutory law relating to the transfer of human property and the right of a testator to emancipate a slave, Marshall ruled that the executors could not reverse David's emancipation to meet obligations to creditors. The creditor Snead, however, could seek relief in Chancery, and David, as a beneficiary of the will, might well be required to satisfy the debt. Given that David's sole asset was his labor, he might well be committed to involuntary servitude in order to satisfy the debt, reversing the emancipation in fact if not in law. But that was a matter for Chancery, and Marshall withheld his thoughts.

During much of his tenure on the Court of Appeals, Marshall served as a professor of law at Transylvania University in Lexington (1836–1850). His elected term on the Court of Appeals ended in 1856, and Marshall returned to private practice. In 1866, Yale honored Marshall by conferring upon him the degree of doctor of laws. During that same year, Chief Justice Simpson died, and Marshall was appointed by the governor to complete the term as chief justice. In 1867, Marshall retired to private life, after performing that last public service for the state of Kentucky. He died in 1871, at the age of seventy-seven.

Sara L. Zeigler

References and Further Reading:

Levin, H., ed. 1982. *The Lawyers and Lawmakers of Kentucky*. Easley, S.C.: Southern Historical Press.

Lockwood, Evelyn. 1983. *Index to Kentucky Legal History: References to Selected Sources of Information concerning the Eighteenth and Nineteenth Centuries*. Frankfort, Ky.: The State Law Library.

"Marshall, Thomas Alexander." The Biographical Directory of the United States Congress: 1774–present. Available at <http://bioguide.congress.gov>.

Marshall Family Papers, 1815–1871. Filsom Club Historical Society, Louisville, Ky.

Wolf, Morris. 1908. "Thomas Alexander Marshall." In *Great American Lawyers: A History of the Legal Profession in America*, Vol. 4, edited by William Draper Lewis. Philadelphia: The John C. Winston Company, 299–327.

MARTIN, FRANÇOIS-XAVIER

(1762–1846)

FRANÇOIS-XAVIER MARTIN
Louisiana Historical Society

FRANÇOIS-XAVIER MARTIN served as judge of the Superior Court, Territory of Mississippi (1809–1810); judge of the Superior Court, Territory of Orleans (1810–1813); attorney general of the state of Louisiana (1813–1815); judge of the Supreme Court of Louisiana (1815–1836); and chief judge of the Supreme Court of Louisiana (1836–1846). From his seat on the bench and through voluminous writings and compilations, Martin helped standardize and Americanize Louisiana's judicial system during the antebellum era.

Born in Marseilles, France, on 17 March 1762, into a successful merchant family, Martin received his education at home under the tutelage of the family's priest. In 1782, Martin traveled to Martinique, where he joined an uncle who supplied provisions for the French navy. After that business failed, Martin ventured in 1784 to New Bern, North Carolina, where he eventually became a printer's assistant and, after a period of training, opened his own printing business. Once that concern was running smoothly, he began studying law. Martin later became a U.S. citizen.

Martin gained a firm knowledge of the common law, was admitted to the North Carolina bar in 1789, hung his shingle, and developed a thriving practice. In his spare moments, he wrote a series of treatises on duties and, in 1802, translated into English Robert Pothier's *Treatise on Obligations Considered from a Moral and Legal View.* Thanks to his success as a printer, the North Carolina legislature hired him to compile the statutes from the state's territorial period and, later, a revised version of the general assembly's acts from throughout its history. In 1806, Martin won his own seat in the House of Commons.

On 7 March 1809, Pres. James Madison appointed Martin superior court judge of the Mississippi Territory. A year later, on 10 March 1810, Madison appointed Martin to the same position in the Territory of Orleans. The Orleans Territory included most of modern Louisiana and consisted of a hodgepodge of cultures, nationalities, and religions plus divergent political and legal traditions.

Martin's most significant actions in Louisiana would revolve around his work in Americanizing the state's judicial system by synthesizing Anglo-American common law practices with French and Spanish civil law traditions. A judicial system based on civil law constrained judges to reach decision by referring only to state-imposed, written law codes. Civil law allowed for little judicial independence and creativity, as judges presented their decisions by listing relevant code citations. Spain and France utilized the civil law system, and it thus had been the primary focus for colonial Louisiana law. Common law, on the other hand, prevailed in the Anglo-American colonies. It flowed from a number of different legal streams—judicial decisions, customs, legislation—and allowed for more freedom and power on the part of judges in creating rulings and through the stare decisis concept, which allowed judicial interpretation of laws and held that judgments rendered became part of the common law. Louisiana's judicial system eventually combined elements of civil and common law, but this outcome was by no means determined in the early 1800s. Creole inhabitants strongly supported a civil form, whereas more recent American transplants favored common law.

The law that created the Orleans Territory had not required usage of the common law, but Pres. Thomas Jefferson wanted the territory to become more like other U.S. states and territories, so he urged Gov. W. C. C. Claiborne to foster the common law's use. Jefferson and Claiborne knew, however, that changing from strictly civilian to strictly common law would create conflict with the inhabitants. Therefore, the territory's first legal compilations emanated from a civil law outlook and included a mixture of French and Spanish precedents with smaller instances of Anglo-American common law. Despite this, common law proponents, most of whom were not Louisiana natives, almost immediately began to institute Anglo-

American practices. American lawyers trained in the common law poured into the territory, and almost all of the judges appointed in that period had trained in the common, not the civil, law.

Martin, as a native of France with technical skill in the common law, proved uniquely qualified to serve as an active participant in the blending of legal traditions. The court he joined in 1810 possessed exclusive jurisdiction in capital cases, jurisdiction in criminal cases with possible prison sentences of more than six years, and original and appellate jurisdiction in civil cases of more than $100. It was the territory's only court of appeals. Judges served four-year terms, held jurisdiction over separate districts, and earned $2,000 per year. The judges traveled among five appellate districts.

The territorial supreme court lacked uniformity and standardization—each of the three judges was entirely autonomous and the code of laws then in force, stemming as it did from complex and varied antecedents, confused more often than it illuminated. Martin found such disorder unsuitable and drew on his past experience as a printer and compiler to publish case reports. The reports allowed judges to know what was going on in each other's courts and also provided much needed information for the general public.

The most important of Martin's early decisions dealt with slavery. The Orleans Territory's sizable population of free persons of color presented legal difficulties with which most other southern states did not have to deal. In *Adele v. Beauregard* (1810), Martin declared that descendants of Indians, of one white parent, or of free black parents could be considered persons of color, as opposed to pure Africans, who were to be presumed slaves. This argument became important in subsequent court decisions, especially in cases of slaves petitioning for freedom.

When the Orleans Territory became the state of Louisiana in 1812, its new constitution called for a state supreme court modeled after other U.S. state courts. This new court consisted of between three and five judges (they were not referred to as justices), appointed by the governor, who served until retirement or removal and earned $5,000 per year. The new court had no jurisdiction over criminal matters, but it did establish rules for bar admissions. The court met in one of two districts: the eastern, headquartered in New Orleans, and the western, based originally in Opelousas. Martin served on the committee to create the rules and regulations of the court.

Martin became Louisiana's first attorney general in 1813. He did, however, go before the court at its very first meeting to be admitted, along with seven other lawyers, as an inaugural member of the state bar. Following the resignation of one of the original members, Martin became a judge of the Supreme Court on 1 February 1815.

At the time of Martin's appointment, the War of 1812 had just ended, and Gen. Andrew Jackson controlled New Orleans. Jackson had declared martial law, and his declaration led directly to Martin's earliest ruling. Even after the British threat to New Orleans faded, the general had ordered arbitrary arrests and imprisonments, arrested federal district judge Dominick Hall, and attempted to stop the Louisiana Supreme Court from meeting. In Martin's first ruling from the court, he judged that Jackson's martial law was illegal and represented nothing more than a usurpation and suspension of powers granted the courts by the people.

In 1816, the Louisiana legislature called for the first comprehensive compilation of territorial and state laws, and Martin, experienced in this sort of task, took the job. Within a year, he produced the three-volume *A General Digest of the Acts of the Legislature of the Late Territory of Orleans and of the State of Louisiana, and the Ordinances of the Governor under the Territorial Government*. The *General Digest* included all ordinances issued by territorial and state governors, all legislative acts, and pertinent public documents. Martin arranged the laws by topic while maintaining their original wordings. The book came out in both French and English and, like his earlier reports, is yet another example of Martin's emphasis on uniformity.

The continued search for judicial and legal uniformity can also be seen in Martin's case reports. Since arriving in Louisiana, he had collected copies of other courts' decisions and made notes on his own. He later added these to his series of case reports, the *Orleans Term Reports* and *Louisiana Term Reports*, which contained the Supreme Court's judgments, the former for the territorial period and the latter for the state. Each report included a case summary, arguments made, and decision rendered. The first two volumes had been completed by 1813, when he took a break while serving as attorney general. He resumed his task following his appointment as Supreme Court judge. By 1830, he published another seventeen volumes. Martin saw the reports as a way of combating the lack of uniformity in addition to sheer lack of knowledge about judicial decisions, and the *Reports* became vastly useful: Judges and lawyers used them to establish precedents, and legislators used them as references while creating laws.

By 1830, the state's growth and the court's expanded jurisdiction made the job increasingly difficult. In 1836, Martin, by then completely blind, replaced George Mathews as chief judge of the Louisiana Supreme Court.

Besides helping to standardize and unify the Louisiana judiciary through his writings, as a judge of the Supreme Court, Martin participated in the bringing of Anglo-American common law practices to Louisiana's judicial system. Perhaps more than any other instance, Martin's ruling in *Reynolds v. Swain* (1839) solidified the dominance of the common over the civilian law and helped define the role of the judiciary in Louisiana.

Reynolds v. Swain established the judiciary's role in light of the Louisiana Code of 1825 and certain statutes of 1828 that had repealed all laws preceding the 1825 code. The case centered on a verbal agreement for the rental of a New Orleans tenement. Although the details of the case are not particularly relevant today, what is important is that the district court judge used *Christy v. Casanave* (1824) as a precedent in a favorable ruling for Reynolds. Swain et al. appealed to the Louisiana Supreme Court, where Thomas Slidell presented their case. Although Slidell presented a technical argument that the verbal agreement should not have been binding, his more important argument said that the *Christy v. Casanave* precedent could not have been used by the district court because it preceded the 1825 code and the repealing statutes that had disavowed all previous law. The big question facing the Martin court in 1839 was this: Did Louisiana judges have to base their decisions only on the Louisiana Code of 1825? In other words, would civil law triumph, or would the common law be maintained?

Martin, knowing the future implications of the court's actions, wrote the decision himself. After quickly dispensing with Slidell's first argument, the chief judge turned his attention to the second, and more important, matter. Martin said that, although the 1825 code and the 1828 repealing statutes had indeed nullified all previous laws, they only extended to those laws directly addressed by them. He also declared that the code and statutes only applied to laws, not previous judicial decisions.

Thus, in one decision, Martin not only upheld the lower court's decision but also validated the idea that, although law codes were important for judicial decisions, they did not provide the sole authority for decisions. The *Reynolds v. Swain* decision ended any notion that the court should be restricted by a civilian code. In reality, the decision did not change much in the court's actual proceedings; it really only justified what the court had been doing for decades. It provided the most enduring legacy of Martin's tenure as chief judge of the court and proved to be the culmination of the Louisiana judiciary's Americanization in the antebellum period.

For all of his earlier positive impact on the Louisiana judiciary, and although he rendered perhaps his most important decision in 1839, in his later years Martin proved an obstacle to progress. By February 1839, retirements left Martin as the only judge on the court. His solitary position, in addition to basic procedural flaws and a rapidly increasing caseload in the wake of the Panic of 1837, led to a logjam on the court's dockets. Even the appointment of two young and enthusiastic judges, George Eustis and Pierre Adolph Rost-Denis, in early 1839, could not speed up the situation. Eustis and Rost-Denis gave up considerable economic enticements to join the court, but, facing Martin's obstinate refusal to reform the court's operations, they both resigned within a few months of their appointment. Martin, once a path breaker in judicial matters, had become so conservative and set in his ways that he refused to accept change.

Eventually, with the appointment of several capable judges in late 1839, the court's business sped up somewhat, but not enough to diminish the mountain of pending cases. Public outrage over the overwhelming caseload led, in part, to the calling of a constitutional convention in 1845. The new constitution restructured the state's judicial system, instituting an eight-year limit on judges' terms. On 18 March 1846, the date of the reconstituted court's first meeting, Martin retired from the bench. Nine months later, on 12 December 1846, he died.

Besides his importance from a legal and judicial standpoint, Martin led a life marked by intellectual and pecuniary pursuits. He received honorary doctorates from both the University of Nashville and Harvard University and was a member of the Order of Ancient Free and Accepted Masons and the Academy of Marseilles. Outside the courtroom, Martin's interest in history led to the publication of his *History of North Carolina* (1806–1807) and the *History of Louisiana from the Earliest Period* (1827–1829).

Martin lived a miserly existence. Stern and serious by temperament, his appearance tended toward the slovenly and unkempt. Contrary to his spendthrift look, however, Martin exhibited a talent for accumulating material wealth. He had extensive real estate holdings in New Orleans, made interest-bearing loans to friends and associates, and even used his influence as a judge to pressure the state to buy copies of his *Digests* and *Reports*. By the time he died in 1846, Martin had amassed a fortune of $400,000.

Martin's wealth, combined with his blindness, led to the extension of his influence on Louisiana judicial traditions even after his death through a dispute over his will. A lifelong bachelor with no children, Martin left everything he owned to his brother, Paul Barthelemy Martin, also of New Orleans, by means of an olographic (written in his own hand) will. The will created unexpected problems for Paul Martin, however. Louisiana attorney general William A. Elmore filed a motion to have the will invalidated, claiming that Paul had faked the will, that François-Xavier could not have written it himself due to his blindness, and that François-Xavier had actually planned on leaving his wealth to relatives in France. Elmore argued that the will had been created to get around an 1842 law that provided for a 10 percent tax on estate wealth distributed overseas; Paul had been set up as sole heir so that he could redistribute the money to their French relatives without having to pay the tax. After witnesses for both sides testified, Judge E. A. Canon, on 15 March 1846, ruled that the attorney general had been correct in challenging the ruling, that François-Xavier Martin could not have written the olographic will without help, and that he had intended to evade the estate tax law.

Ellen Morphonious (1929–)

Although presidents appoint federal judges with the advice and consent of the Senate, many state judges are elected. Candidates for judgeships are frequently able to appeal to the sentiment of the public, often disgusted and frightened by rising crime rates, by stressing how hard they will be on criminals. Ellen Morphonious appears to be such a judge.

Born Lydia Ellen James in a small wooden house without running water or indoor plumbing in North Carolina in 1929, Ellen grew into a beautiful blond woman who modeled and participated in beauty contests before serving as a legal secretary in Florida. It was in that position that she decided to become an attorney, obtaining entrance to the University of Miami Law School, as was then possible, despite the fact that she had not received an undergraduate education.

Despite three pregnancies in law school resulting in two sons and one stillbirth, Morphonious (by then using the name of her first husband) graduated and joined former Florida governor Fuller Warren as a junior law partner. Her first case, before the Florida Supreme Court, involved a suit over her scores on the second bar exam (she failed the first time), which had apparently been lowered by one of Warren's enemies to keep her from passing; these scores were invalidated, and Morphonious passed on her third try.

Defeated in her first campaign for a judgeship in 1960, Morphonious continued work in politics and hosted a radio program, where she vented her conservative views. She subsequently became an assistant district attorney in Dade County, Florida. When she ran in 1970 for a judgeship of a felony court, she succeeded and quickly obtained notoriety for dispensing quick and stiff penalties. She kept a model

(continues)

Paul Martin's attorneys appealed the case to the Louisiana Supreme Court, where Justice Pierre Adolph Rost-Denis wrote the decision: Despite his blindness, François-Xavier Martin indeed could have written the will, and Paul Martin was the sole heir. Rost also admonished the government for bringing suit. Even from the grave, François-Xavier Martin influenced Louisiana's legal and judicial practices.

Michael S. Martin

References and Further Reading:

Billings, Warren M. 1984. "A Judicial Legacy: The Last Will and Testament of François-Xavier Martin." *Louisiana History* 25: 277–289.

Bullard, Henry A. 1997. "A Discourse on the Life and Character of the Honorable François-Xavier Martin, Late Senior Judge of the Supreme Court." In *An Un-*

(continued)

of an electric chair in her chambers as "a symbol of the ultimate form of justice and retribution" (Morphonious 1991, 261). She tried presiding over civil trials for a time but found that she enjoyed criminal work much more.

Known variously as "the Hanging Judge," "Maximum Morphonious," and "the Time Machine" for her stiff sentences, she had a way of capturing the public's attention both by what she did and said in the courtroom and by a tempestuous personal life. Married and divorced three times, Morphonious not only admitted to, but also described, a number of her extramarital affairs in a book written with the help of an editor of the *Miami Herald* (Morphonious 1991).

Being a woman at a time when women attorneys and judges were relatively rare might have made it more difficult to obtain a job as a prosecutor and win her first election. Morphonious admitted, however, that she once got a campaign supporter to persuade an opponent not to run against her when she ran for reelection by asking, "You don't want to get your ass whipped by a woman, do you?" (Morphonious 1991, 210).

Morphonious believes that her life experiences mellowed her during her years on the bench. She still takes pride in her judgments and believes that, although often tough, they were, for the most part, fair. She relishes the story of a man on trial in her court for attempted rape. The prosecutor was questioning the man's accuser: "And where did you shoot the defendant?" The woman answered, "In the groin." Morphonious's short response was not necessarily that of a typical judge. She replied, "Nice shot" (Morphonious 1991, 16).

Reference:

Morphonious, Ellen, with Mike Wilson. 1991. *Maximum Morphonious: The Life and Times of America's Toughest Judge*. New York: William Morrow.

common Experience: Law and Judicial Institutions in Louisiana, 1803–2003, The Louisiana Purchase Bicentennial Series in Louisiana History, vol. 13, edited by Judith Kelleher Schafer and Warren M. Billings. Lafayette: The Center for Louisiana Studies, 691–707.

Dart, Henry P. 1997. "The History of the Supreme Court of Louisiana." In *An Uncommon Experience: Law and Judicial Institutions in Louisiana, 1803–2003*, The Louisiana Purchase Bicentennial Series in Louisiana History, vol. 13, edited by Judith Kelleher Schafer and Warren M. Billings. Lafayette: The Center for Louisiana Studies, 566–611.

Ellis, T. C. W. 1997. "The Louisiana Bar, 1813–1913." In *An Uncommon Experience: Law and Judicial Institutions in Louisiana, 1803–2003*, The Louisiana Purchase Bicentennial Series in Louisiana History, vol. 13, edited by Judith Kelleher Schafer and Warren M. Billings. Lafayette: The Center for Louisiana Studies, 657–675.

Fernandez, Mark F. 1987. "From Chaos to Continuity: Early Reforms of the Supreme Court of Louisiana, 1845–1852." *Louisiana History* 28: 19–31.

———. 2001a. *From Chaos to Continuity: The Evolution of Louisiana's Judicial System, 1712–1862*. Baton Rouge: Louisiana State University Press.

———. 2001b. "Introduction: Louisiana Legal History: Past, Present, and Future." In *A Law unto Itself? Essays in the New Louisiana Legal History*, edited by Warren M. Billings and Mark F. Fernandez. Baton Rouge: Louisiana State University Press, 1–22.

Gaspard, Elizabeth. 1987. "The Rise of the Louisiana Bar: The Early Period, 1813–1839." *Louisiana History* 28: 183–197.

Jumonville, Florence M. 2001. "'The People's Friend—The Tyrant's Foe': Law-Related New Orleans Imprints, 1803–1860." In *A Law unto Itself? Essays in the New Louisiana Legal History*, edited by Warren M. Billings and Mark F. Fernandez. Baton Rouge: Louisiana State University Press, 40–57.

Pearson, Ellen Holmes. 2001. "Imperfect Equality: The Legal Status of Free People of Color in New Orleans, 1803–1860." In *A Law unto Itself? Essays in the New Louisiana Legal History*, edited by Warren M. Billings and Mark F. Fernandez. Baton Rouge: Louisiana State University Press, 191–210.

Pritchett, Carla Downer. 2001. "Case Law Reporters in Nineteenth-Century Louisiana." In *A Law unto Itself? Essays in the New Louisiana Legal History*, edited by Warren M. Billings and Mark F. Fernandez. Baton Rouge: Louisiana State University Press, 58–75.

Schafer, Judith Kelleher. 1994. *Slavery, the Civil Law, and the Supreme Court of Louisiana*. Baton Rouge: Louisiana State University Press.

———. 1995. "Roman Roots of the Louisiana Law of Slavery: Emancipation in American Louisiana, 1803–1857." *Louisiana Law Review* 56: 409–422.

———. 1999. "Martin, François-Xavier." In *American National Biography*, vol. 14, edited by John A. Garraty and Mark C. Carnes. New York: Oxford University Press, 591–592.

Wall, Bennett H., et al. 1990. *Louisiana: A History*. 2d ed. Arlington Heights, Ill.: Forum Press.

Wiethoff, William E. 1997. "The Logic and Rhetoric of Slavery." In *An Uncommon Experience: Law and Judicial Institutions in Louisiana, 1803–2003*, The Louisiana Purchase Bicentennial Series in Louisiana History, vol. 13, edited by Judith Kelleher Schafer and Warren M. Billings. Lafayette: The Center for Louisiana Studies, 374–386.

MCGOWAN, CARL EUGENE

(1911–1987)

Carl Eugene McGowan
Courtesy of Josephine P. McGowan Gardner

In her remarks at Judge McGowan's memorial service, Chief Judge Patricia M. Wald described McGowan in the following manner. "He was a Judge for all seasons: a worldly man who understood both government and politics, an intellectual who successfully examined every premise, a philosopher in search of principles to resolve the dilemmas of a modern Democratic society; a writer who knew how to say what he wanted his readers to know; a revered colleague steadfastly moving the court towards common ground" (Wald et al. 1988b, LXXXIX).

Many scholars consider the United States Court of Appeals for the District of Columbia Circuit to be second in importance only to the United States Supreme Court. Pres. John F. Kennedy appointed McGowan to this court in 1963. McGowan became the strong center of this court in the 1960s and 1970s. During that time the court confronted such landmark issues as freedom of the press and the Pentagon papers; national integrity and the Watergate prosecutions; the revolution in criminal defendants' rights; the restructuring of U.S. administrative law; the rights of congressional plaintiffs; tensions within the separation of powers; the reach of the president's treaty powers; and the privacy of presidential papers (Wald et al. 1988b, LXXXIX).

Supreme Court justice Lewis F. Powell Jr. noted that the Court of Appeals for the District of Columbia was a court widely respected as an authority on federal criminal law and procedures. Justice Powell went on to say that "during that period, Judge McGowan established a reputation as a thoughtful and philosophically neutral judge, whose informed vote often proved decisive on the issues at hand" (Powell et al. 1988, 681).

John H. Pickering, a member of the District of Columbia and New York bars, called McGowan a true "Washington lawyer" because of his experiences; his recognized expertise in public, administrative, and regulated law; and his deep conviction that private lawyers have public responsibilities. His expertise and scholarship made him a perfect choice for the District of Columbia Circuit where the principal focus is on the regulatory interplay between the public and the private sectors (Wald et al. 1988a, 222–223).

Carl E. McGowan was born on 7 May 1911 in Hymera, Indiana, to James W. and Gertrude Cooper McGowan. James McGowan was a grain miller by trade. In 1920 the McGowan family moved from Hymera to Paris, Illinois, where Carl completed elementary and high school, graduating as valedictorian of his high school class. He earned degrees from Dartmouth College in 1932, where he was elected to Phi Beta Kappa, and from Columbia Law School in 1936, which he attended on a full scholarship.

Carl McGowan married Josephine Perry of Boston, Massachusetts, in 1944. He and Josephine had four children—three daughters, Mary, Rebecca, and Hope, and one son, John.

McGowan began his legal career working for the Manhattan law firm now known as Debevoise and Plimpton from 1936 to 1939. In 1939 he left the law firm to join the faculty of the Northwestern School of Law in Evanston, Illinois. He served on the faculty until 1942, when he enlisted in the naval reserve. He was assigned to the Navy Department in Washington, D.C., where he worked with Adlai Stevenson. After the war, he briefly went into private practice in Washington, D.C. In 1948, he and his family moved back to Illinois, where he again joined the faculty at the Northwestern Law School. From 1949 to 1953 he served as counsel to the governor of Illinois under Adlai Stevenson. McGowan and Bill Blair were the co-architects of Stevenson's 1952 presidential campaign. In 1953 McGowan moved to Chicago and joined Ross, McGowan, Haries and O'Keefe, where he specialized in regulated industries. He remained with the firm until his appointment to the appeals court. McGowan also served as general counsel to the Chicago and North Western Railway from 1957 to 1963.

John F. Kennedy nominated Carl McGowan to the United States Court of Appeals for the District of Columbia Circuit on 15 January 1963. He was confirmed by the Senate on 15 March 1963 and received his commission on 27 March 1963. McGowan served as chief judge in 1981 and assumed senior status on 31 August 1981, serving in this capacity until his death on 21 December 1987.

McGowan served on the United States Court of Appeals for the District of Columbia Circuit during tumultuous times in the 1960s and 1970s. During those two decades the court ruled on a wide range of issues including freedom of the press, criminal defendants' rights, separation of powers, and privacy of presidential papers. Through all these decisions Judge McGowan quickly established himself as a centrist and pragmatic jurist whose nearly 500 opinions "were illumined by clear reason, lucid expression, sure wisdom and, not infrequently, surprising wit" (Wald et al. 1988b, LXXXIX). In addition to authoring some 500 opinions while on the court, McGowan also wrote twenty-five articles and ten book reviews for various law journals.

During his twenty-five-year tenure on the Court of Appeals for the District of Columbia, Judge McGowan sat on panels that decided issues involving four of the six presidents under whom he served. He sat on Watergate-related cases such as *United States v. Hunt*, 514 F.2d 270 (D.C. Circuit 1975); *Mitchell v. Sirica*, 502 F.2d 375 (D.C. Circuit 1974); and *Senate Select Committee on Presidential Campaign Activities v. Nixon*, 498 F.2d 725 (D.C. Circuit 1974). McGowan wrote the opinion in *Nixon v. Administrator of General Services*, 408 F. Supp. 321 (DDC 1976), which was later affirmed by the Supreme Court, 433 U.S. He also authored such important administrative law decisions as *Industrial Union Department, AFL-CIO v. Hodgson*, 499 F.2d 467 (D.C. Circuit, 1974) (Wald et al. 1988a, 214).

One of Judge McGowan's earliest, and one of his better-known, opinions was in *Luck v. United States* in which he questioned the fairness of impeaching criminal defendants who testified by automatically introducing evidence of other prior crimes. McGowan ruled that a trial court must weigh the prejudicial impact of the admission of a criminal defendant's record of prior crime in determining whether to admit that evidence to impeach the credibility of his testimony (Powell et al. 1988, 681–682).

Luck v. United States raised two issues. The first issue was the voluntariness of the defendant's admission to the police as testified to by the police officer when it was apparent that the defendant's counsel was about to raise an objection. Judge McGowan ruled that the handling of the issue of voluntariness raised by the counsel's objections did not comport with the procedural standards prescribed by the Supreme Court in *Jackson v. Denno*, 378 U.S. 368, 84 S.Ct. 1774, 12 L.ed.2d 908 (1964).

The second issue raised was the automatic introduction of a prior conviction by the prosecutor for impeachment purposes. The defendant argued that the prior conviction should not have been introduced on the grounds that the defendant had been a juvenile at the time of the earlier crime and that the conviction could not be introduced in evidence for any purpose including impeachment of credibility. The government contended that because at the time of the 1961 offense the juvenile court had waived jurisdiction over the appellant and he had been treated as an adult in the district court and sentenced under the Youth Corrections Act, this prior conviction was admissible for impeachment purposes. Judge McGowan ruled that the court agreed with the government that juveniles tried as adults could have their convictions introduced as evidence in a subsequent trial. The court disagreed, however, with the notion that the prosecution is always entitled to introduce an earlier conviction to impeach a defendant's testimony.

> To the extent, however, that the Government's position implies that the prosecution is always entitled to introduce a juvenile's earlier conviction as an adult following upon waiver of jurisdiction over him by the Juvenile Court, we do not agree. Section 305 is not written in mandatory terms. It says in effect, that the conviction "may," as opposed to "shall" be admitted; and we think the choice of words in this instance is significant. The trial court is not *required* to allow impeachment by prior conviction every time a defendant takes the stand in his own defense. The statute, in our view, leaves room for the operation of a sound judicial discretion to play upon the circumstances as they unfold in a particular case. (*Luck v. United States*, 348 F.2d 763 [1965])

The *Luck* Doctrine, as it came to be called, ultimately was adopted by a majority of the other circuits, and the trial court's discretion is now incorporated in Rule 609 of the *Federal Rules of Evidence* (Powell et al. 1988, 682).

Another one of McGowan's rulings that had national consequences was *Nixon v. Administrator of General Services*, decided in 1976. Former president Richard Nixon sued in federal court over the ownership and access to his presidential papers. In particular, he claimed that the Presidential Recordings and Materials Preservation Act, which was designed to allow public access to papers whose ownership he claimed, was unconstitutional on numerous grounds. These grounds included separation of powers, executive privilege, right to privacy, freedom of speech, freedom of association, equal protection under the law, and violation of the Bill of Attainder clause prohibiting legislative punishments without benefit of a trial.

A three-judge panel headed by Judge McGowan held that the act did not impinge separation of powers and did not violate any claim of the former president to executive privilege; that any intrusion on the former president's constitutional right to privacy was outweighed by the legitimate government objectives served by having the former president's materials screened by archivists; that any intrusion on the former president's freedoms of speech and association was more than balanced by the governmental interest involved; that the act did not deny equal protection to the former president; and that the act neither constituted a bill of pains and penalties nor a bill of attainder. In writing his opinion, Judge McGowan emphasized that the question before the court was narrow—"Is the regulatory scheme enacted by Congress unconstitutional without reference to the content of any conceivable set of regulations falling within the scope of the Administrator's authority under section 104(a)?" (*Nixon v. Administrator of General Services*, 408 F. Supp. 321 [1976]). The United States Supreme Court upheld Judge McGowan's ruling (433 U.S. 425, 1977).

Judge McGowan was also a legal scholar, writing twenty-five articles for various law journals during his tenure on the court. His scholarly focus was the role of the appeals court and the separation of powers among the three branches of government. His articles included one on presidents and their papers. The article traced the development and modification of the concept of private ownership of presidential papers, summarizing the historical development of the concept and the resultant problems. The article also reviewed the events and issues surrounding President Nixon's resignation and subsequent attempts to maintain ownership of his presidential papers. Finally, McGowan discussed Congress's attempt to resolve the question of private ownership through the passage of the Presidential Records Act and then described the problems that remained. In spite of these problems, McGowan believed that the Presidential Records Act of 1978 was important. He hoped that the preservation of papers relating to the federal government would also be good for Congress and for judges (McGowan 1983, 409–437).

McGowan's study of the appellate system and the expansion of its duties is especially relevant given the Court Reform Act of 1970. That act transformed and expanded the duties of the United States Court of Appeals for the District of Columbia Circuit. The law transferred trial and review of local civil and criminal cases to a newly enlarged and revitalized local District of Columbia court system. The law further gave the District of Columbia Circuit review over a vast number of federal administrative agencies' decisions that had previously been handled in other courts.

McGowan viewed the role of the appeals court with its functions of reviewing district court decisions and agency regulations, as well as adjudication of cases raising issues on which the Supreme Court had already spoken, as central to the court system.

> The role of the courts of appeals in resolving novel issues of constitutional law, however, is only half of the picture. Equally important is the appeals courts' adjudication of cases raising issues on which the Supreme Court has already spoken. Because the High Court can only sketch the broad outlines of constitutional DOCTRINE, it remains for the lower courts to apply prece-

dent, elaborate or clarify it, and extrapolate from it. Because appeal from the district courts to the appeals court is right and because most litigation never reaches the Supreme Court, it is in the courts of appeals that the Supreme Court's sketch is worked into a fully drawn landscape. (McGowan 1986c, 1942)

Several of McGowan's articles in the 1970s dealt with the relationship between Congress and the courts. Pointing out that, with the exception of the limited original jurisdiction reposed in the Supreme Court by the Constitution, the business of the federal courts depended on the affirmative action of Congress, McGowan described how the trend toward enlarging the duties of the courts was vastly accelerating. His own court had become increasingly preoccupied with civil litigation involving the federal government. This expansion of the duties of the appellate court, especially in the District of Columbia, had come about when Congress made broad delegations of authority to department heads or new commissions to implement regulations with provision for judicial review. Judicial review was tied to variously articulated standards—arbitrariness, rational basis, or substantial evidentiary support in the record (McGowan 1976, 1588–1589).

Judicial review of agency actions has become an important part of the appellate courts' activities. McGowan believed this role to be important in the checks and balances of power of the federal government. In a response to Judge Loren A. Smith, who described and criticized a trend toward "judicialization," McGowan defended the courts' role in review of agency actions, noting that the courts actually interfere with agency proceedings infrequently.

> What purpose does judicial review of agency action serve? The answer to this question is simple and clear. Judicial review serves as a check on the power of the administrative agencies. Given that Congress has the power, as in *Chaney*, to abolish judicial review in some areas of administrative law, the path chosen by Congress seems clear. Rather than directly controlling the agencies, Congress largely has chosen to use the courts as a check on administrative power. (McGowan 1986b)

Although McGowan agreed with the role of the courts in review of agency actions, he was also concerned with the growing caseload of the appellate courts with no corresponding increase in resources. In the late 1970s and early 1980s, Judge McGowan wrote several articles examining the increasing caseloads of the appellate courts while the Supreme Court was limiting the number of cases reviewed. In the late 1970s, Congress was considering legislation to reduce the caseloads in the appellate courts. The proposal was to abolish diversity jurisdiction of the appellate courts, whereby these courts heard civil cases between citizens of different states. Judge McGowan agreed with this concept, stating that the state courts could handle these types of cases.

A second trend, limiting access to the appellate courts by restricting the reach of federal habeas corpus, concerned McGowan, however. He observed that "elimination of federal diversity jurisdiction would enable a shift toward a more appropriate distribution of judicial power for our contemporary situation. But retrenchment in the area of federal authority over cases involving federal law should proceed with caution" (McGowan 1978, 544).

Judge McGowan also wrote about the relationship of the executive branch with the other two branches of government. In 1986, McGowan analyzed the scope of the presidential veto power, reviewing the history and debate surrounding the design of the veto clauses and highlighting the veto's role in U.S. political and legal history. The article also examined the pocket veto, about which the District of Columbia Circuit had made an important ruling that the United States Supreme Court has yet to confirm or overrule. McGowan concluded that the veto power continued to play an important role in the separation-of-powers scheme of our political system.

> The veto is really but one single check in our separation of powers scheme. As an instrument of conflict, it has many salutary effects on our political system; it focuses the public eye on disputes between the executive and Congress; it provides a check on the legislature's tendency to dominate our tripartite government; and it serves as a countervailing policy tool for the President. The veto does not create conflict simply for conflict's sake. Disputes arising out of the veto keep our government running on an even keel, even though the waters are sometimes rough. For the most part, however, the veto power has admirably performed its function. (McGowan 1986a, 820)

Judge Carl McGowan's service on the United States Court of Appeals for the District of Columbia Circuit came at a time of great turmoil and change in U.S. history. His reputation as a pragmatic jurist and a legal scholar enabled him to navigate through a wide range of potentially divisive issues. His decisions and his articles continue to provide guidance to judges and scholars who continue to confront these matters.

Myra Norman

References and Further Reading:

Luck v. United States. 348 F.2d 763 (1965).

McGowan, Carl. 1976. "Congress and the Courts." *ABA Journal* 62: 1588–1591.

———. 1977. "Congress, Court, and Control of Delegated Power." *Columbia Law Review* 77, no. 8 (December): 1119–1174.
———. 1978. "Federal Jurisdiction: Legislative and Judicial Change." *Case Western Law Review* 28, no. 3 (Spring): 517–555.
———. 1982a. "Federalism—Old and New—and the Federal Courts." *The Georgetown Law Journal* 70: 1421–1432.
———. 1982b. "The View from an Inferior Court." *San Diego Law Review* 19: 659–674.
———. 1983. "Presidents and Their Papers." *Minnesota Law Review* 68: 409–437.
———. 1986a. "The President's Veto Power: An Important Instrument of Conflict in Our Constitutional System." *San Diego Law* Review 23, no. 4 (July–August): 791–821.
———. 1986b. "A Reply to Judicialization." *Duke Law Review* 1986 (April): 217–237.
———. 1986c. "United States Courts of Appeal." In *Encyclopedia of the American Constitution*, vol. 4, edited by Leonard W. Levy, Kenneth Karst, and Dennis J. Mahoney. New York: MacMillan, 1939–1942.
Nixon v. Administrator of General Services. 408 F.Supp. 321 (1976).
Nixon v. Administrator of General Services. 433 U.S. 425 (1977).
Powell, Lewis F., Jr., et al. 1988. "In Memoriam: Judge Carl McGowan." *The George Washington Law Review* 56, no. 4–5 (May–August): 681–702.
"Presentation of the Portrait of the Honorable Carl McGowan." 1984. *Federal Reporter*, 761 F.2d (1984): 69–91.
Wald, Patricia M., et al. 1988a. "In Memoriam: Carl McGowan, 1911–1987." *Northwestern University Law Review* 82, no. 2 (Winter): 213–225.
———. 1988b. "In Memoriam: Honorable Carl McGowan, 1911–1987." *Federal Reporter*, 852 F.2d (1988): 75–95.

MEDINA, HAROLD R.

(1888–1990)

Harold R. Medina
Bettmann/Corbis

Harold Raymond Medina became the most famous federal trial judge in the mid-twentieth century by presiding over two great political trials: *United States v. Foster* (1949), which became known on appeal as *Dennis v. United States* (1950–1951), and *United States v. Morgan* (1953). He was also a distinguished member of the United States Court of Appeals for the Second Circuit (1951–1980) and the first known Hispanic to reach either level of the federal judiciary.

His persona is essential to understanding his contributions and controversial standing as a jurist. "Bright, able and a ham actor," as his student Justice William O. Douglas described him, Medina was a born teacher and colorful showman whose warmth and humor converted classrooms and courtrooms into live theater (Howard 1989, 15). He loved public attention and worked to get it, too. The Hollywood presence he projected—good looks, strong physique, dapper clothes, snazzy cars, volatile temper, and huge ego—tended to overshadow his serious side. He was a religious man, an erudite collector and reader of great literature in several languages, and a systematic perfectionist at work and play. Abstract subjects and theories, such as economics, jurisprudence, and political science, bored him. Because he thought and taught by talking aloud and telling stories, he was attracted to English styles of trial by colloquy. Even this exuberant individualist sometimes wondered if he had the requisite judicial temperament.

Medina was born on 16 February 1888 in a middle-class section of Brooklyn, New York. The elder son of Joaquin Adolfo Medina and Elizabeth Fash Medina, he was reared in that same section of Brooklyn. Family and assimilation values were strong in his upbringing. His father, a prosperous Mexican importer and naturalized citizen who came from an affluent planter family in Merida, Yucatan, was educated at Seton Hall Academy in New Jersey and spoke unaccented English. His mother, a New York Episcopalian of Dutch ancestry, banned Spanish and Catholicism from the house.

Harold Medina attended public school No. 44 in Brooklyn, where he was called a "greaser" during the Spanish-American War, and finished high school in 1905 at the private Holbrook Military Academy in Ossining, New York. A very intelligent and diligent student, he graduated from Princeton University in 1909, tenth in his class, with an A.B. degree, a Phi Beta Kappa key, and highest honors in French. At Princeton, he made two life-shaping decisions. Overcoming feelings of being an outsider and fierce rejections by a protective mother, he successfully wooed his mate, Ethel Forde Hillyer, a beautiful woman from a socially prominent family, who became his gyroscope. He also chose his vocation and picked Columbia to be near his fiancée.

At Columbia Law School (1909–1912), he discovered his legal talents and never looked back. He showed exceptional gifts in grasping distinctions, digesting cases, organizing them into whole subjects, and teaching others what he knew. He made the law review, married in 1911, and passed the bar exam before graduating in 1912 as co-head of his class.

Ambitious and energetic, he became a leader of the New York City bar between the two world wars in a "three-ring circus" of teaching, scholarship, and private practice—plus numerous sideshows. Each began modestly but interacted powerfully in his personal and professional development. As a part-time associate professor at Columbia Law School, he taught New York procedure and practice and wrote authoritative works on that hypertechnical subject. Only Harold Medina could have called those Saturday morning eight o'clocks "my Jolly Classes" ("Special Session" 1990, CI). He also created and taught at night a systematic bar review cram course. From 1914 to the early 1940s, roughly 90 percent of New York City lawyers took this course at thirty-five dollars apiece, earning him a small fortune.

In his main act of private practice (1912–1947), he rose slowly from an ill-paid law clerk and bungling novice to a well-respected advocate and senior member of a Manhattan firm, Medina and Sherpick. He was best known as a "lawyer's lawyer" who handled colleagues' tough work on appeal. In that period he argued over 1,300 appeals, mostly in New York courts.

Having learned what not to do from appeals, he emerged in the Depression and war years as an independent general practitioner and bar association leader in the public eye. He matched wits with such stars as John W. Davis, Joseph M. Proskauer, and Max D. Steuer and a future justice, John Marshall Harlan II. Medina became a vice president of the prestigious Association of the Bar of the City of New York, a director of the American Judicature Society, and president of Manhattan's Lawyers Club. Bucking trends toward specialization, his forte became complex litigation, from trial through appeals, requiring a mastery of both grand strategy and exact details. Central to his style as a combative scrapper were a powerful memory and speaking without notes, traits he gradually developed after watching the great Samuel Seabury wreck an important argument in Albany by fumbling his note cards. For big cases Medina practiced before two witnesses that never lied: his mirror and his wife.

As an advocate he experienced hostile audiences in several highly politicized trials. These cases included *People v. Marcus* in 1932–1933 following the largest bank collapse of the Great Depression; *MacAdams v. Cohen* in 1932, a defeat that led to Fiorello La Guardia's election as mayor; and *Fay v. New York* in 1947, an attack on blue-ribbon juries in which a five–four majority of the United States Supreme Court rejected his trail-blazing argument that intentional discrimination by class, race, or sex could be inferred from statistical patterns. This issue returned to him on the bench and reverberates still in affirmative action suits.

Medina's greatest triumph at the bar was his intrepid defense of Anthony Cramer against charges of treason for harboring Nazi saboteurs in World War II. Serving as assigned counsel without pay or expenses for three years in *Cramer v. United States* (1945), he fought doggedly from trial through two oral arguments at the Supreme Court and persuaded a narrow majority to reverse Cramer's conviction under the two-witness rule of the U.S. Constitution. Cramer's case was the first and foremost treason case decided by the Supreme Court on the merits and the tribunal's sole decision in World War II that enforced and enlarged constitutional limits on national war powers. The decision set a standard that led officials to charge lesser offenses during the Cold War and perhaps the current war on terrorism. Medina's battle ranks among the great episodes in American history in which a prominent lawyer braved personal and public hostility to defend the rights of a popularly despised accused. His brilliant oral argument in the first hearing before the justices impressed several Court insiders as the finest they had ever heard. His adversary, solicitor general Charles Fahy, placed Medina among the century's great appellate advocates who grasped the secret of oral argument: "Be oneself" (Howard 1966, 57).

In 1947 Pres. Harry S. Truman nominated Medina to be a federal judge in the Southern District of New York, the nation's oldest and busiest federal trial court. The Senate confirmed him unanimously, and he took office at age fifty-nine. His selection was the only victory for a new bar association strategy to recommend qualified nominees for lifetime federal judgeships as an alternative to those sponsored by politicians. Though his supporters played racial cards to block rivals, his ethnic origins figured little in the decision. Hispanics were a small minority at the time. His appointment was hailed as a triumph of professionalism over politics—the best since Augustus Hand—while the self-styled political babe-in-the-woods rejoiced that his long dream for a judgeship had come true without lifting a finger or incurring political debts (Howard 1989). Initially euphoric, Medina echoed traditional theory that judges best learn their roles as lawyers en route to the bench. The work, he said, was "just what my whole career has fitted me to do" ("Special Session" 1990, CII). Soon, he felt like an inexperienced freshman grappling with unfamiliar problems of patents, sentencing, and administrative regulation. The greatest irony was that within eighteen months Judge John Knox assigned his fresh, apolitical heavyweight two of the most politically significant megatrials in the twentieth century: *United States v. Foster* (1949), better known as *Dennis v. United States* (1950–1951) and also known as the *Communist Conspiracy* case, and *United States v. Morgan* (1948–1953), also known as the *Investment Banking* case. Each dispute involved a major conspiracy theory in U.S. politics, taken to court after Congress and executive officials failed to resolve it. Both trials challenged fair process as well as Medina's physical and moral stamina. Overlapping in time, they dominated his first six years on the bench and made him a controversial national celebrity and symbol of integrity. Few if any federal trial judges in American history had a greater impact on society in so short a span.

The *Communist Conspiracy* case was a controversial show trial and landmark in the law of free political speech. As the Cold War darkened in 1948, Truman's Justice Department charged twelve top leaders of the Communist Party USA under the Smith Act with knowingly conspiring both to advocate violent overthrow of the U.S. government and to organize and be members of a political party that propagated Marxist-Leninist doctrines of violent revolution. One goal was to settle long-standing legal conflicts over the scope of federal power to combat subversive advocacy, propaganda, and fifth columns. The criminal charges and the evidence followed Federal Bureau of Investigation director J. Edgar Hoover's strategy of fighting ideology with ideology.

The result was a sensational trial in which both sides engaged in a propaganda battle over the meaning of Marxist-Leninist ideas, and the defense tried to put the court on trial before the world. These embers smoldered while Medina, inexperience showing, let a challenge to the jury selection system go on too long. His close supervision of the voir dire jury selection process produced a mixed jury straight out of central casting, led by an African American forewoman. He was discomfited by charges of putting books on trial but accepted them technically as tools of conspiracy under witness Louis F. Budenz's theory that the writings of Marx, Lenin, and Stalin were Aesopian language for revolution. Obtuse debates over party dialectics bewildered Medina. Fireworks erupted over concrete proofs of secret organization, internal dictatorship, tight discipline, and false names in party cells as presented by surprise undercover agents, especially Herbert A. Philbrick, whose exploits fascinated the country in a best-seller and a 1952 television series entitled *I Led 3 Lives*.

Almost as dramatic were Medina's struggles to control his court. His persona offered a ripe target for judge baiting and reversible error. Supported by noisy pickets outside and delegations within, defense lawyers attacked his motives, ignored his orders, and demonstrated in court. He endured most of this with studied calm but sometimes stalked off the bench, face red with fury, to calm down. Increasingly he gave them tit for tat. Less noticed was how he would cool off after such blow-ups and start over. By summer, he had full control and withstood external pressures such as a Peekskill riot in which a defendant was injured. In the late 1940s, when Americans were naive about communism and even the defendants wore suits and neckties, the specter of radicals ganging up on a federal judge was deeply shocking. Congressman Emanuel Celler, Medina's Columbia classmate, demanded his impeachment for losing control. The mass media depicted him as Judge Patience fighting evil at high noon in Foley Square. Even intimates saw untapped reservoirs of courage and gumption. His biggest worry was nervous collapse.

The most important event in his judicial career, Medina thought, was his charge to the jury. He could easily have ducked the First Amendment issues in his first criminal case. Judge G. Murray Hulbert in preliminary hearings had already ruled out the membership charge as unconstitutional (a view Medina shared) and upheld the advocacy and organizing charges under the "bad tendency" test of *Gitlow v. New York* (1925), a test that the Second Circuit had recently reaffirmed. Offering leadership instead, Medina wrote the best summary of the defense position in print, took judicial notice of dangers in subversive advocacy, and saved the Smith Act by a compromise between clashing free-speech doctrines known as the "incitement to future action" test. Rejecting "bad tendency" as too restrictive and Justice Brandeis's "no time for counter-speech" standard as impractical in these circumstances, he ruled that the government could curb advocacy that was specifically intended to incite unlawful action as speedily as circumstances would permit. Many contemporaries praised this standard as a statesmanlike advance in free speech principles during dangerous times.

The jury convicted all defendants, and the judge sentenced them to five years in jail, except for war hero Robert Thompson, who got three. In a swift surprise, he charged five defense attorneys and Eugene Dennis (who acted as his own counsel) for conspiring to obstruct justice and impair his health, convicted them himself, and sentenced them to jail for contempt of court.

This trial made Medina the most famous trial judge in the United States, if not the world, and a folk hero to millions. Lionized by newspaper and magazine chains and demonized on the Left, he remained a controversial figure for decades. He was criticized for making arbitrary rulings, stifling free speech, contributing to the fray, punishing counsel vindictively, fanning anticommunist hysteria, and courting publicity in his many posttrial speeches (Belknap 1977; Kutler, 1982). The Court of Appeals and the Supreme Court affirmed his rulings by divided majorities in *Dennis v. United States* (1951) and in *Sacher v. United States* (1952). On 11 June 1951 President Truman nominated Medina to succeed the great jurist Learned Hand on the United States Court of Appeals for the Second Circuit, and the Senate unanimously affirmed. Meantime, Medina remained by designation on the *Morgan* case.

The largely forgotten *Investment Banking* case (*United States v. Morgan*), which took over four years to litigate, tested Progressive–New Deal theories of a Wall Street money trust in a huge civil antitrust trial without a jury. In what many regarded as the most important lawsuit in Wall Street history, the Justice Department charged seventeen top investment banks, including Morgan Stanley, Goldman Sachs, Lehman Bothers, and every partner, with conspiring from 1915 to 1947 to restrain trade, monopolize, and fix prices in negotiated underwriting of new securities, thereby controlling the large corporations they financed and the U.S. securities markets. The central premise was that the Glass Steagall Act of 1934 and the Securities and Exchange Commission (SEC) had failed to prevent the "Club 17" from recovering former clients and excluding competitors after commercial and investment banks were separated in 1935. For want of incriminating contracts or agreements, the conspiracy had to be inferred from unwritten customs and norms of the trade by constructing a legal realist mosaic composed of thousands of evidentiary pieces from documents, office memos, and depositions regarding syndicate agreements plus statistical patterns of continuous banker-client relations. Every public offering of stocks and bonds handled by the defendants between 1915 and 1947 was potentially in this "history of the industry" case, totaling an estimated 100,000 pages of printed documents at the start.

Jose Alberto Cabranes (1940–)

The first Puerto Rican ever appointed to a court on the U.S. mainland, Jose Cabranes has served on both a United States District Court for Connecticut and on the United States Court of Appeals for the Second Circuit. Born in 1940, Cabranes's family moved to the Bronx when he was five. Cabranes attended public schools. He then graduated from Columbia University in 1961 and from Yale Law School in 1965 and received an M.Litt. degree from Queens' College, Cambridge, in 1967.

Cabranes worked with Casey, Lane and Mittendorf in New York City after returning to the United States before becoming a law professor at Rutgers University. From there he became a special counsel to the governor of Puerto Rico and then a general counsel at Yale University, where he also lectured at the law school. It was in 1979 that Cabranes was nominated by Pres. Jimmy Carter to the United States District Court in Connecticut. Fifteen years later, Pres. Bill Clinton appointed Cabranes to the Court of Appeals.

Cabranes established himself in the district court as "a skilled, pragmatic trial judge" (Tabor 1994, 5). As he was strongly supported by the Hispanic community, many had hoped that he might be appointed as the first Hispanic judge on the United States Supreme Court to replace Justice Harry Blackmun in 1994, but that appointment went instead to Justice David Breyer. Although once a registered Democrat, Cabranes has developed a reputation for defying "ideological labels" (5). One of his best-known decisions was a Connecticut case in which he invalidated the state's closed primary law that limited voting to registered party members.

A strong critic of what he has regarded as overly prescriptive federal sentencing guidelines, Cabranes has supported the rights of minorities while also warning against "victim mentality" (Tabor 1994, 5). In 1979, Cabranes wrote a book, *Citizenship and the American Empire*, dealing with the citizenship of Puerto Ricans, and he has written other articles in law journals. Cabranes has been active in community affairs, serving as one of five judges appointed in 1988 to a Federal Courts Study Committee.

References:

"Cabranes, Jose Alberto." Judges of the United States Courts. Available at <http://air.fjc.gov/history/judges_frm.html>. Accessed 18 January 2003.

"President Clinton Names Judge Jose Cabranes to Serve on the Federal Appellate Bench." The White House, Office of the Press Secretary, 24 May 1994. Available at <http://clinton6.nara.gov/1994/05/1 . . .2nd-district-court-of-appeals.html>. Accessed 22 February 2002.

Tabor, Mary B. W. 1994. "Opportunities' Knocks Put Judge High on List." *New York Times*, 9 May, 5.

Though great issues of power and money were at stake, the litigation had a strong procedural cast. The main goal of the Antitrust Division of the Department of Justice was replacing negotiated underwriting of new securities with public competitive bidding as the prime method of capitalizing big business and foreign governments. The SEC thought that the competitive bidding process was unworkable. Medina's tribunal struggled continuously over the best way to litigate the dispute. In a triumph for rising judicial opposition to the Antitrust Divisions's legal realist techniques, the proceeding produced the most thorough official airing of these oft-investigated charges—and a total defeat for the idea of a Wall Street conspiracy in the U.S. political economy (Carosso 1970, 1973). *Morgan* was the only defeat for Thurman Arnold's famous antitrust initiative in the late New Deal, when Arnold headed the Antitrust Division of the Department of Justice.

Procedural leadership was Medina's main contribution to the case. A strong champion of pretrial discovery, he skillfully negotiated compromises in "powwows" that substantially reduced the documentary intake and improvised imaginative time savers, which became normal practice. Most important, his unorthodox rulings to meld the government's legal realist approach with traditional narrative methods and his activist style of trial by colloquy broke the case apart. And it exposed a new dimension in enduring debates over personal predilections in judging: To what degree may judges shape the way a case is presented to suit the way they think?

Lawyers likened *Morgan* to 1,500 little trials under one tent. Medina's decision to subject each bit of evidence to microscopic examination produced an exhaustive and exhausting trial punctuated by blowups, makeups, and brilliant debates. He again feared a nervous breakdown, and the government formally charged him with personal bias (Kramer 1988, 46, 59–60). Inexorably, theories fell as facts were found, for a very simple reason. Prosecutors, having prepared to build a legal realist mosaic by aggregation of documentary phrases and statistics, were woefully unprepared to show that each piece of the mosaic was sound, much less narrate a full story of collusion in various public offerings in the common law way. The judge required all these standards to prove conspiracy by customs. Even the two prosecution witnesses, railroad magnate Robert R. Young and bond leader Harold L. Stuart, refuted key conspiracy charges. The fatal flaw was weak theory leading to weak facts.

Medina's lengthy opinion was extolled as an important state paper, became required reading in business schools, and enhanced his reputation as a great judge. To insulate the decision from direct appeal to the Supreme Court, he maximized facts and minimized law and excised a furious blast at the Antitrust Division for abuse of process. The incoming Eisenhower team did not appeal, and the great Wall Street conspiracy theory faded into history. Medina was content. An economic conservative, more interested in process than legal theory or public policy, he believed above all in the common law tradition. His credo was: Get the facts and justice of the case right, then the law will grow naturally (a summary of his sentiments as expressed in an interview with the author of this entry on 3 December 1979).

This outlook partly explains why Medina never matched the performances of Learned Hand or his own successor, Henry J. Friendly, on the Court of Appeals. Few did. Also, he spent only five years in active service before taking senior status in 1958 with reduced seniority and workload. Then, too, appellate work is collective, not solo, and his prime audiences were practitioners more than intellectuals.

Still, he had a distinguished appellate career. Medina classified his circuit opinions into three groups. First were institutional cases that significantly affected public law. The most influential were *Lawrence v. Devonshire Fabrics, Inc.* (1959), which advanced arbitration as a legal alternative to adjudication in resolving disputes; and *Eisen v. Jacquelin & Carlisle* (1968), allocating the costs of notifying parties in class action lawsuits, an increasingly important form of group action via litigation. Second were "stinkers," his term for opinions that clarified complex factual disputes. A dramatic instance was *United States v. Ortega* (1972), a drug smuggling case that figured in a hit movie, *The French Connection*. Third were maverick decisions giving justice a human face. In *Wolff v. Selective Service Local Board* (1967), he proudly asserted jurisdiction over draft board reclassifications of students who protested the Vietnam War. Fine work, such as *In re Franklin National Bank Securities Litigation* (1978), continued to the end.

As he aged, colleagues regarded a mellowed Medina with affectionate respect. They valued his vast experience and thoroughness at work and admired his contagious zest in the art of living. He was a social leader on the court, translating Latin legal documents with Learned Hand for fun and arranging rousing entertainments at circuit conferences. He heard his last cases on his ninety-second birthday, the oldest federal judge in service. He retired on 30 April 1980 looking forward to new life and projects: translating *Don Quixote*, cruising on the *QE II*, and gleefully leading Princeton Parades in a golf cart in his late nineties. He died of heart failure on 14 March 1990 at age 102 in a nursing home at Morristown, New Jersey, and is buried next to his wife near their home in Westhampton, Long Island.

Over his long career Medina received twenty-five honorary degrees from colleges and universities, including Columbia, MIT, Princeton, and Tulane, plus scores of awards, citations, and medals. A faculty chair and a classroom are named in his honor at Columbia Law School. He was especially proud of two symbols of his lifestyle: a record of three consecutive Medina generations making the law review at Columbia and a baseball signed by all the

Brooklyn Dodgers, which Jackie Robinson gave him in 1952 when Medina and the lawyers took a break to reduce tension in the *Investment Banking* case.

In the final reckoning, his talents were probably better suited for the reactive functions of trial courts than for the reflective functions of deciding appeals. The *Dennis* case, for good or ill, was a major watershed in the history of free speech. In hindsight the Justice Department bears prime responsibility for taking an ideological approach to controlling a quasi-legal, quasi-underground organization of Stalinists bankrolled by Moscow, which led to needless sacrifice of principle. Though Medina was naive about communism, his charge did not retreat from what free speech law was but rather from what civil libertarians wanted it to be: the clear and present danger test. And even that formula offered no escape from the trap of forecasting perils that courts are ill equipped to gauge. Just as he upheld federal power to punish subversive advocacy, so his emphasis on specific intent and incitement substantially advanced constitutional protections for free speech in the teeth of perceived crisis—an uncommon event in history. The Warren Court reaffirmed this standard in *Yates v. United States* (1957) and moved the bar closer to action during calmer times in *Brandenburg v. Ohio* (1969). Medina should have requested another judge to hear his contempt charges (as he initially decided to do), but he did not do so for fear of crippling judicial power in future political trials. Though Judge Julius J. Hoffman ignored his advice in the Chicago Seven trial (*United States v. Dellinger* 1972), Judge John J. Sirica cited his example in the Watergate scandal.

Medina was a pragmatist who found truth in particulars. In *Morgan*, he never would have dreamed of condensing a great antitrust case with a general theorem like Learned Hand's famous Bull Moose dictum—bigness is bad—in *United States v. Aluminum Company of America* (1945). Medina's piecemeal way in *Morgan* nevertheless settled a major public controversy over financing big business and legitimated a subtle form of competition in an increasingly global economy. If he talked and taught too much publicly about his experiences, Medina comforted and inspired millions in troubled times as a cheerleader of American values. As he confessed, "I'm a rah-rah boy myself" ("Special Session" 1990, CIX).

J. Woodford Howard Jr.

References and Further Reading:

Belknap, Michal R. 1977. *Cold War Political Justice*. Westport, Conn.: Greenwood Press.

Carosso, Vincent P. 1970. *Investment Banking in America*. Cambridge: Harvard University Press, 458–495.

———. 1973. "The Wall Street Money Trust from Pugo through Medina." *Business History Review* 47: 421–437.

Hawthorne, Daniel. 1952. *Judge Medina: A Biography*. New York: Wilfred Funk.

Howard, J. Woodford, Jr. 1966. "The *Cramer* Treason Case." *Journal of Supreme Court History* 1: 49–60.

———. 1989. "The Amateurs Win: Harold R. Medina's Appointment as a Federal District Judge." *New York State Bar Journal* 61: 14–22.

Kramer, Victor H. 1988. "The Trial of the Investment Banking Case: United States v. Morgan." *Litigation* 14: 43–60.

Kutler, Stanley I. 1982. *The American Inquisition*. New York: Hill and Wang, 152–182.

Medina, Harold R. 1954. *Judge Medina Speaks*. New York: Matthew Bender.

———. 1959. *The Anatomy of Freedom*. New York: Henry Holt.

"Special Session, U. S. Court of Appeals for the Second Circuit, in Memory of the Honorable Harold R. Medina." 917 F.2d, XCI-CXIV (1990).

MIKVA, ABNER J.

(1926–)

ABNER J. MIKVA
Ellis Richard/Corbis Sygma

ABNER J. MIKVA, CONGRESSman and White House counsel, was a judge on the United States Court of Appeals for the District of Columbia Circuit. Because of its jurisdiction over policies set by most federal agencies and departments, the court is considered the second most important court in the country after the United States Supreme Court. Mikva was born in Milwaukee, Wisconsin, on 21 January 1926, the son of Ukrainian immigrants. The family was on welfare for a number of years during Mikva's youth until his father was able to obtain a job with the Works Progress Administration in 1937, a fact that explains Mikva's political ideology. After graduating in 1943 from Washington High School in Milwaukee, he briefly attended the University of Wisconsin before enlisting in the Army Air Corps. In 1945, he returned to the University of Wisconsin and then studied at Washington University in St. Louis from 1946 to 1947. Mikva married Zorita "Zoe" Wise in 1948; they had three daughters.

In 1951, Mikva graduated with honors from the University of Chicago School of Law, where he served as editor of the law review. He clerked for U.S. Supreme Court justice Sherman Minton in 1951–1952. A reform Democrat running against Chicago mayor Richard Daley's machine, Mikva was elected to the Illinois House of Representatives in 1956 in spite of Daley's opposition. In 1966, Mikva unsuccessfully challenged a Democratic incumbent for the U.S. House of Representatives. By 1968, the incumbent no longer enjoyed Daley's support, and Mikva was elected with Daley's assistance. He subsequently lost Daley's support after voicing concerns about the mayor's tactics during the turbulent 1968 Democratic convention in Chicago. In 1971, the Illinois legislature redrew congressional districts, putting Mikva in a congressional district represented by another popular Democrat. Mikva moved from the south side of Chicago to Evanston, Illinois, to run in an open seat in a very affluent district. Republican Sam Young defeated him in 1972. In the wake of Watergate, Mikva defeated Young by a slim margin in 1974 to return to Congress. He was reelected in 1976 and 1978, both times by very small margins. In the Illinois legislature and the U.S. House of Representatives, Mikva was known as a leading advocate of handgun control. For this reason, the National Rifle Association (NRA) exerted great effort to block his reelection efforts.

After the 1978 general election, Mikva had tired of exhausting and expensive congressional campaigns. He asked Pres. Jimmy Carter to be considered for appointment to a federal judgeship. Congress had passed the Omnibus Judgeship Act in 1978, creating 152 new federal judgeships, so the president was able to honor the congressman's request. Carter nominated Mikva to the United States Court of Appeals for the District of Columbia Circuit in 1979.

As a member of Congress, Mikva had the respect of many of his colleagues, including many Republicans. This bipartisan support was evident during the confirmation hearings held by the Senate Judiciary Committee. The committee received letters from ex-president Gerald Ford, a former Republican leader in the House. Other endorsements came from former attorney general Edward H. Levi, dean of the University of Chicago School of Law when Mikva was a student, as well as Reps. Robert Michel of Illinois and John J. Rhodes of Arizona.

Several conservative members of Congress opposed Mikva's nomination because they were concerned about his ability to separate the job of a legislator from that of a federal judge. During the debate on the Senate floor preceding the confirmation vote, Sen. Strom Thurmond of South Carolina argued: "I do not think he will exercise the proper judicial restraint. . . ." Thurmond continued: "Mr. Mikva is not only an advocate, but an uncompromising one, a partisan, firmly committed to his personal preconceptions of the Constitution" (*Congressional Record*, 25 September 1979, S 26030). Sen. Gordon Humphrey of New Hampshire reported that, in a legal industry newspaper, the nominee identified the court system as "an important nonlegislative road to reform" (*Congressional Record*, 25 September 1979,

S 26045). Several conservatives revisited the failed nominations of Judges Clement Haynsworth Jr. and G. Harrold Carswell to the United States Supreme Court earlier in the decade. Sen. Humphrey pointed out that Mikva believed that judges sometimes have to operate outside of popular opinion, "judges who swim upstream" (*Congressional Record*, 25 September 1979, S 26033). The senator reminded other senators that liberals believed Haynsworth and Carswell were out of the mainstream, and the two men were not confirmed. The same judicial activism argument also was lodged against Patricia Wald, President Carter's nominee for the other new seat on the District of Columbia Circuit Court.

More vigorous opposition came from Mikva's nemesis, the National Rifle Association. Because of his support of gun control legislation, the NRA spent more than $1 million in a six-month lobbying effort to block Mikva's nomination (Dold 1996). The NRA's message was that groups like it would not receive a fair hearing in a court with Mikva sitting as a judge. The NRA also argued that he was constitutionally disqualified from taking the judgeship. The group claimed that because Mikva was a member of Congress when the Omnibus Judgeship Act was passed, the Constitution's Article 1, section 6, clause 2 prohibited him from filling one of the vacancies created by the law. In addition, he was a member of Congress who voted for a judicial pay increase to take effect in 1979. The NRA's campaign, and the constitutional question, almost worked. The Senate Judiciary Committee voted by a slim margin (nine to six) to send Mikva's confirmation to the floor. Despite sharp debate on the Senate floor, with Sen. James McClure of Idaho declaring, "Mr. Mikva will go to any length to get your guns and my guns" (*Congressional Record*, 25 September 1979, S 26038), Mikva was confirmed on a fifty-eight–thirty-one vote. Seventeen Republican senators voted to confirm, and nine Democrats voted no.

The confirmation fight continued for two more years. Senator McClure filed a lawsuit on the day of the confirmation vote, challenging the constitutionality of Mikva's appointment. A federal district court rejected the suit because McClure lacked standing. McClure had authored the law on which he based his claim in the lawsuit that he filed. The United States Supreme Court denied the senator's appeal (see *McClure v. Carter*, 513 F. Supp 265 [D. Idaho 1981], aff'd sub. nom. *McClure v. Reagan*, 454 U.S. 1025 [1981]).

In 1979, Mikva joined a court in transition. Conservatives in Congress and the Nixon administration stripped the District of Columbia federal courts of criminal jurisdiction in reaction to a series of rulings that expanded criminal defendants' rights issued by the District of Columbia Circuit Court under the leadership of Chief Judge David Bazelon. By the end of the 1970s, the Court of Appeals primarily heard cases arising out of the actions of federal regulatory agencies. The court had always had jurisdiction over appeals of administrative decisions, but in the 1970s, public interest groups began to look to the court to protect the environment, consumers, and workers. Through their rulings, judges rewrote administrative regulations.

Court personnel changed rapidly after Mikva joined the court, largely as judges appointed by Presidents John F. Kennedy and Lyndon Johnson retired. Patricia Wald was President Carter's first appointee to the court; Mikva was the second. In 1980, two more Carter appointees joined the pair: Harry Edwards replaced Bazelon and Ruth Bader Ginsburg filled the vacancy caused by the death of Judge Harold Leventhal.

Former California governor Ronald Reagan defeated President Carter in 1980, a significant event in Mikva's career on the bench. The Reagan administration was elected on a platform that included a promise to appoint less activist judges to the federal bench. From 1982 through 1987, eight judges, primarily conservatives, were appointed to the court: Robert Bork (1982), Antonin Scalia (1982), Kenneth Starr (1983), Laurence Silberman (1985), James Buckley (1985), Stephen Williams (1986), Douglas Ginsburg (1986), and David Sentelle (1987). According to some observers, as the number of conservative judges grew, rancor among the judges increased (see Banks 1999).

Judge Mikva was involved in an incident that almost led to a physical confrontation over ideological differences. Banks related that "it became so turbulent in the court that the *New York Times* reported that Judge Laurence Silberman threatened to assault Judge Mikva over a particularly contentious affirmative action case" (1999, 7). Silberman did not actually assault Mikva, but reports of the outburst probably prevented the Bush administration from nominating Silberman to a Supreme Court vacancy.

Mikva downplayed the court's ideological conflict in a 1989 law review article. He made the observation that "it was never sweetness and light at this court" (Mikva 1989a, 1063). Despite the perception that the court deals largely with dry, administrative matters, the rules and regulations it decides can become issues in an ideological conflict. The article, actually an introduction to a symposium reviewing the court's term, provided an enlightening exposition on the jurisdiction and history of the District of Columbia Circuit Court. Mikva concluded the article by observing: "pick a controversial subject in our democracy, and you can find at least two points of view expressed by judges of the D.C. Circuit" (1068). Differences of opinion were to be expected (1068).

In 1991, Mikva became chief judge of the District of Columbia Circuit after Patricia Wald stepped down two years before the end of her term. Federal law prescribes that the longest-serving judge who is not yet sixty-five years old becomes chief for seven years or until age seventy. Judge Wald stepped down just before Mikva's sixty-fifth birthday. Some observers speculated that the action was meant to deny Judge Silberman the position, but Mikva said Wald had made a promise to take this action when President Carter appointed them in 1979.

During his sixteen years on the bench, Mikva wrote over 300 decisions. A number of these decisions dealt with government regulation of speech. One such ruling, *U.S. Southwest Africa/Namibia Trade & Cultural Council v. United States* (708 F.2d 760 [D.C. Cir. 1983]), dealt with the refusal of the Federal Aviation Administration to approve an advertisement as suitable for public display at Washington National Airport and Dulles International Airport. Despite the willingness of the Trade and Cultural Council to pay for the space and the availability of space, the ad was rejected as a political message. Mikva ruled, "In the absence of demonstrably compelling, countervailing reasons, the government may not ban political advertisements from the display advertising areas at National and Dulles Airports." Judges Wald and Wright joined him in the unanimous decision (774).

A more controversial decision involved the National Highway Transportation and Safety Administration (NHTSA) rule-making process on automobile air bags. In *State Farm Mutual Automobile Insurance Co. v. Department of Transportation* (680 F.2d 206 [D.C. Cir. 1982]), Mikva ruled that the NHTSA had exceeded its delegated authority when it rescinded rules requiring air bags as standard equipment in cars. The rule change was one attempt by the Reagan administration to reduce regulation of U.S. industry. The United States Supreme Court agreed with Mikva's decision that the administration needed congressional authority to rescind the rule (*Motor Vehicle Manufacturers Association v. State Farm Mutual Automobile Insurance Co.*, 463 U.S. 29 [1983]). Mikva's opinion curbed the ability of the Reagan administration to dismantle the regulatory structure in the country without congressional approval.

One example of a routine administrative law question with a political outcome was *Steffan v. Aspin* (8 F.3d 57 [D.C. Cir. 1993]). Joseph Steffan was a midshipman at the United States Naval Academy who was expelled from the academy and denied a commission as an officer after informing a superior officer that he was a homosexual. The academy applied a Department of Defense rule specifying that a service member must be discharged if he or she admits to being a homosexual. Writing for a unanimous three-judge panel, Mikva ruled Steffan's expulsion was "not rationally related to any legitimate goal" (70) and was, therefore, unconstitutional. According to F. Bruce Dold (1996), Mikva told him that he took great pride in overturning the Defense Department rule, even though his ruling was reversed by the whole court meeting *en banc* (*Steffan v. Perry* 41 F.3d 677 [D.C. Cir. 1994]).

Public interest groups criticized Mikva's ruling in *Public Citizen v. United States Trade Representative* (5 F.3d 549 [D.C. Cir. 1993]). Public Citizen, an environmental public interest group, sued under the provisions of the Administrative Procedures Act (APA) to force the president to file an environmental impact statement on the North American Free Trade Agreement (NAFTA). The APA allows citizens and groups to sue if they believe a federal agency's final action in a matter is harmful to the public good. Actions by the president are exempted from the APA, however. Mikva wrote for a unanimous three-judge panel when he found that the court had no jurisdiction in the matter because NAFTA was an action by the president and not by a federal agency. The decision reversed a lower court ruling. Shortly thereafter, Congress approved NAFTA, and the Supreme Court denied certiorari in Public Citizen's appeal.

Mikva worked to improve the public image of the judiciary, and the legal system in general, throughout his career and into his retirement. In 1985, he became the chairman of the Section on Individual Rights and Responsibilities of the American Bar Association (ABA), the only sitting federal judge to head an ABA section. His goal was to increase the size of the section using political campaign tactics. This activity became controversial for the judge when the conservative Washington Legal Foundation filed a complaint against Mikva, claiming that his leadership of the section conflicted with his judicial responsibilities. As a result of the complaint, he stepped down as chairman before the end of his term.

He expressed concern about the role of television, especially the genre of television court shows, in providing a picture of U.S. legal processes. In an article published in *TV Guide*, Mikva critiqued *The People's Court* and the activities of Judge Joseph A. Wapner. He wrote, "Judge Wapner prepares his viewers for a knowledgeable discourse on American law about as much as the doctors on *M*A*S*H* prepared their audiences to perform surgery" (1989b, 14). Mikva's verdict was that the show "does for the law what *Dynasty* was doing for monogamy" (14).

Mikva's name was often mentioned as a possible Supreme Court nominee. He would have accepted a nomination if offered, but twelve years of Republican presidents frustrated his ambitions. After Pres. Bill Clinton's election in 1992 brought the Democratic Party back into power in the executive branch, Mikva told reporters, "I'm too old, too white, too male, and too liberal" to be nominated (Adelman 1997, 31). The closest he got to serving on the Supreme Court was portraying a chief justice swearing in the new president in the 1993 feature film *Dave*.

In 1994, President Clinton named Mikva to the post of White House counsel, the legal adviser to the president. To take the post, he retired from a lifetime appointment on the bench. While Mikva was working for President Clinton, one of his adversaries was Kenneth Starr, his former colleague and the newly appointed independent counsel leading the investigation of the Clintons' failed Whitewater real estate deal. After an exhausting year of long hours in the Clinton White House, Mikva retired from public service in 1995. He returned to Chicago as a visiting professor at the University of Chicago School of Law. In a long career, Abner Mikva served in all three branches of the federal government.

John David Rausch Jr.

REFERENCES AND FURTHER READING:

Adelman, Ken. 1997. "Hat Trick." *Washingtonian*, March, 31.

Andrews, James H. 1993. "Government's Judicial Watchdog." *The Christian Science Monitor*, 6 December, 6.

Banks, Christopher P. 1999. *Judicial Politics in the D.C. Circuit Court*. Baltimore: The Johns Hopkins University Press.

Dold, F. Bruce. 1996. "Dissenting Opinion." *The University of Chicago Magazine*, August. Available at <http://magazine.uchicago.edu/9608/9608Mikva/html>. Accessed 11 January 2003.

Jasperse, Patrick. 1995. "From the Poor House to the White House." *Wisconsin Magazine*, 29 October, 7.

Kiernan, Laura. 1979. "Mikva Could Shape U.S. Court's Future." *Washington Post*, 23 July, C1.

Kondracke, Morton. 1979. "Good Judgment." *The New Republic*, 24 March, 12–14.

Lewis, Neil A. 1991. "Presiding as Ideas Clash in Capital Appeals Court." *New York Times*, 1 February, B4.

Mikva, Abner J. 1989a. "Sturm und Drang at the D.C. Circuit." *George Washington Law Review* 57: 1063–1068.

———. 1989b. "The Verdict on Judge Wapner." *TV Guide*, 22 April, 12–14.

Morris, Jeffrey Brandon. 2001. *Calmly to Poise the Scales of Justice: A History of the Courts of the District of Columbia Circuit*. Durham, N.C.: Carolina Academic Press.

MITCHELL, WILLIAM

(1832–1900)

WILLIAM MITCHELL
National Archives

JUSTICE WILLIAM MITCHELL wrote over 1,600 opinions during his tenure on the Minnesota Supreme Court, the quality and clarity of which placed him among the most accomplished judges of his generation.

William Mitchell was born on 19 November 1832 to John and Mary Henderson Mitchell, Scottish immigrants who had settled in Welland County, Ontario, just over the U.S. border near Niagara Falls, New York. The first of eleven children, Mitchell was raised on the couple's farm and educated in Canada. He attended college in the United States, graduating from Jefferson College in Cannonsburg, Pennsylvania, in 1853.

While at Jefferson College, Mitchell became close friends with fellow student Eugene Wilson, whose father practiced law in Morgantown, Virginia (now West Virginia). Upon graduation, Mitchell and Wilson returned to Morgantown, where the two men "studied the law" under Eugene's father. (Instead of attending law school, prospective lawyers at that time learned their craft by studying and serving as an apprentice to an established practitioner. This process, called "studying the law" or "reading the law," is still recognized by a few states, but it is exceedingly rare for a person to be admitted to the bar in this manner.)

Mitchell stayed in Morgantown for four years, studying law and teaching in a local school. In March 1857, he was admitted to the bar in Virginia. Unlike the situation today, in which a lawyer must be admitted to practice in each state where he or she wishes to work, bar admission at that time in Virginia meant the ability to practice law in any state. Mitchell and Wilson took advantage of this fact and headed west. In April 1857, the two young lawyers traveled by steamboat up the Mississippi River to the frontier town of Winona, in the territory that would soon become the state of Minnesota. The two liked what they saw, stayed, and quickly established a law partnership in the city's downtown district.

The Wilson and Mitchell law partnership did not last long, because Eugene Wilson was soon appointed to serve as a U.S. district attorney. Wilson would go on to have a notable career in public service, both in the Minnesota legislature and the U.S. Congress. In fact, many of Mitchell's law partners and colleagues became distinguished public servants. Mitchell's next partner, Daniel S. Norton, was elected to the U.S. Senate not long after the partnership was formed. Mitchell then joined with William H. Yale, a former lieutenant governor, in creating the law firm of Mitchell and Yale, which lasted until Mitchell was appointed to the bench in 1881.

Mitchell quickly distinguished himself as a smart, hardworking, and fair-minded attorney. He labored tirelessly at his law practice and in community service, serving a term in the state legislature, a term as county attorney, and several years on the Winona city council. He also served on various public and private boards and was a founding member of the Winona Bar Association. He became the first president of the newly formed Winona and Southwestern Railroad Company as well as president of the newly incorporated Winona Savings Bank. Indeed, Mitchell participated in and guided the growth of the town during a time of significant expansion.

Shortly after establishing his law practice, Mitchell returned to Morgantown to marry Jane Hanway Smith, a widow with one child. The couple returned to Winona and had three daughters. The marriage survived ten years, until the death of Mrs. Mitchell in 1867. Mitchell married again in 1872, to Frances Merritt Smith, also a widow with one child. William and Frances Mitchell had two children, a daughter who died in infancy and a son, William DeWitt Mitchell, who would also become a distinguished law practitioner and public servant.

The Mitchell family lived in downtown Winona, a few blocks from his law office. During his years of practice, Winona matured from a frontier town with few businesses and city services to a large, bustling barge city on the Mississippi River. The economic development of Winona and other river and frontier communities set the stage for many of the issues that William Mitchell would soon face as a judge. The United States was growing and changing as the railroads facilitated the increasing industrialization of the nation and made it easier for its population to move westward. Judges in the post–Civil War era, particularly state judges, were often called upon to oversee this unprecedented growth by resolving questions regarding land rights; railroad rates, subsidies, and regulations; employer/employee relations; ownership and use of natural resources, particularly waterways; contract interpretation rules; and the developing theory of negligence liability in tort law.

In 1874, Mitchell was elected to serve as judge of the District Court of the Third Judicial District of Minnesota, an area that covered much of present-day southeastern Minnesota. His first service on the Minnesota Supreme Court occurred shortly thereafter in 1877, when he was specially appointed by the governor to hear the case of *State of Minnesota v. Young,* concerning the use of parole (oral) evidence to complete a sealed agreement. At that time, the Minnesota high court consisted of only three justices. Two of the justices had previously participated in the case and had to recuse themselves for the appeal. Mitchell and attorney Samuel Lord were appointed to take the place of the recused justices. Mitchell wrote the opinion of the court, which was well received in the legal community (Jaggard 1909, 394–395). Consequently, when the state legislature voted to increase the size of the Supreme Court in 1881, Gov. John S. Pillsbury appointed Mitchell to one of the two new seats as associate justice, a position to which he would twice be reelected and would hold until 1900.

Justice Mitchell's tenure on the bench can be characterized first as prolific. He routinely worked seven days a week, completing several opinions a week, during his entire nineteen-year Supreme Court career. He wrote all of his own opinions, as well as required factual summaries and accompanying documents, without the benefit of typewriters or secretaries, let alone computers and word processing programs. An early biographer of Mitchell credited his work ethic to his Scottish and Protestant upbringing, which stressed hard work, clean living, and dedication to pubic service (Jaggard 1909, 388, 395–396). Although Mitchell was not a member of any particular church, he demonstrated these values in both his personal and professional life. During his rare times of relaxation, he pursued fishing, hunting, and gardening—three endeavors that remain extremely popular in Minnesota today.

Although the quantity of Mitchell's opinions was impressive, it was their consistent quality, as judged by his peers, that distinguished Mitchell's judicial tenure. His opinions are characterized by a strong command of statutory and common law, common sense, and a clear, accessible writing style. Mitchell was widely regarded as a brilliant judge with an enviable grasp of the historical development of the law, but his opinions did not show intellectual elitism or arrogance. They were written in a concise, straightforward manner that was generally understandable to laypersons. He explained rules of law so that those who needed to use them could follow them, a fact that was especially important given the numerous areas of emerging law that the Supreme Court was asked to interpret.

Mitchell's approach to oral arguments was similarly nonelitist. He treated attorneys with respect, listened to them attentively, and did not interrupt arguments to make observations or force his views upon counsel (Lees 1920, 381). He was perceived, both as a lawyer and a judge, as scholarly, fair-minded, reserved, and exceptionally courteous—a model country lawyer who did not forget his roots, even when his intellect and reputation propelled him to the state capital and service on the state Supreme Court.

Many of Justice Mitchell's opinions for the Supreme Court announced new legal principles. This was not because Mitchell was an "activist" judge, bent on creating new law—far from it. Rather, his opportunity to create new law, or to clarify confused existing law, stemmed from the time in which he served, during which the law expanded and changed in a number of substantive areas. In short, Mitchell's opinions reflected the realities of late-nineteenth-century life. Like many judges of his time, Mitchell was called upon to decide numerous railroad land grant cases that analyzed the rights of the states both to give land to railroad companies and subsequently to regulate and tax them; riparian rights cases governing how individuals could use and develop water resources on their land; and "freedom of contract" cases governing the relationship between employers and employees as well as between businesses and their competitors.

Mitchell's approach to these cases, and to his docket generally, was rather conservative. He neither believed in substituting judicial opinions for legislative judgments nor was likely to recognize new individual rights. But Mitchell was not a dogmatic practitioner of judicial restraint. He embraced new rules when the old ones became obsolete or could no longer be justified given current conditions. For example, he rejected the widely held rule that a landowner who suffers damage to his property could sue only in the county in which his land was located, noting that the rule, while well established, made little sense in modern times (*Little v. Railroad Company*; Jaggard 1909, 421). He also upheld the state's Sunday business closing laws but rejected the traditional reliance on Christian practices as the justification for them. Instead, Mitchell argued, such laws must be created and defended in secular terms, as an exercise of the state's police power (the inherent power of state government to ensure the protection and to promote the well-being of its citizens). Minnesota had the power to force certain businesses to close on Sunday, but this power could be exercised only for legitimate, nonreligious

Robert Gollmar: A Wisconsin Country Judge (1903–1987)

Although he spent most of his time as a judge on the bench in rural Wisconsin, Judge Robert Gollmar presided over some bizarre trials. These included the trial of Edward Gein, who was convicted of decapitating a woman and whose murder served as inspiration for one of Gollmar's books as well as a novel by Robert Bloch and a Hitchcock film, both entitled *Psycho* ("Robert H. Gollmar").

The son of a circus operator, Gollmar attended law school at the University of Wisconsin in 1925 and practiced in Baraboo, Wisconsin, until he was elected as a Sauk County judge in 1956. He subsequently became a state circuit judge in 1961 and served in that capacity until his retirement in 1973. Thereafter, he worked in Milwaukee as a criminal court reserve judge and later as an acting judge in the Twenty-Fifth Circuit, from which he retired.

Despite handling a number of cases involving multiple murders and other heinous crimes, Gollmar prided himself on his humor, which is evident in his books. He noted that a man who had threatened his life in the courtroom was later released by prison psychiatrists. They noted that "this man has incurable homicidal tendencies. We can do nothing for him, and we, therefore, are returning him to society" (Gollmar 1979, 52). On another occasion he pointed with irony to the note of optimism in the report of a social worker who observed that a defendant who had been convicted and released after attacking a small girl had subsequently been convicted for attacking an older one: "We are making real progress with this young man. Now he is attacking girls of his own age" (53). On another occasion, he reported that an elderly doctor who acted as the coroner in a murder case, when asked whether he had performed an autopsy, responded with surprise, "What for? She was dead, wasn't she?" (80).

Reflecting on more than twenty-five years of service as a judge, Gollmar cited Lord Chancellor Lyndhurst's definition of a good judge and followed with a comment of his own:

> "First, he must be honest. Second, he must possess a reasonable amount of industry. Third, he must have courage. Fourth, he must be a gentleman. And then if he has some knowledge of law it will help."
>
> If I fulfill that definition, I am satisfied. (Gollmar 1979, 187)

References:

Gollmar, Robert H. 1979. *Tales of a Country Judge*. Delavan, Wis.: Chas. Hallberg and Company.

"Robert H. Gollmar." Contemporary Authors Online. The Gale Group, 2000. Available at <http://www.galenet.com/servlet/BioRC>. Accessed 5 March 2002.

purposes (*State v. Petit;* Jaggard 1909, 403). Similarly, Mitchell found unconstitutional the state's attempt to build a grain elevator under the guise of the police power, holding that the state had exceeded the scope of that power by using it for this purpose (*Rippe v. Becker;* Jaggard 1909, 413).

Many, if not most, of Justice Mitchell's opinions were based on the common law. The common law is a body of law—made by judges incrementally in their opinions—that is based upon history, tradition, and local practice. In his groundbreaking 1977 book *The Transformation of American Law, 1780–1860*, Harvard historian Morton Horwitz argued that many nineteenth-century judges used the common law as a tool to shape the development of the rapidly industrializing nation and specifically to facilitate economic growth through decisions that favored the use of natural resources and adopted contract, tort, and workplace rules that favored business over labor. The classic example offered by Horwitz to support his argument was the demise at the hands of common law judges of the long-held legal rule protecting the "first user" of property (particularly waterways) from interference by others. Through a series of judicial decisions, that rule eventually gave way to a new legal rule favoring those who put property to a "reasonable" (that is, productive) use. Horwitz argued that, in adapting this and other established legal rules to meet the demands of industrialization, state judges embraced an "instrumental" use of the law to promote economic development and expansion, an approach they maintained throughout the nineteenth century.

Although Horwitz's analysis focused largely on state judges from the eastern United States, one might apply his analysis to Justice Mitchell as well. In a sense, Mitchell was a conservative justice in that he did not perceive any role for the judiciary in announcing public policy or extending civil rights and liberties. In another sense, however, Mitchell was progressive in that he embraced his common law duties and was not afraid to adapt existing legal principles to the changed circumstances of the late nineteenth century (Lees 1920, 383–386). In doing so, he often adopted the views of his earlier East Coast counterparts who, in Horwitz's view, may not have been as neutral in their judicial orientation as they believed themselves to be.

On the other hand, Justice Mitchell was at various times accused of being both a Jacksonian and a Populist. Although he had started out as a member of the Republican Party, Mitchell changed his affiliation to the Democratic Party during Reconstruction. This decision did not affect his reelection to the bench in 1888 and 1894, when he was renominated by both parties and subsequently reelected. In 1900, he failed to win the endorsement of the Republican Party, however, although he did receive the nomination of the Democratic and Populist Parties. The state Republicans behaved in a particularly partisan manner that year; Mitchell was at the same time opposed by "great vested interests [in the party], because of his supposed populistic rulings" and also by "radicals [in the party], because of [his] imaginary corporate leanings" (Jaggard 1909, 398–399). Perhaps as a consequence, he narrowly lost his reelection bid that year and retired to private law practice with his son. Not even a year into his retirement, William Mitchell died of a stroke on 21 August 1900.

Mitchell had other judicial opportunities during his lifetime. He was nominated by President Harrison to serve on the Eighth Circuit Court of Appeals, but the nomination was later withdrawn. After losing reelection to the Minnesota Supreme Court, he was offered the chief justiceship of Puerto Rico, which he declined. He was also slated to become the dean of the new St. Paul College of Law, in St. Paul, Minnesota, but died prior to assuming the office.

Thus, Mitchell's entire judicial career was served on state benches. This fact, however, does not diminish his accomplishments, for he was widely considered among the top judges of the nation, federal or state, during his tenure. Renowned Harvard law professor James Bradley Thayer, for example, called Mitchell "one of the best judges in this country" and observed that "[o]n no court in the country today is there a judge who would not find his peer in Judge Mitchell" (Jaggard 1909, 398).

Mitchell's son, William DeWitt Mitchell, honored his father's legacy by becoming an accomplished lawyer in his own right. The younger Mitchell graduated from Yale University and the University of Minnesota School of Law. He practiced law in St. Paul for a number of years and was eventually appointed U.S. solicitor general by Pres. Calvin Coolidge and U.S. attorney general by Pres. Herbert Hoover. He declined nomination to the Supreme Court in 1933, supporting soon-to-be justice Benjamin Cardozo. In 1934, the Supreme Court made him chair of its advisory committee for developing the Federal Rules of Civil Procedure, through which he has had a lasting impact. The family legacy continued with William Mitchell's grandchildren, who also became distinguished members of the bar (Heinlen 2000, n.p.).

In 1956, the original St. Paul College of Law and the Minneapolis–Minnesota College of Law merged to form William Mitchell College of Law. Although William Mitchell did not live to become dean of the St. Paul College of Law, his name and legacy are carried on in the distinguished alumnae and alumni of this law school, who include U.S. Supreme Court chief justice Warren Burger and many prominent state and federal judges, attorneys, and elected officials.

Kathleen Uradnik

George Robertson (1790–1874)

George Robertson distinguished himself as a member of Congress, as a representative in the Kentucky legislature, as a professor at Transylvania University, and as a member of the Kentucky Court of Appeals. He served in that court from 1828 until 1843, all but his first year as chief justice, and again from 1864 until 1871, the last year of which he was again chief.

Born in Mercer County, Kentucky, in 1790 to pioneers Alexander and Margaret Robinson, George Robertson received an education under the tutelage of Joshua Fry and subsequently attended, but did not graduate from, Transylvania University. After a plan to go to Princeton proved futile, he read law under Samuel McKee, a representative to Congress, and was licensed to practice by the age of nineteen. Married that same year, Robertson's early years were financially difficult, and he often supplemented his meager earnings by winning at cards, which he believed helped him to learn about human nature (Wilson 1908, 376).

In about 1812, he was appointed as a prosecuting attorney in Garrard County, and in 1814 he became a tax assessor. With a growing legal reputation, he was elected to Congress in 1816, but apparently his success was due at least as much to his ability to play the fiddle as to his oratory (Wilson 1908, 380). Publishing a widely heralded essay opposing a new gubernatorial election, Robertson entered Congress in 1817 and was twice reelected, although he did not serve out his third term. He appears to have taken notable positions on a number of key issues of the day, including the organization of the Arkansas Territory and slave presence there, the sale of public lands, and recognition of South American countries (Coulter).

Ever desirous of returning to the law and earning income for his family, he was instead elected in 1823 to the state House of Representatives from 1824 to 1826 and off and on until 1853. During three years he served as house speaker. Appointed to the Court of Appeals in 1828, he served there until 1843, later being again elevated to that position in his final years. Robertson was a professor at Transylvania from 1835 until 1858, teaching law to more than 1,200 lawyers (Wilson 1908, 388) at a time when Transylvania was one of the main training grounds for the legal profession west of the Alleghenies.

Robertson had only two other colleagues on the court, and the burden of his work required that he write his opinions quickly, but his opinions were still known for their lucidity as well as for occasional rhetorical flourishes. Joseph Story and James Kent were among those who commended the quality of his court's written opinions (Wilson 1908, 393).

Robertson, who favored blending common law with civil law principles, believed in the "malleability" of the common law. As he explained:

> An adjudged point, unreasonable or inconsistent with analogy or principle,

(continues)

(continued)

> should not be regarded as conclusive evidence of the law, unless it shall have been long acquiesced in, or more than once affirmed—and unless, on a survey of all material considerations, you feel that it is better to adhere to it than, by overruling it, to produce uncertainty and surprise. *Stare decisis* should be thus, and only thus, understood and applied. Stability and uniformity require that authority, even when conflicting with principle, should sometimes decide what the law is. But, in all questionable cases, follow the safer guides—reason and the harmony of the law in all its parts. (Quoted in Wilson 1908, 398)

Elsewhere referring to "the onward spirit of the age" and to "the expanded and still expanding genius of the common law," Robertson went on to cite reservations that portrayed judges in a more conservative light:

> We know that a zealous and inconsiderate spirit of innovation and improvement requires the vigilance and restraint of both reason and law. We are fully aware, also, of the fact that, when such a spirit is abroad, private rights are in peculiar danger, unless sternly guarded by the judiciary; and we are not sure that such guardianship is not most needed in a government where whatever is popular is apt to prevail, at first and often at last, only because it is *vox populi*. (Quoted in Wilson 1908, 399)

Robertson appears to have introduced innovations into a number of areas of the law. He wrote a decision in *Griswold v. Hepburn* (opposing payment of paper money for prior debts incurred by the government) that was first affirmed and later overturned by the United States Supreme Court in the *Legal Tender Cases*. He wrote innovative decisions on the liability of employers for fellow-servants, on the law of mental illness, on domestic relations, and on cases where ignorance of the law, or intoxication, might serve as mitigating factors (Wilson 1908, 400–401).

Although he initially opposed emancipation (Coulter), Robertson—who had once spoken eloquently in opposition to the doctrine of states' rights laid down in the Kentucky Resolution of 1798—remained loyal to the Union. He appears, however, to have accepted his second term of service on the court largely to beat out the candidate supported by the state's military government.

Identified in William Draper Lewis's *Great American Lawyers* (1908) as one of the great lawyer/judges of his age, Robertson has slipped into relative obscurity. He appears nonetheless to have been a good example of a competent and conscientious lawyer and judge who often put service to the bench over the financial rewards that he might have achieved had he devoted himself solely to the bar.

References:

Coulter, Ellis Merton. "George Robertson." *Biography Resource Center*. Available at <www.Galenet.com>.

Wilson, Samuel Mackay. 1908. "George Robertson." In *Great American Lawyers*, vol. 4, edited by William Draper Lewis. Philadelphia: The John C. Winston Company, 365–406.

References and Further Reading:

Heinlen, James F. 2000. "William Mitchell School of Law Celebrates Centennial." *Winona Post*, 29 November, sec. "Area News."

Horwitz, Morton J. 1977. *The Transformation of American Law, 1780–1860*. Cambridge: Harvard University Press.

Jaggard, Edwin Ames. 1909. "William Mitchell." In *Great American Lawyers: A History of the Legal Profession in America*, vol. 8, edited by William Draper Lewis. Philadelphia: The John C. Winston Company.

Lees, Edward. 1920. "William Mitchell." *Minnesota Law Review* 4: 377.

MORRIS, LEWIS

(1671–1746)

LEWIS MORRIS
Library of Congress

LEWIS MORRIS WAS A TRAILblazer of early American law and politics. As a jurist he attained greatness for his steadfast belief in justice above all things. Morris's most influential decision was a dissent, delivered in the case of *King v. Van Dam*, holding that a royal governor could not create a court of equity simply to serve his own purposes. The publication of that dissent led to his dismissal as chief justice of the New York Supreme Court and to the infamous trial of newspaper publisher Peter Zenger that stands as a testament to the importance of an independent judiciary.

Lewis Morris was born on 15 October 1671 in New York City. He was the only child of Richard and Sarah Pole Morris, who had emigrated to the colonies from Barbados in 1670. Both of his parents died only a year after his birth, in 1672, and soon after his uncle, Lewis Morris Sr., came to New York and took charge of raising him and managing the Morris estate in New York. Although Lewis Sr. was seventy-two years old when he took control of the Morris estate, he was active in the New York and East Jersey business community, and the estate grew quickly. Lewis Sr. was also politically active and was appointed to both the New York and East Jersey Council and Court of Common Right. These political connections eventually helped young Lewis in his own political career. Lewis Sr. was a devout Quaker, and he raised young Lewis Morris in a strict Quaker home. During the early part of his lifetime the younger Morris was also an active churchman, serving from 1697 to 1700 as a vestryman of Trinity Church and encouraging the Society for the Propagation of the Gospel in its missionary enterprises.

When he was eighteen, Morris rebelled against the strict household maintained by his aunt and uncle and left home. He traveled throughout the colonies and into the Caribbean, where he eventually settled, working as a scrivener, or one who drew up legal documents, in Jamaica for about a year. Upon his return to New York in 1691, both of Lewis's adopted parents passed away within a year, and he assumed control of the Morris estate. By that time, the estate was one of the largest in the provinces of New York and East Jersey, comprising a 6,200-acre estate in East Jersey, known as Tinton Manor; a 1,920-acre manor in New York City, later known as Morrisania Manor; and a 1,500-acre tract of land on Long Island. His position as a landed aristocrat played a large role in his political and judicial philosophy, and throughout his life he defended both the interests of property owners and the Crown. Later in 1691, he married Isabella Graham, daughter of a New York City political power broker and relative to several high-ranking members of the British parliament and military. The two remained married for over fifty-five years, and during that time, Isabella gave birth to fifteen children. Morris was a devoted father and family man, but he spent little energy on business affairs, preferring the fields of law and politics.

Morris was a noted man of both letters and science and quickly accumulated one of the largest private libraries in the colonies. He also considered himself a poet. His first known poem, in which he contrasted the brave and principled patriot's opposition to a tyrant, foreshadowed his future battles against the English governors (Sheridan 1981, 13–14).

Young Morris quickly began to establish his life in politics. In 1692, at the young age of twenty-two, he accepted the first political appointment of his half-century political career when he became a member of the East Jersey Council of Gov. Andrew Hamilton and a judge on the Court of Common Right. On his first day on the bench, Morris faced the case of *Fullerton v. Jones*, involving proprietary property rights. At that time the province of New Jersey was split into two portions, East and West New Jersey. A small council of land proprietors, who owned title through royal grant, politically controlled each region. In *Fullerton*, a New Jersey group of proprietary property rights holders were seeking to eject a subsequent patentee who had been given possession of the land by a New York governor (Sheridan 1981, 23). After two years of argument, Morris and his fellow justices sent the case to the jury with instructions to annul the rights of the subsequent property holders in order to protect the proprietary rights of the landed aristocracy. The jury nullified this instruction, however, and upheld the dwellers' property rights. Morris and the other judges on the East Jersey court would not abide being overruled by a jury composed of nonlanded individuals and reversed the jury's decision. Ironically, forty years later Morris was the financial backer of a group that argued for jury nullification in the landmark slander case against John Peter Zenger.

Morris was both ambitious and contentious. In 1698, he became embroiled in the first of many disputes with colonial governors. He contested the appointment of Jeremiah Basse as Andrew Hamilton's successor as governor of New York and East Jersey and was eventually removed from both his position on the Governors Council and on the Common Court. Morris protested Basse's appointment on the ground that the choice had been made by only ten of the required sixteen land proprietors. After his dismissal, he and his fellow former judges staged a protest of Basse's newly formed Provincial Court that almost ended in bloodshed and resulted in Morris's arrest and fine for denying the authority of the new court. Morris's combativeness continued throughout a career in which Morris placed his principles over possible political consequences.

After this political setback, Morris traveled to England to promote the transfer of the power to choose governors from the council of land proprietors to the Crown. This policy switch was in direct contrast with his previous support of the land proprietors in the provinces, but it was not without purpose. For at the same time, he promoted himself to be first royal governor of the newly created province of New Jersey. His effort to become governor failed, but Queen Anne ended the proprietary system of political control and renewed Crown control over the province. In exchange for this transfer of power, Morris garnered the confirmation of the proprietors' rights to the land of New Jersey against all other patentees (Stelhorn and Birkner 1982, 55). The contacts that Morris made on his trip had both long- and short-term benefits for his career. Upon his return, Morris subsequently mounted a vigorous offensive against the new governor, Lord Cornbury. Despite these protests, he was named to Governor Cornbury's council in 1703. Of course his constant attack on Cornbury's policies led to his removal in 1704. Morris evidenced his view that owning property was an undeniable right in this assault on Cornbury, and this view soon became engrained in the American philosophical lexicon. For example, Morris continually assailed Cornbury for undermining the colonists' *liberties* as that term referred to title to land. Morris and the assembly censured Cornbury for invading the "rights" of the proprietors of the colony, those "rights" being their "Title to their Lands and Rents, violently and Arbitrarily forced from them . . ." (Hutson 1994, 214). Morris was reinstated to the Council upon appeal to the queen, but shortly thereafter, Cornbury removed him again.

Cornbury was removed from office and was replaced by Robert Hunter in 1710. Morris became the most prominent supporter of the newly appointed governor, even naming a son after him. Morris's connections to Hunter led to Morris's appointment as chief justice of the Supreme Court of New York in 1715. In that role, he became the first native-born chief justice of the colony. He also continued to serve upon the Governor's Council for New Jersey. His relationship with Hunter was very close, and in fact in 1714 he collaborated with Governor Hunter on the production of the first play written and published in a British colony (Sheridan 1981, 117). Morris's relationship with Hunter demonstrates that he objected not to English authority but to arbitrary and unchecked authority. Moreover, Morris was a vociferous and constant supporter of the Crown, despite the limits on liberty imposed by the British on the early colonists.

Morris's dichotomies were reflected in his views on slavery. During his tenure as chief justice, Morris took the opportunity in a case to hold that slaves were men and that a slave had the right to take the life of a white man who threatened the life of his master or mistress. Despite this view, he owned about sixty slaves who worked on his manors until he relinquished control of his estates to his son upon being appointed governor of New Jersey in 1738.

Morris's views of factionalism were also inconsistent with his own practice. In the March 1727 Supreme Court term, he charged a grand jury to be wary of the dangers of political factionalism, which he equated with unwarranted or irresponsible criticism of the administration in power:

> The Histories of all Nations abound with melancholy Instances of the terrible effects of Faction; which, when let loose, has been like an impestuous Torrent, capable of overturning all that lay in its Way; and those of our own Country are not without flagrant Examples, what small Sparks seditious Arts have blown into Flame, not easily to be extinguished, and not long since endangered the Constitution it self; therefore no Care or Caution can be too much, to check such Things in their first Appearance. (Sheridan 1981, 139)

Given this caution concerning faction, it is no small irony that he helped plant the seeds of the American Revolution. Morris's conflict with Governor Cosby, which was rife with seditious and factional railings against authority, led directly to the trial of Peter Zenger and was described by Morris's own grandson Gouveneur Morris as "the germ of American freedom, the morning star of that liberty which subsequently revolutionized America" (Few 1997, 46).

By the time newly appointed Governor Cosby arrived in New York in 1732, Chief Justice Lewis Morris was one of the greatest political figures of his time. He was also already the center of the opposition to Cosby's administration. Morris had used his position as chief justice to consolidate his position as the center of anti-executive political machination even before Cosby's arrival. Morris was experienced in the ways of provincial politics, and it was said of him, "tho' he was indolent in the management of his private affairs, yet, thro' the love of power, he was always busy in matters of a political nature, and no man in the colony equaled him in the knowledge of the law and the arts of intrigue" (Moglen 1994, 1506).

Almost immediately, Cosby fell prey to Morris's political machine. Cosby demanded half the pay that senior New York Council member Rip Van Dam had received as acting governor in 1731 during the year before Cosby's arrival. Van Dam countered that he would only share half of his salary if Cosby would split any money received as prerequisites of his office from the time of Cosby's appointment in 1731 until his arrival in New York. Cosby refused this offer and filed suit in the New York Supreme Court, asking the court to sit as a Court of Exchequer, or equity. This would have avoided a jury trial in which a jury of New York colonists, more likely to be sympathetic to Van Dam, would have sat in judgment of their new governor. Many colonists, including Morris, despised courts of equity as arbitrary tribunals composed of high government officials reminiscent of the Star Chamber. Historically, equity courts were generally not sympathetic to common men who were not well connected to the government. Believing that the governor's request was an unlawful creation of a court of equity, Morris refused to hear the case.

His opinion in *King v. Van Dam* describing the case's jurisdictional error has been described as more polemical than legal (Sheridan 1981, 156), but his reasoning was sound. He argued that since the king himself could not create a court of equity without the consent of Parliament, then the king could not delegate that power to a provincial governor, without legislative constraint. Morris's opinion traced the history of judicial powers in the provinces and as a result even called into question the validity of the courts of chancery (Morris [1733] 1929, 2–8). He concluded that only the legislature could create courts and set the limits of their jurisdiction. The combination of the executive branch with the judicial branch of government would result in tyranny. As a result he concluded that "no less or other authority than that of the whole Legislature can erect a court of equity" (Morris [1733] 1929, 2). Subsequently, Morris published his opinion and distributed it throughout the province with a bluntly worded letter addressed directly to Governor Cosby. He stated:

> If Judges are to be intimidated so as not to dare to give any opinion, but what is pleasing to the Governour, and agreeable to his private Views, the People of

> this Province, who are very much concern'd, both with respect to their lives and Fortunes, in the Freedom and Independence of those who are to judge of them, may possibly not think of themselves so secure in either of them as their laws and his majesty intends they should be. (Morris [1733] 1929, 15)

When the Supreme Court reconvened, and Morris learned that his opinion was in fact the minority voice on the three-member panel, he stormed out of the courtroom, describing his peers as "mean, weak and futile" (Sheridan 1981, 152). After Morris departed, Cosby suspended Morris as chief justice, and two days later replaced him with James DeLancey. Van Dam's lawyers objected to the court's continuing to hear the case on the ground that Morris's removal was invalid because Supreme Court justices should be commissioned *quam diu se bene gesserint* (as long as they proved to be honest, or in good behavior) rather than *quam diu nobis placuerit* (at our pleasure). The objection was overruled, and Van Dam was ordered to pay Cosby his money in equity. Morris never again served as a judge.

Morris used the momentum gained from the case to expand his political party. Leaders of the Anti-Cosby Morrisites were Lewis Morris, Rip Van Dam, and Van Dam's two lawyers, James Alexander and William Smith. In Peter Zenger and his newly founded paper, the *New York Weekly Journal*, they saw an opportunity to broaden the impact of their diatribes against the governor. Zenger, eager for their business, became their willing pawn. Soon anonymous letters written by Morris, Van Dam, and others, criticizing the governor, filled Zenger's paper. The journal was an early form of the *Drudge Report*, filled with scandal and satire largely attacking Governor Cosby. This article, attributed to Morris, calls on the citizens of New York not to fall prey to the easy answer of joining the Governor's cause:

> Let this wiseacre (whoever he is) go to any country wife and tell her that the fox is a mischievous creature that can and does do her much hurt, that it is difficult if not impracticable to catch him, and that therefore she ought on any terms to keep in with him. Why don't we keep in with serpents and wolves on this foot? Animals much more innocent and less mischievous to the public than some Governors have proved. A Governor turns rogue, does a thousand things for which a small rogue would have deserved a halter; and because it is difficult if not impracticable to obtain relief against him; therefore it is prudent to keep in with him and join in the roguery. . . . (*New York Weekly Journal* 1734)

Cosby was so incensed that he publicly burned issues of the *Weekly Journal*. Eventually he had Zenger arrested for libel and put on trial. The information on which Zenger was tried echoed Morris's dissent in *King v. Van*

Dam: "I think the law itself is at an end; we see . . . men's deeds destroyed, juries arbitrarily displaced, new Courts erected without consent of the Legislature, . . . by which it seems to me, trials by juries are taken away when a Governor pleases" (Glendon 1996, 50). Although the writings in the weekly journal were printed anonymously, this excerpt truly represents the Morrisite philosophy.

The new chief justice, DeLancey, set bail for Zenger at £400, a virtually unheard-of amount. Zenger's supporters, including Morris, were very wealthy and could have easily raised the bail, but poor Zenger was worth more to the cause as a symbol of the governor's tyranny, so they left him in jail. Their strategy was to base Zenger's defense on the truth of the *Journal* articles, thereby trying Cosby in the process. Zenger's lawyer Andrew Hamilton made an impassioned plea to the jury in support of the liberty to expose and oppose tyranny by speaking and writing the truth without fear of prosecution. Hamilton admitted that Zenger had published the statements in question, but he asserted that the printer could not be convicted of libel for printing the truth. His novel argument was that the jury should determine not only whether Zenger had printed the statements but also whether the statements were legally libelous. These contentions were unsupported by English common law, in which truth was not a defense for libel. Judge DeLancey agreed that truth was not a defense and instructed the jury that it was to determine only whether Zenger had published the statements, leaving the legal determination of libel to the court. In fact, in a murder trial before the New York Supreme Court in 1716, Morris himself had noted of a charge to the jury that the jury "must" return particular verdicts if it finds specified facts to have been proven (*King v. Andrew Broostead* [New York 1716]). Zenger was eventually acquitted and released, signifying one of the first known cases of jury nullification. In 1733, the Morrisites won sweeping victories in various local elections. Morris himself defeated a Cosby appointee in an election as representative of Westchester County to the Provincial Assembly.

After the trial, Lewis Morris left New York in November 1734, accompanied by his son, Robert Hunter Morris, and spent a futile eighteen months in London seeking vindication and reinstatement to judicial office by the Privy Council. Morris pointed out the dangers to the property and liberties of the subjects created by arbitrary removal of judges. Morris hoped that the gubernatorial power of removal in the colonies would be restricted in the future and made to conform to the laws of England. He urged that judicial independence required a royal declaration that judges would not be removable at the pleasure of a governor but only at the pleasure of the Crown. These requests largely fell on deaf ears. The lords of the Board of Trade in London, however, later declared that Morris's removal had been illegal

(Finkelman 1994, 31). This removal remains the only specific removal from judicial office by a governor that is recorded in the entire controversy over judicial tenure in the American colonies (Smith 1976, 1116).

Morris's political career was revived in 1738 when the Crown severed the political connection between New York and New Jersey, and he became governor of New Jersey. His appointment, which made him the first appointed American provincial governor, was based largely on his previous contacts with the Crown as well as the fact that he had been a constantly squeaking wheel in the ear of the Crown. Unfortunately, his administration was not successful. It was marked by confrontations with the general assembly over taxation, support of the militia, issuance of bills of credit, and validity of land titles. Though he had challenged the royal prerogative as represented by Cornbury and Cosby, he permitted no questioning of his own authority or of his royal charge. He frequently lectured the provincial assembly on its duties and complained to the lords of trade in 1740 that the legislators "fancy themselves to have as much power as a British House of commons, and more" (Sheridan 1991, 23). He allowed no criticism of Parliament, noting that "a British Parliament can abolish any Constitution that they deem inconvenient or disadvantageous to the trade of the nation or otherwise" (Stelhorn and Birkner 1982, 56).

In 1739 Gov. Lewis Morris, with the unanimous advice of his Council, appointed his son, Robert Hunter Morris, as chief justice of the Supreme Court. Perhaps with his own experience in mind, he specifically designated Robert's appointment to last during good behavior. Morris's heirs reflected his contentious nature and belief in principle over consequences. When his grandson Lewis Morris was about to sign the Declaration of Independence, his brother cautioned that his signature could cost him all his property. Morris, a plainspoken founder, responded, "Damn the consequences, give me the pen" (Hawke 1976, 210).

Lewis Morris died on 21 May 1746 in Kingsbury, New Jersey. His belief in the need for an independent judiciary laid the foundation of the current system of separation of powers that serves to guarantee freedoms and liberties from executive excesses. It is appropriate that the name Morris derives from the Welsh *mawr* and *rys*, meaning "brave man," as he was one of the first of a long line of great American patriots and judges who bravely stuck to their principles in the face of great personal costs.

Andrew G. Braniff

References and Further Reading:

Alexander, James. 1972. *A Brief Narrative of the Case and Trial of John Peter Zenger.* 2d ed. Edited by Stanley N. Katz. Cambridge: Belknap Press of Harvard University Press.

Few, John 1997. "Citizen Participation in the Legal System." *South Carolina Lawyer* 46 (July/August): 46–48.

Finkelman, John 1994. "Politics, the Press, and the Law: The Trial of John Peter Zenger." In *American Political Trials*, edited by Michael R. Belknap. Westport, Conn: Greenwood Press, 21–42.

Glendon, William R. 1996. "The Trial of Peter Zenger." *New York Bar Journal* 68 (December): 48–52.

Hawke, David Freeman. 1976. *Honorable Treason*. New York: Viking Press.

Hutson, James H. 1994. "The Emergence of the Modern Concept of Right in America, The Contribution of Michel Villey." *American Journal of Jurisprudence* 39: 185.

Katz, Stanley. 1968. *Newcastle's New York: Anglo-American Politics, 1732–1753*. Cambridge: Harvard University Press.

Moglen, Eben 1994. "Considering Zenger: Partisan Politics and the Legal Profession in Provincial New York." *Columbia Law Review* 94: 1495.

Morris, Lewis. [1733] 1929. *The Opinion and Argument of the Chief Justice of the Province of New York, concerning the Jurisdiction of the Supream Court of the Said Province, to Determine Causes in a Court of Equity*. New York: Sold by J. P. Zenger. Reprint, Boston: Massachusetts Historical Society.

New York Weekly Journal. 1734. 21 January.

Sheridan, Eugene. 1981. *Lewis Morris, 1671–1746: A Study in Early American Politics*. Syracuse. N.Y.: Syracuse University Press.

Sheridan, Eugene, ed. 1991. "*The Papers of Lewis Morris, Governor of the Province of New Jersey, Vol. I- IV.*" New Jersey Historical Society.

Smith, Joseph A. 1976. "An Independent Judiciary: The Colonial Background." *University of Pennsylvania Law Review* 124: 1104.

Smith, L. M., and L. Hershkowitz. 1972. "Courts of Equity in the Province of New York: The Cosby Controversy, 1732–1736." *American Journal of Legal History* 16: 1.

Stelhorn, Paul, and Michael Birkner, eds. 1982. *The Governors of New Jersey*. New Jersey Historical Commission.

MOTLEY, CONSTANCE BAKER

(1921–)

CONSTANCE BAKER MOTLEY
Library of Congress

IN ADDITION TO WINNING NINE of ten civil rights cases that she argued before the United States Supreme Court, Constance Baker Motley was the first African American woman to serve in the New York state senate, the first to serve as president of the Manhattan borough, and the first to fill a seat on the federal judiciary in the United States. Appointed by Pres. Lyndon B. Johnson to the United States District Court for the Southern District of New York in 1966, she became chief judge of that court in 1982 and took senior status in 1986.

Born to an immigrant family from the island of Nevis in the West Indies, Constance Baker was born in New Haven, Connecticut, in 1921 as one of twelve children of Willoughby Alva Baker and Rachel Huggins Baker. Her father was a chef at a Yale University fraternity. Although New Haven was far more hospitable to African Americans than was the Deep South, Constance's early years were not free from discrimination, as when she was denied access to a local beach. A tall girl who took on a number of leadership positions within the local African American community, she came from a family that did not have the financial means to send her to college and that expected her to become a hairdresser. Instead, a white businessman, Clarence Blakeslee, who heard Constance give a speech, was so impressed that he agreed to finance her college education. She began her undergraduate education by heading south to Fisk University in Nashville and finished her degree in economics at New York University. She then earned her law degree from Columbia, where she was one of the few women enrolled.

Thurgood Marshall, one of the twentieth century's greatest litigators and most important civil right lawyers (who would also become the nation's first African American United States Supreme Court justice), subsequently employed her as a clerk at the Legal Defense Fund of the National Association for the Advancement of Colored People (NAACP), and Motley, who has also looked to Florence E. Allen (another federal judge) as a role model, continues to regard Marshall as one of her most important mentors and role models. Motley gradually rose in the ranks of the Legal Defense Fund, arguing cases involving equal pay for African American schoolteachers in the South and opening up colleges and universities to African Americans, including James Meredith, whom she helped get admitted into the University of Mississippi. She argued her first case in a southern courtroom that displayed a gigantic mural of splendidly attired white plantation owners and their wives in hooped shirts on one side and black slaves on the other (Brenner 1994, 68), but even in such circumstances she was rarely intimidated.

Especially in the South, Motley was considered something of an oddity because it was unusual for individuals of both her race and her gender to be lawyers, and courts were often packed with observers who came to see the "New York" lawyer in action. Motley was among the lawyers who helped with the briefs for the case of *Brown v. Board of Education* (1954) that overturned *Plessy v. Ferguson* (1896) and declared that the doctrine of "separate but equal" would no longer be tolerated in the area of racial relations, and especially in public schooling. She was often the only female counsel in the major civil rights cases of her era. She got to know Dr. Martin Luther King Jr. and defended him and other civil rights leaders who engaged in peaceful "sit-in" demonstrations.

Although she never received the recognition and adulation that Thurgood Marshall and a number of other lawyers from that era received from the black community, her profile was sufficient to enable her to run successfully for a seat in the New York state senate in 1964, and she was subsequently selected by the New York City Council to serve as Manhattan borough president. The first day she went as part of her job to attend a meeting of the Board of Estimate, she was stopped by a policeman, who—observing her color and not knowing her job—warned her that there would be "no picketing today, lady" (Barron 1999, B2). In the meantime, her legal work had come to the attention of Atty. Gen. Ramsey Clark and New York senator (himself a former attorney general) Robert Kennedy. Although Kennedy apparently later moderated his support over a political controversy, they recommended her for a judicial nomination.

Shirley Mount Hufstedler: Appellate Judge and Secretary of Education (1925–)

United States Supreme Court justice Ruth Bader Ginsburg has singled out Shirley Mount Hufstedler as one of three women pioneers on the lower federal bench (the others Ginsburg listed were Florence Ellinwood Allen and Burnita Shelton Matthews, who are covered elsewhere in these volumes). Shirley Mount was born in Denver, Colorado, in 1925 and earned her undergraduate degree at the University of New Mexico before graduating at the top of her law class at Stanford Law School. She subsequently married Seth Martin Hufstedler in 1949, entered private practice, and worked in the Los Angeles firm of Beardsley, Hufstedler and Kemble from 1951 to 1961. In 1960, she worked with the California attorney general in a complex case involving litigation over the Colorado River, a case that eventually made its way to the United States Supreme Court. The next year she was appointed to the Los Angeles Superior Court, a trial court, and in 1966 to the California Court of Appeal.

In 1968, Pres. Lyndon Johnson appointed Hufstedler to the United States Court of Appeals for the Ninth Circuit, and she served in that capacity for eleven years. Pres. Jimmy Carter appointed her in 1979 to head the newly created Department of Education. Hufstedler served in that capacity for two years, leaving a reputation for professionalism that was important to the new department.

After leaving that post, Hufstedler resumed private practice but continued her concern with public affairs, including arms control and the establishment of closer relationships with Eastern European nations (Ginsburg and Brill 1995, 287). Hufstedler has received numerous honorary degrees, and she chaired a U.S. Commission on Immigration Reform in 1996–1997.

Justice Ginsburg noted that, although Hufstedler was thought for a time to be a prime candidate for an appointment to the United States Supreme Court, "she never tailored her opinions to please the home crowd, or the White House crowd" (Ginsburg and Brill 1995, 286). Ginsburg noted that Hufstedler was a particularly passionate defender of the right to privacy and an opponent of myths of inferiority that are designed to undervalue the contributions of groups of citizens.

References:

Ginsburg, Ruth Bader, and Laura W. Brill. 1995. "Women in the Federal Judiciary: Three Way Pavers and the Exhilarating Change President Carter Wrought." *Fordham Law Review* 64 (November): 281–290.

"Shirley Mount Hufstedler." *The Complete Marquis Who's Who*. 2001. Reproduced in Biography Resource Center, Farmington Hills, Mich.: The Gale Group. Available at <http://galenet.galegroup.com/servlet/BioRC?ste=36&helppg=marquis.htm&LocID=tel_middleten>.

President Johnson initially recommended Motley to the Second United States Court of Appeal, but faced with strong objections from Mississippi's Senator John Eastland and others who had long opposed civil rights, Johnson withdrew her nomination to the Second Circuit and nominated her instead for the post of a United States district judge. Still pressured by Eastland and other southern opponents of civil rights, the Senate took its time, but it confirmed her in this post, which she assumed in 1966. At the time, the only other women federal judges were Sarah Hughes of Dallas, Bonita Matthews (in the District of Columbia), Florence Allen on a United States Court of Appeals, and Mary H. Donlon, a New York City customs judge (Motley 1998, 214). Even though the New York Southern District Court was the largest such court in the nation, with twenty-four judges, at the time of her appointment Motley was the only woman or minority to serve on that court (210). Apparently unaware of her reputation for professional dress as an attorney, two men from the Queens Bar Association wanted to know whether she would appear on the bench in "one of those bright flowered dresses that women wear" and were relieved to hear her respond, "Of course not" (218).

Most stories about Motley, as well as her own remembrances, concentrate on her exciting and tireless years as a civil rights advocate. With her experience arguing such cases as a federal judge, it is not surprising that she appears to have amassed a solid record as a United States district judge as well. She has been showered with honorary degrees by many universities and by awards from civil rights organizations.

United States district judges are trial judges, and they hear a variety of criminal and civil cases. Motley has proved to be no exception. In 1982, she presided over a case in which she sentenced a number of Croatian nationalists to long jail terms for murder, arson, and extortion. She had previously given careful consideration to the legitimacy of search warrants that police officers had used to obtain evidence in this case as well as police use of an alleged confession. Motley's consideration of each issue individually (she accepted the legitimacy of the search warrant based in part on testimony from an informant but concluded that the confession should be suppressed) demonstrated a careful weighing of each issue (see *United States v. Ljubas et al.*, 1982). Similarly, although she ruled that the ABC television network had not, in writing its show "The Greatest American Hero," infringed on "Superman" works owned by Warner Brothers, Motley also ruled in a follow-up case that the suit had not been frivolous and that ABC was not therefore entitled to an award of lawyers' fees (*Warner Brothers v. ABC*, 1982).

In 1987, Motley delivered a powerful blow for the rights of defendants when she declared that police could only detain suspects for twenty-four hours before charging them with an actual crime ("Constance Baker Motley," *Encyclopedia of World Biography Supplement*). That same year, Motley ruled on behalf of a black carpenter, Samuel Richards, who had been passed up for promotion to a foreman's position by the New York Board of Education. Although the white individual who had received the promotion had a slightly higher civil service score, Motley was able to show that Richards was better qualified by education and experience, that the board bypassed its own procedures for choosing among the top three candidates in such circumstances, that it failed even to conduct the requisite interview, and that its decision in Richards's case was part of a more pervasive pattern of discrimination and failure to implement affirmative action hiring policies that demonstrated discriminatory intent (*Richards v. New York City Board of Education*, 1987).

In 1988, Motley was generally credited for her no-nonsense handling of the so-called Wedtech bribery case. It involved multiple defendants and dozens of witnesses. Completing such a complicated case within a five-month period was regarded as a significant achievement (French 1988, 32). A reporter noted that Motley was known for her "daunting glare and sharp rebuke she gives to any lawyer who oversteps courtroom bounds" (32). She rebuked one lawyer by stating that "what you just said to me indicates that you are either not familiar with this court, or you are trying to pull my leg" (32). She has been described as "judicial, formal, [and] precise" (Brenner 1994, 66). That observer has further noted that "unlike many of the civil-rights activists of her generation, she is far more comfortable discoursing on the history of the Fourteenth Amendment than delivering an impassioned speech" (66).

In 1991, Motley had a major impact on academic life when she delivered a powerful award for punitive damages against Kinko's Graphics Corporation. Motley found in *Basic Books Inc. et al. v. Kinko's Graphics Corporation* that the "course packs" that Kinko's was preparing for classes went far beyond "fair use" and were designed not so much to spread knowledge to students as to impair legitimate copyright rights of individuals and companies who had published scholarly articles. In her decision, she made it clear that she was awarding punitive damages with the clear intent of stopping Kinko's from continuing the practice.

In 1994, Motley applied principles from civil rights litigation to the issue of women's rights. At issue was the case of Dr. Cynthia Fisher, who had been denied tenure in the Vassar Biology Department. In a meticulous review of the facts, Motley was able to show that over a thirty-year period the department had never tenured a married woman but had penalized them, presumably because many, like Dr. Fisher, had taken some time from their scholarly studies in order to raise their families. Dissecting the evidence regarding research and publication, teaching, and other university contributions on which the department and the college had denied Fisher tenure, Motley found that Dr. Fisher had credentials that exceeded those of male colleagues who had been tenured during the same time period. Motley further found that the department's proffered reasons for denying tenure to Fisher were "disingenuous, pretextual and clearly made in bad faith" (*Fisher v. Vasser College*, 1202). In ruling that Dr. Fisher should either be awarded her job and back pay or the difference between what she was then making as a social worker (a career she had chosen after being denied tenure) and what she would have made had she been given tenure, Motley noted that "[i]n the case at hand, plaintiff has presented evidence of a virtual smoking gun" (1229).

In a still more recent case involving education, Motley ruled that the Board of Education of New York was still not making sufficient efforts to provide education, especially special education programs, for individuals who were incarcerated on Rikers Island (Forero 2000, B3). Motley also ruled in a recent case that Pam Martens and Judith Mione, who had raised charges of sexual harassment against brokerage house Smith Barney, had to abide by their own contracts and submit their own claims to an arbitration process (Chapelle, "Smith Barney Wins Boom-Boom Round").

Motley learned to be tough and meticulous as a lawyer, and this same toughness and thoroughness appears to have characterized her judicial rulings. She and her husband, real estate broker Joel Motley, have a son who graduated from Harvard Law School and is a practicing lawyer. Numerous civil rights organizations and colleges have honored Motley for her work as a litigator and a judge. Motley believes that the legal profession remains open to persons of color. She notes that "lawyers are natural leaders and activists in the black community. More and more blacks will become involved in policy making agencies, in government, in politics, in business and diplomacy—in areas where blacks have not been before and where decisions and changes are going to be made" (quoted in "Constance Baker Motley," *Notable Black American Women*). Motley has written a number of law review articles as well as her autobiography, *Equal Justice under Law*. She is critical of Justice Clarence Thomas, the second African American Supreme Court justice, for his opposition to affirmative action and, despite her optimism about the role that African Americans can play in the U.S. legal system, remains concerned that the nation is suffering a reaction against African American progress similar to that which occurred after the period of Reconstruction (Motley 1998, 229–247).

John R. Vile

Note

Special thanks are due to Thad Smith for background research on this essay.

References and Further Reading:

Barron, James, with Jonathan P. Hicks and Alex Kuczynski. 1999. "Public Lives." *New York Times*, 20 October, B2.

Basic Books Inc. et al. v. Kinko's Graphics Corporation. 1991 U.S. Dist. LEXIS 19930.

Brenner, Marie. 1994. "Judge Motley's Verdict." *The New Yorker* 70, 16 May, 65–71.

Chapelle, Tony. "Smith Barney Wins Boom-Boom Round." 1 June 2002. Securities Data Publishing on Wall Street. Accessed through LexisNexis web service.

"Constance Baker Motley." *Encyclopedia of World Biography Supplement*. Vol. 18. Gale Research, 1998. Accessed through Biography Resource Center on Internet.

"Constance Baker Motley." *Notable Black American Women*. Book I. Gale Research, 1992, as found on the Internet Biography Resource Center.

Fisher v. Vassar College. 852 F. Supp. 1193 (1994).

Forero, Juan. 2000. "Judge Tells City to Assure Schooling in Jail." *New York Times*, 13 January, B3.

French, Howard W. 1988. "Guiding Wedtech Trial, a Sure Hand." *New York Times*, 7 August, sec. 2, pt. I, p. 32.

Motley, Constance Baker. 1998. *Equal Justice under Law: An Autobiography*. New York: Farrar, Straus and Giroux.

Polhmann, Marcus. 2001. "Motley, Constance Baker." In *Great American Lawyers: An Encyclopedia*, vol. 2, edited by John R. Vile. Santa Barbara, Calif.: ABC-CLIO, 511–516.

Richards v. New York City Board of Education. 668 F. Supp. 259 (1987).

United States v. Ljubas et al. 1982 U.S. Dist. LEXIS 11097.

Warner Brothers v. ABC. 1982 U.S. Dist. LEXIS 15339.

MURRAH, ALFRED P.

(1904–1975)

Alfred P. Murrah
AP Photo

As one of the youngest federal judges ever appointed to the bench, Murrah became a fixture in the Tenth Circuit Court of Appeals. Murrah is known mostly for his work as an administrator, attempting to improve the judicial system, and as the second director of the Federal Judicial Center.

Alfred Murrah was one of the pioneers of the last frontier in the United States, the state of Oklahoma. Murrah was born in Oklahoma on 27 October 1904, three years before the Oklahoma territory became a state. His father, George Washington Murrah, had five children by his first wife, Lucy, and a single child, Alfred, by his second wife, Lanora. Alfred's mother died when he was eight, and his childhood involved hard work, as his family had few financial resources. After graduating from high school, Murrah entered the University of Oklahoma in 1922, graduating with a law degree in 1928. During his college years Murrah struggled to finance his education, being forced to work at a variety of jobs to pay the bills. After graduation, Murrah established a law firm, partnering with Luther Bohannon. The firm focused on workmen's compensation cases, a growing field in the 1930s. At the same time Murrah met and married Agnes Milam in

1930. The Murrahs had three children, a boy and two girls. His son, Paul, also attended law school and worked as an attorney.

As his law practice expanded and became centered in Oklahoma City, Murrah moved beyond the legal realm into the political realm, participating in state politics. He helped manage both state legislative races and federal congressional races. One such race saw him supporting Josh Lee, who ran in 1936 for U.S. senator. Lee won and when given the opportunity to recommend a man for an open federal court vacancy in Oklahoma, he chose Murrah. After a flurry of internal fighting among Oklahoma Democrats, Franklin Roosevelt sent up the nomination and Murrah was confirmed. Murrah took his seat on 12 March 1937, becoming a federal district judge at the age of thirty-two.

Murrah served in that position for four years. During that period Murrah earned a reputation as a prolabor judge, not surprising for a Roosevelt appointee. In one important decision that reached the Supreme Court, *Williams v. Jewel Tea* (1940), Murrah argued for a broad interpretation of the federal commerce power and sought to uphold the Fair Labor Standards Act. The Supreme Court agreed with Murrah, using the *Williams* case to support broad congressional power to regulate the economy.

Most cases heard by Murrah, though, did not become national precedent. In the late 1930s, Oklahoma had a frontier image, with the state and federal governments having difficulty controlling the population. One area of contention was the production and sale of liquor in Oklahoma, which was a dry state at the time. The large number of cases and the difficulty in trying them led Murrah to play the unusual role of judge and defense counsel in one case. Murrah argued before a jury on behalf of a defendant. The defendant was convicted; then Murrah returned to his position as judge and sentenced the defendant. Playing these two roles was an example of how the legal system was just beginning to develop in the state and how Murrah was able to act in a judicious manner.

His abilities soon earned him a reputation in the sparsely populated state. With the retirement of a judge from the Tenth Circuit Court of Appeals, Murrah was mentioned and then appointed to the vacancy. He became one of the youngest appeals court judges on 9 September 1940. He was only thirty-six years old. It would be from this position that Murrah would serve nearly thirty years and earn a national reputation as a reformer of the federal judicial process.

The Tenth Circuit Court of Appeals heard cases originating in Colorado, Kansas, New Mexico, Oklahoma, Utah, and Wyoming. The court had its main center in Denver, Colorado, though the judges would travel throughout the states to decide appeals. When Murrah became a judge, he had three colleagues, and by the time he retired in 1970, there were seven. The growth of the court's membership matched the growth in population in the Rocky Mountain states. The Tenth Circuit, as with all federal appeals courts, heard appeals of decisions from federal district trial courts. The cases before the appeals courts usually involved federal law or an interpretation and application of the U.S. Constitution.

In 1940 the Tenth Circuit was only a decade old, and the types of cases it was hearing were disputes over the new federal labor and commerce regulations passed by Congress during the New Deal. Murrah and his colleagues, three of four being Roosevelt appointees, tended to rule in favor of national regulations and those agencies created to enforce the law. The Tenth Circuit also heard numerous Indian cases involving land disputes and disagreements over who owned mineral wealth beneath the land. Many of the cases handed down by the judges involved interpretation of complex laws and contracts that brought little attention to them.

During that time Murrah proved to be the type of judge favored under the Roosevelt administration. He refused to involve the federal courts in economic or property rights issues but was active in using the judiciary in other individual rights or civil liberties cases. This stance earned Murrah a reputation as a rising young jurist. It also earned him the friendship of his colleagues, who were twenty to thirty years older. The small size of the court, only four judges, was also conducive to close working relationships.

In 1949, the number of judges was increased to five. The change in membership was followed by a change in the focus of the court. As courts accepted New Deal laws, challenges to economic regulations diminished. At the same time, following the lead of the Supreme Court, the Tenth Circuit heard more appeals of cases involving civil liberties issues.

One case authored by Murrah in 1956 has particular significance in modern times. A U.S. citizen, William Colepaugh, was arrested in the United States during World War II. He was charged with acting with the German government to commit sabotage in the United States. Under direct presidential order, Colepaugh was named an enemy combatant and tried before a military court, where he was found guilty and sentenced to death.

In the case of *Colepaugh v. Looney* (1956), which was an appeal of that decision, Murrah asserted the right of Colepaugh to appeal to the civil courts the decision handed down by the military tribunal. At the same time Murrah, writing for two other judges, recognized the president's power as commander in chief to define war crimes against the United States, to charge people under those crimes, and to use military commissions to convict them. Although the case did not receive widespread attention at the time, the decision to uphold the president's war power and use military tribunals for enemy combatants could serve as precedent and argument for future action.

Robert L. Williams (1868–1948)

Born on a farm in Pike County, Alabama, in 1868, Robert L. Williams would become a moving force in the constitutional convention that drafted Oklahoma's constitution, its first chief justice, and its third governor. He was then appointed as a United States district judge for the Eastern District of Oklahoma and finally served on the United States Tenth Circuit Court of Appeals.

Educated in rural Alabama schools, Williams enrolled in Southern University at Greensboro, Alabama, where he earned his bachelor's degree. After an intensive six months of reading law under Col. William S. Thorington in Montgomery, Alabama, and passing the bar, Williams moved briefly to Oklahoma, only to return to Alabama. Converted under the evangelism of Samuel (Sam) Porter Jones, he returned to Southern University to earn a master's degree in theology and serve for a time as a minister of the Methodist Episcopal Church. Apparently relatively unsuited to the job and perhaps disappointed by his failure to win the hand of a woman, Williams returned to the Indian Territory in what is today Oklahoma. There he entered into a law partnership and quickly established himself as a leading attorney in Durant, in partnership with William Elbert Utterback.

An ardent Democrat (who supported Williams Jennings Bryan and a variety of Populist and Progressive measures while strongly opposing socialism and later resisting elements of Franklin D. Roosevelt's New Deal), Williams rose quickly in party ranks and became a national committeeman. He helped push for Oklahoma statehood, favoring a single new state combining the Oklahoma and Indiana Territories rather than two separate entities. One of 112 delegates elected to the constitutional convention that met in Guthrie, Oklahoma, he favored such Progressive measures as the initiative and referendum, taxation of railroad properties, and the direct primary. In conjunction with the men who were to become the state's first governor (a position that Williams himself coveted) and the state's first speaker of the House of Representatives, Williams appears to have had a major impact on the drafting of the constitution, serving as chair of the Committee on Railroads and Public Service Corporations and as a member of several other important committees.

After Oklahoma was admitted into the Union as the forty-sixth state, Williams was elected to the state Supreme Court, whose other four members unanimously selected him as their chief. In just over six years on the court (1908–1914), he wrote more than 500 opinions. These included a decision upholding an innovative banking law; a ruling (later overturned by the United States Supreme Court) upholding Oklahoma's grandfather clause (Williams, who had taken Robert E. Lee's last name as his middle name as a youth, never appears to have sought the black vote and held rather conventional paternalistic southern views of African Americans) and the decision (reaffirmed by the United States Supreme Court in *Coyle v. Smith)* permitting Oklahoma to move its state capital from Guthrie to Oklahoma City, thus giving it an equality with previously admitted states. While serving on the high bench, Williams prepared and published an annotated state constitution.

(continues)

(continued)

In 1914, Williams began his successful quest to serve as Oklahoma governor and took his oath in early 1915. Known in his first two years chiefly for applying business principles to gain efficiency and maintain fiscal austerity in government, Williams also supported the use of prison labor and worked diligently to help the U.S. cause during World War I.

Limited to one term, Williams was appointed by Woodrow Wilson to the United States District Court for the Eastern District of Oklahoma in 1919. An opponent of Prohibition, Williams, who had health problems and had given up drinking upon ascending the bench, nonetheless found that much of his caseload consisted of such cases. Often brusque and almost always willing to speak his mind, he frequently attacked the Women's Christian Temperance Union, once saying: "Under a monarch of Europe a man may distill his liquor, but in America the laws have strangled initiative. There is less liberty in this country today than under a monarchy" (quoted in Dale and Morrison 1958, 294). Williams appears to have allowed many first-time small-time offenders to go free rather than enforce the letter of the Prohibition law. On other occasions, Williams permitted fathers to whip their sons with a leather strap so that they would not be forced to send them to reform school.

Williams's district included many Indian claims; in one case, determination of a Native American's rightful heirs required more than 20,000 pages of testimony (Dale and Morrison 1958, 306). Williams was typically merciful to first offenders and harsh with hardened criminals. He sentenced one such offender to death under the Lindbergh Kidnapping law for kidnapping a police officer who was wounded but did not die as a result of the experience. Behind the scenes, Williams appears to have continued to influence Oklahoma politics.

In 1937, Franklin D. Roosevelt appointed Williams as a judge for the United States Tenth Circuit Court of Appeals with the understanding, which Williams honored, that he would retire at the age of seventy. Williams became a strong friend and supporter of Judge Alfred P. Murrah during that time.

An unmarried man with a brusque exterior, Williams was a strong supporter of the Methodist Church and of other causes that he favored. Once, responding to critics who referred to him as an old bachelor, Williams replied that he was "married to Oklahoma" (quoted in Dale and Morrison 1958, 359). He served on the board of directors of the Oklahoma Historical Society from 1915 to 1948 and helped establish both a historical journal and a building for housing and researching Oklahoma historical documents. He served as president of the Historical Society from 1938 until his death in 1948.

A competent businessman who became a fairly large landowner and whose estate was valued at about $400,000 at the time of his death, Williams, who put great emphasis on initiative, thrift, and self-help, did not always please his tenants, but he appears to have tried to treat them fairly. Although he held more offices than most contemporaries, his strengths and weaknesses appear fairly representative of many other frontier jurists who helped to settle the West.

Reference:

Dale, Edward Everett, and James D. Morrison. 1958. *Pioneer Judge: The Life of Robert Lee Williams*. Cedar Rapids, Iowa: The Torch Press.

The early 1950s saw Murrah write decisions in two cases that would become Supreme Court precedent. In *Lee Optical v. Williamson* (1954), Murrah agreed with his two colleagues in striking down part of a law that treated ophthalmologists and optometrists differently than opticians in fitting people for eyeglasses. *Lee* was a rare case in the 1950s in which the federal courts struck down a state economic regulation. The Supreme Court proceeded to overturn the Tenth Circuit's opinion, refusing to become involved with regulation of the economy by the state.

Although *Lee* represented one of the last economic liberty cases decided by the federal courts during the period, the Tenth Circuit decided two cases that steered a new direction for the federal courts. The issue was that of segregation of public schools and universities. In *McLaurin v. University of Oklahoma* (1948), Murrah was one of three judges who ruled that a university policy of refusing McLaurin into its graduate school based on his race violated the Fourteenth Amendment. The Tenth Circuit followed Supreme Court precedent in banning such blatant segregation and ordered that McLaurin be admitted.

The university then segregated McLaurin in every aspect of his education ranging from the classroom to the cafeteria. McLaurin challenged the new form of segregation in 1950, but three judges of the Tenth Circuit, including Murrah, upheld the university policy as following the separate but equal doctrine found in the Court precedent of *Plessy v. Ferguson* (1896). The United States Supreme Court disagreed with the Tenth Circuit, ruling that the University of Oklahoma's segregation of McLaurin was unconstitutional and requiring the state to integrate him within the graduate program. In both of the McLaurin cases, Murrah and his colleagues played the role of federal judges in applying Supreme Court cases and following those decisions.

McLaurin proved to be the major school desegregation case heard by the Tenth Circuit during Murrah's tenure there. Unlike the southern circuits, the Eleventh and the Fifth, the Tenth Circuit was spared many of the political confrontations associated with federal judges attempting to operate public schools. As the 1960s began, the Tenth Circuit began to focus more on civil liberties and cases involving the rights of criminal defendants. At the same time Murrah began a new job within the Tenth Circuit, that of chief judge.

Although all judges within a circuit court of appeals are considered equals, the chief judge of a circuit has greater responsibilities, including assigning lower court judges and determining which colleagues will sit on which appeals. Murrah obtained that post in August 1959. During his decade-long service as chief judge, Murrah found himself embroiled in political controversies while at the same time earning a national reputation as a judicial reformer.

Murrah was instrumental in getting his former law partner, Luther Bohannon, appointed to a district court judgeship in Oklahoma. Murrah had to spend nearly a year lobbying his home state senators, the Senate itself, and the American Bar Association to get Bohannon the nomination and confirmation. It was during this fight that Murrah displayed his political abilities.

He was less effective in handling a dispute with Stephen Chandler, another federal district judge in Oklahoma. The problems began with a dispute over Chandler's presiding in a case involving Occidental Petroleum. The circuit judges agreed that Chandler should remove himself from the case, but the judge disagreed and went to court to have his colleagues' opinion overturned. The fight turned nasty as Chandler clashed frequently with the other judges, forcing them to strip him of all the cases he was hearing at that moment and prohibit him from hearing any future cases. Chandler went to court to challenge this decision, arguing that the Tenth Circuit judges had abused their power. The case worked its way slowly through the federal judicial system. During that time, Chandler and his colleagues exchanged accusations and verbal attacks. The case reached the Supreme Court and was decided in 1970, after Murrah had left the court. In *Chandler v. Tenth Circuit*, the Supreme Court ruled for the circuit judges, upholding their decision to strip the district judge of his power to hear and decide cases. The entire episode was a black mark on the judiciary and the Tenth Circuit. Unlike his many other ventures, this time Murrah proved unable to fashion a compromise or use his political skills to defuse a conflict.

With controversy dogging the internal workings of the Tenth Circuit during most of his years as chief judge, Murrah also had to serve as a judge deciding appeals. The 1960s saw a deluge of appeals from criminal defendants who were taking advantage of the Supreme Court's rulings that applied the Bill of Rights to state governments. The Tenth Circuit decided many cases involving search and seizure, right to counsel, self-incrimination, and juvenile rights. Murrah applied those rulings, though few reached the Supreme Court on appeal. Overall, Murrah authored over 800 opinions for the Tenth Circuit during the almost thirty years of his tenure. As the 1960s came to a close, retirement beckoned for Murrah. After almost thirty years on the Tenth Circuit and more than thirty years as a federal judge, the time was ripe for him to move off of the bench. But Murrah's reputation as a judicial reformer opened another job for him, that of director of the new Federal Judicial Center.

Murrah's job as director was tied to his previous efforts on the Tenth Circuit. As chief judge he had administrative responsibilities within the circuit. But Murrah also was involved in attempting to improve courtroom procedure throughout the entire judicial system. Starting in the mid-1950s,

Murrah headed a judicial commission that studied trial procedure and produced a booklet on the issue for federal judges to use when faced with prolonged cases. He also led a committee examining how to improve pretrial procedures in order to shorten trials. To accomplish his goal, Murrah was forced to use all of his political skills by lobbying Congress, testifying before a Senate committee, and overseeing passage of a federal statute on the issue. Murrah also worked on creating a standard set of sentencing guidelines for judges in order to make sentences fairer. All of Murrah's efforts earned him a national reputation among his fellow judges. He also became friends with several justices, including William Douglas and Byron White, and worked with another judicial reformer, Warren Burger, who would become chief justice and one of the judges who would pick Murrah for the job as director of the Judicial Center.

Murrah became director of the three-year-old center in 1970. The Judicial Center was created by Congress to improve the federal judicial system by helping train judges and staff members, including court clerks, mediators, and probation officers. The center also conducted studies of the federal judiciary, attempting to discover problems and devise solutions. Under Murrah the center became active in running seminars for judges, helping them work through difficult issues of administering the courts and effectively running trials.

As director, Murrah also had senior status. Retiring from full-time work on the Tenth Circuit, he still occasionally served as a judge, pinch-hitting when there was a vacancy or an additional judge was needed. Murrah remained active as a judge and administrator until his death on 30 October 1975.

Murrah's contribution to the law could be found both inside and outside the courtroom. He was recognized as one of the most important legal figures in Oklahoma, serving as a lawyer and district judge as Oklahoma found its legs as a state. His legacy was continued with the naming of the law library at the University of Oklahoma and of the federal building in Oklahoma City. It was the Alfred P. Murrah federal building that was destroyed by a terrorist bomb in April 1995.

Douglas Clouatre

References and Further Reading:

Creel, Von Russell, Bob Burke, and Kenny Franks. 1996. *American Jurist: The Life of Alfred P. Murrah.* Oklahoma City: Western Heritage Books.

Hellman, Arthur. 1991. *Restructuring Justice.* Ithaca, N.Y.: Cornell University Press.

Songer, Donald. 2000 *Continuity and Change on the United States Courts of Appeals.* Ann Arbor: University of Michigan Press.

PARKER, ISAAC C.

(1838–1896)

Isaac C. Parker
National Archives

As federal judge for the United States District Court in the Western District of Arkansas, Isaac Parker was notorious across the United States. He exercised sole authority over the largest federal judicial district in the United States, sentenced 161 men to the gallows, and engaged in a public and bitter controversy with the Supreme Court and the U.S. attorney general. Although Parker's contemporary reputation was based on his fame as the "hanging judge," his role in U.S. judicial history is more complex. His actions initiated public debate over the role of appellate courts in capital cases. Appeals from his court created a body of Supreme Court decisions protecting the right to self-defense. And Parker's decisions in the court at Fort Smith, which had jurisdiction over Indian Territory, extended federal law at the expense of Native American tribal sovereignty.

Born 15 October 1838 in Belmot County, Ohio, Isaac Charles Parker was the youngest son of Joseph and Jane Shannon Parker. Influenced by his maternal uncle, the governor of Ohio, Parker at age seventeen chose the legal profession as a career. His legal training consisted of reading, self-study, and apprenticeship with a local attorney. He passed the bar in 1859, moved to St. Joseph, Missouri, and joined the firm of another maternal uncle, D. E. Shannon. Parker opened his own office in 1861 and the same year was elected to the first of three terms as city attorney. After he switched to the

Republican party in 1864, voters elected him county prosecutor for the Ninth Judicial Circuit. Four years later, Parker defeated a Democratic incumbent and became judge of the Twelfth Missouri circuit (Tuller 2001, 14–26).

Parker was politically ambitious and served only two years of his judicial term. He clearly intended to use the law as a means of political advancement. In 1870 and 1872 voters elected him to the U.S. House of Representatives for the Seventh Congressional District. Parker proved a loyal party man, and when the Democratic majority in Missouri gerrymandered his district, President Grant rewarded him with a presidential appointment. Parker requested the United States Court for the Western District of Arkansas, a scandal-ridden bench whose corruption had made national headlines (Tuller 2001, 36–40).

Parker's appointment was the direct result of Reconstruction politics. Arkansas was recovering from the aftermath of the Brooks-Baxter war, a violent controversy between factions of the Republican party in Arkansas. The previous judge was a corrupt politician who accepted bribes, seldom held court, and allowed his marshals to embezzle from the federal government. Parker was a political appointee: He had minimal experience, but he was not from Arkansas, he was loyal to Grant and the Stalwarts, and he had never faced corruption charges. The Senate unanimously confirmed Parker in March 1875. On 10 May, eight days after his arrival in Fort Smith, Parker opened court (Tuller 2001, 49–51).

Parker inherited a unique court. It was the largest federal judicial district in the United States and the costliest to run, since it covered 74,000 square miles and included the Indian Territory. The court was the busiest criminal court in the federal system. In addition to its jurisdiction over statutory offenses and federal law over the American Indians, it possessed common law jurisdiction over U.S. citizens in the Indian Territory, an area infested with fugitive criminals. Parker thus had a high proportion of criminal cases on his docket. The most unusual feature of Parker's court was the power granted to its sitting judge. Due to congressional oversight, the district court at Fort Smith also had circuit court powers. This meant that Parker, as circuit judge, sat in appeal over cases coming out of his own district court. Only during the last third of his tenure did Parker become subject to the same appeals process as other federal jurists (Tuller 2001, 42–46, 93–96, 162; Burton 1995, 47–50; Stolberg 1988a, 7).

Parker immediately set to work reforming his court. Parker viewed federal law as the agent of "civilization" in Indian Territory and frequently juxtaposed the "order and tranquility" of the law with the "savageism and brutality" of the lawless. He believed that certain punishment and definite retribution prevented and halted crime. Parker's ideal criminal court was "vigorous, impartial, just, and most efficient" (Stolberg 1988b, 21; see also Tuller 2001, 4–5). Parker broke sharply with the practice of his corrupt predecessor. He held court six days a week from eight in the morning to sundown. He tried, convicted, and sentenced quickly. He increased the efficiency of the court and doubled law enforcement efforts in Indian Territory. In his first term he executed six murderers in public hangings. Parker quickly reversed the image of the court at Fort Smith and gained a national reputation for the swift punishment of lawbreakers (Tuller 2001, 52–69; Stolberg 1988b, 11–12).

Most of the court's business arose from its jurisdiction over Indian Territory. The most commonly prosecuted offense in the Parker court was introducing liquor into Indian Territory in violation of the 1834 Indian Intercourse Act. Violent crime constituted one-fourth of the court's business. Despite Parker's efforts, crime always exceeded punishment in Indian Territory. From 1875 to 1896, grand juries issued 3,942 indictments for murder alone. Only 161 of the alleged killers were finally convicted and sentenced. Even though the sheer size of the Western District inhibited the efficient enforcement Parker sought, he still disposed of more than 12,000 criminal cases during his tenure (Tuller 2001, 104–110, 159–163).

Parker's national notoriety stemmed from his seemingly frequent use of the gallows. In his twenty-one years at Fort Smith, Parker sentenced 161 men to death, and seventy-nine of these were executed, many of them publicly and in groups of two or more. No other federal judge in history executed as many men; no other saw as many capital cases. But Parker's fame rested on cases representing less than 1 percent of his docket. And in his capital trials, an inflexible federal statute usually tied his hands. In U.S. courts during Parker's tenure, the mandatory sentence for murder and rape was death by hanging. The federal statute provided no distinction between degrees of murder (Burton 1995, 47; Tuller 2001, 64–65). Parker himself was ambivalent toward the death penalty; he wept in court the first time he sentenced a man to die, never attended an execution, and later in life told a reporter that he favored abolishing executions provided there was certainty of punishment.

Throughout his tenure, Parker advocated a prison system geared toward rehabilitation and reform of criminals. Acting against Justice Department mandates, he sent men to prisons in Michigan and Illinois rather than closer institutions he believed were poorly run. He consistently sent young boys to reformatories instead of prisons, even when they were over the maximum age. In a letter to the attorney general in 1885, Parker argued that men were "largely criminals from surrounding circumstances" (Stolberg 1988b, 22–23). He believed the "object of punishment is to lift the man up, stamp out his bad nature and wicked disposition, that his better and God-given traits may assert themselves, and so govern and direct him that he becomes a good citizen, of use to himself and his fellow men" (22–23).

Parker often aided citizens and lawyers who sought executive clemency, the sole recourse for capital convicts in the early years of the Parker court. From 1875 to 1880, the majority of Parker's death sentences were not carried out. Lawyers and citizens used the pardon process to prevent many of the scheduled executions. Parker himself supported many of the applications for clemency, and the president tended to follow the recommendations of the district judge, either for or against clemency (Tuller 2001, 67–83).

Although much of Parker's judicial work involved common law cases, he also presided over important cases involving the court's jurisdiction over Indian Territory. In his rulings Parker consistently upheld U.S. sovereignty over tribal lands and limited the power of tribal courts. In several instances, Parker claimed jurisdiction over cases involving adopted citizens of Indian nations. In *Ex Parte Morgan* (1883), he denied Indian tribunals the authority to extradite. The judge did rule against settlers who tried to encroach on Indian land or government land set aside for Indians in *U.S. v. D.L. Payne* (1881) and *Ex Parte Rogers* (1885), but his real concern in these cases was upholding federal authority. He made this point forcefully in *Cherokee Nation v. Southern Kansas Railway* (1888). Congress had given the railroad permission to build a line across the Cherokee nation provided the Cherokee were justly compensated. The Cherokees, asking for an injunction against construction, argued that their nation was sovereign under federal treaty and therefore Congress could not grant the right of way. Parker ruled for the railroad and argued that the United States had ultimate sovereignty over all lands within its borders (Burton 1995, 67–68; Tuller 2001, 115–118).

Parker also initiated a judicial instruction that is important in trial procedures today. The members of a jury returned and told Parker they were deadlocked. Parker instructed the jurors candidly to reexamine their opinions; jurors on each side should consider if the other side was right. Deadlocked juries today are often given similar instructions, known as the "Allen charge," after the case over which Parker presided (Kopel 2000, 316).

Parker's last sixteen years on the bench were embroiled in controversy. In the 1880s, Congress gradually reduced Parker's jurisdiction and amended the appeals process. Congress cut Parker's jurisdiction in half in 1883, but this did little to reduce his caseload. The white population in Indian Territory continued to grow, and with it grew the court's criminal business. Fort Smith remained the most expensive court in the federal judicial system and did more business in 1886 than before 1883. In 1889, Congress drastically reduced the judge's power. The jurisdiction of his court was again curtailed, but more important, the Criminal Appeals Act stripped him of his circuit court powers and gave persons convicted of capital offenses the right of appeal to the Supreme Court. This subjected Parker to the same appeals process as any other district judge in the United States and ended his status as the most powerful judge in America (Tuller 2001, 122–137; Stolberg 1988a, 14).

What developed in the wake of these reforms was a battle between Parker and the Supreme Court. Between 1891 and 1897, the Supreme Court heard appeals in forty-four of Parker's capital convictions. Thirty-one of these were reversed and only twelve upheld. The Court, whose opinions were increasingly critical of the judge, believed Parker continuously erred on several points. First, Parker continued the antebellum practice of giving jury charges that instructed the jury on the verdict. His charges, some of them ranging from forty to seventy typed pages, commented not only on specific points of law but on the merits of the evidence. In some charges he clearly favored the prosecution and implied that the defendant was probably guilty. Second, the Court took issue with Parker on two points of law: flight from the scene of a crime and self-defense (Stolberg 1988a, 17; Murphy 1939, 77–79; Tuller 2001, 79–80, 138–143).

From 1893 to 1896, the Supreme Court handed down a series of decisions, some of them written by John Marshall Harlan, arising from the Parker court on the issue of self-defense. Of the nine cases from Parker's court, eight won reversals. The cases became an important body of decisions that laid the foundation for a 1921 opinion that upheld and extended the right to armed self-defense (Kopel 2000, 294–298). In *Beard v. United States* (1895) and *J. Rowe v. United States* (1896), the Court reversed Parker. In both cases, Parker had instructed the jury that the defendants had the duty to retreat and try to avoid in every way possible taking the assailant's life. The Court ruled that there was no duty to retreat before using deadly force (306, 317–318). In addition, the Court in *Rowe* held that Parker, rather than allowing the jury to evaluate the facts, had improperly told the jury what conclusion to reach. The Court reversed Parker on self-defense in *Thompson v. United States* (1894) and *Gourko v. United States* (1896). In both cases, Parker had instructed the jury that carrying a handgun could be considered evidence of deliberation and a premeditated intent to kill (299–303).

The Court became increasingly irritated with Parker as he continued practices they had already ruled in error. In *Starr v. United States* (1894), the Court reversed Parker because, quoting Proverbs, he told a jury that flight should be considered evidence of guilt. The Court ruled that flight was one of several circumstances a jury could consider but was not alone sufficient proof of guilt. The opinion rebuked Parker for ignoring Court corrections on similar cases (Shirley 1988, 182–183; Kopel 2000, 302,

311–312). But Parker again issued similar instructions to a jury and was again reversed in *Alberty v. United States* (1896).

Parker, for years unregulated by higher courts, had missed the evolution of the law. In the antebellum era, judges often instructed juries on the verdict. On his deathbed, Parker said, "I have been accused of leading juries. I tell you a jury should be led . . . if they are guided they will render justice" (Tuller 2001, 156). But after the Civil War, there was a trend toward greater regulation of judicial behavior, greater standardization, and a more technical appellate procedure. A judge's written charges addressed only specific points of law. Since Parker's decisions were not subject to appeal from 1875 to 1889, he missed these legal developments. Parker continued the common law traditions of an earlier age in U.S. legal history and would not adapt when challenged (Tuller 2001, 154–155; Stolberg 1988a, 8, 20). Thus the Supreme Court continually chastised Parker for his "animated arguments" and his invasion of the "appropriate province of jury fact-finding" (Kopel 2000, 308–309).

Parker publicly lashed out against the Supreme Court and became embroiled in a bitter public feud with the attorney general. In 1895, Cherokee Bill, whom Parker had sentenced to death but whose case was on appeal, shot a guard while trying to escape the Fort Smith jail. Parker, in an interview with the *St. Louis Globe-Democrat,* blamed the Supreme Court for the guard's death. Cherokee Bill was still in the jail because he was waiting for the outcome of his appeal. Parker then attributed the upsurge in murders in the Indian Territory to the number of Supreme Court reversals. He told the reporter that the Court released convicted murderers on the "flimsiest of technicalities" (Tuller 2001, 148). Supreme Court justices, according to Parker, did not have enough experience in criminal cases to overrule the decisions of trial judges. The number of reversals impaired justice because they undermined public belief in the courts' responsiveness and the "certainty of punishment" that was central to deterring crime (148; see also Shirley 1988, 156–157; Stolberg 1988b, 21). The next year, Parker wrote an article for the *North American Review* in which he argued that a recent increase in crime was due to the corruption of the appeals process. His suggested two reforms for appellate courts: judges who were experienced in criminal law and speedy consideration of cases. But his central suggestion was the following: "I would brush aside all technicalities that did not affect the guilt or innocence of the accused. I would not permit them to act on a partial record, or on any technical pleas concocted by cunning minds. I would provide by law against the reversal of cases unless upon their merits innocence was manifest. The guilt or innocence of the party should be the guide" (Parker 1896, 667–674).

The "Hanging Judge"—The Popular Image of Judge Isaac Parker

Isaac Parker served as a federal district judge for twenty-one years at Fort Smith, Arkansas. During his tenure, the Western District of Arkansas had jurisdiction over crimes involving American citizens and violations of federal law in the Indian Territory. This unusual jurisdiction led to an extraordinary situation, with the court nearly overwhelmed with criminal trials; in the twenty-one years Parker served, the court processed over 13,000 cases. As part of his duties, the judge handed a mandatory death sentence to those defendants who were found guilty of the crimes of murder or rape. Of the 161 people who received the death sentence from Judge Parker, seventy-nine took the final plunge of justice from the gallows, often in multiple executions, which received nationwide attention (Burton 1995, 46–71).

Following the termination of the court's jurisdiction over Indian Territory, and the death of Judge Parker in 1896, only a few years passed before the first book detailing the judge's career was published. A collaborative effort between an attorney who defended cases against Parker, a former juror, and a former hangman, *Hell on the Border* was released early in 1899. A 700-page murder novel, the book provided a short overview of the court and focused primarily on the men executed on the gallows and other famous individuals associated with the court. S. W. Harman, a former juror in the court, intended the book to promote the career of George Maledon, a part-time hangman during Parker's tenure. In the process, *Hell on the Border* set the standard interpretation of Judge Parker as a strict but kind-hearted jurist, a friend to Native Americans, sent by President Grant to clean up the Indian Territory (Harman [1898] 2001, 87). The men behind the book did not hesitate to promote themselves; J. Warren Reed, a Fort Smith attorney who had defended a number of famous criminals before the judge, was consistently depicted as the lawyer who never lost his cases (106–115). Maledon's role as hangman was elevated from part-time status to the "Prince of Hangmen" (106–115). Even with self-professed exhaustive research, the authors of *Hell on the Border* perpetrated considerable errors in the course of the book, ranging from errors in dates and the number of executions, to using dime novels as primary sources. Poorly received following its initial publication, the book was largely forgotten until a heavily condensed reprint was published in the 1950s. In addition to creating the Parker image, *Hell on the Border*'s significance comes from its extensive use by over a century of authors.

After languishing in local obscurity for nearly fifty years, Judge Parker reemerged on the national scene through works such as *Hanging Judge*, *He Hanged Them High*, *Court of the Damned*, *Law West of Fort Smith*, and others. With the exception of *Hanging Judge*, by Fred Harvey Harrington (the first book with this title), all of these were popular works, focusing on the more sensational aspects of Parker's career. Each of these books echoed the sentiment of and borrowed heavily from *Hell on the Bor-*

(continues)

(continued)

der. Homer Croy, a Missouri journalist, wrote the most influential of these books, the nationally distributed *He Hanged Them High*. Croy's work did not stop with the already established elements of the Parker myth but substantially added to them. Among his inventions were the "facts" of Judge Parker's watching each execution from his office window and crying each time he sentenced a man to die and the depiction of Isaac Parker as a zealot, a "fanatical judge who hanged eighty-eight men" (Croy 1952, 12).

Beginning in the 1960s, Judge Parker and the federal court at Fort Smith became popular subjects in the genre of Western literature. Depending on the plot and narrative needs of the individual author, authors depicted Parker and the court at Fort Smith through both the traditional and fanatical stereotypes. The majority of these modern-day dime novels fall within the predictable confines of the genre, mirroring the sources used in composing the work: witness such titles as *Hanging Judge* by Elmer Kelton (1969), *Zeke and Ned* by Larry McMurtry and Diana Ossana (1997), and *Hell on the Border* by J. M. Thompson and Fred Bean (2002). Throughout most of these fictional works, the judge is little more than a judicial boogeyman, used to great dramatic effect, as in a scene in *Johnny Blue and the Hanging Judge* in which the main characters appear in court before Judge Parker, and in attendance are Belle Starr heckling from the audience and Buffalo Bill Cody waiting to testify (West 2001, 198). In many of these books the judge is depicted along hauntingly similar lines to the other so-called hanging judge of the West, Roy Bean (who does not in fact ever appear to have presided over a hanging). The fanatical stereotype of the judge, as a man bent on justice no matter the cost, is the most popular use of Judge Parker; even while decrying other writers for portraying the judge as mean spirited, most authors use the very same stereotype. A self-published book took Homer Croy's image of the fanatical judge one step further and depicted Judge Parker as a religious fanatic who condemned men to die in order to bring them to salvation (Moore 1998, 6).

A small number of fictional works rise from the masses to challenge the prevailing stereotypes. The most famous fictional work written about Judge Parker is Arkansas native Charles Portis's novel, *True Grit*. Published in 1968, the book was almost immediately turned into a motion picture starring John Wayne. In *True Grit*, Judge Parker is depicted fairly distantly but in the traditional fashion (Portis 1968, 39–56). Although in reality there were almost no female employees in the court, author

(continues)

The Justice Department and the Supreme Court did not concede that Parker was being overruled on mere technicalities. In 1896, Solicitor General Edward B. Whitney decided not to pursue appeals in which Parker had plainly not corrected earlier instructions from the Supreme Court and began to file confessions of error. Outraged, Parker published a letter attacking Whitney, whom he accused of providing "security to criminals" (Tuller 2001, 150). Whitney responded in a public letter stating that Parker refused

(continued)

Georgia di Donato provided a woman's perspective on the frontier venue of Judge Parker's court in *Woman of Justice*. The main character, Temperance Smith, a circuit judge assigned to Parker, strongly disagrees with capital punishment (di Donato 1980, 39). The positive role of African Americans is conveyed in *Black Marshal*, a fictional telling of the life of deputy marshal Bass Reeves, in which both the title character and Judge Parker are viewed as valiant servants of justice (Burchardt 1981, 181).

Universally remembered as "the Hanging Judge," Isaac Parker's popular image in film and print is a blending of fact and folklore. Depicted as a strong, well-meaning defender of justice, or as a fanatical zealot bent on hanging 100 outlaws, Isaac Charles Parker's legacy has in many ways come down to how he is remembered and not for the accomplishments of his lengthy career.

Eric Leonard

References:

Allen, Eric. 1971. *Fury in Old Fort Smith*. Fort Smith, Ark.: Eric Allen.

Burchardt, Bill. 1981. *Black Marshal*. Garden City, N.Y.: Doubleday.

Burton, Jeffrey. 1995. *Indian Territory and the United States, 1866–1906: Courts, Government, and the Movement for Oklahoma Statehood*. Norman: University of Oklahoma Press.

Croy, Homer. 1952. *He Hanged Them High: An Authentic Account of the Fanatical Judge Who Hanged Eighty-eight Men*. New York: Duell, Sloan and Pearce.

di Donato, Georgia. 1980. *Woman of Justice: A Novel about the First Lady Judge in the West*. Garden City, N.Y.: Doubleday.

Harman, S. W. [1898] 2001. *Hell on the Border: He Hanged Eighty-Eight Men*. With an introduction by Julie Galonksa. Reprint, Fort Washington, Pa: Eastern National.

Harrington, Fred Harvey. 1951. *Hanging Judge*. Caldwell, Idaho: Caxton Printers.

Jones, Douglas C. 1979. *Winding Stair*. New York: Holt, Rinehart and Winston.

Kelton, Elmer. 1969. *Hanging Judge*. New York: Forge.

McMurtry, Larry, and Diana Ossana. 1997. *Zeke and Ned: A Novel*. New York: Simon and Schuster.

Moore, Lonnie W. 1998. *Gates of Hell: The Wrath of Judge Isaac Parker*. Kearney, Nebr.: Morris Publishing.

Portis, Charles. 1968. *True Grit: A Novel*. New York: Simon and Schuster.

Thompson, J. M., and Fred Bean. 2002. *Hell on the Border*. New York: Signet.

Wallman, Jeffrey. 1999. *The Western: Parables of the American Dream*. Lubbock: Texas Tech University Press.

West, Joseph A. 2001. *Johnny Blue and the Hanging Judge*. New York: Signet.

Wright, Will. 1975. *Sixguns and Society: A Structural Study of the Western*. Berkeley: University of California Press.

to accept instructions and was "ignorant and careless" with the law (151). This brought in the attorney general, who admonished Parker for his legal and personal conduct. He reprimanded Parker for insubordination and said his jury charges were continually open to criticism for being misleading and declaratory (151–152).

On 17 November 1896, soon after his exchange with his superiors and just before his court's jurisdiction over Indian Territory expired, Parker died

George Jeffreys (c. 1645–1689)

In the United States, federal judges are appointed by the president with the advice and consent of the Senate, but once in office, judges can attain considerable independence. For all practical purposes, there are few if any rewards that a president can confer upon a lawyer other than nomination for a judicial office, and once an individual reaches the Supreme Court, there is no higher honor that a president can bestow. By contrast, kings in early England could extend many rewards to lawyers and judges whom they favored. One of Thomas Jefferson's complaints in the Declaration of Independence centered on the lack of an independent judiciary.

One example of such royal influence on judging is illustrated by the career of George Jeffreys. Born sometime between 1645 and 1648 and later attending Trinity College at Cambridge, Jeffreys was subsequently admitted for law training at the Inner Temple, where he spent five years. In 1671 London elected Jeffreys as a common sergeant, a position in which he apparently recognized that he could gain further advancement by furthering the interests of the king, Charles II. In 1678, Jeffreys became recorder of London, during which time he enhanced himself in royal eyes by prosecuting the Popish Plot and later presiding over the "Bloody Assizes" of 1685 in which he meted out strong punishments (including many sentences to death) to individuals who had participated in Monmouth's Rebellion. Elevated in 1683 to chief justiceship of the King's Bench and in 1685 to the chancellorship of England, Jeffreys helped James II control the Church of England through an Ecclesiastical Commission on which Jeffreys sat, before James II fled the nation after the arrival of Holland's King William and his wife Mary, who subsequently took over the throne. Jeffreys was arrested and sent to the Tower of London, where he died of complications apparently brought on by the gall and/or kidney stones that had long

(continues)

in Fort Smith at the age of fifty-eight (Tuller 2001, 157). His other accomplishments, and his duel with the Supreme Court, were soon obscured by his reputation as the "hanging judge." A sensational book appeared shortly after his death, entitled *Hell on the Border,* which served as the basis for most work on Parker until the 1990s. Books and films, including *True Grit* and Clint Eastwood's *Hang 'em High,* cared little for historic accuracy in their portrayal of Parker and the court at Fort Smith. Because the Parker court tried so many famous outlaws, many books ostensibly on Parker focused on the lurid details of crime in Indian Territory rather than on the judge's work. Recent scholarship is beginning to correct this problem, however, as more scholars look beyond the gallows in their portrayal of this controversial and complex judge.

Lorien Foote

(continued)

troubled him and that might have contributed to his reputation for heavy drinking and bad temper.

Jeffreys was generally regarded as an able lawyer, but his royalist bias often affected his conduct and rulings on the bench. He lived at a time during which hanging followed by drawing and quartering (or, in the case of women, burning at the stake) was a fairly standard punishment for treason, and, particularly in retrospect, many of his judgments look barbaric. Convicted of perjury for testimony given during the Popish Plots, Titus Oates is said to have received over 2,250 lashes as a result of one of Jeffreys' judgments (Hyde 1948, 201).

Jeffreys was known for his invective from the bench. An observer once described Jeffreys as behaving himself "more like a jack-pudding than with that gravity which beseems a judge" (quoted in Hyde 1948, 99). Jeffreys once silenced a woman witness by saying "Nay, prithee, mistress, be not so full of tattle, so full of clack" (168), and he upbraided an attorney who was rubbing in a point that he had made by comparing him to a hen: "Lord, sir, you must be cackling too. We told you your objection was very ingenious, but that must not make you troublesome. You cannot lay an egg but you must be cackling over it" (176). When asked how he "came off" after an appearance in Jeffreys' courtroom, a defendant commented: "I am escaped from the terrors of that man's face which I would scarce undergo again to save my life; and I shall certainly have the frightful impression of it as long as I live" (quoted 261).

Described by one writer as "the very worst judge that ever disgraced Westminster Hall" (quoted in Hyde 1948, 14), Jeffreys serves as testimony to the value of an independent judiciary and as an example of what can happen when judicial judgments are clouded by the desire to please a king for personal advancement.

References:

Hyde, H. Montgomery. 1948. *Judge Jeffreys*. London: Butterworth and Co.

Walker, David M. 1980. *The Oxford Companion to Law*. Oxford: Clarendon Press.

References and Further Reading:

Burton, Jeffrey. 1995. *Movement for Oklahoma Statehood*. Norman: University of Oklahoma Press.

Harrington, Fred Harvey. 1951. *Hanging Judge*. Caldwell, Idaho: The Caxton Printers.

Kopel, David B. 2000. "The Self-Defense Cases: How the United States Supreme Court Confronted a Hanging Judge in the Nineteenth Century and Taught Some Lessons for Jurisprudence in the Twenty-first." *American Journal of Criminal Law* 27 (Summer): 294–327.

Murphy, James Oakley. 1939. "The Work of Judge Parker in the United States District Court for the Western District of Arkansas—1875–1896." Master's thesis, University of Oklahoma.

Parker, Isaac. 1896. "How to Arrest the Increase of Homicides in America." *North American Review* (June), 667–674.

Shirley, Glenn. 1988. *Law West of Fort Smith: A History of Frontier Justice in the Indian Territory, 1834–1896*. Lincoln: University of Nebraska Press.

Stolberg, Mary M. 1988a. "The Evolution of Frontier Justice: The Case of Judge Isaac Parker." *Prologue* 20, Spring, 7–23.

———. 1988b. "Politician, Populist, Reformer: A Reexamination of 'Hanging Judge' Isaac C. Parker." *Arkansas Historical Quarterly* 47 (Spring): 3–28.

Tuller, Roger H. 2001. *"Let No Guilty Man Escape": A Judicial Biography of "Hanging Judge" Isaac C. Parker*. Norman: University of Oklahoma Press.

PARKER, JOHN JOHNSON

(1885–1958)

John Johnson Parker
Library of Congress

John J. Parker served for thirty-three years as judge and, from 1931 to his death in 1958, as presiding (senior) judge of the United States Court of Appeals for the Fourth Circuit. During that time he was a nominee for associate justice of the United States Supreme Court as well as a legal reformer and leader in federal judicial administration. An exponent of the "New South," he developed a pre-New Deal southern constitutionalism protective of the region's economic development, upheld key components of the New Deal's recovery program, grappled during World War II with civil liberties issues ignited by Jehovah's Witnesses and with the beginnings and burgeoning of the civil rights movement, and, during the Cold War, presided over important Smith Act and presidential power cases.

Parker was born on 20 November 1885 in Monroe, North Carolina, the eldest of four children. His well-educated mother, Frances Ann Johnston of Edenton, North Carolina, was a descendant from William Bradford of Plymouth Colony, a line of early North Carolina governors, and United States Supreme Court associate justice James Iredell (1790–1799).

The daughter of an Episcopal clergyman, she married John Daniel Parker, who eked out a living as an independent grocer.

The younger John Parker worked his way through the University of North Carolina, where he came under the enduring influence of maverick philosophy professor Horace H. Williams and won academic prizes and student government offices prior to receiving his A.B. degree in 1907 and his LL.B. degree in 1908. The six-foot Parker, somewhat reserved in demeanor, had a genial personality and a low-key sense of humor. On 23 November 1910 he married Maria Burgwin Maffitt, a member of an old and prominent Wilmington family. They had three children.

His law practice began in 1908 with David Stern in Greensboro followed by a brief solo practice in his hometown. Thereafter he formed a partnership with Amos M. Stack in Monroe (1910–1919), becoming senior partner in the firm of Stack, Parker and Craig (1919–1922). He moved to Charlotte in 1922 where, until 1925, he headed the firm of Parker, Stewart, McRae and Bobbitt. Both firms developed large general civil and criminal practices in the Carolinas. Parker skillfully argued cases in state and federal trial and appellate courts. Among them was the legendary Peacock murder case wherein Parker's adroitness won acquittal by reason of insanity for his physician client who had shot to death in broad daylight the police chief of Thomasville, North Carolina. Parker successfully represented southern country banks warring against the Federal Reserve Bank's "par clearance" system that discriminated against them. Parker's renown as a criminal lawyer and litigator resulted in his appointment as special assistant to the U.S. attorney general (1923–1924) prosecuting alleged frauds in World War I government contracts.

Parker's path to a federal judgeship coursed through state Republican politics. He joined that party in 1908 when he cast his lot with the dominant "lily-white" and anti-Bryan "business respectables" faction that promoted North Carolina's economic development. Climbing the political ladder, he carried the Republican banner in losing races for congressman (1910), state attorney general (1916), and governor (1920) and also served as GOP national committeeman and delegate-at-large to the Republican National Convention (1924). He supported a myriad of typical progressive reforms as well as tariff protectionism and woman's suffrage. And in 1920, to counter the state Democratic party's customary race-baiting strategy, he publicly disavowed the support of black Carolinians, proclaiming that African Americans did not care to participate in politics and the Republican party did not want them to.

To fill the vacancy created by the death of South Carolinian Charles A. Woods, Pres. Calvin Coolidge gave Parker a recess appointment to the

United States Court of Appeals for the Fourth Circuit on 3 October 1925 and nominated the forty-year-old attorney on 8 December 1925; the Senate confirmed him on 14 December. Following Herbert Hoover's 1928 electoral triumph, Parker received consideration for the solicitor and attorney generalships prior to his nomination on 21 March 1930 to fill the Supreme Court vacancy caused by the sudden death of Associate Justice Edward T. Sanford. Hoover's nomination reflected political, sectional, and jurisprudential considerations. The youthful nominee's "paper trail" of 184 published opinions received little attention with a single exception—*United Mine Workers of America v. Red Jacket Consolidated Coal and Coke Co.* (18 F. 2d 839 [4th Cir., 1927]). That opinion ignited massive opposition from members of organized labor and their putative allies in academe, the press, and the Senate. Although the constitutionality of antiunion "yellow-dog" employment contracts could not then be challenged, however loudly decried, the scope of the original injunction, modified by Parker, against United Mine Workers of America (UMWA) organizing efforts was targeted. Additionally, acting National Association for the Advancement of Colored People (NAACP) director Walter White led a frenetic grassroots lobbying campaign, primarily through black churches, against the nomination. No evidence of Parker's alleged racism emerged either from his judicial opinions or from his associations, which included membership on the North Carolina branch of Will W. Alexander's Commission on Interracial Cooperation. Rather, the NAACP's case rested solely on Parker's 1920 political statement. Thus transmogrified by his opponents' stereotyping, Parker suffered defeat of his nomination in the Senate (forty-one–thirty-nine) on 7 May 1930, and his quests for appointments in 1941, 1942–1943, 1945, and 1954 proved futile.

On the three-judge Court of Appeals, Parker initially sat with ex-Virginia readjuster and senior judge Edmund Waddill Jr. and John C. Rose of Baltimore. His later colleagues included such distinguished jurists as Morris Ames Soper and Simon E. Sobeloff, Armistead M. Dobie and Clement F. Haynsworth Jr. On that court and on three-judge district courts, he heard more than 4,000 arguments and wrote opinions in approximately 1,500 cases, many found in volumes 8–253 of the *Federal Reporter, Second Series*. His opinions reflected a pronounced ability to grasp complicated issues of fact and law and to apply his belief that law was the life principle of society, which itself was an ever-changing organism. Law therefore was not static. "It is," he wrote in *Marshall v. Manese*, "based on reason, arises out of the life of the people, and must change as the conditions of that life change" (85 F. 2d 944, 948 [1936]). Yet he eschewed the role of "judicial legislator," recognizing legislators as preeminent law makers and the subordinate place of an intermediate appellate court judge in the judicial hierarchy. Ambiguity or gaps in the law or cues that a Supreme Court shift was at hand encouraged his exercise of judicial discretion.

Parker early developed a constitutional jurisprudence supportive of the emerging public service state and of regional economic development. Thus he regarded exercises of reserved state police powers as conducive to economic progress, not as threats to private property. That Lincolnton, North Carolina, directed a railroad to replace its wooden bridge, formerly stipulated by ordinance, with a concrete structure impressed him as reasonable and not violative of the Constitution's obligation of contract, commerce, or due process clauses (*Carolina & Northwestern Ry. v. Lincolnton*, 33 F. 2d, 719 [4th Cir., 1929]). Similar self-restraint marked his treatment of Virginia's "Cedar Rust" law designed to protect the state's valuable apple crops by destroying cedar trees that hosted the deadly fungus disease. To Fourteenth Amendment substantive due process arguments, Parker asserted that the state law "does not authorize the taking of one man's property for another man's benefit, but it is a reasonable regulation of the use of property in furtherance of the public welfare" (*Kelleher v. French*, 22 F. 2d 341, 343 [W.D.Va., 1927]). And he looked benignly on exercises of state taxing powers albeit constrained by Supreme Court decisions favoring injunctive relief for taxpayers.

Parker's embrace of governmental regulation of business was tempered by a distinct regional bias favorable to southern economic development. He viewed railroad freight rates fixed by the Interstate Commerce Commission (ICC) as constituting a national internal tariff system that discriminated against southern producers, shippers, and consumers. High ICC-approved interstate rates encouraged him to discover "independent movements" of freight subject to lower state-fixed intrastate rates (*Atlantic Coast Line R.R. v. Standard Oil Co.*, 12 F. 2d 541 [4th Cir., 1926]). Conversely, lowered ICC rates for northern carriers in the Great Lakes bituminous coal trade could threaten the survival of southern mine operators distant from ultimate markets in the North. ICC suspension of similarly lowered "Lake Cargo Coal" rates by the southern carriers led Parker to probe the agency's motives and to hold that neither statutes nor even the Constitution's commerce clause empowered the ICC to equalize intersectional industrial as distinguished from transportation conditions (*Anchor Coal Co. v. United States*, 25 F. 2d 462 [S.D.W.Va., 1928]). The controversial *Red Jacket* case likewise reflected Parker's perception of the deleterious impact on southern mine operators and their labor forces, once their competitive edge in distant coal markets had been dulled by national labor standards associated with unionization. Adhering to prevailing Supreme Court precedents respecting federal jurisdiction, he enjoined the union from persuading miners under "yellow dog" employment contracts to break their contracts (join the union while remaining in the employer's workforce). The faltering southern bituminous industry soon spiraled into deep depression, however, causing Parker to lament "the plight of those engaged in the coal industry, whether as operators or miners"; but he was compelled to hold a producer cartel an unlawful monopoly (*United States v. Appalachian Coals, Inc.*, 1 F. Supp. 339, 349 [S.D.W.Va., 1932]). Emerging in the twilight of an expiring economic order, Parker's constitutionalism was marked by a combination of realism and optimism, by a sober reflection on the painful economic plight of the region, and by eternal optimism about the future of the South's human and natural resources.

That in the depths of the Great Depression the national government might aid the South and its people resonated with Parker's Hamiltonian proclivities. Early in 1934 he publicly declared that there existed "no reason why [the] national government should not foster the healthy growth and development of [the] nation by encouragement to agriculture, industry, education, road building, and other activities essential to the national welfare. . . ." "There is," he continued, "nothing in our constitutional theory which prevents the national government using its powers for the relief of suffering and to place industry again on its feet" (Parker 1934, 382). Constitutional theory became practice in March–April 1935 when Depression-induced revisions in the Bankruptcy Act reached his court. Holding congressional power over the subject to be plenary and capable of meeting the exigencies of modern debtor-creditor relationships, he upheld the constitutionality of the Corporate Reorganization Act (*Campbell v. Alleghany Corp.* 75 F. 2d 947 [4th Cir., 1935]) and the Frazier-Lemke Farm Mortgage Moratorium Act (*Bradford v. Fahey*, 76 F. 2d 281 [4th Cir., 1935]), only to be subsequently whipsawed by the Supreme Court in construing the latter act (*Wright v. Vinton Branch of Mountain Trust Bank*, 85 F. 2d 973 [4th Cir. 1936], rev. 300 U.S. 440 [1937]). Parker's "Buzzard's Roost" opinion came down in February 1936. Over conservative colleague Morris Soper's dissent, Parker upheld that portion of the National Industrial Recovery Act authorizing federal loans to state and local governments for public works, in this instance a public electric power plant. He rejected Tenth Amendment limitations on Congress's constitutional power to tax and spend as well as delegation of powers and substantive due process arguments raised by Duke Power Co. (*Greenwood County v. Duke Power Co.*, 81 F. 2d 986 [4th Cir. 1936]). Parker also favorably construed the Railway Labor Act in June when he held that Congress could bring within its collective bargaining provisions even "backshop employees" not directly involved in interstate commerce and rejected the railroad's "liberty of contract" argument (*Virginian Railroad Co. v. System Federation* 40, 84 F. 2d 641 [4th Cir. 1936]).

Judge Robert Satter on the Differences between Trial and Appellate Judging

In a reflective book, Judge Robert Satter of the Connecticut Superior Court, a statewide trial court of general jurisdiction, reflected on the difference between judging at the trial level, where judges weigh both the law and the facts, and the appellate level, where judges typically focus on the legality of prior proceedings. Noting that a friend on the Connecticut Supreme Court viewed judges as more "detached," Satter said that such detachment is not as easily achieved at the trial level and tried to describe how he did come to his decisions:

> In the appeals court the parties are faceless abstractions, the passions of the trial muffled in the printed appeal record. But to me on the trial bench the litigants have names I remember, personalities that engage me, emotions that involve me. Clearly I do not decide a case on the basis of my liking one party more than the other. But I am keenly conscious of the impact of my decision on the lives and fortunes of flesh-and-blood people. The cases that stimulate me the most are not the ones that are challenging intellectually, as much as I enjoy them, but the ones about whose outcome I care very much. (Satter 1990, 78)

Satter believes that judges must seek both to "apply the law" and "also strive for justice." He explained: "In that regard he is like an artist as to beauty. An artist does not paint beauty. He paints a picture and hopes to create beauty. A judge does not decide justice. He decides the cases before him and hopes to achieve justice. I do this in every one of my cases" (78–79).

Later in his book, Satter told about a law professor, an appellate judge, and a trial judge who go duck hunting and agree that the first to kill a duck will get ten dollars, but whoever shot another kind of bird would lose five. Satter continued:

> By a flip of a coin, the professor went first. A winged creature flew over; the professor took aim and hesitated: "It has the markings of a water fowl; it may be a duck, but on the other hand. . . ." By then it had

(continues)

Parker, encouraged by economic conservative Soper, initially hesitated to depart from the Supreme Court's direct-indirect commerce clause test that prevailed prior to the high court's 1937 "switch-in-time" with respect to the National Labor Relations (Wagner) Act and the Public Utility Holding Company Act. Parker did approve federal support for agriculture under the commerce power but not under the taxing power, unless exercised to raise revenue. So too Parker approved national power to control rivers and streams within states.

Parker believed courts existed to curb governmental excesses and to assure government's role as a liberating rather than an oppressive force in

(continued)

> vanished. The appellate judge went next. Spotting a flapping animal in the sky, he said, "It could be our prey, but let me check this bird catalog." By then it was gone. Now it was the trial judge's turn. As a fowl came into sight, the judge shot and shouted, "It's a bird; I hope it's a duck." (1990, 93)

Satter observed that "I'm afraid on the bench I have shot many a buzzard that way" (93).

Satter noted that one difference between trial judges and judges of the United States Supreme Court is that decisions of trial judges and lower appellate judges can be reversed on appeal. Satter further noted that reversal of a trial judge is more personal than a lawyer's loss:

> There is a difference between lawyers losing a case and judges being reversed. Lawyers try the cases that come their way. They are stuck with whatever the facts are on their side of the dispute. Moreover, they have to contend with unreliable witnesses, opposing counsel, and intractable law.
>
> They have plenty of legitimate excuses for not winning. A trial judge, however, has no place to hide. He determines the facts from the evidence, chooses the legal principles to apply, and makes a decision that is his own and for which he must take complete responsibility. His professional pride always rides heavily on how he fares under appellate court scrutiny. (Satter 1990, 228)

Despite these observations, Satter went on to observe that trial court judges' "'batting averages' before the appeals courts have little effect on their reputation with the bar or their colleagues" (231). Satter explained:

> The judge with few reversals may take only easy cases and decide them strictly in accordance with black letter law. The judge with many reversals may be willing to take difficult and involved cases, which other judges are eager to avoid, and he may courageously fashion thoughtful opinions that seek to extend the boundaries of the law. A judge of the latter kind is one of the most respected members of the Connecticut trial bench. (231)

REFERENCE:

Satter, Robert. 1990. *Doing Justice: A Trial Judge at Work*. New York: Simon and Schuster.

economic life. When the government condemned a water power site, he thought that there was "no reason in law, in justice or in common honesty that it should not pay compensation" based on such projected use (*United States v. Twin City Power Co.*, 215 F. 2d 592, 601 [4th Cir., 1954]). The Supreme Court disagreed (350 U.S. 222 [1956]), as did the Roosevelt Court in flatly rejecting Parker's determination in *Hope Natural Gas Co. v. Federal Power Commission* that the agency's valuation of the enterprise resulted in a rate base that he deemed "arbitrary and unreasonable," saying that it deviated from "statutory requirements and [was] violative of the due process clause of the Fifth Amendment . . ." (134 F. 2d 287, 300 [4th Cir., 1943];

rev. *FPC v. Hope Natural Gas Co.*, 320 U.S. 591 [1944]). Even in National Labor Relations Board cases, he asserted that where the board deviated from law, acted arbitrarily or unreasonably, or abused its discretion, the court was justified "in refusing enforcement of an order entered by the Board in exercise of the power entrusted to it by Congress" (*Newport News Shipbuilding & Dry Dock Co., v. NLRB*, 101 F. 2d 841 [4th Cir., 1939]). Yet his opinion in *NLRB v. Highland Park Mfg. Co.* (1940) upholding the board's finding of bad faith on the employer's part led Sen. Robert Wagner, author of the labor act, to praise Parker's opinion as "an exhaustive and brilliant analysis of the collective-bargaining process . . ." and to insert its full text into the *Congressional Record* (86 *Cong. Rec.* pt. 14 [76th Cong., 3d sess.], 1484 [1940]).

Important issues of civil liberties came before Judge Parker in the 1940s and 1950s to which he applied various reason-based pragmatic balancing tests. The war years saw him challenged by Selective Service cases brought by Jehovah's Witnesses seeking classifications as "ministers" rather than as conscientious objectors, in which classification they would be exempt even from "work of national importance" (*Smith v. United States*, 148 F. 2d 288 [4th Cir., 1945]). However unfavorably Parker came to regard the Witnesses' claims via habeas corpus writs for exemptions from a general secular law, he took a different view of the plight of Witness children who sought an exemption from West Virginia's compulsory flag salute law. In the face of eroding Supreme Court precedent upholding such a law, he weighed asserted religious freedom against the state's interest and found the latter wanting. "The salute to the flag," he opined, "is an expression of the homage of the soul. To force it upon one who has conscientious scruples against giving it, is petty tyranny unworthy of the spirit of this Republic and forbidden . . . by the fundamental law" (*Barnett v. West Virginia Board of Education*, 47 F. Supp. 251, 255 [S.D.W.Va. 1942]).

Especially dangerous to national security during the Cold War era was international communism. Influenced by his experience as alternate American judge at the International Military Tribunal in Nuremberg, Germany (1945–1946), where he materially contributed to development of the critical conspiracy issue, Parker echoed the Supreme Court's decision in *Dennis v. United States* (341 U.S. 494 [1951]) respecting the inutility of the "clear and present danger" test when there existed evidence of a conspiracy to overthrow the U.S. government by force and violence. The associations and advocacy of six Maryland communist leaders were, he warned, "pregnant with potential evil, which, while hidden from view in normal times, is likely to assert itself as an irresistible force when some national crisis presents an opportunity for a putsch or a coup d'etat" (*Frankfeld v. United States*, 198 F. 2d 679, 682 [4th Cir., 1952]). The subsequent and notable prosecution of Junius Scales under the Smith Act's membership clause again found Parker viewing the case through the prism of conspiracy theory derived from *Dennis* and *Frankfield,* both of which rested on indictments under the act's advocacy provision (*Scales v. United States,* 227 F. 2d 587 [4th Cir., 1955]).

Parker deferred to state powers over crime control. He eschewed incorporating provisions of the Bill of Rights into the due process clause of the Fourteenth Amendment, thus rendering them applicable to state criminal procedures. He consistently treated alleged errors in such proceedings with a due process–based "fair trial" rule. Deference to state prerogatives in crime control surfaced in his repeated attempts in his judicial and administrative capacities to curb the use of writs of habeas corpus collaterally to attack final decisions of state supreme courts.

A rising volume of race relations cases confronted Parker beginning in the 1940s. The first wave involved employment discrimination cases pitting black railroad workers against labor unions and employers in *Tunstall v. Brotherhood of Locomotive Firemen and Enginemen* (1944). Heeding the Roosevelt Court's restraint on judicial interference with labor policy, the Fourth Circuit denied jurisdiction under the Railway Labor Act in a case involving blatant union racial discrimination. High court reversal encouraged a predisposed Parker to approve a class action lawsuit against the union in 1945 and to enjoin its discriminatory policies and award back pay to the black firemen in 1947. Analogous job discrimination cases brought by black employees against railroads and rail unions received similarly favorable treatment from Parker.

Black public schoolteachers suffering employment discrimination likewise received a favorable reception from Parker. As early as 1940 in *Alston v. School Board of City of Norfolk,* he had struck down on Fourteenth Amendment grounds salary schedules that set lower pay for black teachers who were equally as qualified as higher-paid whites. Following arguments including those by Thurgood Marshall and William H. Hastie, he stated: "that an unconstitutional discrimination is set forth . . . hardly admits of argument" (112 F. 2d 992, 995 [4th Cir., 1940]). In the midst of court-ordered school desegregation seventeen years later, he assailed a South Carolina statute barring NAACP members from state employment. A schoolteacher challenge to the public employment exclusion law split a three-judge district court wherein two judges favored abstention. Parker vehemently dissented, arguing that the court had a duty to take jurisdiction. Distinguishing the Smith Act cases, he declared: "The right to join organizations which seek by lawful means to support and further what their members regard as in the public interest . . . is protected by the constitutional guarantees of free speech and freedom of assembly; and such right is one of the bulwarks of liberty and social progress" (*Bryan v. Austin*, 148 F. Supp. 563, 569 [E.D.S.C. 1957]).

Political rights asserted by black citizens also received powerful judicial support from Parker. He held the white South Carolina Democratic party primary unconstitutional in *Rice v. Elmore* (1947) as denying every black South Carolinian "any effective voice in the government of his state and his country" (165 F. 2d 389). Subsequently, in *Baskin v. Brown* (1949) he enjoined a further attempt by the Palmetto State to elude the Fourteenth Amendment's "state action" doctrine by privatizing the party primary process. Although Parker suggested future close scrutiny of state poll taxes in *Michael v. Cockerell* (1947), in *Lassiter v. Taylor* (1957) he treated literacy tests warily when evidence of their discriminatory administration was lacking.

Parker accorded a high value to state power when social relations between the races were involved as in public parks and elementary and secondary public education. An abiding concern with maintaining interracial peace and recognition of his role as an intermediate court judge with limited "law-making" capacity also suggested prudence. That the Supreme Court in the then recent *Sweatt v. Painter* case (1950) had refused to reconsider the prevailing "separate and equal" doctrine derived from *Plessy v. Ferguson* (1896) cautioned Parker when confronted with direct constitutional challenges to that doctrine in *Boyer v. Garrett* (public parks) (1950) and in *Briggs v. Elliott* (1951). Unlike dissenting District Judge J. Waties Waring (E.D.S.C.), in the latter case, Parker adhered to stare decisis and ordered the Clarendon County South Carolina school board to equalize but not to eliminate segregated educational facilities. Supreme Court reversal in *Brown v. Topeka* returned the case to the Fourth Circuit. Ever seeking to promote peace and reason in an emotive domain, Parker construed *Brown* to mean that "[n]othing in the Constitution or in the decision of the Supreme Court takes away from the people freedom to choose the schools they attend. The Constitution . . . does not require integration; it merely forbids discrimination. It does not forbid segregation as it occurs as the result of voluntary action, but forbids the use of governmental powers to enforce segregation" (*Briggs v. Elliott*, 132 F. Supp. 776, 777 [E.D.S.C., 1955]). The Parker Doctrine constituted a reasonableness test to be met by state officials. State-mandated administrative procedures to be exhausted by plaintiffs prior to federal judicial proceedings met the test unless such procedures offered mere exercises in futility intended merely to delay compliance with *Brown*. Thereafter the court, in the face of Virginia's Massive Resistance strategy, issued *per curiam* decisions in the last months of Parker's life, ordering specific steps aimed at desegregating the state's school systems.

Although Parker preferred changes in race relations fostered by a Christian spirit rather than by changes spawned by legal coercion, he faithfully performed his constitutional duty. As with economic regulation and labor cases, so with race relations cases—he sometimes stood a step ahead of a changing Constitution in the hands of the Supreme Court and sometimes a short step behind that Court. His well-supported and carefully crafted opinions written in crisis times constitute the legacy of a jurist who perceived both the powers of and limitations on a judge of a court "in-between" trial and supreme courts.

As acting or regular presiding judge, Parker administered his circuit and was a member of the national policymaking Judicial Conference of the United States (1930–1958). He served on sixteen conference committees, including the Advisory Committee, and chaired several. His efforts aided enactment of the Administrative Office of the U.S. Courts Act of 1939, Federal Court Reporters Act of 1944, Federal Youth Corrections Act of 1950, and the Interlocutory Appeals Act of 1958. They also contributed to preservation of broad federal diversity of citizenship jurisdiction and to compensation of counsel and public defenders for indigent defendants provided for by law.

Parker was active in the American Law Institute and the American Bar Association (ABA). His service on the latter's committees began in 1931 and reflected an abiding interest in law reform, judicial administration, criminal law, and international law and relations. As a leader in the ABA Section of Judicial Administration (1934–1958) and in the Judicial Conference and as judicial adviser to the U.S. high commissioner for Germany (1949), Parker promoted judicial reforms to reduce popular influence over courts and expand judges' control of judicial proceedings, to enhance institutional autonomy of the judiciary, and to unify, simplify, and centralize intrajudiciary procedures and administration.

From numerous public platforms, Parker advanced his optimistic view that Americans as individuals and as a nation could surmount all obstacles and master their environment. He worked tirelessly as a member of the University of North Carolina (UNC) Board of Trustees (1921–1958) and as a firm supporter of the North Carolina College for Negroes in Durham. He served as a member of the UNC presidential search committee that nominated Frank Porter Graham. Parker thereafter became a stalwart supporter of the president—a leading southern liberal. The judge urged on the board racial integration of UNC's professional schools in the 1950s; after *Brown II* in 1955, he called on the board to reverse its segregation policies forthwith.

Parker served his state as a member of the North Carolina Constitutional Commission (1931–1932). The proposed constitution reflected Parker's administrative theory through its provisions for flexible legislative taxing power and a stronger executive with budget and veto powers as well as an appointed council of state and a unified judicial system under control of the chief justice of the supreme court. He also performed important extrajudicial services for the nation, sitting with Judges Learned Hand (Court of Appeals, Second Circuit) and Joseph C. Hutcheson Jr. (Court of Appeals, Fifth Circuit) on the Advisory Board on Just Compensation to the War Shipping Administration. Appointment to the International Military Tribunal attested to Parker's rising prominence as a spokesman for "internationalism." He became an early advocate of a United Nations organization, led by the United States and equipped with military capabilities. As the Cold War waxed, he publicly warned against Communist-bloc military power, warmly endorsed aid to Greece and Turkey in 1947, and supported both universal military training and the North Atlantic Treaty Organization. Isolationism manifested in the Bricker Amendment to limit the president's power to make treaties and to enter into executive agreements evoked Parker's sharp public criticism. Nevertheless, in *United States v. Capps* (1953), he held that inherent presidential power to make executive agreements was limited by express constitutional grants of power to Congress, especially when Congress had enacted laws on the basis of such grants.

Parker was a devout and active member of the Protestant Episcopal Church. He served as the denomination's delegate in 1945 to the National Study Conference of the Commission on a Just and Durable Peace of the Federal Council of Churches chaired by John Foster Dulles, and in November 1957 he became chairman of the General Crusade Committee of the Billy Graham Charlotte Crusade. Judge Parker was felled by a heart attack on 17 March 1958 at the Mayflower Hotel in Washington, D.C., while attending the Judicial Conference.

Peter G. Fish

References and Further Reading:

Burris, William C. 1987. *Duty and the Law: Judge John J. Parker and the Constitution*. Bessemer, Ala.: Colonial Press.

Capel, Wint. 1998. *Dethronement of Reason: The Travails of North Carolina's Murderous Dr. J. W. Peacock*. Chapel Hill, N.C.: Cape Corporation Press.

Fish, Peter G. 1977. "Guarding the Judicial Ramparts: John J. Parker and the Administration of Federal Justice." *Justice System Journal* 3: 105–125.

———. 1985. "Judge Parker and the Public Service State." *Duke Law Magazine* 2: 37–44.

———. 1987. "Red Jacket Revisited: Saga of the Case that Unraveled John J. Parker's Appointment to the U.S. Supreme Court." *Law and History Review* 5: 51–104.

———. 1989. "Torchbearer for Pre–New Deal Southern Economic Development: Judge John J. Parker of the U.S. Court of Appeals for the Fourth Circuit." In *An Uncertain Tradition: Constitutionalism and the History of the South*, edited by Kermit L. Hall and James W. Ely Jr. Athens: University of Georgia Press, 253–295.

Goings, Kenneth W. 1990. *"The NAACP Comes of Age": The Defeat of Judge John J. Parker*. Bloomington: Indiana University Press.

"In Memoriam Honorable John Johnston Parker, 1885–1958: Proceedings in the United States Court of Appeals for the Fourth Circuit, April 22, 1958." 1958. *Federal Reporter* 253, 2d Ser., 3–55.

Maltese, John Anthony. 1995. *The Selling of Supreme Court Nominees*. Baltimore: John Hopkins University Press, 52–69.

Medina, Harold R. 1960. "John Johnson Parker, 1885–1958." *North Carolina Law Review* 38: 299.

Parker, John J. 1934. "The Crisis in Constitutional Government." *Commercial Law Journal* 39: 378.

PARSONS, THEOPHILUS

(1750–1813)

THEOPHILUS PARSONS
Library of Congress

THEOPHILUS PARSONS SERVED as the chief justice of Massachusetts from 1806 until his death in 1813. A well-known Federalist, Parsons was appointed to the court by Gov. Caleb Strong, who sought a jurist who possessed the virtues of independence, firmness, and respect for the vital role of the court in developing principles of law. Chief Justice Parsons proved to be such a jurist.

Theophilus Parsons was born to Moses Parsons and Susan (Davis) Parsons in Byfield, Massachusetts, in 1750. His father was a minister; he completed a degree at Harvard in 1736 and devoted his life to the study of theology. Susan Parsons was an active participant in parish activities and was known for her love of books and learning. Both the love of learning and the solid religious grounding were passed on to Theophilus (the name means "lover of God"), who demonstrated interest in a variety of academic fields and whose respect for religious knowledge formed a major theme of his official charges to juries delivered from the bench.

Parsons followed his father's educational path, graduating from Harvard in 1769. Shortly after graduation, he founded a school at Falmouth and served as the sole teacher. He continued as a teacher through 1773 while studying the law with an eminent Falmouth lawyer who shared his first name—Theophilus Bradbury. Parsons's legal career began in July 1774 when he was admitted to practice. He practiced in Falmouth until the town's destruction in the 1775 attack by British forces under the leadership of Adm. Samuel Graves. At that point, Parsons returned to the town of his birth and resumed his legal career.

Parsons then became active in Massachusetts politics. At approximately the same time that Thomas Jefferson was drafting the Declaration of Independence, the leaders of Massachusetts began to draft a constitution. Upon the recommendation of the state House of Representatives, each town selected delegates to draft a constitution. The constitution was duly drafted and was rejected by the people by an overwhelming margin. Parsons, a conservative, strongly opposed the proposed constitution, fearing that the liberties granted therein might easily degenerate into license. He, along with other prominent citizens, was appointed to a committee charged with the duty of preparing a report on the proposed constitution. This "convention" took place in Essex County in 1778 and produced a document known as the Essex Result. Contemporaries credited Parsons with its authorship. The report contained compelling arguments favoring separation of powers, the creation of a Bill of Rights, and (unsurprisingly) judicial independence. The text of the writing reflected a pragmatic grasp of the need for an efficient and powerful government, combined with an understanding of the ways in which corrupt officials might abuse such power. Parsons wrote at length on the issue of judicial independence, insisting that judges should hold office during good behavior and that the power of removal be divided between the executive and legislative branches.

When a new convention was created to draft a state constitution in 1779, Theophilus Parsons served as part of the Essex delegation. Although John Adams (who later became the nation's second president) drafted the new constitution, the principles expressed by Adams's fellow Federalists in the Essex Result were incorporated. By the time of his marriage to Elizabeth Greenleaf in 1780, Parsons was a prominent citizen and well-established lawyer, with a flourishing Essex County practice. He was thirty years old.

According to the memoirs compiled by his son, Parsons, who was a delegate to the Massachusetts ratifying convention, also played a prominent role in developing the first amendments to the U.S. Constitution, collectively referred to as the Bill of Rights. Despite the fact that the amendments were drafted as a means of pacifying the anti-Federalists, the twenty-five-man committee charged with drafting the amendments was composed entirely of Federalists. Although the authorship of the propositions that became the Bill of Rights was never conclusively established, the younger Parsons believed that his father played a pivotal role. He summarized his father's political convictions as follows:

> My father stood firmly and consistently, in every word and act of his life among them who desired a well and wisely balanced government, which should be strong enough to guard liberty from license and anarchy on the one hand and from the iron hand of oppression on the other. His natural proclivity was certainly to the extreme of conservatism . . . but when called upon to express or form a solemn determination, he seems to me to have labored . . . to find and stand upon the just medium. (Parsons [1859] 1970, 106)

After the framing of the U.S. Constitution, Parsons retreated from public life, focusing upon his legal practice and his many hobbies. An enthusiastic scholar, he was fascinated by the sciences, particularly mathematics, astronomy, and optics. Articles on these topics appear in his manuscripts, suggesting that his level of knowledge was significant. Parsons's son (also named Theophilus Parsons) related numerous anecdotes concerning the neighbors' reactions to his father's more outlandish hobbies. The elder Parsons conducted experiments, some of which involved the use of lenses to cast inverted images on the opposite wall. He apparently so frightened one servant that his wife insisted that he change the room used for his experiments so that images would be cast into the garden rather than onto the street, where passers-by might be alarmed (Parsons [1859] 1970, 277). This love of academic pursuits, combined with a propensity for scientific precision, was characteristic of Parsons and was reflected in his approach to the law. He valued succinctness, adherence to established principles, and fact-based argumentation. He was the stereotypical scholar, paying little attention to his appearance. The younger Parsons explains: "He was inattentive to his dress, to the last degree and scarcely seemed to know what he had on, or how it was put on; and was as much under the constant supervision of my mother as one of her younger children" (328).

As a lawyer, Parsons showed little interest in the rhetorical flourishes valued by other members of the Massachusetts bar. As a judge, he demonstrated a decided impatience with lawyers who insisted upon appealing to the emotions and prejudices of juries.

Parsons's first judicial appointment to the Supreme Judicial Court at age fifty-six was also his last. Harvard conferred the degree of doctor of laws upon Parsons in 1804, acknowledging the public respect that made his appointment to the bench possible. Brown University took slightly longer to recognize Parsons's accomplishments, conferring a degree in 1809, after Parsons had served as chief justice for three years. He was elevated from the rank of lawyer to judge in 1806, when Governor Strong appointed him to succeed Chief Justice Francis Dana as the leader of the Massachusetts Supreme Judicial Court. Bypassing such eminent jurists as Theodore Sedgwick, who sat on the court, Governor Strong sought an "outsider" who would be free to reform the administration of the judicial system. Some of the most intractable problems were those that continue to plague the legal system—protracted proceedings, backlog, long-winded lawyers. Parsons's skill in pleadings and logic, combined with his utter intolerance for lengthy diatribes, did much to streamline legal proceedings in Massachusetts.

Many were surprised when Parsons accepted the appointment as chief justice. He was not a wealthy man—his sizable family, his library, and his experiments consumed discretionary income. As a practicing lawyer, he refused to accept payment from widows or clergymen, representing them without charge (and undoubtedly attracting them as clients). According to one estimate, Parsons took an 85 percent cut in pay when he accepted the chief justiceship (Oesterle 1992, 128n. 8). Perhaps this explains Parsons's later insistence upon increases in judicial salaries, backed by threats to leave the bench in the absence of such increases.

As chief justice, Parsons was not afforded the luxury of hearing only cases of pressing political and legal import. In the early nineteenth century, judges rode circuit, traveling across the state to hear the trials of jury cases in every county of the commonwealth. Parsons, not a young man at fifty-six and fondly regarded by family members as a hypochondriac, was obliged to cover a substantial territory. He took this aspect of his job seriously, relishing the opportunity to educate jurors on the sanctity and significance of the law. His instructions to the grand jury, read in each county, contained reflections about the vital role to be played by the citizenry in upholding and protecting the rule of law. The charge to the grand jury, which consumes four pages of very small print in the younger Parsons's memoirs of his father, emphasized the same values Parsons expounded throughout his public career. In clear and forthright language, he outlined the need for a well-educated and watchful citizenry, informed by religious morality and motivated by a love of liberty, to hold their officials accountable through a thoughtful use of the electoral process. Without noting the incongruity of judicial appointment, Parsons reminded the jurors of their solemn duty to uphold the law without preference or prejudice.

Parsons was also respectful of the jurors' time, allowing lawyers to waste none of it. In a letter from Zachariah Eddy, provided to Parsons's son for use in the memoirs, the prominent member of the Massachusetts bar described Parsons's courtroom demeanor:

> Judge Parsons was very provident of time. He would not permit it to be uselessly spent. He had not much patience with counsel or client who had not his case prepared; nor would he hear impertinent or irrelevant testimony, or groundless argument. He said the multitude of cases called for promptness, as did the finances of the county. When a term ended, he would enjoin counsel

to be better prepared in their cases in time to come (and sometimes, to *read their books*), that the time and money of the county might not be wasted. (Parsons [1859] 1970, 172)

Lawyers did not bear this treatment in silence. When one beleaguered lawyer, who had heard Parsons argue cases, protested that "Your Honor did not argue your own cases in the way you require us to," Parsons had a ready reply. Wrote Theophilus Jr.: "'Certainly not,' was the reply; 'but that was the judge's fault, not mine'" (Parsons [1859] 1970, 208). Parsons even threatened to jail a dear friend who insisted upon presenting arguments directly to the jury without submitting them to the court's prior scrutiny for evidentiary relevance. Efficiency was the hallmark of Parsons's courtroom.

Parsons's accomplishments were not limited to administrative reforms. His legal opinions and commentaries were collected into a volume entitled "Commentaries on American Law." These decisions influenced some of the most important decisions relating to the power of government to regulate private economic institutions. Massachusetts was a national leader in economic development, particularly with regard to corporate charters. In fact, Massachusetts was the first state to enact a statute of incorporation. Although many charters were granted in the late eighteenth and early nineteenth centuries, the legal meaning of incorporation was ambiguous. When disputes arose, judges had few places to seek guidance. A landmark Massachusetts case, *Wales v. Stetson* (2 Mass. 143, 1806), served as precedent for Story's opinion in *Dartmouth College v. Woodward* (17 U.S. 518). The issue was the same in both cases—although legislatures had routinely amended corporate charters without the assent of the firm prior to 1806, the issue was first adjudicated in this case. Parsons wrote the opinion, deciding in favor of the corporation. He wrote, "We are satisfied that the rights legally vested in this, or any corporation, cannot be controlled or destroyed by any subsequent statute, unless a power for that purpose be reserved to the legislature in the original act of incorporation" (2 Mass. 144).

As his son attested, Parsons sought the middle ground. Although he felt compelled to limit the power of the legislature arbitrarily to amend charters, he gave precise instructions as to how the legislature might accomplish its purpose and avoid coming before the court in the future. Under Parsons's leadership, the Massachusetts Supreme Judicial Court also infused the corporation with legal personhood, allowing it to sue and be sued in a court of law (Oesterle 1992, 146). Parsons balanced his Federalist preference for a strong central government against the knowledge that legislatures, left unchecked, would not honor its contracts. The advantage was ultimately to the legislature, which could amend charters if fair warning were provided. As the executors of the public will, that was as it should be.

Parsons served as chief justice until his death in 1813, establishing a reputation as an activist and reformer. In the year of his appointment to the bench, he was chosen as a fellow of Harvard College, serving as an active member of the College Corporation until he became too ill to work. During the last two years of his tenure as chief justice, he was plagued by illness that was not a manifestation of his tendency to predict his imminent demise with every ache. Although he fulfilled his duties without fail, family members noticed a change in demeanor, a lessening of Parsons's usual vigor and enthusiasm. According to the younger Parsons, his father's many physicians diagnosed "hydrocephalic apoplexy" or an accumulation of water upon the brain. In November 1813, Theophilus Parsons died.

The younger Theophilus Parsons, whose memoirs provide such a thorough account of his father's life, was sixteen when the elder Parsons died. He followed his parent's career path, pursuing the study of law and rising to prominence in his own right. Unlike Parsons Sr., the son never ascended to the bench and pursued his own scholarly interests in academia, as a professor of law at Harvard University, the institution so beloved by his father.

Sara L. Zeigler

References and Further Reading:

Commonwealth v. Union Fire and Marine Insurance Company. 5 Mass. 230 (1809).

Hoeflich, M. H. 1992. "Theophilus Parsons and the Culture of Practical Value." In *The History of the Law in Massachusetts: The Supreme Judicial Court, 1692–1992*, edited by Russell K. Osgood. Boston:. Supreme Judicial Court Historical Society, 117–125.

Oesterle, Dale A. 1992. "Formative Contributions to American Corporate Law by the Massachusetts Supreme Judicial Court from 1806 to 1810." In *The History of the Law in Massachusetts: The Supreme Judicial Court, 1692–1992*, edited by Russell K. Osgood. Boston: Supreme Judicial Court Historical Society, 127–153.

Osgood, Russell K. 1992. "The Supreme Judicial Court, 1692–1992: An Overview." In *The History of the Law in Massachusetts: The Supreme Judicial Court, 1692–1992*, edited by Russell K. Osgood. Boston: Supreme Judicial Court Historical Society, 1–23.

Parsons, Theophilus, Jr. [1859] 1970. *Memoir of Theophilus Parsons*. New York: De Capo Press.

Wales v. Stetson. 2 Mass. 13 (1806).

PENDLETON, EDMUND

(1721–1803)

Edmund Pendleton
Library of Congress

Judge Edmund Pendleton was the head of the Virginia judiciary from its professionalization upon independence from Great Britain until his death. It was in his court and under his eye that John Marshall, Bushrod Washington, St. George Tucker, Spencer Roane, and the other lawyers of the first period of republican Virginia refined their legal skills. His steady example influenced in one way or another a remarkable generation of lawyers and judges.

Edmund Pendleton was born on 9 September 1721 in Caroline County, Virginia. His parents, Henry Pendleton (1684–1721) and Mary Taylor (1688–1770), were both members of the gentry; they were educated and solvent but not wealthy. Edmund learned the law as an articled, or apprentice, clerk to Benjamin Robinson (1689–1761), the clerk of Caroline County. The clerk of the county was a lawyer who attended to the procedure of the county court and kept the lay justices of the peace on the proper procedural course during litigation in their court. Thus, an apprenticeship to a clerk of court was equivalent to that to a practicing lawyer.

After being "strictly" examined by Edward Barradall (1704–1743), attorney general of Virginia, Pendleton was licensed to practice law in the county courts of Virginia on 25 April 1741. He began his practice in the County Court of Caroline County and in the neighboring counties and was soon appointed king's attorney (the public prosecutor) of nearby Essex County. In 1746, he moved his practice to the General Court in Williamsburg and rapidly distinguished himself in competition with a talented and well-educated bar. From 1751 until the end of the colonial era, Pendleton also sat regularly and faithfully on the County Court of Caroline County.

After becoming established at the bar, Pendleton taught law to a succession of local boys who were apprenticed to him. The two most famous of these were two of his own cousins, John Penn (1740–1788) and John Taylor of Caroline (1753–1824). Penn moved to North Carolina to practice law and was a signer of the Declaration of Independence. Taylor practiced law in Caroline County and Richmond but is better known for his writings on agricultural and political theory.

Pendleton was also active in politics, serving continuously in the Virginia House of Burgesses, the lower house of the General Assembly, from 1752 until the end of the colonial period. He was then elected to the newly formed House of Delegates in 1776 and was made its first speaker. He also represented Virginia in the Continental Congress in 1774 and 1775. He, George Wythe (1726–1806), and Thomas Jefferson (1743–1826) were appointed a committee of the General Assembly, upon independence, to revise the statute law of Virginia in the light of the new Constitution. He was chosen to preside over the Virginia Constitutional Convention of 1788. Though politically conservative, Pendleton actively supported independence from Great Britain and the adoption of the federal Constitution.

After independence, the county courts were retained, but a new system of high courts at the capital was needed. These new high courts were to be filled by professionally trained lawyers, rather than by laymen, as the colonial courts had been.

In 1778, the new Court of Chancery and the new General Court were created. The initial judges on the Court of Chancery were Pendleton, the presiding judge; George Wythe, who sat there until his death in 1806; and Robert Carter Nicholas, who died in office in 1780. Pendleton's next judicial post was president of the Court of Appeals. Thus he served as the head of the Virginia judiciary from 1778 until his death in 1803.

As the spokesman of the court, he must have had a permanent effect on the new Virginia bench and bar not only in terms of legal philosophy but also as to judicial demeanor and public example. He was a learned lawyer and a skillful advocate. He was a modest person, however, who never felt any need for ostentation. He sought public service but never public honors. He was highly intelligent but never intellectually arrogant. He was always approachable and never haughty. The result was that, after his first election to public office, he was never opposed for reelection, and his positions of public trust were given him without any solicitation on his part because it was well known that he would act in them to the general satisfaction of the general public and not for his personal self-interest.

During his twenty-five years on the appellate bench in Virginia, he sat with several colleagues who also distinguished themselves as jurists. George Wythe (1726–1806) was undoubtedly the best. Spencer Roane (1762–1822) overlapped Pendleton on the Court of Appeals from 1795 to 1803. John Blair (1732–1800) sat with Pendleton from 1780 to 1789, when he resigned to become one of the original justices on the Supreme Court of the United States.

Many of the lawyers who practiced in Pendleton's court and learned from his legal insights and judicial opinions went on to distinguish themselves in their own times. John Marshall (1755–1835) and Bushrod Washington (1762–1829) went on to sit on the Supreme Court on the United States. Edmund Randolph (1753–1813), the attorney general of Virginia, and Charles Lee (1758–1815) were appointed the first and second attorneys general of the United States. St. George Tucker (1752–1827) succeeded Pendleton on the Court of Appeals; he also was the second professor of law at the College of William and Mary, an editor of Blackstone's *Commentaries*, and later the federal judge for the District of Virginia. John Taylor of Caroline (1753–1824) had a very lucrative practice in the Court of Appeals before retiring to devote his time to political philosophy. There were many others who are now no longer remembered outside of Virginia, except perhaps for John Wickham (1763–1839) and George Hay (1765–1830), who argued in the trial of Aaron Burr, which was reported nationally.

Pendleton's judicial opinions were reported by Bushrod Washington (1762–1829) and by Daniel Call (1765–1840), two of the lawyers who regularly practiced in his court, and by John Brown (1750–1810), who was the clerk of his court. John Marshall also reported some of Pendleton's decisions, sixteen of which were printed by Call (sadly, Marshall's manuscript has been lost).

Although no individual case in Pendleton's court stands out as a radical milestone of jurisprudence, an act of the legislature that was signed into law by the governor was declared to be unconstitutional by the Court of Appeals in 1788. Even though it was not a matter of formal litigation between a plaintiff and a defendant, the *Remonstrance* or *Cases of the Judges* was reported in Call's *Reports* at volume 4, page 135. In early 1788, the General Assembly attempted to reorganize the high courts in such a way that it happened that the judges' workload would have been substantially increased (with no increase in pay). The judges on the Court of Appeals declared the act unconstitutional because it interfered with the independence of the judiciary and violated the constitutional provision for the separation of powers within the state government. In response, the governor called the General Assembly into special session to respond to the problem. The result was an amicable compromise. The courts were reorganized in a different way so that no sitting judge would be required to accept additional judicial duties, and the judges voluntarily resigned their commissions in the old courts and accepted new commissions in the new Court of Appeals. Thus, it was established that an act of assembly could neither increase the judicial workload of sitting judges nor remove them from their judicial offices and that this was a matter of constitutional law.

Generally, the Court of Appeals of Virginia, under the guidance of Pendleton, found the locus of sovereignty in republican Virginia to be in the people as a whole. The people of Virginia expressed their political will in the written constitution of 1776. This constitution divided the government of Virginia into three independent branches: the legislature, the executive, and the judiciary. Thus, the constitution was above the government. Interpreting the constitution, a legal document, was a matter of law, and the law, as well as its interpretation, was the function of the judiciary. Thus, the Court of Appeals was to review the acts of the other branches of the government as a matter of constitutional law. One aspect of Virginia constitutional law was the separation of powers among the branches of government, and this required that the judiciary give great deference to the legislature when construing a statute. For the judiciary to legislate would be for the court unconstitutionally to usurp the legislative function of the General Assembly. A corollary to this principle is that when confronted by a constitutional issue in a legislative act, the court should, if it can, resolve the issue without declaring an act of assembly unconstitutional. A good example of this is the case of *Commonwealth v. Caton*, 4 Call 5 (1782). Pendleton and the majority of the court, with impressive legal skill, avoided the constitutional issue (where George Wythe was willing to indulge in an unseemly confrontation with the legislature).

Led by Pendleton, the courts of Virginia applied the common law of England to resolve the cases brought before them for resolution. Although there was some flirtation at the time with abolishing all British institutions, including the common law, and starting all over from first principles, this nonsense was never seriously considered by the Virginia lawyers and judges of Pendleton's generation. In fact, in 1776, an act was passed by the General Assembly stating that the common law of England was the common law of Virginia. Many believed that the war was fought to preserve English law and institutions because they guaranteed the general principle of the rule of law. The common law of England was the guarantee of property rights, which is the foundation of liberty, being a check on the government. To tax or confiscate a private person's property without consent or authority, that is, without representation, is against the law. Thus, the common law was to be preserved as the basis of legal judgments. The English common law had to be applied in republican Virginia in an intelligent way, however, in order to suit the new political order without upsetting settled expectations of property and contract rights. This was accomplished under the firm guidance of Edmund Pendleton in Virginia and passed on to the federal judiciary by Blair, Washington, Marshall, Tucker, and Hay.

Edmund Pendleton was married twice but had no surviving children. He died in Richmond on 26 October 1803 and was buried in his native Caroline County, Virginia.

W. Hamilton Bryson

References and Further Reading:

Hilldrup, Robert Leroy. 1939. *The Life and Times of Edmund Pendleton*. Chapel Hill: University of North Carolina Press.

Mays, David John. 1952. *Edmund Pendleton 1721–1803: A Biography*. 2 vols. Cambridge: Harvard University Press.

Mays, David John, ed. 1967. *The Letters and Papers of Edmund Pendleton 1734–1803*. 2 vols. Charlottesville: University Press of Virginia.

Morris, Thomas Robbins. 1975. *The Virginia Supreme Court: An Institutional and Political Analysis*. Charlottesville: University Press of Virginia.

Nelson, Margaret Virginia. 1947. *A Study of Judicial Review in Virginia: 1789–1928*. New York: Columbia University Press.

Wren, John Thomas. 1988. "Republican Jurisprudence: Virginia Law and the New Order, 1776–1830." Ph.D. diss., College of William and Mary.

POLLACK, MILTON

(1906–)

Milton Pollack
Bettmann/Corbis

With more than thirty-five years on the bench of the Southern District of New York, federal judge Milton Pollack has earned his status among giants, particularly for his handling of the Drexel Burnham Lambert mass class action and other high-profile securities cases.

Milton Pollack was born on 29 September 1906 in New York City, the son of Russian Jewish immigrants. His father was a successful clothing manufacturer. Pollack attended Columbia University, where he graduated from college in 1927 and law school in 1929. Shortly after his admission to the bar, the stock market crashed, bankrupting businesses and banks alike, creating record unemployment, and plunging the United States into deep depression. In this time of financial upheaval, Pollack began his practice with the law firm of Gilman and Unger, representing bankrupted shareholders in lawsuits against their stockbrokers and banks. No one could have predicted that, sixty years later, Pollack would still be handling the same kinds of cases—this time as a federal judge for the Southern District of New York.

In response to the stock market tragedy, and to the misery caused by the ensuing Great Depression, Congress passed landmark legislation to oversee the nation's securities markets. The Securities Act of 1933 and the Securities and Exchange Act of 1934 sought to make the trade in securities more open and honest and thereby to regain investors' confidence in the stock market and the economy generally. Congress created the Securities and Exchange Commission (SEC) to implement this legislation. It was given the primary duty of protecting investors by making and enforcing rules for the offering and trading of securities. Pres. John F. Kennedy's father, Joseph Kennedy, was appointed the first chairman of the SEC.

SEC investigations of brokerage houses and banks generated plenty of litigation to keep the young lawyer busy. Pollack continued his practice with the firm until 1937, when the Gilman and Unger law firm became Unger and Pollack. This partnership lasted until 1944, when Pollack formed his own firm.

By 1967, Milton Pollack had been practicing law for almost forty years, and one might have expected him to begin thinking about retirement. But Pollack had other ideas. On 12 June 1967, Pres. Lyndon B. Johnson appointed him to become a judge on the United States District Court for the Southern District of New York, located in Manhattan. Amazingly, as of this writing, Judge Pollack is still there, actively handling a significant caseload at age ninety-five!

Judge Pollack, however, does not qualify as a great judge on the basis of his longevity alone. He is most famous for presiding over the massive class action and bankruptcy litigation arising out of the failure of the investment banking firm of Drexel Burnham Lambert and the indictment of its managing director, Dennis Levine, and its head of high-yield securities, Michael Milken. Judge Pollack himself considers the resolution of the Drexel Burnham litigation his crowning achievement—and for good reason. The litigation commonly called *Drexel Burnham* actually consisted of over 180 lawsuits, even the smallest of which alleged damages in the millions of dollars. In fact, the total claimed damages for the litigation exceeded 30 *billion* dollars. At the company's request, Judge Pollack also presided over Drexel Burnham's bankruptcy in 1990, which required him to liquidate and distribute billions of dollars of the firm's assets. Yet the *Drexel Burnham* litigation, which many feared would clog the federal courts for a decade or more, was resolved by the judge in only three years, a truly tremendous feat considering its enormous size and complexity (Kennedy 1995, 75).

The investment banking firm of Drexel Burnham Lambert was once a powerhouse of Wall Street. Led by a select group of talented, ambitious, and ultimately unscrupulous managers and traders, the firm developed and championed what came to be known in the 1980s as the "junk bond" market. The 1980s were a time of unprecedented mergers and acquisitions, in which large companies would attempt to purchase other companies, often against their will. Although corporate mergers are not unusual, the number and scope of mergers in the 1980s were. For a time it seemed as if every major U.S. corporation was either a pursuer or a target; large, well-established companies were swallowed up, sometimes by much smaller, lesser-known competitors. Companies that did not wish to be acquired by others were forced to fight off the "corporate raiders" for their survival.

This flurry of mergers and acquisitions activity was made possible in large part by the use of "junk bonds." Bonds are issued by both public and private entities as a way to raise money. An investor purchases a bond from the entity, which promises to pay it back with interest. The government and various credit agencies rank bonds by, among other things, the likelihood that they will be paid back. *Junk bond* is the colloquial term for a bond that has received a low rating, indicating that its purchaser is assuming significant risk that the bond will not be paid. In exchange for taking that risk, the investor is promised a significantly higher interest rate on his or her investment. But, as the name implies, junk bonds are not for most investors and are by that rating considered below investment grade.

During the first half of the decade, corporate mergers were often funded with these bonds. Investment banking and brokerage houses made tremendous amounts of money by issuing junk bonds to investors on behalf of corporate raiders, who would then use the proceeds to fund their acquisitions in a process known as the leveraged buyout or LBO. The money generated by this process became far too tempting for Wall Street brokers and deal makers, who sought advantage in the market by, among other things, trading on inside information about the raiders and their targets. Eventually, the approach of taking over companies through leveraged buyouts began to crumble, like a giant pyramid scheme, when the debts that came due could not be paid.

The beginning of the end of the junk bond era came in 1986, when the U.S. government began to indict the first in a series of Wall Street financial leaders, charging them with crimes ranging from securities fraud and insider trading to perjury and racketeering. At the same time, investors who had lost billions in the collapse of the junk bond market began civil lawsuits against their brokers, brokerage houses, banks, and anyone else who had had a hand in their losses. Most of these lawsuits were filed in the Southern District of New York, the district that includes Wall Street, although suits appeared across the country.

To handle the myriad of civil lawsuits against Drexel Burnham arising out of these complex events, the federal judicial Panel on Multi-District Litigation consolidated and directed all of the cases to Judge Pollack. The judge, with his many years of securities practice experience, plus his years of handling securities cases on the bench (an inevitability for any federal judge who sits in Manhattan), was a natural choice. As described earlier, the litigation consisted of nearly 200 cases, with hundreds of thousands of plaintiffs, ranging from individual and corporate investors to the U.S. government itself, claiming billions of dollars in damages. The fact that

Louis H. Pollack (1922–)

Judge Louis H. Pollack of the United States District Court for the Eastern District of Pennsylvania has enjoyed a distinguished academic and judicial career. Pollack was born in New York City on 7 December 1922. He attended Harvard College, graduating in 1943. Upon graduation, he served in the United States Army until the end of World War II. He entered Yale Law School in 1946. After receiving his law degree, Pollack served as a law clerk to Supreme Court justice Wiley B. Rutledge.

During the 1950s, Pollack held a variety of legal positions, working as an associate attorney for a major law firm, a special assistant to U.S. ambassador-at-large Philip C. Jessup, and the assistant counsel for the Amalgamated Clothing Workers. In 1955, he joined the faculty of the Yale Law School. He served as dean of the school from 1965 to 1970. In 1974, Pollack left Yale to join the faculty at the University of Pennsylvania Law School. He served as its dean from 1975 to 1978.

Pollack is widely considered one of the nation's leading constitutional law scholars. He has authored numerous law review articles on American legal history and constitutional law, including studies of distinguished legal figures such as Justices Thurgood Marshall and Felix Frankfurter. He is the author of *The Constitution and the Supreme Court: A Documentary History* (1966).

Pollack has also written on and worked extensively for civil rights issues. Before his appointment to the bench, he served for many years as vice president of the Legal Defense Fund of the National Association for the Advancement of Colored People. While at Yale, Professor Pollack helped to broker a settlement of the famous Birmingham, Alabama, civil rights boycott of 1963. In 1977, he served as an international observer at the inquest examining the death of South African antiapartheid activist Steven Biko, founder of the country's Black Consciousness Movement. As a judge, Pollack participated in a historic rehearing of *Plessy v. Ferguson* and a tribute to the original litigants in *Brown v. Board of Education*, both sponsored by Harvard Law School.

Pres. Jimmy Carter appointed Pollack to the district court, and he was sworn in on 8 September 1978. Even after his appointment to the bench, Pollack has continued to publish regularly in legal journals and law reviews. He comments frequently on the role of the judge, judicial and legal ethics, and legal professionalism. In the

(continues)

Judge Pollack was now in his mid-eighties might have caused some to question his selection; for Judge Pollack, however, it was never an issue.

No litigation like it had ever been seen before or has been seen since. Judge Pollack worked tirelessly through countless evenings and weekends to organize the litigation and bankruptcy and move them forward. He certified the civil lawsuits as a class action and worked with the parties toward

(continued)

mid-1990s, for example, he participated as a witness before the Commission on Separation of Powers and Judicial Independence, created by the American Bar Association to examine the nature and extent of judicial independence in the federal and state courts and to investigate potential threats to that independence.

During his long judicial tenure, Pollack has become one of the nation's most widely respected federal judges. He has handled a number of high-profile cases, including the civil rights litigation arising out of the city of Philadelphia's 1985 attempt to raid a row house inhabited by members of the antigovernment group MOVE (the Christian Life Movement). When the members dug in, the city's Police Department, with authorization from the mayor, dropped a bomb on the group's rooftop gun turret in an attempt to create a hole large enough to allow officers to drop teargas canisters into the building. The roof caught fire, and the fire went quickly out of control. It burned an entire city block, killing eleven people (including five children) and leaving over 250 people homeless.

More recently, Judge Pollack caused a sensation when he ruled that Federal Bureau of Investigation (FBI) fingerprint identification (matching) procedures were too subjective and therefore not reliable as evidence. He concluded that the identification process known as "ridgeology" did not conform to accepted scientific standards as set forth by the Supreme Court in *Daubert v. Merell Dow Pharmaceuticals, Inc.*, 509 U.S. 579 (1993). Judge Pollack backed up his decision with a carefully constructed forty-nine-page opinion that detailed the flaws in fingerprint identification methods.

The FBI and the Justice Department immediately asked for a rehearing on the issue, and after the presentation of extensive testimony and other evidence on the bureau's procedures, Judge Pollack reversed his earlier ruling (*U.S. v. Llera-Plaza,* No. 98–362–10. E.D. Pa., 13 March 2002). Even though the judge changed his mind, however, he showed both courage and independence in refusing to accept such evidence as a matter of course. By putting the government to its proof, he publicized the shortcomings in fingerprint identification processes; it is clear in the aftermath of the case that the debate started by the judge on this issue is far from over.

Judge Pollack elected senior status in 1991. He has not, however, elected to slow down. To this day, he continues to maintain an active and impressive schedule of judicial service, academic writing, and teaching.

Kathleen Uradnik

obtaining a single, global settlement of claims. In 1991, he approved a settlement in excess of $2 billion for Drexel Burnham's creditors in the bankruptcy. In 1992, he approved a $1.3 billion settlement in the class action against over 200 officers and directors of Drexel Burnham and the firm's related entities. It was an incredible judicial achievement, one that would not have been possible without Pollack's knowledge, organizational skills, dogged persistence, and commitment to achieving a complete and equitable resolution of all claims.

One might think that, given the lessons investors learned in the 1980s, a situation like that of Drexel Burnham would never happen again. Far from it. In 2001, Judge Pollack threw out a lengthy, high-profile complaint filed by disgruntled investors against prominent stock analyst Mary Meeker and her employer, Morgan Stanley Dean Witter. The eight related class action lawsuits sought damages against Meeker and the firm arising out of losses from the precipitous drop in value of numerous Internet company stocks, including Amazon.com and eBay.com. Judge Pollack dismissed the complaint in a curt three-page opinion. Said Pollack: "I got so mad reading that complaint . . . [the plaintiffs] had no business saying the nasty things that they did" (Neumeister 2001, n.p.). Pollack admonished plaintiffs for their "irrelevant" and "inflammatory" claims, which may have allowed the investors to vent their frustrations, but which were not grounded in law (n.p.). Pollack observed that the same phenomena he saw while practicing law at the time of the 1929 stock market crash was repeating itself yet again: Investors caught up in the fury of profit making during times of economic boom seek to blame others after their money is lost in times of economic bust. These losses may permit legal action, as they did in the Drexel Burnham litigation, but, as the judge recognized, a legally cognizable cause of action does not accompany every bad investment.

The *Drexel Burnham* case, although the biggest, was not the only milestone in Judge Pollack's long career. The judge himself identified his most noteworthy cases upon receiving the Devitt Award in 1995 (Pollack 1995, 71). They include *Chris Craft v. Piper Aircraft Corporation* (determining whether an unsuccessful corporate bidder for a company can sue for damages under securities laws), *Miller v. Wells Fargo Bank International Corporation* (deciding that a bank was not a secured creditor of a bankrupt corporation), *Corbin v. Federal Reserve Bank* (challenge to receiver arising from the insolvency of the then twentieth-largest bank in the United States), *Rodman v. Grant* (dismissing a trustee's lawsuit against former officers and directors of a bankrupt corporation), *Gartenberg v. Merrill Lynch* (dismissing shareholders' derivative lawsuit alleging excessive compensation for management of mutual fund), *Curtiss-Wright v. Kennecott* (denying a preliminary injunction to prevent a corporation from terminating a tender offer), *SEC v. Banca Della Svizzera Italiana* (compelling a foreign bank to reveal information pertinent to the SEC's prosecution of an insider trading lawsuit), *Seagram v. St. Joe Mineral Corporation* (granting an injunction against a corporation that would rather dissolve itself than allow hostile takeover), *Standard & Poor's v. Commodity* (enjoining the latter's unlicensed use of the S &

P 500 Stock Index), and *Moss v. Morgan Stanley* (dismissing securities and racketeering claims against the brokerage house). As these cases indicate, Judge Pollack has spent much of his judicial career deciding novel and complex legal issues arising out of the rise and fall of some of the nation's largest corporate and financial institutions.

The Devitt Award, given annually to the federal judge who has made the greatest contribution to justice, is only one of a host of awards received by Judge Pollack. In addition, he received the John Jay Award from his alma mater, Columbia University; the Ford-Stein Prize; the New York County Lawyers' Distinguished Service Award; the French Legion of Honor Chevallier; the Proskauer Award from the Federation of Jewish Philanthropies; and the Learned Hand Award (Pollack 1995, 71). Among a host of philanthropic endeavors, the judge and his wife, Moselle Erlich Pollack, have endowed scholarship, loan, and award programs for college and professional students. The judge has proved a loyal Columbia graduate as a past alumni director, alumni president, and guest lecturer.

Apart from his work on the bench, Judge Pollack is highly regarded for his work in judicial administration. While serving on the Panel for Multi-District Litigation, he helped to create many of the rules and procedures he would later use with much success in the *Drexel Burnham* litigation. He was a member of the Judicial Conference of the United States, serving for nearly twenty years on its Committee on Court Administration. He also served on its Trial Practice and Techniques Committee, Subcommittee to Examine Possible Alternatives to Jury Trial in Complex Civil Cases, and on various personnel committees. He was a member of the Board of Editors of the *Manual for Complex Litigation*. He also participated actively in various Southern District committees to revise its various rules of court.

In 1983, Judge Pollack elected senior status on the court. Senior status enables a judge nearing retirement to reduce his or her caseload with no concomitant reduction in salary. Of course, a judge could simply choose to retire and continue to draw his or her full salary. Increasingly, however, federal judges are choosing to keep working instead of retiring, thereby donating their time to the judiciary. Judge's Pollack's gift in this regard has been enormous, as he has served as a senior judge for almost twenty years and has continued to maintain a full (and current) caseload throughout. As of this writing, he is ninety-five years old, thirty years past his retirement age and still working his standard fifty-hour weeks. Said the judge in 2001: "Having a daily occupation keeps me alive, and I have no plans to leave" (Markon 2001, n.p.). Thus the judge's highly regarded and distinguished career continues—indefinitely.

Kathleen Uradnik

References and Further Reading:

Bruck, Connie. 1989. *The Predators' Ball: The Inside Story of Drexel Burnham and the Rise of the Junk Bond Raiders*. New York: Penguin Books U.S.A.

Jebsen, Per. 2001. "Analysts Can Breathe Easier after Meeker Ruling." *The Industry Standard*, 22 August 22 (Reuters News Service release).

Kennedy, Anthony. 1995. "Remarks of Justice Anthony Kennedy at the Presentation of the Devitt Award to the Honorable Milton Pollack." 909 F. Supp. LXIX.

Markon, Jerry. 2001. "Elderly Judges Handle 20 % of United States Caseload." *Wall Street Journal*, 8 October, n.p.

Neumeister, Larry. 2001. "Judge Has Long Memory of Downturns." *Cincinnati Enquirer*, 23 August, n.p. (Associated Press release).

Pollack, Milton. 1995. "Vita." Contained in Dedication of the Devitt Award to the Honorable Milton Pollack. 909 F. Supp. LXIX (1995).

Stewart, James B. 1991. *Den of Thieves*. New York: Simon and Schuster. (This Pulitzer Prize–winning journalist's book details the rise and fall of the junk bond market and its Wall Street proponents.)

POSNER, RICHARD A.

(1939–)

Richard A. Posner
Reuters NewMedia Inc./Corbis

Richard Posner is the most influential and prolific judge to sit on the court of appeals bench in the last two decades. A distinguished, prolific, and inventive scholar, Posner has had a significant impact on American intellectual life. Posner has brought the law and economics approach to judicial decisionmaking, especially in the key doctrinal areas of contracts and torts.

Education and Professional Activities before Appointment to United States Circuit Court of Appeals

Posner was born on 11 January 1939 in New York City. The family moved to the suburb of Scarsdale in 1948. His father began in the jewelry business, attended law school, became a criminal defense lawyer, and gained wealth as a moneylender in the New York slums. His mother politically was a communist.

Posner graduated from Yale in 1959, *summa cum laude*, and was elected to Phi Beta Kappa. An English major, he wrote a senior honors thesis on Yeats's poetry and briefly considered a career as an English professor (MacFarquhar 2001, 84). He graduated first in his class at Harvard Law School in 1962, was president of the *Harvard Law Review*, and earned additional honors.

Following graduation Posner clerked for United States Supreme Court justice William J. Brennan Jr. After that he worked in Washington, D.C., during the Kennedy and Johnson administrations. From 1963 to 1965 he was assistant to Commissioner Philip Elman of the Federal Trade Commission and from 1965 to 1967 he assisted two solicitor generals of the United States, Erwin Griswold and future Supreme Court justice Thurgood Marshall. Posner served as general counsel of President Johnson's Task Force on Communications Policy. He also was a member of a task force on economic issues and a commission to study the Federal Trade Commission (1969).

He has been married to the former Charlene Horn for forty years, and they have two sons and three grandsons. Son Kenneth is a securities analyst in New York, and Eric, a law professor at the University of Chicago, also writes on law and economics.

For many years, Posner considered himself a liberal democrat. While serving as an associate professor of law at Stanford, however, Posner met several conservative economists from the University of Chicago and was surprised to discover that he agreed with them. He moved to the University of Chicago in 1969 (MacFarquhar 2001, 86). "For the past ten years or so, Posner has called himself a pragmatist, meaning that he believes that there is no objective way to choose between incompatible moral positions. Pragmatism has a bracingly impious air that he finds exhilarating"(88). He taught law full-time at Chicago until his appointment in 1981 to the Seventh Circuit Court of Appeals, also in the Windy City.

Among the most distinguished and prolific scholars ever to sit on a United States Court of Appeals, before joining the bench Posner wrote several books, including *The Economics of Contract Law* (1978), *Antitrust Law: An Economic Perspective* (1980), the classic *Economic Analysis of Law*—now in its fifth edition—and *The Economics of Justice* (1981). He also wrote numerous articles, most exploring the application of economics to such diverse legal subjects as antitrust, public utility and common carrier regulation, torts, contracts, and procedure. He called for major reforms in antitrust policy, proposed and tested the theory that judges use the common law to promote economic efficiency, urged wealth maximization as a goal of legal and social policy, contributed to the economic theory of regulation and legislation, and extended economic analysis into such fields as family law, primitive law, racial discrimination, jurisprudence, and privacy. He founded and edited the *Journal of Legal Studies*, was a research associate of the National Bureau of Economic Research (1971–1981), and was the first president (1977–1981) of Lexecon Inc., a firm that provided economic and legal research in antitrust, securities, and other litigation.

Posner continues to teach part-time at the University of Chicago. He is known for his "freakish productivity" (MacFarquhar 2001, 78). To date, Posner has written thirty-one books, more than 300 articles, and nearly 1,900 judicial opinions (78). In early 2002 Posner heard his 4,000th case. Posner wrote, "To say that all 4,000 cases have been interestingly different would be a bit of an exaggeration, but only a bit; that is what makes the job fun" (Posner, "Diary," 15 January).

The titles of the books he has published since becoming a judge demonstrate the continuing breadth of his interests. They include *Cardozo: A Study in Reputation* (1990), *The Essential Holmes* (1992), *Sex and Reason* (1992), *Private Choices and Public Health: The AIDS Epidemic in an Economic Perspective* (1993), *Overcoming Law* (1995), *Aging and Old Age* (1995), a second edition of *The Federal Courts* (1996), *Law and Legal Theory in England and America* (1996), a revised and enlarged edition of *Law and Literature* (1998), *An Affair of State: The Investigation, Impeachment, and Trial of President Clinton* (1999), *The Problematics of Moral and Legal Theory* (1999), a second edition of *Antitrust Law* (2001), and *Public Intellectuals* (2001).

As the most notable proponent of the law and economics approach to legal theory and practice, Richard Posner is a primary opponent of normative, philosophical approaches to the law, as best exemplified by philosopher Ronald Dworkin. Posner is a public intellectual. His articles, commentary, and book reviews appear in prestigious journals in law, economics, and social sciences as well as in popular journals of opinion.

Prior to becoming a federal judge, Posner had offered expert testimony before a wide range of congressional committees and government agencies. Since becoming a judge, Posner has appeared before a congressional committee to discuss administrative issues facing federal courts (Posner 1996). In 1999 Posner was selected to mediate the government's antitrust lawsuit against Microsoft. Case managers apparently thought that Microsoft would accept him "because of his hostility to antitrust law" and the government "because of his hostility to cartel-like behavior that threatened a free market" (MacFarquhar 2001, 87).

Posner enjoys making controversial arguments, especially in his books: "Posner likes to take topics, like sex and race, that are normally accorded a certain sentimental deference and treat them with jarring candor. In *Sex and Reason* (1992), he argued that the sex drive was subject to the control of rational calculation" (MacFarquhar 2001, 81). "He once argued . . . that a higher proportion of black women than white women are fat because the supply of eligible black men is limited, thus black women find the likelihood of profit from an elegant figure too small to compensate for the costs of dieting" (78). Posner admits to thriving on arguing against the conventional wisdom of the day:

John T. Noonan Jr.
(1926–)

Some judges gain almost as much recognition for their writing off the court as for their decisions on the bench. John T. Noonan Jr. is a good example. Like Benjamin Cardozo, Richard Posner, and Henry Friendly, Noonan is the epitome of the scholar judge.

Born in Boston, Massachusetts, in 1926, the son of a lawyer, Noonan proceeded to earn an undergraduate degree at Harvard, pursue graduate study at Cambridge University, earn master's and doctor's degrees from Catholic University, and then get a law degree from Harvard. After serving on the staff of the National Security Council and as a member of a Boston law firm, Noonan became a law professor at the University of Notre Dame. He subsequently moved to the University of California, where he also served as chair of the Department of Religious Studies. He married Mary Lee Bennett, an art historian, and they have three children. He fit comfortably into academic life and won a number of high academic honors (including grants to study at Princeton, the Woodrow Wilson Center in Washington, D.C., and Stanford) before Pres. Ronald Reagan nominated him in 1985 to the United States Ninth Circuit Court of Appeals (headquartered in San Francisco). Despite some opposition from prochoice proponents, he was confirmed by the U.S. Senate and has been serving ever since. He is currently the senior judge on that court.

A recognized scholar of Catholic canonical law, prior to his appointment to the bench Noonan had published such classic studies as *The Scholastic Analysis of Usury* (interest), *The Church and Contraception*, *The Morality of Abortion*, *Persons and Masks of the Law*, and *The Antelope: The Ordeal of the Recaptured Africans in the Administrations of James Monroe and John Quincy Adams* ("John T[homas] Noonan, Jr."). Noonan continues to lecture widely, and his appointment to the bench appears to have done little to slacken his scholarly production. In 1986, an enlarged version of his earlier study of *Conception: A History of Its Treatment by the Catholic Theologians and Canonists* was published. Since being

(continues)

> Negligible work rarely attracts much criticism; it's simply ignored. Only when a work gets under people's skin do they bother to criticize it, and the deeper under the skin it gets the shriller the criticism. Often the reason a work gets under one's skin is that it shakes one's faith in oneself, one's values, or one's career. . . . When academics step outside the ring of critical fire that is one of the glories of the academic culture at its best, the risk of their falling flat on their faces is very great. (Posner, "Diary" 17 January)

Posner has received numerous honorary degrees. He is a fellow in the American Academy of Arts and Sciences, the American Law Institute, and the British Academy.

(continued)

appointed to the bench, he has also published *The Believer and the Powers That Are: Cases, History, and Other Data Bearing on the Relation of Religion and Government* (1987), *The Responsible Judge* (1993), and *The Lustre of Our Country: The American Experience of Religious Freedom* (1998). A more recent book, *Narrowing the Nation's Power: The Supreme Court Sides with the States*, is critical of recent United States Supreme Court decisions expanding state sovereign immunity. Noonan also has criticized recent United States Supreme Court decisions that narrow congressional authority under Section 5 of the Fourteenth Amendment and, in Noonan's judgment, unduly increase the Court's own authority (Greenhouse 2002).

A committed Roman Catholic who has served on a number of church commissions, Noonan nonetheless believes that canonical law, like other forms of law, develops over time. Although he remains a strong opponent of the United States Supreme Court decision in *Roe v. Wade* (1973) legalizing abortion, Noonan has taken a more liberal position on the issue of birth control and on other issues than has the church as a whole. Despite the failure of many of his views to prevail, Noonan has maintained an optimistic view of the future of Catholicism in the United States (McGreevy 2002).

An observer has argued that as a jurist Noonan has not completely satisfied either conservatives or liberals. Thus, he has expressed deep reservations about the death penalty, opposed the deportation of a Salvadoran refugee who feared persecution in her native land, and written a strong opinion in 1995 (later affirmed by the United States Supreme Court) opposing assisted suicide (McGreevy 2002). Noonan's clerks note that he addresses individuals who appear before him, even noncitizens, by their full names in an attempt to treat them respectfully (McGreevy 2002).

References:

Greenhouse, Linda. 2002. "Beyond Original Intent: The Supreme Court's Majority Has Given Up on Strict Construction, a Judge Asserts." *New York Times*, 18 August, 8.

"John T(homas) Noonan, Jr." *Contemporary Authors Online*. The Gale Group, 2001.

McGreevy, John T. McGreevy. 2002. "A Case of Doctrinal Development—John T. Noonan: Jurist, Historian, Author, Sage." *Commonweal* 127, 17 November, 12.

Posner provided a glimpse of his variegated life in a diary that he wrote for *Slate.com* during the week of 14 January 2002:

> I have a busy week ahead—a day of hearing appeals, three two-hour classes on the law of evidence, an after-dinner speech Tuesday on civil liberties and national security and a priority for Sunday was finishing up the draft of my speech. And finishing up a short paper on the economics of international law. And working on two articles that I am writing with an economist, one on presidential pardons . . . and another on copyright law, focusing on an issue of considerable theoretical interest: Should copyrights be perpetual, rather than limited to the lifetime of the author plus 70 years? And on a book on legal

pragmatism and democratic theory. And on a sixth edition of a textbook-treatise on economic analysis of law, my specialty. (Posner "Diary," 14 January)

Service on the United States Circuit Court of Appeals, Seventh Circuit, Chicago, Illinois

Ronald Reagan nominated Richard Posner in October 1981 to a seat on the Seventh Circuit Court of Appeals, which Phillip Willis Tone had vacated. The Senate quickly confirmed Posner, who served as chief judge from 1993 to 2000.

Larissa MacFarquhar portrayed Posner as a lighthearted and joyful participant in daily proceedings on the bench. Posner compared himself to his cat—as "cold, furtive, callous, snobbish, and playful, but with a streak of cruelty" and "like an imperfectly housebroken pet" (MacFarquhar 2001, 79–80). MacFarquhar described Posner as a "Bench Burner," "the most mercilessly seditious legal theorist," and "one of the most powerful jurists of the generation." She continued, "He comes up with what strikes him as a sensible solution, then looks to see whether precedent excludes it" (78). She described Posner in court as "harsh, but not nasty" but "frequently bored by the arguments the lawyers presented, and tending to lead the discussion in the direction of issues that interested him" (81).

Posner has criticized contemporary judges who rely on their clerks to write their opinions. He explained that "it's a mistake on a number of grounds: The more you write, the faster you write; only the effort to articulate a decision exposes the weak joints in the analysis; and the judge-written opinion provides greater insight into the judge's values and reasoning process and so provides greater information not least to the judge" (Posner "Diary," 14 January).

Judicial Decisionmaking as an Exemplar of Pragmatism

Blomquist characterized *Dower v. United States* (1981), Posner's first written opinion, as "remarkable" for its discussion of facts in a story form similar to "fiction or good journalism" (2000, 685). Posner's early opinions "exhibit an overarching attention to policy concerns; what might be viewed as the purpose of rules, the pragmatic functioning of relevant legal doctrine, or the advisability of choosing one body of potentially applicable principles over another . . ." (690). Posner's pragmatism is central.

In 1999, Judge Posner defined what he meant by pragmatic adjudication: "'Pragmatist' judges always try to do the best they can do for the present and the future, unchecked by any felt *duty* to secure consistency in principle with what other officials have done in the past . . ." (Posner 1999, 241). A pragmatic judge is concerned "with securing consistency with the past only to the extent that deciding in accordance with precedent may be the best method for producing the best results for the future" (241) Responding to criticism that a pragmatist judge is unprincipled and fails to take past decisions into account, Posner distinguished the way in which the past is more important for the pragmatist judge than for the "judicial positivist." To the pragmatist, the past provides "sources of information" that can (and should) be used to inform one's opinion but are not "authorities," ensuring that the judges act directly in accord with their dictates (242). In *Overcoming Law,* Posner wrote, "Pragmatism would treat decision according to precedent . . . as a policy rather than as a duty" (1995, 4). For Posner, the wisdom of the prior rule can only be determined by looking at empirical information of the application rules in the past, the facts in the case, and the possible effects of continuing or modifying the rule in the future. Posner rejects judicial minimalism for its own sake. He does not think that courts should be restrained from a particular ruling just because the legislature or the Supreme Court has previously ruled otherwise.

For Posner, the pragmatist judge can be an activist problem solver who facilitates societal progress: "The pragmatist believes in progress without pretending to be able to define it, and believes that it can be effected by deliberate human action" (Posner 1995, 5). Therefore courts can be an important venue for progress in society. Progress is a process; it is not defined in principled terms as more democracy and citizen participation, or more access to political process, or based on some moral theory of equality or fair distribution of goods.

Because judges cannot know absolute truth, pragmatic judges will search for facts and keep skeptical, flexible minds. A good judge gathers as much information as possible about a case while being skeptical of finding the one absolutely true and good decision. Posner believes that judges must not be dogmatic and must view the world outside the court as social and as contextual, not as natural (Posner 1995, 6–7).

Posner acknowledged that pragmatist judges seek to optimize certain values. Rejecting the idea of reasoning "top-down" from moral or constitutional theory as Dworkin, John Hart Ely, and other legal scholars have advocated, Posner argues that the pragmatist judge understands the common law as based "on the 'as if' assumption that judges try to maximize the wealth of society" (Posner 1992, 434). Posner seeks to demonstrate the importance of reasoning from the bottom up, through empirical evidence and the close analysis of a particular case. At the core of his view of judicial decisionmaking is what Posner calls "interpretation." In responding to Dworkin, Posner wrote,

I agree there isn't much bottom-up reasoning. We don't ever really "start" from a mass of cases or from a statute or from a clause of the Constitution. To read a case, to read a statute, a rule, or a constitutional clause presupposes a vast linguistic, cultural, and conceptual apparatus. . . . And, if, as is so common, the case or statute or other enactment is unclear, and maybe even when it seems quite clear, the reader, to extract or more precisely to impute its meaning, must *interpret* it; and interpretation, we know, is as much creation as discovery. (435)

Posner summarized: "I would abandon, however, as too ambitious, too risky, too contentious, the task of fashioning a comprehensive theory of constitutional law, an 'immodest' top-down theory intended to guide judges. At the same time I would allow judges to stretch clauses—even such questionable candidates as the Due Process Clause—when there is a practical case for intervention" (446–447).

In *Slate.com*, Judge Posner further explained his pragmatic approach:

Applied to law, it asks judges to weigh consequences rather than to steer by abstractions such as "property," "liberty," "rights," "justice," "fairness," and "equality." The judge who thinks he can reason his way to what is "just" and "fair," a self-appointed moral virtuoso, is unlikely to think seriously about the practical consequences of his decisions. May we be spared those judges, as well as the ones who shirk responsibility for their decisions by imagining themselves a mere transmission belt for conclusions reached hundreds of years ago by the all-knowing framers of the Constitution. The judge is a *responsible* official, not an oracle; and his responsibility is to use the resources of text, history, and precedent to help him reach practical results that are responsive to the needs of the present day. (Posner "Diary," 17 January)

Posner distrusts morality as a motivational force. He has observed that "knowing the moral thing to do . . . furnishes no motive, and creates no motivation, for doing it" (MacFarquhar 2001, 84). Only through the imposition of prohibitions and penalties, though incentives, can the law alter what an individual will actually do in a given situation. Linda Fisher identified the core elements of Posner's pragmatism:

He is highly empirically oriented, with the goal of producing those legal rules and decisions that are best for society. . . . Justice and morality are not defined by reference to an absolute standard, but rather by social norms and traditions. He [Posner] . . . retains his previous emphasis on economics as a policy since par excellence, along with its goal of wealth maximalization, but subordinates that specific goal to the overall pragmatic goal of rendering decisions to improve society. (2001, 456)

As a founder of the law and economics theory of jurisprudence, Posner's opinions reflect the goal of wealth maximization. Fisher argued, however, that he subordinates this goal to "the overall pragmatic goal of rendering decisions that improve society" (2001, 456). Fisher identified Posner with an "[a]ttitude rather than a dogma; an attitude whose 'common denominator' is a future-oriented instrumentalism that tries to deploy thought as a weapon to enable more effective action" (5).

Posner's court opinions also demonstrate "his broad search for empirical information that can usually inform decision making . . . his openness and candor . . . [and] the wide scope of issues he believes to be appropriately addressed in legal decisions" (Fisher 2001, 465–466). Fisher observed that "at their best, these efforts can produce strongly reasoned decisions that are supported by a combination of logic, good policy, relevant factual information, and, where appropriate, precedent and applicable text" (466–467).

Posner has written over 1,900 court opinions. More of his cases have appeared in law school casebooks than those of any other United States Court of Appeals judge; in this area, Posner is one of two "Giants in a World of Pygmies" (Gulati and Sanchez 2002). Mitu Gulati and Veronica Sanchez counted the number of opinions by federal court judges who were active from August 1995 to August 1997 that appeared in 300 casebooks in use in U.S. law schools from June 1999 to May 2000. Such casebooks included 118 of Posner's opinions. By comparison, 45 percent of the judges studied had zero to five opinions in casebooks and 44 percent of the circuit court judges studied had six to nine. The two closest judges to Posner, Judges Easterbrook and Winter, had 56 and 35 cases in lawbooks, respectively. Posner had an entry rate of 6.94 cases per casebook; Easterbrook's entry rate was 4.92, and Wood's was 3.00 (Gulati and Sanchez 2002, 1155, 1166). When the number of Posner's and Easterbrook's torts and contracts opinions in casebooks are compared with those of prior circuit court giants—Cardozo, Friendly, and Hand—only Cardozo comes close to Posner (1179). The reasons that Posner and these other judges dominate the legal "canon" include their role in the academy and the fact that they write opinions that are "clear, concise, fully theorized, innovative, irreverent, placed in historical context, illustrative, and humorous" (1153). Fellow judges also frequently cite Posner's decisions. In a sophisticated study of the citations of 205 individual judges sitting on the courts of appeals in 1992 with six or more years of tenure at the end of 1995, Posner topped the list (Landes, Lessig, and Solimine 1998, 288–292).

Posner's Impact on Case Law

Posner has impacted areas as diverse as First Amendment freedom of speech, criminal law, intellectual property, social insurance, and labor law. Jeffrey Stempel argued that Posner's background in economics creates blind spots that vary from field to field: "On insurance cases . . . Posner is almost without judicial peer. But where the topic is employment discrimination or civil rights, Posner's econominalism plays an arguably counterproductive role and insensitivity often replaces sensitivity" (2000/2001, 10). Stempel cited Posner as an example of "the 'cerebration' of insurance law—increased focus and in-depth analysis of not only policy language but the intent, purpose, and context of insurance arrangements as well as the role of risk and insurance in the modem world" (12).

Stempel identified ten dominant aspects of Posner's insurance jurisprudence. They are (1) neutrality between insurance companies and policyholders, (2) application of pragmatism rather than morality, (3) lack of emotional involvement in cases and issues, (4) emphasis on the good faith obligation of contract for all parties in a case, (5) respect for literal contract interpretation without slavish adherence to it, (6) emphasis on "the purpose of the transaction and the context of the dispute" (2000/2001, 17), (7) "a moderate, reasonable and nuanced view of the ambiguity doctrine," (8) acknowledgment "that insurance law remains largely a matter of state law but also accounts for the growing body of a federal common law of insurance in ERISA cases" (20), (9) "considerable self-consciousness about both his own jurisprudential approach and the implications of legal theory and judicial approach for real case outcomes," and (10) writing characterized by "clarity, wit, and distinctively memorable prose" (23).

Stempel contrasted his admiration of Posner's decisionmaking in insurance cases with criticism of Posner's bias toward commercial entities in contract and labor law. There he believed "Posner's jurisprudence is interesting, arguably correct, but disturbingly resistant to the rights of workers at the expense of opposing commercial entities" (2000/2001, 42). To illustrate this criticism, Stempel cited *Herzberger v. Standard Insurance Co.* (2000) involving "the issue of when ERISA plans have discretionary authority over health benefits claims" (43). Posner sought to create a uniform national rule for deciding these cases. Stempel stated, "Posner's system seems slanted toward employer prerogatives at the expense of fair treatment of workers and beneficiaries" (45).

Similarly, Leonard Bierman concluded that "Judge Posner views labor unions as 'worker cartels' designed to raise the price of labor above the competitive level" (Bierman 1985, 881). Through an analysis of Posner's National Labor Relations Board (NLRB) cases, Bierman demonstrated that Judge Posner is all too willing "to override the Board's decisions whenever necessary to enforce the spirit of neutrality expressed in the Taft-Hartley amendments" (884). Because Posner believes that the NLRB has been pro-union rather than a neutral player, "Posner has ignored the Board's administrative expertise and readily overturned several Board decisions" (906).

In employment discrimination cases, Stempel contended that Posner's generally excellent opinions have underappreciated "workplace realities" and read antidiscrimination laws too narrowly. Acknowledging that Posner's opinions occasionally display "appreciation for the grittiness of the real world" and that his voice is "helpfully informative," Stempel thought that "in employment cases Posner's sensitivity runs toward the employer" (2000/2001, 49–50, 62).

In explaining Posner's economics-based decisionmaking, Eric Beal pointed to Posner's philosophy that "economists speak in terms of incentives, not of moral character" (Beal 2000/2001, 85). Beal demonstrated that in insurance contract cases Posner views "moral hazard [as a] malleable concept which should be applied to both sides of an agreement and that allocates the risks of uncertain future events" (102). Still, Beal concluded, "Posner's decisions are laudable for giving thoughtful and thorough treatment of insurance and moral hazard issues" (102).

Beatrice Beltran argued that Posner believes that "tort law is intended to serve more as a deterrence mechanism versus a compensatory mechanism. Therefore, the tort system should not be regarded primarily as a form of insurance" but "as a means of deterring behavior that society deems risky and undesirable" (2000/2001, 157–158).

A good example of Posner's view of tort law is *Pomer v. Schoolman* (1989), involving a farmhand, Pomer, whose legs were seriously mangled by a farm machine. Although Pomer may not have been informed of the dangerousness of the machine, Posner held that "Pomer knew that the accident was caused only by his momentary lapse of judgment. . . . Thus in terms of deterrence, Pomer was in the best possible position to prevent this accident. It would be in error to shift the responsibility for this gruesome accident onto other parties who were in no position to prevent the accident" (Beltran 2000/2001, 172–173).

With regard to contract law, Lawrence Cunningham demonstrated that Posner's law and economics approach to law emphasizes efficiency as a value over virtue, which Cardozo emphasized in such decisions. Consequently, Posner's ultimate concern is "to promote contract relationships that in turn 'promote the efficient allocation of resources'" (1995, 1413). Cunningham wrote:

> Posner is more apt to locate the basis of contract in reliance and has employed that doctrine in clever ways to limit the scope of liability in contract. He brings to contract law an interpretive literalism that resists implication or the construction of standards of conduct based on traditional norms such as good faith as unjustifiable paternalism. Posner is deeply, philosophically committed to freedom of contract and seizes on judicial opportunities to advance this principle. (1455)

Posner has supported free speech in some notable decisions. In *American Amusement Machine Association v. Kendrick* (2001), Posner invalidated an Indianapolis ordinance blocking minors' access to violent video games. Posner agreed that the Indianapolis ordinance was a content-based speech restriction and that the language in the ordinance was "unconstitutionally vague" (Calvert 2002, 4). Characteristically, Posner based his decision not on previous precedent or principle but on historical and sociological data. His opinion also demonstrates his rhetorical flair for sociocultural commentary: "Violence has always been and remains a central interest of humankind and a recurrent, even obsessive theme of culture both high and low. It engages the interest of children from an early age . . ." (5).

Linnemeir v. Board of Trustees of Purdue University Fort Wayne (2001) involved a suit brought against Purdue University, Fort Wayne, by Republican state legislators who opposed the performance of the play *Corpus Christi*. They believed it was blasphemous. Posner upheld the lower federal court decision permitting the play to be staged. Posner disagreed, however, with the trial court's ruling that the theater was a limited public forum (Harrison 2002, 187). Instead, Posner wrote, "the school authorities and the teachers, not the courts, decide whether classroom instruction shall include work by blasphemers" (187). This might allow censorship based on university standards of "decency."

Critics of Posner's pragmatism and empiricism argue that they result in fewer restrictions on judges and less principled decisions. Linda Fisher wrote, "The costs of his [Posner's] approach . . . however, on both theoretical and practical levels, can include a lack of restraint that might give the pragmatic judge more power than a formalist judge, or at least substitute empirical formalism for analytical formalism" (2001, 467).

Fisher chose *United States v. Shannon* (1997) and *United States v. Thomas* (1998), which involved whether statutory rape should count as a "violent" act, to make her critique (2001, 475). Instead of basing his opinion on the Wisconsin state statute that applied in *Shannon*, Posner looked into other state statutes and empirical evidence (477). He rejected the view that just because sex occurred under a particular age, it should be considered violent. Instead, he focused on empirical fact. Posner ultimately decided that sex with a thirteen-year-old was "a crime of violence" for sentencing purposes (478). He used a similar technique in *Thomas* to reach the opposite conclusion. *Thomas* involved the statutory rape of a sixteen-year-old as a violent offense, which would have added fifteen years to a burglar's sentence. Although Illinois had set the age of consent at seventeen, Posner relied on sociological and medical data supporting the increased independence and maturity of a sixteen-year-old girl to make decisions and to consent to sex.

Conclusion

Posner is one of the nation's most influential judges. His impact stems not simply from his numerous decisions but also from his genius as a scholar of unmatched brilliance, productivity, breadth, and depth and from his prodigious efforts to fulfill the role of public intellectual. Although his brilliance and influence are rarely questioned, his pragmatic approach remains quite controversial.

Ronald Kahn

References and Further Reading:

Beal, Eric L. 2000/2001. "Posner and Moral Hazard." *Connecticut Insurance Law Journal* 7: 81–102.

Beltran, Beatrice A. 2000/2001. "Note and Commentary: Posner and Tort Law as Insurance." *Connecticut Insurance Law Journal* 7: 153–193.

Bierman, Leonard. 1985. "Judge Posner and the NLRB: Implications for Labor Law Reform." *Minnesota Law Review* 69 (April): 881–908.

Blomquist, Robert F. 2000. "Playing on Words: Judge Richard A. Posner's Appellate Opinions 1981–1982—Ruminations on Sexy Judicial Opinion Style during an Extraordinary Rookie Season." *University of Cincinnati Law Review* 68 (Spring): 651–682.

Bryn, Brenda. 1987. "Refusals to Cross Picket Lines and the Wealth Maximization Principle: An Economic Analysis of the Views of the NLRB and Judge Posner." *University of Miami Law Review* 41 (January): 533–590.

Calvert, Clay. 2002. "Violence, Video Games, and a Voice of Reason: Judge Posner to the Defense of Kids' Culture and the First Amendment." *San Diego Law Review* 39 (Winter): 1–30.

Cunningham, Lawrence A. 1995. "Cardozo and Posner: A Study in Contracts." *William and Mary Law Review* 36 (Spring): 1379–1457.

Fisher, Linda E. 2001. "Content: Pragmatism Is as Pragmatism Does: Of Posner, Public Policy, and Empirical Reality." *New Mexico Law Review* 31 (Summer): 455–492.

Gulati, Mitu, and Veronica Sanchez. 2002. "Giants in a World of Pygmies? Testing the Superstar Hypothesis with Judicial Opinions in Casebooks." *Iowa Law Review* 87 (May): 1141–1212.

Harrison, Lindsay. 2002. "The Problem with Posner as Art Critic: Linnemeir v. Board of Trustees of Purdue University Fort Wayne." *Harvard Civil Rights–Civil Liberties Law Review* (Winter): 185–206.

Landes, William M., Lawrence Lessig, and Michael E. Solimine. 1998. "Judicial Influence: A Citation Analysis of Federal Courts of Appeals Judges." *Journal of Legal Studies* 27 (June): 271–332.

MacFarquhar, Larissa. 2001. "The Bench Burner: How Did a Judge with Such Subversive Ideas Become a Leading Influence on American Legal Opinion?" *The New Yorker*, 10 December, 78–89.

Posner, Richard A. 1992. "Exchange; The Concept of Unenumerated Rights; Legal Reasoning from the Top Down and from the Bottom Up: The Question of Unenumerated Constitutional Rights." *University of Chicago Law Review* 59 (Winter): 433–450.

———. 1995. *Overcoming Law*. Cambridge: Harvard University Press.

———. 1996. *The Federal Courts: Challenge and Reform*. 2d ed. Cambridge: Harvard University Press.

———. 1999. *The Problematics of Moral and Legal Theory*. Cambridge: Harvard University Press.

———. "Diary: A Weeklong Electronic Journal." Slate.com. 14–18 January 2002.

Sheehy, Barbara A. 2000/2001. "An Analysis of the Honorable Richard A. Posner's Social Security Law." *Connecticut Insurance Law Journal* 7: 103–151.

Slania, Laura J. 1987. "Dynamics Corp. of America v. CTS Corp.: Posner's Plan for Poison Pills." *Wisconsin Law Review* 1987 (July/August): 711–735.

Stempel, Jeffrey W. 2000/2001. "An Inconsistently Sensitive Mind: Richard Posner's Celebration of Insurance and Continuing Blind Spots of Eco Nominalism." *Connecticut Insurance Law Journal* 7: 7–79.

POUND, CUTHBERT WINFRED

(1864–1935)

CUTHBERT WINFRED POUND
Library of Congress

CUTHBERT POUND SERVED FOR almost thirty years on the courts of the state of New York—for ten years on the Supreme Court (the trial court in the state system)—and for just under twenty years on the New York Court of Appeals, the state's highest appellate court. His years on the Court of Appeals (1915–1934) closely coincided with the tenure on that court of Benjamin Cardozo. That was a period in which the judiciary faced repeated constitutional attacks on legislation aimed at protecting workers, tenants, and consumers against the economic dominance of employers and property owners, with the constant need to reexamine and reshape common law doctrines that were no longer suited to the needs of the twentieth century. Pound committed himself to meeting these challenges with dedication and conviction and consistently resisted the efforts of the economically powerful members of society to use the courts to preserve their power in the face of demands for change. A scholarly analysis of his judicial career concluded that he "was close to preeminence in his ability to differentiate between the interests of the privileged class to which judges belong and the interests of society, in his prevailing impulse to protect the interests of the unprivileged" (Edgerton 1935, 45).

Judge Pound was born in June 1864 in Lockport, New York, a city that he regarded as his home throughout his life. His parents, Alexander Pound and Almina Whipple Pound, were longtime residents of the area, and his older brother, John Pound, was for many years a leading attorney in the city. Judge Pound studied history and political science at Cornell University for three terms after his graduation from high school in Lockport, leaving Cornell in 1884 to study law in his brother's law office. He was admitted to the New York bar in 1886 and practiced law with his brother until 1895, when he joined the faculty of the law school at Cornell. While in Lockport, he was city attorney from 1889 to 1891; he served in the state senate for one term in 1894–1895 but was not reelected. He was an active legislator in his brief period of service, most notably responsible for leading the successful effort in the senate to win approval of the state constitutional amendment to provide for women's suffrage, adopted by the legislature in 1895. He was appointed to the state Civil Service Commission in 1900 by Gov. Theodore Roosevelt and remained on the commission for four years, serving as its president from 1902 to 1904. He was a member of the Cornell faculty for nine years, resigning in 1904 on the death of his brother, to return to Lockport to take over his brother's practice. He remained deeply devoted to Cornell all his life, however, and he was a member of its Board of Trustees from 1913 until his death.

Pound became counsel to Gov. Frank Higgins in 1905, and Higgins appointed him in 1906 to fill a vacancy on the state Supreme Court. Pound was elected to a fourteen-year term on that court in the following year. In 1915, Gov. Charles Whitman appointed Pound to serve on the Court of Appeals as an auxiliary judge because of a backlog on the court's docket, and he was elected to a fourteen-year term on that court in 1916. He was reelected in 1930; in 1932, when Benjamin Cardozo, then chief judge, was appointed to the United States Supreme Court, Gov. Franklin Roosevelt appointed Pound to succeed Cardozo. Later in that year he was elected to that position, but he was only able to serve as chief judge for two years before reaching the mandatory retirement age of seventy in 1934. His death resulted from a cerebral hemorrhage suffered while he was speaking at a dinner in his honor in Ithaca, New York, shortly after his retirement. He died the next day, 3 February 1935.

Judge Pound's judicial approach was characterized by a refusal to be tightly bound by legal forms developed in previous centuries, particularly as these impeded the attainment of social justice, and by a readiness to accept legal change where it served to promote the public welfare. He emphatically rejected the idea that the meaning of state and federal constitutions was frozen in time and could not be reinterpreted in later eras to accommodate the different needs of those eras and the new demands placed on government by the recognition of those needs. He expressed his philosophy forcefully in a 1923 lecture:

> The world cannot be run forever on the lore of Coke or Mansfield or Eldon. Justice, not law, is the greatest interest of man on earth and we may be sure that as a constitution is nothing but a law, emanating from the people, not imposed upon them from above, the people . . . will not hesitate to prefer a constitution of common right to a constitution of mere legalism. . . . Good government, therefore, rests on the will of the constituent sovereign people and not on the temporary written expression of such will. The constitution is the slave, not the master of its creator. (Pound 1923, 410–411)

Perhaps no judicial opinion he wrote in his career more clearly reflected his beliefs or received greater recognition than one he wrote while still on the state Supreme Court, prior to his elevation to the Court of Appeals. In 1910, he became the first U.S. judge to uphold the constitutionality of a workmen's compensation statute, in this case a New York law modeled after the English Workmen's Compensation Act of 1897, that overrode the common law rules under which an employee could not recover from an employer for job-related injuries unless he could prove negligence or other fault on the part of the employer. For Pound, the enactment raised no serious constitutional questions. The common law, he wrote, was always subject to alteration or abrogation by the legislature, which had here done nothing more remarkable than shift liability for injuries resulting from the hazards of certain types of employment from the employee to the employer. And placing liability for damages on the employer when he was not at fault did not constitute a deprivation of property without due process of law, for due process did not withdraw from the legislature "power to pass all manner of necessary and wholesome acts for the protection and well being of the public, although such acts may interfere with personal liberty and the right to do what one will with his own" (*Ives v. South Buffalo Railway Co.* 1910, 923–924).

Judge Pound's decision was promptly reversed by the New York Court of Appeals, which held that the due process clause of the state constitution, if not also the U.S. Constitution, prohibited the legislature from altering the common law to place liability for job-related accidents on an employer who was free from fault (*Ives v. South Buffalo Railway Co.* 1911). But, as Pound might have predicted, the Court of Appeals did not have the last word either. In his 1923 lecture, he observed: "When the courts push limitations on legislative power to a 'dryly logical extreme' unpopular decisions are not infrequently followed either by constitutional amendments or by decisions more in keeping with the spirit of the times" (Pound 1923, 410). So it was in this case. The New York constitution was amended two years after the ruling of the Court of Appeals to empower the state legislature to enact workmen's compensation laws. With regard to the U.S. Constitution, the Supreme Court, in a series of decisions culminating in the *Arizona Employers' Liability Cases* in 1919, held, over the vigorous objections of a conservative minority, that such laws did not violate the due process or equal protection clauses of the Fourteenth Amendment, thus providing support for Pound's judgment that "that which the people deem just and necessary they will have. . . . Historical backgrounds, constitutional precedent and the traditions of the fathers will be appealed to in vain as against a determined desire for an extension of the powers of government" (410).

Upon his elevation to the New York Court of Appeals, Pound continued to decline to impose constitutional barriers to economic regulations "which the people deem just and necessary," even though these might affect the traditional property rights of employers and landlords. His nineteen years of service on that court covered a period when judges commonly saw themselves as indispensable protectors of vested property rights and actively employed constitutional doctrines such as substantive due process to frustrate legislative efforts to ameliorate some of the social injustice that could result from the unfettered exercise of economic power. But Pound was not one of their number. And, somewhat surprisingly, given the conservative inclinations of the judiciary in those years, he frequently found his position affirmed by a narrow majority of the United States Supreme Court, as had been the case with regard to workmen's compensation. A well-known instance was his majority opinion upholding the New York emergency housing laws of 1920, in which the legislature sought to deal with the housing crisis in the major cities caused by the migration of population in World War I and the cessation of housing construction during the war. The law temporarily prevented landlords in those cities from dispossessing tenants whose leases had expired and who were willing to pay a fair and reasonable rent, rather than the exorbitant rents that the landlords, under the existing conditions, were able to demand. In response to the argument that these restrictions deprived landlords of their property without due process of law, Pound declared: "Either the rights of property and contract must when necessary yield to the public convenience, advantage and welfare, or it must be found that the state has surrendered one of the attributes of sovereignty for which governments are founded and made itself powerless to secure to its citizens the blessings of freedom and to promote the general welfare" (*People ex rel. Durham Realty Corp. v. LaFetra* 1921, 443). A month after this decision, the United States Supreme Court, by a vote of five to four, upheld the New York housing laws on appeal in a separate case brought in federal district court (*Marcus Brown Holding Co. v. Feldman* 1921).

Another instance was a famous case in the early New Deal period. In 1933, the New York legislature, faced with a crisis in the dairy industry caused by the inability of milk producers to obtain a price for their product equal to the cost of its production, passed a series of laws to regulate the sale and distribution of milk, including setting a minimum price for the retail sale of milk to consumers. A due process challenge to the laws had precedent on its side because the United States Supreme Court, in a series of cases in the 1920s, had held that price-control regulations were violative of due process except with regard to "businesses affected with a public interest," a category in which the dairy industry did not appear to fall. Judge Pound, speaking for all but one of the participating members of his court, was undeterred. He had no doubt that the legislature's authority included the power to control prices in order to avert the destruction of an industry vital to the state's economy or that "[t]he policy of non-interference with individual freedom must at times give way to the policy of compulsion for the general welfare" (*People v. Nebbia* 1933, 272). The decision to uphold the law was affirmed, five to four, by the United States Supreme Court, which held that "[t]he phrase 'affected with a public interest' can . . . mean no more than that an industry, for adequate reason, is subject to control for the public good" (*Nebbia v. New York* 1934, 536).

Judge Pound's willingness to support the political branches in their efforts to attain their social goals did not, however, extend to legislative efforts to abridge civil liberties, particularly the right of political dissidents to freedom of speech and assembly. In one case, a city ordinance prohibited meetings or assemblages on the public streets without a permit from the mayor, who denied an application for a permit for a Socialist meeting, stating that he would grant no permits to Socialists. The Court of Appeals sustained a denial of habeas corpus relief, and Pound alone dissented. Regardless of the constitutionality of the ordinance on its face, he contended, application of the law to silence groups whose views were disapproved by the mayor was "unauthorized, arbitrary and oppressive" and thus a violation of the constitutional guarantees of free speech and assembly (*People ex rel. Doyle v. Atwell* 1921, 107–108). Although Pound conceded the constitutionality of the ordinance on its face, the United States Supreme Court, when it became receptive to free speech claims in the following decade, was to hold void on their face laws that granted standardless discretion to public officials to issue or deny permits for meetings or for the distribution of literature, on the ground that such laws invited discriminatory application (*Hague v. C.I.O.* 1939).

In the historic case of *Gitlow v. New York*, the defendants had distributed a manifesto advocating mass action in support of revolutionary socialism and were convicted under the New York Criminal Anarchy law, which prohibited advocacy of overthrow of organized government by force or violence. The Court of Appeals in 1922 sustained the convictions. Because the United States Supreme Court had only recently upheld the constitutionality of convictions under the federal Espionage and Sedition Acts for the distribution of revolutionary literature (*Abrams v. United States* 1919), to dissent in the *Gitlow* case, as did Judge Pound, joined by Judge Cardozo, required an approach not based on constitutional law. Therefore, Pound instead argued that the New York law only forbade the advocacy of anarchy, that is, the absence of government, and, since revolutionary socialism called for a totalitarian dictatorship of the proletariat, its advocacy was not a violation of the statute (*People v. Gitlow* 1922, 154–158). The majority of the Court of Appeals refused to read the law so narrowly, and a majority of the United States Supreme Court upheld its constitutionality, with Justices Oliver Wendell Holmes Jr. and Louis Brandeis dissenting (*Gitlow v. New York* 1925).

Shortly after he joined the Court of Appeals, Judge Pound published a brief law review article questioning whether what were regarded in the law as "voluntary" confessions were in fact voluntary. At the time, the law in New York was that confessions were considered voluntary, and thus admissible as evidence, if they had not been induced by threats or by the assurance that one would not be prosecuted. But Pound saw that that statutory rule did not provide an adequate measure of the voluntariness of a confession. Suppose, he wrote, that an accused who is illegally in custody and has neither been arraigned nor allowed access to counsel is questioned for long hours without food or rest, and finally confesses. For Pound, the fact that he had neither been threatened nor given assurance that he would not be prosecuted did not establish that the confession was voluntary. He was likely to have confessed simply "because he hoped to end the inquisition. . . . [A]nd whether the statement be true or false, our sense of justice revolts at a conviction based [solely] on a finding by the jury that such a statement is voluntary" (Pound 1916, 80). If there were independent evidence to corroborate the statements in the confession or to prove guilt, Pound would not reverse a conviction on the ground that a confession had been illegally obtained (*People v. Trybus* 1916). But where there was indisputable evidence that a confession had been obtained by violence (although it was rare to find indisputable evidence because police and prosecutors routinely concocted explanations to cover their wrongdoing regardless of the strength of the evidence of it), he would hold it inadmissible as a matter of law and not allow the question of its voluntariness to be given to the jury. In 1930, he wrote for a unanimous court ordering a new trial where a murder conviction was based on a confession obtained after a lengthy interrogation—occurring after the district attorney had left the suspect "in the hands of three police officers"—from which the suspect emerged with severe bruises and a blackened eye, as corroborated by the testimony of an examining physician and by a nude photograph of him that was ordered taken by a judge over the objection of the district attorney. Pound angrily declared that such "[l]awless methods of law enforcement should not be countenanced by our courts even though they may seem expedient to the authorities in order to apprehend the guilty" (*People* v. *Barbato* 1930, 178). But an effective judicial corrective for these practices had to await the Warren Court.

During the years in which Pound served on the bench, courts had to contend with common law rules that had developed in other eras and that had become inappropriate for the new economic and social realities of the modern industrial age. Pound was considerably more willing to abandon these outmoded rules than his colleagues, who were generally reluctant to do so because departing from existing rules went against the normal desire of judges to maintain stability in the law. Therefore, he frequently had difficulty in persuading the court to join him in setting old rules aside. In one striking instance, Pound expressed intense exasperation when the Court of Appeals, on the basis of the common law fiction that a husband and wife were a legal unity, held that a wife could not bring a tort action against her husband. Pound responded: "When time makes ancient rules of personal rights and remedies uncouth, illogical and productive of harm, they need not be inexorably insisted upon" (*Allen* v. *Allen* 1927, 575).

Karl Llewellyn, in his exhaustive study of the ways in which appellate courts perform their function in a common law system, ranked Pound among the finest of the common law judges and described him as "a judge with a consistent record of craftsmanship, forthrightness, and earthy common sense" (1960, 106). The case Llewellyn chose as an example of these qualities was another in which Pound dissented when the Court of Appeals insisted on clinging to obsolete rules. It involved a suit against a municipality by a householder whose family had contracted typhoid fever from contaminated water piped into his home by the city. The city demurred, pointing out that it had never expressly warranted that its water was pure and wholesome, and the majority of the court sustained the demurrer, noting that, under the common law, "a private water company or a municipality is not an insurer nor liable as a guarantor of the quality of the water it furnishes to its customers." Pound sharply and succinctly rejected that conclusion. "I fail to comprehend," he argued, "how we can escape the application of the doctrine of implied warranty of wholesomeness," since the householder should be entitled to rely on the purity of the water delivered by the city (*Canavan* v. *City of Mechanicville* 1920, 476, 481).

But there were areas in which Pound had greater success. Early in his tenure on the Court of Appeals, he wrote a majority opinion (only one judge dissenting) that narrowed the doctrine of contributory negligence, under which an employer could escape liability for a work-related injury to an employee if the employee was also at fault. Pound held that it was the employer's duty "to exercise reasonable care for the safety of the employee" and that, where "the employer's negligence causes the dangerous conditions," he can be held liable even if he gave generalized warnings of the existence of danger, unless the employee was guilty of gross negligence (*Larkin* v. *New York Telephone Co.* 1917, 32). And he wrote for a unanimous court holding that statutes abrogating the "fellow-servant" rule and providing for the liability of an employer even where the injury to an employee was caused by the negligence of a co-worker also applied where the injury was caused by the willful misconduct, as opposed to the negligence, of the co-worker, if the wrongful act was "intended and believed to be for the interest of the [employer]" (*Encarnacion* v. *Jamison* 1929, 223–224).

Judging was Cuthbert Pound's life, and when he was obliged to retire from the bench on 31 December 1934, having reached the mandatory retirement age, he stepped down only with great reluctance, remarking in the "Concerning the Alumni" section of the *Cornell Alumni News* that "I would be guilty of the grossest hypocrisy if I said that this was anything more than the saddest moment of my life. The play is done, the curtain drops, and I say farewell with the deepest regret" (17 January 1935, 10). Ironically, he was to die just over one month later.

Dean Alfange Jr.

References and Further Reading:

Abrams v. United States. 250 U.S. 616 (1919).
Allen v. Allen. 246 N.Y. 571; 159 N.E. 656 (1927).
Arizona Employers' Liability Cases. 250 U.S. 400 (1919).
Canavan v. City of Mechanicville. 229 N.Y. 473; 128 N.E. 882 (1920).
Edgerton, Henry W. 1935. "A Liberal Judge: Cuthbert W. Pound." *Cornell Law Quarterly* 21 (December): 7–45.
Encarnacion v. Jamison. 251 N.Y. 218; 167 N.E. 422 (1929).
Gitlow v. New York. 268 U.S. 652 (1925).
Hague v. C.I.O. 307 U.S. 496 (1939).
Ives v. South Buffalo Railway Co. 124 N.Y.S. 920 (1910).
Ives v. South Buffalo Railway Co. 201 N.Y. 271; 94 N.E. 431 (1911).
Larkin v. New York Telephone Co. 220 N.Y. 27; 114 N.E. 1043 (1917).
Llewellyn, Karl N. 1960. *The Common Law Tradition: Deciding Appeals*. Boston: Little, Brown.
Marcus Brown Holding Co. v. Feldman. 256 U.S. 170 (1921).

Nebbia v. New York. 291 U.S. 502 (1934).
People v. Barbato. 254 N.Y. 170; 172 N.E. 458 (1930).
People v. Gitlow. 234 N.Y. 132; 136 N.E. 317 (1922).
People v. Nebbia. 262 N.Y. 259; 186 N.E. 694 (1933).
People v. Trybus. 219 N.Y. 18; 113 N.E. 538 (1916).
People ex rel. Doyle v. Atwell. 232 N.Y. 96; 133 N.E. 364 (1921).
People ex rel. Durham Realty Corp. v. LaFetra. 230 N.Y. 429; 130 N.E. 601 (1921).
Pound, Cuthbert W. 1916. "Inquisitorial Confessions." *Cornell Law Quarterly* 1 (January): 77–81.
———. 1923. "Constitutional Aspects of American Administrative Law." *American Bar Association Journal* 9 (July): 409–416.

REHNQUIST, WILLIAM H.

(1924–)

William H. Rehnquist
Dane Penland, Smithsonian Institution, Collection of the Supreme Court of the United States

Born on 1 October 1924 in Milwaukee, Wisconsin, William Hubbs Rehnquist was the son of a first-generation Swedish American, William B. Rehnquist. Although his father never attended college, his mother Margery held a degree from the University of Wisconsin and was fluent in five foreign languages (Jenkins 1985, 31). Graduating from high school in 1943, Rehnquist won a scholarship to Kenyon College in Gambier, Ohio. After only one semester, however, he chose to leave school and join the Army Air Corps as a weather observer. After he returned from Africa following the war, he enrolled in Stanford University and graduated Phi Beta Kappa with a degree in political science in 1948 (U.S. Senate Committee on the Judiciary 1971, 2, 7, 12, 56–57; Shapiro 1978, 109; Martz, McDaniel, and Malone 1986, 20; Lord and Work 1986, 18). Rehnquist then pursued and received an M.A. degree in political science from Stanford and a second M.A. in government from Harvard.

Rehnquist decided to return to Stanford to enter law school, where he graduated first in his class in 1952 (U.S. Senate Committee on the Judiciary 1971, 12; Martz, McDaniel, and Malone 1986, 20; Lord and Work 1986, 18). Sandra Day O'Connor, appointed to the Supreme Court in

1981, sometimes dated Rehnquist at Stanford. In reflecting upon their law school days, O'Connor noted, "He quickly rose to the top of the class and, frankly, was head and shoulders above all the rest of us in terms of sheer legal talent and ability" (U.S. Senate Committee on the Judiciary 1971, 12). During the 1971 Senate confirmation hearings on the appointment of Rehnquist to the Supreme Court, a former law school professor recalled, "As a student he was nothing short of brilliant, dogged in his determination to achieve excellence and persistent in his expectation of excellence on the other side of the podium" (John B. Hurlbut, letter to Sen. James O. Eastland, 28 October 1971, in U.S. Senate Committee on the Judiciary 1971, 8). Following his graduation from Stanford Law School, Rehnquist served an eighteen-month clerkship term under Supreme Court justice Robert H. Jackson. In 1953, Rehnquist moved to Phoenix, Arizona, where he was associated with the firm of Evans, Kitchel and Jenckes. He won widespread respect among his colleagues for his integrity, diligence, unusual intellectual abilities, and professional competence. One professional colleague in 1971 remarked, "He is an outstanding lawyer, completely thorough, scholarly, perceptive, articulate, and possessed of the utmost integrity as well as a keen wit" (Jarrel F. Kaplan, letter to Sen. Edward W. Brooke, 27 October 1971, in U.S. Senate Committee on the Judiciary 1971, 8).

In February 1969, Pres. Richard Nixon appointed Rehnquist as assistant attorney general in the Office of Legal Counsel, U.S. Department of Justice. He was responsible for the resolution of most of the legal questions that did not relate to litigation. In this position, he became highly respected among his colleagues. In 1971, President Nixon nominated Rehnquist, then age forty-seven, as an associate justice of the Supreme Court (*Report of the Standing Committee* 1971, 132; Shapiro 1978, 110).

From Justice to Chief Justice

Despite his outstanding legal record and considerable reputation, Rehnquist's nomination to the Supreme Court did not receive uniform approbation. Those who questioned his nomination were predominantly civil libertarians concerned about his past support of various conservative causes. In describing his judicial philosophy, Rehnquist alluded to the importance of construing the Constitution in light of the framers' original intent, determined from available sources (see, for example, Shapiro 1978, 19, 55, 81–82, 138, and 167). Judicial conservatism has remained a guiding principle for Rehnquist ever since.

Although Rehnquist is widely recognized as one of the brightest and most efficient justices on the Court, his influence on the Court took time to develop. In 1986, University of Virginia law professor A. E. Dick Howard observed: "No one on the Court writes with more style, force or assurance. It is hard to match his agility in shaping a record and marshaling arguments to reach a conclusion" (Lord and Work 1986, 18). For a decade after his coming onto the Court, however, the Court's majority seemed unsympathetic to Rehnquist's entreaties from the right. Rehnquist seemed perfectly comfortable in disagreeing with many of the Court's decisions. Gradually, however, Rehnquist's keen intellect and insights began to influence the Court. By the 1980s, a more conservative Court had begun to emerge with Justices Byron R. White, Lewis F. Powell Jr., Sandra Day O'Connor, and Chief Justice Warren E. Burger often voting with Rehnquist. By 1982, long before the retirement of Chief Justice Burger, Yale law professor Owen Fiss was calling Rehnquist the "leader" of the Court (Lord and Work 1986, 18; Fiss and Krauthammer 1982, 14). Following Burger's retirement in June 1986, Pres. Ronald Reagan nominated Rehnquist as the sixteenth chief justice of the Supreme Court. After numerous acrimonious hearings, the U.S. Senate confirmed his nomination on 17 September 1986.

Rehnquist is credited with reducing the size of the Court's docket, deciding only seventy-five cases in 1995, less than half of the number in the 1984 term and the lowest number since the 1953 term. Some have criticized Rehnquist's reduction of the docket as enabling him to gain greater control of the Court. Because he limited the number of civil rights cases and increased cases that reopen the issues of federalism, Rehnquist is seen as shifting the Court from a somewhat liberal agenda to a more conservative one (Davis 1999, 146). Nevertheless, Rehnquist is generally appraised as efficient and effective in his leadership of the Court. According to his Court colleagues, his relaxed but professional style brings calm and stability to a body of jurists dealing with many of the most emotion-laden issues of the day. He also received high marks for fairness in presiding over the 1998 U.S. Senate impeachment proceedings of Pres. William Clinton.

Rehnquist's Judicial Philosophy

Among the commentators who have closely scrutinized his written opinions and voting patterns, considerable agreement emerges concerning certain distinctive doctrines that guide Rehnquist in his decisionmaking. A selective examination of three of these key doctrines—strict constructionism, judicial deference, and an advocacy of states' rights—will serve to depict Rehnquist in a wider judicial context.

Strict Constructionism

A common way of analyzing judges relates to methods of construing the Constitution. Judges differ not only as to the meaning of constitutional provisions but also as to the interpretive approaches they employ. There are essentially two models of constitutional interpretation: the strict constructionist and the evolutionist.

The evolutionist model permits changes in the scope of constitutional provisions as contemporary thinking and social conditions shed new light on constitutionally expressed norms. Under the evolutionist interpretation, what is constitutional in one era may become unconstitutional in the next, and vice versa (Kleven 1983, 3). Evolutionism departs, then, in varying degrees, from the specific intent of the framers, although it may not be totally fair to suggest, as Rehnquist has, that evolutionist decisions are in no way "tied to the language of the Constitution" (Rehnquist 1976, 698).

The model of strict constructionism holds that "judges deciding constitutional issues should confine themselves to enforcing norms that are stated or clearly implicit in the written Constitution" (Ely 1980, 1). In modern parlance, this model is referred to as "interpretivism." Although the name is new, the theory is not. Its roots go back at least to Supreme Court justice Joseph Story (1811–1845).

Professor Ronald Dworkin has suggested that the strict constructionist model is premised on two positive tenets: that law is objectively determinable and that law is logically separate from moral values that are arbitrary or subjective (1977, 14–22). Dworkin's description is succinct and insightful and can readily be discovered in Rehnquist's writings. Judges who depart from the constitutional text cease being judges and become, in Rehnquist's estimation,

> [a] small group of fortunately situated people with a roving commission to second-guess Congress, state legislatures, and state and federal administrative officers concerning what is best for the country. . . .
>
> Beyond the Constitution and the laws in our society, there simply is no basis other than the individual conscience of the citizen that may serve as a platform for the launching of moral judgments. (Rehnquist 1976, 693, 704)

In other words, a judge's function is to adhere to the text and abstain from making moral judgments. Such judgments are, according to Rehnquist, better left to the legislator who, even though no wiser than the judge, is at least more democratically accountable in a majoritarian-based republic. Such was the rationale for Rehnquist's dissent in *Roe v. Wade*, 410 U.S. 113 (1973). The Court majority enunciated a "right of privacy" arising out of various constitutional amendments that would be applied to the states through the Fourteenth Amendment, but Rehnquist objected on the grounds that such a right "was apparently completely unknown to the drafters of the Amendment . . . the drafters did not intend to have the Fourteenth Amendment withdraw from the States the power to legislate with respect to this matter" (*Roe* 1973, 198, 200).

Judicial Deference

Deference reflects a judge's view of the role of the courts in relation to other branches of government. At one extreme, a judge could take the perspective that a court should decide anew the wisdom of every governmental action coming before it. By contrast, a judge could go to the opposite extreme and totally defer to all decisions made by other branches of government. That no judge does this in practice demonstrates that all judges to some degree are activists. If, for example, the popular branches of government exceed the limits of their constitutional powers, judges must become, in Rehnquist's words, "the keepers of the covenant" (Rehnquist 1976, 698). In placing proper limitations upon the other branches of government in keeping with the Constitution, the judge becomes (appropriately, by all accounts) an activist.

Rehnquist's dissent in *Furman v. Georgia* (408 U.S. 238 [1972]) illustrates his adherence to the principle of judicial deference to decisions of state governments. Reacting to the Court majority's decision to invalidate the Georgia death penalty as cruel and unusual punishment, Rehnquist protested: "The Court's judgments today strike down a penalty that our nation's legislators have thought necessary since our country was founded" (*Furman* 1972, 465). Although admitting that "overreaching the legislative and executive branches may result in the sacrifice of individual protections that the Constitution was designed to secure against action of the State," he insisted that the "judicial overreaching" evident in the decision sacrificed "the equally important right of the people to govern themselves" (*Furman* 1972, 470).

The same deference theme was expressed by Rehnquist in his dissent from a five-to-four decision in *Trimble v. Gordon* (430 U.S. 762 [1977]), which invalidated an Illinois law prohibiting interstate inheritance by illegitimate children from their fathers. Rehnquist reasoned that policy decisions are to be made by the people through their elected representatives, not by judges. He added that the "Constitutional Convention in 1787 rejected the idea that members of the federal judiciary should sit on a council of revision and veto laws which it considered unwise" and that the "Civil War Amendments did nothing to alter that decision" (*Trimble* 1977, 778).

Federalism

On the question of the balance of power between the federal and state governments, Rehnquist is a strong proponent of state sovereignty and the limitation of congressional power in regard to states' rights. In *Trimble v.*

Gordon (430 U.S. 762 [1977]), Rehnquist argued that the framers presumed that all power resided in the people of the states and was only delegated in limited spheres to the federal government. All authority that was not explicitly delegated by the Constitution was reserved for the states and citizens of the states (*Trimble* 1977, 777–778).

Rehnquist might be expected to ground his principles of federalism in the text of the Constitution or in established precedent. One might expect a search of historical data for answers to questions about the relationship between the states and the federal governments. To the contrary, Rehnquist's opinions are often marked by a structural mode of analysis, not unlike the structurism used by those who view the Constitution as an evolving document. His departure from historical interpretation is particularly evident in *Usery* (Davis 1989, 150).

Perhaps the centerpiece of Rehnquist's theory of federalism is his majority opinion in *National League of Cities v. Usery* (426 U.S. 833 [1976]), an opinion later overruled in *Garcia v. San Antonio Metropolitan Transit Authority*, 105 S. Ct. 1005 (1985) but still viewed by some scholars as the centerpiece of Rehnquist's federalism (Powell 1982, 1325). In *Usery*, the Court held that Congress could not require state or local governments to pay the minimum wages applicable to individuals. Rehnquist wrote that the structure of the Constitution withheld from Congress any power to regulate the operating of "states as states" (*Usery* 1976, 845). *Usery* reintroduced into the Court's jurisprudence the long-absent doctrine of state sovereignty and discredited the conventional wisdom that there was virtually no enforceable judicial limit on congressional power. Although the *Usery* case has not been followed in later Supreme Court cases, it remains central to Rehnquist's constitutional jurisprudence.

In order to preserve the "original understanding at Philadelphia," Rehnquist minimizes the impact of the Civil War amendments. Of particular note is his systematic rejection of the Court's doctrine of selective incorporation first adopted in *Gitlow v. New York* (268 U.S. 652 [1925]). Rehnquist referred to the doctrine as "the mysterious process of transmogrification by which [a guarantee of the Bill of Rights] was held to be 'incorporated' and made applicable to the States by the Fourteenth Amendment" (*Carter v. Kentucky* 1981, 309). He further labeled incorporation as a "judicial building block" used by the Court to construct constitutional doctrine with an "increasingly remote" and even "incomprehensible" connection to the Constitution text (*Snead v. Stringer* [102 S. Ct. 536 (1981)]).

Rehnquist's continuing defense of a federalist position can be seen in several recent Court decisions. In *U.S. Term Limits, Inc. v. Thornton*, Justice Clarence Thomas, joined by Justices Antonin Scalia, O'Connor, and Rehnquist, wrote the dissenting opinion, in which he argued that "nothing in the Constitution deprives the people of each State of the power to prescribe eligibility requirements for the candidates. . . . The Constitution is simply silent on this question. And where the Constitution is silent, it raises no bar to action by the States or the people" (*U.S. Term Limits* 1995, 845). In *New York v. United States*, 505 U.S. 144 (1992), the Rehnquist Court held that "[t]he Federal Government may not compel the States to enact or administer a federal regulatory program" (*New York* 1992, 188).

With regard to the First Amendment, Rehnquist has been willing to approve of its incorporation into the Fourteenth Amendment only in a limited sense. In *Buckley v. Valeo*, Rehnquist stated:

> I am of the opinion that not all of the strictures which the First Amendment imposes upon Congress are carried over against the States by the Fourteenth Amendment, but rather that it is only the "general principle" of free speech, that the latter incorporates.
>
> Given this view, cases which deal with state restrictions on First Amendment freedoms are not fungible with those which deal with restrictions imposed by the Federal Government. . . . (*Buckley v. Valeo* [424 U.S. 291 (1976)])

In a 2000 case, Rehnquist again adopted a federalist position in negotiating the space between free speech rights and state police powers, thus emphasizing the limited application of the Fourteenth Amendment. In *Hill v. Colorado*, the Court ruled by a six-to-three majority to limit the free speech in certain areas surrounding health clinics and the people attempting to enter such clinics. In this case, he joined, not the usual Thomas and Scalia, but rather Justices John Paul Stevens, David H. Souter, Ruth Bader Ginsburg, Stephen G. Breyer, and Sandra Day O'Connor (George).

One of the most significant Rehnquist-era developments is the Court's extensive alteration of established standards for interpretation of the First Amendment's religion clauses. The result has been a movement of the Court from a strong separationist view toward a more conservative position that carves out significantly more space in the public sphere for governmental accommodation of religion. It is probably a mistake, however, to view Rehnquist as essentially "proreligion." Rather, this development more likely reflects his view that governments at all levels should be entitled to formulate their own policies on religion (see D. Davis 1991).

Rehnquist's use of these three principles—strict constructionism, judicial deference, and federalism—serves his understanding that the constitutional framers intended to disfavor federal interference with state sovereignty, a principal justification for a number of commentators to characterize Rehnquist as a judicial activist (Powell 1982; Fiss and Krauthammer, 1982; Boles

Sandra Day O'Connor (1930–)

As of the beginning of 2003, 113 individuals had served on the United States Supreme Court. Of these, only two have been women. Republican president Ronald Reagan appointed the first woman, Sandra Day O'Connor, in 1981 (the 106th justice to serve on the Court), and Democratic president Bill Clinton appointed the second woman, Ruth Bader Ginsburg (the 112th justice) in 1993.

Reagan's appointee, Sandra Day O'Connor, was born in El Paso, Texas, in 1930 and spent most of her early life with her parents and younger siblings on a large Arizona ranch and, during the school year, with a grandmother who lived in El Paso. After graduating from high school at the age of sixteen, Day earned her undergraduate and law degrees at Stanford in five years, serving on the *Stanford Law Review* and graduating third in her law school class (future chief justice William Rehnquist was first). Declining an offer as a legal secretary at a time when women were not always welcomed into the legal profession, O'Connor became a deputy county attorney in San Mateo, California. She later joined her husband, John O'Connor, in an overseas military assignment with the Judge Advocate General's Corps in Germany, where she worked as a civilian lawyer for the Quartermaster Corps. After the couple returned to Arizona, O'Connor temporarily put full-time employment on hold as she raised three sons and participated in a variety of volunteer jobs and political activities.

In 1965, O'Connor served as an Arizona assistant attorney general, and she was appointed in 1969 to the Arizona Senate, to which she was twice reelected. In 1972 she became the first woman ever to be elected as the majority leader of such a body. Two years later, O'Connor won election to the

(continues)

1987). Rehnquist claims that history demonstrates the congruence of his states' rights theory with the intent of the framers and excludes alternative interpretations (*Trimble v. Gordon* 1977, 777). State sovereignty and limited federal government are authentic expressions of a central strand of U.S. constitutional philosophy. As noted by legal scholar Jefferson Powell, in the Jeffersonian tradition, the transcendent goal of freedom is unattainable unless the national government is kept as small and unobtrusive as possible (1982, 1364). "This vision of limited government has haunted our history from its beginning," said Powell, "and is reflected frequently . . . in the opinions of Justice Rehnquist" (1364). Even the patron saint of strong national government Abraham Lincoln found it necessary to invoke Jefferson and his ennobled ideals, stating that "the principles of Jefferson are the definitions and axioms of a free society" (Abraham Lincoln, letter to Committee of Boston Republicans, 16 April 1859, quoted in Powell 1982, 1364). Rehnquist's constitutional theory taps into this almost sanctified tra-

(continued)

Maricopa County Superior Court, and in 1979, the Arizona governor appointed O'-Connor to the Arizona Court of Appeals. In 1981 President Reagan fulfilled a campaign promise to find a qualified woman for the job by appointing her to the United States Supreme Court to replace Potter Stewart, who was retiring from that body. During her confirmation hearings, O'Connor responded to how she would like to be remembered by saying that she would like for her tombstone to read "Here lies a good judge" (Cushman 1995, 509). She was confirmed by a ninety-nine–to–zero vote; although her record of prior judicial service was relatively slender, she had served in all three branches of state government and was the only member of the Court to have held elective office.

On the Supreme Court, O'Connor has affirmed her prior reputation as a moderate conservative. When Justice Lewis Powell was on the Court, the two often voted together; today, she often votes with Justice Anthony Kennedy. O'Connor's votes have been particularly important in cases involving affirmative action, in cases involving states' rights, and in matters of church and state. In *Planned Parenthood of Southeastern Pennsylvania v. Casey* (1992), Justice O'Connor joined Justice Anthony Kennedy in a concurring opinion authored by Justice David Souter arguing that the Court's controversial decision legalizing most abortions in *Roe v. Wade* (1973) should not be overturned.

Conservative in temperament and in judicial philosophy, O'Connor has nonetheless proved to be a trailblazer for other American women, and she is widely admired as a judicial role model.

References:

Abraham, Henry J. 1999. *Justices, Presidents, and Senators: A History of the U.S. Supreme Court Appointments from Washington to Clinton*. Lanham, Md.: Rowman and Littlefield Publishers.

Cushman, Clare, ed. 1995. *The Supreme Court Justices: Illustrated Biographies, 1789–1995*. Washington, D.C.: Congressional Quarterly.

dition in U.S. intellectual history, says Powell, and it is that which gives his federalism such appeal.

Derek H. Davis

References and Further Reading:

Boles, Donald E. 1987. *Mr. Justice Rehnquist, Judicial Activist: The Early Years*. Ames: University of Iowa Press.

Buckley v. Valeo. 424 U.S. 1 (1976).

Carter v. Kentucky. 450 U.S. 288 (1981).

Davis, Derek. 1991. *Chief Justice Rehnquist and the Course of American Church-State Relations*. Buffalo, N.Y.: Prometheus Books.

Davis, Sue. 1989. *Justice Rehnquist and the Constitution*. Princeton, N.J.: Princeton University Press.

———. 1999. "The Chief Justice and Judicial Decision-Making: The Institutional Basis for Leadership on the Supreme Court." In *Supreme Court Decision-Making,* edited by Cornell W. Clayton and Howard Gillman. Chicago: The University of Chicago Press, 135–154.

Dworkin, Ronald. 1977. *Taking Rights Seriously*. Cambridge: Harvard University Press.

Ely, John Hart. 1980. *Democracy and Distrust: A Theory of Judicial Review*. Cambridge: Harvard University Press.

Fiss, Owen M., and Charles Krauthammer. 1982. "A Return to the Antebellum Constitution: The Rehnquist Court." *New Republic* 185, 10 March, 14.

Furman v. Georgia. 408 U.S. 238 (1972).

George, Robert P. "The Supreme Court 2000: A Symposium." *First Things* 10. Available at <http://www.firstthings.com/ftissues/ft0010/articles/symposium-george.html>. Accessed 6 October 2000.

Gitlow v. New York. 268 U.S. 652 (1925).

Hodel v. Indiana. 452 U.S. 314 (1981).

Hodel v. Virginia Surface Mining & Reclamation Association. 452 U.S. 264 (1981).

Jenkins, John A. 1985. "The Partisan: A Talk with Justice Rehnquist." *New York Times Magazine*, 3 March, 28–35, 88, 100–101.

Kleven, Thomas. 1983. "The Constitutional Philosophy of Justice William H. Rehnquist." *Vermont Law Review* 8 (Spring): 3.

Lord, Lewis J., and Clemens P. Work. 1986. "From Lone Dissenter to Chief." *U.S. News and World Report*, 30 June, 18.

Martz, Larry, Ann McDaniel, and Maggie Malone. 1986. "A Pair for the Court; Rehnquist and Scalia Seem to Be Two of a Tory Kind." *Newsweek*, 30 June, 20–22.

National League of Cities v. Usery. 426 U.S. 833 (1976).

New York v. United States. 505 U.S. 144 (1992).

Powell, H. Jefferson. 1982. "The Complete Jeffersonian: Justice Rehnquist and Federalism." *Yale Law Journal* 92: 1317–1370.

Rehnquist, William H. 1976. "The Notion of a Living Constitution." *Texas Law Review* 54 (May): 693–706.

Report of the Standing Committee on the Federal Judiciary of the American Bar Association, 2 November 1971.

Roe v. Wade. 410 U.S. 113 (1973).

Shapiro, David L. 1978. "William Hubbs Rehnquist." In *The Justices of the United States Supreme Court: Their Lives and Major Opinions*, edited by Leon Friedman. New York: Chelsea House Publishers, 109–141.

Snead v. Stringer. 102 S. Ct. 535 (1981).

Trimble v. Gordon. 430 U.S. 762 (1977).

U.S. Senate Committee on the Judiciary. 1971. *Hearings before the Committee on the Judiciary on Nominations of William H. Rehnquist, of Arizona, and Lewis F. Powell, Jr., of Virginia, to Be Associate Justices of the Supreme Court of the United States*. 92d Cong., 1st sess., 3–4 November 1971.

U.S. Term Limits, Inc. v. Thornton. 514 U. S. 779 (1995).

RIVES, RICHARD

(1895–1982)

RICHARD RIVES
Library of Congress

JUDGE RICHARD RIVES SERVED during a pivotal period of U.S. judicial history. His appointment to the Fifth Circuit Court of Appeals in New Orleans dropped him into the maelstrom that was the effort by the federal judiciary to integrate southern society. Rives joined his colleagues in enforcing the rulings of the Warren Court and suffered under the general opprobrium of southern politicians and the public.

Richard Rives was born on 15 January 1895 in Montgomery, Alabama. Rives avoided most of the formal education required of modern lawyers. After attending Tulane University in 1913, he studied under a local lawyer and passed the bar exam at the ripe age of nineteen. He spent several years in the courtroom as a lawyer and served as the president of the Montgomery and the Alabama Bar Associations. He befriended Hugo Black, helping in one of the senator's election campaigns. This connection made him a prominent figure in the national Democratic Party and within judicial circles in Washington once Black was appointed to the United States Supreme Court. Rives even argued a case before the justice, his only before the Supreme Court.

Rives was also involved in the many political battles of the Alabama legislature during the 1940s. Although he was not a legislator himself, he testified frequently before committees in favor of or in opposition to certain legislation. During the 1940s he worked in the campaigns of various Alabama gubernatorial candidates. He also represented a local county government in a voter discrimination case. During the early days of the Truman administration he was mentioned as a possible appointee to the Fifth Circuit Court of Appeals although he had no judicial experience at the state or federal level. The death of his son delayed that appointment, but in May 1951 he was confirmed and took his seat as a federal appellate judge.

At the time of Rives's arrival, the Fifth Circuit was one of the largest appeals courts in terms of geography. It stretched across the Deep South and included Alabama, Florida, Georgia, Louisiana, Mississippi, and Texas. Cases involving federal law or the national Constitution that originated in those states could be appealed to the Fifth Circuit court located in New Orleans.

As with other federal appeals courts, the Fifth Circuit heard most of its cases in three-judge panels, with different groupings of judges for each case. This tradition required Rives to work with different colleagues, most of them southerners, some supportive of integration in the South, others not. But during his nearly thirty years as a federal judge, Rives participated in some of the most important cases, making decisions that either broke new ground in the law or enforced the decisions already handed down by the United States Supreme Court.

Rives's early years on the court were quiet, but as the federal courts became more involved in the civil rights movement and southern judges were given the job of enforcing new integration decisions handed down by the Supreme Court, Rives found himself involved in increasing controversy. One of the most important of those United States Supreme Court opinions was in *Brown v. Board of Education* (1954), which struck down the segregation of public schools and the separate but equal doctrine. The result of this decision was a series of political acts that directly challenged the legal structure in the South and led to court cases eventually appealed to the Fifth Circuit.

One of those cases was *Browder v. Gayle* (1956). Rives sat as one of three judges hearing an appeal of a lower court decision. In *Browder*, Alabama laws requiring segregation in bus travel in the state were challenged as unconstitutional. A bus boycott in Montgomery, Alabama, challenged the same ordinance and made the case a legal and political issue of the first order. Browder's attorneys argued before Rives and two other judges that the *Brown* decision had struck down all segregation statutes as unconstitutional under the Fourteenth Amendment.

The court split in the decision. Rives wrote for himself and another judge. In his decision he stated that the separate but equal doctrine that was used to segregate public facilities had been struck down in *Brown* and should also be struck down for the use of buses. In *Browder*, Rives moved beyond the Supreme Court decision, taking it to its logical end and using judicial power to strike down a law.

The *Browder* decision drew different reactions from white and black leaders. The bus boycotts broadened in Alabama as boycott participants were emboldened by the support given them by the court decision, whereas white politicians in the state and throughout the South denounced Rives and his colleagues. After *Browder*, Rives would find that many of his old friendships and political connections ceased, and he was shunned in his hometown.

Rives's decisions showed that he was willing to use his opinions to carry out Supreme Court decisions. This boldness would be necessary in another series of cases involving the controversy over the integration of public schools and implementation of the *Brown* decision.

Beginning in the late 1950s, formerly segregated school districts were required to integrate. A flurry of court cases followed, with lower district court decisions being appealed to the Fifth Circuit by the losing side. One such set of appeals originated in the New Orleans school district. The series of court arguments and rulings in this area earned Rives a reputation as a strict enforcer of integration.

The New Orleans School District had been ordered to integrate by a federal judge but had refused. The school board was backed by a series of special laws passed by the Louisiana legislature delaying integration, declaring school holidays, and threatening to shut down the entire school district if integration were attempted. Lower courts struck the laws down, and the state appealed. Rives heard these appeals along with Judge Herbert Christenson and Judge Skelly Wright.

The hearings before the three judges had a circus atmosphere to them. The Louisiana attorney general denounced the judges in open court and stomped from the room. He was cited for contempt. After the hearing the three judges unanimously struck down several state laws they saw as undermining their order to desegregate. The ruling placed integration back on the fast track. At the same time the judges assumed almost total power over the New Orleans school system. They issued injunctions against every high state official in Louisiana, ranging from the governor to all district attorneys in the state to mayors and sheriffs, prohibiting all of them from any involvement in the New Orleans school district. This blanket prohibition was unprecedented and drew action from the one institution not covered by the judges, the Louisiana legislature.

Several special legislative sessions followed with passage of laws allowing the state to take control of the New Orleans school district. The legislators also created a school holiday for the first day partly integrated schools were to open. Judge Rives and his two colleagues reacted immediately, striking down all of the legislators' works in the strongest possible language. Rives entered the fray for the first time by writing the court's opinion and accusing the Louisiana legislature of using the old secessionist doctrine of nullification. The lawmakers, according to Rives, had attempted to use state law to override the Constitution as interpreted by the Fifth Circuit.

The result of this was a stiffening of the opposition and a political furor that did little to enhance the reputation of the Fifth Circuit, the state legislature, or the effort to integrate southern schools. Rives silently agreed to Wright's opinions but in that silence he showed his support for strong judicial efforts to integrate schools. It was only with the intervention of the federal government that the standoff between New Orleans and the Fifth Circuit was settled.

Efforts to integrate state universities in the South also produced legal controversy. The best known of these was the attempt by James Meredith to enroll as the first black student at the University of Mississippi. The governor of Mississippi, Ross Barnett, refused to allow the admission and was found in contempt. The order was appealed to the Fifth Circuit. Barnett demanded a jury trial in his contempt hearing, an issue that complicated the case.

The judges of the Fifth Circuit sat *en banc* for the case, meaning all of the judges of the court, rather than simply a panel of five, heard oral arguments and wrote a decision. Rives participated in the hearing and decision, questioning the constitutional reasoning used by the governor in refusing to follow the judiciary's decisions. The court split on whether Barnett was to receive a jury trial for his contempt hearing. Rives joined three colleagues in denying that right while four other justices upheld Barnett's constitutional right to have a jury decide his case.

Rives also sat in a case in which a three-judge panel of the Fifth Circuit overruled a federal judge in Savannah, Georgia, who refused to allow integration to occur in the Savannah school district. That judge, Frank Scarlett, refused to enforce the *Brown* decision and struck down repeated attempts by the Savannah district to integrate. His order was overturned by Rives.

Rives's work on the Fifth Circuit was the product of efforts of several of his colleagues, many of whom shared his belief in using judicial power to order public officials to do what they saw as their constitutional duty. During the 1950s, the South was solidly Democratic, but several judges of the Fifth Circuit were Republicans who sought to open the political processes in the region and make the South competitive for the Republican Party. Three of the judges, Elbert Tuttle, John Minor Wisdom, and John Brown, were Republicans who had supported Dwight Eisenhower for president. Tuttle was from Georgia, Wisdom from Louisiana, and Brown from Texas. Each of the three worked to create pro-Eisenhower delegations to attend the 1952 Republican convention. These delegations helped Eisenhower earn the nomination, then go on to win the presidency. The three men's efforts were not forgotten, and as openings occurred on the Fifth Circuit, they earned appointments to the court.

The three Republicans joined the Democratic Rives to form "the Four." This name was given the group of judges who voted consistently to require integration of the South. At the same time they refused to allow federal judges to delay reforms of voting rights and equal education.

Yet Rives did not have the same close relationship and level of agreement with all of his Fifth Circuit colleagues. Some of the Democratic judges on the court took issue with Rives's views on judicial power, states' rights, and integration. Judge Benjamin Cameron wrote several opinions castigating Rives and his opinions. Rives responded in private letters to Cameron and his colleagues. Although the immediate controversy died down after a short time, there remained a residue of tension between the two, particularly over legal issues.

One area of disagreement among all of the judges was the pace and method of desegregating public schools in the South. The Republican judges, including Judges Tuttle and Wisdom, supported broad-based policies; Rives approved a slower approach. In his rulings he allowed local school districts in Alabama to make reassignments of individual students to achieve a level of integration even if it was not complete. Rives's views were different than the policies created in the 1970s in which judges had large groups of students transported by buses to suburban and urban school districts.

Rives also reflected during his later career the turn away from judicial decisions in all cases involving integration. He became part of the growing trend away from judicial control and oversight of every decision made by local governments. In the 1970 case of *Thompson v. Palmer,* Rives rendered a decision for a closely divided Fifth Circuit court. The *Thompson* case involved the closing of all public swimming pools in Jackson, Mississippi. The decision was made after the city was ordered to integrate the pools. The full court of appeals, all fifteen judges, heard the arguments that the closing represented racial discrimination. Eight judges disagreed, with Rives in the lead. Rives upheld the closures as nondiscriminatory, noting that whites and blacks were both denied access to public pools. Rives refused to create group rights based on race, and his decision in *Thompson* was upheld by the Supreme Court in *Palmer v. Thompson* (1971). Rives's usual supporters in the Fifth Circuit, Judges Wisdom and Tuttle, dissented in the case, arguing for group rights.

Judge Rives also avoided a controversy involving the nomination of a Fifth Circuit judge to the United States Supreme Court. G. Harrold Carswell was Richard Nixon's second choice to fill the judicial vacancy created by the resignation of Abe Fortas. The judges of the Fifth Circuit, where Carswell had been serving, signed a letter of support for Carswell, but once it was presented to the Senate, Judges Tuttle and Wisdom withdrew their support. Their action and comments drew the court into a typical Washington political battle and did not help the Fifth Circuit in appearing to be nonpartisan.

After nearly fifteen years on the Fifth Circuit, Rives retired, retaining senior status. That position allowed him to work part-time as a judge on that court. He continued to sit in three-judges panels when needed and occasionally with the entire circuit court. During his last years of service Rives had a more limited calendar, and in October 1981 he was reassigned to serve on the newly created Eleventh Circuit that split off from the Fifth Circuit and included the states of Alabama, Florida, and Georgia. He served briefly in the Eleventh, dying on 27 October 1982 in his hometown of Montgomery, Alabama.

Judge Richard Rives had a considerable impact on U.S. law and the political issues of his era. As a judge on the Fifth Circuit Court of Appeals he was faced with enforcing the Supreme Court's desegregation decisions against uncooperative state officials. In doing so he strained the powers of the federal courts, using them to force state officials to carry out the law as he saw it. Rives operated within a society fighting change and disdainful of anyone who tried to make those changes.

Douglas Clouatre

References and Further Reading:

Bass, Jack. 1981. *Unlikely Heroes: The Dramatic Story of the Southern Judges of the Fifth Circuit Who Translated the Supreme Court's Brown Decision into a Revolution for Equality*. New York: Simon and Schuster.

Peltason, Jack W. 1971. *Fifty-eight Lonely Men: Southern Federal Judges and School Desegregation*. Urbana: University of Illinois Press.

Songer, Donald. 2000. *Continuity and Change on the United States Courts of Appeals*. Ann Arbor: University of Michigan Press.

ROANE, SPENCER

(1762–1822)

SPENCER ROANE
Courtesy of the Library of Virginia

A POLITICAL AND LEGAL LEADER in Virginia during his twenty-six years on the Virginia Court of Appeals (1795–1822), Spencer Roane often clashed with the Marshall Court on the scope of federal and state judicial power.

The early years of the American republic witnessed some of the greatest debates about the scope and reach of federal and state power. Many of the issues of that day were debated within the courts. The main supporter of federal power was Chief Justice John Marshall of the United States Supreme Court. One of his chief rivals and a representative of state power was Judge Spencer Roane of the Virginia Court of Appeals. During the first two decades of the Marshall Court (1801–1835), Roane offered the arguments for greater state independence from the federal government. Although Roane found himself on the losing side of the federal-versus-state debate, he contributed greatly to it, offering an alternative to expanding federal power.

Spencer Roane was born in Essex County, Virginia, northeast of Richmond, on 4 April 1762; his father, William Roane, was a leader in the American Revolution and a political leader in Virginia. Roane was part of the state's gentry with a political career before him. He attended William and Mary with two future Supreme Court justices, Bushrod Washington and John Marshall, and heard George Wythe lecture on the law, lectures that he supplemented with self-study. Roane was admitted to the bar in 1782 and served briefly in the Virginia House of Delegates, where he was a colleague of John Marshall and Patrick Henry. Henry had considerable influence on Roane, who grew to distrust centralized government and worried about the loss of states' rights under the new Constitution. Roane followed Henry when he became governor, serving on the Council of State, an advisory board for the governor.

Roane's political career, though, was limited. In 1787 and 1788 he participated in the Virginia debate over ratification of the newly written constitution. He stated in letters and articles that the national government was provided with too much power under the constitution. These beliefs followed him through his subsequent judicial career.

That career began in 1789 when Roane was elected by the Virginia legislature to serve on the general court, the main trial court in the state. Roane was active in asserting the independence of the courts from political influence. In 1792 he issued a decision in which he struck down a state law that attempted to limit judicial power. Roane reasoned that the state constitution was fundamental law and could not be overridden by the Virginia legislature. Roane's conception of judicial review and the power of the courts was adopted by the federal courts a decade later by Roane's chief judicial rival, John Marshall.

Roane's abilities earned him attention from Virginia legal circles. When an opening occurred in the Virginia Court of Appeals, Roane earned the nod, taking his seat in 1795 at the age of thirty-three. The court of appeals was the highest court in the state and one of the main forums for those favoring state power over federal power in Virginia and the South. The battles between the federal and Virginia state courts prompted many important legal rulings during the first three decades of the Constitution.

The Alien and Sedition Acts presented one of the earliest clashes between federal and state power. The second of these acts prohibited seditious speech criticizing the national government and leaders. Leaders in Virginia, particularly James Madison and Thomas Jefferson, offered the Virginia and Kentucky Resolutions as a response. The resolutions rejected the right of the national government to limit political speech in such a manner and reserved for the states the authority to refuse to enforce a federal law that went against the constitutional powers of government.

Roane agreed with the resolutions though he had no role in their construction. He was most influenced by the call of state nullification of federal laws that were unconstitutional. This declaration of state sovereignty and power would be offered up by Roane during subsequent constitutional cases when Virginia claimed that the federal courts could not overrule state courts.

The election of Jefferson as president promised a changed relationship between the national and state governments. It has been subsequently suggested that Roane was Jefferson's choice to be Supreme Court chief justice after the resignation of Oliver Ellsworth. But the outgoing president, John Adams, appointed John Marshall to that position. His rise to chief justice in 1801 marked the beginning of a two-decade duel between the United States Supreme Court and the Virginia Court of Appeals, between John Marshall and Spencer Roane.

John Marshall was the consummate federalist, a man who agreed with the Hamiltonian idea of a national state bound together by commerce. He also saw state legislatures and politicians as the greatest threat to the economic development of the country. Marshall sought to expand judicial power to protect property rights. It was inevitable he would clash with the judges in the highest court of the largest and most powerful of southern states. Several Marshall Court cases originated in Virginia, and others prompted loud disagreements from Roane.

One decision, though, that did not draw Roane's ire was Marshall's decision in *Marbury v. Madison* (1803), which is recognized as having established judicial review, that is, the power to examine and strike down unconstitutional acts of federal legislation. Roane supported the power of federal judges to void national laws that were unconstitutional; moreover, because the decision in *Marbury* referred to federal power, it did not threaten the state sovereignty so jealously guarded by the judge. Another case, though, struck at the power of the state and its courts.

The first great clash between Roane and Marshall originated in a dispute between British loyalists and revolutionaries in Virginia. One such loyalist, Lord Fairfax, had his estate seized and sold by the state of Virginia. Fairfax's heirs claimed ownership of the same land, selling that interest to several Virginians, including John Marshall. The heirs claimed that the dispute over the land had been settled by the Jay Treaty, which protected the property of British loyalists from government seizure.

The case reached the Virginia Court of Appeals, which upheld the seizure of the land. That decision was overturned by the federal Supreme Court, which ruled the Jay Treaty took precedence over any state law. The case then returned to the Virginia Court of Appeals where Roane issued a decision directly challenging the power of the federal courts. Roane stated in a sweeping opinion that the Supreme Court had no power to overturn a state court decision. He ruled that the federal law that granted it that power, the Judiciary Act of 1789, was unconstitutional in granting the Supreme Court jurisdiction over state court decisions. Roane's argument in *Martin v. Hunter's Lessee* (1816) was one of the most direct attacks on federal judicial power and one in a series of arguments that the Constitution was composed by the states, which retained considerable independence, including the functioning of their courts systems separate from the federal courts.

Roane's arguments had little effect on the Supreme Court when *Martin* was appealed to the justices for a second time. In his response, Justice Joseph Story ruled that under the Constitution and the law, federal courts could overrule state courts in matters involving federal law or treaties. According to Story, the federal Constitution was supreme over the states, and because the federal courts were granted the power to interpret that Constitution, their interpretation would always be final.

The dispute over the power of state courts in *Martin* established the supremacy of the federal courts and placed state judges under the authority of federal judges when considering the reach of federal law and treaties. Roane saw his claim of state court independence completely rejected by the Supreme Court.

Although his public battles with the Marshall Court are better known, Roane was also involved in interpreting the Virginia constitution and the transformation of Virginia from a British colony to a sovereign state. One of the major issues in Virginia during Roane's life was the role of religion in the new society. While a legislator, Roane had opposed a religious assessment against Virginians. This tax would have been used to fund the state church. As a judge on the Court of Appeals, Roane was asked to rule on a law that was meant to disestablish the Episcopal Church as the official religion of the state.

The 1802 law allowed Virginia to seize abandoned church property and sell it. The reasoning for the seizure was that as an established church, the property had been purchased with state funds. Under the new Virginia constitution and with a series of resolutions that ended the state church in Virginia, the state was no longer able to maintain church property at its own expense. The Episcopal Church went to court, arguing that the law violated the constitutional prohibition against seizure of property.

Roane wrote for the court in the case of *Turpin v. Locket* (1804) and upheld the state law as a proper disestablishment of religion. The land could be seized because the state of Virginia had decided that there would be no state church. The Episcopal Church appealed to the Supreme Court, which overruled Roane and struck down the law. This decision, though, did not draw a response from the judge either in his court writings or in his other favorite forum, the Richmond newspaper he had helped to create.

Holding strong views and having served in a political office, Roane sought forums for stating his constitutional views on state power and the federal Constitution. That forum was the newspaper that Roane helped create along with others who agreed with his views. Roane was a member of the most prominent and politically connected trio of Virginians, known as the Richmond Junto. Thomas Ritchie and William Brockenbrough joined Roane in opposing the federal judiciary and the broad reading of constitutional power favored by Marshall. Ritchie was the publisher of one of the more strident and influential states' rights newspapers in the South. He cofounded the *Richmond Enquirer* with Roane, and the men used its pages to express their opinions about many of the important Marshall Court opinions. William Brockenbrough was also a judge in the lower Virginia courts. He used his opinions to express his states' rights views and also wrote in the *Enquirer*.

As Roane and Marshall clashed, the judge found another prominent ally in Virginia. The retired Thomas Jefferson grew professionally closer to Roane, offering his own letters and published comments in support of Roane's views. Roane served on a commission that chose to locate Jefferson's University of Virginia on the grounds of Center College. He also participated in the debate with Jefferson over the establishment of the entire educational system in Virginia. In this debate, Roane displayed his usual concern for individual rights and protection against state coercion. He disagreed with Jefferson's call for a literacy requirement to vote and with Jefferson's views on religion. These disagreements over Virginia politics did not sour their agreement on national politics, though Jefferson was heard to say at the opening of the University of Virginia that Roane could not have taught at the university because of his lack of scholarship.

Spencer Roane served on the Virginia Court of Appeals until his death in 1822. It was during his last years on the court that the greatest dispute over federal and state relations broke into the open. The Marshall opinion in *McCulloch v. Maryland* (1819), creating a broad congressional power to create agencies to carry out federal laws, drew an anonymous response from Roane. Writing under the name of Hampden, a figure in British history, Roane used the pages of the *Richmond Enquirer* to take issue with the *McCulloch* decision. Roane argued that the case represented an aggrandizement of congressional power to such a degree that there was no limit on the type of laws that Congress could pass. Because *McCulloch* overturned a state law, Roane worried that Congress had been made supreme to state law and that state independence was being taken away. Roane's Hampden essays drew a response from Marshall defending his decision.

In 1821, Roane directly clashed with Marshall and his Court. The case, *Cohens v. Virginia*, dealt with a federal lottery. Cohens sold tickets for the federal lottery in Virginia, which had a state law against such lotteries. He was charged with violation of the law and fined. Cohens appealed to the Virginia Court of Appeals, which took the stand that the state law banning lotteries overrode the federal law in Virginia. Cohens's appeal to the United States Supreme Court drew an immediate response from Roane.

Roane argued that Cohens's case could not be heard by the Supreme

Court. According to Roane, the Eleventh Amendment, which prohibited individuals from suing a state in federal court, prohibited appeals of state court decisions in federal courts. Hence the Virginia Court of Appeals would be the last court to hear and decide Cohens's case.

Chief Justice Marshall and the Court disagreed. Marshall stated that the Eleventh Amendment did not apply to appeals because appeals established the supremacy of the federal courts over state courts when ruling on federal law. *Cohens* was a partial victory for Roane in that Marshall upheld Cohens's conviction under state law (deciding that Congress had not intended for residents of the District of Columbia to sell tickets in states where such sale was illegal), but the ruling on federal judicial power served as another defeat in Roane's crusade to limit the ability of federal courts to overturn state decisions.

Roane's response to the *Cohens* decision proved to be his last battle with Marshall. Using the *Enquirer,* Roane wrote five essays under the name Algernon Sidney. In his writings, Roane criticized Marshall's opinion as sophistry, arguing that by making the federal courts supreme he was ignoring the checks and balances system of the Constitution. Roane noted that the Constitution represented a compact between the states that allowed for state sovereignty. According to Roane, *Cohens* was another example of aggrandizement of federal power at the expense of the states.

Roane died at home on 4 September 1822 after an extended illness. Interestingly enough, he had spent his last years living on a property that was next to John Marshall's estate. Yet these two neighbors had been unable to bridge the differences in their constitutional views. With his death, many of Roane's views on states' rights were adopted by others less interested in constitutional theory than in asserting political goals of secession.

Roane's role in the development of constitutional theory in the formative years of the Constitution tended to be negative. Most of his arguments for state judicial supremacy were rejected by the Supreme Court and the American public. Roane is best remembered as a polemicist rather than a legal scholar. Yet Roane's judicial writings extended beyond the major Supreme Court cases. Many of his state rulings protected individuals from excessive state power. At the same time, the theme of his arguments for less government decentralization became more popular during the final decades of the twentieth century as states began to reassert their own authority.

Douglas Clouatre

References and Further Reading:

Davis, Richard. 1964. *Intellectual Life in Jefferson's Virginia*. Chapel Hill.: University of North Carolina Press.

Hobson, Charles F. 1996. *The Great Chief Justice: John Marshall and the Rule of Law.* Lawrence: University Press of Kansas.
Horsnell, Margaret. 1986. *Spencer Roane: Judicial Advocate of Jeffersonian Principles.* New York: Garland Publishing.
Malone, Dumas. 1981. *Jefferson and His Times: The Sage of Monticello.* Boston: Little, Brown.
Smith, Jean Edward. 1996. *John Marshall: Definer of a Nation.* New York: Henry Holt and Co.

RUFFIN, THOMAS

(1787–1870)

THOMAS RUFFIN
National Archives

THOMAS RUFFIN IS REGARDED as one of the antebellum South's most important judges. After he had served on the North Carolina Superior Court from 1816 to 1818 and from 1825 to 1829, the state legislature selected Ruffin to serve on the state Supreme Court, where he stayed from 1829 to 1852. He spent the years from 1833 to his retirement from the bench as chief justice. During his time on the bench, which included an additional year of service from 1858 to 1859, he rendered decisions in about 1,500 cases (Morris 1999, 45). Prior to being appointed a judge, Ruffin had established himself as an accomplished, albeit aggressive, attorney, and he was active in North Carolina politics, especially during his early career. As a judge, Ruffin's opinions were noted for their "pragmatism" and their "flexibility" (Huebner 1999, 131).

Thomas Ruffin was born to Sterling and Alice Roane Ruffin in King and Queen County, Virginia, in November 1787. His mother was a first cousin of Virginia judge Spencer Roane. When Thomas Ruffin was relatively young, his family moved to North Carolina, where Ruffin attended school before going to the College of New Jersey, today's Princeton University. On his return, Ruffin read law under Archibald D. Murphey, a prominent attorney in the Piedmont area of North Carolina whose advocacy of "educational advancement, internal improvements, and constitutional reform" undoubtedly influenced Ruffin (Huebner 1999, 133). Ruffin gained admission to the bar in 1808, marrying Annie M. Kirkland of Hillsboro the next year. In 1813, Ruffin was elected to the North Carolina House of Commons where, in three years, he became speaker. A Jeffersonian Democrat, he also served as a presidential elector for James Monroe and as a later supporter of William Crawford (after which he appears to have become fairly disillusioned with politics). He was widely respected and also served for a time as president of the State Bank of North Carolina, apparently rescuing it from probable bankruptcy.

After his appointment to the North Carolina Supreme Court, Ruffin moved to Alamance County. He was a successful planter who owned more than 100 slaves whom he employed on plantations in Rockingham and Alamance Counties (Morris 1999, 45). Although he never formally opened a law school, Ruffin also mentored many North Carolinians seeking entrance to the bar (Heubner 1999, 134). An active Episcopalian, Ruffin was generally considered to be a southern gentleman who was "hard-working, warm, humane, and religious" (Yanuck 1955, 460), but his personal beliefs did not always translate into policies, especially toward slaves, that individuals would today associate with Christianity.

Ruffin is, in fact, probably best known for his decision in the case of *State v. Mann* (1829). Faced in this decision with a master who had shot and wounded a slave as she fled from chastisement and refused to heed his call to stop, Ruffin refused to convict the slave owner of battery. Focusing on what he believed to be the societal benefits of slavery, Ruffin concluded that "the power of the master must be absolute to render the submission of the slave perfect" (quoted in Yanuck 1955, 462). Like other judges from the period who noted that there was sometimes a disjunction between law and justice when slavery was at issue, Ruffin went on to justify his view that the master's violence was limited only by state law with the observation that

> as a principle of moral right every person in his retirement must repudiate it. . . . But in the actual condition of things it must be so. There is no remedy. This discipline belongs to the state of slavery. They cannot be disunited, without abrogating at once the rights of the master, and absolving the slave from his subjection. It constitutes the curse of slavery to both the bond and free portions of our population. But it is inherent in the relation of master and slave. (Quoted 462–463)

Ruffin thus subordinated his views of morality to what he believed to be the necessities of a slave economy.

In other cases, Ruffin did somewhat modify the severity of his judgment. In particular in *State v. Hoover* (1839), Ruffin was willing to convict a slave owner who had cruelty tortured and killed a slave. In yet another case, however, *State v. Caesar* (1849), Ruffin was the only one of three judges who was unwilling to mitigate the punishment for an attack by a slave on whites who were abusing a fellow slave. Ruffin reasoned that slaves were expected to behave in an obsequious manner, consistent with their status (Heubner 1999, 150–151). In other decisions involving slavery, Ruffin was more understanding, commending a trustee who decided to sell slave children from a single family as a group rather than splitting them apart and also allowing slave owners to manumit their slaves (Yanuck 1955, 469–470).

Although Ruffin's language in *State v. Mann* had suggested that he viewed slavery as a moral evil, as the slavery debate progressed, Ruffin actually argued, in conjunction with other slave apologists, such as Judge William Harper, that the system of "mixed labor" in the South was superior to that elsewhere. As one of Ruffin's most able commentators has explained, "by the middle of the 1850s, Ruffin believed that paternalistic slavery was the highest ideal to which southern society could aspire. In simplest terms, slavery served the public good—the interests of whites and blacks" (Heubner 1999, 153).

Fortunately, Ruffin's legacy extended beyond his arguments on behalf of slavery. One of his positive legacies was his fight for judicial independence. Faced shortly after his election with a decrease in judicial salaries—which troubled Ruffin not so much for its effect on his own finances as for its effect on the independence of the judicial branch—he was able to assert some judicial authority in *Hoke v. Henderson* (1833). North Carolina had adopted legislation requiring that judicial clerks, who had previously been appointed, now be elected. When clerk Henderson refused to resign, in an opinion that stressed the importance of judicial service during good behavior, Ruffin was able to vindicate his claim by holding that the office constituted a type of property and that the legislature had no authority to deprive individuals of such property (Huebner 1999, 136–137). An astute observer of Ruffin's life observed that this decision appeared to mark a turning point, after which the state began to grant courts greater independence and treat them with greater respect (137).

Although industrialization is more frequently associated with the nineteenth-century North than the South, the South too was facing issues dealing with the expansion of new industries and modes of transportation. At about the same time that Chief Justice Roger Taney was modifying earlier rulings by the Marshall Court on property to accommodate progress (most notably in the 1837 case of *Charles River Bridge v. Warren Bridge*), state judges were coping with similar issues. Lemuel Shaw, the chief justice of the Massachusetts Supreme Court, is often credited with allowing states to appropriate property under their right of eminent domain, which provides that owners of such condemned property be given "just compensation." Ruffin also contributed to this development, issuing an opinion in *Wellington, et al., Petitioners* (1834) that upheld the right of the state legislatures to facilitate progress by permitting such appropriations. Ruffin's decision apparently went even further in its reasoning than did Shaw's in recognizing that, even when railroads were privately owned, their construction contributed to a legitimate "public purpose" (Heubner 1999, 138–139). Significantly, Ruffin was willing to allow five men to decide on the value of the property seized by the government rather than requiring a jury of twelve, as some thought the Constitution required (140).

Many of Ruffin's cases involved criminal law, and in this area, Ruffin had a reputation for toughness. He refused to require "malice aforethought" in convicting a man of biting off an enemy's ear in a fight (Heubner 1999, 142). Similarly, he refused to exonerate individuals who provoked opponents into a fight and then killed them under the guise of self-defense. In one case he observed that "To follow a person and seek a combat with him for the purpose of killing him, and covering the act with the pretense of a dangerous resistance to a moderate assault, is nothing less than wreaking a diabolical vengeance" (*State v. Martin,* 1841, as quoted 143).

Comparing Ruffin to other southern judges of the time period, Timothy Heubner has noted that he resembled them "in accumulating a substantive record upholding the convictions of violent criminals. Relying on North Carolina precedent and established common-law authorities, Ruffin consistently upheld the instructions of trial judges that involved the distinctions among murder, manslaughter, and excusable homicide" (1999, 145).

Although many judges choose to die in harness, Ruffin retired from the Supreme Court in 1852 and resumed his life as a planter (serving from 1854 to 1860 as president of the North Carolina Agricultural Society) while maintaining an interest in the preservation of judicial independence. As war approached, Ruffin first tried to seek compromise, and he was one of the most elderly men who attended the Old Gentleman's, or Peace, Convention in 1861 in Washington, D.C., in an attempt to avoid civil war. Ruffin initially proclaimed that "I came to maintain and preserve this glorious Government! I came here for Union and peace!" and that "I was born before the Constitution was adopted. May God grant that I do not outlive it" (quoted in Huebner 1999, 155). Faced with intransigence by both pro- and antislavery forces, however, Ruffin's attitude hardened during the course of the convention. Although never as vehement in support of the southern cause as his firebrand cousin, Virginia's Edmund Ruffin, Ruffin nonetheless viewed the war as a legitimate exercise of the right of revolution.

At the end of the war Ruffin succeeded in obtaining a pardon from Pres. Andrew Johnson. Although Ruffin opposed the more liberal constitution

George Lewis Ruffin (1834–1886)

George Lewis Ruffin was the first African American to graduate from the Harvard Law School or from any law school in the United States. He was the oldest of eight children born to George Washington Ruffin and Nancy Ruffin, free blacks then residing in Richmond, Virginia. Mrs. Ruffin (apparently with her husband's consent) later moved with her children to Boston, largely in the hopes of securing a better education than would be possible for them in the South. George had moved to Boston at age seventeen the previous year. After graduating from the public schools of Boston, Ruffin became a barber.

In 1864 Ruffin attended the First National Convention of Colored Men, held in Syracuse, New York. Inspired in part by Frederick Douglass, Ruffin began to study in the law offices of Harvey Jewell when he returned to Boston. He entered the Harvard Law School in 1868 at the age of thirty-four and graduated after two semesters.

In 1870 Ruffin was elected to the Massachusetts legislature, and although he was defeated as a Labor candidate for the position of state attorney general during his second term, he placed as the fourth of seven candidates (Smith 1995, 218). Ruffin, who was later elected to the Boston Common Council, practiced law in Boston. He was a strong supporter of the presidency of Ulysses S. Grant and wrote the introduction to Frederick Douglass's autobiography.

Although Ruffin had continued to support the Republican candidate for governor after Benjamin Butler had switched parties and run for that post as a Democrat, the victorious Butler nonetheless nominated Ruffin to fill a vacancy in the state district court for Charleston. After confirmation by the executive council, the governor proudly swore in Ruffin. Ruffin noted: "I can only account for this action

(continues)

drawn up by a Reconstruction government, in 1870 he advised his son against joining the Ku Klux Klan, believing that "the whole proceeding is against law and the civil power of government and assumes to supersede by taking the power of trying, condemning, and punishing in their own hands" (Heubner 1999, 159). Ultimately, then, Ruffin acknowledged greater allegiance to the rule of law than to the southern system that he had tried so long to uphold.

John R. Vile

References and Further Reading:

Brady, Patrick S. 1978. "Slavery, Race, and the Criminal Law in Antebellum North Carolina: A Reconsideration of the Thomas Ruffin Court." *North Carolina Central Law Journal* 10: 248–260.

(continued)

of his excellency on the ground that he wished to testify, in a complimentary manner, his pleasure that a representative of my race had at length been confirmed for the position" (quoted in Smith 1995, 230).

Only two other African Americans in Massachusetts had previously held judicial posts, one as a justice of the peace and the other as a county magistrate (Smith 1995, 230–231). Ruffin's tenure was cut short by death from kidney failure three years after his appointment as a judge. His wife, Josephine St. Pierre Ruffin, became a leader in the women's movement.

Often discouraged by the hypocritical rhetoric of American freedom when compared to the treatment that African Americans received, Ruffin identified with members of his race who had not been born free and who had not been accorded the opportunities he had received. The author of the most comprehensive article on Ruffin noted that

> George Lewis Ruffin, born free, could have determined that his stature as the descendant of free black parents separated him from the plight of his people. He might have determined that a Harvard law degree lifted him above the obligation to assist his people to fight for a better social and political position in America. On the contrary, Ruffin made the plight of black people his plight and used his Harvard law degree to fight for the liberation of black people from the badges of slavery. He never turned his back on his people. He impressed the world with his brilliance; the tongues of white and black people across the country spoke of it, forever sealing his name in the history of Harvard Law School, in America's legal and political history, in African-American history, and in the history of Boston, freedom's birthplace. (Smith 1995, 235)

REFERENCE:

Smith, J. Clay, Jr. 1995. "In Freedom's Birthplace: The Making of George Lewis Ruffin, the First Black Law Graduate of Harvard University." *Howard Law Journal* 39 (Fall): 201–235.

Huebner, Timothy S. 1999. *The Southern Judicial Tradition: State Judges and Sectional Distinctiveness, 1790–1890*. Athens: The University of Georgia Press.

Morris, Thomas D. 1999. "Ruffin, Thomas." In *American National Biography*, vol. 19, edited by John A. Garraty and Mark C. Carnes. New York: Oxford University Press, 45–46.

Yanuck, Julius. 1955. "Thomas Ruffin and North Carolina Slave Law." *The Journal of Southern History* 21 (November): 456–475.

RYAN, EDWARD GEORGE

(1810–1880)

EDWARD GEORGE RYAN, LAWYER, publisher, politician, orator, and —from 1874 to 1880—third chief justice of the Wisconsin Supreme Court, was a man of extraordinary legal ability. Appointed 16 June 1874 by Gov. William Taylor, Ryan was sixty-four years old when he replaced retiring Chief Justice Luther S. Dixon. Although Ryan's legal skills as an attorney were well admired, he had no judicial experience. The wisdom of Taylor's decision, however, was quickly reaffirmed when Ryan, a lifelong Democrat running unopposed in a dominantly Republican state, was popularly elected on 16 April 1875.

EDWARD GEORGE RYAN
Wisconsin Historical Society

From 1874 to 1878 Ryan's presence dominated the three-man court. In addition to issuing his own opinions, often on the most complex cases, he also supplied the legal reasoning and arguments for many cases assigned to fellow justices Orasmus Cole and William P. Lyon.

The quantity of the work was astonishing. In 1875, for example, the court, convening two terms each year, heard 228 cases. By July, Ryan had lost fifteen pounds from the strain and labor (all opinions were hand written by the justices themselves) (Beitzinger 1955, 593). Harlow Orton, who would, with David Taylor, soon become a justice himself—when the legislature, in 1878, expanded the court to five members—wrote of Ryan that year: "He brings all the learning and all the law . . . His opinions are not only conclusive, but exhaustive of all the subjects embraced" (594; Beitzinger offered a complete discussion of the Ryan court justices). Legal historian and lawyer Joseph A. Ranney, describing, more than a century later, the experience of reading a Ryan declamation, noted, "one feels as though one is listening to an irascible but brilliant pedagogue examine the topic at hand from all angles, like a toy, and then produce a decision that seems at the time definitive and unanswerable" (Wisconsin's Legal History: Part II. Available at <www.wisbar.org>).

Edward George Ryan was a complex personality of unfathomable and irreconcilable themes. He himself judged his life, excepting his judicial labors, a failure. Possessed of a querulous and splenetic spirit of pathological proportion, his existence was an endless fuse of destructive petty quarrels woven from the combative threads of suspicion, arrogance, and intolerance. When ignited by some random spark from his mercurial temperament, all would abruptly explode.

Few were unaware of this dark facet of Ryan's character. William Vilas, friend and future Wisconsin senator, noted that Ryan's temper "made him terrible to his friends as well as his enemies; tyrannical, perhaps sometimes cruel . . . violent and hostile where he should have been friendly." It should be noted, however, that Ryan's demon temper never reduced him to incoherence; he never lost control on the bench; and the passion for perfection, which his temper betrayed, motivated the court to a higher standard.

Other aspects of Ryan's character were tragic. A deeply religious man who authored his own prayers and recited them daily—"Give me grace to bear patiently, to consider diligently, to understand rightly and decide justly" read one, in part (Winslow 1912, 313)—he nonetheless possessed little tolerance for those less gifted than himself. A champion of the individual over all combinations of power—economic, political, military—his wellspring was *passion against* privilege and its consequent injustice, not *compassion for* fallible human beings.

An Irish émigré, born and raised in a country without racial strife, Ryan was, nonetheless, an avowed racist. His private library, some 1,400 volumes, contained the treatises on ethnology and anthropology that had persuaded him that blacks were "an inferior and degraded" race. Mankind, he held, was a hierarchy of white intelligence at the top and black physicality at the bottom. Slavery was "a great social evil," and, although he profited nothing from the "peculiar institution," still, by the terms of his evolutionary view, it was "a necessary evil" (Beitzinger 1960, 56).

If blacks occupied the base of Ryan's social caste system, women occupied the apex. But the Ryan schema produced the same effect for both groups—

a kind of "frozen" exclusion by some principle of "otherness" that removed them from the fluid and privileged domain of white maleness.

Despite these tragic flaws of character, his contemporaries—supporters and detractors alike—acknowledged Justice Ryan as one of the nation's leading jurists. His aggressive passion forged and distilled creative decisions in Wisconsin tax law, the conduct of railroad and insurance industries, the emerging area of corporate tort liability, government regulation and oversight, legal ethics, and the relationship of federal and state courts. Justice John Winslow wrote that Ryan's life had "added vastly to the standing and prestige of (the) Court"; that his legal opinions "left a monument to his memory more enduring than brass or marble" (Winslow 1912, 306). On questions of the power of the state to control its own creations, the great corporations, Ryan helped to rebalance the equation between the controlling effect of industrial wealth and the free agency of human beings.

Edward George Ryan was born 13 November 1810 at New Castle House estate, near the village of Enfield, Meath County, Ireland. The second son of Edward and Abby (Keogh) Ryan, and one of ten children, young Edward was "born and educated in full sight of wealth but inheriting no share of it beyond its refining influence" ("Ryan Obituary" 1880). The family, initially prosperous, lost everything when their landholding fell into debt. An annuity set aside by the Keogh grandfather, however, guaranteed the education of all the Ryan children. Young Edward, from 1820 to 1827, attended an all-boys Jesuit boarding school, Clongowes Wood College, in Kildare.

In 1830 Ryan emigrated to the United States. For six years he lived in New York City, reading law, teaching school, and immersing himself in the Democratic politics of Tammany Hall. He was naturalized 9 April and admitted to the bar 13 May 1836. Both events were easy formalities for those with Tammany Hall patronage. That same year he relocated to Chicago.

In Chicago, often ill, he practiced law. He served briefly, in 1841, as state's attorney for the Seventh Judicial Circuit. He also published, from 4 April 1840 to 22 August 1841, a Democratic newspaper, the *Chicago Tribune* (not the precursor of today's *Chicago Tribune*). Often embroiled in fisticuffs, but never as victor, he once challenged an adversary to a duel, only to be disdainfully dismissed. Prof. Alfons Beitzinger, the authoritative voice on Ryan's life, wrote, "Ryan was . . . recognized as a singularly rare character—an Irishman who could not fight. 'Who hasn't licked Ryan?' became a byword in Chicago" (1960, 12).

In 1842 Ryan married Mary Graham, of Dixon, Illinois, and moved to Racine, in territorial Wisconsin. In 1846 he gained prominence as a delegate to the first state constitutional convention, authoring the radical antibanking provision that ultimately defeated the constitution. But with the untimely death of his wife in 1847, Ryan, with two infant children, moved

Reah Mary Whitehead (1883–1972)

Washington State's first female judge, Reah Mary Whitehead, was born in Kansas City, Missouri, in 1883 and moved to Seattle in 1890. She began work as a legal stenographer in Alaska at the age of sixteen and subsequently enrolled at the School of Law at the University of Washington. She graduated and passed the bar in 1904. Initially working as a clerk for a judge and then for a prosecutor, she was appointed in 1909 as the first woman prosecutor in the state of Washington but was initially largely consigned to office work. She ran for the office of justice of the peace for the King County, Washington, Seattle District Court in 1914 and won the election over nine male competitors.

As a judge, Whitehead's cases were limited to civil matters involving no more than $100, but she also adjudicated criminal matters. Reporters were often so taken with the novelty of a female judge that their reports primarily focused on what she wore and how she looked. Whitehead believed that it was important for women to serve as judges. During a reelection campaign, she once said:

> There is no sex in brains. I didn't originate that statement, I simply adopted it in setting forth my belief that a woman is just as mentally capable as a man and that the State of Washington and King County in particular should have a woman superior court judge to even up matters. Don't get the idea that I think that I or any other woman can do judicial work better than a man. That's just the point at issue. It's that a woman's viewpoint plus a man's viewpoint equals the human viewpoint. And that is what our courts need. (Bragg 1998, 154)

Whitehead married a retired grocer named Frank Sidney Harrison in 1931, but she retained her maiden name, and they later divorced.

Whitehead retired after seven terms on the bench and was replaced by another woman. Whitehead died in 1972.

Reference:

Bragg, L. E. 1998. *More than Petticoats, Remarkable Washington Women*. (Helena, Mont.: Falcon Publishing, 149–157.

to Milwaukee. In 1848 he opened a law firm. (Today, twenty-five name changes later, its descendant is Michael Best and Friedrich LLC, the 150th largest law firm in the nation. Its client list, overcoming the Ryan antibanking stand, has included the five largest banks in Milwaukee.)

In 1850 Ryan married Caroline Willard Pierce, of Massachusetts. This union produced seven children, three of whom died before the age of three.

During the next quarter century Ryan was a commanding presence in the legal history of the new state. He appeared, from 1849 through 1874, in 375 cases (eighty-two before the Wisconsin Supreme Court, eleven before the United States Supreme Court; see Beitzinger 1956, table). In 1853 he argued for the impeachment of Judge Levi Hubbell, for accepting bribes; in

1854 he argued *In re Booth*, a high-profile fugitive slave law and states' rights controversy; in 1855, against his own party's interest, he represented Republican Coles Bashford's successful challenge, on grounds of fraud, of Democrat William Barstow's gubernatorial election (by a plurality of 157 votes), where Ryan's high-profile nonpartisanship impressed and calmed an inflamed state.

In 1862 Ryan authored *Address to the People by the Democracy of Wisconsin*. Called "the Ryan address," it attacked the "unconstitutional" aspects of the Lincoln administration's conduct of the war. The resultant storm, however, ended any possible political career for Ryan. Many branded him a copperhead and a traitor. In 1863, with Republicans carrying the elections, Ryan, buried in opprobrium, sank into oblivion. From 1866 to 1869 he participated in only fifteen legal cases. Finally, in April 1870, financially impoverished and repudiated by the Democratic Party, Ryan sought and was elected to the post of Milwaukee city attorney on the independent Citizens ticket. Reelected in 1871 and 1872, he lost the 1873 election.

On 16 June 1873, with the young Robert La Follette in the audience, Ryan addressed the graduating class of the Wisconsin Law School. In this famous address, he sculpted the ethical obligations of all members of the legal fraternity. He also warned of "vast corporate combinations of unexampled capital" where "money [took] the field as an organized power . . . [and] the question [arises] . . . which shall rule—wealth or man; which shall lead—money or intellect; who shall fill public stations—educated and patriotic free men, or the feudal serfs of corporate capital" (1873, 31–32).

The following June Ryan took his seat on the state supreme court.

Edward George Ryan, age seventy, died 20 October 1880, at his Madison home. The last years of his life were difficult. Estranged from wife and family, he, as Judge Jenkins noted, "Died as he lived, grand, gloomy and peculiar, wrapped in the solitude of his own originality" (Clark 1895, 250).

Christened a Roman Catholic, Ryan had, in the 1850s, become an Episcopalian. Taken by train to Milwaukee, he was buried there from St. James Episcopal Church. Having died in near penury, Ryan rested in an unmarked grave for many years. In 1909 the state bar of Wisconsin raised funds for the white granite obelisk that now delineates his resting place at the Forest Home Cemetery.

Most judges are best known by their cases. A brief summary of some notable Ryan cases follows.

Attorney General v. Chicago & Northwestern R. Co. (1874) was Ryan's first and greatest decision. It covered eighty-five pages and took almost four hours to deliver orally. It established the principle that corporations are subordinate to the state.

Ryan's exhaustive treatment of all issues involved—the power of the legislature to effect original charter, the state constitutional grant of original jurisdiction, the use of injunction as a prerogative writ—was breathtaking. Roscoe Pound, noted Professor Beitzinger, wrote that Ryan's opinion was "the leading American decision for the visitatorial jurisdiction of courts over corporations at the suit of the state" (1960, 120; see also 113–122).

Wight v. Rindskopf (1877) was a sharply worded decision decrying the exchange of immunity for evidence in a case—"corruption in the administration of public justice beyond justification" was Ryan's characterization (Winslow 1912, 350). He wrote that an attorney's retainer was a "sacred confidence" imposing "a duty" on him that his "professional learning and skill," his true strength, be practiced in "open contest" (350). A lawyer's "forensic ability is the only true professional influence on the course of justice," he said, concluding, "a lawyer may devote himself professionally to the legitimate business of his client; but he cannot be retained in whatever may not be rightfully and lawfully done. He may defend a wrong done in the past, but he cannot be privy to the doing of a wrong in the present. The profession is not sinless but its sins are all unprofessional" (350).

State ex rel. Drake v. Doyle (1876) involved Wisconsin's power to impose conditions on out-of-state corporations wishing to do business in the state. Collaterally, it involved a clarification of state and federal court jurisdiction. The United States Supreme Court, in *Insurance Company v. Morse* (1874), had found an 1870 Wisconsin statute, which prohibited a foreign company from removing actions brought against it in state courts to U.S. courts, unconstitutional and the licensing agreement made with respect to it void. Subsequently, a new 1872 Wisconsin law provided that if any foreign company licensed in Wisconsin petitioned to remove an action pending against it to a federal court, its license to do business in the state would be revoked.

Ryan wrote in *State ex rel. Drake v. Doyle*, "the State, having power to exclude entirely foreign corporations, had necessarily power to license them to enter the state upon condition of their forbearing to exercise a right, and revoke that license upon their attempting to exercise it" (Winslow 1907, 110). Later, the United States Supreme Court, in *Doyle vs. Continental Insurance Co* (1876), essentially upheld Ryan's reasoning.

In the Matter of the Motion to Admit Goodell (39 Wis. 232, 1875), the remarkable Lavinia Goodell, Wisconsin's first female lawyer, admitted to the Rock County bar on 17 June 1874, was denied admission to the Wisconsin State Supreme Court bar. Seen through the prism of today's urgent concerns for sexual equality of the workplace, it is the most well known and notorious of Judge Ryan's decisions. In 1875 it also met with national criticism (see Cleary 1991).

Ryan wrote,

> There are many employments in life not unfit for female character. The profession of the law is surely not one of these. The peculiar qualities of womanhood, its gentle graces, its sensibility, its tender susceptibility, its purity, its delicacy, its emotional impulses, its subordination of hard reason to sympathetic feeling, are surely not qualifications for forensic strife. . . . Womanhood is moulded for gentler and better things. (39 Wis. 245)

Then, deserting all caution, he opined,

> The law of nature destines and qualifies the female sex for the bearing and nurture of the children of our race and for the custody of the homes of the world and their maintenance in love and honor. And all life-long callings of women, inconsistent with these radical and sacred duties of their sex, as in the profession of law, are departures from the order of nature; and, when voluntary, treason against it. (245)

Craker v. Chicago & North Western Railway Co. (1875) held that a corporation is not liable for punitive damages for the willful acts of the employee unless it ratifies them. Called the Kissing Case, Ryan's gracefully piercing, sarcastic Irish wit was well displayed. A railroad, sued by a woman kissed against her will by its conductor, opined, in its defense, that the woman might have had a claim against it for assault if a third party had kissed her, as the conductor's protection against such an event would have been faulty. The railroad argued, however, that it was not liable, since it was its own employee that made the assault.

Ryan responded,

> It is contended . . . that if one hire out his dog to guard sheep against wolves, and the dog sleep while the wolf makes way with a sheep the owner is liable; but if the dog play wolf and devour the sheep himself, the owner is not liable. . . . The carrier's contract is to protect the passenger against all the world. The appellant's construction is that it was to protect the passenger against all the world *except* the conductor whom it appointed to protect her, reserving to the shepherd's dog a right to worry the sheep. No subtleties in the books could lead us to sanction so vicious an absurdity. (Winslow 1907, 112)

Kevin Collins

References and Further Reading:

Attorney General v. Chicago & Northwestern R. Co. 35 Wis. 425 (1874).

Beitzinger, Alfons J. 1955. "Chief Justice Ryan and His Colleagues." *Wisconsin Law Review* 1955: 592.

———. 1956. "Edward George Ryan—19th Century Lawyer." *Wisconsin Law Review* 1956 (March): 248

———. 1960. *Edward G. Ryan: Lion of the Law.* Madison: The State Historical Society of Wisconsin.

Clark, Gilbert J. 1895. *Life Sketches of Eminent Lawyers.* Vol. 2. Kansas City, Mo.: Lawyers International Publishing.

Cleary, Catherine B. 1991. "Lavinia Goodell, First Woman Lawyer in Wisconsin." *The Wisconsin Magazine of History* 74: 243–271.

Craker v. Chicago & North Western Railway Co. 36 Wis. 657 (1875).

Doyle v. Continental Insurance Company. 94 U.S. 535 (1876).

Hinton, John W. 1880. *Memorial Address on Edward G. Ryan, Late Chief Justice of Wisconsin, Delivered by John H. Hinton before the Moot Court of Milwaukee, November 4, 1880.* Milwaukee: The Court (located in the Wisconsin Historical Society Pamphlet Collection).

In the Matter of the Motion to Admit Goodell. 39 Wis. 232 (1875).

Insurance Company v. Morse. 87 U.S. 445 (1874).

Ryan, Edward G. 1873. *An Address Delivered before the Law Class of the University of Wisconsin, June 16, 1873.* Madison, Wis.: Democrat Co. Book and Job Printers.

"Ryan Obituary." 1880. *Milwaukee Sentinel*, October 20.

State ex rel. Drake v. Doyle. 40 Wis. 175 (1876).

Winslow, John Bradley. 1907. "Edward George Ryan." In *Great American Lawyers*, vol. 6, edited by William Draper Lewis. Philadelphia: The John C. Winston Company, 77–119.

———. 1912. *The Story of a Great Court.* Chicago: T. H. Flood and Company.

Wight v. Rindskopf. 43 Wis. 244 (1877).

SCHAEFER, WALTER VINCENT

(1904–1986)

WALTER VINCENT SCHAEFER
Illinois Issues, *University of Illinois at Springfield*

OFTEN NAMED ALONG WITH his friend Chief Justice Roger Traynor of the California Supreme Court as one of the leading scholar-judges on state courts, Walter Schaefer served on the Illinois Supreme Court from 1951 to 1976, before returning to the private practice of law and to the classroom at Northwestern University Law School where he had taught before being named to the bench. While serving as a state supreme court justice, Schaefer collected numerous accolades and honorary degrees and delivered some of the most prestigious lectures in the leading law schools, including the Oliver Wendell Holmes lectures at the Harvard Law School.

Schaefer was born in Grand Rapids, Michigan, in 1904 and received both his bachelor's and law degrees from the University of Chicago. Schaefer characterized his performance at Chicago as "pretty good" though "no world beater" (Jenner 1979, 694) and by all accounts devoted considerable time to his third-base position on Chicago's baseball team (before Chicago's president Robert M. Hutchins decreed that it would abandon varsity athletics) and its tennis team. The tennis team on which Schaefer played won the Big Ten championship two years in a row, and Schaefer's doubles partner went on to play on a Davis Cup team (694). Schaefer's devotion to intercollegiate athletics was such that when, during his junior year, he was in danger of having enough credits to graduate, he simply switched his major so he could return his senior year and serve as captain of the tennis team (Schaefer 1986, 1154).

Admitted to the Illinois bar in 1928, Schaefer spent the next two years drafting statutes for the Legislative Reference Bureau in the state capital, Springfield. It was there that he developed a passion for clarity and brevity, two traits that marked his later judicial decisions (Ward 1979, 1153). His experience as a legislative draftsman led directly to one of the seminal events both of his early career and of the legal history of the state of Illinois.

In 1931, a number of young Illinois lawyers, including Walter Schaefer and Albert Jenner (founding partner of the Chicago firm Jenner and Block), formed the Younger Members Committee on Amendment of the Law along with other lawyers who had, like Schaefer, served in the Legislative Reference Bureau. With the blessing of the senior members of the Chicago Bar Association, the Younger Members Committee set about to reform the law in Illinois. For the next several years, the committee drafted, introduced, and orchestrated the passage of acts that reformed and codified the law in the probate, mortgage, and criminal law (Jenner 1979, 694–695).

At about the same time, a distinguished group of scholars was completing a statute intended to replace Illinois's common law pleading system with a modern pleading and practice statute. The Illinois Bar Association then became involved, and its young members Jenner and Schaefer were dispatched to compare the draft against the Illinois Revised Statutes. By mid-October 1931, they had finished their work and made recommendations to the Drafting Committee; the revised draft was then sent to practitioners and judges for comment. After further discussion, the draft was submitted to the Illinois General Assembly in 1933, and Jenner and Schaefer were dispatched to aid the assembly as the bill made its way through the legislative process. The new Civil Practice Act was signed into law in 1933 and took effect the following year. But Jenner and Schaefer's role was not yet complete. Not only did they annotate the act, they also toured the state with the new president of the state Bar Association making presentations and otherwise explaining the new act. The two young lawyers, now close friends, then prepared the new rules for the Illinois Supreme Court and even taught a night class for lawyers wishing to become conversant with its intricacies. Owing to his experiences in Illinois, Schaefer was then invited to assist Yale Law School dean Charles Clark in preparing the Federal Rules of Civil Procedure (Jenner 1979, 697–698).

Following his work in New Haven, Schaefer left for Washington, D.C., one of many bright young lawyers attracted to the energy and excitement surrounding the first New Deal. Schaefer worked for the Agricultural Adjustment Administration (headed for a time by future federal judge Jerome

Frank) and the Reconstruction Finance Corporation. He then returned to Illinois to work as assistant corporation counsel for the city of Chicago (Jenner 1979, 698–699).

In 1940, Schaefer joined the faculty at Northwestern University's law school, a position that he held—excepting only a two-year interlude as a bankruptcy referee occasioned by the war-induced drop in law school enrollment—until 1951, when he was appointed to the state high court. At Northwestern Schaefer taught, among other courses, civil procedure and evidence. His former students fondly remembered him as an individual possessed of "an almost biblical pragmatism" (Allen 1979, 692). Former colleagues at the law school commented not only on Schaefer's unabashed enthusiasm for "the Kids," as he called his students, but also for his wise and patient mentoring of junior faculty members (Allen 1986, 1149–1150). As one former colleague reflected upon the occasion of Schaefer's retirement from the Illinois Supreme Court:

> His kindly and agreeable manner, his solid stock of legal learning, his tenacious patience in trying to communicate that learning to others, his capacity for useful and stimulating reflection about the larger ends of the law, his ability to relate established legal principles to the realities of the moment and to identify the resulting tensions and their possible solvents, his willingness to contemplate, and actively to forward, evolution and development of those principles by the uses of reason—all served as badges of his value in the classroom as well as visible precursors of the great judicial career which ultimately was to be his. (McGowan 1979, 679)

Schaefer's judicial career was due in large part to serendipity. Illinois has an elective judiciary, and the mid-century Illinois constitution provided that the governor could fill vacancies on the state supreme court only if they occurred in the final year of the occupant's term. Such a contingency occurred in March 1951, and Gov. Adlai Stevenson appointed Schaefer to fill the vacancy. According to one friend of both men, upon learning of the vacancy, Governor Stevenson exclaimed "Now I can have Walter!" (McGowan 1986, 1151). Almost immediately after Schaefer began serving, however, he had to run in the June election. The election was not a shoo-in, as Schaefer was in a district composed of Cook County and neighboring counties not known for their support of Democratic candidates. Nevertheless, the head of the Cook County Democratic organization, future Chicago mayor Richard J. Daley, was persuaded to mobilize his base to elect Schaefer. "To him," wrote one commentator, "must go most of the credit for assuring Walter's judicial career" (1151). Thereafter, Schaefer won reelection to the bench until his retirement in 1976.

Perhaps the most famous case in which Justice Schaefer participated was that of *People v. Escobedo* (190 N.E.2d 825 [1963]), in which the Illinois Supreme Court held that a suspect's confession to the crime of murder was admissible despite the fact that the suspect's lawyer was denied the opportunity to advise his client while in police custody. The United States Supreme Court disagreed, found that Escobedo's right to legal counsel was violated when the police refused him access to his lawyer, and held that his confession should have been excluded (*Escobedo v. Illinois*, 378 U.S. 478 [1964]).

The *Escobedo* case was controversial, as was the later *Miranda* case, in which the Supreme Court held, among other things, that when placed under arrest, a person had to be apprised of his right to remain silent and his right to an attorney. Critics of the Warren Court decisions complained that the decisions placed too many restrictions on law enforcement officers, with public safety suffering as a result.

Justice Schaefer was among these critics. Soon after being appointed to the bench, Schaefer was asked to deliver the prestigious Oliver Wendell Holmes Lectures at the Harvard Law School for 1956. There, he sounded a cautionary note about the Supreme Court's apparent, though still nascent, desire to nationalize constitutional criminal procedure (Schaefer 1956). But his criticisms were not the simplistic "law and order" polemics that were the staple of politicians and pundits during the 1960s. Schaefer often criticized the Court's constitutional pronouncements for promising more than the Supreme Court—or any court for that matter—could deliver.

For example, he criticized the Supreme Court's decision in the *Miranda* case for giving insufficient attention to the likely effects of a defendant's choice to remain silent. He faulted that decision for failing to "fairly advis[e] the suspect of all of the relevant considerations that bear upon his choice," for example, the fact that whether or not adverse commentary upon a decision to remain silent is permitted, "not even the Supreme Court can prevent the judge or the jurors who are trying the case from drawing adverse inferences from the silence of a defendant, whether at a trial or before it" (Schaefer 1969, 10). Although he agreed "that a suspect should not be compelled to answer and that a defendant should not be required against his will to take the witness stand," it was his opinion that "it is entirely unsound to exclude from consideration at the trial the silence of a suspect involved in circumstances reasonably calling for explanation, or of a defendant who does not take the stand. It therefore seems to me imperative that the privilege against self-incrimination be modified to permit comment upon such silence" (Schaefer 1966a, 520).

He was also a critic of the exclusionary rule that rejected evidence seized in violation of the Fourth Amendment. But again his criticism was of a different flavor than most. Schaefer felt that the rule was deficient because of its underinclusiveness. He noted that "it is available only to those who are formally charged with criminal offenses. It does not bear at all upon the overzealous officer whose victims never appear in court. Thus, it does little to curb the obvious potential for evil in the promiscuous use of stop and frisk as a technique of harassment" (Schaefer 1969, 14).

His other writings focused on the technique of judging. In 1955, for example, he delivered the Ernst Freund lectures at the University of Chicago Law School. There, he discussed analogical reasoning used by common law judges to keep the law supple by enabling it to adapt to changes in circumstances. He went on to ask whether such reasoning by analogy was not also appropriate when dealing with statutory materials, given the growing involvement of legislatures in law reform and their disinclination to keep their work product up-to-date (Schaefer 1966b). Another perennial concern of Schaefer's was with how the Supreme Court handled the implementation of its decisions: whether it would make new constitutional rules retroactive or whether they would operate only prospectively (Schaefer 1982, 1967).

In recognition of his contributions to the bench and bar, Schaefer was awarded the American Bar Association's medal for service to the cause of American jurisprudence. He was similarly feted by the American Judicature Society and the Illinois Bar Association, both in 1977. In addition to the distinguished lectures he gave at Harvard, Chicago, Northwestern, and New York University, Schaefer was the recipient of honorary degrees from Northwestern, the University of Chicago, John Marshall Law School, Lake Forest College, Notre Dame University, and DePaul University. He was also a member of the American Law Institute and the American Academy of Arts and Sciences. Justice Schaefer died in 1986 at the age of eighty-two.

Brannon P. Denning

References and Further Reading:

Allen, Francis A. 1979. "In Honor of Walter V. Schaefer." *Northwestern University Law Review* 74: 691–693.

———. 1986. "In Memoriam: Walter V. Schaefer." *Northwestern University Law Review* 80: 1149–1150.

Jenner, Albert E. 1979. "In Honor of Walter V. Schaefer." *Northwestern University Law Review* 74: 693–700.

McGowan, Carl. 1979. "In Honor of Walter V. Schaefer." *Northwestern University Law Review* 74: 678–682.

———. 1986. "In Memoriam: Walter V. Schaefer." *Northwestern University Law Review* 80: 1151–1152.

Schaefer, Nancy. 1986. "In Memoriam: Walter V. Schaefer." *Northwestern University Law Review* 80: 1154–1155.

Schaefer, Walter V. 1956. "Federalism and State Criminal Procedure." *Harvard Law Review* 70: 1–26.

———. 1965. "Chief Justice Traynor and the Judicial Process." *California Law Review* 53: 11–24.

———. 1966a. "Police Interrogation and the Privilege against Self-Incrimination." *Northwestern University Law Review* 61: 506–521.

———. 1966b. "Precedent and Policy." *University of Chicago Law Review*. 34: 3–25.

———. 1967. "The Control of 'Sunbursts': Techniques of Prospective Overruling." *New York University Law Review* 42: 631–646.

———. 1969. "The Fourteenth Amendment and the Sanctity of the Person." *Northwestern University Law Review* 64: 1–17.

———. 1970. "Unresolved Issues in the Law of Double Jeopardy: *Waller* and *Ashe*." *California Law Review* 58: 391–404.

———. 1982. "Prospective Rulings: Two Perspectives." *Supreme Court Review*:1–24.

Ward, Daniel P. 1979. "In Honor of Walter V. Schaefer." *Northwestern University Law Review* 74: 702–705.

SEABURY, SAMUEL

(1873–1958)

Samuel Seabury
Library of Congress

In the year 1873 in the city of New York, wealth was in the hands of a few and government in the hands of criminals. In that year on Washington's birthday, 22 February, Samuel Seabury was born in the rectory of the Church of the Annunciation on West Fourteenth Street. He would dedicate his life to fighting poverty and governmental corruption.

One of Seabury's ancestors, another Samuel Seabury, was the first Episcopal bishop in America and an obstreperous loyalist during the Revolution. Seabury's father, William Jones Seabury, was a professor of canon law; his mother was Alice Van Wyck Beare Seabury. Seabury was always interested in his genealogy and held with pride to his family's tradition of strong moral conviction.

At age eleven Seabury went to England with his father and saw the Inns of Court. The experience soon had him speaking of a career as a lawyer. But old and distinguished in America as his family was, its members were not wealthy, and when he entered New York Law School in 1891, he had to support himself. He graduated in 1893, but not yet being twenty-one and so ineligible to take the bar examination, he took postgraduate courses, hearing lectures by future president Woodrow Wilson and future president and United States chief justice Charles Evans Hughes. Seabury was admitted to the bar in 1894 and practiced with the firm of Seabury and Pickford. He enjoyed good success in the several years that he practiced.

The writings of, and Seabury's acquaintance with, economist Henry George exerted a profound early influence on Seabury's political beliefs. George's essential idea was that although each human being properly owns his own labor and the economic value that flows from it, it is unjust that persons are born into a world where others already have appropriated all the raw material (which he called "land") upon which that labor might be exercised. His solution was for society to regard land as a common good, with its possessor paying a tax that would function as a sort of rent on the unimproved value of the land. Because there was to be no other tax, George's followers were sometimes called "single taxers." Although George's view might today be regarded as close to economic libertarianism and therefore not especially concerned with the plight of the poor, it was in fact intended as a solution to the problem of poverty and in its day was regarded by many as dangerously socialistic. Seabury became an enthusiastic convert.

In 1899 the Independent Labor Party, later joined by the Republican and other parties, nominated the twenty-six-year-old Seabury for justice of the City Court. This court handled civil (noncriminal) cases in which the amount in controversy did not exceed $2,000. The notorious political machine of Tammany Hall was powerful in the city then, and the standard bribe for Tammany endorsement for a judgeship on the lower courts was $10,000; for the Court of Appeals, $25,000. Seabury and his fellow reform candidates hoped to break this system. Although he spent less than forty dollars on the campaign, it attracted some attention in the press. Seabury campaigned on the themes of the single tax and opposition to corruption. But Tammany was too well entrenched, and Seabury and his fellow reform candidates were defeated. From that time forward his critics tried to characterize him as a dangerous radical, a tactic made easier by his blunt, outspoken public statements.

The next year Seabury married. Maud Richey was not quite the girl next door—she lived down the street in the house in which Clement Clarke Moore had written "A Visit from St. Nicholas"—but their fathers both were professors at the General Theological Seminary and the two families were close. The wedding took place on 6 June1900, their fathers and one other minister presiding. Maud was a quiet but strong woman, and the marriage would prove a happy one, though childless. They lived in an inexpensive house in the city; later they would have a house in East Hampton, Long Island, with a large library, and Seabury would write a "Historical Sketch" of the town that would be "published for the community" in 1926.

In 1901 Seabury ran for the City Court again, as candidate of the Citizens Union Party. He and his fellow reform candidates campaigned for governmental honesty; corruption in the Metropolitan Street Railway Company received particular mention. He long would champion the cause of public ownership of such natural monopolies as utilities and urban transportation networks; he later collected his thoughts on the subject in *Municipal Ownership and Operation of Public Utilities in New York City* (1905). This time Seabury was elected, becoming the youngest justice of the City Court up to that time, at a salary of $10,000 a year for a term of ten years.

Seabury found that his position required him to address the problems both of the litigants before him and of the court itself. He discovered that the clerks of the court were embezzling the fees owed to jurors and sheriffs. The chief clerk was an officer in the Tammany organization and refused to act on Seabury's information. Seabury had to expose the matter to the press before the chief clerk would remove the thieves from their offices.

Seabury discovered too that the Metropolitan Street Railway Company, whose corruption had been an issue in the campaign, had an arrangement with the court clerk to have one of its employees sit on juries in cases where it was a party, to influence the jurors in favor of the company, and that the company also paid outright bribes to jurors. The man impersonating a juror was convicted, and five clerks were removed, but Seabury's efforts to procure additional prosecutions were impeded by an uncooperative district attorney.

Seabury's work product was prodigious. He worked remarkably long hours, and his written opinions are notable for their clarity and logical rigor. On one occasion another judge had fallen behind in writing his opinions and Seabury volunteered to write them for him. The judge in question was pleased with them, but under influence from Tammany changed the result in one, a suit for recovery of fees for boarding horses, while keeping most of the same text that Seabury had written. Seabury disagreed with the new outcome and as a result wrote both the majority and dissenting opinions in the case (*Bailey v. Kraus*, 39 Misc. 845 [1903]).

In addressing the range of human affairs that came before his court, Seabury began to reveal his style of judging and his judicial philosophy. His rather formal demeanor served him well as a judge, and though on a personal level some found him rather remote, he unquestionably had a capacity for subtle humor. His philosophy of legal interpretation was that the reading of the law should be flexible enough to reflect changing social realities. He consistently favored freedom and the rights of labor. His continuing activity in the Henry George Society prompted the *New York Sun* to comment that the "Boy Judge . . . does not act on the theory that persons holding judicial office should either be reticent or inactive in political matters."

In 1905 Seabury maneuvered to avoid receiving the mayoral nomination of the Municipal Ownership League, putting forth instead a political ally, the muckraking journalist William Randolph Hearst. Seabury ran for justice of the Supreme Court, in New York the highest trial court. Hearst lost the election, probably through fraud, and Seabury too went down to defeat. But in the election of 1906, in which Hearst was defeated in his race for governor, Seabury was elected to the Supreme Court as the candidate of both the Democratic Party and the Independence League (a successor to the Municipal Ownership League). He was thirty-three years old. Just before assuming his new duties he completed *The Law and Practice of the City Court of the City of New York,* which long served as a standard reference work.

He was distinctly unimpressed with his colleagues on the Supreme Court, whom he regarded in the main as pompous, poker-playing political hacks. With his outspokenness it was not long before some of them became his enemies. They could not fail to be impressed, however, by his output of opinions.

His progressive tendencies continued unabated. He ruled that the police could not search premises on mere suspicion of criminal activity in *Fairmont Athletic Club v. Bingham,* 113 N.Y.Supp. 905 (1908), and upheld the attempt of the fire commissioner to require owners of tenements to install fire-prevention equipment in *Lantry v. Hoffman,* 55 Misc. 261, 105 N.Y.Supp. 353 (1907). In a case that garnered considerable attention, he ordered the reinstatement of a fired schoolteacher, a married woman, on the ground that her absence from work to have a child could not be considered "neglect of duty" (*People ex rel. Peixotto v. Board of Education,* 82 Misc. 684, 144 N.Y.Supp. 87 [1913]; *rev'd,* 160 App. Div. 557, 145 N.Y.Supp. 863; *aff'd,* 212 N.Y. 463, 106 N.E. 307 [1914]). Though his ruling was reversed by the Supreme Court's Appellate Division and that reversal was upheld by the Court of Appeals, in the end the commissioner of education agreed with Seabury and voluntarily reinstated the teacher.

Seabury apparently was amused by a suit to collect $200 for the sale of a set of forty-two volumes of the works of the French philosopher and writer Voltaire, in which the defendant claimed that the contract was invalid because the works in question were obscene (*St. Hubert Guild v. Quinn,* 64 Misc. 336, 118 N.Y.Supp. 582 [1909]). The defendant objected specifically to *The Philosophical Dictionary* and *The Maid of Orleans.* Seabury conceded that the works, especially the latter, did contain some material offensive to modern tastes. He noted, however, that a contract for sale of a book could not be declared illegal "unless its sale or publication violates the criminal law" (118 N.Y.Supp., 584) and concluded that "[u]nder no reasonable construction can our law be held to declare the sale or publication of the works of Voltaire a crime" (584). The defendant was perhaps unfortunate in the judge assigned to the case; a year or two earlier Seabury had himself written some rather turgid verse in praise of the "Mocker, scoffer, sceptic" Voltaire.

A case receiving intense scrutiny was that of Charles Becker, a police lieutenant at whose behest several gangsters (all with names like "Lefty Louie") killed a gambler who was about to testify in court about Becker's involvement in a gambling enterprise. Becker's first conviction was reversed, and Seabury presided at the second trial. His impartiality was such that the *New York World* said that he looked "as if his face had been carved out of stone." Becker was again convicted, and this time the result stood on appeal. In 1915 the state electrocuted him.

Seabury broke with Hearst, believing that the publisher was more interested in personal ambition than the public good, but he continued his political involvement. He successfully intervened in favor of Morris Quasha, a Jew whom the bar's "character committee" refused to approve for the practice of law, though he had passed the bar examination and provided thirty testimonials as to his character, with no evidence against him. In 1913 Seabury received the Progressive Party's nomination for the Court of Appeals, New York's highest court, along with the renowned jurist Learned Hand, but without the endorsement of a major party the cause was hopeless, and both men lost. Early in 1914 Gov. Martin Glynn was to appoint a new justice to that court to fill a vacancy, and the candidates came down to Seabury and Benjamin Cardozo. The governor vacillated endlessly, repeatedly telling first one man and then the other that he was his choice, until the matter became a standing joke between the two judges. Finally Cardozo received the nod. But later that year Seabury, with the backing of both the Progressive and Democratic Parties, won election to the Court of Appeals himself.

He was to serve on this court for barely a year and a half. His opinions in that short time were characteristic of him. In *People ex rel. Somerville v. Williams*, 217 N.Y. 40, 111 N.E. 252 (1916), he held that a state employee could not be fired for refusing to make a political contribution. An important dissent of his favored the rights of workers. At issue was the interpretation of the relatively new workmen's compensation law. These laws were enacted to provide compensation for work-related injuries, as against the old system in which various legal doctrines such as assumption of the risk and contributory negligence generally shielded employers from liability. Seabury argued that the statute was "a new step in the field of social legislation" that should be "interpret[ed] in accordance with the spirit which called it into existence" (*In re Carroll v. Knickerbocker Ice Co.*, 218 N.Y., 445, 113 N.E. 507 [1916]). Thus, common law rules restricting what evidence the worker could offer should not apply. Though his view did not prevail on the court, it influenced the legislature (435).

In 1916 former president Theodore Roosevelt told Seabury that he would support him for the gubernatorial nomination of the Progressive Party, which Roosevelt controlled. In reliance on this promise, Seabury secured the nomination of the Democratic Party for governor. Confidently expecting to receive the Progressive endorsement as well, he resigned from the court. Roosevelt then announced that "no Progressive should vote for Mr. Seabury." Without that party's nomination, Seabury's chances were ruined, but he campaigned vigorously nonetheless, losing to Charles Whitman. Privately he told Roosevelt to his face that he was a "blatherskite" (an inane, babbling person), an incident he recounted often later in life.

Seabury never returned to the bench. His later career was marked by further unsuccessful political action, including chimerical hopes for the Democratic presidential nomination in 1932 and the Republican gubernatorial nomination in 1934. He achieved great success, however, in investigations into city corruption in the 1930s.

His beloved wife, Maud, died in 1950, leaving him bereft. He declined seriously in the 1950s and was declared incompetent to handle his affairs in 1955 due to senile dementia. He died on 7 May 1958 at age eighty-five. His funeral drew hundreds of people who knew at first hand of his unflinching integrity.

Tim Hurley

REFERENCES AND FURTHER READING:

Chambers, Walter. 1932. *Samuel Seabury: A Challenge*. New York: The Century Company.

Mitgang, Herbert. 1963. *The Man Who Rode the Tiger: The Life and Times of Judge Samuel Seabury*. New York: Fordham University Press (the best book on Seabury and the most important source for this entry).

Northup, William B., and John B. Northrup. 1932. *The Insolence of Office: The Story of the Seabury Investigations*. New York: G. P. Putnam's Sons.

Seabury, Samuel. 1901. *A Review of the Labor Laws Relative to the Rate of Wages and the Hours of Labor in the State of New York*. New York: E. R. Mantz.

———. 1905. *Municipal Ownership and Operation of Public Utilities in New York City*. New York: Municipal Ownership Publishing Co.

———. 1950. *The New Federalism*. New York: E. P. Dutton and Co.

SEWALL, SAMUEL

(1652–1730)

SAMUEL SEWALL
Library of Congress

SAMUEL SEWALL IS BEST KNOWN as one of the judges in the Salem witch trials of 1692, but his real contribution to history lies in his thirty-six-years' service on the Supreme Court of Judicature of Massachusetts, including ten years as chief justice. He was widely esteemed as a man of honor and integrity and as one of the first to speak out against slavery and for the rights of Native American Indians.

Sewall was born in Bishop Stoke, Hampshire, in England, the son of Henry Sewall Jr. and Jane Dummer. His father had been sent to Massachusetts in 1635, as a twenty-year-old, to establish a plantation for his family in Newbury; Sewall's mother had emigrated at age nine. The two of them, along with her parents, returned to England in 1646, where Henry served as the minister for North Baddesley until he returned to settle permanently in Massachusetts in 1659. Samuel, his mother, and his siblings followed in 1661.

Sewall's formal education began in England. He learned to read at the petty school in North Baddesley before being sent to a grammar school in Romsey, where he started learning Latin. After his arrival in Newbury, he continued his education under Thomas Parker, a highly educated minister with an M.A. from Oxford and a Ph.D. from Franeker University in the Netherlands. When Sewall was fifteen, his father took him to Harvard, where he was tested in his knowledge of Latin and Greek. Having passed the entrance exam and completed a transcription of the university's laws, he became a student in 1667. He received his A.B. in 1671 and his M.A. in 1674. His master's thesis was entitled "An Peccatum originale sit & Peccatum & Poena" (Whether Original Sin Is Both Sin and a Punishment).

After completing his M.A., Sewall returned home, where he refused an offer to become the minister at Woodbridge, New Jersey. At that time he married Hannah Hull, daughter of John Hull, one of the wealthiest merchants and landowners in Boston. He and Hannah had fourteen children, six of whom lived to adulthood; three of them survived Sewall. His son Joseph became a minister at the Old South Church and was later chosen as president of Harvard. Sewall's wife died in 1717. He married Abigail Tilley in 1719; she died in 1720, and he married Mary Gibbs in 1722. He had no children with either of these women.

Sewall joined his father-in-law in business, and in 1681, the General Court appointed him to manage the colony's printing press, a position he held for three years. In 1683, he was elected as a member of the General Court, representing the same town his father-in-law had represented; after Hull's death, Sewall took his place on the Court of Assistants, a combination legislature, executive council, and criminal court. When Massachusetts lost its charter in 1684, Sewall turned his attention back to business matters.

The loss of the charter threatened many colonists' land titles; in an attempt to secure his rights, Sewall sailed to England in November 1688, where he learned that James II had been overthrown. Sewall spent a year in England, taking care of business and unofficially helping Increase Mather, who was there trying to get the colony's charter restored. Upon Sewall's return to Boston, he was almost immediately reelected to the General Court.

By the time the new governor, Sir William Phips, arrived in 1692, over 100 people were in jail in Salem, accused of witchcraft. Phips set up a Special Court of Oyer and Terminer to deal with the cases and appointed Sewall to that court. His fellow judges included William Stoughton, who served as chief justice, Bartholomew Gedney, John Hathorne, John Richards, Nathaniel Saltonstall, Peter Sergeant, and Wait Winthrop. When Saltonstall resigned in disgust after the first trial, he was replaced by Jonathan Corwin. Sewall's brother Stephen served as court clerk. The Salem witch trials are one of the most notorious episodes in American history, not only because nineteen defendants were convicted and hanged (including Sewall's friend from Harvard, George Burroughs) and one other defendant, Giles Corey, was pressed to death for refusing to plead, but also because the court allowed the admission of spectral evidence—testimony by the so-called afflicted girls as to the identities of the apparitions they claimed were tormenting them. Sewall may have had misgivings during the trials, but his diary, which is otherwise a valuable source, is relatively silent about the trials and his reactions to them. In the midst of the trials, he did write his cousin in England that he was "'perplexed p[er] witchcrafts: six persons have already been condemned and executed in Salem'" (Winslow 1964, 127). Beyond that hint, however, we know little of his feelings at the time.

The trials ended in September; Sewall seemed relieved. Soon afterward, he was one of those on the General Court who pushed for a colony-wide day of fasting and repentance to atone for the harm caused by the trials; the measure failed for several years before finally passing. Sewall drafted the proclamation, and the day was set for Thursday, 17 January 1697. At the Old South Meeting House that day, Sewall passed a note to his minister, Samuel Willard (who had vehemently opposed the use of spectral evidence during the trials) for Willard to read to the congregation. This declaration read, in part, "Samuel Sewall, . . . being sensible, that as to the Guilt contracted upon the opening of the late Commission of Oyer and Terminer at Salem . . . is, upon many accounts, more concerned than any that he knows of, Desires to take the Blame and shame of it" (Sewall 1973, 367). The statement then went on to ask both man's and God's forgiveness. It is a remarkable admission on the part of Sewall, who had become convinced that the deaths of two of his children in 1696 were God's punishment for his role in the trials. Sewall was the only one of the Salem judges to apologize, and his experience on this court was to have a profound effect on the rest of his life: It almost certainly influenced his concern over proper procedure and due process as a Superior Court judge and may well have influenced his efforts to help Native American Indians and to persuade his fellow colonists to end slavery.

The Salem witch trials have been the subject of many books, plays, and films, most famously Arthur Miller's *The Crucible,* which he adapted for the screen in 1996. Sewall does not appear in the play but is a character in the film. Because so little is known of the judges' words or actions during the trials, any claims as to Sewall's conduct during the trial are pure speculation. More seriously, though, the leading judge in *The Crucible* is Thomas Danforth, who was not one of the judges of Oyer and Terminer at the time.

Governor Phips's return not only resulted in the Court of Oyer and Terminer, but it also restored legitimate government to Massachusetts, as Phips brought with him the colony's new charter. As part of this charter, a new legislative body was created, and Sewall was elected to the upper house, the Governor's Council. Members of the council were elected by votes cast both in the council and in the General Court, or lower house. It was not uncommon for council members to hold multiple positions; Sewall was a member of the council from 1692 until 1725 and combined his activities on the council with several other public positions, including Superior Court judge.

In addition to setting up the new legislature, Governor Phips set up a proper court, the Superior Court of Judicature, and Sewall became one of the first judges. He was joined on the court by several of his fellow Salem judges: William Stoughton, John Richards, and Wait Winthrop. In theory, the governor had the authority to appoint the judges. In practice, however, "the advice and consent of the [Governor's] Council took the form of an actual vote" (Flaherty 1989, 117). Like his fellow judges, Sewall had no formal legal training. (The first formally trained lawyer on the court was not appointed until 1712; by 1718, he had been joined by two others.) On his trip to England in 1688–1689, Sewall had observed several court sessions and had asked some relatively technical questions of lawyers and judges. Back in Boston, he began importing English legal manuals and made a real effort to acquire a working knowledge of the law. By the time he died, he had acquired a collection of at least twenty-six volumes of Massachusetts, English, and colonial law, all of which he seems to have studied and used. Sewall's efforts to educate himself in the law were typical of the period; it was common for judges to learn from experience, books, colleagues, and lawyers who appeared before them.

Massachusetts law in that period was not just a carbon copy of English common law, however; it was based on a combination of common law, Biblical precepts, statutes, and local custom. Sewall's behavior on the bench reflected this amalgam. Although he upheld Puritan beliefs about the Sabbath, drunkenness, theater, and proper attire, he was also concerned with ensuring that defendants received due process regardless of their social status.

One of the most revealing examples of this concern occurred in 1700, when Sewall became disturbed by the conduct of a fellow Superior Court judge, John Saffin. Saffin had entered into a written contract with a black servant, promising to release him after seven years. At the end of the period, Saffin refused to release the servant, Adam, claiming that Adam had not fulfilled his end of the bargain. Sewall was critical of Saffin's actions, both in refusing to release the man (against Sewall's order) and for engineering his elevation to the Superior Court, where he refused to recuse himself from his own case. The servant, Adam, was eventually released, but the case prompted Sewall to write a tract against slavery, *The Selling of Joseph*. According to Winslow, this was the "first public plea" against enslaving blacks, and Sewall continued to distribute copies of it for years, despite its cool reception (Winslow 1964, 162). In 1719, he wrote to a fellow judge who was to hear a case of a white man accused of killing his slave, reminding him that "the poorest Boys and Girls within this Province, such as are of the lowest condition; whether they be English, or Indians, or Ethiopians. They have the same right to Religion and Life, that the Richest Heirs have" (167).

The Judge and Jury from Hell

Many students of literature will be familiar with Stephen Vincent Benet's fictional story "The Devil and Daniel Webster," in which Webster successfully defends Jabez Stone from the terms of a contract he has made with Satan. Benet described the jurors, all Americans but all literally from hell, as follows:

> For there was Walter Butler, the loyalist, who spread fire and horror through the Mohawk Valley in the times of the Revolution; and there was Simon Girty, the renegade who saw white men burned at the stake and whooped with the Indians to see them burn. His eyes were green, like a catamount's, and the stains on his hunting shirt did not come from the blood of The deer. King Philip was there, wild and proud as he had been in life, with the Great gash in his head that gave him his death wound, and cruel Governor Dale, who broke men on the wheel. There was Morton of Merry Mount, who so vexed the Plymouth Colony, with his flushed, loose, handsome face and his hate of the godly. There was Teach, the bloody pirate, with his black beard curling on his breast. The Reverend John Smeet, with his strangler's hands and his Geneva gown, walked as daintily as he had to the gallows. The red print of the rope was still around his neck, but he carried a perfumed handkerchief in one hand. One and all, they came into the room with the fire of hell still upon them, and The stranger named their names and their deeds as they came, till the tale of Twelve was told. (Benet 1942, 40)

With bravado, Webster commented on his disappointment at not seeing Benedict Arnold but was informed that he was "engaged upon other business" (Benet 1942, 41).

As judge, the devil had selected "Justice Hathorne," whom he described as "a jurist of experience." Hathorne, who had presided over some of the Salem witch trials, was none other than one of the forebears of the novelist Nathaniel Hawthorne.

In Benet's tale, the jury ultimately acquitted Stone, noting that "even the damned may salute the eloquence of Mr. Webster" (Benet 1942, 43).

Reference:

Benet, Stephen Vincent. 1942. *Selected Works of Stephen Vincent Benet*. Vol. 2: *Prose*. New York: Farrar and Rinehart.

Sewall also used his dual positions on the council and on the bench to try to protect Native Americans. In 1699 he had become the treasurer of the Society for the Propagation of the Gospel in New England, a group dedicated to Christianizing the Indians. Sewall was inspired in part by a belief that the Indians were one of the lost tribes of Israel and spent both time and money to see that churches were built to serve the Indians. He was also motivated by simple humanity, and in 1705, he managed to alter the wording of a bill that outlawed marriages between blacks and whites; the original draft of the bill had included Indians, but Sewall warned that he feared such a measure would "be an Oppression provoking to God and that which will promote Murders and other Abominations" (he added that he had managed to include a clause allowing blacks to marry one another) (Sewall 1973, 532.). Sewall wrote in 1716 that he had tried to prevent blacks and Indians being "rated with Horses and Hogs, but could not prevail" (822). Sewall was also one of the first to propose a formal and permanent boundary between Indians and whites (something the Indians also wanted) on the grounds that such a boundary was the only way to prevent further war and bloodshed. Although he retained Puritan beliefs about proper conduct and dress, he was well ahead of his time on other issues.

Sewall was also willing to uphold a defendant's legal rights, even when the other party in the case was rich and powerful. In 1705 two carters, Thomas Trowbridge and John Winchester Jr., had allegedly refused to move their carts out of the road and allow Governor Dudley's carriage to pass. An altercation broke out, though the governor and the two carters each told different versions of the events; when a justice of the peace arrived, the governor had the two carters arrested. Despite the objections of the governor and his son the attorney general, Sewall insisted that the men be allowed bail on the grounds that only those charged with felonies or treason were to be denied bail. Sewall wrote in his diary that he was happy to have "been instrumental" in getting the men released (Sewall 1973, 536).

Dudley did not stop there, though. Prior to the trial, he tried to influence the outcome of his case by reading a statement of his version of events at a council meeting on 12 January 1706. (Like Sewall, several of the Superior Court judges who were to hear the case were also council members.) Dudley also accused Sewall of preparing to report that "quarts of blood [were] running out of Trowbridge's horses." Sewall denied the accusation but did argue that the justice of the peace who had been present when the carters were arrested should not have drawn his sword; the governor defended the justice of the peace. When the case finally came to trial in November 1706, the two defendants were acquitted (Flaherty 1989, 127; Winslow 1964, 146–147). Sewall's actions in this case are even more remarkable given the fact that Superior Court judges served only at the pleasure of the Crown (Flaherty 1989, 121).

Sewall was sworn in as chief justice of the Superior Court in April 1718, following the death of Wait Winthrop. Governor Shute had intended to appoint Paul Dudley, the attorney general and son of the former governor, to the position, but the governor was successfully convinced by Sewall that as a man of standing in the community and as the only judge to have served since 1692, he deserved the position. He also reminded the governor that he had "'not miss'd Bristol Circuit for more than Twenty years together'" (Flaherty 1989, 119). Sewall held the position of chief justice until he resigned from it in July 1728 at the age of seventy-six. At the time of his resignation, he had served on the Superior Court for thirty-six years, traveling throughout the colony several times a year.

In 1722, Sewall once again intervened to protect the rights of Indians. At a council meeting, he voiced his concerns over a plan to arrest leaders of an Indian rebellion and to force them to pay for the costs of the uprising. If the leaders were unwilling to cooperate, the plan called for them to be captured and brought to Boston. Sewall expressed his doubts about the legality of this move; such was Sewall's reputation and influence that the scheme was postponed (Flaherty 1989, 125).

Sewall's public life began winding down in 1725, when he resigned his position on the Governor's Council, despite the pleas of a deputation sent to change his mind. He resigned as probate court judge for Suffolk County in 1728, a position he had held since 1715. He also resigned from the Superior Court in 1728. During his thirty-six years as a Superior Court judge, Samuel Sewall worked to ensure that the law was administered fairly and honestly. He personified the behavior that he believed all judges should exhibit: "May the Judges always discern the Right, and dispense Justice with a most stable, permanent Impartiality" (Sewall 1973, 714). Sewall died on 1 January 1730.

Carol Loar

References and Further Reading:

Chamberlain, N. H. 1897. *Samuel Sewall and the World He Lived In*. Boston: De Wolfe, Fiske, and Company.

Flaherty, David H. 1989. "Chief Justice Samuel Sewall, 1692–1728." In *The Law in America, 1607–1861*, edited by William Pencak and Wythe W. Holt Jr. New York: The New York Historical Society, 114–154.

Hoffer, Peter C. 1996. *The Devil's Disciples: Makers of the Salem Witchcraft Trials*. Baltimore, Md.: Johns Hopkins University Press.

Sewall, Samuel. 1973. *The Diary of Samuel Sewall*. Edited by M. Halsey Thomas. New York: Farrar, Straus and Giroux.

Strandness, T. B. 1967. *Samuel Sewall: A Puritan Portrait*. Lansing: Michigan State University Press.

Washburn, Emory. 1840. *Sketches of the Judicial History of Massachusetts*. Boston: C. C. Little and J. Brown.

Winslow, Ola E. 1964. *Samuel Sewall of Boston*. New York: Macmillan.

SHARSWOOD, GEORGE

(1810–1883)

George Sharswood
Library of Congress

From the earliest colonial times through the end of the nineteenth century, the city of Philadelphia was, as one writer phrased it, "the cynosure [that is, guiding star] of the legal profession in [America's] early national period" (Nash 1965, 205). Steeped in English legal tradition, Philadelphia's lawyers, many of whom had had years of study in Great Britain's Inns of Court, were the sons of the elite of the city. The Philadelphia bar was thought to be the equal of the bar of Westminster Hall. "I have never met a body of men more distinguished by acuteness and extensive professional information than the members of the Philadelphia bar," wrote British scholar and diarist Thomas Hamilton in 1833 (205).

George Sharswood, the son of a lumber salesman, was a product of this august legal tradition. He was a legal scholar, lecturer (1836–1883) and law professor (1850–1868), Pennsylvania legislator (three terms), district court judge (1845–1867, including nineteen years as presiding, or "president," judge), and Pennsylvania Supreme Court justice (1867–1882, four years of which he served as chief justice). A lifelong resident of Philadelphia, he was one of America's most outstanding jurists. On 8 January 2002, the Philadelphia Bar Association, marking its bicentennial, enshrined Sharswood in its Hall of Fame, noting, "Sharswood was considered by lawyers to be a great judge. He had a reputation for being extremely practical, decisive, rigidly impartial, quick to grasp facts, firm in controlling the courtroom, and lucid in his jury charges."

Sharswood was a prolific author and annotator. His first published work, an article on the Revised Code of Philadelphia, was written when he was but twenty-four. An expert in many areas of the law, his writings often became standard textbooks in the U.S. law schools of the period. His 1859 edition of *Blackstone's Commentaries on the Laws of England, with Notes and a Life of the Author,* written with special reference-use for U.S. lawyers, was his best-known work. Here, and in other writings, can be found one of the central tenets of his judicial philosophy: "Civil liberty, the great end of all human society and government, is that state in which each individual has the power to pursue his own happiness according to his own views of his interests and the dictates of his conscience, unrestrained except by equal, just and impartial laws" (Ransier).

An incomplete list of his other books includes *Roscoe on Criminal Evidence* (1835), *Leigh on Nisi Prius* (1838), *Stephens on Nisi Prius* (1844), *Russell on Crimes* (1844), *English Common Law Reports* (in 1847 he indexed, with George W. Biddle, volumes 1–47; in 1853 he annotated volumes 66–90), *Byles on Bills of Exchange* (1852), *The Common Law of Pennsylvania* (1855), *Lectures on Commercial Law* (1856), *Lectures Introductory to the Study of the Law* (1870), *Tudor's Leading Cases in Mercantile and Marine Law, with American Notes and References* (1873), *Starkie on Evidence* (1876), and *Smith on Contracts* (1879). Many of these books saw multiple revised editions throughout his lifetime. His most influential work, *Essay on Professional Ethics* (1854), is still referenced today. In 1907 it became the basis for the American Bar Association's first ethical code, *The Canons of Professional Ethics*.

Sharswood's commitment to teaching began in his twenties. He lectured, intermittently, at the Law Academy of Philadelphia for forty-seven years. The academy, a professional social and debating society for lawyers and students, founded in 1821, made him a vice-provost (1835–1853) and then provost (1836–1883). He also served one term (1836–1837) as its president. His last address, delivered 13 March 1883, two months before his death, chronicled the history and aims of that institution.

At the University of Pennsylvania, where he taught for eighteen years, Sharswood was instrumental in guiding the state's transitional period in legal education from an office-apprenticeship system (two to three years of study and clerkship under the guidance of a practicing attorney, called a "preceptor") to a two-year program of systematic university training. Constituting a faculty of one, Sharswood accepted the position of professor of law on 2 April 1850. At that time there were only fourteen other law schools in the United States. His initial class, including practicing attorneys, numbered fifty.

In 1852 Sharswood became the Law School's first dean. He increased the faculty to three, adding professors Peter McCall, a future Philadelphia mayor, and Elihu Spencer Miller, a published scholar and colleague from the Law Academy. He continued to lecture, twice a week, in international, constitutional, commercial, and civil law. Although the "preceptor" system of legal education continued, by 1856 the Law School's bachelor of law degree sufficed to meet all requirements for admission to the bar. From 1872 to 1883 Sharswood was a trustee of the university and president of the Alumni Society.

When Columbia University and New York University established law schools in 1858, they both granted Sharswood honorary LL.D. degrees. In the 1860s Sharswood, with George W. Biddle, organized a political economy club. For years it met twice a month, with various members delivering papers on the works of economists Adam Smith, John Stuart Mill, David Ricardo, and others.

George Sharswood, the sixth generation of American Sharswoods, was born in Philadelphia, 7 July 1810, to George and Esther (Dunn) Sharswood. The elder Sharswoods had left England in 1665, settling in New London, Connecticut. Subsequently, they moved to Cape May, New Jersey, before settling in Philadelphia, about 1706.

When his father died, tragically, on 2 February 1810 at the young age of twenty-two—some five months before his son's birth—the burden of young George's upbringing fell to his widowed mother, Esther, and his paternal grandfather, James. Grandfather Sharswood, an educated man of considerable accomplishment, effected young George's primary education. A captain in the American Revolution, he had amassed a considerable fortune in lumber, had served as a state legislator, and had authored newspaper articles critical of the first Bank of the United States.

In 1825, at the age of fifteen, Sharswood enrolled, as a sophomore, at the University of Pennsylvania. He studied in the Classical Department and graduated 31 July 1828 with highest honors, delivering the salutatory address in Latin. That August he began the study of law in the office of Joseph R. Ingersoll, his preceptor for three years. Sharswood later recalled this experience as one of the best of his life. He was admitted to the bar 5 September 1831 at the age of twenty-one. Forsaking active legal practice, however, he continued his scholarly pursuits. In 1834 he delivered "An Address upon the Rights of the States" to the States Rights Association of Pennsylvania, articulating his opposition to governmental proscription of personal liberties and actions.

A lifelong Democrat, Sharswood began his political career in 1837 with his election to the Pennsylvania legislature. Leaving the legislature, he was elected, 1838–1840, to successive terms on the Select Council of Philadelphia. He closed his political career with reelection to the legislature in 1841 and 1842. In 1841, as a member of the judiciary committee that also included the ardent abolitionist Thaddeus Stevens, he debated a proposal to abolish imprisonment for debt—a subject, at the time, of intense and bitter feelings. The measure became law.

That same year, Sharswood accepted a position as secretary on a committee of bank shareholders formed to examine the failure of the second Bank of the United States. The bank, established in 1816, collapsed amid great political entanglements in 1836. At the demise of the second bank, president Nicholas Biddle, a Philadelphian, incorporated, at a cost of $6 million, its Philadelphia branch bank. Highly questionable and risky operations, however, squandered the new state bank's reputation and credit, and in 1841 it also failed. Sharswood authored two highly respected reports (the second a critical rejoinder) that demonstrated a remarkable grasp of the entire complicated financial affair. Missouri senator Thomas Hart Benton, an implacable foe of the second bank, in his autobiographical memoir *Thirty Years View,* reproduced the report with admiration and agreement (1856, chap. 87).

Democratic governor Francis R. Shunk nominated Sharswood for the position of associate judge of the District Court for the City and County of Philadelphia on 8 April 1845. Unanimously confirmed by the Senate, Sharswood was not yet thirty-five when he took his seat. Subsequently, with the resignation of president judge Joel Jones, Sharswood became the new president judge on 1 February 1848.

On 27 November 1849, Judge Sharswood married Mary Chambers, the daughter of Pennsylvania State Supreme Court justice George Chambers of Chambersburg.

In 1850 the judiciary became elective, specifying ten-year terms for District Court judges. Elected president judge in 1851, Sharswood was the unanimous and independently nominated candidate of all five existing political parties. In 1861 his reelection was again without opposition.

The District Court's docket in 1848 had a backlog of 1,600 cases, with new filings numbering more than a thousand a year. The delay between filing and hearing was about one year. With the concurrence of Associate Justices John Innis Clark Hare and George M. Stroud, Sharswood's court set itself a Herculean task; meeting ten months a year, it resolved that a trial should be finished on or before midnight of the day it began. Thus, by precariously balancing the notion of "due consideration" with the dictum "justice delayed is justice denied," the court, by 1855, reduced its arrears to about a stable 600 cases a year, even as the number of new cases filed annually increased dramatically (Biddle 1883, 12; Dickson 1907, 136).

During Sharswood's career on the District Court bench, he wrote more than 4,000 opinions, many of them, of necessity, concise and brief. Many more were delivered orally. Testimony exists that litigants were consistently satisfied with the fairness of their hearings, and the legal quality of the court's decisions was astonishing. Of 156 Sharswood decisions appealed to the State Supreme Court, only thirty-two were reversed. His opinions from 1850 to 1868 are contained in volumes 1–6 of *The Philadelphia Reports*.

In 1862 the federal government passed the Legal Tender Act, issuing "greenbacks" (not convertible to metal on demand) to defray the cost of the Civil War. The act's constitutionality was brought before Sharswood's court in *Borie v. Trott* (5 Philadelphia Reports, 366). The court found the act legal; but in a fifteen-page dissenting opinion, relying on a strict interpretation of the Constitution's grant of limited powers and meticulously citing all relevant cases and history, Sharswood found the new federal notes to be not "money" but "bills of credit" and not "legal tender." The Constitution, he said, sanctioned only coins or metallic money. The thoroughness of his opinion became the classical expression, in future arguments, for all those who opposed "paper money."

In this century, Sharswood's views on "hard money" appear antiquated. Taken in a larger historical context, however, they are not. In the nineteenth century the debate over "hard money" versus "paper money" was, after slavery, the second most hotly debated national topic. Metal money was, by its nature, of limited supply—its value more stable. Paper money, easily printed, fluctuated with the supply on hand. Established states, like Pennsylvania, and their banks—conservative, well established and able to be lending institutions—had a vested interest to be protected by *in specie* repayment (value loaned should be repaid in equal value). On the other hand, frontier "emerging" states, with their speculative entrepreneurial efforts, wars, and revolutions, benefited more by borrowing at stable value (hard money) and repaying in inflated paper money of inferior purchasing power.

The economist John Kenneth Galbraith wrote that the basic tension between *in specie* and paper money was the monetary mechanism that established our economy and developed our entire nation (1971, chap. 3). Beneficial within limits, but destructive when uncontrolled, paper money functioned as a taxation of the established where actual taxation would have been unacceptable. Because it had the immoral virtue of losing some of its worth as more of it was printed, it provided, in effect, a discount on the repayment of debt. The opposition of these two "money" policies, he wrote, was a very beneficial dialectic for the development of America.

All accounts of Judge Sharswood's life portray him as a kindly and agreeable man. One wonders, however, if his sense of humor would have embraced an incident that occurred in 1736 when Pennsylvania was an "emerging" state. Benjamin Franklin, a fellow Philadelphian, was an enthusiastic supporter and printer of paper money. When his press was so busy in 1736 printing paper money that his *Pennsylvania Gazette* was not published on time, Franklin once printed an apology, explaining that he had been busy "laboring for the publick Good to make Money more plentiful" (Galbraith 1971, 54).

The debate between metal and paper money interests was, in fact, a debate about money supply and not merely the "form" that money should take. Judge Sharswood's decision, based on a conservative constitutional view, was a well-reasoned legal argument for a tight money supply. Today, those debates take place among money supply theorists at the Federal Reserve Bank—and, in paper money.

In 1867 Sharswood was elected to a fifteen-year term as associate justice of the Pennsylvania Supreme Court, besting the Republican candidate, Henry W. Williams (Williams would later join him on the court). Because the court met in Philadelphia, Harrisburg, and Pittsburgh, Sharswood resigned from the university, giving his last lecture on 30 April 1868.

Eleven years later, on 6 January 1879, he became, by priority of commission, the court's chief justice, occupying the vacated chair of George W. Woodward. He retired, with the expiration of his term, in January 1883.

Sharswood's decisions are cataloged in volumes 57–102 of the *Pennsylvania State Reports*. Three, of historical interest, are cited here. Others, encompassing other areas of law, are addressed in Biddle (1883, 25–37).

In *Audenried v. Philadelphia and Reading Railroad* (68 Pa. St. 377), the correct function of a preliminary injunction was a matter of discussion. Sharswood, noting that an injunction, as a measure of mere temporary restraint, should not be used as a tool to accomplish other ends, wrote, "A tribunal that finds itself unable directly to decree a thing, ought never to attempt to accomplish it by indirection" (378). His conservative view of injunction is clearly at odds with that of Illinois federal judge Thomas Drummond (1809–1890).

In December 1871 Justice Sharswood wrote the opinion in *Carrie S. Burnham v. Louis Luning, George Lewis, and Joseph Haughton* (9 Phil. Rep. 241). Burnham, a twenty-one-year-old female resident of Philadelphia, sued election officers for "refusing her vote" under the definition of a "freeman." The suit was denied, Sharswood reasoning that "under the word 'freeman' in the constitution of Pennsylvania, Article III, sec. 1, the right of voting is confined to citizens of the male sex" (241).

In 1879 the court heard *Kane v. Commonwealth* (89 Pa. St. 522). The question at issue was whether a jury's duty was to judge the law as well as the facts in a criminal case. In deciding affirmatively, Sharswood said, "the power of the jury to judge of the law in a criminal case was one of the most valuable securities guaranteed by the Bill of Rights" of Pennsylvania (527).

Justice George Sharswood died at his Philadelphia residence, 322 South Thirteenth Street, early on the morning of 28 May 1883. He was seventy-three years old and had spent the final fifteen years of his life quietly resigned to the chronic and severe physical pain associated with the fistula that claimed his life. (He once confessed to a friend that he had not experienced a single conscious pain-free hour during all of those years.)

He had also suffered the loss of his entire household. Mary, his beloved wife of only eight years, had died 8 November 1857. Their only son, a lawyer, but also a fragile consumptive for many years, had passed away shortly before Sharswood's retirement. His devoted mother, Ester, had predeceased him in 1865.

In addition to having been past president of the Philadelphia Institution for the Deaf and Dumb, Sharswood, a Presbyterian, had been a member and trustee of Philadelphia's Tabernacle Presbyterian Church, a trustee of the Presbyterian General Assembly, and a director of the Theological Seminary at Princeton.

Today, a commemorative medallion and inscription honoring Justice George Sharswood grace the Thirty-fourth Street entrance of the Law School's Silverman Hall in Philadelphia.

Kevin Collins

References and Further Reading:

Benton, Thomas Hart. 1856. *Thirty Years View*. Vol. 2. New York: D. Appleton and Company, chap. 87.

Biddle, George W. 1883. *A Sketch of the Professional and Judicial Character of the Late George Sharswood*. Philadelphia: The Law Association of Philadelphia.

Clark, Gilbert J. 1895. *Life Sketches of Eminent Lawyers*. 2 vols. Kansas City, Mo.: Lawyers International Publishing.

Dickson, Samuel. 1907. "George Sharswood." In *Great American Lawyers*, vol. 6, edited by William Draper Lewis. Philadelphia: The John C. Winston Company.

Galbraith, John Kenneth. 1971. *Money: Whence It Came, Where It Went*. Boston: Houghton Mifflin, chap. 3.

Hart, Charles Henry. 1882. "State Celebrities—George Sharswood." *The Philadelphia Press*, 30 March.

———. 1884. *Memoir of George Sharswood*. Philadelphia: The Numismatic and Antiquarian Society of Philadelphia.

Nash, Gary B. 1965. "The Philadelphia Bench and Bar, 1800–1861." *Comparative Studies in Society and History* 7, no. 2 (January).

Ransier, Alonzo J. "Neglected Voices: Speeches of African American Representatives Addressing the Civil Rights Bill of 1875." Available on-line at <http://www.law.nyu.edu/davisp/neglectedvoices/RansierJan051874.html>. Accessed 15 January 2003.
"Sharswood Obituary." 1883a. *Legal Intelligencer*, 1 June.
"Sharswood Obituary." 1883b. *New York Times*, 29 May.

SHAW, LEMUEL

(1781–1861)

Chief justice of the Supreme Judicial Court of Massachusetts from 1830 to 1860, Lemuel Shaw wrote approximately 2,200 opinions. These opinions covered a broad scope of jurisprudence, with the exception of admiralty, and no state judge's work so profoundly shaped not only his own times but the path of American law for generations to come. Bernard Schwartz, in *A Book of Legal Lists* (1997, 130), ranked Shaw as the greatest non–Supreme Court judge in U.S. history. Shaw's main biographer, Leonard W. Levy, concluded: "No other state judge through his opinions alone had so great an influence on the course of American law" (1957, 3).

Lemuel Shaw
Social Law Library, Boston

Shaw was born on 9 January 1781 in Barnstable, Massachusetts, the second son of the Reverend Oakes Shaw, an Episcopalian minister, and his second wife, Susanna Hayward. Oakes Shaw educated his son at home, except for a few months at a private school in Braintree. Lemuel Shaw entered Harvard in 1796 and graduated four years later with high honors. He studied law with David Everett and entered practice in Boston in November 1804. His practice was lucrative; his political life was active.

Shaw became engaged in 1802 to Nancy Melville, daughter of Maj. Thomas Melville of Boston, but she died before they were married. On 6

January 1818 Shaw married Elizabeth Knapp, daughter of Josiah Knapp of Boston. She died in 1822, leaving a son and a daughter. The latter became the wife of acclaimed author Herman Melville, nephew of Shaw's former fiancée. Melville is believed to have modeled at least one fictional character on Shaw, namely the lawyer figure in "Bartleby," an essay that appeared in *Putnam's Monthly* in 1853. As Shaw would do in *Brown v. Kendall* (1850), the lawyer in the essay emphasized the word *prudent*. Other literary critics believe that Melville's portrait of Guinea in *White-Jacket* reflected Shaw's ambivalence on slavery. Still other critics believe Shaw influenced Melville's treatment of substantive and procedural criminal matters in *Billy Budd*, and they find links particularly with Shaw's approach to guilt and innocence in his charge to the jury in *Commonwealth v. Webster* (1850). In any event, on 29 August 1827 Shaw married Hope Savage, daughter of Dr. Samuel Savage, and with her had two sons.

Shaw had a wide and varied political career that prepared him well for service on the bench. He was elected to the Massachusetts General Court and served in 1811–1814, 1820, and 1829 and in the Senate in 1821–1822. He was also elected to the Massachusetts constitutional convention in 1820, where he played a leading role. He drafted the first charter for the city of Boston and held a number of offices for the city prior to beginning his service on the bench.

Gov. Levi Lincoln appointed Shaw to the position of chief justice of the Supreme Judicial Court on 30 August 1830. Immediately, his salary dropped from $20,000 a year to $3,500, but by that time Shaw had amassed considerable wealth and was eager to join the state's highest court. He served three decades, resigning on 21 August 1860 to the overwhelming acclaim of the Massachusetts bar.

During Shaw's time the chief justice sat not only to hear appeals but to try cases as well. In both areas, Shaw left an indelible impression on American law. The smaller of his judicial tasks involved presiding over trials, several of which became landmarks in U.S. legal history. As a trial judge, Shaw earned a reputation for thoroughness, patience, and an unexcelled capacity to charge juries.

Those skills were tested in the 1834 trial of anti-Catholic rioters who destroyed the Ursuline convent in Charlestown (*Commonwealth v. Buzzell*, 33 Massachusetts Reports 153). At the trial of the rioters, who were convicted, Shaw was scrupulously fair, even when faced with virulent anti-Catholic prejudice. During the trial, Shaw noted that "witnesses of all religious persuasions are placed on the same footing, each is to stand on his own individual character" (Levy 1957, 268).

Shaw also presided over other highly visible criminal trials. Perhaps the most notorious was the 1850 proceeding against Prof. John White Webster, of Harvard University, who was convicted of murdering Dr. George Parkman (*Commonwealth v. Webster*, 59 Massachusetts Reports 295 [1850]). Webster, the editor of the *Boston Journal of Philosophy and the Arts*, had borrowed extensively from Parkman, perhaps the best-known man in Massachusetts. When Parkman learned that Webster was attempting to borrow money on already-mortgaged property, he demanded immediate payment and threatened to have Webster removed from his prestigious faculty position. Webster retaliated by killing Parkman, butchering his body, and stuffing part of it down a laboratory privy. The case generated enormous public interest and considerable criticism of Shaw, notably for his decision to allow the courtroom audience to change every ten minutes, which permitted more than 60,000 people to glimpse the proceedings, and, even more important, for his three-hour charge to the jury. That charge, which has been the subject of heated debate among legal scholars, effectively placed the burden on Webster to prove his innocence rather than on the Commonwealth to prove his guilt.

Controversy followed Shaw into other areas of the law, especially matters involving race and slavery. There is no doubt that Shaw had an unstinting commitment to a free society. For example, in the case of *Commonwealth v. Aves* (18 Pickering 193 [1836]), Shaw addressed the question of whether a six-year-old slave girl, Med, who had traveled from New Orleans with her female master, had become a free person as a result of having journeyed into the free territory of Massachusetts. Thomas Aves, the father of the owner, kept the young girl during her stay in Boston. Antislavery groups in the city sought a writ of habeas corpus to have the girl freed, but Aves refused to release her, claiming that he had a duty to return her to her owner, his daughter. The question posed to Shaw was whether a slave brought temporarily into a free state could become permanently free.

Shaw forthrightly condemned slavery. He held that the peculiar institution could not exist in the commonwealth and that it was "contrary to natural right, to the principles of justice, humanity and sound policy" (18 Pickering 210). With those ringing words, Shaw ordered Med freed and laid down the principle that slavery could only exist by local, positive law. Antislavery advocates in Boston greeted the decision enthusiastically, but Shaw's actions in freeing Med only partially captured the reality of his beliefs. Shaw also had substantial doubts about the capacities of African Americans, and as a matter of law, he also supported the rights of owners of fugitive slaves.

In the home state of abolitionist leader William Lloyd Garrison, there had been substantial progress directed toward improving the condition of the African American population. Massachusetts, for example, by 1849 had rescinded a law that prohibited interracial marriage and passed another that ended the practice of Jim Crow segregation on railroads. Several cities in the commonwealth had also abolished separate schools for African American students, although Boston was not one of them. To that end, Charles Sumner in 1849 argued before Shaw and his colleagues that such schools should be abolished in the city, where they had existed for more than half a century.

Shaw spoke for a unanimous court in *Roberts v. City of Boston* (5 Cushing 198 [1849]), holding that the school committee that operated the Boston schools had the power to impose segregation by race. Shaw noted that the plaintiff had access to an existing African American school and that it was as well prepared to serve the children who attended as were the all-white schools in the city. The committee that ran the schools, Shaw continued, had the authority to decide who might attend a particular school, whether on the grounds of race, color, or religion. Shaw agreed not only that the committee had the power to decide the matter but also that it had the capacity to decide what was in the best interests of the citizens and the children in doing so. If it believed that schools segregated by race were appropriate, then so be it. Shaw recognized that prejudice existed in society, but he also concluded that there was nothing that the law and courts could do about it. That prejudice, he noted, "is not created by law, and probably cannot be changed by law" (Levy 1957, 115). What Shaw did require, in light of an equal protection clause in the Massachusetts constitution, was that all schools provide for their students in the same way. In short, Shaw read the concept of "separate but equal" into the American law of race relations.

That concept had greater vitality nationally than it did in Massachusetts. In the case of the latter, the state's legislature in 1855 responded to abolitionist demands by eliminating race, color, or religious opinions as a basis to determine entry into a public school. Nationally, however, the concept of separate-but-equal enjoyed considerable longevity, and southern legislators and judges regularly cited Shaw's opinion in *Roberts*, even after adoption of the Fourteenth Amendment, to sustain a segregated social order. The Supreme Court of the United States finally discredited the doctrine in *Brown* v. *Board of Education of Topeka* (347 U.S. 483 [1954]).

Antislavery and abolitionist criticism of Shaw reached a crescendo in 1851 when he refused to issue a writ of habeas corpus to free Thomas Sims, purportedly a slave owned by a rice planter in Chatham County, Georgia. Under the authority of the Fugitive Slave Act of 1850, the U.S. magistrate in Boston took Sims into custody and imprisoned him in the jury room of the Boston Court House. As the magistrate initiated proceedings against Sims before federal magistrate George Ticknor Curtis, Samuel E. Sewall, an antislavery advocate, asked Shaw to issue the writ to bring Sims before the Supreme Judicial Court on the ground of illegal detention.

In *Sims Case* (7 Cushing 285 [1851]), Shaw seemingly reversed course from his earlier decision involving the slave child Med, much to the chagrin of Boston's militant antislavery forces. After briefly consulting his associates, Shaw refused to help free Sims. He concluded that his court lacked any authority to decide the question of whether Sims was a freeman or a slave; that question, under the 1850 federal law, properly belonged to the federal magistrate. In effect, Shaw, an opponent of slavery, gave preference to his ideas about the role of a judge, which stressed the need to follow the law, even if it meant that he had to subordinate his personal and political views to do so. The abolitionist leader Wendell Phillips denounced Shaw "in terms that a gentleman would hardly apply to a pickpocket" (Levy 1957, 95). Recent historians have been equally as critical, charging that Shaw preferred to use the mask of the law as a way of hiding his moral duty to do everything he could to undermine the evil of slavery.

Shaw established his greatness through a strong sense of duty as a judge, his fidelity to the law as he understood it, and his resoluteness in the face of hostile opponents. These qualities became particularly clear in his capacity as an appellate judge. Shaw did not achieve distinction based on the literary quality of his opinions, which were often verbose and overwrought; instead, Shaw's greatness stemmed from the reasoned majesty of those opinions. He managed through them not only to accommodate the law of the commonwealth but U.S. law more generally to the rise of market-driven capitalism.

The court's 1842 term was among its most important, and during that term Shaw gave expression to two enduring concepts in U.S. labor law: the fellow servant rule and the legality of labor unions.

Lemuel Shaw did not originate the idea of the fellow servant rule, which courts in both England and South Carolina had articulated earlier. What Shaw did, however, was to take the existing weak rule and turn it into something greater. The rule held that a servant, or employee, injured through no fault of his or her own by a fellow servant could only seek an action for damages against the employee ("fellow servant") who had done the injury, not against the employer of that person. The rule, which Shaw articulated in *Farwell v. Boston and Worcester Railroad* (4 Metcalf 49 [1842]), relieved American capitalism, at a critical moment in its development, of the direct costs associated with industrial accidents and shifted those costs to the workers. The decision was widely cited both in the United States and in England.

Shaw's other significant decision in 1842 involved the law of labor conspiracies. Since the middle of the fourteenth century, English law had made it a crime to conspire to organize workers with the goal of improving their conditions of labor. As a result, trade unionism was severely restricted; those who engaged in collective organizing efforts faced criminal prosecution, fines, and jail. Early American courts had adopted the concept as well.

Most American judges subscribed to the so-called wage-fund theory that held that there was only a fixed amount of national income available for wages, which meant that employers had to be free to hire whomever they wanted and at a level dictated by the balance sheet. More than a dozen cases had ended in convictions between 1806 and 1842, when Shaw issued his opinion in *Commonwealth v. Hunt* (4 Metcalf 111 [1842]).

The case began in 1840 when Jeremiah Horne, a member of the Boston Journeymen Bootmakers' Society, refused to pay a fine to the society for doing extra work without compensation, a practice that violated the society's rules. Even after his employer agreed to pay the fine, Horne remained resolute, and largely because he feared a strike by other workers, his employer discharged him from his position. Horne then complained to the district attorney in Boston, Samuel D. Parker, who sued the society as a criminal conspiracy. The society members were found guilty, but they appealed to Chief Justice Shaw and his court.

Shaw's achievement in *Commonwealth v. Hunt* was to exercise fidelity to established doctrine involving the law of labor while giving trade unionists the legal support they needed to organize. Shaw recognized that in some instances trade unions might conspire to serve bad purposes, but the mere act of being part of a union did not constitute a conspiracy. Moreover, Shaw concluded, a union might appropriately engage in activities that would provide assistance to its members in time of trouble, improve intellectual or social conditions, improve their craftsmanship, and even raise their wages. Since these were lawful ends, it was also appropriate, and lawful, to form a union with just such purposes and to have it operate as a closed shop, one in which the union could require that only its members be employed by an owner.

The decision in *Hunt* came at particularly critical moment in the history of labor and the law. On the one hand, labor was busy with an increasingly active agenda of organizing its growing ranks; on the other hand, legal reformers were pressing for wholesale codification of the common law, a development that Shaw opposed. In this instance, Shaw was able to adapt the law to the growing realities of the industrial labor market while retaining the prerogative of judges to invoke the common law process to promote social change. Shaw, in the end, wanted to make certain that he and his fellow judges, not just legislators enacting codes, retained the power to change and adapt the law to new social circumstances.

Shaw's skill at adapting settled law through the judicial process resulted a year later in another enduring milepost, *Brown v. Kendall* (6 Cushing 292 [1850]). The emerging American market economy depended on rewarding people who were willing to take risks and engage in ventures for productive ends. The traditional rules covering torts—civil wrongs—provided that a person acted at his or her own peril. What the emerging market economy needed, however, was a rule that put greater emphasis on blameworthiness. That meant the law had to be structured in such a way that the injured person had to show why the law should shift the loss onto the one who caused the injury. Liability became a necessary condition of fault instead of being the indiscriminate product of all acts that caused an injury.

Shaw's opinion in *Kendall* held that a plaintiff had to demonstrate either that the intention of the defendant who caused the injury was unlawful or that he or she was at fault. If the injury was unavoidable and the defendant had acted without blame, then there could be no liability. What Shaw decided, what he read into American law, was that those who engaged in economic activity should not be exposed to liability for the consequences of pure accidents, unless a prudent person could have foreseen the possibility of harm. As a result, risk-creating enterprises were viewed as less hazardous than they had been under the common law.

A year later, Shaw added to his view that the law and courts should assist entrepreneurs. At the heart of doing so was the definition of the state's police powers—those powers of the legislature to deal with health, safety, morals, and welfare. In *Commonwealth v. Alger* (7 Cushing 53 [1851]), Shaw broadly defined the scope of those powers.

The case involved a defendant, Alger, who had erected a wharf in violation of legislative boundary lines. Alger claimed that since he had built the wharf entirely on his property the law had no application and was invalid. His legal counsel insisted that the state could only interfere with Alger's property rights if it compensated him justly when doing so. Shaw, however, took a dramatically different tack. He emphasized that public rights took precedence over private rights and that all private property was subject to restraint in its use for the public good. Shaw noted that the legislature has the power "of defining and securing the rights of the public" and "to make such reasonable regulations as they judge necessary to protect public . . . rights" (7 *Cushing* 104). For the next century, the aggressive view of the police power struck by Shaw would gradually prevail over a strict laissez-faire ideology. The rise of the police powers also fitted with one of Shaw's other goals: placing courts and legislatures in the position of building the strength of the commonwealth by constantly balancing individual rights against the need for government to shape the public good.

Shaw was an important and influential judge because he combined a respect for the development of public policy through the courts with a belief that his responsibility was to interpret the law as he understood it. Thus Shaw left a legacy of judging in which he once observed that "[i]t is not enough to say, that the law is so established. . . . The rule may be so good a rule. . . . But some better reason must be given for it than that, so it was enacted, or so it was decided" (Levy 1957, 334). He managed, therefore, to fix what he deemed enlightened public policy at the root of all legal principles, and that approach made it possible for him to domesticate the received common law of England and to make the result compatible with the practical realities of a rapidly expanding economy and growing state power. Oliver Wendell Holmes Jr., himself one of the nation's most eminent jurists, observed about Shaw that "[f]ew have lived who were his equal in their understanding of the grounds of public policy to which all laws must be ultimately referred" (1881, 106).

Kermit L. Hall

References and Further Reading:

Chase, F. H. 1918. *Lemuel Shaw, Chief Justice of the Supreme Judicial Court of Massachusetts, 1830–1860*. Boston: Houghton Mifflin.

Cover, Robert. 1975. *Justice Accused: Anti-Slavery and the Judicial Process*. New Haven, Conn.: Yale University Press.

Hall, Kermit L. 1989. *The Magic Mirror: Law in American History*. New York: Oxford University Press.

Holmes, Oliver Wendell, Jr. 1881. *The Common Law*. London: Macmillan.

Levy, Leonard W. 1957. *The Law of the Commonwealth and Chief Justice Shaw*. New York: Oxford University Press.

Osgood, Russell K., ed. 1992. *The History of the Law in Massachusetts: The Supreme Judicial Court, 1692–1992*. Boston: Supreme Judicial Court Historical Society.

Schwartz, Bernard. 1997. *A Book of Legal Lists*. New York: Oxford University Press.

SIRICA, JOHN JOSEPH

(1904–1992)

JOHN JOSEPH SIRICA
Bettmann/Corbis

JOHN J. SIRICA WAS THE UNITED States district court judge whose persistence in presiding over the Watergate cases led to Pres. Richard Nixon's resignation. Sirica's order that tape recordings of White House conversations about the Watergate break-in be made available to prosecutors set him on collision course with President Nixon, who invoked executive privilege to argue that the tapes were not subject to judicial scrutiny. In a historic ruling the Supreme Court upheld Sirica's order in *United States v. Nixon* (1974), precipitating Nixon's fall from power. Sirica was known as a tough, unpredictable trial judge. His stubborn pursuit of the facts during the Watergate cases, however, made him a national celebrity. Several colleges conferred honorary degrees on him, and *Time* magazine named him "Man of the Year" in 1973.

John Sirica was born in Waterbury, Connecticut, 19 March 1904. He was the son of an Italian immigrant father, Ferdinand Sirica, and a second-generation Italian American mother, Rose Zinno. According to Sirica's own account, his childhood was the "sad odyssey" of a poor immigrant family during Depression-era America (Sirica 1979, 19). The family moved from town to town, his father failing in one business venture after another, until finally settling in Washington, D.C., in 1919, where his father made a modest living as a pool hall operator and barber. Others have disputed this account, however, noting that the Siricas wintered in Florida and were buying property in Miami even at the height of the Depression. The senior Sirica had been arrested for violation of the Volstead Act. Although the charges were later dropped, there is some evidence that the pool hall and barber shop he operated may have been fronts for illegal bootlegging and gambling (Adler 2000).

Whichever account is accurate, Sirica's youth was not one of privilege, and he began working early to support himself. He was a mechanic's helper, a garbage man, a life guard, and a boxing instructor at the local Young Men's Christian Association (YMCA). The latter skill he put to use on more than one occasion while helping his father with unruly customers at the pool hall. In 1921, he graduated from Columbia Preparatory School with what he said was the equivalent of two or three years of high school. In those years only a high school diploma was needed for law school, and Sirica, encouraged by his father and his uncle, Fonzi Sirica, entered George Washington School of Law. Unprepared for the rigors of law school, however, Sirica dropped out after a few weeks. The following year he applied and was admitted to Georgetown Law School, but again he gave up after only a month. Finally, in 1923, Sirica was readmitted to Georgetown and persevered, graduating in the middle of his class three years later in June 1926.

While in law school Sirica began fighting exhibition bouts to earn extra money. Unsure of his ability to make it in the legal profession, he considered becoming a professional prize fighter. In July 1926, while waiting for the results of the bar exam, he fought his only professional bout, winning a ten-round welterweight match in Miami. After the fight his parents were furious with the younger Sirica and convinced their son to stick with the law and return to Washington, D.C., to look for work.

Sirica was turned down by most of the city's major law firms. Eventually, in 1926 he landed a job practicing criminal law in the office of a friend of one of his former YMCA sparring partners. For the next few years he apprenticed to Bert Emerson, a skilled trial lawyer and one of Sirica's closest friends. Sirica's early legal career lacked promise. He struggled to make it through law school, and once in practice, he lost his first thirteen court-assigned felony cases. He barely made enough money to pay his rent. Once, in desperation, he punched a vice squad policeman during an argument in the prosecutor's office.

In 1930, Sirica was offered a job by another former sparring companion, Leo Rover, who had been appointed U.S. attorney by President Hoover. A condition for becoming an assistant U.S. attorney, however, was obtaining the endorsement of two Republican members of Congress. Up to that point, Sirica had been uninterested in politics and unconcerned with party labels. Through family connections he was able to secure the endorsements of two Republican members of Congress and the position. During the next three and a half years, Sirica gained valuable trial experience prosecuting nearly 200 cases. More important, this position cemented his political affiliation. His father had been a staunch Democrat who disliked Hoover, but the junior Sirica later said that he "never forgot" the favor Republicans had done for him, and from that point on politics became "sort of a hobby" (Sirica 1979, 33–36).

With Franklin Roosevelt's election, Sirica left the U.S. attorney's office in 1934 and began his own law office. For the next fifteen years Sirica survived with a meager practice. One of his few important cases during that period was a defense of journalist Walter Winchell against a libel suit. The law business, however, was scarce, and Sirica turned to promoting prize fights to help his financial situation. The venture failed, but Sirica developed a lifelong friendship with the former heavyweight champion Jack Dempsey. He and Dempsey briefly toured the country selling war bonds during World War II, and Dempsey later became best man at Sirica's wedding to Lucile Camalier in 1952.

While waiting for work in his private practice, Sirica became increasingly active in Republican politics. He later wrote that "I had it in the back of my mind that some day I'd like to be a federal judge, and thought that my work in politics might help" (Sirica 1979, 37). In 1940 he was elected to the Republican state committee in Washington, D.C., and actively campaigned for Wendell Willkie in 1940, Thomas Dewey in 1948, Robert Taft in 1952, and Dwight Eisenhower and Richard Nixon in 1956.

His politicking paid off. Sirica soon developed close friendships with influential members of the Washington establishment, including Federal Bureau of Investigation director J. Edgar Hoover and Sen. Joseph McCarthy. He served as general counsel to the House Select Committee to Investigate the Federal Communications Commission in 1944, and in 1949 he was offered the chief counsel position for a McCarthy committee investigating communist infiltration of the government. That same year, however, Sirica accepted a position with Hogan and Hartson, a large Washington law firm that needed an attorney with trial experience and was impressed by Sirica's growing political connections. For the first time in his life Sirica was making a comfortable salary. Fortunately, his wife, Lucile, convinced him to pass on the McCarthy job, which, in the event, went to Roy Cohn. Had Sirica accepted the position, it would have undoubtedly ended any opportunity he had for becoming a federal judge.

Sirica was offered, but declined, an appointment by Eisenhower in 1956 to be a commissioner of immigration. The following year Judge Henry A.

Schweinhaut retired from the United States District Court for the District of Columbia. This time Sirica called in his political favors. His friendship with officials in the Eisenhower Justice Department, including Deputy Attorney General William Rogers, the official charged with screening the administration's judicial nominees, secured him the appointment. He was nominated by President Eisenhower on 25 February 1957, received his commission on 28 March, and was sworn in as a federal district court judge on 2 April 1957.

During the next fifteen years Sirica's work on the bench was routine, though not particularly distinguished. He had a relatively high rate of reversal by the court of appeals, and his opinions were known neither for their erudition nor legal craft. In fact, in a court "known for its thoughtful and progressive jurists, he was regarded near the bottom in depth of legal knowledge" (Sussman 1974, 131). In those years, because of its territorial status, district court judges in Washington, D.C., acted both as federal judges and, in some ways, as state court judges, hearing large numbers of relatively minor criminal cases. Sirica quickly developed a reputation for being tough on crime. His working-class background, his experience as a prosecutor, and a lingering lack of confidence in his own legal acumen shaped his approach to judging. He was known as an outspoken judge who did not allow traditional ideas of courtroom procedure or legal technicality to thwart his search for the truth. He often questioned witnesses himself, he was uninhibited when instructing juries, and he was quick to reject plea bargains if he felt defendants were getting off too easily. Local reports nicknamed Sirica "Maximum John" because of his willingness to impose stiff sentences (Barnes 1992).

In 1971, Sirica assumed the role as chief judge of the District of Columbia District Court, a position based on seniority. A year later, while presiding over a grisly murder trial, Sirica learned of the Watergate break-in. Seven men were arrested for breaking into the headquarters of the Democratic National Committee in the Watergate complex. At least three of these individuals—E. Howard Hunt, G. Gordon Liddy, and James McCord—had clear ties to the Nixon campaign. As chief judge, Sirica knew that assigning the case posed a dilemma. If it were tried by a Republican-appointed judge, there would be charges of cover-up, but if it went to a Democratic appointee, there would be charges of overzealousness. With a reputation as a publicity hound, Sirica eventually decided to take the case himself.

The original trial of the Watergate burglars ended in January 1973 with convictions of the men on relatively minor charges for the break-in and conspiracy. The defendants, however, remained silent about any involvement by higher officials in the Nixon administration. Sirica's handling of the trial was criticized in the press. During the trial he had ignored standard procedures in selecting a jury; he issued, but then reversed, a pretrial order that sought to gag nearly all press coverage of the case; and he jailed the Washington bureau chief of the *Los Angeles Times* for refusing to turn over information from interviews conducted by the newspaper (Sussman 1974, 131–133).

Sirica himself later recounted his frustration with the trial. His instincts told him that there was more to the case than a botched burglary by low-level operatives in the Nixon administration. In an unusual move, Sirica ordered presentencing investigations for the seven defendants but let the convicted men know that the severity of their sentences would depend heavily on whether they cooperated with ongoing investigations by Congress and other federal prosecutors. Within weeks James McCord delivered a letter to Sirica, which the judge read aloud in open court. The letter charged that perjury had been committed in the initial trial and that bribes had been made to the defendants in exchange for their silence. Sirica was outraged and later recounted that he found the "whole thing disgusting." He deferred sentencing McCord but imposed stiff provisional sentences of up to forty years on the remaining defendants, leaving open the possibility of reduction for those who decided to cooperate (Sirica 1979, 84–90).

From that point on the Watergate scandal quickly began to unravel. During subsequent federal grand jury and congressional investigations the existence of the White House tapes became known. The tapes revealed that Nixon had approved plans for a cover-up just six days after the Watergate break-in. When Sirica issued a subpoena for the tapes, a long legal battle ensued in which the president claimed the tapes were protected by executive privilege. Attorneys for Nixon pressured Sirica, arguing in court that what was at stake was "nothing less than the continued existence of the presidency as a functioning institution" ("Man of the Year," 15). Sirica disagreed. In an opinion praised by legal scholars as unexpectedly erudite, he argued that the president's lawyers had failed to provide "any reason for suspending the power of courts to get evidence and rule on questions of privilege in criminal matters simply because it is the President of the United States who holds the evidence" (15). On 24 July 1974, a unanimous Supreme Court upheld Sirica's order. Faced with certain impeachment in the House of Representatives, Nixon announced his resignation fifteen days later.

Sirica went on to preside over the trials of several top Nixon aides, including H. R. Haldeman, John Ehrlichman, and former attorney general John Mitchell, each of whom was found guilty. In all, more than nineteen top administration officials were convicted or pled guilty to violations of the law. Sirica reduced the sentences of most who cooperated with prosecutors but handed down tough sentences on those who remained recalcitrant.

Critics contend that Sirica's handling of the trials was arbitrary and that he overstepped his judicial role. His heavy-handed questioning of witnesses from the bench and his use of the provisional sentencing procedure was criticized by legal scholars. Philip Kurland, from the University of Chicago, called it "a form of extortion" and something for which Sirica deserved to be censured ("Man of the Year"). Despite the criticism, Sirica's tactics were upheld on appeal. Upholding G. Gordon Liddy's conviction on conspiracy and burglary charges, United States Court of Appeals judge Harold Leventhal in *United States vs. Liddy* (509 F. 2d 428 [1974]) wrote: "Judge Sirica's palpable search for the truth in such a trial was not only permissible, it was in the highest tradition of his office as a federal judge" (442).

Sirica's courage and tenacity in getting to the truth during the Watergate affair also won him deep public respect. In choosing him "Man of the Year" in 1973, *Time Magazine* wrote: "Exposure of wrongdoing is, of course, the first requisite in achieving justice—and Sirica deserves the prime credit for taking those vital initial steps." Perhaps more broadly, his handling of the Watergate cases was seen as an important "vindication of the legal system at a time of great stress" and national peril ("Man of the Year").

Within a year of concluding the Watergate cases, Sirica retired as chief judge of the district court and assumed senior status. Countless books have been written and movies produced about Watergate. Most focus on the actions of the Nixon White House or those involved in investigating the scandal. In 1979 Sirica wrote his own book, entitled *To Set the Record Straight*, detailing his experience during the trials. He retired from the bench in 1986. He died 14 August 1992.

Had it not been for Watergate, John Sirica's career probably would be unworthy of historical note. Nevertheless, if great cases make great judges, Sirica is an extraordinary example. Whether his career exemplifies what is wrong, or what is right, with the U.S. judicial system has been debated. Sirica's nomination to the bench was a reward for political service to the Republican Party, his educational background was mediocre at best, and he was known as a careless and irritable trial judge. Nevertheless, at time of great constitutional peril, John Sirica rose to the occasion. He has been called "a tough, tenacious, patriotic Harry Truman of the Bench" ("Man of the Year"). His refusal to bend against the full panoply of power of the president of the United States during a moment in history established him as a lasting symbol of the American judiciary's insistence on the rule of law.

Cornell Clayton

References and Further Reading:

Adler, Renata. 2000. "A Court of No Appeal." *Harper's Magazine*, August, 45–56.

Judy Sheindlin (1942–)

Best known as the outspoken star of television's *Judge Judy*, Judy Sheindlin was born in Brooklyn, New York, in 1942 and was hired in 1972 as a prosecutor of juvenile delinquents. Ten years later, New York City mayor Ed Koch appointed Sheindlin to preside over a family court in the Bronx. Judy's second husband (whose last name she now shares) was also appointed to a criminal court, with Judge Judy subsequently being made Manhattan's supervising judge and her husband elevated to the New York Supreme Court (Sheindlin 1997, 5).

Judge Judy has strong opinions on every topic she addresses. She opposes what she believes is undue regard for "victims," many of whom have brought problems upon themselves. She frequently refers to juveniles as "punks" and believes that delinquents should find their first experience in court to be "an excruciating experience they will never want to repeat" (Sheindlin 1997, 37). She opposes the use of probation and thinks that even juveniles with public defenders should have to pay some of their fees. She is a harsh critic of the foster care system, especially when it pays relatives for supporting children, and she believes that fathers and mothers should, whenever possible, share custody of children of divorce. She prides herself on awarding custody to men in cases where their wives have unjustifiably accused them of sexual abuse.

Sheindlin has noted that there are "two kinds of judges." She explained:

> Some liken their jobs to that of an umpire; they sift through information that lawyers provide. Then they make decisions based on that information.
>
> I am generally unhappy with that approach, unless the lawyering is superb, be-

(continues)

Barnes, Bart. 1992. "John Sirica, Watergate Judge, Dies." *Washington Post,* 15 August, A01.

"Man of the Year. Judge John J. Sirica: Standing Firm for the Primacy of Law." *Time Magazine* (7 January 1974), 14–20. Available at <http://www.time.com/time/special/moy/1973.html>. Accessed 12 January 2003.

Sirica, John J. 1979. *To Set the Record Straight: The Break-in, the Tapes, the Conspirators, the Pardon.* New York: W. W. Norton.

Sussman, Barry. 1974. *The Great Coverup: Nixon and the Scandal of Watergate.* New York: Crowell.

(continued)

> cause without quality information you can make mistakes.
>
> In life, as on the bench, you are either passive or active. I prefer the second kind of judging—where the court actively seeks the truth. I ask a lot of questions. (1997, 161)

Sheindlin advocates an open judicial system but seems to betray concern over public opinion in a story about a prosecutor who asked for "an adjournment in contemplation of dismissal" in the case of a fourteen-year-old accused of sodomizing a four-year-old, who was too traumatized to testify. Noting that "I could just see the headlines: SLAP ON WRIST BY SOFT FAMILY COURT JUDGE RESULTS IN TRAGEDY," Judge Judy instead asked the prosecutor to call his first witness, and when he was unable to do so, he had to withdraw charges, thus succeeding in helping her dodge "the potential media bullet" (Sheindlin 1997, 206).

Sheindlin summarized her views of personal responsibility as follows:

> If you want to eat, you have to work.
> If you have children, be prepared to take care of them.
> If you break the law, it is your fault. Be prepared to pay.
> If you tap the public purse, be prepared to account. (1997, 238)

In addition to calling for increased responsibility, Judge Judy enjoys telling stories of her career. Once, facing a father whose denials of paternity conflicted with a blood test, she asked how he could be so certain. He responded, "Because I was wearing a condominium." Judge Judy replied that "his condominium obviously had a hole in the roof" (Sheindlin 1997, 19).

REFERENCE:

Sheindlin, Judy, with Josh Getlin. 1997. *Don't Pee on My Leg and Tell Me It's Raining: America's Toughest Family Court Judge Speaks Out.* New York: HarperPerennial.

STONE, GEORGE WASHINGTON

(1811–1894)

George Washington Stone
Alabama Department of Archives and History

Alabama Supreme Court justice George Washington Stone built his reputation on hard work and conscientious attention to detail. During his twenty-eight years on the bench he wrote over 2,400 opinions extending through volumes 40–100 of the official reports of the court (the *Alabama Reports* for 1856–1865 and 1876–1894). By the time of his death he had, in the words of the *Albany* (New York) *Law Journal*, helped make the Alabama Supreme Court "one of the ablest in the country" (Huebner 1999, 185).

Born 24 October 1811 in Bedford County, Virginia, one of ten children of Micajah and Sarah (Leftwich) Stone, George Washington Stone moved to Lincoln County, Tennessee, at the age of six. Micajah Stone prospered there but died when George was only sixteen, making it impossible for his son to attend college. George instead used his small inheritance to study law with James Fulton, a member of the bar in Fayetteville, Tennessee, after completing his schooling in old-field (privately subscribed) schools and local academies.

In 1834 he married Mary Gillespie of Franklin, Tennessee, and the couple immediately moved to Talladega County, Alabama. Within months

Stone had been admitted to the Alabama bar, and five years later he joined the state's Supreme Court bar. He was to spend twenty-six of the next sixty years in private legal practice, eighteen of those years in partnership with men who, like Stone himself, would serve as justices of the Alabama Supreme Court.

Described by a contemporary as a "laborious and careful" attorney, Stone proved to be a master of chancery court practice although he was "never very successful before juries," owing to his plain oratory (Caffey 1909, 169). This lack of oratorical skills and his "somewhat austere demeanor" kept Stone from achieving widespread personal popularity, and he seldom succeeded as candidate for elected office. He was, however, "universally respected and by his intimates much beloved" (191).

Stone began his legal career in Sylacauga, Alabama, serving also for a time as the town's postmaster. He moved next to the town of Talladega, where from 1840 to 1843 he practiced law with William P. Chilton, the first of Stone's law partners who later became a justice of the Alabama Supreme Court.

Following the death of his first wife in 1849, Stone married Emily Moore and relocated to her home in Lowndes County, where he worked in partnership with Thomas J. Judge, whom he succeeded on the Supreme Court in 1856. After the disorder of Reconstruction forced Stone off the court in 1865, he practiced in partnership with David Clopton and James H. Clanton in Montgomery. In 1876 Stone was reappointed to the Supreme Court, where David Clopton joined him in 1884.

Stone, a firm supporter of Andrew Jackson, had become active in the Democratic party in Talladega County soon after he began his career there, and he later helped organize the first bar association in the county. In August 1843, Gov. Benjamin Fitzpatrick appointed Stone judge of the Ninth Circuit Court to fill an unexpired term. The legislature elected him to a full six-year term in December of that year, but Stone chose not to stand for election after the death of his first wife, retiring from the bench in 1849.

In 1856 the General Assembly elected Stone an associate justice of the Supreme Court, a position to which he was reelected in 1862. The first legislature that convened after the defeat of the Confederacy called on Stone and J. W. Shepherd, editor of the *Alabama Reporter,* to prepare a revised penal code for the state that incorporated the postwar changes in the criminal code. Stone continued to serve on the Supreme Court until Provisional Gov. Lewis E. Parsons removed all three members of the court from office in 1865.

In March 1876 the first legislature that convened after the redemption of the state by the Democratic party once again selected Stone to a vacancy on the Supreme Court, this one caused by the death of his former law partner,

Thomas J. Judge. Stone was elected by the people to a six-year term on the court in 1880 and was appointed chief justice in 1884 by Gov. Edward A. O'Neal, a position to which the people reelected him in 1886 and 1892. He remained chief justice until his death on 11 March 1894 at the age of eighty-three, becoming one of the longest-serving justices in Alabama history.

Stone's importance to the judicial history of Alabama does not rest on his length of service, however, but on the number and quality of the decisions that he wrote and on his contribution to the professionalization of the practice of law in the state. Although Stone was neither well educated nor particularly brilliant, his opinions were, his contemporaries noted, "clear and vigorous" ("Chief Justice George W. Stone" 1970, 165) and marked by "sturdy common sense" (Caffey 1909, 183).

During his first term on the court, Stone wrote 491 opinions, an average of 49 per year. Between 1876 and 1894 he wrote 1,958 opinions, an average of 109 per year. "The numbers are more remarkable," a contemporary noted, "when it is known that he never employed a stenographer but wrote very slowly in his own hand" (Caffey 1909, 182). Although rendered in the midst of the political turmoil of the Civil War, two of Stone's decisions concerning conscription laws enacted by the Confederate government marked him as a moderate on the issue of states' rights. In reaching these decisions he relied on opinions rendered earlier by the United States Supreme Court, and that Court later cited Stone's wartime decisions in its own opinions.

In *Ex parte Hill in re Willis v. Confederate States* (1864), Stone recognized a dividing line between the rights of local and general governments that had to be "kept distinct" (38 Alabama 455). While conceding that the line was "sometimes difficult of ascertainment," he nonetheless argued that it "must when discovered be respected" (455). Stone also maintained that if an officer of either government exercised its legitimate power erroneously, correction could only come from courts within that government. Conversely, Stone held, a state or national court could give redress only when an officer of the other government clearly exercised power outside that government's jurisdiction (38 Alabama 429).

In *State ex rel. Dawson, in re Strawbridge and Mays* (1864), Stone, unlike some other Confederate judges, followed previous rulings by the United States Supreme Court that when there was a conflict between state and federal law, and each acted within its own legitimate domain, national law took precedence (39 Alabama 367). In both decisions Stone clearly acknowledged an inviolable domain for both state and national governments, whether federal or confederate.

In a speech to the Alabama Bar Association in 1889, Stone spoke glowingly of the contributions of modern technology to social progress and urged judicial science "to keep pace with the necessities of this progress"

Stone 1889, 112). In numerous post–Civil War cases, Stone himself, drawing on United States Supreme Court decisions such as the *Slaughter House Cases* and *United States v. Cruikshank*, helped develop what his first biographer called "an excellent body of corporation law in Alabama" (Caffey 1909, 185).

In *Perry v. New Orleans, Mobile and Chattanooga Railroad Company* (1876), for example, Stone wrote that state legislatures (but not, in this case, the city of Mobile) were entitled to use their police power to facilitate projects in the public interest, including railroads (55 Alabama 425). In other cases he conferred on corporations all the rights of a natural person, and on more than one occasion he struck down state laws that treated railroads or other companies differently from individuals. Stone thus brought Jacksonian antimonopoly and antiprivilege ideology forward into a period of economic and corporate transformation, thereby becoming a participant in what Timothy Huebner has described as the "maturing national legal culture" (Huebner 1999, 184).

Stone penned his most influential opinions in a series of cases restricting the use of self-defense arguments in murder cases. Beginning with the 1860 case *McManus v. State*, he "set the tone for thirty years of decisions by the Alabama Supreme Court in the area of manslaughter, homicide, and self-defense" (Huebner 1999, 176). In that case Stone not only denounced the southern code of honor that promoted violence but also unequivocally asserted that "an insult, or an assault, or an assault and battery, which does not endanger life or member, furnishes no excuse for taking life" (36 Alabama 293).

The common law doctrine of a "duty to retreat" lay at the heart of Stone's arguments. In *Ex parte Nettles* (1877) he explicitly rejected an earlier, more lenient decision by the Mississippi Supreme Court, which he linked with a growing "carnival of manslaughter" (58 Alabama, 274). In *Bain v. State* (1881), Stone drew on Blackstone's *Commentaries* to establish unambiguous criteria for justifiable homicide: The defendant must not "provoke or encourage the difficulty"; the defendant must be "so menaced . . . as to create a reasonable apprehension of the loss of his life"; and there must be no "reasonable mode of escape" for the defendant (70 Alabama, 7). In *Myers v. State* (1878), Stone reiterated his contention that encouraging or provoking a fight nullified self-defense (62 Alabama 599); and in *Cleveland v. State* (1888), he put the "burden on the defendant to show that he had no alternative" to murder (86 Alabama 10).

Stone also worked to limit the application of the state's concealed carry law (*Polk v. State*, 62 Alabama 237) and the use of the insanity defense (*Shorter v. State*, 63 Alabama 129). During Stone's lifetime his campaign to curtail brutality in the state often put him at odds with many of his fellow southern justices. But in the next century Justice Oliver Wendell Holmes Jr. cited several of Stone's opinions on self-defense as precedent in cases before the United States Supreme Court, reflecting a new distaste for legalized violence.

The scholarly inclinations and meticulous craftsmanship displayed in Stone's opinions, along with his own high professional and personal standards, made him a natural leader in the movement to elevate the standing of the bench and bar in the state. He began in 1841 by helping organize a bar association in the community in which he had just entered practice, and in 1879 he played a central role in organizing the Alabama Bar Association. During his last years on the Supreme Court he used the association's annual meetings to advocate judicial reform, especially consolidation of common law and equity jurisdiction into a single court system and simplification of pleadings in civil suits. Although he saw little progress toward these goals during his lifetime, in the 1950s Alabama adopted most of the reforms that Stone had advocated.

Stone moved to Montgomery after his first appointment to the Supreme Court and lived there until his death, a period of thirty-eight years. His second wife died in 1862, and in 1866 he married Mary (Harrison) Wright, who along with three children, George Washington Stone, Martha S. Griffin, and William J. Stone, survived him. He played the violin entirely by ear and in his later years enjoyed employing his instrument to entertain his children and grandchildren in his Montgomery home, where he also spent many hours cultivating an extensive flower garden.

Like several other justices before him, Stone enjoyed writing verse, and in 1871 he published a small volume of his work. A contemporary who read the book later remarked that he was amazed that "such meritorious judicial opinions and such unmeritorious verse . . . could have been written by the same man" (Caffey 1909, 188). Today, however, his poetry places him squarely if peripherally in the mainstream of late-nineteenth-century humorous poetry.

The year before his death the Alabama Bar Association organized a celebration in honor of his fiftieth anniversary on the bench and presented him with a silver cup. When he died on 11 March 1894, Alabama's attorney general, William L. Martin, paid tribute to Stone in the official report of the Supreme Court as "an able and reliable lawyer and a learned and upright judge" ("Memorial" 1893, xx). Following Stone's burial in Oakwood cemetery in Montgomery, Gov. Thomas G. Jones declared in an official proclamation: "No man ever lived in Alabama who did her more honor; and none ever died within her borders whose loss was a greater calamity to the state" (Caffey 1909, 167).

Thus ended George Washington Stone's half-century of service to Alabama. He had achieved his success not by brilliance or personal magnetism but by diligence and devotion to his profession during a career spanning five decades, from Andrew Jackson to William Jennings Bryan.

Ellen Barrier Garrison

References and Further Reading:

Adkinson, Janis Faye. 1991. "George Washington Stone and Alabama Criminal Law: A Battle against the Southern Legal Tradition." Master's thesis, University of Florida.

Brantley, William H., Jr. 1943. *Chief Justice Stone of Alabama*. Birmingham, Ala.: Birmingham Publishing.

Caffey, George. 1909. "George Washington Stone, 1811–1894." In *Great American Lawyers*, vol. 6, edited by William Draper Lewis. Philadelphia: John C. Winston, 165–193.

"Chief Justice George W. Stone." 1970. *Alabama Lawyer* 31: 165.

Huebner, Timothy S. 1999. *The Southern Judicial Tradition: State Judges and Sectional Distinctiveness 1790–1890*. Athens: University of Georgia Press.

"Memorial." 1893. 100 *Alabama Reports*, ix–xx.

Merchant, Alice. 1957. "The Historical Background of the Procedural Reform Movement in Alabama." *Alabama Law Review* 9 (Spring): 284–292.

Stone, George W. 1889. "Judicial Reform." *Proceedings of the Alabama State Bar Association:* 108–121.

———. Papers. Alabama Department of Archives and History, Montgomery, Alabama.

STONE, HARLAN FISKE

(1872–1946)

Harlan Fiske Stone
Harris & Ewing, Collection of the Supreme Court of the United States

Harlan Fiske Stone was an associate justice of the United States Supreme Court from 1925 to 1941 and chief justice from 1941 to 1946. Pres. Calvin Coolidge nominated Stone as the replacement for Justice Joseph McKenna on 5 January 1925. Stone was the first Supreme Court nominee to appear before the Senate committee, which was examining his qualifications. Stone effectively responded to the questions posed by the committee's members and was subsequently confirmed by a seventy-one–six Senate vote on 5 February 1925. When Chief Justice William Howard Taft resigned in 1930, many expected Stone to succeed him. Taft, however, fearing that Stone would be unable to persuade the justices to decide cases unanimously or coalesce behind a single rationale, did not recommend Stone for the position. Taft's concern prompted President Hoover to appoint Charles Evans Hughes instead. Stone served as an associate justice until 12 June 1941, when Pres. Franklin Roosevelt nominated him to replace Hughes as chief justice. The U.S. Senate unanimously confirmed Stone as chief justice on 27 June 1941. Stone, a Republican, was one of only two chief justices nominated to the position by a president from the other political party (Edward D. White was the other) and was one of only three chief justices elevated from the rank of associate justice (White and William H. Rehnquist were the others).

Stone was born in Chesterfield, New Hampshire, on 11 November 1872 to Frederick Lawson Stone and Ann Sophia (Butler) Stone. He grew up on the family farm, where he acquired his independence, diligence, and sense of civic obligation. Although his rural New England upbringing was a significant influence on his development, he eventually chose a college education over the farm life. He took his B.A. (1894) and M.A. (1897) degrees from Amherst College, where he graduated Phi Beta Kappa and served as class president three times. He taught high school to finance his law school education at Columbia. He completed his law degree at Columbia in 1898 and was admitted to the New York bar the following year. Stone began his legal practice with the New York firm of Sullivan and Cromwell in 1899 and eventually became head of its litigation division. Among his clients was the banker J. P. Morgan. While he developed his own Wall Street practice at Sullivan and Cromwell he also served on the law faculty at Columbia. In 1910 he was named dean of Columbia Law School. Stone engaged in the academic life in addition to maintaining his law practice, and he published frequently in law reviews and other professional journals. During his tenure as dean, Columbia gained prominence as one of the country's leading schools of legal realism jurisprudence. He married Agnes Harvey in 1899, a marriage that lasted forty-seven years, until his death. Stone and his wife had two sons.

Calvin Coolidge, who succeeded to the presidency on the death of Warren Harding in 1923, was Stone's friend and Amherst classmate. Coolidge brought Stone to Washington the following year to replace U.S. attorney general Harry Daugherty, whose tenure as head of the Justice Department had been severely damaged by corruption, including the Teapot Dome scandal. Coolidge not only wanted the scandal fully investigated but also wanted to restore the image of the Justice Department. Coolidge needed someone with extraordinary leadership skills as well as unquestioned integrity. Stone clearly possessed both of these attributes. Stone was "less concerned with finding proof of past abuses, grave as these were, than with establishing standards for the future" (Mason 1956, 149). Although Stone held the position of attorney general for only a year prior to his appointment as associate justice, he was able to effect substantial organizational changes in the Justice Department and rebuild its institutional stature. He made a number of personnel changes within the Justice Department, one of which was to name J. Edgar Hoover to head the Federal Bureau of Investigation. Under Stone's predecessor, the government's legal business had been badly handled. Stone required that the department's permanent legal staff prepare and argue all cases "and in major cases the brief presented by the Attorney General himself" (167). Because he enforced the law "'without fear or favor,' especially his 'overzealous' activity in purging the Justice Department of corruption and his efforts to enforce the anti-trust laws," some believed Stone to have been "kicked upstairs" when he was appointed to the Supreme Court (Mason 1956, 182). Alpheus T. Mason, author of the definitive biography on Stone, rejected this explanation. He concluded instead that Coolidge's decision to appoint Stone was prompted by Stone's record, one "marked by fearlessness and independence, as head of the Justice Department, achievements that excited the admiration of even its traditional critics; his political services during the 1924 campaign, and personal friendship" (182–185).

In 1925 Stone joined a conservative Court headed by William Howard Taft. The Court included the "Four Horsemen"—Justices Pierce Butler, James McReynolds, George Sutherland, and Willis Van Devanter—whose views led them categorically to oppose the New Deal initiatives a decade later. Many expected Stone to join the conservative majority. Almost immediately, however, Stone became the third member of the Court's moderate-liberal bloc, joining Oliver Wendell Holmes Jr. and Louis Brandeis. As a member of the Hughes Court, Stone was often found with Justices Brandeis and Benjamin Cardozo on the minority side in many significant economic regulation rulings. As was true of Holmes and Brandeis, Stone advocated the judicial self-restraint view. He believed that policy matters are the exclusive domain of the legislative branch, and Stone sought not to substitute his own policy preferences for those of elected legislators.

Stone embraced such principles as judicial self-restraint long before he began his service on the Supreme Court. He offered a series of lectures at Columbia in 1915 that were subsequently published as a book entitled *Law and Its Administration* (1967). The views contained in the volume were considered conservative, but he supported using the Fourteenth Amendment to extend federal Bill of Rights guarantees to the state level. He spoke of the Fourteenth Amendment as a "powerful and efficient agency in the protection of civil liberty from encroachment of state governmental action and from the injustice of special and class legislation" (Stone 1967, 147). He saw the "popular desire for justice" as the foundation of a "just and adequate legal system." "True law reform" began, in his view, "with the stimulation in the public mind of the love of justice, its education as to the nature of law, and the grave importance of delegating its administration only to those who are fit to bear that responsibility" (194). He adhered to many of these views throughout his judicial career but continually adapted his jurisprudence at the same time. He admitted in 1938 that he would be "surprised if there were not many things in *Law and Its Administration* with which I do not agree today" (Mason 1956, 124).

Stone had no previous judicial experience when Coolidge first nominated him for the Supreme Court. Nonetheless, he provided invaluable guidance for judges in his insightful opinions. Stone was a strong proponent of judicial deference to legislative judgment. Stone was a partisan Republican and was privately critical of Franklin Roosevelt and much of his New Deal. As a restraintist, however, he chose not to impose his own political preferences on elected legislators. One of Stone's greatest opinions came in his dissent in *United States v. Butler* (1936). The case involved review of the Agricultural Adjustment Act of 1933, which attempted to stabilize prices of agricultural products and provide financial benefits to U.S. farmers. The plan was to pay farmers not to produce on some of their acreage. The benefit payments were to come from revenues raised by a tax imposed on processors of various farm commodities. A six-justice majority struck down the measure as an unconstitutional infringement of the sovereign powers of the states.

Stone's dissent in *Butler* was grounded on his restraintist outlook. To Stone, the majority in *Butler* read the Constitution too narrowly. In an emergency such as the Great Depression, judges ought not question the means chosen by Congress to put its delegated powers into effect. Stone offered two "guiding principles of decision which ought never be absent from judicial consciousness." One was that courts are "concerned only with the power to enact statutes, not with their wisdom." The second was that although unconstitutional exercise of power by the legislative and executive branches of the government is subject to judicial restraint, "the only check upon our own exercise of power is our own sense of self-restraint." Stone argued that the Court had not followed these guidelines in deciding *Butler*. The food processing tax was struck down, he suggested, not because Congress could not levy a tax to defray public expenditures, "but because [of] the use to which its proceeds are put is disapproved" (297 U.S., 78–79).

Judicial self-restraint was again evident in Stone's majority opinion in *United States v. Darby Lumber Co.* (1941), which upheld the Fair Labor Standards Act (FLSA) of 1938. Many observers regarded the FLSA as Congress's last New Deal enactment. The ruling reversed *Hammer v. Dagenhart* (1916), and Justice Stone spoke for a unanimous Court. Interstate commerce, Stone contended, "should not be made the instrument of competition in the distribution of goods produced under substandard labor conditions." The "motive and purpose" of a regulation of interstate commerce "are matters for the legislative judgment upon the exercise of which the Constitution places no restriction and over which the courts are given no control" (*Darby Lumber*, 312 U.S., 115). The goods produced and marketed by the lumber company, Stone concluded, were part of a stream of commerce and were clearly within the reach of the federal commerce power. Stone argued that the Tenth Amendment's reserve clause "states but a truism that all is retained which has not been surrendered." There is nothing about the amendment or its origin to suggest that its purpose "was other than to allay fears that the new government might seek to exercise powers not granted" (*Darby Lumber*, 124). Until relatively recently, this portion of Stone's *Darby* opinion put into cold storage the Tenth Amendment jurisprudence known as "dual federalism," which had been used effectively to restrict the commerce power.

Stone remained on the minority side of most split decisions until the Court's doctrinal change of 1937. As a result of this change, Stone became part of the moderate-liberal majority until he became chief justice. During the infamous "court-packing" controversy of 1937, Stone indicated to Roosevelt that he did not support changing the Court's size. At the same time, he understood Roosevelt's frustration with the Court and was active behind the scenes in urging appointment of justices with the judicial philosophy of Justices Brandeis, Cardozo, and himself. After 1937, the Court essentially deferred to economic regulation initiatives both at the federal and state level. The new consensus on government power to regulate the economy did not generalize to all other constitutional issues, however. Cases containing civil liberties questions became more frequent as World War II neared, and these issues would prove to be even more divisive than economic questions. The Roosevelt appointees on the Court were more than willing to speak their minds on these matters, causing Stone to refer to justices such as Hugo Black, William Douglas, and Frank Murphy as "wild horses." Stone's relations with most of the Roosevelt-appointed justices, both before and after his elevation to chief justice, were "strained" at best. The duties of chief justice took their toll on his judicial opinions—his best opinions came prior to his elevation to chief justice.

Perhaps Stone's greatest contribution to U.S. law came in his majority opinion in *United States v. Carolene Products Co.* (1938). In *Carolene Products*, the Hughes Court upheld a federal law that prohibited the interstate shipment of so-called filled milk, which was skimmed milk mixed with animal fats. What made this opinion significant was the famous Footnote 4, where Stone suggested that there may be a "narrower scope for operation of the presumption of constitutionality when legislation appears on its face to be within a specific prohibition of the Constitution such as those of the first ten amendments . . ." (304 U.S. 152). He offered an exception to the doctrine of judicial self-restraint. The Court should subject statutes dealing with civil liberties and discrimination issues to a more searching examination than laws pertaining to economic matters. This opinion clearly suggested a "double standard." It affirmed the self-restraint approach except when personal liberties are affected by government actions. Paradoxically, the *Carolene Products* opinion suggested that statutes that restrict individual rights should be subject to a closer scrutiny because the rights protection provisions of the Bill of Rights and the Fourteenth Amendment occupy a "preferred position." Although the legislature should be allowed to correct its own mistakes in other contexts, the directive must not apply when legislative bodies cannot take corrective action. Federal court judges continue to cite the *Carolene* footnote, and the doctrine retains analytic value when courts are considering constitutional limits on government.

The analytic power of the "preferred freedom" approach was immediately evident in Stone's dissent in *Minersville School District v. Gobitis* (1940). The Court ruled in *Gobitis* that the country could ask its citizens to engage in such patriotic behavior as saluting the flag. The Jehovah Witnesses challenged compulsory participation in flag salute exercises by school children on free exercise of religion grounds. Justice Frankfurter said for the majority that "conscientious scruples" cannot relieve citizens from obedience to "general law not aimed at the promotion or restriction of religious beliefs" (310 U.S., 594). Stone was the only justice to disagree. He argued that the "very essence of the liberty" protected by the First Amendment "is the freedom of the individual from compulsion as to what he shall think and what he shall say. . . ." If the Bill of Rights guarantees are to have meaning, he continued, "they must be deemed to withhold from the state any authority to compel belief or expression of it where that expression violates religious convictions, whatever may be the legislative view of the desirability of such compulsion" (604). Heeding his "preferred freedoms" directive, he concluded that "careful scrutiny of legislative efforts to secure conformity of belief and opinion by a compulsory affirmation of the desired belief, is especially needful if civil rights are to receive any protection" (606). The position Stone advanced in *Gobitis* was sufficiently compelling that when the Court reexamined the compulsory flag salute issue less than three years later, five members of the Court joined Stone to overrule *Gobitis* in *West Virginia State Board of Education v. Barnette* (1943).

His five-year tenure as chief justice began just before Pearl Harbor and concluded less than a year after the end of World War II. Although Stone was regarded as one the great contributors to U.S. law, he was strikingly ineffective as chief justice. His elevation had been universally praised, but his distaste for administrative work and his inability to unify his fractious Court diminished his reputation and produced a decline in the public's perception of the Court's dignity and authority. In many ways, the chief justiceship was an unhappy ending to Stone's otherwise illustrious public life. In the minds of some of his colleagues, the basic problem was his inability to resolve conflict among the members of the Roosevelt Court he was chosen to lead.

Stone is not regarded as a successful chief justice because that term includes the capacity to lead the Court. Stone was almost sixty-nine when he succeeded Hughes, and he would serve only a comparatively brief time as chief justice. Nonetheless, most constitutional scholars rank him as one of the great associate justices to sit on the Court. He was an intellectual with an open mind and clear sense of justice. The thinking contained in his insightful opinions had a profound influence on the Warren Court and its expansion of constitutional rights during the 1960s. He served as chief justice until he suffered a stroke on 22 April 1946. He was stricken as he completed his dissent in *Girouard v. United States*, and he died in Washington, D.C., of a cerebral hemorrhage later that day.

Peter G. Renstrom

References and Further Reading:

Abraham, Henry J. 1992. *Justices and Presidents: A Political History of Appointments to the Supreme Court*. 3d ed. New York: Oxford University Press.

Johnson, John W. 1994. "Harlan Fiske Stone." In *The Supreme Court Justices: A Biographical Dictionary*, edited by Melvin I. Urofsky. New York: Garland, 425–434.

Konefsky, Samuel J. 1946. *Chief Justice Stone and the Supreme Court*. New York: Macmillan.

Mason, Alpheus Thomas. 1956. *Harlan Fiske Stone: Pillar of the Law*. New York: Viking.

———. 1969–1978. "Harlan Fiske Stone." In *The Justices of the Supreme Court, 1789–1969: Their Lives and Major Opinions*, edited by Leon Friedman and Fred L. Israel. New York: Chelsea House, 1099–1116.

Minersville School District v. Gobitis. 310 U.S. 586 (1940).

Morehead v. New York ex rel. Tipaldo. 298 U.S. 587 (1936).

Stone, Harlan Fiske. 1967. *Law and Its Administration*. New York: AMS Press.

United States v. Butler. 297 U.S. 1 (1936).

United States v. Carolene Products Co. 304 U.S. 144 (1938).

United States v. Darby Lumber Co. 312 U.S. 100 (1941).

Urofsky, Melvin I. 1997. *Division and Discord: The Supreme Court under Stone and Vinson*. Columbia: University of South Carolina Press.

White, G. Edward. 1976. *The American Judicial Tradition: Profiles of Leading American Judges*. New York: Oxford University Press.

STORY, JOSEPH

(1779–1845)

Joseph Story
Library of Congress

In his thirty-five years on the United States Supreme Court, from 1811 to his death in 1845, Joseph Story made a more profound mark on American law than any other associate justice. Despite his appointment by a Republican president, Story joined with Federalists John Marshall and Bushrod Washington to craft a strongly nationalist jurisprudence in an age of centrifugal sectionalism. At the same time, his scholarly treatises on equity, commercial law, and constitutional law, written from his perch as Dane Professor at the Harvard Law School, shaped U.S. lawyers' understanding of common law, making Story an American Blackstone. He was a bastion of New England legal conservatism. Andrew Jackson—who had a different constitutional vision—called him "the most dangerous man in America" (McClellan 1971, 55).

Story was born on 18 September 1779 in Marblehead, Massachusetts. His father, a physician, participated in the Boston Tea Party; was a Son of Liberty; fought at Lexington, Concord, and Bunker Hill (afterward tending to the wounded); became a surgeon in the revolutionary army; and served with Washington at Long Island, White Plains, and Trenton. Story thus grew up with stories of revolutionary heroism and a native ardor for the new Republic.

On Sundays, the Story household attended a Congregationalist (Puritan) Church, where his Uncle Isaac preached the fallenness of man and the need for repentance and regeneration in the spirit of New Light Calvinism. At home, there were twice-daily prayers, but his father's theology inclined more toward the doctrines of Enlightenment Christianity with its less pessimistic view of human nature. Later, at Harvard College, Story would convert to Unitarianism and still later serve as national president of that denomination—which did not keep him from lecturing (in opposition to fellow Unitarian Thomas Jefferson) that Christianity is part of the common law.

After studying at Harvard College (where, as class poet, he wrote an embarrassingly bad graduation anthem, called "Reason"), he read law with Samuel Sewall in Marblehead and later with Samuel Putnam in Salem. In 1801, he opened a law office in Salem, a Federalist stronghold, and after a slow start became a leading advocate. The high point of his private practice was representation of the Massachusetts purchasers of Yazoo properties, leading to his one and only argument before the Supreme Court, *Fletcher v. Peck* (1810). The side that Story represented prevailed in the opinion that Chief Justice John Marshall authored.

Story also became active in Democratic-Republican (then often still called anti-Federalist) politics. Nicknamed "Orator Jo," he was a popular speaker at Republican rallies, as a result of which he was physically assaulted by a Federalist bully and—more seriously—lost the hand of his first love, whose family could not stomach his politics or his religion. He was elected to the Salem Town Committee, to three terms in the state House of Representatives, and to a partial term in the U.S. Congress, where he offended party leaders by opposing President Jefferson's trade embargo. His political career ended when President Madison appointed him to the Supreme Court, after three other candidates turned down the job. At thirty-two years of age, Story was the youngest justice ever to serve.

In light of Story's early warm support of Washington and Adams and later alliance with Marshall, Webster, and the lingering Federalist establishment of Massachusetts, his affiliation with the party of Jefferson calls for some explanation. Part of the explanation surely lies with his father's Republicanism, Story's religious heterodoxy, and his youthful enthusiasm for Rousseau. Part lies with the fact that greater opportunities seemed to present themselves with up-and-coming Republican merchants than with the hidebound and exclusive Federalist aristocracy of Massachusetts. But the deeper explanation probably lies with the peculiar antinationalist turn taken by New England Federalists after the Adams presidency, culminating in the Hartford Convention. Story, always the nationalist, had little patience with the Federalists' unprincipled opposition to the Louisiana Purchase and was infuriated by the disloyalty of many New Englanders during the troubles with England, including flirtation with secession. In many respects, however, Story never accepted Republican orthodoxy—especially its attacks on the judiciary. Even before his appointment to the bench, Jefferson called Story a "pseudo-republican" (Newmyer 1985, 59).

Although presumably appointed to be a counterweight to John Marshall's Federalist jurisprudence, Story quickly became the chief justice's friend and close ally. That is not to suggest, however (as some have thought), that Story became a mere acolyte to the great Virginian. Story maintained a surprising degree of independence, dissenting seven times between 1812 and 1816—more than any other justice, including William Johnson, the first "great dissenter." Off the Court as well, in his capacity as Dane Professor at Harvard Law School and as a prolific writer of legal scholarship, Story expounded the principles of nationalistic constitutionalism and of capitalistic common law—though it should be noted that his capitalism was one in which corporations were strictly required to meet their contractual obligations, seamen (the laborers of the leading industry of New England) were protected from cruelty and exploitation, and the treaty rights of Indians were protected. In a lecture to his Harvard students, Story commented: "The oppressor may belong to the very circle of society in which we love to move" (Newmyer 1985, 153).

As a nationalist and a supporter of a powerful and independent judiciary, Story's zeal exceeded even that of Marshall. On circuit, he crafted opinions expanding the implied power of the executive to control foreign affairs and the implied authority of federal courts to punish common law crimes, and on both issues was reversed by the full Court, including Marshall.

It should be stressed that although Story and Marshall championed an expansive view of congressional powers—for example, in *McCulloch v. Maryland* (1819), upholding the Bank of the United States, and in *Gibbons v. Ogden* (1824), affirming congressional authority over interstate transportation—this was not in service of a national regulatory agenda (though the precedents were later cited in support of the New Deal). Rather, Story and Marshall used national power to unleash entrepreneurial activity from the constraints of state mercantilism and populism. To Story and Marshall, the promise of the Union was one of a great, commercially dynamic common market, in which merchants, industrialists, and the forces of early modern capitalism would flourish and contracts would be held sacred. Thus, it is significant that in *McCulloch*, the Court spared a privately owned, nationally chartered bank from disruptive state taxation, and in *Gibbons*, the Court enabled a competitive carrier to avoid the monopolistic policy of the state of New York.

Story's most celebrated and important opinion was *Martin v. Hunter's Lessee* (1816). The case concerned ownership of extensive tracts of land in northern Virginia. One set of claimants traced title to Lord Fairfax, a Loyalist who fled the country during the Revolution. (These claimants included John Marshall, who did not sit in the case, as well as other members of the Marshall family.) The other claimants traced title to Virginia confiscation statutes and an interpretation of Virginia common law under which foreigners could not inherit property. In *Fairfax's Devisee v. Hunter's Lessee* (1813), the Supreme Court upheld the Fairfax claims, overturning a contrary decision of the high court of Virginia. In a provocative opinion, Story declared that the Virginia court had erred in its interpretation of common law and the meaning of a Virginia statute. Story also held that Virginia law was preempted by federal treaties with Britain guaranteeing the property rights of British citizens.

On remand, the Virginia Court of Appeals, led by the redoubtable Judge Spencer Roane, Marshall's next-door neighbor in Richmond and the intellectual leader of the Virginia states' rights movement, declined to comply with the Supreme Court's ruling. The Virginia Court of Appeals held that the statute giving the Supreme Court authority to review state court decisions involving federal issues—Section 25 of the Judiciary Act of 1789—was unconstitutional. Nowhere in the Constitution was the Supreme Court explicitly granted appellate jurisdiction over state courts. The Virginia Court of Appeals agreed that it was bound by the federal Constitution and laws but denied that it was bound to obey the Supreme Court's interpretations of them. According to the Virginians, the two systems of courts—state and federal—were instrumentalities of separate sovereigns, not answerable one to the other.

On appeal, the case—now styled *Martin v. Hunter's Lessee*—became a disquisition into the very nature of sovereignty in the U.S. constitutional system. Story, writing again for the Court in the absence of the chief justice, found that Congress had power "by necessary implication" to grant jurisdiction to the Supreme Court in cases involving federal law. Such appellate authority was essential to ensure uniformity of decisions interpreting federal law and to overcome "State prejudices, state jealousies and state interests." Moreover, Story maintained that Congress is *required* to do so. "The judicial power must therefore be vested in some court, by Congress: and to suppose that it was not an obligation binding on them, but might, at their pleasure, be omitted or declined, is to suppose, that, under the sanction of the constitution they might defeat the constitution itself; a construction which would lead to such a result cannot be sound" (14 U.S. 326, 347, 329).

In asserting jurisdiction over state courts, Story struck a mighty blow for uniformity of U.S. law. Without a single tribunal to resolve conflicting interpretations, federal law would be different in every state. Moreover, in light of the weakness of federal administrative institutions in the early years

Early United States Supreme Court Justices and Circuit-Riding Duties

In an attempt to make justice more accessible, some state supreme courts are required to hold sessions in different parts of the state, but justices typically have access to modern forms of transportation and find themselves housed in appropriate buildings wherever they meet. By contrast, circuit riding greatly added to the strain on the life of judges in early America (and later on the frontier), particularly those, including Supreme Court justices, who had the responsibility of "riding circuit" over large areas relatively distant from the nation's capital—which was first located in New York and Pennsylvania. The Southern Circuit, for instance, comprised North and South Carolina and Georgia.

Supreme Court justice James Iredell, who served on the United States Supreme Court from 1790 to 1799, reported having traveled more than 1,900 miles on a single tour of his circuit where he would join with U.S. district judges to render circuit court decisions. He described passing through barren land, encountering flooding, being the victim of highway robbery, and having to seek lodging in private houses where inns were either nonexistent or filthy and boisterous. Iredell noted that his circuit duty made him "a Post Boy" and complained about "perpetual traveling, and almost continual absence from home" (quoted in Fish 2002, 21).

The author of an excellent recent history of federal justice in the mid-Atlantic states noted that the Southern Circuit, "characterized by great geographical distances, places of court located in the remote interior, a poor transportation system and sparse public accommodations, posed special hardships" (Fish 2002, 20). The presence of Supreme Court justices in the hinterlands may, however, have helped to keep the early justices in contact with the people and may have in turn served to educate the people in the principles of the new Constitution.

Reference:

Fish, Peter G. 2002. *Federal Justice in the Mid-Atlantic States: United States Courts from Maryland to the Carolinas, 1789–1835*. Washington, D.C.: Administrative Office of the United States Courts.

of the Republic, it is hard to see how the federal government could achieve its purposes without the ability to use the apparatus of state judicial enforcement.

In a more theoretical respect, too, Story's opinion in *Martin* struck a blow for constitutional union. Addressing the Virginia court's contention that "such an appellate jurisdiction over State Courts is inconsistent with the genius of our governments and the spirit of the constitution" because "the latter was never designed to act upon State sovereignties, but only upon the people"—an argument still alive and well in modern federalism theory—Story responded that it was "a mistake" to suppose that "the constitution was not designed to operate upon States in their corporate capacities. It is crowded with provisions which restrain or annul the sovereignty of the States in some of the highest branches of their prerogatives" (14 U.S. 342–343). Thus Story boldly contradicted the very heart of states' rights constitutional theory.

Did Story go too far? Unlike his mentor, Marshall, who knew when to retreat as well as when to advance, Story tended to press his theories to their logical extent, without regard to opposition. *Martin* was a mighty blow for federal judicial power, but perhaps it was too ambitious. Congress has never accepted the view that it is obliged to vest the full judicial power of the United States in federal courts, and even the Supreme Court has retreated from the view that it has authority to overturn state court interpretations of state law in cases within its appellate jurisdiction.

In a similar vein, Story's opinion for the Court in *Swift v. Tyson* (1842) established the power of federal courts in diversity cases to create a national common law in commercial matters—a decision reversed about a century later, in *Erie Railroad v. Tompkins* (1938). He also expanded the powers of the federal courts over maritime and admiralty cases—a jurisdiction they continue to exercise. Had Story's constitutional vision prevailed—sweeping federal court jurisdiction armed with federal common law for commercial and other civil matters, crimes, and admiralty—the federal courts might well have superseded both states and Congress as the primary lawmaking authority for the nation.

Also notable were Story's majority opinion in *Terrett v. Taylor* (1815) and concurrence in *Dartmouth College v. Woodward* (1819), both of which protected private corporations from state alteration of their charters. These decisions laid the framework not only for private corporate enterprise but also for an independent sector of religious, educational, and charitable institutions. *Terrett* involved a Virginia statute asserting state ownership of the "glebe lands"—income-producing property for the support of the parish minister—held by the Episcopal Church, which had been the established church of the Virginia colony. *Dartmouth College* involved a state takeover of a college founded by royal charter, with the benefit of land grants. In both contexts, Story found that these mixed public-private institutions had become irreversibly "private" and that the state no longer had authority to seize control over their property.

Story's most enduringly problematic decision was *Prigg v. Pennsylvania* (1842), striking down Pennsylvania's personal liberty law, which enabled putative slaves to challenge their status before a jury before being carried back to the South as fugitives. He ruled that this law conflicted with the fugitive slave clause, which, he said, was a fundamental part of the bargain that had stitched together the original Union. The opinion was greeted with satisfaction in the South and excoriated by abolitionists. But there was another side to the coin. Under the theory of *Prigg,* state governments were not permitted to interfere with slave recovery, but they also could not be required to assist in it. Some—including Story's son—have argued that *Prigg* was a victory for freedom in disguise. In most respects, Story was a strong advocate of moderate antislavery measures, such as exclusion of slavery from the territories and suppression of the slave trade. But in its inattention to the problem of due process for free blacks wrongly accused of being slaves, the *Prigg* opinion seems to betray those principles.

In addition to his judicial career, Story was one of the most influential and prolific legal scholars in the nineteenth-century United States and thus the model for the scholar-judge. In 1829, at a time when Harvard Law School had dwindled to a single student, he reluctantly moved to Cambridge and became a professor and head of the law school, which he reformed and revitalized. Based on his lectures, Story published major treatises: *Bailments* (1832), *Bills of Exchange* (1843), *Promissory Notes* (1845), *Conflict of Laws* (1834), *Equity Jurisprudence* (1836), and *Equity Pleading* (1838). His most famous and enduring scholarly effort, the three-volume *Commentaries on the Constitution* (1833), was the leading work on the subject for decades and has been cited frequently by the Supreme Court. Written in opposition to the increasingly radical states' rights theories of such thinkers as John C. Calhoun and John Taylor of Caroline, who envisioned the Constitution as a compact among sovereign states, Story forcefully expounded the nationalist theory of constitutional union. Sovereignty, according to Story, devolved upon the entire people of the United States after independence—and not on the states. The people, in turn, formed a "more perfect Union" in 1787 without intercession from the state governments. That theory was controversial in 1833, and it remains contested today.

The third volume of Story's *Commentaries* contained a clause-by-clause explanation of each part of the Constitution—the first of its kind—with citations to relevant opinions, mostly of the Marshall Court. Perhaps most interestingly, Chapter 5 set forth nineteen "rules of interpretation" to guide judicial construction of the fundamental charter. It reflected Story's aspiration to create a "science" of law and thus to distinguish the objective arena of legal decisionmaking from the realm of politics. This was the birthplace of constitutional law as a serious field of study. Whether Story succeeded in his attempt to establish legal objectivity—indeed, whether any such enterprise can ever succeed—is the question at the heart of constitutional theory now as it was when it was written.

Michael W. McConnell

References and Further Reading:

McClellan, James. 1971. *Joseph Story and the American Constitution*. Norman: University of Oklahoma Press

Newmyer, R. Kent. 1985. *Supreme Court Justice Joseph Story: Statesman of the Old Republic*. Chapel Hill: University of North Carolina Press.

Presser, Stephen B. 1983–1985. "Joseph Story." In *The Guide to American Law*. St. Paul, Minn.: West Publishing, 406–413.

Story, Joseph. 1833. *Commentaries on the Constitution of the United States, with a Preliminary Review of the Constitutional History of the Colonies and States before the Adoption of the Constitution*. 3 vols. Boston: Hilliard, Gray, and Company.

White, G. Edward. 1988. *The Marshall Court and Cultural Change, 1815–1835*. New York: Macmillan.

TANEY, ROGER BROOKE

(1777–1864)

Roger Brooke Taney
Library of Congress

Had his reputation not been irrevocably blemished in old age by his leading role in enunciating the infamous *Dred Scott* decision, Roger Brooke Taney (pronounced "Tawney") would probably be considered one of the most eminent judges ever to sit on an American bench. Certainly he was one of the most influential.

Taney entered the world on 17 March 1777, the second of four sons born to Michael Taney, who owned a large tobacco plantation located on the Patuxent River at the mouth of Battle Creek in Calvert County, Maryland. Taney's mother, Monica, was the daughter of Roger Brooke, a wealthy neighbor. A Federalist and a leading member of the Maryland General Assembly, Taney's father was a hard-drinking, impetuous, domineering outdoorsman who was a strong Roman Catholic. In his seventies he stabbed a neighbor to death in a quarrel over a woman and fled to Virginia, where he died two years later after being thrown from a horse (Swisher 1961, 8–14, 103–104).

Roger Taney graduated from Dickinson College at Carlisle, Pennsylvania, in 1795 at the age of eighteen after only three years of residence. He was the valedictorian of his class of twenty-four graduates. After a year spent largely in foxhunting, he began reading law in the office of Judge Jeremiah T. Chase of Annapolis and was admitted to the Maryland bar on

19 June 1799, after which he opened his own law office, also being elected in October 1799 to the House of Delegates as a Federalist (Lewis 1965, 3–35).

In 1800 a Jeffersonian landslide swept many Federalists, including Taney, out of public office. He then relocated his law practice in March 1801 to the little town of Frederick in western Maryland, where there was less competition for business. As his practice rapidly expanded, he gradually overcame an innate shyness and greatly grew in self-confidence. On 7 January 1806 he married Anne Phebe Charlton Key, the sister of a former college classmate, Francis Scott Key. Anne, born on 13 June 1783, gave Taney six daughters (all raised as Episcopalians like their mother) and one son, who died in infancy (Lewis 1965, 37–45).

During the period from 1803 to 1812, Taney was repeatedly a candidate for public office, but without success. Finally in 1816 he was elected to the state senate. Meanwhile, despite a frail physique that at times forced him to take to his bed after arguing a difficult case, he began to win a reputation for diligence, honesty, mastery of the most complicated features of the law, and a disposition to represent unpopular clients, some of whom he was convinced were guilty, in order to assure them an adequate defense. For example, in 1811 he defended Gen. James Wilkinson, accused of committing treason against the United States, at a court martial trial that culminated in a not guilty verdict (Swisher 1961, 45–49, 59–60, 73–74; Lewis 1965, 74–75).

Taney's most momentous achievement during that period was his successful defense in March 1819 of the Reverend Jacob Gruber, a Methodist minister from Pennsylvania who was indicted in Washington County for allegedly inciting slaves "to commit acts of mutiny and rebellion" while preaching to a crowd estimated at 3,000 persons, including at least 400 Negroes. Taney's opening statement in Gruber's behalf cogently expressed his own views on the subject of slavery. "Mr. Gruber," Taney declared,

> did quote the language of our great act of national independence, and insisted on the principles contained in that venerated instrument. He did rebuke those masters who, in the exercise of power, are deaf to the calls of humanity; and he warned them of the evils they might bring upon themselves. He did speak with abhorrence of those reptiles who live by trading in human flesh and enrich themselves by tearing the husband from the wife and the infant from the bosom of the mother; and this, I am instructed, was the head and font of his offending. . . . So far is he from being the object of punishment, in any form of proceeding, that we are prepared to maintain the same principles and to use, if necessary, the same language here in the temple of justice and in the presence of those who are the ministers of the law. . . .

> A hard necessity indeed compels us to endure the evil of slavery for a time. . . . It cannot be easily and suddenly removed. Yet, while it continues, it is a blot on our national character; and every real lover of freedom confidently hopes that it will be effectually, though it must be gradually, wiped away. (Lewis 1965, 76–79)

At the time of his marriage Taney himself owned at least three slaves and acquired others thereafter. By 1821, however, he appears to have emancipated all but two of them, who were too old to care for themselves. Although he represented slave owners in several runaway slave cases, he also held the office of vice president of the American Colonization Society, of which his brother-in-law, Francis Scott Key, was one of the founders, and he fully supported the objective of the society, which was to establish a haven for freed Negroes in Liberia (Steiner 1970, 55–56, 376; Lewis 1965, 44, 76).

In February 1823 Taney relocated his law office to Baltimore, which was then the second-largest city in the United States. Two years later he began arguing cases in the United States Supreme Court, the first significant one of which was *Etting v. Bank of the United States* (1826). Accusing officials of the Bank of the United States of corruption, Taney eventually obtained a settlement for his Maryland clients, despite the opposition of Chief Justice John Marshall and two of the five other Supreme Court justices. This initial encounter with the Philadelphia-based banking behemoth and his own association with Maryland state banks whose directors tended to resent the Bank of the United States as an arrogant monopoly foreshadowed Taney's future support of Pres. Andrew Jackson's "war" against the federal bank (Lewis 1965, 86–89).

On 3 September 1827, Maryland's governor appointed Taney to the post of state attorney general, an office whose duties were arduous although the pay was pitiful. Taney probably owed his selection to having ably represented the state government in the Supreme Court case of *Brown v. Maryland* (1827), resulting in a landmark decision by Chief Justice Marshall that under the interstate commerce clause of the U.S. Constitution, no state could tax imports from a foreign country or from another state. Although Taney lost this initial battle with mercantile interests, his ardent defense of states' rights versus federal power presaged many of his own later opinions from the bench (Swisher 1961, 114–115).

In 1831, largely because of the Peggy Eaton affair (in which President Jackson rose to the defense of the wife of his secretary of war, who had been snubbed by the wives of some of his cabinet members), vacancies materialized in President Jackson's cabinet. Old Hickory then prevailed upon Taney to become U.S. attorney general, in which capacity he provided Jackson with many of the arguments presented in Jackson's 10 July 1832 message to Congress vetoing a bill to extend the charter of the Bank of the United States. Oddly, in view of Taney's later opinions on the subject of judicial authority, Jackson's veto message asserted that despite the precedent of *M'Culloch v. Maryland* (1819), a decision of the Supreme Court upholding an act of Congress was not binding upon the chief executive if he believed such an act to be unconstitutional. Moreover, regarding the question of whether an act of the federal government was necessary and proper and therefore constitutional, Taney (through Jackson) put the greatest emphasis on the word *necessary,* in contrast to the much greater weight placed upon the word *proper* by Chief Justice Marshall (Lewis 1965, 129–165).

After Jackson was reelected in November 1832, he decided that the U.S. Treasury deposits should be removed from the Bank of the United States and transferred to state-chartered banks. When Secretary of the Treasury William J. Duane refused to do this, Jackson removed him from office and replaced him with Taney, who promptly issued the removal order. In June 1834, however, Taney's nomination as treasury secretary became the first cabinet appointment ever rejected by the Senate. He was therefore forced to resign his office (Lewis 1965, 178–180; Swisher 1961, 286–289).

On 15 January 1835 a grateful Jackson nominated Taney to fill a vacancy on the United States Supreme Court. The Senate, dominated by anti-Jackson Whigs, promptly rejected the appointment. But a determined president seized the opportunity provided by the death of Chief Justice Marshall late that year once again to nominate Taney to the Court. This time the Senate, after considerable debate, approved the appointment on 8 April 1836, thus enabling Taney, at the age of fifty-nine and in precarious health, to begin a tenure of twenty-eight years as chief justice of the United States (Lewis 1965, 239–251).

Despite frequent illnesses of one kind or another and an onerous requirement to ride circuit, a duty of Supreme Court justices not eliminated by Congress until 1869, Taney still managed in his methodical fashion to write approximately 300 Supreme Court opinions, only seven of which were dissents. In only twenty-six cases did he differ from a majority of the justices without writing a formal dissent. And he participated, of course, in hundreds of additional cases, the written opinions in regard to which he generously assigned to fellow justices (Steiner 1970, 448; Lewis 1965, 314, 337).

When Taney joined the Court, he inherited from a divided Marshall Court a controversy involving a legislative charter to build a bridge, the so-called Warren Bridge, across the Charles River at Boston. The construction of the new bridge was opposed by the Charles River Bridge Company, whose own toll bridge had been chartered in 1786. The essence of the plaintiffs' argument was that the state had violated a contract embodied in the original charter, which they maintained had conferred by implication an exclusive privilege to build and operate such a facility. The issue, then, was whether the construction of the new bridge violated the contract clause of the U.S. Constitution and the Marshall Court's ruling in *Dartmouth College v. Woodward* (1819), which had held that state legislative charters creating corporations were contracts that could not afterward be legislatively altered, even for the public good (Swisher 1974, 73–81).

In delivering the decision of the Supreme Court in *Charles River Bridge v. Warren Bridge* (36 U.S. 420, 1837), Taney drew heavily upon Marshall's opinion in the case of *Providence Bank v. Billings* (29 U.S. 514, 1830), which stipulated that a corporation's privileges "do not flow necessarily from the charter, but must be expressed in it, or they do not exist" (562). Since "the object and end of all government is to promote the happiness and prosperity of the community by which it is established," Taney declared, such a government would be of little value "if by implications and presumptions, it was disarmed of the powers necessary to accomplish the ends of its creation" (548). The entire community, Taney asserted, "have a right to require that the power of promoting their comfort and convenience, and of advancing the public prosperity, . . . shall not be construed to have been surrendered or diminished by the State, unless it shall appear by plain words that it was intended to be done" (449–450). Thus, by requiring that state contracts be construed strictly, the Taney Court facilitated national economic development and provided protection for community rights over corporate property rights. Years later Justice John Archibald Campbell was to declare in regard to the Charles River Bridge decision that "no opinion of the Court more fully satisfied the legal judgment of the country, and consequently none has exerted more influence upon its legislation" (Lewis 1965, 289; see also Kutler 1977, 87–89, 114–119).

Also important in limiting the power of corporate monopolies was the Taney Court's decision in *West River Bridge v. Dix* (1848), in which it upheld the right of eminent domain, allowing state legislatures to appropriate corporate property for public use with just compensation (Swisher 1974, 471).

As government at the state and local level became more democratic during the Jackson era, the Taney Court handed down decision after decision supporting the constitutional right of state legislatures to enact social welfare laws even at the expense of private interests. Chief Justice Marshall had ruled in *Fletcher v. Peck* (1810) that a state legislature had no right because of the limitations of natural law to void a private contract, even if such an instrument was the product of extensive public corruption. Thus he implicitly recommended the judicial process as a weapon that private economic interests might use against governmental interference with their activities. But Taney, who never mentioned the law of nature as limiting legislative activity, consistently ruled that only the most narrow restrictions applied to such activity, and these were to be largely decided by state courts, not by federal tribunals (Newmyer 1968, 64–68; Smith 1973, 122–123).

Taney's support for community rights over corporate rights was not unlimited. In rendering the Supreme Court's decision in *Ohio Life Insurance & Trust Co. v. Debolt* (1854), he maintained that the will of the sovereign people of a state, expressed contractually in a corporate charter, created a constitutional obligation that could not afterwards be impaired by a legislative act attempting to invalidate it, even if the power to enter into the original contract had been "indiscreetly and injudiciously exercised" (Lewis 1965, 120–123). And in its decision in *Bank of Augusta v. Earle* (1839), the Taney Court ruled that if a corporation chartered in one state was permitted by that instrument to do business in another state, it could do so because of the comity clause in the Constitution, unless expressly prohibited by law in the other state (Swisher 1974, 115–121).

When it came to setting boundaries for the exertion of federal authority over the states, Taney was less hesitant than when dealing with issues involving corporate privilege. To the chief justice, a state's innate police power was ordinarily supreme over federal authority within that state. Perhaps the most cogent of his many rulings in this vein was his opinion in the *License Cases* (46 U.S. 504, 1847) in which he defined state "police powers" as "nothing more or less than the power of government inherent in every sovereignty" (583). In almost every case in which state regulatory laws were challenged in the United States Supreme Court while Taney was chief justice, on the ground that they usurped federal authority under the interstate commerce clause, Taney voted to sustain the legislation of the states. His emphasis upon the broad reach of the police power of the states and his insistence that a state might enact laws affecting interstate commerce as long as they did not conflict with federal legislation exercised a dominant influence upon future court decisions for years to come (Smith 1973, 130–139).

There was one notable exception to Taney's emphasis on states' rights, illustrated by his opinion in the landmark case of *Propeller Genesee Chief v. Fitzhugh* (1852), in which he ruled that a state's authority did not override that of the federal government on the navigable waters of the American interior. Departing from English admiralty law, whose precedents extended inland only as far as waterways were affected by the tides of the sea, Taney declared that the maritime jurisdiction of U.S. admiralty courts extended to all navigable streams and lakes, whether affected or not by ocean tides. In view of the enormous amount of commerce affected by this judgment, perhaps Justice John Catron was not in error when he wrote to future president James Buchanan that the *Genesee* decision and a clarifying companion, *Fretz v. Bull*

(1852), had "in their practical consequences . . . more in them than any fifty others ever made by the Supreme Court." (Swisher 1974, 446). As noted in a contemporary law journal, the *Genesee* decision provided that all disputes involving "every stream of any importance in the United States" must be decided not in state tribunals but in federal courts. One of Taney's biographers asserted that the Genesee opinion was his "most important contribution to jurisprudence" (Steiner 1970, 292–296; see also Swisher 1974, 442–447).

Notwithstanding the enhancement of federal jurisdiction provided by the *Genesee* decision, Taney and a majority of his colleagues endeavored throughout his tenure as chief justice to formulate a doctrine less favorable to federal power over interstate commerce than that expressed by Chief Justice Marshall in *Gibbons v. Ogden* (1824), in which Taney's predecessor broadly interpreted the meaning of the word *commerce* insofar as it applied to the exercise of federal power upon the waterways of a state. Dissenting in a five–four decision entitled the *Passenger Cases* (48 U.S. 283, 1849), Taney maintained that under the Constitution the Congress lacked the power to compel a sovereign state to admit any person "whom it might deem dangerous to its peace" (466) or to "abridge the power of taxation in the States" (480). And writing the Court's majority opinion in *Luther v. Borden* (48 U.S. 1, 1849), he ruled that federal courts must "adopt and follow the decisions of the State courts in questions which concern merely the constitution and laws of the State" (40). The United States Supreme Court, "the final appellate power," as Taney declared in *Ableman v. Booth* (62 U.S. 520, 1859), whenever any question arose regarding the legitimacy of an act of Congress, would stand behind the rights of the states (Lewis 1965, 130–134; Kutler 1977, 101–105, 110–113).

It would so stand in regard to the most controversial issue in all of U.S. history—that of human bondage. In the *Ableman* decision the Court upheld the Fugitive Slave Act of 1850, widely hated in the North, "in all of its provisions." No state could interfere with the operation of that detestable law. Taney's insistence that public officials in nonslave states were obligated to enforce it had already been made clear in a partial dissent in *Prigg v. Pennsylvania* (1842). Despite his insistence upon limiting narrow property rights expressed in such decisions as that involving the Charles River Bridge, he maintained in Prigg that the obligation "of the state authorities to protect the master when he is endeavoring to seize a fugitive from his service" was "necessarily implied" (Kutler 1977, 110–113, 149).

Five years later the Supreme Court was again confronted with the fugitive slave problem. Its decision in *Jones v. Van Zandt* (1847) upheld the constitutionality of the original Fugitive Slave Act, which provided heavy penalties for harboring or concealing a runaway slave, even if state laws encouraged such forms of defiance. In response to this decision, Salmon P.

Kirby Benedict (1810–1874)

Kirby Benedict is not well known today, but he was an associate of Abraham Lincoln in Illinois and served terms as both an associate judge and a chief justice of the Judicial Court in New Mexico when it was still a territory. Born in Kent, Connecticut, in 1820, Benedict went to Ohio when he was twenty-one and subsequently read law in Natchez, Mississippi, under John Anthony Quitman, where he also appears to have acquired knowledge of French and Spanish. First admitted to the bar in Ohio, he later settled in Illinois, where he served for six years as a probate judge of Macon County, a county that he also represented for a time in the state legislature. Riding circuit in Illinois, Benedict came to know Abraham Lincoln, Stephen Douglas, and David Davis (who later served on the United States Supreme Court).

In 1853, Pres. Franklin Pierce appointed Benedict to be an associate judge of the Third Judicial District of New Mexico, a job that included work on the Supreme Court for the territory. Although three judges were supposed to be there, Benedict often found himself as the only judge on call. He moved his family to New Mexico in 1855 and appears to have served conscientiously. In 1857, Pres. James Buchanan appointed Benedict to serve as chief justice, a term that he began in 1858. During his time in New Mexico, Benedict wrote more Supreme Court decisions than did any of his colleagues (Hunt 1961, 122). As chief justice his work was primarily exercised in the first district. Known for having far more dramatic oratory than Lincoln, in one case where Benedict found a man guilty of first-degree murder, he ended a long speech with:

> The Court was about to add, Jose Maria Martin, "May God have mercy on your soul," but the Court will not assume the responsibility of asking an allwise Providence to do that which a jury of your peers has refused to do.
>
> The Lord will not have mercy on your soul! (Quoted in Hunt 1961, 81)

Benedict, who had already gained knowledge of Spanish, apparently also learned the customs of the people he gov-

(continues)

Chase of Ohio, later to become Taney's successor as chief justice, passionately protested against its requirement that free men in free states must actively assist slaveholders to repossess their human property. Senator Chase even went so far as to declare that Congress was in no way bound to accept the Supreme Court's interpretation of the Constitution (Pfeffer 1967, 147–149).

Then came Taney's ruling in *Dred Scott v. Sandford* (1857), which invalidated the 1820 Missouri Compromise, which had banned slavery from the Northwest Territories. The *Dred Scott* decision energized antislavery opinion in the North, thus becoming one of the principal causes of the Ameri-

(continued)

erned; in an early case, he had to resolve a conflict over which of two Native American tribes was entitled to a disputed portrait of St. Joseph. At the time of his arrival, peonage (whereby an individual could contract out his or her own, and in some cases, his or her children's services in payment for debt), albeit not chattel, slavery was legal in New Mexico and continued into effect in 1867. Although slavery was sanctioned for a time, Benedict remained faithful during the Civil War to the Union, and remembering his old friendship, Lincoln reappointed Benedict as a chief justice in 1862. Benedict was one of three men who revised and codified the territory's laws in 1865. Writing to Lincoln in July 1864, Benedict described the kind of men that were needed in the territory: "Send us good men. A narrow and mischievous mind and spirit should never be sent here. No one should be sent here who is not courageous, persevering, and of the highest integrity. He should have manners, deportment, and the bearing of a gentleman with good sense enough to make no wanton or unprovoked controversies" (quoted in Hunt 1961, 168).

Benedict helped found the Historical Society of New Mexico and was an active Mason. Opponents accused him of demagoguery and drunkenness (both charges of which appeared to have elements of truthfulness), and Pres. Andrew Johnson replaced Benedict with Col. John P. Slough. Slough was subsequently shot, and Benedict was among the lawyers who successfully defended his killer. Showing contempt for the court in a later case, Benedict was disbarred and refused to apologize for three years. His reapplication to the bar brought inquiry into his behavior, including intemperate articles attacking public officials that he had published as editor of the *New Mexico Weekly Union*. Benedict withdrew his application for reinstatement and died shortly thereafter in 1874. He had become indebted by his many years of service, and his property was sold at auction. Benedict's wife returned virtually penniless to Illinois.

Reference:

Hunt, Aurora. 1961. *Kirby Benedict: Frontier Federal Judge: An Account of Legal and Judicial Development in the Southwest, 1853–1874, with Special Reference to the Indian, Slavery, Social and Political Affairs, Journalism, and a Chapter on Circuit Riding with Abraham Lincoln in Illinois*. Glendale, Calif.: The Arthur H. Clark Company.

can Civil War. In *Dred*, Taney reiterated his opinion that the Constitution protected a slaveholder's right freely to possess his human property in all the territories of the United States. The widespread outrage over this decision ranged from the outright rejection of its validity by such antislavery men as Chase and Horace Greeley of the New York *Tribune* to a reluctant obedience among such moderate Republicans as Sen. William Seward of New York and Abraham Lincoln of Illinois, both of whom suggested that a future Supreme Court would adopt a contrary view (Swisher 1974, 599–650).

Late in 1860 slave states began to leave the Union, and early in 1861 the Civil War began. At once Taney's domination of the Supreme Court began to diminish. When he declared in *Ex Parte Merryman* (1861), a circuit opinion, that Pres. Abraham Lincoln's suspension of the writ of habeas corpus in Taney's home state of Maryland was an unconstitutional usurpation of congressional power, Lincoln simply then and thereafter ignored the rulings of the chief justice. It became evident that Taney's authority had vanished in the chaos of war. Lincoln, moreover, was soon able to add four new justices to the Supreme Court, drastically altering the ideological balance on that tribunal to the point that Taney, in declining health and entirely opposed to the administration's military assault against the South, had little influence on jurisprudence during his final years on the bench (Newmyer 1968, 145).

Exemplifying the chief justice's shrinking stature was his dissent in the *Prize Cases* (1863), which dealt with (1) whether the president could constitutionally institute a naval blockade of the southern coastline in the absence of a congressional declaration of war, and (2) whether, if an actual war existed, it was a conflict between sovereign nations or merely an armed rebellion against a national government. In a five–four decision, with Taney in the minority, the Supreme Court ruled that an actual war had existed at the time that Lincoln (with Congress not in session) had proclaimed the blockade and that such a state of war had created a "military necessity" that allowed Lincoln to exercise vast powers as commander in chief of the nation's armed forces. It was not, however, such a war as would justify foreign nations in granting formal recognition to the southern Confederacy as a sovereign nation; it was in this sense merely a domestic rebellion allowing the South only limited belligerent rights. Taney thought otherwise, concurring in the dissenting declaration of Justice Samuel Nelson that the conflict could not have become an actual war until legitimized by Congress and that absent such a legal war, the blockade could not be legal either (Swisher 1974, 884–892; Kutler 1977, 161–164; Newmyer 1968, 145–146).

Remaining to the last a strict constructionist opposed to any appeal to "natural law" or to "necessity," Taney consistently demanded even during the desperate days of the Civil War that the exercise of federal power be limited to what was explicitly allowed by the actual wording of the Constitution. His emphasis on state sovereignty was exemplified by his decision in the case of *Kentucky v. Denison* (1861). The governor of Kentucky had requested a mandamus ordering the governor of Ohio to deliver one Willis Largo, accused of trying to aid a slave to escape from Kentucky, for trial. Taney ruled for an unanimous Court that the Constitution granted the executive authority of a state in which a crime had been committed, once the alleged perpetrator had been "charged in the regular course of judicial proceedings," to demand that the executive authority of "the State in which he is found" turn over the accused, "without any reference to the character of the crime charged, or to the policy or laws of the State to which the fugitive has fled." Neither the Constitution nor the Fugitive Slave Act, however, provided any "means to compel the execution of this duty, nor inflict any punishment for neglect or refusal." Indeed, the right to exercise such a power through the agency of a federal court ruling "would place every State under the control and domination of the general government," something clearly not allowed by the Constitution. Thus, in his last important Supreme Court decision, Taney continued to insist on a severely limited federal authority over the states, which was consistent with his opinion that the southern slave states had a constitutional right to secede from the Union and could not be compelled by force to stay (Steiner 1970, 438–442, 449–450).

Deeply depressed at the horrors of the North-South conflict and at his own helplessness, as demonstrated by the *Merryman* case, in the face of what he considered were the unconstitutional acts of the Lincoln administration, Taney rapidly declined in health as the Civil War progressed and hardly left his house during the final months of his life. He died on 12 October 1864 at the age of eighty-seven and was buried next to his mother in the Jesuit cemetery in Frederick, Maryland (Steiner 1970, 518–521).

Taney's greatest judicial achievement had been to bring U.S. jurisprudence "into accord with the political and economic currents of the Age of Jackson" by making "a substantial body of decisional law" inherited from the Marshall Court relevant to the new era (Newmyer 1968, 90). He was a man of great personal integrity, modesty, simplicity, and courtesy; diligent and devoted to his duty as he saw it. He was much admired for his unceasing struggles against chronic ill health to achieve mastery of the most intricate aspects of the law applicable to whatever case he had been called upon to judge. Unfortunately his stubborn tendency to look backward to the uncertain lessons of the distant past, rather than to adjust his thinking to the insistent requirements of a rapidly changing and expanding nation, ensured that he would confront increasing opposition, bringing down upon himself "a tempest of aspersions" that ultimately blemished his place in history (Steiner 1970, 538). Especially for removing the Treasury deposits from the Bank of the United States, for ruling in the *Dred Scott* decision that all of the western territories must be open to slavery, and for publicly and privately denouncing as unconstitutional many of the measures taken by President Lincoln to preserve the American Union, Taney was at the end of his life the object of much obloquy and his death was viewed "as the removal of a barrier to human progress" (Steiner 1970, 539). Yet the great majority of his constitutional decisions have been almost universally judged to have been "sensible and sound," and the modern consensus is that—in the words of one of his best biographers—"He was a great judge and a good man" (Steiner 1970, 320–325, 522–542; see also Newmyer 1968, 90–94).

Norman B. Ferris

References and Further Reading:

Kutler, Stanley I., ed. 1977. *The Supreme Court and the Constitution: Readings in American Constitutional History*. New York: W. W. Norton.

Lewis, Walker. 1965. *Without Fear or Favor: A Biography of Chief Justice Roger Brooke Taney*. Boston: Houghton Mifflin.

Newmyer, R. Kent. 1968. *The Supreme Court under Marshall and Taney*. Arlington Heights, Ill: AHM Publishing.

Pfeffer, Leo. 1967. *This Honorable Court: A History of the United States Supreme Court*. Boston: Beacon Press.

Siegel, Martin. 1987. *The Taney Court, 1836–1864*. New York: Associated Faculty Press.

Smith, Charles W., Jr. 1973. *Roger B. Taney: Jacksonian Jurist*. New York: Da Capo Press.

Steiner, Bernard C. 1970. *Life of Roger Brooke Taney, Chief Justice of the United States Supreme Court*. Westport, Conn.: Greenwood Press.

Swisher, Carl Brent. 1961. *Roger B. Taney*. Hamden, Conn.: Archon Books.

———. 1974. *History of the Supreme Court of the United States*. Vol. 5: *The Taney Period*. New York: Macmillan.

TRAYNOR, ROGER JOHN

(1900–1983)

ROGER JOHN TRAYNOR
California State Archives

CONSIDERED ONE OF THE MOST influential jurists of the twentieth century, Roger John Traynor established various protocols on tort and product liability law, and he helped to establish the principle that some defendants could be held liable in the absence of fault. Born in 1900 in Park City, Utah, Traynor received his bachelor's, doctorate, and jurist degrees from the University of California at Berkeley. He taught political science and law at Berkeley from 1926 to 1940 before accepting a position as justice on the California Supreme Court, a position he held for thirty years. He became chief justice in 1964, a position he held for six years. During his tenure on the court, Traynor wrote more than 900 opinions and became known as an innovator who abandoned earlier precedents, particularly in the expansion of rights for criminal defendants. At his death, at the age of eighty-three, he had contributed to many of the major doctrinal developments in contract law.

Traynor's tenure on the California Supreme Court marked unprecedented change, not only in the state of California but also in the United States as a whole. The years 1940 to 1970 were historically important since these were the decades in which the New Deal, the New Frontier, and the Great Society each had an impact on social and judicial norms. His thirty years on the court mirrored the major demographic and technological changes in the country as a whole, but particularly reflected the trends in California. Traynor, as both jurist and chief justice, reflected the concern that government, whether at the state or national level, should be a principal agent of change. At the beginning of his career in 1940, the concept of affirmative government was just getting off the ground, and by the time he retired in 1970, the movement for affirmative government had reached its peak. During his thirty-year quest for judicial change, Traynor attempted to force government to make an affirmative response to social problems; in many ways, therefore, he was an activist in a world of affirmative government, but one who thought that such activism could be consistent with rationality and impartiality.

In order to explain the judicial process more clearly, Traynor often used metaphors associated with the clearing of a forest. He would compare legal precedents to trees, with the obscure ones blocking out the light and barring progress and the more secure ones providing guidance and nurture to the soil. The task of the judge would be to prune carefully, removing the diseased wood without cutting down all the trees. Therefore, Traynor wanted to prune the underbrush, and he felt that brush clearing would induce progress without violence to other structures. By limiting the unjust features of an application (pruning), or overruling (chopping it down), Traynor felt he could make some judicial headway.

This sort of academic comparison marked many of Traynor's judicial opinions and resembled his application of scholarly analysis to many of his decisions. In fact, he published frequently, including essays such as "The Ways and Meanings of Defective Products and Strict Liability" and "War and Peace in the Conflicts of Laws," which led to Traynor's changes in the common law for California and set precedents across the nation. For example, his opinion in the defective products case *Escola v. Coca Cola Bottling Company* created the principle that a manufacturer whose "defective" product injures another is liable for injuries that could be traced to the product's defectiveness. This case set a precedent for subsequent liability cases, and by the 1960s, the authors of the *Restatement of Torts*, as well as numerous jurisdictions, had adopted Traynor's approach. Today, consumers injured by "defective" products sue manufacturers directly in tort in most areas, directly following Traynor's lead. In considering the conflict of laws, Traynor wrote in "War and Peace": "When there is no clearing, [the judge] must chop his way through, however clumsily, and hope that scholars will speed their reinforcements." With this in mind, Traynor applied the theory of interest analysis, and its emphasis on the law of "forum state," which reserved choice of law questions for those situations in which the forum state did not have an interest in policy application. Traynor applied this policy to two decisions later in his career, *Bernkrant v. Fowler* (55 Cal. 2d 588, 1961) and *Reich v. Purcell* (67 Cal. 2d 551, 1961).

Traynor refused to follow protocol, and by the time he began his tenure as a justice, the concept of judicial deference had overtaken the judicial system, the limitations of which Traynor acknowledged. Traynor felt that the basic responsibility of lawmaking review remained with the court system, as he noted in an essay, "The Unguarded Affairs of the Semikempt Mistress," in which he argued that both legislative and judicial lawmaking are in a constant state of change. The relationship between the two types of lawmaking is often symbiotic rather than competitive; once a court followed through with an application, the legislature might revise the court's ruling if found to be offensive. In essence, Traynor created a common law rule patterned on the treatment of those who execute the law. Traynor felt that the legislative process only furthered his zeal for action; he wanted to determine a way that judges could make optimal use of legislative statutes. Traynor was guided by a results-oriented approach, despite the criticism given to this approach; he felt that rationality linked the dispassionate judge and the "results-oriented" judicial decision that critics often viewed as one sided. Traynor expounded upon this belief in "Statutes Revolving in Common Law Orbits," by arguing that the "primary internal characteristic of the judicial process is that it is a rational one." A judge, Traynor argued, should not simply "write up" a person's feelings, and if one bases a decision on personal opinion, then this is hardly being impartial for an office that prides itself on impartiality. The real concern, therefore, seems to be not only in remaining impartial but also in avoiding arbitrariness. Impartiality, Traynor argued, served as a constraint on judicial decisionmaking, by making certain that decisions would not be biased. Traynor advocated a more moralistic approach, specifically concentrating on the facts-based, rational approach, rather than an arbitrary approach that relied on one-sided opinions.

In keeping with this rational-based approach, and not one that relied on public sympathy, Traynor was instrumental in the *Alien Land Law* cases and other immigration cases. For example, in the case of *Sei Fujii v. State of California,* which covered the land claims of Sei Fujii, and its precedent, the case of Kajiro Oyama and his family, Traynor made headlines. The original case, surrounding Kajiro Oyama and his family, who sought permission in 1937 to borrow $4,000 to finance the subsequent crop growth, originated with the concept of Japanese internment. In 1942, Oyama and his family were removed from the West Coast as part of the World War II containment policies, but in 1944, the state of California filed a petition to revert the Oyama property to the state. In the subsequent 1946 California Supreme Court case, the California Supreme Court upheld the action of the state to "escheat" the land, or revert the property to the state. In cases

James Wickersham: A Judge in Frontier Alaska (1857–1939)

Law is generally regarded as a civilizing influence, and much is owed to those who are the first to bring law to the frontier. Few frontiers could have been much wilder than the one that arose in Alaska as a result of gold finds there at the end of the nineteenth century. One of the pioneer judges is that area was James Wickersham.

Born in Patoka, Illinois, in 1857, Wickersham had studied law under Gov. John McAuley Palmer in his office in Springfield. Wickersham subsequently practiced law in the Washington territory from 1883 until 1900, serving as a probate judge of Pierce County from 1884 to 1888 and later as the Tacoma city attorney and a member of the Washington state house of representatives. Pres. William McKinley appointed Wickersham as a United States district judge for Alaska in 1900, a position that he held until 1908. He resigned in 1908 to serve as an elected delegate to Congress from Alaska and served in that capacity from 1909 to 1921 and from 1931 to 1933.

Much like early American Supreme Court justices, Wickersham had to "ride circuit" in Alaska (although the flyleaf to his book is more accurate in referring to his court as a "floating" court), beginning in Eagle City (his headquarters was later moved to Fairbanks) and moving from one town to another in mainland Alaska and the Aleutian Islands to dispense justice. Much of his work centered around thefts, murders, and mining claims (such matters were often settled before his arrival by lynch law), his most famous case being that to the title of the Kennecott copper mine. In a number of towns he was responsible for building the first courthouses and jails, often largely financed by license fees from saloons. In Nome, Wickersham succeeded Judge Arthur Noyes, who had been removed for colluding with shysters and claim jumpers to cheat miners out of their legitimate claims and whose court had a serious backlog of cases, which Wickersham worked diligently to complete. When he arrived to preside over the court, Wickersham did much to clear the air by announcing that he would no longer meet privately with attorneys but that all business would be done in open court (Wickersham 1938, 366). As a judge Wickersham compiled and edited the first seven volumes of the *Alaska Territory Law Reports* as well as *A Bibliography of Alaskan Literature*.

Not all of Wickersham's cases involved criminal law or mining. His very first case after assuming the Alaskan bench was to return a dog that had been stolen from an Indian chief, who took great care first to

(continues)

in which such petitions are upheld, they usually involve a decedent who has died intestate, without the possibility of inheritance, a profile that did not fit Oyama. Escheat may also be used to cover cases of abandonment of property, but not in the case of Oyama since he and his family had no choice but to move. Oyama appealed to the United States Supreme Court,

(continued)

ascertain that there was no greater white chief than Wickersham in the area (Wickersham 1938, 43–44). In another case, Wickersham helped an Indian who had shot what he believed to be a moose only to discover that he had instead killed a "white man's moose," namely a mule (200).

Wickersham delighted in the geography of Alaska and filled his life story with descriptions of his travels and of the terrain and customs of the area. He was in the first group that unsuccessfully attempted in 1903 to scale the heights of Mt. McKinley and later introduced a bill in Congress to establish the Mt. McKinley National Park (Wickersham 1938, 202). Wickersham appeared to have taken delight in rustic circumstances that would have intimidated many others with his legal background and education.

As a territorial judge, Wickersham served for a four-year term. Decisions involving high-value mining claims often brought Wickersham enemies. He noted that:

> There was never a closed season for protection of the district judges in Alaska as there was for brown bear and other varmints. Most of our early Alaska judges were removed from office upon secret charges without notice or a hearing; all of them were maliciously assailed and more or less intimidated in the performance of their judicial duty without an opportunity to defend their judicial acts or character from the secret malice of disappointed litigants. (Wickersham 1938, 434)

Himself investigated by an assistant, W. A. Day, in the U.S. attorney general's office, Wickersham was vindicated, with Day reporting that he was

> an able, honest, and upright judge; that he administers justice promptly and firmly; that he possesses the confidence of the people of his division; that his long residence in western communities and his familiarity with mining laws and customs peculiarly fit him for the position he holds; that he deserves reappointment, and that the best interests of the people of the third division,—and of all Alaska for that matter,—would be subserved by his continuance in office. (Quoted 441)

Still, Wickersham's reconfirmation was blocked by filibusters, and Roosevelt gave him four recess appointments before he was finally reconfirmed for his second judicial term.

Wickersham's subsequent election is a testament to the confidence that those who knew him had in his character. Wickersham eventually made his home in Juneau.

Reference:

Wickersham, James. 1938. *Old Yukon: Tales—Trails—and Trials*. Washington, D.C.: Washington Law Book Co.

and its 1948 ruling justified the right of the Oyama family to its land. Similarly, the *Sei Fujii v. State of California* (38 Cal. 2d 718) case of 17 April 1952 resulted in the ability of a noncitizen to purchase and own property in his own name. California Supreme Court chief justice Phil S. Gibson, along with support from fellow justice Traynor and Justices Carter and

Edmonds, wrote the majority opinion, essentially following on the heels of the *Oyama v. California* case. In 1948, Fujii had purchased an undeveloped lot in East Los Angeles, and after that time the United States Supreme Court had ruled in *Oyama v. California* that noncitizen parents who were ineligible for citizenship could purchase land as gifts for their children who were born as citizens. Fujii, who had graduated from the University of Southern California Law School, wanted to test the law, and the state of California tried to take his property, a motive favored by Superior Court judge Wilbur C. Curtis. After Fujii appealed to the California Supreme Court, Traynor and fellow judges overruled the lower court's decision. Both the *Fujii* and *Oyama* cases resulted in the declaration of the Alien Land Law as unconstitutional on 4 November 1956.

In conjunction with the upholding of integrity, while Traynor was chief justice he created a Code of Judicial Conduct. As head of a committee first formulated by the American Bar Association, Traynor felt that all judges should be evaluated equally, hence the code of conduct. The canons included the following: (1) that a judge should uphold the integrity and independence of the judiciary, (2) that a judge should avoid impropriety and the appearance of impropriety in all of his or her activities, and (3) that a judge should perform the duties of his or her office impartially and diligently. Traynor wanted to avoid contention, yet at the time, he also wanted to legitimize the public office in which he firmly believed.

It was in the field of tort law, the law of accidents and personal injury, that Traynor distinguished himself. Traynor distinguished between acts of an administrative or legislative discretion that had been immune from tort liability and acts that led to government tort liability. In *Johnson v. State of California* (69 Cal. 2d 782, 293 [1968]), the issue of the California Tort Claims Act, which provided that a public entity was not liable for an injury or failure to adopt an enactment, reached the court. In this case, the state upheld a suit against the California Supreme Court for failure to warn foster parents about the dangerous tendencies of those children under their care. Similarly, in 1963, Traynor authored *Greenman v. Yuba Power Products Inc.*, the first case to adopt the doctrine of strict liability in tort. Previous cases, such as *Henningsen v. Bloomfield Motors, Inc.*, a 1960 New Jersey court case, had moved liability from contract law to tort law. When Justice Traynor issued the *Greenman* decision in 1963, the American Law Institute was involved in the revision of tort law.

Similarly, in an appeal case, *Paul Robert Cohen v. California*, entered 22 October 1969, the appellant was charged with "engaging in tumultuous and offensive conduct" that violated the peace-keeping statute of California. The appellant was sentenced to thirty days in the county jail, but after appeal to the Superior Court, the decision was reversed, thereby allowing the state to petition for a rehearing. This resulted in the reversal of the judgment of conviction, and the state again petitioned. After the fifth appeal, the appellant filed a petition for rehearing, although the petition was denied on 13 November 1969. The appellant then filed a petition for hearing before the California Supreme Court, although this petition was denied on 17 December 1969 by a four-to-three vote, with Chief Justice Traynor as one of the three dissenters. The case returned to the appellate courts, making any judgment on the appellant level the highest possible, since Traynor's Supreme Court refused to hear the case. This case brought into question whether the use of a four-letter word with sexual connotations worn on a jacket in relation to the draft should be referred to as "offensive conduct," since the appellant did not engage in, or threaten, any acts of violence. Ultimately, the United States Supreme Court overruled the lower court, deciding that this was an example of permissible speech that fell within neither the category of "fighting words" nor of "obscenity," since it was neither directed toward a specific individual nor erotic in nature.

Jennifer Harrison

References and Further Reading:

Field, Benjamin T. 2000. "Justice Roger Traynor and His Case for Judicial Activism." Ph.D. diss., University of California.

Roth, Elizabeth. 1983. "The Two Voices of Roger Traynor." *American Journal of Legal History* 27, no. 3: 269–301.

Traynor, Roger J. 1987. *The Traynor Reader: Nous Verrons*. San Francisco: O'Brien Center for Scholarly Publications.

TUCKER, ST. GEORGE

(1752–1827)

ST. GEORGE TUCKER
Courtesy of the Library of Virginia

LONG BEFORE *Marbury v. Madison* was decided, Virginia jurist St. George Tucker embraced a conception of judicial review fully consistent with the views of Chief Justice John Marshall. For instance, as an attorney, he wrote in his unpublished notes in support of his argument as *amicus curiae* in the 1782 *Commonwealth v. Caton* case: "[The judiciary] alone . . . can decide what is or is not Law and consequently . . . on the validity or nullity of different Laws contradicting each other" (Treanor 1994, 523). In his opinion as judge in the 1788 *Kamper v. Hawkins* case (3 Va. 20, 23), he said, "[T]he judiciary are bound to take notice of the constitution, as the first law of the land; and . . . whatsoever is contradictory thereto, is not the law of the land" (81). That Tucker's views were consistent with those of Marshall is shown by the wording of the opinion of the Supreme Court by Chief Justice Marshall in *Marbury v. Madison* (1 Cranch [5 U.S.] 137): "[I]f a law be in opposition to the constitution; if both the law and the constitution apply to a particular case, so that the court must either decide that case conformably to the law, disregarding the constitution; or conformably to the constitution, disregarding the law; the court must determine which of these conflicting rules governs the case. This is of the very essence of judicial duty" (178). Although Tucker was not alone in his early endorsement of judicial review, his articulation of this constitutional principle as early as 1782 places him among the first advocates of this far-reaching judicial power.

At the beginning of the nineteenth century, St. George Tucker was recognized as one of the most distinguished jurists and legal scholars in America. He served as a member of Virginia trial and appellate courts from 1788 to 1811 and as a United States district judge in Virginia from 1813 until his retirement in 1825. For more than thirteen years, beginning in 1790, he held the chair of professor of law and police at the College of William and Mary, previously occupied by George Wythe. Tucker had studied law under Wythe's supervision, as had such prominent public figures as Thomas Jefferson, John Marshall, and Spencer Roane.

Although widely recognized as an outstanding judge and law professor, St. George Tucker was probably best known as the editor of an American edition of William Blackstone's *Commentaries*. In the postrevolutionary generation, law students and practicing attorneys in America relied heavily on Blackstone's *Commentaries on the Laws of England*. In an effort to make this indispensable source more relevant to the needs of practitioners, Tucker expanded Blackstone's four-volume treatise by "Americanizing" the text through extensive annotations and by adding a number of essays on important aspects of American constitutional and political thought. With the publication of his five-volume edition in 1803, Tucker became known as the American Blackstone.

During his long career of public service, St. George Tucker held a number of other important public positions. For example, he served as a member of the Virginia Council of State in 1782, as a delegate to the Annapolis Convention of 1786, and as an active participant on a committee charged with the responsibility of revising the laws of Virginia in 1792. In addition, immediately prior to his appointment as professor of law and police, Tucker served briefly as rector of the College of William and Mary.

Tucker's significant accomplishments were not confined to the field of law. He displayed considerable literary talent as the author of over 200 poems, several plays, and a number of literary essays. He wrote widely (and often satirically) on a number of divisive political issues including the Jay Treaty, which he opposed, and the Louisiana Purchase, which he approved. A true "renaissance man," he was also an inventor, amateur astronomer, and avid gardener.

In a brief biographical sketch, it is impossible to do full justice to the range and depth of St. George Tucker's life and work. But even a brief summary of his most important judicial opinions and observations on the federal Constitution makes it clear that Tucker's contribution to the formative years of the American republic deserves the attention that has long eluded him.

St. George Tucker was born near Port Royal on the British-held island of Bermuda on 10 July 1752. The given name "St. George," passed down from generation to generation, was introduced into the family when the Englishman George Tucker of Milton in Kent married Elizabeth St. George around 1600. The Tucker family emigrated to Bermuda in the mid-1600s and, long before St. George's birth, had achieved prominence on the island. The youngest of six children of Henry Tucker and Anne Butterfield Tucker, St. George showed an early interest in entering the legal profession.

After two years of literary and classical study in a private school operated by the Reverend Alexander Richardson, St. George began reading law in 1770 under the direction of his uncle, John Slater, the attorney general of Bermuda. The original plan was for St. George to study law at the Inns of Court in London, but his father's financial reverses led to the less expensive, alternative choice of the College of William and Mary in Virginia. Entering the college late in 1771, St. George graduated after completing a general course of study the following year. He then undertook an individualized course of legal study under the supervision of the prominent Williamsburg attorney (later law professor and judge) George Wythe. Tucker was admitted to the legal profession in 1774, but his practice of law was soon interrupted by the outbreak of the American Revolution.

In the spring of 1775, Tucker began working with his father and a number of Virginia leaders to establish favorable commercial relations between America and Bermuda. For roughly the next three years, he engaged in a number of highly lucrative trading ventures, smuggling salt and ammunition to Virginia in exchange for corn, indigo, and other products produced on the mainland. Through these efforts, he soon gained financial independence. In September 1778, he married the widow Frances Bland Randolph, one of whose three sons later gained political prominence as John Randolph of Roanoke. Tucker participated actively in the education of his stepsons and assumed responsibility in helping to manage his wife's three large plantations. By the late 1770s, Tucker, still in his late twenties, had become a member of Virginia's planter elite.

During the final stages of the American Revolution, St. George Tucker saw military action as a militia volunteer. Appointed major of cavalry, he took part in the Battle of Guilford Courthouse in North Carolina early in 1781, receiving a minor leg wound in an effort to prevent one of the American regulars from retreating. Promoted to the rank of lieutenant colonel, he was present at the siege of Yorktown, where he was asked to serve on the governor's staff as a French translator, facilitating communications between American officers and members of Lafayette's staff. During the final stages of the siege, Tucker kept a diary in which he recorded the daily movements of the army. His account is now recognized as an important source of firsthand information on the final stages of the campaign that led to the surrender of General Cornwallis.

With the end of hostilities, St. George Tucker returned briefly to plantation life but soon launched his legal career. He rapidly gained prominence as a leader of the Virginia bar. In October 1782, he presented an argument before the Virginia Court of Appeals in Richmond in opposition to the conviction of three prisoners for violation of Virginia's treason statute. Serving as *amicus curiae* rather than as a representative of the prisoners, Tucker argued that the treason statute was in conflict with the state constitution and that the Virginia Court of Appeals should invalidate it. Tucker argued that conflicts between the constitution and statutes should be resolved in favor of the former. He referred to "those Fundamental Principles of our Government, of which the Judiciary Department is constituted the Guardian" (Treanor 1994, 526). Although the Virginia Court of Appeals did not invalidate the statute in this case, two members of that tribunal, George Wythe and James Mercer, expressed support for judicial review. Among those present during the argument of this highly publicized case was John Marshall, then a twenty-seven-year-old attorney practicing law in Richmond. Marshall was obviously aware of Tucker's views as well as those of Edmund Randolph, who also argued in support of judicial review in the *Case of the Prisoners*. This may help to explain Marshall's later endorsement of judicial review at the Virginia Ratifying Convention of 1788 and his confident assertion of that power in *Marbury v. Madison*.

Tucker's law practice flourished during the 1780s, and early in 1788, the General Assembly elected him to a seat on the General Court, a tribunal with statewide original jurisdiction. This professional triumph was offset by personal tragedy. Shortly before his judicial appointment, Tucker's wife, Frances, died a few weeks after giving birth to their sixth child. Later in 1788, Tucker moved his family to Williamsburg, where he spent most of the remainder of his life. In October 1791, he married Lelia Skipwith Carter, daughter of Sir Peyton Skipwith, widow of George Carter, and mother of two children.

For more than a decade beginning in 1790, Tucker divided his professional attention between his teaching and research duties at William and Mary and his judicial responsibilities on the General Court. He soon became a recognized leader of that tribunal, as evidenced by his scholarly opinion in the 1793 case of *Kamper v. Hawkins* (1 Va. Cas. 20 [1793]). In seriatim opinions, all five judges of the court agreed in holding unconstitutional a state law that sought to give equitable powers to judges of the District Court. At that time, a sharp distinction existed between chancery courts and courts of law. A Virginia statute of 1792 granted district judges the equitable power to issue injunctions, authority previously exercised only by judges of the Chancery Court.

Reflecting his strong commitment to judicial independence, Tucker concluded in *Kamper v. Hawkins* that this statute clearly violated the Virginia constitution. In his view, the constitution "provided that the judiciary department should be arranged in such a manner as not to be subject to legislative control" (3 Va. 23). The constitution, Tucker maintained, expressed the sovereign will of the people. The judge had a duty to invalidate a legislative act if, in the course of deciding a case, he concluded that the act conflicted with the constitution. The parallel between Tucker's reasoning and that of Marshall in *Marbury v. Madison* is obvious. Tucker's opinion in *Kamper* provided strong support for Marshall's conclusion *Marbury v. Madison* that "it is emphatically the province and duty of the judicial department to say what the law is" (1 Cranch 177). (For other examples of Tucker's position on judicial review, see *Woodson v. Randolph*, 1 Brockenbrough and Holmes Reports 128 [General Court 1796] and *Turpin v. Locket*, 6 Call Reports 113 [Court of Appeals, 1804].)

In 1796, Tucker wrote an essay entitled "A Dissertation on Slavery: With a Proposal for the Gradual Abolition of It, in the State of Virginia." He sent this essay to the Virginia General Assembly, which courteously acknowledged its receipt but took no action on Tucker's proposal. In a letter dated 28 August 1797, Tucker's friend, Thomas Jefferson, who himself had previously advocated the gradual abolition of slavery, thanked Tucker for providing him with a copy of the "pamphlet" and expressed general support for Tucker's proposal (Ford 1904, 334–336). Although both Tucker and Jefferson were slaveholders who by no means endorsed the principle of racial equality, it is significant that they and other southern leaders in the late eighteenth century were willing to go on record in opposition to the institution of slavery.

The seminal publication of Tucker's American edition of Blackstone's *Commentaries* in 1803 was followed early the next year by his controversial election to the Virginia Court of Appeals and by his resignation from the William and Mary faculty. Because of a long-standing disagreement with the William and Mary administration, Tucker welcomed the opportunity to sever his connection with the college. The administration had objected to Tucker's practice of teaching his law students at home where he had full access to his law library. He viewed the administration's efforts to require him to teach on campus and to meet regularly with students in their rooms at the college as degrading and showing a lack of confidence in a person of his professional attainments (for discussion, see Cullen 1987, 140).

The Virginia Assembly elected Tucker to fill a vacancy on the Court of Appeals resulting from the death of Judge Edmund Pendleton on 23 October 1803. Tucker, who was identified with Virginia's eastern establishment, was actively opposed by Judge Archibald Stuart, a colleague on the General Court, who resided in the western part of the state. Before the legislators voted, however, Tucker was compelled to deal with unsubstantiated allegations of attempted bribery. Thomas Bailey made these allegations in writing shortly after his gambling conviction in Staunton, Virginia, in early September 1803. Tucker and his colleague, Judge Joseph Jones, had presided at Bailey's trial. In essence, Bailey asserted that Tucker had offered to rule in his favor in exchange for 100 guineas. Tucker, who "had a reputation as a 'hanging judge' in gambling cases" (Cullen 1987, 166), was enraged by this accusation and immediately took steps to refute it. He gathered numerous affidavits from prominent residents of Staunton attesting to his excellent character and to Bailey's reputation as a "liar," "swindler," and "cheat." Tucker demanded that the Virginia House of Delegates investigate Bailey's charge and, after a "select committee" considered this request along with a petition from Bailey restating his allegation, the General Assembly unanimously accepted the committee's report exonerating Tucker. On 6 January 1804, the General Assembly elected Tucker to the Court of Appeals by a vote of 115 to 82 (for additional background, see Cullen 1987, chap. 9).

St. George Tucker served as an active and influential member of the Virginia Court of Appeals from 1804 until 1811. Most of his opinions were fact specific, dealing with disputes over such matters as land titles, wills, and estates. He avoided an opportunity to address an important constitutional issue when he recused himself from participating in an 1810 decision reversing one of his own earlier rulings broadly interpreting the scope of the federal treaty power. Significantly, the United States Supreme Court, in 1813, reversed the Virginia Court of Appeals and reaffirmed Tucker's original interpretation. Tucker's broad view of the federal treaty-making power is particularly striking in light of his strong states' rights orientation as a Jeffersonian-Republican (for background, see Golove 2000, 1075).

Expressing dissatisfaction with the increasing workload of the Court of Appeals and what he regarded as unconstitutional legislative encroachments on the court's independence, Tucker resigned his life-tenured judgeship in 1811. Vowing never again to hold public office, Tucker returned to private practice in Williamsburg. In 1813, however, he accepted an appointment by Pres. James Madison to serve as United States district judge for the district of Virginia.

In addition to work at the trial level, United States district judges during that period shared Circuit Court duty with United States Supreme Court justices. In this capacity, Tucker frequently sat with Chief Justice John Marshall, whose circuit included Virginia. On one notable occasion in June 1813, Tucker filed a Circuit Court memorandum addressing an interesting constitutional question. He maintained that a provision authorizing treble damages for violation of a federal patent statute was a penal measure. According to Tucker, "a prosecution by a private person for a penalty that is three times more than its real damages cannot be distinguish'd in principle from a criminal prosecution . . ." (Hobson 1993, 7:410). He concluded that such a penalty amounted to an ex post facto law in violation of the federal Constitution (*Evans v. Jordan & Morehead;* see Hobson 1993, 7:409–411). The Supreme Court had previously held that the ex post facto restriction was limited to criminal cases. Adhering to this view, John Marshall disagreed with Tucker's expansive interpretation. The Supreme Court later affirmed Marshall's position. Tucker's view on this question underscored his strong commitment to the broad protection of individual rights.

St. George Tucker resigned from the United States District Court in 1825. He retired to the home of his son-in-law, Joseph C. Cabell, in Nelson County, Virginia, where he died on 10 November 1827. Throughout his career as judge and legal scholar, he emphasized the importance of judicial independence, limited government, and individual liberty. His influence as a champion of states' rights was significant prior to 1860. The nationalist views advanced by Alexander Hamilton, John Marshall, Joseph Story, Daniel Webster, and Abraham Lincoln, however, became dominant in the aftermath of the Civil War, and the judicial opinions as well as the legal commentaries of St. George Tucker were soon forgotten.

Late in the twentieth century, however, a number of legal scholars began to express renewed interest in Tucker's work. In addition to his contribution to the early development of judicial review, his lengthy 1803 essay, "View of the Constitution of the United States," endorsed a view of civil liberties in many respects consistent with contemporary interpretation. For example, Tucker's understanding of the "right of the people to keep and bear arms," embodied in the Second Amendment, represents an increasingly influential perspective. He saw this right as broad and unconditional, observing that "this may be considered as the true palladium of liberty. . . ." "The right of self-defense," he added, "is the first law of nature: in most governments it has been the study of rulers to confine this right within the narrowest limits possible. Wherever standing armies are kept up, and the right of the people to keep and bear arms is, under any color or pretext whatsoever, prohibited, liberty, if not already annihilated, is on the brink of destruction" (Tucker 1999, 238–239). In addition, Tucker accorded broad scope to federal and state constitutional provisions guaranteeing freedom of speech and the press.

St. George Tucker made significant contributions to early American constitutional development at state and federal levels. He was also an influential legal scholar and educator. He was a prolific writer, not only on legal subjects but on political and literary themes as well. Future scholarship should include a full-scale biography of this extraordinary individual.

Otis H. Stephens

References and Further Reading:

Coleman, Mary Haldane. 1938. *St. George Tucker: Citizen of No Mean City*. Richmond, Va.: The Dietz Press.

Cullen, Charles T. 1987. *St. George Tucker and Law in Virginia, 1772–1804*. New York: Garland Publishing.

Ford, Paul Leicester, ed. 1904. *The Works of Thomas Jefferson*. Vol. 8, Federal Edition. New York: The Knickerbocker Press.

Golove, David M. 2000. "Treaty-Making and the Nation: The Historical Foundations of the Nationalist Conception of the Treaty Power." *Michigan Law Review* 98 (March): 1075.

Hobson, Charles F. 1996. *The Great Chief Justice: John Marshall and the Rule of Law*. Lawrence: University Press of Kansas.

Hobson, Charles F., ed. 1993. *The Papers of John Marshall*. Vol. 7: *1807–1813*. Chapel Hill: The University of North Carolina Press.

Shevory, Thomas C. 1994. *John Marshall's Law: Interpretation, Ideology, and Interest*. Westport, Conn.: Greenwood Press.

Treanor, William Michael. 1994. "The Case of the Prisoners and the Origins of Judicial Review." *University of Pennsylvania Law Review* 143 (December): 491–570.

Tucker, St. George. 1999. "View of the Constitution of the United States." In *View of the Constitution of the United States with Selected Writings*, edited by Clyde Norman Wilson. Indianapolis, Ind.: Liberty Fund.

White, G. Edward. 1991. *The Marshall Court and Cultural Change, 1815–1835*. Abridged ed. New York: Oxford University Press.

TUTTLE, ELBERT PARR

(1897–1996)

ELBERT PARR TUTTLE
Library of Congress

JUDGE ELBERT PARR TUTTLE served as judge on the Fifth and Eleventh Circuit Courts and as chief judge on the United States Court of Appeals for the Fifth Circuit from 1961 to 1968. It was in this position that Tuttle, the grandson of a Civil War veteran who fought for the Union, brought about the integration of the University of Georgia and contributed to the desegregation of the South as only part of his illustrious career.

Elbert Tuttle was born 17 July 1897 in Pasadena, California, to parents Guy Harmon Tuttle and Margie Etta Tuttle (née Parr). Before entering college, he studied at Punahou Academy in Honolulu, Hawaii. While the family was living in Honolulu on the island of Oahu, Tuttle became a charter member of the now-famous Outrigger Canoe Club of which his father was president. The Tuttle family—Elbert, his father, and his brother Malcolm—were among the first nonnative Hawaiians to take up the sport of surfing.

Tuttle left Hawaii to begin college at Cornell University, where he earned an A.B. in 1918. While there he served as president of his senior class. Two years later when he went on to Cornell Law School, he was Order of the Coif and editor in chief of the law review, earning an LL.B. in 1923 and finishing first in his class. He was also awarded two honorary LL.D. degrees: one from Emory University in 1958, the other from Harvard University in 1965.

Elbert Tuttle met his wife, Sara Sutherland Tuttle, in 1917 in Jacksonville, Florida. Unable to afford the trip home to Hawaii for the summer, Tuttle decided to stay with the family of a fraternity brother, Strawn Perry, for the summer. On the day he arrived in Jacksonville, Elbert met Sara Sutherland at a swimming party, and the two were inseparable thereafter. During the same trip, Elbert met another individual who would be important in his life: Sara's brother, Bill Sutherland, with whom Elbert would later enter into a partnership to practice law. Tuttle once remarked that "my entire life was shaped by the Cornell circumstances that originally brought me to Florida, since marrying a Florida girl and becoming acquainted with the south are the circumstances that caused me to decide to move to the south after graduating from law school in 1923" (Aman 1996, 2).

Between graduating from college and making the decision to enter law school, Tuttle worked as a journalist in New York for the *New York Sun* and in Washington, D.C., for the *American Legion Weekly*. Tuttle had worked his way through college at Cornell working on the *Cornell Daily Sun* with such individuals as E. B. White and Sam Howe, and pursuing journalism seemed to him to be the natural next step in his career. He gave up journalism in 1920, however, to enter law school at Cornell and pursue a different career.

Elbert Tuttle and Sara Sutherland were married during his time at Cornell Law School and later had two children, Elbert and Jane. When he graduated from law school, the couple chose to settle in Atlanta, Georgia, owing largely to the fact that Sara's family lived in the South and her brother, Bill, was practicing law in Atlanta as well. Elbert was admitted to the Georgia bar in 1923. He joined an established firm in Atlanta, Anderson, Rountree and Crenshaw, but his real desire was to go into partnership with his brother-in-law Bill Sutherland. The opportunity came in 1924 when Sutherland won a case in the Georgia Supreme Court, earning a fee of $2,500. The two believed that this would be enough money to cover their expenses for a year and so formed the law firm of Sutherland and Tuttle.

World War II brought an interruption to Tuttle's legal career. He had enlisted in the army during World War I and became a Flying Cadet in the Observation Corps of the United States Field Artillery. The use of airplanes by the army was new and untried and required much training. World War I ended while Tuttle was still engaged in that training. He served in the

Georgia National Guard until the United States entered the conflict of World War II. He served as a combat soldier in World War II, commanding a battalion of the Seventy Seventh Infantry Division of the United States Army, which took part in the invasions of Guam, Leyte, and Okinawa. Tuttle suffered several wounds and was heavily decorated for his service. He was awarded the Legion of Merit, the Purple Heart with Oak Leaf Cluster, and the Bronze Star. He was discharged in 1946 as a colonel and entered the United States Army Reserves as a brigadier general for the 108th Airborne Division.

After the war, Tuttle returned to the practice of law in Atlanta until 1953, when he took the position of general counsel to the U.S. Department of the Treasury. He was working for the Department of the Treasury when he was appointed to the United States Court of Appeals for the Fifth Circuit in 1954. The Fifth Circuit was made up of Georgia, Florida, Alabama, Louisiana, Mississippi, and Texas. At the time of Tuttle's appointment, six judges sat on the Fifth Circuit, and traditionally one judge was appointed from each of the six states encompassed. Tradition also dictated that when a judge died or resigned, his replacement would be chosen from his home state. In 1954, however, Congress created a seventh judicial seat for the growing Fifth Circuit, and the president in office was Dwight Eisenhower, for whom Tuttle had worked as a campaign strategist. Eisenhower nominated Tuttle to the new seat on 7 July 1954, and his confirmation proceeded without incident. The Senate confirmed his nomination on 3 August 1954. Thus, Tuttle became the only Republican on the Fifth Circuit at the time and also the only member who had not been raised in the South among its deep-seated racial prejudices. In 1961, Tuttle was elevated to chief judge of the Fifth Circuit, and he served in that capacity until 1968, a time period that encompassed the peak of the civil rights movement. He continued to serve as a judge on the Fifth Circuit until 1981 when the circuit was split into the Fifth and Eleventh Circuits, at which time he became a member of the Eleventh Circuit Court.

Admired by his peers for many things, Judge Tuttle is respected for his willingness to try new things, such as the sport of golf, which he took up at the age of sixty-nine. Although he started playing much later in life than most golfers, he became an avid and accomplished golfer, taking advantage of his travel on the court circuit to play at different courses.

Of course, Judge Tuttle is most admired for his accomplishments in his legal career, throughout which he showed great character, integrity, and decisiveness. A revealing example of these virtues is Tuttle's argument as an attorney before the Supreme Court in the case of *Johnson v. Zerbst*, perhaps the most frequently cited decision in the constitutional law of criminal procedure. When a marine accused of counterfeiting was not informed by the trial judge that he had a right to counsel, the American Civil Liberties Union (ACLU) asked Elbert Tuttle to handle the appeal. When the Fifth Circuit Court of Appeals held that there was no affirmative duty of the trial court to inform an accused of his right to counsel, Tuttle continued to pursue the case despite the fact that the ACLU had no more money to spend on counsel or court costs. When Tuttle finally argued the case before the Supreme Court, having spent his own money to progress that far, he won by a six–two decision, with the Court holding that trial of an accused without a knowing waiver of the right to counsel violated the due process clause of the U.S. Constitution.

In his career as a judge, Tuttle often held fast to his dissenting opinions, refusing to be swayed by the majority or by popular opinion. In fact, several of Judge Tuttle's dissents ultimately became law upon appeal. For example, in *Wesberry v. Vandiver* in 1962, the Fifth Circuit held that the issue of the constitutionality of Georgia's county-unit system was a political question that the court could not decide. Judge Tuttle disagreed, stating in his dissent that he thought the issue was fully justiciable and that the county-unit system was clearly unconstitutional, and the Supreme Court, in a majority decision penned by Justice Black, agreed with him. The same happened again in 1966 in *Bond v. Floyd* when the Supreme Court once again agreed with Judge Tuttle's dissent and ruled that the Georgia legislature could not refuse to seat an elected state representative because of his public lack of support for the Vietnam War.

One of Judge Tuttle's most famous decisions, however, was one that he made while sitting alone as chief justice of the United States Court of Appeals for the Fifth Circuit. In the struggle to desegregate southern universities, and particularly those in Georgia, black leaders had chosen several promising high school students over a course of years to represent the cause. As colleges such as the University of Georgia fought their efforts, each case in turn became moot as the students were forced to pursue their educations at traditionally black universities. When Charlayne Hunter and Hamilton Holmes applied for admission at the University of Georgia (UGA) in an effort led by the National Association for the Advancement of Colored People, they were in danger of the same fate as their predecessors. UGA had used numerous delay tactics before finally denying both students admission, and almost two years had passed before Judge Tuttle heard the case.

In September 1960, these two students filed suit, more than a year after their initial applications for admission. Judge William A. Bootle, a United States District Court judge for the Middle District of Georgia, heard the case and decided that the matter required a full trial to determine whether UGA had denied Hunter and Holmes admission because they were black. After a full trial, Judge Bootle ruled in favor of the plaintiffs on 6 January

1961, only three days before registration for the coming term closed. Hunter and Holmes would have to register for classes within three days or allow the university another school term to find new ways to fight, possibly with the help of the Georgia legislature, which had previously shown a willingness to engage in creative legislation to preserve segregation. But when the state presented its motion for a stay of the order pending appeal, Judge Bootle granted that motion at 9:30 A.M. on Monday, 9 January, the very day that registration would close.

Constance Baker Motley, one of the attorneys representing the plaintiffs, called Judge Tuttle's office asking how soon he could hear an appeal of the order to stay the decision. Tuttle agreed to hear the matter in Atlanta that afternoon at 2:30 if she could have the notice of appeal filed by that time. Judge Tuttle was troubled by the matter of authority: He knew that the Court of Appeals could lift Judge Bootle's stay, but could he do so sitting alone, as there was no time to convene a panel of three judges? Tuttle set his clerks to work on this question and then dove into the research himself, finally finding the authority to act in statute. Having done so, Judge Tuttle took the bench at exactly 2:30, knowing that the criticism and anger that would surely come out of the day's proceedings would rest on his shoulders alone. In a short opinion, Tuttle reversed the order of stay, emphasizing that the stay would allow the ongoing denial of a constitutional right for the two students. With the stay lifted, Hunter and Holmes were able to register for classes that very afternoon, and they began classes at the University of Georgia on Wednesday, 11 January 1961, thus desegregating the institution.

Certainly Judge Tuttle was instrumental in this and many other civil rights cases, several of them quite notable. His influence is as apparent in the sheer number of cases he heard, however, as it is in the importance of some of those cases. During his career as a judge, Tuttle sat more often than most other judges, turned out opinions more promptly than most judges, and wrote more opinions each year than most judges. In fact, he wrote over 1,400 opinions in his career. It has also been said that Judge Tuttle was always prepared for each case that came before him for oral argument, often asking the questions that were the key to the case's outcome.

Judge Tuttle's work ethic and willingness to do for himself the work that most judges would assign to a clerk are perhaps best exemplified by an incident observed by Anne Emanuel, one of his clerks from 1975 to 1976. During the energy crisis, she observed that he personally placed upon each light switch in the office a sticker reading, "Turn Off the Light When Not in Use," and then proceeded to turn off each light (Aman 1996, 8). Tuttle was also heavily involved in the Atlanta community, serving as president of the Atlanta Chamber of Commerce, president of the Atlanta Bar Association, president of the Lawyer's Club of Atlanta, trustee of the Atlanta Community Chest and the Atlanta Planning Council, director of the Atlanta Children's Home and Piedmont Hospital, and trustee on the boards of Atlanta University, Morehouse College, and Spellman College as well as of his alma mater, Cornell University.

At the end of a very distinguished career for which President Carter awarded him the Presidential Medal of Freedom, Elbert Parr Tuttle passed away on 23 June 1996. He was ninety-eight years old and was still sitting on the United States Court of Appeals for the Eleventh Circuit.

Brandi Snow Bozarth

References and Further Reading:

Aman, Alfred C., Jr. 1996. "Elbert Parr Tuttle." *Cornell Law Review* 82 (November): 1.

Bass, Jack. 1998. "Faces Turned to the Future." *Houston Law Review* 34 (Spring): 1492.

Bond v. Floyd. 385 U.S. 116 (1966).

Chase, Harold, Samuel Krislov, Keith O. Boyum, and Jerry N. Clark. 1976. *Biographical Dictionary of the Federal Judiciary*. Detroit, Mich.: Gale Research.

Emanuel, Anne S. 1996. "Lynching and the Law in Georgia circa 1931: A Chapter in the Legal Career of Judge Elbert Tuttle." *William and Mary Bill of Rights Journal* 5 (Winter): 215.

———. 1999. "Turning the Tide in the Civil Rights Revolution: Elbert Tuttle and the Desegregation of the University of Georgia." *Michigan Journal of Race and Law* 5 (Fall): 1.

"Excerpts from Elbert Tuttle Portrait Ceremony and Eleventh Circuit Historical Society Ceremony." 1983. *Cornell Law Review* 68 (January): 158.

Wesberry v. Vandiver. 206 F. Supp. 276 (N.D. Ga. 1962).

VANDERBILT, ARTHUR T.

(1888–1957)

Arthur T. Vanderbilt
Bettmann/Corbis

Arthur T. Vanderbilt was the nation's leading judicial reformer during the middle decades of the twentieth century. As chairman of the New Jersey Judicial Council from 1930 to 1947, he advocated fundamental changes in the New Jersey court system, ultimately succeeding when New Jersey adopted a new constitution with a revised judicial article in 1947. As president of the American Bar Association from 1937 to 1938, he made reform of the administration of justice his top priority. In 1939 he helped draft the statute creating the nation's first body dedicated to judicial administration, the U.S. Administrative Office of the Courts. Two years later, he helped draft the Federal Rules of Criminal Procedure, which were designed to simplify procedures, increase fairness, and eliminate expense and delay. Appointed chief justice of the newly created New Jersey Supreme Court in 1948, he used his position to establish the state's court system on a firm foundation, transforming what had been regarded as the nation's worst court system into one of its best. While serving as chief justice, he founded the Institute of Judicial Administration, which was dedicated to the task of promoting judicial reform nationwide, and he remained president of the institute until his death. Thus, one can view Arthur Vanderbilt's service as chief justice (1948–1957) as the culmination of a lifelong commitment to improving the administration of justice.

Arthur Vanderbilt was born in Newark, New Jersey, on 7 July 1888. After graduating from Wesleyan University in 1910 and Columbia University School of Law three years later, he returned to Newark and entered private practice. Until he became a judge, Vanderbilt maintained a highly successful law practice. But he was far more than a distinguished attorney. In 1914, as his law practice was getting established, Vanderbilt began teaching evening classes at New York University Law School, and he continued teaching on a part-time basis for twenty-nine years. Appointed dean of the New York University (NYU) Law School in 1943, he dramatically enhanced the school's flagging reputation by creating the NYU Law Center, now housed in a building that bears his name. In 1921 Vanderbilt was appointed county counsel for Essex County (New Jersey), an office that he held for twenty-six years. He was appointed to Wesleyan University's Board of Trustees in 1934 and continued in that position until his death in 1957. Finally, as noted, Vanderbilt actively campaigned for judicial reform in New Jersey and nationwide.

Vanderbilt was also a major political figure in New Jersey. Following his graduation from law school, Vanderbilt became identified with the Republican reformers advocating "clean government" in Essex County. Ironically, given his opposition to Democratic political machines and in particular to Mayor Frank Hague of Jersey City, the boss of the Hudson County machine, Vanderbilt developed into something of a political boss himself. He served as president of the Essex County Republican League, and his leadership of the Essex County Clean Government organization gave him a power base that enabled him to play a role as "kingmaker" in the state. In 1946 he endorsed Alfred Driscoll as the Republican candidate for governor, and Clean Government's strong support for Driscoll was decisive in securing him the Republican nomination and a victory in the general election in November.

Ever eager to promote judicial reform, Vanderbilt had extracted from Driscoll as the price of his support a promise to make constitutional reform the centerpiece of his administration. Governor Driscoll called for a constitutional convention in his inaugural address, and one was convened in June 1947. Because he was recuperating from a stroke suffered in May of that year, Vanderbilt did not attend the 1947 constitutional convention. He avidly followed the proceedings, however, especially the activities of the Committee on the Judiciary. Governor Driscoll had consulted Vanderbilt about who should serve on the committee, and the committee's leadership shared Vanderbilt's commitment to modernization of the New Jersey judiciary. The committee endorsed and the convention adopted many of the recommendations that Vanderbilt had initially proposed through the New Jersey Judicial Council. Among these was the creation of a new court, the New Jersey Supreme Court, to replace the state's antiquated Court of Errors and Appeals.

When Governor Driscoll appointed Vanderbilt as the first chief justice of the New Jersey Supreme Court, Vanderbilt recognized that this was a unique opportunity to implement his reform agenda. The 1947 constitution designated the chief justice as "the administrative head of all the courts in the State," and Vanderbilt likened his position "to that of chairman of the board and president of a business concern" (Vanderbilt 1955, 98). He devoted his energies to asserting managerial control over New Jersey's courts and making them more efficient. Prior to 1947, each of New Jersey's various courts had operated autonomously, developing its own rules and procedures and managing its own caseloads. With Vanderbilt this changed. As chief justice, his first priority was to introduce a "simplification of procedure, so that technicalities and surprise may be avoided, and so that procedure may become a means of achieving justice rather than an end in itself" (10). In 1948 he took the first step toward that end by standardizing judicial procedure throughout the state, promulgating rules of procedure based on the Federal Rules of Civil Procedure. The rules of practice and procedure remained a concern for Chief Justice Vanderbilt, however, who insisted that they be continually reassessed to determine how effectively they promoted justice. In fact, he completely revised New Jersey's rules of procedure only five years after their initial adoption.

When Vanderbilt became chief justice, another problem demanding attention was delay in New Jersey's trial courts. Vanderbilt aggressively attacked the problem of case backlogs. He moved judges from their normal assignments to assist in courts plagued by heavy caseloads and congestion. He also demanded greater productivity from the state's judges. Court rules were adopted prescribing the number of hours per week that a judge should sit on the bench. Vanderbilt required each judge to submit to the New Jersey Administrative Office of the Courts a weekly report listing the cases and motions heard and the cases still unresolved. Vanderbilt personally reviewed these reports, and judges who failed to dispose of cases expeditiously could expect to be contacted by the Administrative Office of the Courts or by Vanderbilt himself for an explanation. The chief justice also published these weekly reports, using publicity to put pressure on laggard judges to mend their ways. Many judges resented the loss of their traditional autonomy, but Vanderbilt's methods worked. By 1950 the case backlogs had disappeared, and New Jersey's courts were among the nation's most efficient.

Because these and other changes met with resistance from many New Jersey judges, Vanderbilt had to devote considerable effort to persuasion and arm twisting. Indeed, he estimated that his administrative responsibilities consumed one-third of his time. He was also forced to fight a continuing battle with political forces in the state legislature that sought to limit the judiciary's independence by asserting legislative control over judicial rule making. This battle culminated in Chief Justice Vanderbilt's most important and most controversial decision, *Winberry v. Salisbury* (74 A.2d 406 [NJ 1950]).

Winberry raised a question crucial to the autonomy of New Jersey's reconstituted judiciary: Did the supreme court or the state legislature have ultimate control over the rules of judicial procedure? The New Jersey legislature insisted that it had authority to revise by statute the procedural rules adopted by the supreme court, because the constitution of 1947 gave the supreme court its rule-making power "subject to law." Writing for a five-member majority, Vanderbilt disputed this interpretation, asserting that

> The only interpretation of "subject to law" that will not defeat the objective of the people to establish an integrated judicial system and which will at the same time give rational significance to the phrase is to construe it as the equivalent of substantive law as distinguished from pleading and practice. . . . The phrase "subject to law" . . . serves as a continuous reminder that the rule-making power as to practice and procedure must not invade the field of the substantive law as such. While the courts necessarily make new substantive law through the decisions of specific cases coming before them, they are not to make substantive law wholesale through the exercise of the rule-making power. (74 A.2d, 410)

In sum, so long as the supreme court confined its rule making to procedural matters, its exercise of this power could not be overridden by the legislature.

Vanderbilt's opinion was vehemently attacked. Justice Clarence Case refused to join the chief justice's opinion, insisting that it was not necessary to construe the constitutional provision in order to resolve the case. More important, Vanderbilt's opinion appeared to fly in the face of constitutional history. In its report to the convention, the Committee on the Judiciary had expressly indicated that it considered "subject to law" to mean subject to legislation. And Vanderbilt himself, in a letter to the convention objecting to inclusion of the phrase, had interpreted it the same way. Thus, although Vanderbilt's position may have secured the independence of the judiciary and promoted better administration of the courts, it more closely resembled a usurpation than a faithful interpretation of the constitution.

Winberry reveals a great deal about Vanderbilt. It demonstrates his concern for the institutional position of the New Jersey Supreme Court and his willingness to take action to protect it. He later defended judicial rule making by noting that it allowed for reassessment of court procedures "without waiting for stated legislative sessions and without burdening already overworked legislators" (Vanderbilt 1963, 108). Yet it seems likely that a concern to protect the autonomy of the judicial branch, as well as a skepticism about legislative expertise in the area, were far more important in explaining his position. *Winberry* also shows Vanderbilt reaching out to address a politically explosive issue rather than deciding the case on narrow grounds. This willingness, even eagerness, to confront controversial questions is consistent with his more general understanding of the judicial role. In both judicial opinions and extrajudicial writings, Vanderbilt categorically rejected the canons of judicial restraint (134–139). Finally, despite the dubious argument advanced in *Winberry*, the key point is that Vanderbilt prevailed. The reforms of 1947 that Vanderbilt had championed and Vanderbilt's own stature had created a reservoir of support on which he could draw in repelling what he perceived as an attack on the New Jersey Supreme Court. The press and bar unanimously supported Vanderbilt; and in the face of that sentiment, his opponents in the New Jersey Assembly were forced to shelve plans for a constitutional amendment and accept the decision (Tarr and Porter 1988, 193–194).

Another contentious case was *Tudor v. Board of Education of Rutherford* (100 A.2d 857 [1953]). The Gideons International received permission from the Board of Education of Rutherford to distribute copies of the Gideon Bible to students in the borough's public schools, over the objection of Catholic and Jewish parents who complained that it was a sectarian book inconsistent with their beliefs. Speaking for the New Jersey Supreme Court, Chief Justice Vanderbilt agreed. In a scholarly opinion, Vanderbilt reviewed the history of religious conflict within Christianity and the growth of religious toleration. He noted, without attempting to resolve, the continuing controversy over whether the First Amendment was meant to erect a "wall of separation" between church and state. What was indisputable, Vanderbilt emphasized, was that neither the state nor its instrumentalities could show a preference for one religion over another. Reviewing the testimony at trial, Vanderbilt concluded that the Gideon Bible was a sectarian book. Drawing upon a wealth of precedent and testimony, he demonstrated that its distribution by the school amounted to an endorsement of a particular creed and would be perceived as such by students and their parents. Vanderbilt's thoughtful analysis convinced his colleagues on the court and averted political repercussions.

Vanderbilt was, however, less successful in persuading his fellow justices to subject long-established common law doctrines to critical scrutiny. A case in point is *Fox v. Snow* (76 A.2d 877 [1950]), in which Vanderbilt wrote one of his most eloquent opinions. Relying on stare decisis, the majority in *Fox* adhered to a technical rule of law in interpreting a will, despite (in Vanderbilt's words) "the deleterious effects of the rule and the lack of any sound principle to support it" (882). In dissent, Vanderbilt refused to "put the common law in a self-imposed straitjacket" (882). Quoting Justices Oliver Wendell Holmes and Benjamin Cardozo in support of his position, he argued that judges should not hesitate to repudiate doctrines that lacked support in reason or public policy and should "adapt the law to the needs of the living present" (882–883). Thus, Vanderbilt was as willing to jettison outmoded legal doctrines as he was to replace ineffective rules of procedure. He concluded:

> We should not permit the dead hand of the past to weigh so heavily upon the law that it perpetuates rules of law without reason.
>
> Unless rules of law are created, revised, or rejected as conditions change and as past errors become apparent, the common law will soon become antiquated and ineffective in an age of rapid economic and social change. It will be on its way to the grave. (76 A.2d 885)

How does one measure the greatness of a judge? One measure might be the recognition and honors bestowed upon the judge by his contemporaries. Vanderbilt scores well on that measure. His leadership in judicial reform earned him honorary degrees from thirty-two universities as well as awards from (among others) the American Bar Association, the American Judicature Society, and the New Jersey and New York State Bar Associations (Vanderbilt 1976, 216–217). Vanderbilt was avidly sought out as a lecturer: His two books, *The Challenge of Legal Reform* (1955) and *The Doctrine of the Separation of Powers and Its Present-Day Significance* (1963), were based on lecture series given at the University of Virginia and at the University of Nebraska. The Eisenhower administration seriously considered him for a position on the United States Supreme Court, but Vanderbilt's advancing age and his commitment to implementing reform in New Jersey led him to demur.

Another measure of judicial greatness is the legacy that a judge leaves behind. On this measure too, Chief Justice Vanderbilt scores well. Vanderbilt catapulted the New Jersey courts to an unaccustomed position of prominence and respect, and his national reputation helped shield them from political attack. He also furnished the New Jersey Supreme Court with an example and an implicit challenge: namely, how to live up to the tradition of judicial excellence that he had founded and personified. This legacy continues long after Vanderbilt's death: The national prominence of the current New Jersey Supreme Court can be seen as vindicating his efforts. As Chief Justice Robert Wilentz observed in 1982: "The experience of that reform is so strong, and its meaning so clear, that is still moves us substantially in New Jersey" (quoted in Buchsbaum 1982, 33).

Vanderbilt's legacy extended beyond the borders of New Jersey. His agenda for judicial modernization was adopted by reformers throughout the nation, as well as in several foreign countries (Vanderbilt 1976, 217). For example, he created the first state Administrative Office of the Courts, and every state has followed his lead. Indeed, when the National Center for State Courts was established, its first director was Edward McConnell, who had headed New Jersey's Administrative Office of the Courts under Vanderbilt. The Institute of Judicial Administration that he founded has become known nationally and internationally for its services to the administration of justice. Perhaps Justice William J. Brennan Jr., who had served with Vanderbilt before his elevation to the United States Supreme Court, put it best: "He is one of the very great judges of our time. His contribution toward the improvement of judicial administration and substantive law are an imperishable monument to this legacy" (quoted in Gerhart 1980, 296).

G. Alan Tarr

References and Further Reading:

Buchsbaum, Peter. 1982. "The Courts: The 1947 'Revolution.'" *New Jersey Reporter* (November): 33.

Fox v. Snow. 76 A.2d 877 (1950).

Gerhart, Eugene C. 1980. *Arthur T. Vanderbilt: The Compleat Counsellor.* Albany, N.Y.: Q Corporation.

Tarr, G. Alan, and Mary Cornelia Aldis Porter. 1988. *State Supreme Courts in State and Nation.* New Haven, Conn.: Yale University Press.

Tudor v. Board of Education of Rutherford. 100 A.2d 857 (1953).

Vanderbilt, Arthur T. 1955. *The Challenge of Law Reform.* Princeton, N.J.: Princeton University Press.

———. 1963. *The Doctrine of the Separation of Powers and Its Present-Day Significance.* Lincoln: University of Nebraska Press.

Vanderbilt, Arthur T., II. 1976. *Changing Law: A Biography of Arthur T. Vanderbilt.* New Brunswick, N.J.: Rutgers University Press.

Winberry v. Salisbury. 74 A.2d 406 (1950).

WARING, J. WATIES

(1880–1968)

J. Waties Waring
Courtesy of South Carolina Library, University of South Carolina, Columbia

Long before the Warren Court began the modern revolution in civil rights law, a Charleston, South Carolina, federal district judge with impeccable social credentials outraged white citizens of his city, state, and region with decisions requiring equal pay for black and white teachers, outlawing South Carolina's white primary, and rejecting the state's whites-only law school, as well as a vehement dissent decrying segregated public schools as "*per se inequality*" and strident attacks on the southern "slavocracy" in forums throughout the nation. Julius Waties Waring's roots and early life furnished hardly a clue to his later court record. Waring was born on 27 July 1880, an eighth-generation Charlestonian whose father's family had first settled there in 1683, only thirteen years after the city's founding. Following education at a local private academy and the College of Charleston, he read law with a prominent trial lawyer, hung out his shingle, and steadily developed a successful private practice. His social position continued to flourish as well, especially following his marriage in 1913 to Annie Gammell, a well-connected woman with a prestigious Meeting Street home south of Broad Street, an area wherein resided the elite of Charleston society, known to inhabitants and outsiders alike as the "S.O.B.'s."

Waring also became active in Democratic politics, cultivating associations that led to his being named assistant U.S. attorney in 1914. His caseload ran the gamut from a shipboard murder, to counterfeiting, mail fraud, and wartime sabotage, to countless liquor prosecutions under what Waring considered the "terrible" Volstead Act (quoted in Yarbrough 1987, 7). Among his most celebrated prosecutions was one arising from the 1917 sinking of the German freighter *Liebenfels* in Charleston harbor.

When the Democrats lost the presidency in 1920, Waring established a law practice with D. A. Brockington. The firm throve through the 1920s, handling a good deal of real estate law, a large federal practice, and the legal affairs of the city's morning and evening dailies, as well as other business clients.

Waring and Brockington fell on relatively hard times during the Depression. But in 1931, newly elected Charleston mayor Burnet Rhett Maybank invited Waring—his friend and mentor—to join his administration; and the city council appointed the future judge to the post of corporation counsel, or city attorney, a position Waring was to hold until his elevation to the federal bench. Waring also continued to cultivate close ties with South Carolina's low-country segregationist politicians, including the colorful and demagogic Ellison D. "Cotton Ed" Smith, the dean of the U.S. Senate.

In 1942, Waring's political connections paid off handsomely with his appointment as United States district judge for South Carolina's eastern district. Charlestonians were proud of their native son. The *News and Courier* of 19 December 1941 called him "an accomplished and industrious lawyer, of long and successful experience, a man of excellent character." As late as 1945, the College of Charleston awarded its graduate an honorary doctorate of laws. By that point, however, a combination of circumstances was at work that would soon make the judge a pariah even among his family and closest friends.

For the first two years of his tenure, Waring's caseload and decisions were largely uneventful. In 1944, however, he issued the first of several remarkable rulings. In two cases, he ordered the equalization of pay for black and white teachers in Charleston and Richland County (Columbia). Pressed by the judge in another case, the state created a law school for blacks. When South Carolina repealed all its laws regulating party primaries in a campaign to preserve its all-white Democratic primary as a private affair beyond the reach of the Fifteenth Amendment's ban on racial discrimination at the polls, Waring struck the scheme down in *Elmore v. Rice* (72 F. Supp. 516, 1947), inviting South Carolinians "to rejoin the Union" (528).

The next year the Democratic state convention limited party membership to whites only and allowed African Americans to vote in the party's primaries—tantamount to general elections in solidly Democratic South

Carolina—only if they took an oath of allegiance to "states' rights" and segregation. But in *Brown v. Baskin* (1948), the judge rebuffed that stratagem as well. He had also appointed a black bailiff; eliminated a number of discriminatory practices in his court, including the race-coding of jury lists and segregated seating of jurors; and become increasingly hostile on the bench toward counsel for the state.

Waring later attributed what he termed his growing "passion for justice" to a number of factors. In 1945, he had abruptly divorced Annie Gammell, his devoted wife of more than thirty years, to marry Elizabeth Hoffman, a northerner wintering in Charleston with her second husband. The new Mrs. Waring was reportedly shocked at the more sordid aspects of southern race relations, especially the prompt acquittal by a jury in Judge Waring's court of a town police chief who had blinded a young black with his billy club. At Elizabeth's urging, she and the judge began reading Myrdal's *An American Dilemma* and other classic studies of southern racial mores in a campaign to raise their consciousness about the evils of discrimination.

Breaking completely with the judge's segregationist past, the Warings also began entertaining prominent blacks in their Meeting Street home and speaking to African American and racially mixed audiences in Charleston and elsewhere. In a speech to the city's black Young Women's Christian Association (YWCA) branch, Mrs. Waring scorned the "decadence" of southern whites. Shortly thereafter, she reiterated her charges on *Meet the Press* while also condoning interracial marriage. Nor were avowed opponents of racial reform their only targets. Railing against the "false god of gradualism" in speeches around the nation, Judge Waring ridiculed Mississippi editor Hodding Carter, Ralph McGill of the Atlanta *Constitution*, and other southern liberals who opposed immediate desegregation and advocated racial reform through voluntarism rather than federal force. Such gradualists, the judge charged, were more dangerous than unabashed racists.

The Warings had now become almost completely isolated from white Charlestonians. Certain of his relatives and close friends later contended that they had been willing to continue their association with the couple, but the Warings had broken off relations with them. Others expressed outrage at the judge's divorce and harangues against the South, yet denied that Waring's civil rights decisions had influenced their feelings. Following the divorce, the judge had purchased the Meeting Street house from Annie Gammell, who moved into the rented kitchen house of a nearby home. But Charleston whites suspected that Waring had stolen the house from the compliant Miss Annie, relegating her to the humble rooms she would occupy until her death in 1954 while the judge and his new bride enjoyed the comfort of his first wife's home.

Hostile southern reaction to the Warings went well beyond ostracism by friends and relations. On the floor of the U.S. House of Representatives, South Carolina congressman L. Mendel Rivers accused the judge of advocating "force" in the cause of civil rights, according to the Charleston *News and Courier*. Backed by petitions signed by thousands of his state's citizens, Rivers urged the House to impeach Waring. Mississippi segregationist John Rankin went further, exclaiming, as recorded in the *Congressional Record* (1950, vol. 96, pages 4930–4932), that Waring was "crazy" and should be confined to a mental institution. After Mrs. Waring's speech to the YWCA, offensive telephone calls became a nightly occurrence. Youths taunted her as the "witch" of Meeting Street. While the Warings were in New York, a small cross was burned in front of their house. In October 1950, a window pane was shattered and the front-door screen punctured. The Warings claimed that shots were fired and demanded an intensive Federal Bureau of Investigation investigation. But police found only pieces of mortar, and the *News and Courier*, on which the judge's nephew Tom Waring served as managing editor, dismissed the incident as the prank of teenagers.

Concerned that Waring's public statements had exceeded the bounds of judicial propriety, other judges often declined to attend affairs held about the country in the couple's honor. In the eyes of many, however, they were courageous symbols of the struggle for racial justice. Following the stoning incident, supportive blacks and whites from several southern states made a pilgrimage to the Warings' home, offering moral support to the couple. Although not nearly so extensive as Mrs. Waring thought warranted, national press coverage, including profiles in the *New York Post* and *Collier's* as well as the African American press, was overwhelmingly sympathetic. Accepting the Warings' contention that shots had been fired at their home, *Post* columnist Max Lerner described their "lonely vigil amidst the encircling hostile spears" of whites in "darkest Charleston" (12 October 1950). For a time, Tom Waring attempted to persuade friendly national journalists to publish details of his uncle's personal life, but to no avail.

While controversy swirled around the Warings, the judge became involved in another significant civil rights case. The couple now numbered among their friends prominent African American civil rights leaders. Although hardly consistent with the canons of judicial ethics, Waring urged National Association for the Advancement of Colored People (NAACP) executive director Walter White and other association officials to file a suit in his court challenging segregated public schools and what he considered the "sophistry" of the "separate but equal" doctrine the Supreme Court had endorsed in *Plessy v. Ferguson* (1896) (Waring, J. Waties. Papers. 6 January 1950).

Eventually, the case Waring wanted came before him. For several years, Joseph Albert DeLaine, a black teacher and minister in rural Clarendon County, had been seeking modest improvements in educational opportunities for black students in the county's woefully inadequate segregated schools. Subjected to a reign of terror for his audacity, the Reverend DeLaine and his family soon left the state. Later, a suit seeking bus transportation for Clarendon's black students was filed in Judge Waring's court. That case was dismissed on technical grounds. Thurgood Marshall and other NAACP lawyers then persuaded twenty black Clarendon parents to file *Briggs v. Elliott*, contending that the county's black schools were clearly inferior to those provided white students. At a pretrial conference, Judge Waring agreed that it would be easy for the plaintiffs to prove gross inequities in Clarendon's segregated school system. He suggested, however, that the plaintiffs withdraw their suit and file a new one attacking not only the obvious inequalities in the Clarendon County schools but also the constitutionality of segregated education in itself.

In those days, a constitutional challenge to a state policy had to be heard before a three-judge panel. The court chosen to hear the new *Briggs* suit consisted of Judge Waring, appeals court chief judge John J. Parker, and district judge George Bell Timmerman. By southern standards, Judge Parker, a North Carolina Republican, had developed a relatively liberal record on the federal bench. Like most other southern progressives, however, Parker thought it the wiser course to delay desegregation and improve the quality of black schools pending substantial improvements in the economic and social conditions of African Americans. Judge Timmerman was even less likely than Parker to reject segregated education and the *Plessy* "separate but equal" doctrine.

After a trial, the panel voted two-to-one to accept South Carolina's promise to equalize its segregated schools and refused to overturn *Plessy*. In a vehement dissent in *Briggs v. Elliott* (98 F. Supp. 529 [1951]), Judge Waring condemned segregation as nothing more than a remnant of slavery. Citing the testimony of witnesses for the plaintiffs that the "mere fact" of segregation had a "deleterious and warping effect upon the minds of children" (547), he scorned segregated education as "*per se inequality*" (548).

Waring had been deeply disappointed, although hardly surprised, that he was unable to secure Judge Parker's vote to overturn segregation. He was heartened, however, at the generally favorable national reaction to his *Briggs* dissent. Myles Horton of the controversial Highlander civil rights school in Tennessee predicted that Waring's opinion would one day become "the law of the land" (Waring, J. Waties. Papers. 6 June 1951. Horton to Waring). Horton, of course, was prophetic. Albeit in more conciliatory language and without mentioning the controversial Waring's name, Chief Justice Earl Warren essentially tracked Waring's rationale in his unanimous opinion for *Brown v. Board of Education* (1954), *Briggs*, and companion cases.

More than two years before the Supreme Court's desegregation ruling, the Warings had departed Charleston for a life of "exile" in New York. By 26 January 1952, the judge had served ten years on the federal bench and was eligible, given his age, for retirement at full salary. On that date, he sent President Truman and Judge Park letters indicating his intention to retire on 15 February.

For the judge's close associates, the reasons for his decision were not difficult to fathom. His distaste for Judge Parker's *Briggs* opinion and its endorsement of *Plessy* ran so deep that he had declined to serve further on the three-judge panel. He had also become increasingly disenchanted with what he considered to be the timidity of Charleston blacks and their failure to bring more civil rights cases into his court. After the cross burning and stoning incidents, the Warings' circle of black friends had steadily dwindled; and their feelings had been hurt the previous Christmas, when black children who traditionally serenaded prominent white families passed 61 Meeting Street and sang instead at the nearby home of a Waring enemy. Perhaps his retirement, he wrote a friend, would put Charleston blacks "on their mettle," bolstering their courage. Finally, as a retired judge, Waring would be completely free to speak out on civil rights issues, no longer muzzled—if ever he had been—by the dictates of judicial propriety.

On learning of his retirement, admirers praised Waring's record and resolve in letters to newspapers and private correspondence. Undated clippings in the Waring papers show that in an admiring editorial, the *New York Times* termed the judge "a Judge Worthy of Honor" and that even the Charleston newspapers greeted the announcement with what Judge Waring later conceded was "tasteful" restraint. The *Courier* editorialized that "aside from 'crusading' on the Negro question," the judge had compiled an excellent judicial record. When Septima Clark, one of the Warings' closest black friends and a future leader in the modern civil rights movement, asked that the *Courier* reprint the *Times* editorial, Tom Waring readily obliged.

In New York, the Warings enjoyed the adulation denied them by white Charlestonians. When the Supreme Court's desegregation ruling was announced on 17 May 1954, prominent civil rights leaders, including Walter White and NAACP board members, gathered at the Warings' small Fifth Avenue apartment as much to honor their hosts as the Court's ruling. Later that year, the couple returned to Charleston for ceremonies praising the judge's contributions to racial justice, with one speaker comparing Waring's rejection of his segregationist past to the Apostle Paul's conversion.

The Warings would remain in the North until their deaths. During the twilight of his life, the judge continued his efforts in behalf of racial equality, becoming a board member of the American Civil Liberties Union and president of an organization attempting to provide food, clothing, and agricultural supplies to blacks in the rural South. As in the past, he also remained contemptuous of the fainthearted in the struggle for civil rights. When Alabama senator John Sparkman, the Democrats' 1952 vice presidential nominee, appeared to reject the civil rights plank in the party's platform, Waring urged Adlai Stevenson, the party's presidential candidate, to reject his running mate's statements. When a *New York Times* columnist endorsed the 1957 Civil Rights Act as at least a beginning, Waring scorned the statute as more loophole than law. He repeatedly clashed, moreover, with NAACP and other civil rights leaders he considered insufficiently zealous in their pursuit of racial reform.

Nor had white Charlestonians forgiven their native son and his second wife. Judge Waring died on 20 January 1968, Elizabeth in late October the same year. The judge's body was returned to Charleston's Magnolia Cemetery for burial. Over 200 blacks were present, fewer than a dozen whites. Family and friends still considered the judge's rulings and attacks on their society acts of revenge for their refusal to accept his divorce and second wife rather than a reflection of Waring's sincere commitment to civil rights.

But time—and changing political realities—can heal wounds and blur memories. South Carolina's white politicians now vie for black votes. The Warings' African American friends, including Septima Clark and Ruby Cornwell, became active in a variety of biracial civil affairs. In 1981, Charleston's mayor placed a sculpture honoring Waring's memory in the city council chamber, overlooking the federal courthouse.

Tinsley E. Yarbrough

References and Further Reading:

Waring, J. Waties. Papers. Moreland-Spingarn Research Center, Howard University, Washington, D.C.

Yarbrough, Tinsley E. 1987. *A Passion for Justice: J. Waties Waring and Civil Rights*. New York: Oxford University Press.

WARREN, EARL

(1891–1974)

Earl Warren
Harris & Ewing, Collection of the Supreme Court of the United States

Earl Warren was one of only three chief justices of the United State Supreme Court to have an era named after him. The Warren Court (1954–1969) was arguably the most important—and certainly the most written about—since the Marshall Court (1801–1836), and the Warren Court's record of accomplishment far exceeds that of the Taney Court (1836–1859). Whether those accomplishments will endure through the ages or be a momentary liberal aberration in a Supreme Court history dominated by conservatives remains to be seen.

Warren was born to a family of exceedingly modest circumstances in Los Angeles, California, in 1891. His parents, Methias (Matt) and Chrystal (Hernlund) Warren, were émigrés from Scandinavia. Earl Warren lived from the age of three in Bakersfield, a hot, dusty railroad town on the edge of the desert. At the age of seventeen he enrolled at the University of California in Berkeley, where he stayed until he graduated from law school in 1914. Bakersfield provided an enormously formative environment that helps explain his actions and passions decades later as chief justice.

The Warrens moved to Bakersfield in 1894 after Matt was fired and blacklisted by the Southern Pacific Railroad for participating in a strike.

Matt was a rail repairman, car inspector, and eventually a foreman. Apparently the blacklist did not get to Bakersfield, as the Southern Pacific hired Matt there as well. He never made more than a modest salary but, unlike the majority of his peers, did not smoke, drink, or gamble, and he had a passionate interest in education. He also had a reputation as being extraordinarily tightfisted, but as a result he was able to provide a relatively stable home and save enough to send his only son to college. He was disappointed he could not do the same for his daughter, Ethel.

As a young boy Earl himself worked as a railroad caller—running to alert workers when an incoming train needed work. As he related in his memoirs, "I witnessed crime and vice of all kinds countenanced by corrupt government. . . . The things I learned about monopolistic power, political dominance, corruption in government, and their effect on the people of a community were valuable lessons that would tend to shape my career throughout life . . ." (Warren 1977, 31). Matt Warren was murdered in his home in Bakersfield in 1938. His killer was never found.

Earl Warren remembered his train trip from Bakersfield to Berkeley in 1908 as both literally and symbolically refreshing. Feeling the sea breezes for the first time in his life, he resolved to live his life in the Bay area. Warren did not particularly stand out as a student at Berkeley. He had average grades, and although he made numerous friends, he did not run for student government or otherwise show that talent for public office or winning elections he would display later in life. But neither was he particularly docile. Boalt Hall, Berkeley's law school, employed the Socratic method, which required students to dialogue with professors in class. Students often ended up embarrassed or humiliated in these exchanges. Despite a warning from the dean that he might not graduate, Warren refused to participate. Nor did he obey the strict rule against outside employment. It was a breach that could have had him expelled if members of the administration had discovered his work. They never did.

One of the most formative experiences during these years was Warren's decision to join an organization called the Lincoln-Roosevelt League. This was a group made up of members from the Democratic, Republican, and Progressive parties interested in reform politics. Warren offered his services to one of the league leaders, Hiram Johnson, who ran for governor as a reform Republican and won. Johnson remained one of Warren's role models. He was an activist, reform-minded governor who vowed to put an end to the dominance of the Southern Pacific railroad in California politics. The Lincoln-Roosevelt League later changed its name to "Progressives," and although Warren continued to espouse its values of bipartisanship, good government, and public morality, he identified himself, perhaps somewhat lightly, as a Republican. On the other hand, when he later ran for public office he had no qualms about running in the Democratic and Progressive primaries as well as that of the Republican party.

Once he graduated Warren had difficulty finding a career niche. He worked first as an entry-level lawyer for the Associated Oil Company in San Francisco. Unhappy to be treated more like a clerk than a lawyer, he moved within a year to Robinson and Robinson, an Oakland firm. Finding himself once again doing research for other attorneys and with a meager salary, he strategized with two Berkeley classmates to form their own firm. Before they could put it together, the United States entered World War I, and Warren opted to enlist. He served only from September 1917 to December 1918 and never left the country, but during that time he stood out as a good manager of men and was commissioned an officer. After his release from the army, he found a position as staff attorney for the judiciary committee of the state legislature. This was the beginning of a lifelong career in public service.

In 1920 a position as deputy district attorney of Alemeda County (Oakland) opened up. Warren applied and was accepted. Since the pay was low, most deputies had traditionally practiced law on the side and given as little time and energy to their public duties as they could get away with. Warren was different. He began an enthusiastic five years of litigating, opinion writing, and advising the county Board of Supervisors. He quickly became one of two chief deputies. In 1925 the district attorney resigned, and Warren was appointed as acting district attorney. In 1926 he was elected in his own right and served for the next twelve years.

In 1921 the young deputy district attorney met a young widow, Nina Palmquist Meyers; they dated for four years until after Warren was appointed district attorney and felt he was finally making enough money to support a family. They married and had six children: James, a son from Nina's previous marriage whom Earl adopted, and five of their own—Virginia, Earl Jr., Dorothy, Nina Elizabeth (known as Honeybear), and Robert. The image of an "all-American family" certainly helped Warren in his political career, but he and Nina made strenuous efforts to separate their public and private lives, rarely entertained for political reasons, and kept their children sheltered from the battles of political life.

During those years Warren refined his political and management skills: long-range planning, thorough preparation for every case, an exquisite sense of timing, and a keen ability to form and use public opinion. He was affable, gregarious, and tough and tried to emphasize nonpartisan cooperation, an appealing combination that garnered widespread newspaper support. Warren also developed a theme that proved to be extraordinarily popular and led to the development of a statewide reputation: professionalizing law enforcement. Warren pushed for extensive training of police officers and even for courses in California colleges, a radical idea at the time. He also worked for "coordination" among the three major law enforcement groups—sheriffs, local police, and the state's district attorneys—but was careful to insist on the independence of each. In a brilliant stroke Warren developed a lobby group from among these constituencies that became a powerful political force in Sacramento.

Becoming attorney general of California was a natural next step, and in 1938 Warren filed for the nomination in the Democratic, Republican, and Progressive parties. He was selected by all three and won an overwhelming majority of votes. In his *Memoirs*, Chief Justice Warren indicated that he had fully intended to end his career in this position, but several unforeseen events intervened. The first was that he found himself working for a highly partisan Democratic governor, Culbert Olson. As one biographer expressed it, "Olson saw Warren as a Republican and a potential political rival, and consequently as a man to be isolated" (White 1982, 53). The two seemed to clash on every major political issue, and Warren found it exceedingly difficult to maintain his nonpartisan stance. Things came to a head with the attack on Pearl Harbor on 7 December 1941. Governor Olson determined to take all law enforcement into his own hands and as part of his isolation strategy refused even to consult his attorney general. Warren found this personally insulting and dangerous. Although he and the governor actually had similar views on a number of political issues, Warren developed a visceral and lasting dislike of Olson.

The second event was the decision to remove people of Japanese ancestry from the West Coast and relocate them to "internment camps" in the interior of the country. Warren was intimately and intensely involved in that decision—urging military commanders to move quickly and decisively to remove the citizens of Japanese extraction. Although he later regretted this decision as racist and unnecessary, at the time it was popular in California. It reinforced Warren's reputation as a tough, no-nonsense attorney general.

The two events—Olson's continuous efforts to snub and isolate Warren, and his popularity as a result of his law enforcement credentials and war efforts—combined to convince Warren that he should oppose Olson in the 1942 election for governor. Warren won the contest with 57 percent of the vote. He had run as much out of spite and frustration as out of conviction, but at the age of fifty-two Earl Warren found himself governor of California.

Warren's ten years as governor are hard to categorize in standard political terms. He continued to be an amazingly popular politician, being reelected twice by large pluralities. This did not go unnoticed on the national scene, as he was the first Republican star since Roosevelt had swept the Republicans out of power in 1932 and launched the New Deal. But was he liberal or conservative? In fact, he was a bit of both, and a bit of a commonsense visionary as well. He began as governor by cutting taxes and establishing a financial reserve for emergencies. But he also worked for prison reform; he increased spending for higher education and assistance for the elderly and the mentally ill; and most interesting from a twenty-first-century perspective, he pioneered a compulsory health insurance system. Some commentators see a progression from conservative early days as governor to liberalism in his later years, but Warren can be just as easily classified as a pragmatic problem solver who saw government as a means to help those in California who needed help. He continued to have sensitivity for the underdogs in society. Thus while he joined in the anti-Communist crusades after World War II, he was willing to make distinctions and try to protect academic freedom, freedom of speech, and due process. This did make him suspect in the eyes of some and was the basis for decades of distrust between him and Richard Nixon.

Much to Warren's astonishment, Gov. Thomas Dewey of New York asked Warren to run for the office of vice president on the national Republican ticket in 1948. Republican leadership continued to be impressed with Warren's ability to draw voters and also by the Electoral College votes of California. The candidates did not know each other personally before the electoral campaign, and Warren had shown little interest in partisan politics and even less in national issues, but he consented to run because he felt he owed it to the party. When Truman pulled off his famous come-from-behind victory, Warren returned to his governorship with some relief. When he won a third term by over a million votes, however, Warren received extensive national publicity and was touted as presidential material.

The 1952 Republican National Convention was filled with intrigues that led in a roundabout way to Warren's nomination to the Supreme Court. There was a real potential for a deadlock between the two main candidates, Dwight Eisenhower and Robert Taft. Warren was seen as the logical compromise candidate or at least the favorite son who could pledge California's votes to either candidate. But it did not happen. Eisenhower was nominated on the first ballot. Warren genuinely liked Eisenhower and campaigned actively for him. In return, Eisenhower respected Warren's administrative abilities and intimated that he would like him to take a cabinet position. Warren responded that the only position in which he had an interest was a Supreme Court seat. Eisenhower or one of his aides then promised Warren "the first available seat" on the Court, not anticipating that it would be the chief justice position. Chief Justice Fred Vinson died of a heart attack on 8 September 1953. Warren's nomination was announced on 30 September.

The Warren Court was one of the most activist Courts since the founding of the Republic. It had as profound and comprehensive an impact on

U.S. society as any Court in history. Indeed, the Warren Court practically defined political liberalism in the post–World War II era and set much of the national agenda for the next half century. It began with an assault on racial segregation. The Court's unanimous decision in *Brown v. Board of Education* (1954), declaring that legally segregated schools are inherently unequal, is arguably the most important event in race relations since ratification of the Fourteenth Amendment in 1868. It overruled *Plessy v. Ferguson* (1896), a fifty-eight-year precedent, and signaled the Court's willingness to plunge into political thickets where state and federal legislators refused to tread. Technically *Brown* dealt only with education, but its principled argument was sweeping, and dozens of cases followed that outlawed segregated public transportation, public accommodations, housing, employment, and even marital relations.

Nothing reveals Chief Justice Warren's management of the Court more poignantly than the drama behind the scenes while *Brown v. Board of Education* was being decided. The case was originally argued in 1952, but the Court was bitterly divided. Justices Hugo Black, Harold Burton, William O. Douglas, and Sherman Minton favored overruling *Plessy*. Justices Stanley Reed and Tom Clark and Chief Justice Fred Vinson wanted to uphold *Plessy*, and two justices, Robert Jackson and Felix Frankfurter, although expressing personal distaste for segregation, were fearful of the political and social impact of a Supreme Court decision that overturned both precedent and legislation in such a volatile area. Justice Frankfurter prevailed upon the Court to hold the case over until the 1953 term, during which it was reargued. When Chief Justice Vinson died and Warren was appointed, the balance shifted dramatically. Warren let it be known to the other justices that he thought segregation was immoral and would vote to overturn *Plessy*, but he asked them all to consider how this could be done to best serve the country. By his willingness to take suggestions and to compromise—for example, by establishing the principle but delaying implementation until states had an opportunity to propose means to do so in a second case, *Brown v. Board of Education II* (1955), and by using moderate language for the principle and vague language for implementation, ". . . with all deliberate speed"—Warren was able to command unanimity, a remarkable achievement at the time.

Segregation was only the first problem the Warren court addressed. Other issues included (1) forcing state legislatures to reapportion so that each citizen's vote counted as much as every other citizen's (*Baker v. Carr* [1962], *Reynolds v. Sims* [(1964]); (2) limiting the federal government's ability to intimidate and destroy careers and reputations by using its investigative powers (*Watkins v. United States* [1957], *Greene v. McElroy* [1959]); (3) limiting local governments' abilities to require or even allow prayer in public schools

Bruce McMarion Wright (1918–)

Few judges have had more controversial careers than Bruce McMarion Wright. Born in Princeton, New Jersey, in 1918 to a white mother and a black father, Wright attended segregated schools at Princeton and was later told by both Princeton (where he had been awarded a scholarship before his ethnicity was known) and Notre Dame University that his attendance at these universities would be offensive to the large number of southerners who attended. Wright was expelled from Virginia State University when he made fun of religious exercises on the campus and eventually graduated from all-black Lincoln University in Pennsylvania.

Subsequently enrolling at Fordham University law school, Wright was drafted, served in the army in Europe as a private, and was decorated for his service. Insulted when trying to board a ship back to the United States, Wright, who had written some poetry during the war, went absent without leave for eighteen months in Paris, making the acquaintance of Langston Hughes and Leopold Sedar Senghor, who was later to become the president of Senegal.

Reluctantly returning to the United States, whose racism he detested, Wright enrolled at the New York University Law School and became a clerk at a prestigious New York City firm, Proskauer, Rose, Goetz and Mendelsohn, where he was dissuaded from continuing. Wright set up a private practice, much of which involved handling legal matters for prominent African American musicians with whom he often toured both in the United States and abroad. Wright is very open about his own life, which has involved being married to five women (two of whom apparently died during the marriage) and fathering five sons. Wright worked, beginning in 1967, for the Human Resources Administration of New York City.

(continues)

(*Engel v. Vitale* [1962], *Abington School District v. Schempp* [1963]); (4) enhancing the government's power to regulate economic activities to enhance safety, honesty, and fairness (*NLRB v. Gissel Packing Co.* [1969], *Brown Shoe Co. v. United States* [1962]); and (5) most controversial, protecting the rights of those accused of crimes (*Mapp v. Ohio* [1961], *Gideon v. Wainwright* [1963], *Escobedo v. Illinois* [1964], *Miranda v. Arizona* [1966], *Terry v. Ohio* [1968]). It was one of Warren's strengths that he could assign majority opinions, even in major precedent-setting cases, to other justices who might have a particular interest in the issue. Warren liked to win, but he did not need the spotlight.

Aside from race relations, no initiatives of the Warren Court triggered more public reaction than its largely successful effort to protect the rights of criminal defendants. With twenty-two years in California law enforcement, Earl Warren had more experience than all other justices on the bench com-

(continued)

Mayor John Lindsay appointed Wright to the criminal court of New York City in 1970, but Wright's reputation for dealing leniently with criminals and setting low bail for those he believed were not at risk for fleeing was so notorious (he was frequently referred to as "Turn 'em Loose Bruce") that he received numerous threats on his life and was for a time reassigned to the civil court. Frequently investigated and censured at least once by the Judiciary Relations Committee, Wright was regarded as a hero to many African Americans, and he was appointed in 1983 to the New York Supreme Court. The author of works of poetry as well as of two books detailing his career and his views of the differences between justice as it is meted out to blacks and whites in the United States, Wright has often provoked controversy by his speeches. He served for a time as a visiting professor at the Cooper Union for the Advancement of Science and Art.

A judge with a distinct attitude, Wright is a religious skeptic and is definitely not enamored with the American political system. He explains: "I have had a long and passionate love-hate affair with the law. I remain unforgiving of the so-called Founding Fathers, those pious thieves who took over what has become America, while banishing the Indians to remote ghettos we call reservations" (Wright 1996, 206). Wright still professed, however, to be following judicial ideals: "I never thought of myself as a 'liberal,' in any event. My efforts on the bench were, I hope, in the tradition of humanism: honor the presumption of innocence and give everyone, accuser and accused, a fair trial, whether in the civil or criminal side" (203).

References:

Contemporary Black Biography. 1992. Vol. 3. Detroit: Gale Research.

Wright, Bruce. 1993. *Black Robes, White Justice*. New York: Carol Publishing Group.

———. 1996. *Black Justice in a White World, A Memoir*. New York: Barricade Books.

bined and wrote with confidence. Indeed, of the 235 opinions Warren authored, sixty-nine or nearly a third concerned criminal law and procedure. No case caused more controversy than his opinion in *Miranda v. Arizona* in which he laid out guidelines for the famous Miranda warnings that must be read to all criminal suspects at the time of their arrest and before they can be questioned: "You have the right to remain silent; anything you say can be used against you in court; you have the right to talk to a lawyer before questioning and to have a lawyer with you during questioning. You may stop questioning at any time. If you cannot afford a lawyer one will be provided for you." Warren also made clear that evidence gathered in violation of these stipulations could not be used as evidence in a court of law.

Conservatives were apoplectic. "Impeach Earl Warren" signs went up across the country. With the passage of time, scholars have been able to evaluate the impact of the changes in criminal process initiated by the

Warren Court: Neither convictions nor the number of confessions declined measurably. Rarely did a guilty person go free. The most important result of the Warren Court's jurisprudence was increased education and training of police forces across the country. This was exactly the agenda Warren had had as attorney general.

One endeavor in which Warren was not entirely successful was in leading the investigation of Pres. John F. Kennedy's assassination. Appointed to head a commission by Pres. Lyndon Johnson despite his reluctance, Warren wanted to publish a definitive report putting to rest American fears of an international conspiracy. The Warren Commission Report had quite the opposite effect. Much of the blame can be laid on the chief justice himself. Because he wanted a quick report, the commission staff did not vigorously pursue evidence collected by the Federal Bureau of Investigation and the Central Intelligence Agency; did not follow up on alternative theories that more than one bullet was fired, possibly from different locations; and refused to allow graphic pictures to accompany the report. Warren also insisted on a unanimous opinion by committee members and was willing to water down statements to get it. The Warren report was widely attacked as a cover-up or, at best, a sloppy, unprofessional piece of work. Although the commission's results have never been disproved, the damage to Warren's reputation was significant.

Chief Justice Earl Warren was a liberal, activist judge. He saw his role as guiding the judicial system to promote the ethical values imbedded in the Constitution—equality of opportunity; liberty for individuals to speak, read, write, and associate as they saw fit without government censorship; the right of government to regulate businesses for the common good; and protection of those minorities most vulnerable to abusive government power, Negroes and those accused of crime. For all his successes, Earl Warren did not forget the lessons he learned during his early years in Bakersfield. His legal opinions were neither brilliant nor subtle. He argued in clear, simple language buttressed with moral passion. He strove to do what was right for the country and did not hesitate to create new law to make it happen. Warren retired from the Supreme Court in 1969 and died of congestive heart failure on 9 July 1974

Paul J. Weber

References and Further Reading:

Abington School District v. Schempp. 374 U.S. 203 (1963).
Baker v. Carr. 369 U.S. 186 (1962).
Brown v. Board of Education I. 347 U.S. 483 (1954).
Brown v. Board of Education II. 349 U.S. 294 (1955).

Brown Shoe Co. v. United States. 370 U.S. 294 (1962).
Cray, Ed. 1997. *Chief Justice: A Biography of Earl Warren*. New York: Simon and Schuster.
Engel v. Vitale. 370 U.S. 421 (1962).
Escobedo v. Illinois. 378 U.S. 478 (1964).
Gideon v. Wainwright. 372 U.S. 335 (1963).
Greene v. McElroy. 360 U.S. 474 (1959).
Katcher, Leo. 1967. *Earl Warren: A Political Biography*. New York: McGraw Hill.
Lewis, Anthony. 1969. "A Talk with Warren on Crime, the Court, the Country." *New York Times Magazine*, 19 October, 35.
Mapp v. Ohio. 367 U.S. 643 (1961).
Miranda v. Arizona. 384 U.S. 436 (1966).
NLRB v. Gissel Packing Co. 395 U.S. 575 (1969).
Plessy v. Ferguson. 163 U.S. 537 (1896).
Pollack, Jack H. 1979. *Earl Warren: The Judge Who Changed America*. Englewood Cliffs, N.J.: Prentice Hall.
Reynolds v. Sims. 377 U.S. 533 (1964).
Terry v. Ohio. 392 U.S. 1 (1968).
Tushnet, Mark. 1996. *The Warren Court in Historical and Political Perspective*. Charlottesville: University Press of Virginia.
Warren, Earl. 1977. *The Memoirs of Earl Warren*. New York: Doubleday.
——. Oral History Collection, Regional Oral History Office, The Bancroft Library, University of California at Berkeley. Available at <http://bancroft.berkeley.edu/ROHO>. (Primary source material.)
Watkins v. United States. 354 U.S. 178 (1957).
Weaver, John D. 1967. *Warren: The Man, the Court, the Era*. Boston: Little, Brown.
White, G. Edward. 1982. *Earl Warren: A Public Life*. New York: Oxford University Press.

WEINSTEIN, JACK B.

(1921–)

OFTEN CONTROVERSIAL, ALWAYS outspoken, federal district judge Jack B. Weinstein, who was appointed to the United States District Court for the Eastern District of New York in 1967, has spent a career handling the types of cases that give other judges fits.

JACK B. WEINSTEIN
Bettmann/Corbis

Jack B. Weinstein was born on 21 August 1921 in Wichita, Kansas. His grandparents were poor Russian Jewish immigrants who had come to the United States at the turn of the century. His family returned to Brooklyn, his mother's birthplace, in his youth. He was raised in an urban, working-class family; his father was a salesman, his mother a nurse.

He attended Brooklyn College in Brooklyn, New York, graduating in 1943. After serving as a lieutenant in the navy in World War II, Weinstein enrolled in Columbia Law School. He graduated in 1948 and clerked for the Honorable Stanley H. Fuld of the New York Court of Appeals. He began private practice in New York City thereafter. During the next twenty years, he served in a variety of public roles, including special counsel for the New York Joint Legislative Committee on Motor Vehicle Problems, counsel to a New York state senator, research assistant for the New York Senate, consultant for the New York Temporary Commission on Courts, and reporter for the New York Advisory Committee on Practice and Procedure.

In 1952, he became an associate professor of law at Columbia Law School, advancing to full professor in 1956. Upon joining the federal bench, he became an adjunct professor at the law school, a position he still holds. He has also served as an adjunct professor at New York University School of Law, Brooklyn Law School, and George Washington University School of Law in Washington, D.C. In addition, he has served as a visiting scholar and lecturer at many law schools and professional organizations.

Pres. Lyndon B. Johnson appointed Weinstein to the federal bench in the spring of 1967. Interestingly, Judge Weinstein had declined previous offers to serve on the federal judiciary—he had been asked to serve, for example, in the Southern District of New York, which includes Manhattan. This time, however, President Johnson had asked him to serve in the Eastern District—his hometown of Brooklyn—and Weinstein readily agreed. He explained to another judge that the Eastern District (which encompasses Long Island) had been his father's sales territory; it was the right place for him to be (Sifton 1996, 77). Weinstein took his seat at the court on 1 May 1967. He served as chief judge of the district from 1981 to 1988 and became a senior judge in 1993. He continues to serve in the Eastern District.

Weinstein's judicial career has now spanned three and one-half decades. He is perhaps best known for his willingness and ability to manage the most complex cases, particularly mass class action tort litigation. Judge Weinstein has become famous for his work on these high-profile cases, which have included the Agent Orange case, brought by Vietnam veterans exposed to the chemical defoliant during their military service; asbestos litigation, which numbered over 90,000 separate cases; diethylstilbestrol (DES) litigation, brought by women who, having taken the dangerous drug to prevent miscarriages, bore children who had severe birth defects; carpal tunnel (repetitive stress) injury litigation; and a significant portion of the recent antitobacco litigation cases—among others.

Mass class action tort cases are characterized first by their huge number of litigants, which commonly number in the thousands, and even tens of thousands. An army of counsel and their support staff represents these plaintiffs. The defendants, who are typically the manufacturers of products believed to be dangerous or defective, are similarly armed. Added to the fray are the defendants' insurance companies and their lawyers, secondary insurers, and so on. As a result, the number of active participants before the court in such a case can easily number in the hundreds. The main issue in the litigation might seem straightforward—plaintiffs claim that they have been harmed by the defendant's negligence in manufacturing, marketing, or using a product—but proving that claim rarely is. Millions of pages of evidence may be produced; hundreds of depositions taken; hundreds of procedural and evidentiary motions filed. Outcomes often depend on how a jury views the conclusions of competing expert witnesses, who argue over complex scientific research that may or may not link the product to the damage that has been done. Given the risks involved in getting the jury to understand such testimony, and with juries generally, many of these cases are settled out of court, with counsel for plaintiffs typically taking 30 to 40 percent of any award as their contingent fee.

How, then, does an individual plaintiff—one person among thousands who will probably never meet his or her lawyer, let alone appear in court—receive justice? This complicated but essential question lies at the heart of Judge Weinstein's management of complex litigation. In his book, *Individual Justice in Mass Tort Litigation* (1995), Weinstein described the balance the judges must strike between obtaining justice for the injured and resolving these conflicts in a procedurally fair and efficient manner. Weinstein analyzed numerous reform proposals and suggested many of his own, developed over the years from his experiences on the bench.

Weinstein's phrasing of the central questions of his book revealed much about the person and the judge: "How can we provide each plaintiff and each defendant with the benefits of a system in mass torts that treats him or her as an individual person? How can each person obtain the respect that his or her individuality and personal needs should command in an egalitarian democracy such as ours?" (1995, 3). In his work on the bench, in his civic involvements, and in his outspoken stands on controversial political and legal issues, Jack Weinstein has demonstrated a fundamental respect for people and a deep commitment to ensure justice not only for the litigants before him but for society as a whole.

Judge Weinstein's judicial philosophy is not without controversy, of course. Critics consider him an "activist" judge who directs the settlement of cases toward a result that he believes is fair. Lawyers for the tobacco industry, for example, recently watched in dismay as plaintiffs' attorneys used a procedural device for case management called the "consolidated case rule" to steer antismoking lawsuits into his courtroom, a practice that the judge allegedly facilitated (Bradley 2000). Similarly, in *Agent Orange on Trial* (1986), author Peter Schuck portrayed Weinstein as a tough-minded judge intimately involved in pressuring the defendants to settle a case where liability was not clear-cut.

Weinstein, for his part, has not let criticism affect his approach to litigation, which he acknowledges is highly managerial. Weinstein embraces a kind of "hands on" and "roll up the sleeves" approach, a fact best demonstrated by his refusal to wear judicial robes. Instead, he dresses in a suit and tie and, except at trial, sits down with lawyers at the counsel table, rather than addressing them from the bench. Judge Weinstein's official photograph for the Eastern District, hanging among auspicious portraits and photos of judges in their full judicial regality, shows him in that simple suit and tie, his standard judicial attire (Gleeson 1996, 83).

Although Judge Weinstein is best known for adjudicating and writing about mass tort cases, he has been outspoken on numerous other legal issues. For example, in 1993 he briefly refused to accept drug cases in his courtroom, in opposition to the Federal Sentencing Guidelines for drug offenders (and particularly its mandatory minimum sentencing provisions). He is a vocal critic of America's War on Drugs and has argued repeatedly for reform of national drug policy. In an opinion piece for the *New York Times*, for example, Weinstein called the policy "self-defeating" and encouraged the nation to develop an approach that would "reduce the violence, moral degradation, and waste associated with drugs in a more humane, effective, and cost-efficient way" (1993, op. ed.).

In that article, Weinstein noted the high proportion of young African American men jailed for drug offenses, challenging his readers to consider whether this fact is evidence of "an overlooked moral dilemma" in our criminal justice system (op. ed.). Weinstein has also questioned the disparate impact of the death penalty on minority defendants. He adamantly opposes capital punishment, doubting its deterrence value and decrying the procedural shortcomings in death penalty cases, which he has labeled "intolerable." He concluded in a *New York Law Journal* article: "Conditions change. Our view of what is required of a humane and caring people should change with the times. . . . [There is] no excuse for unnecessary cruelty and inhumanity" (2000, n.p.).

In the mid-1990s, Judge Weinstein decided the case of *Ayeni v. Mottola*, which concerned the Secret Service's decision to invite CBS News along as it executed a search warrant in Babatunde Ayeni's home. The Secret Service served the warrant to Mrs. Ayeni, who was wearing only a nightgown, and the agents, with cameras and audiotape rolling, proceeded to tear apart the household in front of a fearful Ayeni and her five-year-old son. Repeated requests by Mrs. Ayeni to stop the taping were unheeded, as the camera crew proceeded to film both the Ayenis and their personal possessions and documents.

Both the criminal case against Mr. Ayeni and the civil case filed by the Ayenis against the Secret Service and CBS News came before Judge Weinstein. The judge first required CBS to produce its videotape and then excluded it as evidence in the criminal matter, concluding that the taping had rendered the search unreasonable. He also allowed the civil lawsuit to continue, rejecting the parties' claim that they were entitled to government immunity. A decision by the Second Circuit Court of Appeals subsequently affirmed Weinstein's decision. After a split in the federal circuit courts emerged, the Supreme Court agreed to hear the similar case of *Wilson v. Layne*, which arose when a *Washington Post* reporter and cameraman accompanied police on a raid of Charles Wilson's home. The high court unanimously held that law enforcement agencies can be sued for bringing the media (or any other third party, for that matter) along on raids and related undertakings. It agreed, as Judge Weinstein had pointed out in *Ayeni*, that in accordance with the Fourth Amendment, the sanctity of one's home must be protected from unreasonable government searches and seizures.

A staunch advocate for social justice and the rights of individuals, Weinstein angered many when he ruled in 2001 that the rights of parents and children in New York City's foster care system were being abridged by the city's inadequate provision and compensation of court-assigned counsel; he subsequently ordered an increase in pay for these Family Court attorneys *(In re Sharwline Nicholson)*. In the case, Weinstein fumed about the city's routine of taking children away from battered mothers, arguing that such a practice ignored the plight of battered women and punished them for being battered. Similarly, Weinstein caused a stir in 2002 when he ruled that the United States cannot deport an immigrant who is a felon unless the government first considers the impact deportation will have on his or her children who remain in this country *(Beharry v. Reno)*. Weinstein also raised the ire of many when he concluded that gun manufacturers could be held liable to the victims of gun violence for the negligent marketing of handguns, a decision that was subsequently reversed on appeal *(Hamilton v. Accu-Tek)*.

Judge Weinstein has had his share of reversals, which apparently bothers him not at all. When asked by the *New York Times* for his opinion of two potential Supreme Court justices, he told the newspaper that both were worthy candidates, noting "I'd be proud to be reversed by either of them" (Gleeson 1996, 83). Although some may quarrel with his rulings, no one disputes the fact that Jack Weinstein is a brilliant, highly organized, and extremely efficient judge. He is widely regarded as a leading expert in civil procedure and evidence. Thousands of law students have encountered Weinstein through the legal casebook of which he is one author, *Evidence: Cases and Materials* (1997), which continues to be the benchmark in the field. He has also written over 100 articles and reports on a wide range of subjects, including not only torts and evidence but also civil procedure, ethics, constitutional law, and Judaism. He has lent his expertise to numerous prominent boards and committees, including the Presidential Commission on Catastrophic Nuclear Accidents (having presided over the legal challenges to the construction of a nuclear power plant in Shoreham, New York); the Carnegie Commission on Science, Technology, and Government Task Force on Science and Technology in Judicial and Regulatory Decision-Making; the Subcommittee on Federal Jurisdiction of the Committee on Court Administration of the Judicial Conference of the United States; and the American Law Institute's Complex Litigation Project.

Over the years, Judge Weinstein has received numerous honorary degrees and legal and civic awards. He was awarded the Stanley H. Fuld Award of the New York State Bar Association (NYSBA) (2000) for his exceptional contributions to commercial law and litigation. He previously had received the NYSBA's Gold Medal Award (1998), the highest honor bestowed by the state bar. He was also awarded the Judicial Recognition Award of the National Association of Defense Lawyers and the William J. Brennan Award of the New York State Association of Criminal Defense Lawyers. He was named the *National Law Journal*'s "Lawyer of the Year" for 1993.

Judge Weinstein also received the Devitt Distinguished Service to Justice Award (1994), presented annually to the federal judge who has made the most significant contribution to justice. In summarizing the decision of the Devitt selection panel, federal district judge Oliver Gasch noted simply that "the breadth of [Weinstein's] judicial service to the cause of justice is incomparable" (1994, 76). In typical fashion, Weinstein donated the $15,000 cash award on behalf of himself and his wife, Evelyn, to the children's playroom at the Long Island College Hospital in Brooklyn. He even refused to accept reimbursement for the travel expenses he incurred to attend the award presentation, because he did not want to appear to accept a gift from the award's sponsor, a prominent legal publishing company. Said Judge Weinstein, "I don't like to take anything of value from anybody" (Schmickle and Hamburger 1995).

In 1993, Judge Weinstein assumed senior status on the district court. Typically used by judges as a transition to retirement, it permits a judge significantly to reduce his or her caseload and judicial duties. Not surprisingly, Weinstein has been a senior judge in title alone, refusing to slow down or shut up. At age eighty-one, he continues to make significant contributions to the federal bench and will likely do so for some time to come.

Kathleen Uradnik

References and Further Reading:

Bradley, Barbara. 2000. "Judge Jack Weinstein." National Public Radio, *Morning Edition*, 5 June.

Gasch, Oliver. 1994. "Remarks of Judge Oliver Gasch at the Presentation of the Devitt Award to the Honorable Jack B. Weinstein." 870 F. Supp. LXIX.

Gleeson, John. 1996. "Remarks of Judge John Gleeson at the Special Session of the U.S. District Court for the Eastern District of New York in Honor of the Dedication of Judicial Portrait Photographs." 938 F. Supp. LXI.

Schmickle, Sharon, and Tom Hamburger. 1995. "Devitt Award Is Prestigious—and Unusual." *Minneapolis Star Tribune*, 5 March.

Schuck, Peter H. 1986. *Agent Orange on Trial: Mass Toxic Disasters in the Courts*. Cambridge: Harvard University Press.

Sifton, Charles P. 1996. "Remarks of Judge Charles P. Sifton at the Special Session of the U.S. District Court for the Eastern District of New York in Honor of the Dedication of Judicial Portrait Photographs." 938 F. Supp. LXI.

Weinstein, Jack B. 1993. "The War on Drugs Is Self-Defeating." *New York Times*, 8 July, op. ed.

——. 1995. *Individual Justice in Mass Tort Litigation: The Effect of Class Actions, Consolidations, and Other Multi-Party Devices*. Evanston, Ill.: Northwestern University Press.

——. 2000. "Death Penalty: The Torah and Today." *New York Law Journal* 224, 23 August, 2.

Weinstein, Jack B., et al. 1997. *Evidence: Cases and Materials*. 9th ed. New York: Foundation Press.

WILKINSON, J. HARVIE, III

(1944–)

J. Harvie Wilkinson III
Courtesy J. Harvie Wilkinson

Judge J. Harvie Wilkinson III, chief judge of the United States Court of Appeals for the Fourth Circuit (with jurisdiction over Maryland, Virginia, West Virginia, and North and South Carolina), was born in New York City on 29 September 1944, the son of J. Harvie Jr. and Letitia Nelson Wilkinson. A Phi Beta Kappa, *magna cum laude* B.A. graduate from Yale University in 1967, he entered the United States Army for two years of service (1968–1969). Subsequently, he became an outstanding student at the University of Virginia's School of Law, where he served with distinction on its law review and became a member of the Order of the Coif, receiving his J.D. in 1972. He was then admitted to the Virginia state bar.

Evincing an early interest in public affairs, he had tried his hand at a political career by running for Congress as a Republican candidate for the U.S. House of Representatives from what was the Third District of Virginia in 1970. Failing in that quest—in a personal interview with Henry J. Abraham he referred to it as a "humblingly unsuccessful campaign" (17 November 1970)—he did, however, receive a three-year appointment to the Board of Visitors (trustees) of the University of Virginia from that state's first Republican governor, Linwood A. Holton. "Jay"

Wilkinson, as he is known to friends and family, was the youngest person ever to have served on that prestigious board.

During the same period, the future judge was asked by Richmond attorney and newly nominated associate justice of the United States Supreme Court, Lewis F. Powell Jr., to become his first clerk upon Powell's confirmation by the Senate in late 1971. Wilkinson would serve Justice Powell with characteristic personal dedication and professional excellence during the latter's first two terms on the highest court in the land. To the young lawyer it would prove to be a defining experience both professionally and personally, the warm relationship between the two men continuing until Justice Powell's death in 1998. At the end of his clerkship in June 1973, Wilkinson married Lossie Grist Noell. Two children, James Nelson and Porter Noell, were born to that union.

The youthful Wilkinson's first post-clerkship position was his 1973 appointment as an assistant professor of law at the University of Virginia, specializing in constitutional law. A mere two years later the popular young teacher was promoted to the rank of associate professor, receiving the coveted Alumni Board of Trustees Teaching Award in 1976. He continued to teach until 1978 when, seeking a new experience, he became the editorial page director for the Norfolk, Virginia, *Virginia-Pilot*. It proved to be an interesting stint for the bright member of the literati, who held the position for three years. He then returned to his erstwhile post at the University of Virginia as professor of law in 1981, serving in that capacity on a full or partial basis until 1984.

During that three-year period he entered federal government service when Pres. Ronald Reagan appointed him deputy assistant attorney general in the Civil Rights Division of the Department of Justice in 1982. He held that post for one year. On 30 January 1984, having resumed full-time teaching at Virginia, Wilkinson was honored and delighted to be nominated by Reagan as a judge on the United States Court of Appeals for the Fourth Circuit.

Given the nominee's versatile and successful career experience, and his broad bipartisan political support in Virginia, confirmation was expected to be smooth. His academic, legal, intellectual, and personal qualifications and characteristics were demonstrably stellar. Indubitably, here was one of the "best and brightest" lawyers in the land. Yet opposition to the nomination surfaced quickly. Beyond customary and predictable quotidian political considerations, it focused on two aspects: one, Professor Wilkinson's lack of trial court experience; the other, and ultimately more contentious and protracted, his conservative political philosophy. A moderate in the Powell tradition, Wilkinson's writings and public statements testified to that philosophical commitment, albeit always in wholly objective, carefully reasoned compass, as his three books penned prior to his nomination demonstrated. Democratic senators launched a prolonged assault on the nominee's Weltanschauung, resorting to a filibuster in late July when Wilkinson's confirmation seemed all but certain. They were aided by the opposition of a few liberal Republicans, notably Senator Arlen Specter (Pa.), whose constituency contained a large number of African Americans, who disapproved of what they viewed as Wilkinson's hostile position on racial busing and aspects of affirmative action. Ultimately, Wilkinson's supporters succeeded in invoking cloture, and confirmation came on 9 August 1984, more than seven months after his nomination.

Written in clear, lucid, elegant language, Judge Wilkinson's books and articles have made major contributions to the realm of public law and policy. His first tome, *Harry Byrd and the Changing Face of Virginia* (1968), written when its author was only twenty-four years old, is a fascinating analysis of the so-long-entrenched powerful political Byrd machine and its inevitable, gradual, and ultimate decline. *Serving Justice: A Supreme Court Clerk's View* (1974) represents an incisive, informative, and warm account of the position of Supreme Court clerks, how they are selected, the range and extent of their labors and influence, and their relationship with "their" justice(s). The Court and its personnel come to life in the book's eminently readable pages, and Wilkinson wisely avoided violating the tribunal's traditional confidentiality, unlike more recent post-clerkship books by his successors. The third volume, arguably his most important prior to his nomination to the Court of Appeals, *From Brown to Bakke: The Supreme Court and School Integration* (1979), constituted a trenchant examination of such contentious issues as racially mandated public school attendance and busing, as well as the ongoing vexatious problems of affirmative action, with its still unsolved questions of constitutionality and legality. Wilkinson's most recent book is his 1997 publication, *One Nation Indivisible: How Ethnic Separatism Threatens America*. It is a sophisticated treatment of the contemporarily daunting issues of diversity, group-centered claims to entitlements, and multiculturalism. Wilkinson has written countless law review articles and manifests an unusually high profile in the popular media, publishing commentaries for national newspapers on the need to support federalism's role for state political power and the importance of maintaining the present size of the U.S. judiciary.

Judge Wilkinson's tenure on the Fourth Circuit has dovetailed neatly with the generally conservative jurisprudence of that Court of Appeals. As a proponent of strong state power, vis-à-vis the federal government, his rulings and opinions have typically coincided with those of the Rehnquist Court. Characteristic of this posture was Wilkinson's concurring opinion in *Brzonkala v. Virginia Polytechnic Institute* (169 F.3d 820 [1999]), in which the

Fourth Circuit invalidated the portion of the Violence Against Women Act (VAWA) that created *civil* remedies in *federal* courts for female victims of violent crimes. Congress had passed the act, including the challenged section in *Brzonkala*, under its interstate commerce power, contending that violence against women had a direct impact on the nation's economy. Wilkinson's concurrence read like a scholarly treatise on judicial restraint and federalism. He distinguished the Fourth Circuit's invalidation of the relevant portion of VAWA from earlier examples of Supreme Court judicial activism during the New Deal and Warren Court eras. He asserted that the Fourth Circuit, and the Supreme Court in its recent pro-state decisions, "preserve[d] Congress as an institution of broad but enumerated powers, and the states as entities having residual sovereign rights" (893). In so doing, Wilkinson argued, the courts temporarily eschewed the preferred position of judicial restraint in order to conserve core constitutional principles. Contrasting the VAWA decision, and other profederalism cases from the 1990s, with activist decisions from the New Deal and Warren Courts, Wilkinson contended that the latter two ruled as they did with favored constituencies and substantive results in mind. He concluded that the judges' role "in this modern era is not as substantive adjudicators, but as structural referees" (895). Although Wilkinson's distinction between modern conservative judicial activism and older versions practiced by preceding courts did not entirely convince liberal commentators, the Fourth Circuit's chief judge proved yet again that he is one of the federal judiciary's most intellectual members. In addition, the United States Supreme Court upheld the Fourth Circuit's ruling in Brzonkala's appeal to the high tribunal. The narrow five-to-four majority, led by Chief Justice William Rehnquist, agreed with Wilkinson's reasoning that Congress had overstepped its interstate commerce authority in creating a civil remedy for women victims of violent crime.

Wilkinson's conservatism was also evident in his narrow reading of the Americans with Disabilities Act (ADA) in *EEOC v. Sara Lee Corporation* (237 F.3d 349 [2001]). He ruled that the act does not require an employer to deviate from its nondiscriminatory seniority policy in order to accommodate a worker, especially when that worker is not substantially limited in a major life activity (the threshold criterion for invoking the ADA). On behalf of the Fourth Circuit, he also refused to allow an ADA suit, for want of subject matter jurisdiction, brought by five purchasers of handicapped parking placards against North Carolina's Division of Motor Vehicles. The plaintiffs claimed that a federal regulation, promulgated under the ADA, prohibited public entities from charging a fee to cover the costs of accessibility programs designed to assist the disabled. Wilkinson concluded that the regulation exceeded Congress's Fourteenth Amendment, Section 5 remedial powers, as interpreted by the United States Supreme Court in *City of Boerne v. Flores* (521 U.S. 507 [1997]).

Judge Wilkinson has been equally abstemious in applying the Individuals with Disabilities Education Act (IDEA) to the question of mainstreaming disabled students. Combining his penchant for judicial restraint with his affirmance of federalism, he has concluded that "the IDEA does not grant federal courts a license to substitute their own notions of sound educational policy for those of local school authorities, or to disregard the findings developed in state administrative proceedings" (*Hartman v. Loudoun County Board of Education*, 118 F.3d 998 [1997]). In addition, Wilkinson has ruled that the IDEA does not provide for compensatory or punitive damages (*Sellers v. School Board of Manassas, Virginia*, 141 F.3d 524 [1998]).

Nevertheless, Wilkinson has been willing to uphold broader constructions of congressional and national power when the legislature is clearly acting under constitutional authority. In validating a Fish and Wildlife Service regulation that limits the taking of red wolves on private land, Wilkinson wrote for the Fourth Circuit that "because the regulated activity substantially affects interstate commerce and because the regulation is a part of a comprehensive federal program for the protection of endangered species[,] [j]udicial deference to the judgment of the democratic branches is therefore appropriate" (*Gibbs v. Babbitt*, 214 F.3d 486 [2000]).

Likewise, Wilkinson has supported what he has described as the clear meaning and intentions of recent congressional acts regulating modern technology. In *Zeran v. America Online, Inc.* (129 F.3d 327 [1997]), he ruled that the Communications Decency Act "plainly immunizes computer service providers like AOL from liability for information that originates with third parties" (328). In a case that came to the Fourth Circuit under the Anticybersquatting Consumer Protection Act, Wilkinson determined that the congressional statute protected Volkswagen from the bad-faith actions of an on-line service provider, Virtual Works, Inc., that had registered the domain vw.net with the intention of selling it to the better-known Volkswagen automobile company (*Virtual Works, Inc. v. Volkswagen of America*, 238 F.3d 264 [2001]).

Modern technology has also impinged on the traditional realm of criminal rights, and the Fourth Circuit has not been immune from suits invoking rights to deoxyribonucleicacid (DNA) testing to determine guilt or innocence in criminal cases. In an opinion written in early 2002, Judge Wilkinson surprised some liberal observers by not opposing a prisoner's access to DNA testing using technology that was unavailable at the time his Virginia conviction for rape became final. Yet holding the line against judicial creation of a constitutional right to such testing, Wilkinson called on legislatures to establish the rules of access to DNA examinations, lest meddlesome courts "deaden the life-force of democracy" (*Harvey v. Horan*, 285 F.3d 298 [2002]).

In civil liberties cases involving church/state issues, Wilkinson has demonstrated an accommodationist stance, ruling against strict separation of religion and government. He wrote the opinion for a unanimous Fourth Circuit panel that cleared the way for Columbia Union College (an institution affiliated with the Seventh-day Adventist Church) to receive aid from the state of Maryland (*Columbia Union College v. Oliver*, 254 F.3d 496 [2001]). The state had argued that the college was "pervasively sectarian" and that to provide it funding would violate the First Amendment's establishment clause. Wilkinson "recognize[d] the sensitivity of this issue and respect[ed] the constitutional imperative for the government not to impermissibly advance religious interests" (510), but he concluded that "by refusing to fund a religious institution solely because of religion, the government risks discriminating against a class of citizens solely because of faith" (510). In this case, "[b]ecause state aid is allocated on a neutral basis to an institution of higher education which will not use the funds for any sectarian purpose, . . . Columbia Union qualifies for [Maryland's] funds" (498).

In another First Amendment case, Judge Wilkinson, voting with the majority in a nine-to-three *en banc* Fourth Circuit decision, reached what might seem to be an ostensibly conservative result with an arguably liberal rationale, which proves how imprecise ideological labels can be. The court ruled that an individual could not be denied the right to erect a Christmas crèche outside the Fairfax County, Virginia, government center because the county banned nonresidents from using the space (*Warren v. Fairfax County*, 196 F.3d 186 [1999]). In his elegantly crafted concurrence, the circuit's chief judge reasoned: "To limit a forum such as this one to those who live within the [Fairfax County] jurisdiction is to balkanize our civic dialogue. . . . Speech in America cannot be that parochial. . . . Surely a speaker is entitled to spread the faith or the political gospel beyond the community in which she lives" (199).

J. Harvie Wilkinson III is frequently cited as a potential nominee to the United States Supreme Court under a Republican administration. His superb academic and professional credentials; keen intellect; talent for fluent, cogent, eloquent writing; and effective leadership skills would make him the ideal candidate for the high bench, including its chief justiceship. Judicial appointment politics, however, especially in the post-Bork era, can derail even the most qualified candidate, particularly one with a public record as extensive as Judge Wilkinson's. Yet given a propitious alignment of political factors, this soft-spoken Virginian might follow in the footsteps of his personal and judicial hero, United States Supreme Court justice Lewis F. Powell Jr.

Barbara A. Perry and Henry J. Abraham

References and Further Reading:

Wilkinson, J. Harvie, III. 1968. *Harry Byrd and the Changing Face of Virginia*. Charlottesville: University Press of Virginia.

———. 1974. *Serving Justice: A Supreme Court Clerk's View*. New York: Charterhouse.

———. 1979. *From Brown to Bakke: The Supreme Court and School Integration*. New York: Oxford University Press.

———. 1994. "The Drawbacks of Growth in the Federal Judiciary." *Emory Law Journal* 43: 1147.

———. 1997. *One Nation Indivisible: How Ethnic Separatism Threatens America*. Old Tappan, N.J.: Addison-Wesley.

———. 2001. "Federalism and the Future." *Southern California Law Review* 74: 523.

Will, George F. "One Judge's Conservatism." *Newsweek* 141 (March 3, 2002): 68.

WISDOM, JOHN MINOR

(1905–1999)

JOHN MINOR WISDOM
Bettmann/Corbis

JOHN MINOR WISDOM WAS A federal appeals court judge who changed the face of education and civil rights in the South in the 1960s as he enforced the Supreme Court's *Brown v. Board of Education* decisions mandating that schools be racially integrated. From 1957 until he took senior status in 1977, Judge Wisdom was the intellectual leader of a groups of judges on the old Fifth District Court of Appeals who decided numerous cases and ordered school districts throughout the South to take affirmative steps to integrate educational facilities.

Judge Wisdom authored nearly 1,500 opinions during his tenure, with his most notable decisions addressing issues of civil rights, school integration, and the Ku Klux Klan. In addition to serving as a Fifth Circuit judge, from 1975 till his death in 1999 he served on the Special Court for the Regional Reorganization of Railroads, serving as the presiding judge from 1986 on. He also was a judge from 1968 to 1979 on the Multi-District Litigation Panel, presiding from 1973 to 1979. Recognized for his many accomplishments, his awards included in 1989 the Devitt Distinguished Service to Justice Award; in 1991 he received the Lewis F. Powell Award for Professionalism and Ethics; in 1993 President Clinton awarded him the Medal of Freedom; and in 1996 he received the American Bar Association's highest award. Finally, in 1994, the Court of Appeals building in New Orleans was named after him.

John Minor Wisdom was born in New Orleans in 1905 and received his B.A. from Washington and Lee University in 1925. He then studied at Harvard University for about a year before attending Tulane Law School, graduating first in his class in 1929. In 1931 he married, and he and his wife, Bonnie, had been married for almost sixty-eight years at the time he died. His wife was a noted Shakespeare and Marlowe scholar, and together they had three children. From 1929 to 1957 he was in private practice, starting his own law firm with a law school classmate. To this day, Stone, Pigman, Walther, Wittmann and Hutchinson remains one of the preeminent law firms in New Orleans. While in private practice John Wisdom successfully handled groundbreaking litigation, including *Schwegmann Brothers v. Calvert Distillers Corporation*, 341 U.S. 384 (1951), an important antitrust case that struck down Louisiana laws that had permitted price-fixing.

In addition to maintaining a legal practice, John Wisdom served in the United States Army during World War II (1942–1946) as a lieutenant colonel working on intelligence matters. He was active in his community, serving as director of the New Orleans Urban League and president of the New Orleans Council of Social Agencies. At a time when Louisiana and the rest of the South were solidly Democratic, John Wisdom helped found and became active in the New Orleans Republican Party. During the 1952 Republican presidential convention, he successfully fought to get Dwight Eisenhower's delegates seated, ultimately helping Eisenhower secure the party's presidential nomination.

In 1953 Wisdom was nominated by President Eisenhower to the federal bench. Wisdom turned him down but eventually accepted a second nomination to the Fifth Circuit Court of Appeals in 1957. In 1957, the Fifth Circuit included Alabama, Florida, Georgia, Louisiana, Mississippi, and Texas. It was split in 1980 into the Fifth and Eleventh Circuits, with the new Fifth including Texas, Louisiana, and Mississippi, and the Eleventh including the remainder of the states from the old Fifth Circuit.

At the time Judge Wisdom was appointed to the court, the federal judiciary in the South was in the midst of enforcing the recently decided *Brown v. Board of Education* decisions that declared the separate but equal doctrine unconstitutional. As a result of the Supreme Court's declaring an end to the racial segregation of schools, school districts in the South bitterly opposed efforts to integrate. This opposition ranged anywhere from ignoring the order or closing schools to, in the case of Alabama and Mississippi, using state national guard troops to keep African American students out. Within the context of the Supreme Court's orders to integrate the schools and under the light of the emerging civil rights movement, Judge Wisdom took the bench and issued his opinions. Those who saw the court's decisions as destroying the southern way of life labeled him and Fifth Circuit judges Elbert Tuttle of Georgia, Richard Rives of Alabama, and John Brown of Texas as "the Four." These four judges, along with federal district court judge Frank Johnson of Alabama, were influential in reshaping the law and civil rights in the South from the 1950s to the 1960s.

Although Judge Wisdom's nearly 1,500 opinions affected many areas of the law, he was most famous in the area of civil rights. Perhaps his most visible opinions were *Meredith v. Fair*, 298 F.2d 696 (5th Cir. 1962) and 305 F.2d 343 (5th Cir. 1962). In the first case, at issue was whether applicants could be required to submit certificates from University of Mississippi alumni regarding their character and fitness for admission to the school. James Meredith applied to the university and indicated in his application that because he was black he could not get the certificates because the school was all-white, and it would be difficult for any of these alumni to support the candidacy of an African American. Judge Wisdom struck down the alumni certificates as unconstitutional and enjoined the school from employing them as an admissions requirement. According to Wisdom:

> We hold that the University's requirement that each candidate for admission furnish alumni certificates is a denial of equal protection of the laws, in its application to Negro candidates. It is a heavy burden on qualified Negro students, because of their race. It is no burden on qualified white students.
>
> The fact that there are no Negro alumni of the University of Mississippi, the manifest unlikelihood of there being more than a handful of alumni, if any, who would recommend a Negro for the University, the traditional social barriers making it unlikely, if not impossible, for a Negro to approach alumni with a request for such a recommendation, the possibility of reprisals if alumni should recommend a Negro for admission, are barriers only to qualified Negro applicants. It is significant that the University of Mississippi adopted the requirement of alumni certificates a few months after *Brown v. Board of Education* was decided. (298 F.2d, 701–702)

These two decisions resulted in James Meredith's being the first African American to be admitted to the University of Mississippi. But that only occurred after four attempts by another judge to stay Wisdom's opinion, after Gov. Ross Barnett of Mississippi personally obstructed Meredith's registration, and after a riot that required use of federal troops and tear gas to maintain order at the school.

Another famous opinion of Judge Wisdom's was that in *United States v. Original Knights of the Ku Klux Klan*, 250 F. Supp. 330 (E.D. La. 1965). This case grew out of events in Bogalusa, Louisiana, where in 1965 militant black activists were confronted by Louisiana's largest klavern of the Ku Klux Klan (KKK). The U.S. Department of Justice moved for an injunction against the Bogalusa Klan to prevent it from interfering with the civil rights of the black activists. But the attorney for the defendants argued that the Klan was a private organization, beyond the reach of civil rights laws. A special three-judge district court headed by John Minor Wisdom issued the requested order. In doing so, his opinion provided a historical overview of the Klan's history of violence and intimidation, concluding that it "otherwise interfered with (1) Negroes exercising their civil rights, (2) persons encouraging Negroes to assert their rights, and (3) public officials, police officers, and other persons seeking to accord Negroes their rights. These acts are part of a pattern and practice of the defendants to maintain total segregation of the races in Washington Parish" (250 F. Supp., 343).

The court not only enjoined the Klansmen from engaging in intimidation and threats but also required the Bogalusa Klan to file monthly reports detailing its meetings and membership. Judge Wisdom's decision both illuminated the scope of activities that the Klan engaged in and provided the basis for future legal strategies by groups such as the Southern Poverty Law Center to cripple the ability of the KKK to harass African Americans.

United States v. Louisiana, 225 F. Supp. 353 (E.D. La. 1963), was another of Judge Wisdom's more important decisions, and it addressed voting rights. The state of Louisiana had a law that required new applicants to vote to be able to understand and orally explain any passage of the U.S. or Louisiana constitution. The law, not surprisingly, systematically excluded new African American applicants from voting. Judge Wisdom described this requirement as a "wall" to registration that must come down:

> A wall stands in Louisiana between registered voters and unregistered, eligible Negro voters. The wall is the State constitutional requirement that an applicant for registration understand and give a reasonable interpretation of any section of the constitutions of Louisiana or of the United States. . . . We hold: this wall, built to bar Negroes from access to the franchise, must come down because it was a violation of the Fifteenth Amendment, and the equal protection clause of the Fourteenth Amendment, as well as several other sections of the Constitution. (225 F. Supp., 355)

It was in the area of school desegregation that Judge Wisdom made his biggest impact, however. For example, *Singleton v. Jackson Municipal Separate School District*, 348 F.2d 729 (5th Cir. 1965) was one of numerous school desegregation cases that Judge Wisdom and the Fifth Circuit decided. Wisdom ruled that the court would attach great weight to the standards for desegregation plans set by the Office of Education of the Department of Health, Education, and Welfare (HEW). More important, Judge Wisdom expressed his impatience with the southern resistance to integration, stating: "The time has come for footdragging public school boards to move with celerity toward desegregation" (348 F.2d, 729).

More important, in *United States v. Jefferson*, 372 F.2d 836 (5th Cir. 1966), *affd per curiam* 380 F.2d 385 (5th Cir. 1967), Judge Wisdom and the Fifth Circuit held that states had an affirmative duty to integrate formerly de jure segregated public school systems by incorporating the HEW standards for a school desegregation plan. According to Wisdom, the only school desegregation plan that meets constitutional standards is one that works (372 F.2d, 847). He called for an immediate dismantling of the old segregated school system, "lock, stock, and barrel" (372 F.2d, 878). The judge declared: "The clock has ticked the last tick for tokenism and delay in the name of deliberate speed" (372 F.2d, 896). Not only was the *Jefferson* opinion significant in articulating an affirmative duty on the part of states to desegregate, but appended to it was a model decree indicating how to implement an integrated school system. This model decree was subsequently used by other courts, and, more important, Wisdom's language in *Jefferson* was employed a year later by the Supreme Court in *Green v. County School Board of New Kent County*, 391 U.S. 430, 442 (1968), a case ordering states to integrate immediately. It also paved the way for *Swann v. Charlotte-Mecklenburg Board of Education*, 402 U.S. 1 (1971), an important decision that eventually gave the federal courts the authority to order busing to achieve racial integration of schools.

Judge Wisdom's jurisprudence often anticipated other trends in civil rights policy. In *Weber v. Kaiser Aluminum & Chemical Corporation*, 563 F.2d 216 (5th Cir. 1977), at issue was whether a private company could voluntarily institute an affirmative action policy to remedy past discrimination in hiring without violating Title VII of the 1964 Civil Rights Act. The Fifth Circuit majority said no, but in dissent Judge Wisdom noted that Kaiser Aluminum had perhaps violated discrimination law in the past through its hiring and argued that if an affirmative action plan, adopted in a collective bargaining agreement, was a reasonable remedy for an arguable violation of Title VII, it should be upheld. Wisdom's dissent in *Weber v. Kaiser Aluminum & Chemical Corporation* formed the basis for the United States Supreme Court's opinion overturning the majority decision in that case. The Court held that an employer and a union could voluntarily agree on an affirmative action plan without violating Title VII (*revd sub nom. United States Steelworkers v. Weber*, 443 U.S. 193 [1978]).

Besides being noted for his crusading decisions on civil rights, Judge Wisdom was a stickler for language and precision. He was noted for precision in writing opinions, and whenever new law clerks began working for him, he would hand them several writing style books, including his own personal list of rules that came to be known as Wisdom's Idiosyncrasies. The judge was a scholar and fluent in several languages, as evidenced by his opinion in *Block v. Compagnie Nationale Air France*, 386 F.2d 323 (5th Cir. 1967), where, in an effort to understand the Warsaw Convention rules regarding the liability of airlines in the event of accidents, he wrote an opinion that flowed from French to English and back to French.

Judge Wisdom took senior status on the Fifth Circuit in 1977, but he remained active and committed to eradicating racial discrimination till his death in 1999. In June 1998 at age ninety-three, less than a year before his death, the judge—in *Valley v. Rapides Parish School Board*, 145 F.3d 329 (5th Cir. 1998)—wrote an impassioned dissent from a panel decision upholding a Louisiana school district's attempt to split the district in two, thus creating an all-white system and an all-black system: "The . . . majority opinion is . . . a blatant attempt to establish a special public school district for whites in a limited area known as the white section of Alexandria. . . . It is incredible that half a century after Brown, one should have to ask for an en banc judgment to prevent the establishment of a school for whites in a public school system" (145 F.3d, 334).

During his tenure as a judge, Wisdom had more than ninety-five law clerks, many of whom rose to high levels of prominence. For example, Lamar Alexander subsequently became governor of Tennessee, secretary of education, a presidential contender, and a U.S. senator. Bill Pryor became attorney general of Alabama, and Ricki Tigert Helfer served as chair of the Federal Deposit Insurance Corporation. Other clerks went on to become law school professors or judges. Overall, Judge John Minor Wisdom's impact on civil rights, the law, and those who worked with him was immense.

David Schultz

References and Further Reading:

Bass, Jack. 1981. *Unlikely Heroes: The Dramatic Story of the Southern Judges of the Fifth Circuit Who Translated the Supreme Court's Brown Decision into a Revolution for Equality*. New York: Simon and Schuster.

———. 1999. "John Minor Wisdom and the Impact of Law." *Mississippi Law Journal* 69 (Fall): 25–37.

Block v. Compagnie Nationale Air France. 386 F.2d 323 (5th Cir. 1967).

Brown v. Board of Education. 347 U.S. 483 (1954).

Brown v. Board of Education II. 349 U.S. 294 (1955).

Clark, Charles. 1999. "John Minor Wisdom: A Brief Overview of His Epoch." *Mississippi Law Journal* 69 (Fall): 39–42.

Green v. County School Board of New Kent County. 391 U.S. 430 (1968).

Meredith v. Fair. 298 F.2d 696 (5th Cir. 1962).

Meredith v. Fair. 305 F.2d 343 (5th Cir. 1962).

Peltason, J. W. 1961. *Fifty-eight Lonely Men: Southern Federal Judges and School Desegregation*. New York: Harcourt, Brace and World.
Schwegmann Brothers v. Calvert Distillers Corporation. 341 U.S. 384 (1951).
Singleton v. Jackson Municipal Separate School District. 348 F.2d 729 (5th Cir. 1965).
Swann v. Charlotte-Mecklenburg Board of Education. 402 U.S. 1 (1971).
United States v. Jefferson. 372 F.2d 836 (5th Cir. 1966).
United States v. Louisiana. 225 F. Supp. 353 (E.D. La. 1963).
United States v. Original Knights of the Ku Klux Klan. 250 F. Supp. 330 (E.D. La. 1965).
United States Steelworkers v. Weber. 443 U.S. 193 (1978).
Valley v. Rapides Parish School Board. 145 F.3d 329 (5th Cir. 1998).
Weber v. Kaiser Aluminum & Chemical Corporation. 563 F.2d 216 (5th Cir. 1977).

WRIGHT, JAMES SKELLY

(1911–1988)

James Skelly Wright
National Portrait Gallery

J. Skelly Wright was one of the most liberal and activist judges ever to sit on the federal bench. He was the first United States district judge in the Deep South to order school desegregation following the United States Supreme Court's decision in *Brown v. Board of Education*, 347 U.S. 483 (1954) that separate schools were unconstitutional. As a member of the District of Columbia Circuit Court of Appeals he made controversial decisions in the areas of affirmative action, campaign spending, environmental protection, business regulation, and judicial review of administrative agency decisionmaking. Apart from those appointed to the United States Supreme Court, Skelly Wright is among the best-known federal judges of the last half of the twentieth century.

James Skelly Wright was born in New Orleans, Orleans Parish, Louisiana, on 14 January 1911 to James E. and Margaret (Skelly) Wright. He was the second of seven children. His mother was of Irish descent, and the children were raised as Roman Catholics. Skelly Wright's uncle, Joseph P. Skelly, was one of the leaders of the Regular Democratic Organization, the machine that ran the city. Joseph Skelly found a job for Skelly Wright's father, a plumber, with the city as inspector for the New Orleans Sewage and Water Board. Despite these political connections, the family was poor and lived in a downtown working-class neighborhood known as the Irish Channel.

Wright attended public schools in New Orleans. He aspired to be a lawyer but could not afford to attend Tulane University, from which many of the leading attorneys of New Orleans, who practiced in large downtown law firms, had graduated. Instead, after winning a scholarship, he enrolled at Loyola University, a Jesuit institution, in the combined undergraduate/law program, a program that allowed him to finish with a law degree in six rather than seven years. He took summer courses at Tulane in order to earn a teaching certificate and transferred to Loyola's night law school so that he could teach mathematics and history during the day at a public high school. He received the bachelor of philosophy (Ph.B.) degree in 1931 and the LL.B. in 1934.

He was unable to find law-related work in the depths of the Great Depression and continued to teach high school until 1936, when he became a lecturer at Loyola University. Wright's first big break occurred in 1937 when he was appointed an assistant U.S. attorney for the Eastern District of Louisiana, a position he held for five years. His uncle, Joseph Skelly, by then a city commissioner, landed him the job. His uncle had approached Allen J. Ellender, the new U.S. senator from Louisiana, whose election had been supported by the Regular Democratic Organization. Wright began his work as a prosecutor in the narcotics section.

During World War II he served as a lieutenant commander in the United States Coast Guard. He spent most of his war service in London as a member of the legal staff of Adm. James Stark. On 1 February 1945, he married Helen Patton, a secretary in the United States Embassy in London. Her father had been a navy admiral and chief of the U.S. Coast and Geodetic Survey, and she had attended Sweet Briar College in Virginia. They had one son, James Skelly Wright Jr., born in 1947, who became a practicing lawyer in Washington, D.C.

In 1945 Skelly Wright resumed his position as assistant U.S. attorney. In 1946 he left New Orleans to engage in the private practice of law in Washington, D.C., his wife's home. He specialized in maritime and shipping cases. He unsuccessfully argued one case before the United States Supreme Court, *Louisiana ex rel. Francis v. Resweber*, 329 U.S. 459 (1947), in which he contended that submitting a convicted murderer to the electric chair twice (the first time the machine had malfunctioned) was "cruel and unusual punishment" in violation of the Eighth and Fourteenth Amendments. In 1947 Wright formed a partnership with John Ingoldsby and Marvin Coles.

Early in 1948, the position of U.S. attorney in New Orleans became vacant. Wright spoke to Senator Ellender to express interest in the position, and later in the year he returned to New Orleans, following his appointment by Democratic president Harry S Truman to the office of U.S. attorney for the Eastern District of Louisiana. Wright remained loyal to Truman, and the president renewed the prosecutor's appointment after his victory in the November election. Most of Wright's Democratic associates in Louisiana had alienated Truman when they supported Strom Thurmond's 1948 third-party Dixiecrat campaign for the presidency.

In June 1949 a vacancy occurred on the Fifth Circuit Court of Appeals. Wright did not contact either of Louisiana's senators because of their support for the Dixiecrats in the last election; instead he went straight to Tom Clark, the U.S. attorney general, and told him that he was interested in the position. Truman was happy to make the nomination. The chief judge of the Fifth Circuit, Joseph C. Hutcheson Jr., objected, however, on the grounds that the thirty-eight-year-old Wright was too young and inexperienced. Hutcheson suggested to Truman that he promote Wayne G. Borah from the district court to the court of appeals and appoint Wright to fill Borah's vacancy. The president agreed.

On 21 December 1949, while Congress was in recess, Truman appointed Wright to the United States District Court for the Eastern District of Louisiana. Truman submitted Wright's nomination to the Senate on 5 January 1950. Although Truman had snubbed them in the nomination process, both of Louisiana's senators, Ellender and Russell Long, supported Wright's candidacy. The Senate confirmed the nomination on 8 March 1950.

The Desegregation of the New Orleans Schools

Wright's role in the elimination of racial segregation made him the most hated man in Louisiana in the 1950s and 1960s. He crossed the Rubicon on segregation just a few months after his confirmation as a federal judge. Following the United States Supreme Court's decision to desegregate the University of Texas Law School in *Sweatt v. Painter*, 339 U.S. 629 (1950), on the grounds that separate law schools could never be equal, a three-judge district court in October 1950 ordered the desegregation of the Louisiana State University Law School. Judge Wright wrote the opinion for the unanimous panel (*Wilson v. Board of Supervisors of Louisiana State University*, 92 F. Supp. 986). Wright acknowledged that the *Wilson* case marked his decision no longer to accept the status quo in race relations in Louisiana.

On 5 September 1952, A. P. Tureaud, a black civil rights lawyer associated with the National Association for the Advancement of Colored People, filed a lawsuit to desegregate the public schools in New Orleans, *Bush v. Orleans Parish School Board*. Wright was in the battle of his life, for Louisiana was determined to maintain racial segregation and was willing to use every method of resistance, short of violence, that it could muster. Between 1954 and 1963, the Louisiana legislature passed more than a hundred resolutions and laws opposing desegregation in defiance of the Supreme Court, more than any other state.

Wright asked Chief Judge Hutcheson to appoint a three-judge district court to hear the case as allowed by section 2281, volume 28, of the United States Code when a plaintiff challenges the constitutionality of a state law in federal court. Hutcheson agreed such a court was required and appointed District Judge Herbert Christenberry and Circuit Judge Wayne Borah to join Wright on the panel. In 1955, in *Brown v. Board of Education II*, 349 U.S. 294, the Supreme Court entrusted the implementation of its decision that segregated schools are unconstitutional to the United States district courts, which were instructed to proceed "with all deliberate speed."

The special three-judge district court convened for the first time on 1 December 1955. Because of the clarity of the Supreme Court's decision in *Brown* that segregated schools violate the equal protection of the laws clause of the Fourteenth Amendment, Christenberry and Borah withdrew from the panel, since no serious constitutional question remained, leaving the case to Wright alone. On 15 February 1956, Wright became the first district court judge within the Fifth Circuit (Texas, Louisiana, Mississippi, Alabama, Georgia, and Florida) to issue an injunction ordering a school board to abolish racial segregation. For Wright his decision was the logical outcome of the South's defeat in the Civil War and the subsequent changes to the U.S. Constitution made during Reconstruction. Wright concluded his opinion, "We are, all of us, freeborn Americans, with a right to make our way, unfettered by sanctions imposed by man because of the work of God" (*Bush v. Orleans Parish School Board,* 138 F. Supp., 341–342).

Wright enjoined the members of the Orleans Parish School Board "from requiring [or] permitting segregation of the races in any school under their supervision" and ordered the board "to make arrangements for admission of children to such schools on a racially nondiscriminatory basis" (138 F. Supp., 342). A spokesman for the board responded to Wright's decision, "We will not integrate" (quoted in Baker 1996, 265). The Louisiana legislature unanimously passed a resolution declaring Wright's decision to be in violation of the U.S. and Louisiana constitutions. The board itself filed thirty-six delaying motions. The only prominent supporter of Wright's desegregation order was Joseph Francis Rummel, archbishop of the Catholic Archdiocese of New Orleans. The intense resistance of the school board, the Louisiana legislature, and the governor made the *Bush* case distinctive, and the conflict became known as "the second battle of New Orleans."

On 15 July 1959, the black plaintiffs returned to Wright's courtroom to demand compliance. In 1958 the Supreme Court had dealt harshly with the attempts by the governor and legislature of Arkansas to delay desegregation in defiance of federal district court orders (*Cooper v. Aaron*, 358 U.S. 1). Wright ruled that there had been too much deliberation and not enough speed and ordered the school board to produce a plan for desegregating the schools by 1 March 1960. He suggested that the board begin by desegregating one grade a year. He called upon the news media, public and private leaders, church officials, and the school board not to excite the white community and produce a violent confrontation with federal authorities similar to that in Little Rock, Arkansas. In October, Wright extended the deadline to 16 May 1960.

When the parties convened on that date, the school board presented no plan to desegregate. Wright decided that he had had enough and that, although other judges might allow still more delay, he was going to force the school board to comply. He came up with his own plan, even though he had no experience in educational administration. He ordered desegregation of the first grade at the opening of the school year in September. Black six-year-old children could attend the formerly all-white elementary school nearest their home. Desegregation would proceed, he ordered, at the pace of one grade per year. Wright thus became the first federal judge in the Fifth Circuit to set a specific date for integration of the public schools. When the governor of Louisiana, Jimmie Davis, threatened to take over the New Orleans schools and close them in order to prevent their desegregation, Wright issued an injunction to him and the attorney general.

The school board requested a postponement of the September date for implementing the court's decision, and Wright granted one until 14 November 1960, six days following the presidential election. He said that the U.S. Justice Department had asked him to delay the order until after the election in order not to embarrass Vice Pres. Richard Nixon's campaign for the presidency. When a committee of the state legislature attempted to take control of the Orleans Parish school system and to shut down the schools in order to evade Wright's desegregation order a few days before its implementation, Wright issued an injunction prohibiting all interference with New Orleans schools by the state of Louisiana. On Sunday, 13 November, facing open rebellion from the state government, Wright took the extraordinary step of issuing a restraining order against the governor, his cabinet, and every member of the state legislature prohibiting any interference with the next day's desegregation. It was the first time that a federal judge had issued an injunction to an entire state legislature.

Nearly all of Wright's New Orleans friends abandoned him and his wife, including his best friend from law school, Emile Wagner, who was now an elected member of the school board committed to maintaining separate schools for the races. Wright, aware that 90 percent of the white people of

New Orleans hated him, kept to himself, ate lunch alone, and stayed at home when not at work. He walked as far from the curb as possible, afraid that a pedestrian would push him into traffic. The Wrights received volumes of hate mail and crank telephone calls. The city posted a twenty-four-hour police guard around the judge's home. An effigy of Wright hung on the grounds of the Louisiana Capitol with a swastika on the back and a hammer and sickle on the front and a label hanging from the neck saying "J. Wrong." There were several cross burnings on his lawn. Nationally, however, he became a hero. *Time* magazine named him to a judicial honor roll, and newscasters referred to him as one of the most courageous judges in the South. His rulings would have ended his judicial career before the age of forty had he been an elected state judge. Because he was a federal judge, however, he was immune from retaliation and became a monument to life tenure.

Wright as an Appellate Judge

Wright's courage was noticed by the Kennedy administration. In the fall of 1961 Atty. Gen. Robert Kennedy telephoned Wright to inform him that Pres. John Kennedy wanted to promote Wright to the Fifth Circuit but that the implacable opposition of both Louisiana's Democratic senators, Allen Ellender and Russell Long, and Mississippi senator James Eastland, chairman of the Judiciary Committee, made it impossible. Then E. Barrett Prettyman retired from the United States Court of Appeals for the District of Columbia, and President Kennedy offered the position to Wright, knowing that southern senators would be happy to get the hated judge out of the South. Wright accepted and Kennedy announced the nomination on 15 December 1961. The Senate Judiciary Committee and then the full Senate confirmed Wright without objection on 28 March 1962. The assassination of President Kennedy in November 1963, however, ended any chance that Skelly Wright would be promoted to the Supreme Court.

During his twenty-five years on the Court of Appeals, Wright was a member of the liberal, activist bloc, which formed a majority until Pres. Richard Nixon began making judicial appointments in 1969. Wright consistently ruled in favor of groups that were politically weak and subjected to discrimination by the majority, including blacks, homosexuals, the criminally accused, environmentalists, and political dissidents. Wright's hero was Supreme Court justice Hugo Black. Wright's method of judging was "result-oriented" as opposed to formalistic. In 1982, he described his judicial thinking process thus: "I want to do what's right. When I get a case, I look at it and the first thing I think of automatically is what's right, what should be done—and then you look at the law to see whether or not you can do it. . . .

I am less patient than other judges with law that won't permit what I conceive to be fair" (quoted in Baker 1996, 493).

Between 1950 and 1962, Wright taught law as an adjunct faculty member at his alma mater, Loyola University. As a circuit judge, he gave numerous speeches, many of which were published in law reviews, in which he defended his controversial judicial views. The best-known case with which Wright was associated during his years on the District of Columbia Circuit Court of Appeals was the Pentagon Papers case, *New York Times v. U.S.*, 403 U.S. 713 (1971). Wright was the sole dissenter on a three-judge panel that issued an injunction to prevent newspapers from publishing stolen classified documents. Wright was vindicated eleven days later when a majority of Supreme Court justices ruled against censorship of the press on First Amendment grounds.

Wright served as chief judge from 1978 to 1981. He assumed senior status on 1 June 1986. His service as a federal judge terminated on 6 August 1988, at the age of seventy-seven, when he died of prostate cancer at his home in Westmoreland Hills, Maryland.

Kenneth M. Holland

References and Further Reading:

Baker, Liva. 1996. *The Second Battle of New Orleans: The Hundred-Year Struggle to Integrate the Schools*. New York: HarperCollins.

Bass, Jack. 1981. *Unlikely Heroes: The Dramatic Story of the Southern Judges of the Fifth Circuit Who Translated the Supreme Court's Brown Decision into a Revolution for Equality*. New York: Simon and Schuster.

Miller, Arthur Selwyn. 1984. *A "Capacity for Outrage": The Judicial Odyssey of J. Skelly Wright*. Westport, Conn.: Greenwood Press.

Miller, Arthur Selwyn, ed. 1984. *On Courts and Democracy: Selected Nonjudicial Writings of J. Skelly Wright*. Westport, Conn.: Greenwood Press.

Peltason, J. W. 1961. *Fifty-Eight Lonely Men: Southern Federal Judges and School Desegregation*. New York: Harcourt, Brace and World.

"Tribute to Judge J. Skelly Wright." 1980. *Hastings Constitutional Law Quarterly* 7: 857–999.

WRIGHT, JONATHAN JASPER

(1840–1885)

Jonathan Jasper Wright
Courtesy of South Carolina Library, University of South Carolina, Columbia

Jonathan Jasper Wright, associate justice of the South Carolina Supreme Court from 1870 to 1877, was the first African American to sit on any state's highest court, and "it would take almost another century for another African-American to be appointed to an American court of last resort" (Walsh 1997, 294). Although Wright was the focus of extensive national attention on attaining the position, his judicial career ended in disgrace and his life in obscurity. Members of the public and scholars essentially ignored his accomplishments for almost a century; in recent decades, however, his reputation and record of public service have been revived and reconstructed.

Wright was born on 11 February 1840 in Luzerne County, Pennsylvania. He was the son of Jane and Samuel Wright, a runaway slave from Maryland. The elder Wright purchased a farm at Springville, Susquehanna County, Pennsylvania, in 1854 and encountered all the economic problems faced by most small farmers (Woody 1933, 115). The younger Wright first attended the local public schools, but at fifteen, he began private studies with abolitionist and former Presbyterian missionary Dr. William Wells Pride. He then attended Lancasterian Academy in New York, where he graduated in 1860.

Wright's first professional position was teaching school at Montrose in his home county while he read law at the offices of Bentley, Fitch, and Bentley. After four years, he moved to Wilkes-Barre to a new teaching position and continued his legal studies at the chambers of Judge O. Collins. He also became active in politics—participating in both Fredrick Douglass's first national convention of African Americans and the Pennsylvania State Equal Rights Convention for Colored People (Gergel and Gergel 2000, 37–38).

In 1864, Wright sought admission to the Pennsylvania bar. Judge Ulysses Mercur informally, but unambiguously, indicated that any effort by Wright to become an attorney would be unsuccessful. Upon this denial, Wright joined the American Missionary Society and was sent to Beaufort County, South Carolina, to establish schools for illiterate black military personnel stationed there. Wright was apparently successful in his efforts as within a year he wrote that all of the men could read the New Testament. In addition, he participated in civic activities and gave public lectures including one to a crowd of 5,000 on the anniversary of emancipation (Gergel and Gergel 2000, 39).

Wright returned to Pennsylvania when he learned that Judge Mercur had departed from the bench, an event that revived Wright's hope of obtaining license to practice law. Indeed, the new judge, B. F. Skinner, gave him the examination and approved the application on 18 August 1866. Wright thus became the first black attorney in Pennsylvania. Not all observers agreed with Judge Skinner's decision, however, and the local newspaper described Wright as impudent for even seeking the opportunity (Gergel and Gergel 2000, 40).

When Wright's attempt to establish his own practice was unsuccessful because of lack of business, he obtained a position with the Freedman's Bureau and returned to South Carolina as a lawyer for the federal government. In February 1867, Wright and William J. Whipper became the first blacks to appear as attorneys in legal proceedings in South Carolina in the case of *United States v. William T. Bennett*, which involved the assault by a white man on a black man (Gergel and Gergel 2000, 40). A year later, Wright, Whipper, and Robert B. Elliott achieved another first when they were the first African Americans to be admitted to the South Carolina bar (Woody 1933, 121).

Wright resumed his political activities and was elected to the state constitutional convention from Beaufort County. His stand on issues before the convention reflected his life experiences. As a former teacher, he strongly advocated public schools, although he did not support either compulsory education or segregated schools. His feeling was that black students would not seek to attend white schools, a prediction that proved correct during the Reconstruction era. As the son of a small farmer, he fought for protection of homesteads from forced sales by creditors and against any limits on state indebtedness in order that the money would be available to help the poor. As the victim of racial bias and the son of a former slave, he opposed life tenure of judges and pointed to Chief Justice Roger Taney, author of *Scott v. Sandford*, as an example of judicial arrogance and isolation (Underwood 2000, 16–17).

Wright served on South Carolina's judiciary committee and thus was instrumental in structuring the constitution's judicial section. It was upon his motion that a three-member Supreme Court was created. He opposed public election of appellate judges and instead supported selection of judges by the legislature as the representatives of the people—the method adopted by the convention—while advocating the election of inferior court judges (Underwood 2000, 16–17).

Wright was elected as state senator from Beaufort, which set up his selection to fill the unexpired term as associate justice of the Supreme Court by a joint session of the South Carolina legislature in 1870. His chief opponent was his former co-counsel and house member, Whipper, who was known as a contentious member of the radical wing of the Republican Party. Wright, more of a centrist, was able to forge a coalition between the more moderate Republicans and Democrats and thus win the position. Later that year, he was elected to a full six-year term (Gergel and Gergel 2000, 44, 46).

Wright joined Chief Justice Franklin D. Moses Sr., "the first Jewish chief justice ever elected by any state," and Associate Justice A. J. Willard, a law school graduate from New York, on the bench (Gergel and Gergel 2000, 46). Woody described the 1870–1877 court as consisting of "Moses, a scalawag, Willard, a carpet-bagger, and Wright, a Negro" (1933, 118), but he offset those harsh comments by identifying Moses as a "man of experience, integrity, and recognized ability" and Willard as a "well-trained lawyer" (118). Contemporary newspapers described the events when Wright first assumed the bench. Chief Justice Moses "turned in his seat, bowed, and shook hands with Wright" while Justice Willard made "no sign of recognition whatever" (*Charleston Daily Courier*, 4 February 1870 and *Charleston Daily News*, 4 February 1870). The antipathy toward Wright's selection was not limited to Willard, but in other quarters, there was great jubilation. Even newspapers that routinely railed against the power of black politicians supported Wright's appointment—if indeed a black was to fill the position.

As a justice, Wright was diligent and participated in nearly all of the cases heard by the court during his tenure. Woody wrote that "he seems to have been assiduous in attention to his duties and to have performed them creditably" (1933, 122). Wright's judicial philosophy has been characterized as formalism or strict adherence to the law, essentially divorcing himself from his personal attitudes and ideology about the subject matter of the litigation. Judicial formalists eschewed making moral or policy decisions, an approach denounced by critics because it favored the elites. In addition, Wright strongly believed in following established precedent. "Judge Wright's adherence to formalism as a jurisprudential method, and perhaps his proclivity not to offend the white establishment, may have influenced him to decide cases before him without emphasizing race, class or community disability or personal standing" (Smith 2000, 77).

Most of the cases reaching the Supreme Court during Wright's service involved debts or property, but the difficulties of Wright's position became immediately apparent when those cases involved matters concerning lingering effects of slavery. For example, in *Calhoun v. Calhoun*, 2 S.C. 283 (1870), the court faced the question of whether debts for the purchase of slaves survived the war and South Carolina's attempt to abolish such debts; Wright concurred in Chief Justice Moses's opinion that the contract underlying the debt was valid. In *Russell v. Cantwell*, 5 S.C. 477 (1875), Russell brought suit for malicious prosecution for events that occurred while he was a slave. Although Wright had declared during the constitutional convention that slavery was always illegal, his opinion as a justice was that, according to the law at the time of the event, Russell could have not brought the suit as a slave and that bar still existed in 1875.

The case that led to Wright's fall from grace began in the contested election of 1878. In the governor's race, former slave owner and Confederate general Wade Hampton was at the top of the Democratic ticket and Daniel Chamberlain, incumbent reform governor, was the titular head of the divided Republican Party. The election was marred by violence and allegations of corruption and resulted in each faction's claiming victory and the establishment of rival legislatures and governors. The Supreme Court dealt with the legislative issue first and found the Democratic body to be legally constituted.

The putative governors each issued pardons to prisoners to provide the test case to move the matter into the courts. In *Ex parte Norris*, 8 S.C. 408 (1877), in the absence of Chief Justice Moses who had been incapacitated by a stroke, Justices Willard and Wright approved the pardon issued by Hampton, effectively recognizing Hampton as governor, although by agreement, the decision was not immediately made public. On 27 February 1877, Willard wrote the order that was endorsed by Wright indicating his concurrence; however, two days later, Wright produced a contradictory order indicating that, upon reflection, he had altered his opinion The Clerk's Office released the original order on 2 March. Speculation immediately swirled as to Wright's motivations and the pressures to which he was subjected; Wright actually fled the state for a time for fear of reprisals (Woody 1933, 122–127).

Within days, efforts to remove Wright from the court solidified with the creation of a house committee to investigate his activities, and on 6 June 1877, Wright was impeached on the grounds of drunkenness, a charge that has since been discounted. Recognizing the probable outcome since other prominent Republicans were being forced from office by the Democratic legislature, Wright resigned in August 1877 (Gergel and Gergel 2000, 64–65).

The next year, Wright's reputation was further tainted during hearings about corruption by former governors Chamberlain and Franklin Moses Jr. From his jail cell, Moses alleged that, during consideration of *William Whaley v. Bank of Charleston*, 5 S.C. 189 (1873), Chamberlain, an attorney in the case, approached Moses to act as broker and to offer Wright a bribe to break the stalemate between Chief Justice Moses and Willard. Wright vehemently denied his participation in the scheme, and the investigative committee was unable to confirm that Wright even had knowledge of the conspiracy (Gergel and Gergel 2000, 66–67).

From 1872 to 1881, Wright served on the Board of Trustees of Claflin College, one of the first institutions of higher education established for black students in South Carolina. Wright himself had been awarded the LL.D. degree from Avery College, Allegheny City, Pennsylvania, shortly after his election and was appointed as Chair of Law at Claflin in 1881. Following his resignation from the bench, Wright combined his professions of teaching and law by establishing his law practice in Charleston and conducting classes for Claflin (Fitchett 1943, 47, 49). Wright's law practice was only moderately successful, owing, in part, to poor health as a result of tuberculosis. He died 19 February 1885 and was buried at the Calvary Episcopal Church, Charleston (Gergel and Gergel 2000, 69–70).

Assessment of the quality of Wright's work on the bench has been mixed. Journalist John Reynolds, a contemporary of Wright's, reported that many thought that Wright was not capable of authoring the opinions credited to him and that they were actually prepared by someone else (Lengel 1997, 41). James Lengel pointed out, however, that Reynolds produced no evidence to support that statement and that opinions attributed to Wright often employed Pennsylvania law as precedent as would be expected of a lawyer trained in that state (44). Woody commented that the opinions in "all the important cases involving novel points of law or large political or economic interests" were produced by either Moses or Willard, although Wright's "written opinions were clearly expressed and judicious in tone" (1933, 121).

Although the early commentaries were not laudatory, Wright's reputation as a jurist has undergone something of a resurgence in recent decades. In his analysis of Wright's work, Chief Justice J. Clay Smith, a law professor at Howard University, argued that although "Wright's ability to influence legal history and create binding precedential authority was severely limited by the small number of cases that he was assigned," Wright remained "one of the finest legal minds . . . [of] Reconstruction" (2000, 75). Of the 426 signed opinions during the seven-year period, Wright authored only ninety or 21 percent, whereas Willard produced 162 opinions or 38 percent and Moses was the most prolific, authoring 175 or 41 percent of the signed opinions. Although extant records do not permit the exact determination of the number of cases assigned to each judge, it appears that the caseload was not divided equally among the three because of the disproportionate number of signed opinions by the other justices (75–76). Jaffe argued that Smith overstated Wright's impact on South Carolina jurisprudence because only eight of Wright's opinions were deemed controlling by later courts and that, although Wright was certainly an important historic figure, he did not rate among the great legal scholars (2001, 11). Instead, "he was a conservative justice who stayed well within the bounds of safe, legal reasoning for his time" (12).

Whatever the evaluation of Wright as a jurist, there is no disagreement on Wright's eminence in the legal history of South Carolina and of the nation. Wright occupies a noteworthy place in American judicial history because of his unique accomplishments. In one of his public addresses, Wright spoke of his dream of leaders noted not for their party, not for their section of the nation, nor their race but for their "ability to perform well the duties to be committed to their charge" (Woody 1933, 131). The restoration of his stature as a leading jurist of Reconstruction has been the product of such assessment.

Susan Coleman

References and Further Reading:

Fitchett, E. Horace. 1943. "The Role of Claflin College in Negro Life in South Carolina." *Journal of Negro Education* 12 (Winter): 42–68.

Gergel, Richard, and Belinda Gergel. 2000. "'To Vindicate the Cause of the Downtrodden.'" In *At Freedom's Door: African American Founding Fathers and Lawyers in Reconstruction South Carolina*, edited by James Lowell Underwood and W. Lewis Burke Jr. Columbia: University of South Carolina Press, 36–71.

Jaffe, Caleb Adam. 2001. "Obligations Impaired: Justice Jonathan Jasper Wright and the Failure of Reconstruction in South Carolina." M.A. thesis, University of Virginia.

Lengel, James H. 1997. "Justice Jonathan Jasper Wright: An African American First." M.A. thesis, Vanderbilt University.

Smith, J. Clay, Jr. 2000. "The Reconstruction of Justice Jonathan Wright." In *At Freedom's Door: African American Founding Fathers and Lawyers in Reconstruction South Carolina,* edited by James Lowell Underwood and W. Lewis Burke Jr. Columbia: University of South Carolina Press, 72–89.

Underwood, James Lowell. 2000. "The South Carolina Constitution of 1868." In *At Freedom's Door: African American Founding Fathers and Lawyers in Reconstruction South Carolina,* edited by James Lowell Underwood and W. Lewis Burke Jr. Columbia: University of South Carolina Press, 1–35.

Walsh, Walter J. 1997. "Introduction: Speaking Truth to Power: The Jurisprudence of Julia Cooper Mack." *Howard Law Journal* 40 (Winter): 291.

Woody, R. H. 1933. "Jonathan Jasper Wright, Associate Justice of the Supreme Court of South Carolina, 1870–77." *Journal of Negro History* 18 (April): 114–131.

WYTHE, GEORGE

(1726–1806)

GEORGE WYTHE *(right)*
Statue at Marshall-Wythe Law School, College of William & Mary. Sculpted by Gordon S. Kray.

GEORGE WYTHE, VIRGINIA lawyer, legislator, and law professor, served as a judge on Virginia's High Court of Chancery from the court's inception in 1778 to his death in 1806.

Wythe, the son of Thomas and Margaret Walker Wythe, was born in Elizabeth City County (now Hampton), Virginia, sometime in 1726. The first Wythes arrived in Virginia about 1680. On his mother's side, Wythe descended from the Pennsylvania pioneer George Keith. Thomas Wythe died in 1729, leaving Margaret Wythe to raise George; his older brother, Thomas; and his younger sister, Anne. Margaret Wythe launched George's education in the Greek and Latin classics, which eventually formed the course of study for Wythe's law students. About 1742 Wythe began to study law with Stephen Dewey, his uncle by marriage and king's attorney for Charles City County. Dewey was apparently an inattentive mentor and left Wythe to master the law on his own.

As a second son, Wythe inherited none of his father's estate.

After completing his legal training, Wythe set out to practice law and make his fortune in the Shenandoah Valley of Virginia. He lived in Spotsylvania County, practiced mainly in Orange County, and was also admitted in Augusta and Caroline Counties. Zachary Lewis, king's attorney for Spotsylvania, chose Wythe as an associate, and Wythe became the busiest lawyer in the area, apart from Lewis himself. Wythe cemented his connection to the Lewis family by marrying Lewis's daughter Anne on 26 December 1747. Both the marriage and the partnership were short lived. Anne Lewis Wythe died on 8 August 1748, and soon after Wythe returned to the tidewater, settling in Williamsburg.

Wythe's cousin by marriage, longtime judge and burgess Benjamin Waller, guided Wythe's entry into the Williamsburg area legal and political establishment. He was admitted to the York and Warwick (now Newport News) County bars in 1748 and established a reputation for exhaustive preparation of cases and spotless integrity. Wythe began his political career in 1748 as clerk of the Privileges and Elections committee and the Propositions and Grievances committee of the House of Burgesses. Wythe reached the top of the legal profession as Peyton Randolph's temporary replacement as attorney general, serving from January 1754 to May 1755.

In 1755 Wythe inherited his brother's estate and married Elizabeth Taliaferro. Her father, Richard, is said to have designed the couple's house on the Palace Green. Wythe's political fortunes rose less steadily than his legal career. He was first elected a burgess for Williamsburg in 1754. He lost elections for an Elizabeth City County seat in 1756 and 1758. William and Mary sent him to the House of Burgesses in 1758, as did Elizabeth City County in 1761 and 1766. Wythe resigned to become clerk of the House of Burgesses in 1768 and the same year served as mayor of Williamsburg. Wythe was at the center of the capital's intellectual and social life. He was an intimate of Lt. Gov. Francis Fauquier and introduced his first law student, Thomas Jefferson, to the upper strata of Virginia society.

Wythe's prominence in Virginia propelled him to the national stage. He was elected to the Continental Congress in 1775 and took his place on the pro-independence side. He returned to Virginia in 1776 and was elected speaker of the House of Delegates in 1777. The same year he helped revise the laws of Virginia with Thomas Jefferson and Edmund Pendleton. Wythe wrote bill 92, establishing an admiralty court (ignored by the legislature), and bill 93, creating a Court of Appeals consisting of the judges of the High Court of Chancery, General Court, and Court of Admiralty (passed by the legislature). In 1787 Wythe returned to Philadelphia as a member of the Constitution Convention. The next year he chaired the Committee of the Whole at the Virginia ratifying convention.

George Mason (1725–1792)

Often assumed to have been a lawyer because of his role in drafting both the Virginia Declaration of Rights and the state's first constitution, Virginia's George Mason of Gunston Hall was a self-educated planter. Despite his lack of legal training, Mason was appointed a commissioner of the peace in Fairfax County, Virginia, in 1747. A scholar explained that "[b]y inheritance Mason belonged to the privileged class of gentlemen justice who were expected to assemble at the courthouse once a month to govern the county and decide lawsuits without compensation of any kind except prestige" (Horrell 1989, 34). Mason was dropped, apparently for poor attendance, in 1752 but rejoined the court in 1764. Perhaps in part because of poor health, Mason continued his record of spotty attendance, even when serving as the court's chief judge. As a commissioner, Mason served as a representative for the "country" party who opposed tax levies that were advocated by the merchants in Fairfax (Mason believed that since commissioners were appointed, albeit now under a constitution that Mason had himself largely authored, this violated the principle of "no taxation without representation").

Accepting a rare appointment as a delegate to the U.S. Constitutional Convention of 1787, Mason gave a strong speech opposing slavery but ultimately opposed the new Constitution both because it lacked a bill of rights and because it provided for what he considered to be the overcentralization of powers. This position led to a sad rift with George Washington, George Mason's longtime neighbor and friend. Mason's decision not to swear allegiance to the new Constitution appears to account for his resignation from his court in 1789. Attempting to account for the fact that Mason clung so long to a judge's chair that he so rarely occupied, one writer has concluded that, however lowly, Mason's office allowed him to serve, as in the Roman republic that he so admired, as "a tribute of the people" (Horrell 1989, 55). Today, there are very few judicial posts left where gifted men like Mason, without formal legal training, can serve.

Reference:

Horrell, Joseph. 1989. "George Mason and the Fairfax Court." In *George Mason and the Legacy of Constitutional Liberty*, edited by Donald J. Senese. Fairfax, Va.: Fairfax County Historical Commission, 32–58.

Wythe's longest-lasting contribution to American law was as a teacher. In December 1779, the board of visitors of the College of William and Mary appointed Wythe the professor of law and police, the first such professorship in the country. From his chair, Wythe launched the careers of the Virginia and American legal and political elite. Wythe's students included several future governors of Virginia, future president James Monroe, and future chief justice John Marshall. Wythe stepped down in 1790, replaced by St.

George Tucker, a future federal district court judge and also a Wythe student. Wythe moved to Richmond in 1791, where he continued to take on law students, among them Henry Clay.

The longest phase of Wythe's career was his tenure as a judge of the High Court of Chancery from 1778 to 1806. The Virginia legislature created the chancery court in 1778 and unanimously elected Wythe, Edmund Pendleton, and Robert Carter Nicholas as the first judges, with Pendleton as the presiding judge. The were sworn in on 6 April 1778. The chancellors also sat on the Court of Appeals. The legislature created a separate Court of Appeals in December 1788, elevating Pendleton and John Blair to the new court and leaving Wythe as sole chancellor. Wythe doubtless could have been promoted to the highest state court or to a federal court if he wanted but preferred to remain at the chancery. By 1802 the caseload was too much for one chancellor to administer justice. That year the legislature divided the High Court of Chancery into three districts, sitting at Staunton, Richmond, and Williamsburg. Wythe served as chancellor for the Richmond district until his death on 8 June 1806.

Wythe's first decade as a judge cannot be completely reconstructed, as the court records burned in 1865. The most important Court of Appeals case in the Wythe era, *Caton v. Commonwealth* (1782), was popularly known as the Case of the Prisoners and was an early instance of judicial review. James Lamb, Joshua Hopkins, and John Caton were convicted of treason on 15 June 1782. The trio appealed to the General Assembly for a pardon. The House of Delegates voted to grant one, but the Senate did not. The Treason Act of 1776 gave the power to pardon traitors to the General Assembly, but the constitution gave the pardoning power to the governor and council of state unless the law directed otherwise. In October, the General Court heard the case and sent it to the Court of Appeals. Pendleton convened the court on 29 October and heard arguments on 31 October. The ultimate decision hung on whether the Court of Appeals could hear the case, whether the court could declare a law unconstitutional, and if so, whether the Treason Act was unconstitutional.

The court rendered its decision on 2 November. According to Pendleton's notes, Wythe "at first doubted of the Jurisdiction but afterward expressed himself satisfied" that the Court of Appeals could hear the case. Wythe went on to argue that "an Anti-constitutional Act of the Legislature would be void, and if so, that this Court must in Judgement declare it so, or not decide according to the Law of the land. However that the Treason Act was not against the Constitution, and therefore the concurrence of the senate was necessary to the Pardon of a Traitor, and this paper not a pardon" (Pendleton 1967, 2:426–427). Daniel Call attributed a longer speech to

Wythe and a more ringing defense of judicial review. Wythe proposed to tell the legislature, "here is the limit of your authority; and hither shall you go, but no further" (quoted in Brown 1981, 249).

As chancellor, Wythe heard equity cases, mostly involving wills, land claims, and payment of debts. The revolution threw each of these into confusion, leaving Wythe no shortage of work. Wythe considered the High Court of Chancery as a dispenser of pure justice. Wythe believed equity courts had an advantage over common law courts, because an equity court could command the execution of an agreement such as a will or deed, whereas a common law court could only assess and grant damages (Wythe 1795, 60). Wythe saw no conflict between equity and common law courts. Equity courts stepped in when the common law could not grant adequate relief; "in proceeding thus, the court of equity maintains a perfect harmony with the court of common law, or is not at variance with it" (33). The equity courts could grant the relief that the common law court "reluctantly withholds," thereby "accomplishing the main design of both, which is the attainment of justice" (33).

The more political instincts of Edmund Pendleton, presiding over the Court of Appeals, frequently frustrated Wythe's quest for pure justice. Wythe's 1795 collection, *Decisions of Cases in Virginia in the High Court of Chancery, with Remarks upon Decrees of the Court of Appeals, Reversing Some of Those Decisions*, is self-explanatory. The collection demonstrated the depth of Wythe's learning, with frequent references to Roman and English law. Wythe also showed his displeasure with the Court of Appeals, casting himself as a scholar thwarted by the baser instincts of his superiors. Wythe complained that he was "bound to accept the decrees of the court of appeals," but did so with "the poignancy which Galileo suffered, when, having maintained the truth of the Copernican in opposition to the Ptolemaic system, he was compelled, by those who could compel him, to abjure the heresy" (44). Pendleton planned to respond but decided against it upon learning that Wythe had sold few copies.

Wythe's most important case as sole chancellor was *Page v. Pendelton and Lyons* in 1793. The case revolved around the politically charged issue of payment of prewar debts to British merchants. In 1783 the Virginia legislature allowed debtors to pay into the state loan office, which would assume the debts and pay them off in worthless paper money. The peace treaty of 1783 prohibited any interference with the collection of prewar debts. Wythe ruled that Virginia had no right either to absolve Virginians of their debts to British merchants or to alter the means by which those debts were to be paid. Again, Wythe cast himself as the agent of pure and impartial justice, having taken "an oath, which no human power can dispense, that he will do equal right to all manner of people" (Wythe 1795, 132). Equal justice to British merchants meant that the paper money from the loan office did not constitute payment of the debts.

One of Wythe's last cases, *Hudgins v. Wright* (1806), demonstrated the problem slavery presented to the political and legal thought of revolutionary Virginia. Three generations of women claimed by Hudgins argued that they were descendants of free woman, and therefore free. Wythe put the burden of proof on the master. As he could not prove the women were slaves, Wythe ruled them free, not only as a matter of law but also as a birthright of all people. Higher courts upheld Wythe on the issue of burden of proof, but not on that of natural right.

Wythe served the law all his life, but in the end it failed him. Wythe had no children and willed his estate to his sister's grandson, George Wythe Sweeney. Sweeney had been forging checks of his granduncle's account and needed money. On 25 May 1806, Sweeney poisoned Wythe's morning coffee. Wythe lingered long enough to disinherit his grandnephew, before dying on 8 June 1806. Sweeney was acquitted for lack of evidence.

Robert W. Smith

References and Further Reading:

Blackburn, Joyce. 1975. *George Wythe of Williamsburg*. New York: Harper and Row.

Brown, Imogene E. 1981. *American Aristides: A Biography of George Wythe*. Rutherford, N.J.: Farleigh Dickinson University Press.

Clarkin, William. 1970. *Serene Patriot: A Life of George Wythe*. Albany, N.Y.: Alan Publications.

Dill, Alonzo Thomas. 1979. *George Wythe, Teacher of Liberty*. Williamsburg: Virginia Independence Bicentennial Commission.

Kirtland, Robert Bevier. 1983. "George Wythe: Lawyer, Revolutionary, Judge." Ph.D. diss., University of Michigan.

Pendleton, Edmund. 1967. *The Letters and Papers of Edmund Pendleton 1734–1803*. 2 vols. Edited by David John Mays. Charlottesville: University Press of Virginia.

Wythe, George. 1795. *Decisions of Cases in Virginia in the High Court of Chancery, with Remarks upon Decrees of the Court of Appeals, Reversing Some of Those Decisions*. Richmond, Va.: Thomas Nicolson.

WYZANSKI, CHARLES E., JR.

(1906–1986)

Charles E. Wyzanski Jr.
Courtesy of Art & Visual Materials, Special Collections Department, Harvard Law School Library

Brilliant, contemplative, and committed to the ideals of democracy and justice, district court judge Charles E. Wyzanski made his mark not only on the law, but seemingly on everyone he met.

Charles Wyzanski was born in 1906 into a well-to-do family in Brookline, Massachusetts, a prosperous suburb of Boston. As a child, he attended prestigious private schools, including Phillips Exeter Academy, that fostered his lifelong love of learning. He attended Harvard University, graduating in 1927 and earning Phi Beta Kappa honors. Through his prestigious family and schooling, Wyzanski became connected to a circle of friends and colleagues that was destined to change American government and law. Its members—ranging from Oliver Wendell Holmes Jr., who encouraged young Charles to go to law school, to Judges Augustus and Learned Hand, to Prof. Felix Frankfurter and the best and brightest minds of Pres. Franklin Roosevelt's New Deal administration—would become giants in their fields, in a period of political and legal creativity the likes of which the United States has not seen since.

Wyzanski's tenure at Harvard Law School was impressive. He earned almost straight A grades, made the law review, and graduated *magna cum laude*. The relationships he built at law school proved seminal in directing his legal, and later his judicial, career. On the recommendation of Prof. Felix Frankfurter, Wyzanski was offered clerkships on the United States Court of Appeals for the Second Circuit with both Augustus Hand and Learned Hand. These judges profoundly influenced the young law graduate. At the conclusion of his clerkships, he went to work for the law firm of Ropes and Gray in Boston. His life in private practice, however, was short lived. Wyzanski refused an assignment to write a brief against an anti-injunction law because he believed that the law was both valid and desirable (Freund 1987, 711). Such defiance could typically result in the discharge of a young associate attorney, but in this case news of Wyzanski's decision made its way through well-connected New England channels all the way to Pres. Franklin Roosevelt. Roosevelt appointed Wyzanski, who was only three years out of law school, to become solicitor of the Department of Labor, serving under labor secretary Frances Perkins, the nation's first female cabinet member.

At first, Wyzanski represented the Department of Labor by helping to draft key New Deal legislation, including the National Recovery Act. He was transferred to the Justice Department in 1935, where he defended the Labor Department in a number of soon-to-be famous New Deal court cases. The most important of these was undoubtedly *National Labor Relations Board v. Jones & Laughlin Steel Corporation* (1937). In *Jones & Laughlin*, the Supreme Court, in a notable departure from its previous approach to New Deal legislation, upheld the National Labor Relations Act and, with it, Congress's ability to address the nation's ongoing economic crisis by regulating interstate commerce and labor-management relations.

In 1941, when Wyzanski was just thirty-five years old, President Roosevelt appointed him to the federal district court in Massachusetts. Wyzanski loved the district court because it gave him independence and allowed him to connect with and educate the lawyers, clients, and jurors who came before him at trial (Freund 1987, p. 712). He turned down offers for the appellate court, choosing instead to stay in his first judicial appointment—which he did for the next forty-five years.

Wyzanski's intellectual brilliance and love of law made him a superlative judge. His judicial philosophy was strongly influenced by Judges Augustus and Learned Hand and Jerome Frank, Justices Oliver Wendell Holmes Jr. and Louis Brandeis, and his former academic mentor–turned–justice Felix Frankfurter. Wyzanski earned a reputation for his extensive and unending reflection on the judge's role. Indeed, his attitude toward judging was not only the product of his background but also of his extensive knowledge of history and philosophy. Wyzanski was extremely well read and had a penchant for including subtle, arcane, and yet adept references to history and literature in his writings and conversations.

Burnita S. Matthews (1894–1988)

Burnita Shelton Matthews was the first woman ever to serve as a United States district court judge. Born in Copiah County, Mississippi, she aspired as a child to be a lawyer (her father was a clerk in a chancery court), but her parents sent her to study piano and voice at the Conservatory of Music in Cincinnati while sending her brother to law school.

During World War I, Matthews moved to Washington, D.C., and worked for the Veterans Administration while attending night school at the National University Law School (now part of George Washington University), where she received her LL.B. degree in 1919 and her LL.M. the following year. As a law student, she joined pickets in front of the White House in favor of woman's suffrage. During her time in law school she married Percy A. Matthews, who was also a lawyer.

Refused entry into the Veterans Administration Legal Department (the local bar association also initially rejected her application for membership), Matthews opened her own office and, in 1920, became the National Woman's Party's lawyer. Unsuccessful in persuading the Supreme Court not to take the party's property across from the U.S. Capitol for the construction of the current Supreme Court building, Matthews is credited with winning a generous allotment for this governmental taking, and she established friendship with a number of U.S. senators.

Matthews taught at the Washington College of Law during the 1930s and 1940s and was appointed to a new United States district court judgeship by Pres. Harry Truman in 1949. Although confirmed, she was given the cold shoulder by her male colleagues, one of whom openly stated that "Mrs. Matthews would be a good judge" except for the fact that "she's a woman" (quoted in Greenhouse 1988, 27). As a woman, Matthews chose females for clerks both in order to show her confidence in them and so that others could not attribute her own legal work to men.

Initially given many of the more technical cases that the male judges did not like, Matthews presided over some high-profile trials, including a 1957 bribery trial of Teamster's vice president Jimmy Hoffa, who was acquitted, and a case involving the rights of Black Muslins to conduct religious services while in prison. Matthews continued to serve until 1968, when she took senior status, thus continuing to try cases before a number of courts. Her husband died the following year, but Mrs. Matthews continued hearing cases until five years before her death, after a stroke, in 1988.

References:

Ginsburg, Ruth Bader, and Laura W. Brill. 1995. "Women in the Federal Judiciary: Three Way Pavers and the Exhilarating Change President Carter Wrought." *Fordham Law Review* 64 (November): 281–290.

Greenhouse, Linda. 1988. "Burnita S. Matthews Dies at 93; First Woman on U.S. Trial Courts." *New York Times*, 28 April, p. 27, col. 1.

"Matthews, Burnita Shelton." Available at <http://air.fjc.gov/servlet/uGetInfo?jid=1506>.

Wyzanski rejected the notion that judges should be social or political activists, yet he also rejected the traditional notion that judges simply "interpret" the law. The distinction between making and interpreting the law was too simplistic for Wyzanski. Rather than engage in a debate over terminology, Wyzanski offered a view not of what the judge should *do*, but rather of what kind of person the judge should *be*. For Wyzanski, the judge had a noble calling and had to be up to the task. That meant he or she should be not only smart and well prepared for such work, but, more important, cautious and humble in undertaking it. He recognized that judges in the U.S. legal system might exercise awesome power; for Wyzanski, the question was whether and under what circumstances they should do so.

Wyzanski argued, for example, that the judiciary has a special role to play in the protection of civil rights and liberties and should act decisively to preserve them. He believed that judges should be courageous in the face of political opposition and criticism. Nevertheless, this fact did not give judges *carte blanche* on the bench, because Wyzanski also and even more strongly stressed the judge's obligation to recognize his or her own limitations. A judge, he pointed out, is not elected and has no special entitlement in deciding matters of policy. A true democrat, Wyzanski argued that the true power of the nation rested not in its judiciary, but in its people. The people, through their elected officials, were the nation's legitimate policymakers; interference or second-guessing by the judiciary was tantamount to substituting a judge's values for the people's. Because Wyzanski recognized that judges to varying degrees would forget or ignore this distinction, he insisted that, as a first requirement, they be careful, contemplative, moral actors who understood both their historical and current roles in the larger system of governance. He was especially concerned that judges, and indeed all participants in the U.S. legal system, recognize its enduring norms and values and aim to set a high, selfless standard in their work.

Wyzanski's philosophy served him well when he received his most famous case, *United States v. United Shoe Machinery Corporation* (1953). Today, this landmark antitrust case is best known for the principle that the federal government has the authority to break up a corporation that has committed antitrust violations. The nature and extent of this power have been explored continually since *United Shoe*. Examples include the breakup of American Telephone and Telegraph (AT & T) into numerous "baby Bell" telephone companies and most recently the federal government's ongoing litigation against Microsoft Corporation, in which it has sought to divide the corporation into smaller independent companies to remedy its alleged monopolistic practices.

The United Shoe Corporation, a manufacturer of the machinery used to make leather shoes, had been in litigation for decades over its business practices before this particular case came before Judge Wyzanski. Competitors argued that United Shoe had been engaging in a long, concerted effort to drive its competition out of business. Rival companies, and then the U.S. government itself, sued United Shoe in a series of cases alleging unfair, anticompetitive, and monopolistic business practices. This particular lawsuit, which came before the judge in the late 1940s and was not ultimately resolved until the 1960s, was by his own admission Wyzanski's favorite, as it posed new, significant, and exciting questions of law.

The case centered on United Shoe's alleged ongoing violations of the Sherman Antitrust Act. The Sherman Act, passed by Congress in 1890, prohibits restraint of trade by a single business or coalition of businesses that act as a monopoly. Recognizing that the case would involve complex economic analysis of the shoe-making industry, including its markets and sales, Judge Wyzanski took the then-unheard-of step of appointing a Harvard economist to be his law clerk. Carl Kaysen, a new assistant professor of economics at Harvard, was recommended to the judge by his Harvard colleagues (Kaysen 1987, 713). Despite opposition from the corporation's counsel, Kaysen served as clerk for two years, during the trial of United Shoe. He attended the trial in person as often as he could; when his teaching schedule conflicted with it, Kaysen received daily trial transcripts by messenger from the judge (714).

The *United Shoe* trial proved long and complex. Throughout the trial, which ended in the summer of 1952, economist Kaysen and Judge Wyzanski discussed the evidence at length. Kaysen wrote an expert report to the judge summarizing his economic analysis of the case. A few months later, in February 1953, Judge Wyzanski ruled that United Shoe had engaged in monopolistic practices in violation of the Sherman Act. With victory in hand, the federal government asked Judge Wyzanski to impose "divestiture" on United Shoe—to break up United Shoe into three separate companies to end its monopoly. Wyzanski refused and instead subjected the company to extensive sanctions and restrictions aimed at reducing its power and making the market for its products more competitive. He issued a remedial order and asked the parties to report on the progress of its implementation.

The United States thus continued to monitor United Shoe's activities under the judge's remedial decree. In 1965, the Justice Department reported to Judge Wyzanski that United Shoe was continuing its monopolistic practices and once again asked that the company be split, this time into two entities. The judge again refused, noting that the government had not met the legal standard that would compel him to alter his earlier remedial order. Disappointed that Judge Wyzanski had once again left United Shoe intact, the government appealed this decision to the United States Supreme Court. In 1968, the high court held that Judge Wyzanski was not, as he had concluded, limited in his ability to change his initial remedial order. Instead, Judge Wyzanski had both the authority and the obligation to change the remedial decree to see that its goals were met. The Court remanded the case to Judge Wyzanski, to determine whether the remedies he ordered had worked and, if not, to modify the decree to see that its goals were met. After the Court's ruling and upon further reflection, Judge Wyzanski finally ordered divestiture.

The *United Shoe* case set the stage for subsequent government attempts to break up what it believed to be monopolistic companies. In 1969, the Justice Department sued International Business Machines (IBM) for antitrust violations, a lawsuit it later dropped. In 1974, it sued AT & T and forced the eventual creation of numerous smaller telephone providers (which, over time, have grown quite large themselves). Finally, in 1990 the government sued the Microsoft Corporation, alleging that it had monopoly power over various technologies, including computer operating systems. In 2000, United States District Court judge Robert Penfield Jackson found for the government and ordered Microsoft's divestiture. Microsoft appealed Jackson's rulings, and the parties involved settled on a resolution that did not require the breakup of Microsoft (Memorandum opinion, *United States of America v. Microsoft Corporation*, Civil action 98-1232, U.S. District of Columbia, November 1, 2002).

Judge Wyzanski is often credited with being the first federal judge to break up a U.S. corporation. That is not entirely correct, as Judge Wyzanski repeatedly refused to impose the ultimate punishment until after the Supreme Court ruled. More accurately, Judge Wyzanski is remembered as a trailblazer in the area of antitrust whose careful and considered approach to *United Shoe* set a very high standard for subsequent attorneys and judges to follow. Indeed, it is a fitting testament to the judge that both the government and Microsoft cited his opinion in *United Shoe* to make their respective cases.

Judge Wyzanski's contributions to federal law are not limited to the field of antitrust. As indicated earlier, he firmly believed that a judge should act courageously to uphold the civil rights and liberties of citizens, even when doing so was politically unpopular. He had the chance to do just that in the case of *United States v. Sisson* (1969). Sisson refused to be inducted into the armed services during the Vietnam War, a violation of the Military Selective Service Act. He argued that the Vietnam War was illegal, immoral, and unjust. But Sisson refused "conscientious objector status" because his beliefs were particular to the Vietnam War, rather than to wars in general. Consequently, he was brought to trial and convicted by a jury of willfully violating his induction order.

Upon motion by Sisson after the trial, Judge Wyzanski set aside his conviction. The judge concluded that Sisson had acted sincerely and according to his conscience. Prior to that time, it was typical for someone seeking conscientious objector status to prove that he or she was precluded from military service by membership in a particular religion. Sisson was not a member of an organized religion but nevertheless claimed the "right of conscience" to excuse him from service. Judge Wyzanski agreed, noting that persons like Sisson, whether religious or not, could be excused from the draft if their objection was based on "profound moral beliefs which constitute the central convictions of their beings" (297 F. Supp., 911).

Predictably, the United States appealed Judge Wyzanski's decision. A divided Supreme Court ultimately held that it had no jurisdiction over the case and could not review the judge's decision because it was tantamount to an acquittal. In setting aside the jury's decision, Judge Wyzanski had effectively acquitted the defendant from criminal wrongdoing, and Sisson was freed. Although ultimately the *Sisson* case did not resolve the issue of whether one can object to specific wars, Judge Wyzanski offered a compelling argument that religious affiliation should not be required for a person who refuses military service on the grounds of conscience.

This case illustrates well Judge Wyzanski's contemplative nature as a judge, as well as his refusal to adjudicate in a politically expedient manner. Other evidence is found in his criticism of the Nuremberg Trials, where he argued that the tribunal and its procedures would not serve as a model for future resolutions of international law and were susceptible to becoming propaganda devices that did not serve the interests of justice (1946). Wyzanski's commentary was controversial, of course, particularly because such contemporaneous remarks were unusual for a sitting judge. But in true Wyzanski fashion, he authored another article a few months later in which he disagreed with himself and made significant counterarguments in support of the proceedings (1947b). In the best lawyerly and scholarly fashion, he argued both sides of the case thoughtfully and convincingly.

Wyzanski kept busy with numerous other endeavors besides judging. A loyal Harvard alumnus, he served as president of the Harvard Board of Overseers and as a senior fellow at the Harvard Society of Fellows. He was a longtime trustee of the Ford Foundation, as well as a counselor of the American Law Institute. He taught law and government at Harvard and law at the Massachusetts Institute of Technology, Stanford, and Columbia. From 1965 to 1971 he served as chief judge of the District of Massachusetts and then assumed senior status on the court. He was still serving on the bench upon his death in 1986 at the age of eighty.

A few years before his death, he and his colleague (now United States Supreme Court justice) Stephen Breyer attended a meeting of the Administrative Office of the Courts, where the presenter explained all of the new forms and paperwork that federal judges would now be required to fill out and described the Office's new telephone number that enabled litigants across the nation to be instantly connected to the Office when they wished to complain about a federal judge. The judges in the audience, of course, were incredulous. But Judge Wyzanski, in his thoughtful way, simply observed that "[S]oon I shall be in judicial heaven, with Learned Hand and Augustus Hand and Jerome Frank; and I won't have to put up with any of this" (Breyer 1987, 710).

Following Judge Wyzanski's death, several tributes to him were included in volume 100 of the *Harvard Law Review*. Authors included Prof. Edward H. Levi, *New York Times* columnist Anthony Lewis, and attorney Elliot Richardson as well as Stephen Breyer, Paul Freund, and Carl Kaysen. In his memorial tribute, Justice Breyer concluded that "it is for giving me a glimpse of that 'judicial heaven,' where he rightly belongs, that I am grateful to the judge" (1987, 710).

Kathleen Uradnik

References and Further Reading:

Breyer, Stephen. 1987. "In Memoriam: Charles E. Wyzanski, Jr." *Harvard Law Review* 100: 707.

Freund, Paul. 1987. "In Memoriam: Charles E. Wyzanski, Jr." *Harvard Law Review* 100: 710.

Kaysen, Carl. 1987. "In Memoriam: Charles E. Wyzanski, Jr." *Harvard Law Review* 100: 713.

United States v. Sisson. 297 F. Supp. 902 (1969).

Wagoner, James. 2001. "Wyzanski, Charles E., Jr." In *Great American Lawyers: An Encyclopedia*, vol. 2, edited by John R. Vile. Santa Barbara, Calif.: ABC-CLIO.

Wyzanski, Charles E. (Jr). 1946. *"Nuremberg in Retrospect." The Atlantic Monthly* 178, no. 6, 56–59.

———. 1947a. "Judge Learned Hand's Contributions to Public Law." *Harvard Law Review* 60.

———. 1947b. "Nuremberg—A Fair Trial? Dangerous Precedent." *The Atlantic Monthly* 177, no. 4, 66–70.

———. 1952. "A Trial Judge's Freedom and Responsibility." *Harvard Law Review* 65: 1281.

———. 1965. *Whereas—A Judge's Premises, Essays in Judgment, Ethics, and the Law.* Boston: Little, Brown.

———. 1973. "Equal Justice through Law." *Tulane Law Review* 47: 951–960.

Joseph A. Wapner: Judge of the People's Court (1919–)

Best known for his role in the popular television series *The People's Court,* Judge Joseph A. Wapner had many years of practical experience as a judge prior to becoming a television celebrity. After earning his diploma at the University of Southern California (USC), Wapner went into the army and served during World War II, during which time he was wounded in action in the Philippines. He subsequently returned to USC and earned a law degree. Appointed as a municipal court judge in 1959, he became a superior court judge in 1962 and served until 1979 (serving pro tem for some time as a justice on the California Court of Appeals), after which he began his television show, in which both parties agree to accept his judgment in small claims matters.

In his book *A View from the Bench,* Wapner stressed the human elements of being a judge. He believes that judges need to embody the virtues of "empathy, intelligence, compassion, deliberation, and courage" (1987, 13). Using as an illustration a case in which he invalidated a police search, Wapner said that "'law and order' begins with everyone following the Constitution—and I mean *everyone,* from policemen to presidents" (38). Wapner also emphasized the need for community, which he believes has been eroding in recent years. Unlike judges who emphasize their toughness on criminals, Wapner said that "'Throw the book at them' is a recipe for an unfeeling society which may function by some kind of casebook or statute book, but doesn't have the kind of human qualities that a working society must have" (66). He added, "In my courtroom, I dealt with human beings" (66).

Wapner is a strong advocate of settling cases prior to trial whenever possible. He often handed out fortune cookies that said, "Lean settlement better than fat lawsuit" (Wapner 1987, 156). Wapner believes that jury settlements are too often like a lottery, and he envisioned himself as an impartial observer who could listen to both sides and "save most of the rigmarole of the formal, drawn-out legal process" (162). He noted that "If my peers from the Superior Court could say only one thing about me, I would hope it would be that Joe Wapner could feel other people's pain enough to know that settlement is a wonderful way to resolve a case" (203).

Again, in contrast to some judges who attack higher courts for broad interpretations of the Constitution, Wapner cited a case in which constitutional law was interpreted and said that "I believe the process of reinterpreting and reinvigorating the Constitution and every kind of legal procedure is so vital that I hardly mind at all being reversed" (1987, 216). He further observed that "The glory is that the American law can accommodate the pain of the people before it, the concern of thousands of judges, who can feel that pain, and then, far more often than not, render justice" (227).

Reference:

Wapner, Joseph A. 1987. *A View from the Bench.* New York: Simon and Schuster.

Appendix A

Great American Judges Listed by Year of Birth

Samuel Sewall (1652–1730)
Lewis Morris (1671–1746)
Edmund Pendleton (1721–1803)
George Wythe (1726–1806)
Robert R. Livingston Jr. (1746–1813)
Theophilus Parsons (1750–1813)
St. George Tucker (1752–1827)
John Marshall (1755–1835)
John Davis (1761–1847)
François-Xavier Martin (1762–1846)
Spencer Roane (1762–1822)
James Kent (1763–1847)
William Cranch (1769–1855)
Roger Brooke Taney (1777–1864)
John Bannister Gibson (1780–1853)
Lemuel Shaw (1781–1861)
Isaac Blackford (1786–1859)
Thomas Ruffin (1787–1870)
Nathan Green Sr. (1792–1866)
Thomas Alexander Marshall (1794–1871)
Joseph Henry Lumpkin (1799–1867)
John Hemphill (1803–1862)
John Appleton (1804–1891)
Samuel Ames (1806–1865)
Thomas Drummond (1809–1890)
Edward George Ryan (1810–1880)
George Sharswood (1810–1883)
George Franklin Comstock (1811–1892)
George Washington Stone (1811–1894)
Stephen J. Field (1816–1899)
Thomas McIntyre Cooley (1824–1898)
Matthew Paul Deady (1824–1893)
Roy Bean (1825–1903)
Hugh Lennox Bond (1828–1893)
Horace Gray (1828–1902)
Charles Cogswell Doe (1830–1896)
William Mitchell (1832–1900)
John Marshall Harlan (1833–1911)
Isaac C. Parker (1838–1896)
Jonathan Jasper Wright (1840–1885)
Oliver Wendell Holmes Jr. (1841–1935)
Walter Clark (1846–1924)
Charles Fremont Amidon (1856–1937)
Louis Dembitz Brandeis (1856–1941)

Judges born in the same year are arranged alphabetically rather than by birthday.

Charles Evan Hughes (1862–1948)
Cuthbert Winfred Pound (1864–1935)
Kenesaw Mountain Landis (1866–1944)
Augustus Noble Hand (1869–1954)
Benjamin N. Cardozo (1870–1938)
Learned Hand (1872–1961)
Harlan Fiske Stone (1872–1946)
Samuel Seabury (1873–1958)
James E. Horton Jr. (1878–1973)
Julius Waties Waring (1880–1968)
Felix Frankfurter (1882–1965)
Florence Ellinwood Allen (1884–1966)
John Johnson Parker (1885–1958)
Hugo Lafayette Black (1886–1971)
Henry White Edgerton (1888–1970)
Harold R. Medina (1888–1990)
Arthur T. Vanderbilt (1888–1957)
Jerome Frank (1889–1957)
Earl Warren (1891–1974)
Richard T. Rives (1895–1982)
Sarah Tilghman Hughes (1896–1985)
Elbert Parr Tuttle (1897–1996)
John Marshall Harlan II (1899–1971)
Roger John Traynor (1900–1983)
Luther Lee Bohanon (1902–)
Henry Jacob Friendly (1903–1986)
William Henry Hastie (1904–1976)
Alfred P. Murrah (1904–1975)
Walter Vincent Schaefer (1904–1986)
John Joseph Sirica (1904–1992)
John Minor Wisdom (1905–1999)
Milton Pollack (1906–)
Charles E. Wyzanski Jr. (1906–1986)
Warren Burger (1907–1995)
David L. Bazelon (1909–1993)
John R. Brown (1909–1993)
Carl Eugene McGowan (1911–1987)
Clement Furman Haynsworth (1912–1989)
Harold Leventhal (1915–1979)
Griffin Bell (1918–)
Frank M. Johnson Jr. (1918–)
William Wayne Justice (1920–)
Constance Baker Motley (1921–)
Jack B. Weinstein (1921–)
Hans A. Linde (1924–)
William H. Rehnquist (1924–)
Abner J. Mikva (1926–)
Robert H. Bork (1927–)
A. Leon Higginbotham Jr. (1928–1998)
Richard Alan Enslen (1931–)
Shirley Schlanger Abrahamson (1933–)
Rose Elizabeth Bird (1936–1999)
Richard A. Posner (1939–)
J. Harvie Wilkinson III (1944–)
Frank Hoover Easterbrook (1948–)
Alex Kozinski (1950–)

Appendix B

Great American Judges Listed by Century

Colonial Times

Lewis Morris (1671–1746)
Samuel Sewall (1652–1730)

Eighteenth Century

Edmund Pendleton (1721–1803)
George Wythe (1726–1806)

Nineteenth Century

Samuel Ames (1806–1865)
John Appleton (1804–1891)
Roy Bean (1825–1903)
Isaac Blackford (1786–1859)
Hugh Lennox Bond (1828–1893)
George Franklin Comstock (1811–1892)
Thomas McIntyre Cooley (1824–1898)
William Cranch (1769–1855)
John Davis (1761–1847)
Matthew Paul Deady (1824–1893)
Charles Cogswell Doe (1830–1896)
Thomas Drummond (1809–1890)
Stephen J. Field (1816–1899)
John Bannister Gibson (1780–1853)
Horace Gray (1828–1902)
Nathan Green Sr. (1792–1866)
John Marshall Harlan (1833–1911)
John Hemphill (1803–1862)
James Kent (1763–1847)
Robert R. Livingston Jr. (1746–1813)
Joseph Henry Lumpkin (1799–1867)
John Marshall (1755–1835)
Thomas Alexander Marshall (1794–1871)
François-Xavier Martin (1762–1846)
William Mitchell (1832–1900)
Isaac C. Parker (1838–1896)
Theophilus Parsons (1750–1813)
Spencer Roane (1762–1822)
Thomas Ruffin (1787–1870)
Edward George Ryan (1810–1880)
George Sharswood (1810–1883)
Lemuel Shaw (1781–1861)
George Washington Stone (1811–1894)
Roger Brooke Taney (1777–1864)
St. George Tucker (1752–1827)
Jonathan Jasper Wright (1840–1885)

Twentieth Century

Shirley Schlanger Abrahamson (1933–)
Florence Ellinwood Allen (1884–1966)
Charles Fremont Amidon (1856–1937)
David L. Bazelon (1909–1993)
Griffin Bell (1918–)
Rose Elizabeth Bird (1936–1999)
Hugo Lafayette Black (1886–1971)
Luther Lee Bohanon (1902–)
Robert H. Bork (1927–)
Louis Dembitz Brandeis (1856–1941)
John R. Brown (1909–1993)
Warren Burger (1907–1995)
Benjamin N. Cardozo (1870–1938)
Walter Clark (1846–1924)
Frank Hoover Easterbrook (1948–)
Henry White Edgerton (1888–1970)
Richard Alan Enslen (1931–)
Jerome Frank (1889–1957)
Felix Frankfurter (1882–1965)
Henry Jacob Friendly (1903–1986)
Augustus Noble Hand (1869–1954)
Learned Hand (1872–1961)
John Marshall Harlan II (1899–1971)
William Henry Hastie (1904–1976)
Clement Furman Haynsworth (1912–1989)
A. Leon Higginbotham Jr. (1928–1998)
Oliver Wendell Holmes Jr. (1841–1935)
James E. Horton Jr. (1878–1973)
Charles Evans Hughes (1862–1948)
Sarah Tilghman Hughes (1896–1985)
Frank M. Johnson Jr. (1918–)
William Wayne Justice (1920–)
Alex Kozinski (1950–)
Kenesaw Mountain Landis (1866–1944)
Harold Leventhal (1915–1979)
Hans A. Linde (1924–)
Carl Eugene McGowan (1911–1987)
Harold R. Medina (1888–1990)
Abner J. Mikva (1926–)
Constance Baker Motley (1921–)
Alfred P. Murrah (1904–1975)
John Johnson Parker (1885–1958)
Milton Pollack (1906–)
Richard A. Posner (1939–)
Cuthbert Winfred Pound (1864–1935)
William H. Rehnquist (1924–)
Richard T. Rives (1895–1982)
Walter Vincent Schaefer (1904–1986)
Samuel Seabury (1873–1958)
John Joseph Sirica (1904–1992)
Harlan Fiske Stone (1872–1946)
Roger John Traynor (1900–1983)
Elbert Parr Tuttle (1897–1996)
Arthur T. Vanderbilt (1888–1957)
Julius Waties Waring (1880–1968)
Earl Warren (1891–1974)
Jack B. Weinstein (1921–)
J. Harvie Wilkinson III (1944–)
John Minor Wisdom (1905–1999)
Charles E. Wyzanski Jr. (1906–1986)

Appendix C

Great American Judges Listed by Birth Year, Years of Life, Nation or State of Birth, Colleges Attended, and Courts over Which They Presided

Name	*Years*	*Nation or State of Birth*	*Undergraduate Education*[i]	*Graduate and/or Legal Education*[ii]	*Service as Judge or Justice*
Samuel Sewall	1652–1730	England	Harvard	M.A. Harvard	MA Gen. Ct. 1683–1684 MA Oyer & Terminer, 1692 Sup. Ct. of Judicature 1692–1718 Chief Justice of Ct. of Judicature, 1718–1728
Lewis Morris	1671–1746	NY	None	None	East Jersey, Court of Common Right, 1692–1698 Chief Justice, Supreme Court of NY, 1715–1733
Edmund Pendleton	1721–1803	VA	None	Read law	VA Court of Chancery, 1778–1779 VA Court of Appeals, President 1779–1803
George Wythe	1726–1806	VA	Tutoring	Read law	VA High Court of Chancery, 1778–1806
Robert Livingston Jr.	1746–1813	NY	King's (Columbia)	Read law	Chief, NY Chancery Court, 1777–1801
Theophilus Parsons	1750–1813	MA	Harvard	Read law	Chief Justice MA, 1806–1813
St. George Tucker	1752–1857	Bermuda	William & Mary	Read law	General Court of Virginia, 1788–1804 Virginia Supreme Court of Appeals, 1804–1811 U.S. District Judge, Virginia, 1813–1825
John Marshall	1755–1835	VA	Tutoring	William & Mary (Wythe) Read law	Chief Justice, U.S. Supreme Ct., 1801–1836
John Davis	1761–1847	MA	Harvard	Read law	Federal Judge, MA, 1801–1841

François-Xavier Martin	1762–1846	France	Tutored	Read law	Superior Court, Mississippi Territory, 1809–1810 Superior Court, Territory of Orleans, 1810–1813 Louisiana Supreme Court, 1815–1846 Chief Judge, Louisiana Supreme Court, 1836–1846
Spencer Roane	1762–1822	VA	William & Mary	William & Mary (Wythe) Read law	General Court of Virginia, 1789–1795 Virginia Court of Appeals, 1795–1822
James Kent	1763–1847	NY	Yale	Read law	Associate Justice, NY Supreme Court, 1798–1804 Chief Justice, NY Supreme Court, 1804–1814 Chancellor, New York, 1814–1823
William Cranch	1769–1855	MA	Harvard	Read law	D.C. Circuit Court, 1801–1855 Chief Judge of D.C. Circuit, 1806–1855
Roger Taney	1777–1864	MD	Dickinson	Read law	Chief Justice, U.S. Supreme Court, 1836–1864
Joseph Story	1779–1845	MA	Harvard	Read law	Assoc. Jus., U.S. Supreme Court, 1811–1845
John Bannister Gibson	1780–1853	PA	Dickinson	Read law	PA Court of Common Pleas, 11th Cir., 1813–1816 PA Supreme Court, 1816–1853
Lemuel Shaw	1781–1861	MA	Harvard	Read law	Chief Justice MA Supreme Court, 1830–1860
Isaac Blackford	1776–1859	NJ	Princeton	Read law	1st Territorial Circuit Ct. of IN, 1814–1816 Supreme Court of IN, 1817–1853 U.S. Court of Claims, 1855–1859
Thomas Ruffin	1787–1870	VA	Princeton	Read law	North Carolina Superior Court, 1816–1818, 1825–1829 North Carolina Supreme Court, 1829–1852, 1858–1859 Chief Justice, NC Supreme Court, 1833–1852

Name	*Years*	*Nation or State of Birth*	*Undergraduate Education*[i]	*Graduate and/or Legal Education*[ii]	*Service as Judge or Justice*
William Harper	1790–1847	Leeward Islands	South Car. College	Read law	Chancellor, Territorial Court of MO, 1819–1823 Chancellor, South Carolina, 1828–1830 Court of Appeals, South Carolina, 1830–1835, 1835–1847
Nathan Green Sr.	1792–1866	VA		Read law?	Tennessee Chancery Court, 1826– Tenn. Supreme Court of Errors & Appeals, 1831–1834 Tennessee Supreme Court, 1834–1852
Thomas A. Marshall	1794–1871	KY	Yale	Read law	KY Court of Appeals, 1835–1856, 1866–1867
Joseph H. Lumpkin	1799–1867	GA	Princeton	Read law	Supreme Court of GA, 1845–1866
John Hemphill	1803–1862	SC	Jefferson College	Read law	Texas District Judge & TX S. Court, 1840 Chief Justice, TX Supreme Court, 1840–1859
John Appleton	1804–1891	NH	Bowdoin	Read law M.A. Bowdoin	Associate, Maine Supreme Court, 1852–1862 Chief Justice, Maine Supreme Court, 1862–1883
Samuel Ames	1806–1865	RI	Brown	Read law Litchfield, CT	Chief Justice, Rhode Island Supreme Ct., 1856–1865
Thomas Drummond	1809–1890	ME	Bowdoin	Read law	U.S. Court of District of Illinois, 1850–1855 U.S. Court for Northern Dis. of IL, 1855–1869 U.S. 7th Judicial Circuit Court, 1869–1884
Edward George Ryan	1810–1880	Ireland	Jesuit Boarding School	Read law	Chief Justice, Wisconsin Supreme Court, 1874–1880

George Sharswood	1810–1883	PA	U. PA	Read law	District Court for Philadelphia, 1845–1867 President Judge of above, 1848–1867 PA Supreme Court, 1867–1882 Chief Justice, PA Supreme Court, 1879–1883
George F. Comstock	1811–1892	NY	Union College	Read law	New York Court of Appeals, 1856–1861
George W. Stone	1811–1894	VA		Read law	North Carolina 9th Circuit Court, 1842–1849 North Carolina Supreme Court, 1856–1865 North Carolina Supreme Court, 1876–1894 Chief Justice, 1884–1894
Stephen Field	1816–1899	CT	Williams College	Read law	California Supreme Court, 1857–1863 Associate Justice, U.S. Supreme Court, 1863–1897
Thomas M. Cooley	1824–1898	NY	Attica Academy High School	Read law	Michigan Supreme Court, 1865–1885 Chair, Interstate Commerce Comm., 1887–1891
Matthew Deady	1824–1893	MD	Barnesville Academy	Read law	Territorial Court of Oregon, 1853–1859 U.S. District Judge, Oregon, 1859–1893
Roy Bean	1825–1903	KY	None	None	Texas Justice of the Peace 1882–1903. Not always there by official appointment or election.
Hugh Bond	1828–1893	MD	New York U.	Read law	Baltimore Crim. Ct., 1861–1867 U.S. 4th Circuit., 1870–1893
Horace Gray	1828–1902	MA	Harvard	Harvard	Mass. Supreme Court, 1864–1882 Chief Justice, MA Supreme Court, 1871–1882 U.S. Supreme Court, 1882–1902
Charles Doe	1830–1896	NH	Harvard: attended Dartmouth: graduated	Read law Harvard	NH Supreme Court, 1859–1896 Chief Justice NH Supreme Court, 1876–1896

Name	*Years*	*Nation or State of Birth*	*Undergraduate Education*[i]	*Graduate and/or Legal Education*[ii]	*Service as Judge or Justice*
William Mitchell	1832–1900	Canada	Jefferson College	Read law	District Court, 3d Circuit, Minnesota, 1874–1881 Minnesota Supreme Court, 1881–1900
John Marshall Harlan	1833–1911	KY	Centre College	Transylvania U.	Franklin County Court, 1858–1861 Associate Justice, U.S. Supreme Court, 1877–1911
Isaac C. Parker	1838–1896	OH	None	Read law	12th Missouri Circuit, 1868–1870 U.S. District Court (W. AK), 1875–1896
Jonathan J. Wright	1840–1885	PA	Lancasterian Academy	Read law	S. Carolina Supreme Court, 1870–1877
Oliver Wendell Holmes, Jr.	1841–1935	MA	Harvard	Harvard	Massachusetts Supreme Court, 1883–1902 Chief Judge of MA Supreme Court, 1899–1902 U.S. Supreme Court, 1902–1932
Walter Clark	1846–1924	NC	U. N. Carolina	Columbia Law School (D.C.)	Superior Court Judge, North Carolina, 1885–1889 North Carolina Supreme Court, 1889–1924 Chief Justice, NC Supreme Court, 1903–1924
Charles F. Amidon	1856–1937	NY	Hamilton College	Read law	U.S. District Court, North Dakota, 1896–1928 Sometimes worked on U.S. 8th Circuit Ct. of Appeals
Louis Brandeis	1856–1941	KY	Annen–Realschule, Germany	Harvard	U.S. Supreme Court, 1916–1939
Kenesaw M. Landis	1866–1944	OH	None	Union College of Law (Chicago)	U.S. District Judge, Northern Illinois, 1905–1922

Charles Evan Hughes	1862–1948	NY	Colgate Brown	Columbia	Associate, U.S. Supreme Court, 1910–1916 Chief Justice, U.S. Supreme Court, 1930–1941
Cuthbert Pound	1864–1935	NY	Cornell	Read law	New York State Supreme Court, 1906–1915 New York Court of Appeals, 1918–1934 Chief Justice, NY Court of Appeals, 1932–1934
Augustus N. Hand	1869–1954	NY	Harvard	Harvard	U.S. District Court (Southern Dist. N.Y.), 1914–1927 U.S. 2d Circuit Court, 1927–1954
Benjamin Cardozo	1870–1938	NY	Columbia	M.A. Columbia Columbia Law	NY Supreme Court, 1913–1917 NY Court of Appeals, 1917–1932 Chief, 1926–1932 U.S. Supreme Court, 1932–1938
Learned Hand	1872–1961	NY	Harvard	M.A. Harvard Harvard	U.S. District Court, New York, 1909–1924 U.S. Court of Appeals, 2d Cir., 1925–1951 Senior Judge, U.S. 2d Cir., 1948–1951 Senior Status, U.S. 2d Cir., 1951–1961
Harlan Fiske Stone	1872–1946	NH	Amherst	Columbia	Associate, U.S. Supreme Court, 1925–1941 Chief Justice, U.S. Supreme Court, 1941–1946
Samuel Seabury	1873–1958	NY		NY Law School	New York City Court, 1901–1906? New York Supreme Court, 1906–1914? New York Court of Appeals, 1915–1916
James Edwin Horton Jr.	1878–1973	AL	Vanderbilt	Cumberland U. Cumberland U	Chancellor, N. Chancery Division of AL, 1915–1917 8th Circuit Court of Appeals, 1928–1935
Julius Waties Waring	1880–1968	SC	College of Charleston	Read law	U.S. District Judge (Eastern, SC), 1942–1952
Felix Frankfurter	1882–1965	Austria	City College of NY	Harvard	U.S. Supreme Court, 1939–1962

Name	*Years*	*Nation or State of Birth*	*Undergraduate Education*[i]	*Graduate and/or Legal Education*[ii]	*Service as Judge or Justice*
Florence E. Allen	1884–1966	UT	W. Reserve	M.A. Western Reserve New York University	Cleveland Ct. of Common Pleas. 1920–1922 Ohio Supreme Court, 1922–1934 U.S. 6th Circuit Ct., 1934–1959
John J. Parker	1885–1958	NC	U. of NC	U. North Carolina	U.S. 4th Circuit Court of Appeals, 1925–1958
Hugo Black	1886–1971	AL		University of Alabama	Police Court, 1910–1911 U.S. Supreme Court, 1937–1971
Henry White Edgerton	1888–1970	KS	U. of Wis. Cornell	Harvard	U.S. Court of Appeals, D.C., 1937–1970 Chief Judge, U.S. Ct. of Appeals, D.C., 1955–58 Senior Judge, U.S. Ct. of Appeals, D.C., 1963–70
Harold Medina	1888–1990	NY	Princeton	Columbia	U.S. District Court (Southern NY), 1947–1951 U.S. 2d Circuit Court of Appeals, 1951–1958 Senior Status, 2d Circuit, 1958–1980
Arthur T. Vanderbilt	1888–1957	NJ	Wesleyan	Columbia	Chief Justice, New Jersey Supreme Court, 1948–1957
Jerome Frank	1889–1957	NY	Chicago	Ph.D. Chicago	U.S. 2nd Circuit Court of Appeals, 1941–1957
Earl Warren	1891–1974	CA	Berkeley	Berkeley	Chief Justice, U.S. Supreme Court, 1953–1969
Richard T. Rives	1895–1982	AL	Tulane	Read law	U.S. 5th Circuit Court of Appeals, 1951–1981 Chief Judge, U.S. 5th Circuit, 1959–1960 Senior Status, U.S. 5th Circuit, 1966–1981 Senior Status, U.S. 6th Circuit, 1981–1982
Sarah T. Hughes	1896–1985	MD	Goucher Col.	Geo. Washington	Texas State District Court, 1935–1962 U.S. District Court, Texas, 1962–1985

Elbert Tuttle	1897–1996	CA	Cornell	Cornell	U.S. 5th Circuit Court of Appeals, 1954–1981 Chief Judge, 5th Circuit, 1961–1968 U.S. 6th Circuit Court of Appeals, 1981–1996
John Marshall Harlan II	1899–1971	IL	Princeton	Oxford NY Law	U.S. 2nd Circuit Court of Appeals, 1954–1955 U.S. Supreme Court, 1955–1971
Roger John Traynor	1900–1983	UT	Berkeley	Berkeley	Justice, California Supreme Court, 1940–1970 Chief Justice, CA Supreme Court, 1964–1970
Luther Lee Bohanon	1902–	AR	U. of OK	U. of Oklahoma	U.S. District Court for Oklahoma, 1969–1974 Senior Judge, U.S. Oklahoma, 1974–
Henry J. Friendly	1903–1986	NY	Harvard	Harvard	U.S. 2d Circuit Court of Appeals, 1959–1986 Chief Judge, 1971–1973 Senior Judge, 1974–1986
William Hastie	1904–1976	TN	Amherst	Harvard	U.S. District Court, Virgin Islands, 1937–1939 U.S. 3d Circuit Court of Appeals, 1950–1976 Chief Judge, 1968–1976
Alfred Paul Murrah	1904–1975	OK	U. of Oklahoma	U. of Oklahoma	U.S. District Court, 1937–1940 U.S. 10th Circuit Court, 1950–1975 Chief Judge, U.S. 10th Circuit, 1959–1970? Senior Status, U.S. 10th Circuit, 1970?–1975
Walter V. Schaefer	1904–1986	MI	Chicago	Chicago	Illinois Supreme Court, 1951–1976
John J. Sirica	1904–1992	CT	Columbia Prep. School	Georgetown	U.S. District Court, D.C., 1957–1986 Chief Judge of D.C. District, 1971–1974 Senior Status, 1977–1986
John M. Wisdom	1905–	LA	Washington & Lee	Tulane	U.S. 5th Circuit Court of Appeals, 1957–1977 Senior Status, U.S. 5th Circuit, 1977–1999

Name	Years	Nation or State of Birth	Undergraduate Education[i]	Graduate and/or Legal Education[ii]	Service as Judge or Justice
Milton Pollack	1906–1999	NY	Columbia	Columbia	U.S. District Court, Southern District NY, 1967–
Charles Wyzanski Jr.	1906–1986	MA	Harvard	Harvard	U.S. District Court, MA, 1941–1986 Chief, 1965–1971 Senior Status, 1971–1986
Warren Burger	1907–1995	MN	U. Minnesota	St. Paul C. of Law	U.S. Court of Appeals for D.C., 1955–1969 Chief Justice, U.S. Supreme Court, 1969–1986
David Bazelon	1909–1993	WI	Northwestern B.S. in law		U.S. Ct. of Appeals for D.C., 1950–1919 Chief Judge, D.C. Appeals, 1962–1978 Senior Judge, D.C. Appeals, 1978–1986
John R. Brown	1909–1993	NE	U. of Nebraska	U. Michigan	U.S. 5th Circuit Ct., 1955–1979 Senior Status, 1979–1991?
Carl McGowan	1911–1987	IN	Dartmouth	Columbia	U.S. D.C. Circuit Ct. of Appeals, 1963–1987 Chief Judge, 1981 Senior Status, 1981–1987
Skelly J. Wright	1911–1988	LA	Loyola U.	Loyola U.	U.S. District Ct., E. LA, 1950–1962 U.S. Ct. of Appeals for D.C., 1961–1988 Chief Judge, D.C. Circuit, 1978–1981 Senior Status, 1986–1988
Clement F. Haynsworth	1912–1989	SC	Furman	Harvard	U.S. 4th Circuit Court, 1957–1989 Chief Judge, 4th Circuit, 1964–1981
Harold Leventhal	1915–1979	NY	Columbia	Columbia	U.S. Court of Appeals, D.C., 1965–1979

Griffin Bell	1918–	GA	GA Southwestern	Mercer	U.S. 5th Circuit Court of Appeals, 1961–1975
Frank M. Johnson	1918–	AL		U. Alabama	U.S. Federal District Judge, 1955–1979 U.S. 11th Circuit, 1979–1996
William Wayne Justice	1920–	TX	U. of Texas	U. Texas, Austin	U.S. District Judge (East Texas), 1968–1998 Chief Judge, 1980–1998 Senior Status, 1998–
Constance Baker Motley	1921–	CT	Fisk NYU	Columbia	U.S. District Judge (Southern NY) 1966– Chief Judge, 1982–1986 Senior Status, 1986–
Jack Weinstein	1921–	KS	Brooklyn College	Columbia	U.S. District (Eastern NY) 1967– Chief Judge, 1981–1988 Senior Judge, 1993–
Hans A. Linde	1924–	Germany	Reed	Berkeley	Oregon Supreme Court, 1977–1990
William Rehnquist	1924–	WI	Kenyon Stanford	MA, Stanford/ Harvard	Associate Justice, U.S. Supreme Court, 1971–1986 Chief Justice, U.S. Supreme Court, 1986–
Abner J. Mikva	1926–	WI	U. Wisconsin Washington U. (St. Louis)	Chicago	U.S. Circuit Court, D.C., 1979–1994
Robert Bork	1927–	PA	Chicago	Chicago	U.S. Circuit Court, D.C., 1982–1988
Leon Higginbotham Jr.	1928–1998	NJ	Purdue Antioch	Yale	U.S. District Court, PA, 1964–1977 U.S. 3d Circuit, 1977–1993 Chief Judge, 3d Circuit, 1989–1991

Name	*Years*	*Nation or State of Birth*	*Undergraduate Education*[i]	*Graduate and/or Legal Education*[ii]	*Service as Judge or Justice*
Richard A. Enslen	1931–	MI	Kalamazoo Col.	Wayne State Univ. VA (LL.M.)	State District Judge, Michigan, 1968–1970 U.S. District Judge (Western MI), 1979– Chief Judge, U.S. District, Western MI, 1999–2001
Shirley S. Abrahamson	1933–	NY	New York U.	Indiana Law School Univ. of Wisconsin	Justice, Wisconsin Supreme Court, 1976–1996 Chief Justice, Wisconsin Supreme Court, 1996–
Rose Elizabeth Bird	1936–1999	AZ	Long Island U.	Berkeley	Chief Justice, California Supreme Court, 1977–1986
Richard Posner	1939–	NY	Yale	Harvard	U.S. 7th Circuit Court of Appeals, 1981– Chief Judge, 1993–2000
J. Harvey Wilkinson III	1944–	NY	Yale	U. Virginia	U.S. 4th Circuit Court of Appeals, 1984–
Frank Easterbrook	1948–	NY	Swarthmore	Chicago	U.S. 7th Circuit Court of Appeals, 1985–
Alex Kozinski	1950–	Bulgaria	UCLA	UCLA	U.S. Court of Claims, 1982–1985 U.S. 9th Circuit Court of Appeals, 1985–

[i] In early years, students sometimes went directly from high school to law programs, so some individuals who received degrees from law schools will not have an undergraduate affiliation listed.

[ii] In colonial times, individuals sometimes served on the bench without any formal college education. Even in the early years of the Republic, when American law schools were scarce or nonexistent, lawyers often "read law" in the offices of attorneys rather than continuing formal legal training in a university setting. George Wythe was among the notable lawyers (and judges) who was known for his work in mentoring new lawyers in this fashion.

Appendix D

United States Supreme Court Justices Listed by Name, Years of Life, Nation or State of Birth, Education, Years of Prior Judicial Service, and Years of Service on the Court

Name	*Years*	*Nation or State of Birth*	*Undergraduate Education*	*Law School*	*Prior Judicial Experience St./Fed./Total*	*Appointing President*	*Yrs. of Ser. U.S. Sup. Ct.*
John Jay*	1745–1829	NY	King's College	Read law	0–2–2	Washington	1789–1795
John Rutledge	1739–1800	SC	None	Read law/Middle Temple	0–6–6	Washington	1739–1800
William Cushing	1732–1810	MA	Harvard	Read law	0–29–29	Washington	1790–1810
James Wilson	1742–1798	Scotland	St. Andrews	Read law	0–0–0	Washington	1789–1798
John Blair Jr.	1732–1800	VA	William & Mary	Middle Temple	0–11–11	Washington	1790–1796
James Iredell	1751–1799	England	None	Read law	0–1/2–1/2	Washington	1790–1799
Thomas Johnson	1732–1819	MD	None	Read law	1–1 1/2–1 1/2	Washington	1793–1806
William Paterson	1745–1806	Ireland	Col. of N.J. (Princeton)	Read law	0–0–0	Washington	1793–1806
John Rutledge*	1739–1800	SC		Read law/Middle Temple	0–6–6	Washington	1795–1800
Samuel Chase	1741–1811	MD	None	Read law	0–9–9	Washington	1796–1811
Oliver Ellsworth*	1745–1807	CT	Yale/Col. of N.J.	Read law	0–5–5	Washington	1796–1800
Bushrod Washington	1762–1829	VA	William & Mary	Read law	0–0–0	Adams	1799–1829
Alfred Moore	1755–1810	NC	None	Read law	0–1–1	Adams	1800–1804
John Marshall*	1755–1835	VA	None	William & Mary	0–0–0	Adams	1801–1836
William Johnson	1771–1834	SC	Col. of N.J.	Read law	0–6–6	Jefferson	1804–1834
Henry B. Livingston	1757–1823	NY	Col. of N.J.	Read law	0–0–0	Jefferson	1807–1823
Thomas Todd	1765–1826	VA	Liberty Hall (W& L)	Read law	0–6–6	Jefferson	1807–1826
Gabriel Duvall	1752–1844	MD	None	Read law	0–6–6	Madison	1811–1835

Joseph Story	1779–1845	MA	Harvard	Read law	0–0–0	Madison	1812–1845
Smith Thompson	1768–1843	NY	Col. of N.J.	Read law	0–16–16	Monroe	1823–1843
Robert Trimble	1779–1828	VA	KY Acad. (Translv.)	Read law	9–2–11	J.Q. Adams	1826–1828
John McLean	1785–1861	NJ	None	Read law	0–6–6	Jackson	1830–1861
Henry Baldwin	1780–1844	CT	Yale	Read law	0–0–0	Jackson	1830–1844
James Wayne	1790–1867	GA	Col. of N.J.	Read law	0–5–5	Jackson	1835–1867
Roger B. Taney*	1777–1864	MD	Dickinson	Read law	0–0–0	Jackson	1836–1864
Philip P. Barbour	1783–1841	VA	William & Mary	Read law	6–2–8	Jackson	1836–1841
John Catron	1786–1865	PA	None	Read law	0–10–10	Jackson	1837–1865
John McKinley	1780–1852	VA	None	Read law	0–0–0	Van Buren	1838–1852
Peter V. Daniel	1784–1860	VA	Col. of N.J.	Read law	4–0–4	Van Buren	1842–1860
Samuel Nelson	1792–1873	NY	Middlebury	Read law	0–22–22	Tyler	1845–1872
Levi Woodbury	1789–1851	NH	Dartmouth	Litchfield	0–6–6	Polk	1845–1851
Robert C. Grier	1794–1870	PA	Dickinson	Read law	0–13–13	Polk	1846–1870
Benjamin R. Curtis	1809–1874	MA	Harvard	Harvard	0–0–0	Fillmore	1851–1857
John A. Campbell	1811–1889	GA	UGA/West Point	Read law	0–0–0	Pierce	1853–1861
Nathan Clifford	1803–1881	NH	None	Read law	0–0–0	Buchanan	1858–1881
Noah H. Swayne	1804–1884	VA	None	Read law	0–0–0	Lincoln	1862–1881
Samuel F. Miller	1816–1890	KY	Transylvania (M.D.)	Read law	0–0–0	Lincoln	1862–1890
David Davis	1815–1886	MD	Kenyon	N. Haven Law (Yale)	0–14–14	Lincoln	1862–1877
Stephen J. Field	1816–1899	CT	Williams	Read law	0–6–6	Lincoln	1863–1897

Name	*Years*	*Nation or State of Birth*	*Undergraduate Education*	*Law School*	*Prior Judicial Experience St./Fed./Total*	*Appointing President*	*Yrs. of Ser. U.S. Sup. Ct.*
Salmon P. Chase*	1808–1873	NH	Dartmouth	Read law	0–0–0	Lincoln	1864–1873
William Strong	1808–1895	CT	Yale	Yale	1–11–12	Grant	1870–1880
Joseph B. Bradley	1813–1892	NY	Rutgers	Read law	0–0–0	Grant	1870–1892
Ward Hunt	1810–1886	NY	Union	Litchfield	0–8–8	Grant	1873–1882
Morrison B. Waite*	1816–1888	CT	Yale	Read law	0–0–0	Grant	1874–1888
John Marshall Harlan	1833–1911	KY	Centre	Transylvania/Read law	0–1–1	Hayes	1877–1911
William B. Woods	1824–1887	OH	Western Res./Yale	Read law	12–0–12	Hayes	1881–1887
Stanley Matthews	1824–1889	OH	Kenyon	Read law	0–4–4	Garfield	1881–1889
Horace Gray	1828–1902	MA	Harvard	Harvard	0–18–18	Arthur	1882–1902
Samuel Blatchford	1820–1893	NY	Columbia	Read law	15–0–15	Arthur	1882–1903
Lucius Q.C. Lamar	1825–1893	GA	Emory College	Read law	0–0–0	Cleveland	1888–1893
Melville W. Fuller*	1833–1910	ME	Bowdoin	Read law/Harvard	0–0–0	Cleveland	1888–1910
David J. Brewer	1837–1910	Turkey	Wesleyan/Yale	Albany	5–14–19	Harrison	1890–1910
Henry B. Brown	1836–1913	MA	Yale	Yale/Harvard	16–0–16	Harrison	1892–1903
George Shiras Jr.	1832–1924	PA	Ohio U./Yale	Yale	0–0–0	Harrison	1893–1895
Edward D. White	1845–1921	LA	Mt. St. Mary's Georgetown	U. of LA (Tulane)	1 1/2–0–1 1/2	Cleveland	1894–1910
Rufus W. Peckham	1838–1909	NY	None	Read law	0–0–0	Cleveland	1896–1909

Joseph McKenna	1843–1926	PA	Benicia Collegiate Institute	Read law	5–5–10	McKinley	1898–1925
Oliver W. Holmes Jr.	1841–1935	MA	Harvard	Harvard	0–20–20	T. Roosevelt	1902–1932
William R. Day	1849–1923	OH	Michigan	Michigan	0–0–0	T. Roosevelt	1903–1922
William H. Moody	1853–1917	MA	Harvard	Harvard/Read law	0–0–0	T. Roosevelt	1906–1910
Horace H. Lurton	1844–1914	KY	Chicago	Cumberland U.	16–10–26	Taft	1910–1914
Charles E. Hughes	1862–1948	NY	Colgate/Brown	Columbia	0–0–0	Taft	1910–1916
Edward D. White*	1845–1921	LA	Mt. St. Mary's Georgetown	U. of LA (Tulane)	1 1/2–16–17 1/2	Taft	1910–1921
Willis Van Devanter	1859–1941	IN	Indiana Asbury (DePauw)	U. Cincinnati	7–1–8	Taft	1911–1937
Joseph R. Lamar	1857–1916	GA	Washington & Lee	Read law	0–2–2	Taft	1911–1916
Mahlon Pitney	1858–1924	NJ	Princeton (B.A. & M.A)	Read law	0–11–11	Taft	1912–1922
James C. McReynolds	1862–1946	KY	Vanderbilt	Virginia	0–0–0	Wilson	1914–1941
Louis D. Brandeis	1856–1941	KY	Annen–Realschule, Germany	Harvard	0–0–0	Wilson	1916–1939
John H. Clarke	1857–1945	OH	Western Reserve	Read law	2–0–2	Wilson	1916–1922
William H. Taft*	1857–1930	OH	Yale	Cincinnati	8–5–13	Harding	1921–1930
George Sutherland	1862–1942	England	Brigham Young	Michigan	0–0–0	Harding	1922–1938
Pierce Butler	1866–1939	MN	Carleton	Read law	0–0–0	Harding	1923–1939
Edward T. Sanford	1865–1930	TN	Tennessee	Harvard (M.A., LL.B)	14–0–14	Harding	1923–1920
Harlan Fiske Stone	1872–1946	NH	Amherst	Columbia	0–0–0	Coolidge	1925–1941
Charles E. Hughes*	1862–1948	NY	Colgate/Brown	Columbia	6–0–6	Hoover	1930–1941

Name	*Years*	*Nation or State of Birth*	*Undergraduate Education*	*Law School*	*Prior Judicial Experience St./Fed./Total*	*Appointing President*	*Yrs. of Ser. U.S. Sup. Ct.*
Owen J. Roberts	1875–1955	PA	Pennsylvania	Pennsylvania	0–0–0	Hoover	1930–1945
Benjamin N. Cardozo	1870–1938	NY	Columbia	Columbia	0–18–18	Hoover	1932–1938
Hugo L. Black	1886–1971	AL	U. Alabama Medical	U. Alabama	0–1 1/2–1 1/2	F.D.R.	1937–1971
Stanley F. Reed	1884–1980	KY	Ky. Wesleyan/Yale	Virginia/Columbia/ Sorbonne	0–0–0	F.D.R.	1938–1957
Felix Frankfurter	1882–1965	Austria	City College of N.Y.	Harvard	0–0–0	F.D.R.	1939–1962
William O. Douglas	1898–1980	MN	Whitman College	Columbia	0–0–0	F.D.R.	1939–1975
Frank Murphy	1890–1949	MI	Michigan	Michigan, Lincoln's Inn Trinity College, Dublin	0–7–7	F.D.R.	1940–1949
James F. Byrnes	1879–1972	SC	None	Read law	0–0–0	F.D.R.	1941–1942
Harlan Fiske Stone*	1872–1946	NH	Amherst	Columbia	16–0–16	F.D.R.	1941–1946
Robert H. Jackson	1892–1954	PA	None	Albany	0–0–0	F.D.R.	1941–1954
Wiley B. Rutledge	1894–1949	KY	Maryville C./Wisconsin	Colorado	4–0–4	F.D.R.	1943–1949
Harold H. Burton	1888–1965	MA	Bowdoin	Harvard	0–0–0	Truman	1945–1958
Fred M. Vinson*	1890–1953	KY	Centre College	Centre College	5–0–5	Truman	1946–1953
Tom C. Clark	1899–1977	TX	V.M.I./ Texas	Texas	0–0–0	Truman	1949–1967
Sherman Minton	1890–1965	IN	Indiana (LL.B.)	Yale (LL.M.)	8–0–8	Truman	1949–1956
Earl Warren*	1891–1974	CA	CA (Berkeley)	CA (Berkeley)	0–0–0	Eisenhower	1953–1969

John M. Harlan II	1899–1971	IL	Princeton	Oxford/NYU	1–0–1	Eisenhower	1955–1971
William J. Brennan Jr.	1906–1997	NJ	U. Pennsylvania	Harvard	0–7–7	Eisenhower	1956–1990
Charles E. Whittaker	1901–1973	MO		U. Kansas City Law	3–0–3	Eisenhower	1957–1962
Potter Stewart	1915–1985	OH	Yale/Cambridge	Yale	4–0–4	Eisenhower	1958–1981
Byron R. White	1917–2002	CO	Colorado	Yale	0–0–0	Kennedy	1962–1993
Arthur J. Goldberg	1908–1990	IL	Crane Jr./DePaul/ NW	Northwestern	0–0–0	Kennedy	1962–1965
Abe Fortas	1910–1982	TN	SW (Rhodes)	Yale	0–0–0	L.B. Johnson	1965–1969
Thurgood Marshall	1908–1993	MD	Lincoln University	Howard	3 3/4–0–3 3/4	L.B. Johnson	1967–1991
Warren E. Burger*	1907–1995	MN	U. Minn.	St. Paul College of Law	13–0–13	Nixon	1969–1986
Harry A. Blackmun	1908–1999	IL	Harvard	Harvard	11–0–11	Nixon	1970–1994
Lewis F. Powell Jr.	1907–1998	VA	Washington & Lee	Harvard	0–0–0	Nixon	1972–1987
William H. Rehnquist	1924–	WI	Stanford	M.A. Harvard/ M.A. Stanford/ LL.B. Stanford	0–0–0	Nixon	1972–1986
John Paul Stevens	1920–	IL	Chicago	Northwestern	5–0–5	Ford	1975–
Sandra Day O'Connor	1930–	TX	Stanford	Stanford	0–6 1/2–6 1/2	Reagan	1981–
William H. Rehnquist*	1924–	WI	Stanford	M.A. Harvard/ M.A. Stanford/ LL.B. Stanford	14–0–14	Reagan	1986–
Antonin Scalia	1936–	NJ	Georgetown/U. Fribourg	Harvard	4–0–4	Reagan	1986–
Anthony M. Kennedy	1936–	CA	Stanford/London Sch.	Harvard	12 1/2–0–12 1/2	Reagan	1988–
David H. Souter	1939	MA	Harvard/Oxford	Harvard	1/2–12–12 1/2	Bush	1990–
Clarence Thomas	1948	GA	Holy Cross	Yale	1/2–0–1/2	Bush	1991–

Ruth Bader Ginsburg	1933	NY	Cornell	Harvard/Columbia	13–0–13	Clinton	1993–
Stephen G. Breyer	1938	CA	Stanford/Magdalen	Harvard	14–0–14	Clinton	1994–

*Indicates that an individual was appointed to serve as a chief justice. In cases where a chief was appointed from within the Court, prior years of experience on the Supreme Court are included in years of experience as a federal judge.

Materials for this appendix were primarily gathered from Henry J. Abraham, *Justices, Presidents, and Senators: A History of the U.S. Supreme Court Appointments from Washington to Clinton* (Lanham, Md.: Rowman & Littlefield Publishers, 1999), see especially pp. 38–40 and 377–381. Information about educational degrees was primarily taken from Lisa Paddock, *Facts about the Supreme Court of the United States* (New York: H. W. Wilson Company, 1996).

How Well Do You Know Your Great American Judges?

Which great American judge:

* Was the only woman to serve on the Wisconsin Supreme Court prior to 1993? [Shirley S. Abrahamson]
* Was the first woman to sit on both a state supreme court and a federal court of general jurisdiction? [Florence Ellinwood Allen]
* Set high standards for publication of appellate court decisions while serving as chief justice of the Rhode Island Supreme Court? [Samuel Ames]
* Served from 1896 to 1921 as the only federal judge in North Dakota? [Charles F. Amidon]
* Pushed for legal and constitutional reform before being named chief justice of Maine? [John Appleton]
* Served on the United States Circuit Court for the District of Columbia and was influential in reshaping the M'Naghton Rule that had applied to insanity? [David L. Bazelton]
* Was a notorious Texas judge ("the law West of the Pecos") who once fined a dead man forty dollars for carrying a concealed weapon and then pocketed the fee? He was also known for telling newlyweds, "And may God have mercy on your souls." [Roy Bean]
* Served as an attorney general in the administration of Pres. Jimmy Carter after having previously stepped down from his position as a judge on the United States Fifth Circuit Court of Appeals? [Griffin Bell]
* Became embroiled in controversy for what were regarded as her liberal decisions as chief justice of the California Supreme Court and was denied reconfirmation by the voters? [Rose E. Bird]

* Was discovered to have been a member of the Ku Klux Klan prior to his appointment to the United States Supreme Court but went on to have an illustrious career arguing that the entire Bill of Rights should be applied to the states through the Fourteenth Amendment? [Hugo L. Black]
* Served for more than thirty-five years on the Indiana Supreme Court and authored a series of notable court reports? [Isaac Blackford]
* Is credited with having done more to shape Oklahoma law in the 1960s and 1970s than any other individual? [Luther Lee Bohanon]
* Served on the United States Fourth Circuit during and after Reconstruction and was known both for defending the rights of African Americans and for promoting economic nationalism and industrial capitalism? [Hugh Lennox Bond]
* Was the solicitor general who carried out President Nixon's order to fire Special Prosecutor Archibald Cox, was subsequently denied a seat on the United States Supreme Court, and is today considered to be a champion of conservative jurisprudence? [Robert H. Bork]
* Was the first Jew to serve on the United States Supreme Court and the man who, prior to his appointment, authored a famous kind of legal brief that still bears his name? [Louis D. Brandeis]
* Was a Texan who became a judicial activist on the United States Fifth Circuit Court of Appeals, where he served from 1955 to 1993? [John R. Brown]
* Was appointed as chief justice of the United States Supreme Court when Earl Warren retired and is well known for his efforts on behalf of streamlining judicial administration? [Warren Burger]
* Made his reputation on the New York Court of Appeals where he served from 1914 to 1932 prior to being appointed to the United States Supreme Court and remains one of the most quoted federal judges in law school casebooks? [Benjamin N. Cardozo]
* Made his reputation as a North Carolina Supreme Court justice for criticizing the federal judiciary and advocating constitutional reforms? [Walter Clark]
* Served on the New York Court of Appeals and was influential in reorganizing Genesee College into Syracuse University? [George F. Comstock]
* Served on the Michigan Supreme Court for twenty years before becoming the first head of the Interstate Commerce Commission? [Thomas M. Cooley]
* Served for fifty years as a member of the Circuit Court of Appeals of the District of Columbia but is more frequently recognized as an early compiler of United States Supreme Court decisions? [William Cranch]
* Served from 1801 to 1841 on a federal district court of Massachusetts, where he developed a reputation for his rulings on admiralty law? [John Davis]

* Served both on the territorial court of Oregon and as the state's first federal judge? [Matthew P. Deady]
* Served for thirty-seven years on the New Hampshire Supreme Court? [Charles C. Doe]
* Served as a federal judge in Illinois during the time that Abraham Lincoln practiced in the state? [Thomas Drummond]
* Is the contemporary judge on the United States Seventh Court of Appeals most closely associated with Judge Richard Posner and his views on law and economics? [Frank H. Easterbrook]
* Served on the United States Circuit Court of Appeals for the District of Columbia and declared racial segregation to be unconstitutional four years before the United States Supreme Court agreed with him in its historic decision in *Brown v. Board of Education* (1954)? [Henry White Edgerton]
* While serving as a federal judge in Michigan has developed a reputation for his work on alternate dispute resolution in federal courts? [Richard A. Enslen]
* Was believed to have been the target of an assassination attempt by a former colleague on the California Supreme Court while serving as a United States Supreme Court justice? [Stephen J. Field]
* Authored *Law and the Modern Mind* before serving for sixteen years as a federal appellate judge? [Jerome N. Frank]
* Was a Harvard law professor and strong supporter of Franklin D. Roosevelt's New Deal before being appointed to the United States Supreme Court, where he surprised many individuals by his conservatism? [Felix Frankfurter]
* Was a onetime law clerk to Supreme Court justice Louis Brandeis who served on the United States Second Court of Appeals and was especially known for his rulings on administrative law? [Henry J. Friendly]
* Served as Pennsylvania's longest-serving Supreme Court justice and once authored a dissenting opinion questioning the doctrine of judicial review whereby federal courts can declare congressional laws to be unconstitutional? [John Bannister Gibson]
* Served as a reporter for the Supreme Judicial Court of Massachusetts before being appointed as an associate justice where he served for seventeen years before being appointed to the United States Supreme court? [Horace Gray]
* Served as chief justice of the Tennessee Supreme Court, a position that was later occupied by his grandson? [Nathan Green Sr.]
* Was a cousin of Learned Hand who helped craft an exception to the Hicklin Test, which was at the time applied to obscenity law? [Augustus N. Hand]
* Was a New York judge who is often cited as the most capable twentieth-century judge who was never appointed to the United States Supreme Court? [Learned Hand]

* Authored the famous dissent in *Plessy v. Ferguson* (1896) in which he opposed the doctrine of "separate but equal" in race relations? [John Marshall Harlan]
* Was the grandson of an earlier Supreme Court justice, also known for his dissents, albeit largely from a liberal court rather than a conservative one? [John Marshall Harlan II]
* Served as a chancellor in both Missouri and South Carolina and was known for his defense of slavery? [William Harper]
* Was a highly successful attorney for the Legal Defense Fund of the National Association for the Advancement of Colored People before being named as the first African American federal judge? [William H. Hastie]
* Was a long-serving judge on the United States Fourth Circuit who was rejected by the Senate for the United States Supreme Court but was eventually honored when the federal courthouse in Greenville, South Carolina, was named after him? [Clement F. Haynsworth Jr.]
* Served as chief justice of both the Republic and the state of Texas and has been likened to John Marshall for the influence he had on law within the state? [John Hemphill]
* Was only the third African American to serve as a chief judge in a federal appellate court and wrote an "open letter" to incoming United States Supreme Court justice Clarence Thomas criticizing his views on civil rights? [A. Leon Higginbotham Jr.]
* Fought and was wounded in the U.S. Civil War, authored *The Common Law*, and went on to become one of the best-recognized and longest-serving United States Supreme Court Justices? [Oliver Wendell Holmes Jr.]
* Was the courageous Alabama judge who overturned a jury verdict in the *Scottsboro Boys* case, lost his bid for reelection, and subsequently retired to his farm? [James E. Horton Jr.]
* Was a former New York governor who resigned from the United States Supreme Court in an unsuccessful bid for the presidency but later served as chief justice during Franklin D. Roosevelt's proposed "court-packing plan"? [Charles Evans Hughes]
* Was the federal district judge in Texas who swore in Lyndon B. Johnson as president after the assassination of Pres. John F. Kennedy? [Sarah Tilghman Hughes]
* Was an activist federal judge who enforced civil rights decisions, ordered reform, and was once told by Alabama governor George Wallace that he needed a "barbed wire enema"? [Frank M. Johnson Jr.]
* Was described as "the law East of the Pecos" and was known for his activism in cases involving Texas public schools, the juvenile justice system, and the treatment of the mentally ill and of prisoners? [William Wayne Justice]

* Is probably better known for his *Commentary on American Law* than for his service as New York chancellor? [James Kent]
* Was born in Romania, serves on the United States Fourth Circuit Court of Appeals, and is well known for his view that commercial speech should be accorded the same constitutional protection as other speech? [Alex Kozinski]
* Was a former United States district judge in Illinois but is best known for his role as a baseball commissioner, in which role he helped restore a reputation of integrity to the sport? [Kenesaw Mountain Landis]
* Served on the United States Court of Appeals for the District of Columbia from 1965 to 1979 and is best known for his decisions involving administrative law? [Harold Leventhal]
* Has served on the Oregon Supreme Court and is best known for championing the view that state judges should consult their own constitutions before looking at the U.S. Constitution? [Hans A. Linde]
* Was the first chancellor of New York, helped negotiate the purchase of the Louisiana Territory, and later became involved in the steamboat monopoly case that led to the famous United States Supreme Court decision in *Gibbons v. Ogden* (1824)? [Robert R. Livingston Jr.]
* Is generally credited with being the most influential individual in establishing the Georgia Supreme Court on a firm foundation? [Joseph Henry Lumpkin]
* Served on the United States Court of Appeals for the District of Columbia during the 1960s and 1970s and often expressed his views in law journals on matters involving separation of powers? [Carl E. McGowan]
* Was a cousin of Thomas Jefferson best known for having been both a participant in, and the decider of, the case of *Marbury v. Madison* (1803), which established the power of the United States Supreme Court to invalidate unconstitutional federal legislation? [John Marshall]
* Was married to the sister of Chief Justice John Marshall, with whom he shared his surname, and served multiple times as chief justice of the Kentucky Supreme Court? [Thomas A. Marshall]
* Served for many years on the Louisiana Supreme Court and is credited with helping to standardize and "Americanize" the Louisiana legal system? [François-Xavier Martin]
* Is best known for presiding over the trial of leading American Communists under the Smith Act in a case later appealed to the United States Supreme Court as *Dennis v. United States* (1951)? [Harold R. Medina]
* Served as a congressman and White House counsel before being appointed to the United States Circuit Court for the District of Columbia? [Abner J. Mikva]

* Was a nineteenth-century judge, first in a United States district court and then on the Minnesota Supreme Court, who subsequently had a law school named after him? [William Mitchell]
* Is best known for having been fired as chief justice of the New York Supreme Court for a dissent denying the power of the royal governor to create a court of equity simply to serve his own purposes? [Lewis Morris]
* Was the first African American woman to serve in the New York state senate and on the federal judiciary? [Constance Baker Motley]
* Was a pioneer in Oklahoma justice who had a federal building named after him that was later the target of domestic terrorists? [Alfred P. Murrah]
* Served in Fort Smith, Arkansas, where he gained the reputation as perhaps the nation's foremost "hanging judge"? [Isaac C. Parker]
* Served on the United States Court of Appeals for the Fourth Circuit, was rejected by the Senate for a nomination to the United States Supreme Court, but continued his strong advocacy for the "New South"? [John J. Parker]
* Served toward the end of his life as chief justice of the Massachusetts Supreme Court, where he was credited with bringing about administrative reforms? His opinions were later collected in a volume called *Commentaries on American Law*. [Theophilus Parsons]
* Headed the Virginia judiciary from 1778 until 1803 and was sometimes involved in controversy with Virginia judge George Wythe? [Edmund Pendleton]
* Has served for more than thirty-five years as a United States district judge in New York, where he is well known for his handling of the Drexel Burnham Lambert mass class action suit and other high-profile cases? [Milton Pollack]
* Is both one of the most prolific writers and most-cited contemporary federal judges in the United States and who also serves as a law professor at the University of Chicago? [Richard A. Posner]
* Served for almost thirty years as a judge in New York and was a colleague of Benjamin Cardozo when both sat on the New York Court of Appeals? [Cuthbert W. Pound]
* Succeeded Warren Burger as chief justice of the United States Supreme Court and is one of only two justices to have presided over an impeachment of a U.S. president in the U.S. Senate? [William H. Rehnquist]
* Was an Alabama native who served on the Fifth Circuit Court of Appeals during the period in which that court made many historic rulings upholding and enforcing United States Supreme Court decisions relating to racial desegregation? [Richard Rives]
* Was a neighbor of Chief Justice John Marshall who articulated a very different view of federalism during his years as a member of the Virginia Court of Appeals? [Spencer Roane]

* Served as a prominent antebellum North Carolina judge who once refused to convict a slave owner who had shot and wounded a slave who fled from his chastisement and refused to stop? [Thomas Ruffin]
* Was born in Ireland and went on to become the third chief justice of the Wisconsin Supreme Court, where he was recognized for his acumen and productivity? [Edward George Ryan]
* Served on the Illinois Supreme Court from 1951 to 1976 and earned a reputation as a leading scholar-judge of state courts? [Walter V. Schaefer]
* Became known as a prominent New York reformer but resigned from his seat on the New York Court of Appeals in the unfulfilled expectation that he would receive Theodore Roosevelt's endorsement for governor? [Samuel Seabury]
* Apologized for his participation in the Salem witch trials and went on to serve for thirty-six years on the Supreme Court of Judicature of Massachusetts, including ten years as its chief justice? [Samuel Sewall]
* Was known for his extensive publications, his work as a law professor, and his service on a Pennsylvania district court and the Pennsylvania Supreme Court? [George Sharswood]
* Wrote Boston's first city charter before serving for thirty years as chief justice of the Massachusetts Supreme Court, where his decisions included the case of *Roberts v. City of Boston* (1849), in which he decided that the Constitution as then written (at that time there was no Fourteenth Amendment) did not prohibit racial segregation? [Lemuel Shaw]
* Became best known for his trial court decision in the Watergate tapes case but had considered becoming a prize fighter and actually participated in a professional welterweight match while he was awaiting the results of his bar exam? [John J. Sirica]
* Served for many years on the Alabama Supreme Court and was known for helping to professionalize the practice of law within the state? He also published humorous poetry, for which, however, his reputation is not as strong. [George Washington Stone]
* Was a former Columbia Law School dean who authored perhaps the most famous footnote in American case law in the *Carolene Products* Case prior to being elevated as chief justice of the United States Supreme Court, where he had previously served as an associate justice? Scholars do not generally credit his skills as a chief justice as much as they do his opinions. [Harlan Fiske Stone]
* Was a colleague of John Marshall on the United States Supreme Court and became known both as a Harvard lecturer and as the author of *Commentaries on the Constitution?* [Joseph Story]
* Was the chief justice who succeeded John Marshall on the United States Supreme Court and was well known for his decision in the *Charles River*

Bridge case prior to what is almost universally regarded as his disastrous decision in the *Dred Scott* case? [Roger Brooke Taney]

* Taught law and political science at the University of California at Berkeley before serving on the California Supreme Court for thirty years (six as chief justice), in which role he is considered to have been one of the most influential judges of the twentieth century? [Roger John Traynor]

* Edited and adapted Sir William Blackstone's *Commentaries on the Laws of England* for an American audience and served on the Virginia Court of Appeals from 1804 to 1811? [St. George Tucker]

* Was the grandson of a Civil War veteran, was born in California, studied in Hawaii, and served from 1961 to 1968 on the United States Fifth Circuit Court of Appeals, where he was a major figure in leading decisions related to racial desegregation? [Elbert Parr Tuttle]

* Served as chief justice of the New Jersey Supreme Court and is widely recognized as one of the leading judicial reformers of the twentieth century? [Arthur T. Vanderbilt]

* Was an eighth-generation Charlestonian whose civil rights decisions as a United States district judge eventually alienated him from most prominent members of that community? [J. Waties Waring]

* Served as governor of California and a Republican vice presidential nominee before becoming one of the most influential United States chief justices in U.S. history? During his service, the Supreme Court issued its historic opinion in *Brown v. Board of Education*. [Earl Warren]

* Has served for more than thirty years as a United States district judge in New York and authored a book entitled *Individual Justice in Mass Tort Litigation?* [Jack B. Weinstein]

* Wrote about his experiences as a clerk to United States Supreme Court justice Lewis Powell before being appointed to the United States Fourth Circuit Court of Appeals, where he has continued to publish scholarly books and articles? [J. Harvie Wilkinson III]

* Is considered to have been the intellectual leader of the judges on the United States Fifth Circuit Court of Appeals who issued major decisions involving civil rights cases from the 1950s through the 1970s? [John Minor Wisdom]

* Was the first United States district judge to order desegregation after the United States Supreme Court's decision in *Brown v. Board of Education* (1954) and was later appointed to the District of Columbia Circuit Court of Appeals, where he continued to issue controversial rulings? [James Skelly Wright]

* Became the first African American ever to sit on a state supreme court, serving on the South Carolina bench from 1870 to 1877? [Jonathan Jasper Wright]

* Served as the first professor of law in America and later as a Virginia chancellor, where he frequently came into conflict with Edmund Pendleton? He counted Thomas Jefferson and Henry Clay among his students before being poisoned by his nephew. [George Wythe]
* Was a prominent member of Franklin D. Roosevelt's "brain trust" before his appointment to a federal district court in Massachusetts, where he served for many years? [Charles E. Wyzanski Jr.]

Questions about judges described in sidebar boxes rather than in full entries: Which American judge:

* Was the first woman to both serve as an assistant U.S. attorney general and preside over a California appellate court? [Annette Abbott Adams]
* Served as a chief justice on both the Nevada and California supreme courts? [William H. Beatty]
* Came to know Abraham Lincoln while riding circuit in Illinois and was later appointed to a federal court in New Mexico, where he helped found the state's historical society? [Kirby Benedict]
* Is an African American judge in Memphis, Tennessee, who has starred in a television program in which he resolves disputes of individuals who appear before him? [Joe E. Brown Jr.]
* Became California's first woman judge? [Georgia Bullock]
* Was the first Puerto Rican ever appointed to a U.S. court on the mainland? [Jose Alberto Cabranes]
* Was born in Milan, Italy, became dean of the Yale Law School, and now serves on the United States Second Court of Appeals? [Guido Calabresi]
* Was a judge on the United States First Circuit Court of Appeals who penned a book entitled *The Ways of a Judge: Reflections from the Federal Appellate Bench?* [Frank M. Coffin]
* Was one of the most prominent English judges and is often associated with the idea that even a nation's highest legislative body is subject to judicial oversight? [Sir Edward Coke]
* Was a New York judge best known for continuing speculation about his unsolved disappearance? [Joseph Force Crater]
* Is a judge of Hispanic background who serves on the United States Fifth Circuit Court of Appeals and was considered for the United States Supreme Court in a nomination that eventually went to Justice Clarence Thomas? [Emilio M. Garza]
* Was the first Jewish woman ever to be appointed to the United States. Supreme Court? [Ruth Bader Ginsburg]
* Presided over a trial that became the basis for the Alfred Hitchcock film *Psycho?* [Robert Gollmar]

* Served on the Texas Supreme Court prior to being chosen by George W. Bush as his chief White House counsel? [Alberto R. Gonzalez]
* Returned to teaching at Hastings Law School after being ousted from the California Supreme Court in the same election that ousted Chief Justice Rose Bird? [Joseph R. Grodin]
* Served as chief of the Colorado territorial bench from 1866 to 1877 and then on the first United States District Court of Colorado from 1877 to 1906? [Moses Hallett]
* Served as chief justice of the Alabama Supreme Court prior to serving as a senator from that state? [Howell Heflin]
* Served as a justice of the Oklahoma Supreme Court and as a mayor of Oklahoma City and later donated his opulent house to the Oklahoma Heritage Association? [Richard A. Hefner]
* Served as the nation's first secretary of education after having previously served on the Ninth United States Circuit Court of Appeals? [Shirley Mount Hufstedler]
* Became the only federal judge siding with the Confederate States of America who was impeached and removed from office? [West H. Humphreys]
* Served in a succession of high English judicial offices and has a reputation for being among that nation's most "bloody" judges? [George Jeffreys]
* Became identified with the title "Golden Rule" when, as a police court judge, he tried to avoid incarcerating anyone? [Samuel Jones]
* Served as a United States district judge in New York, where he decided that James Joyce's *Ulysses* was not obscene and spoke out against Pres. Franklin D. Roosevelt's "court-packing plan"? [John C. Knox]
* Was a Texan long referred to as a "judge," who later became an official "referee" on bankruptcy matters before the United States District Court for the Western District of Texas? [Kirvin Kade Leggett]
* Served as a judge in both Colorado and California and was best known for his outspoken views on behalf of juvenile justice and sex education? [Benjamin B. Lindsey]
* Became the first woman in Georgia to win an elected judicial position to which she had not been previously appointed? [Rufe McCombs]
* Was one of the greatest civil rights litigators of the twentieth century, who went on to become the first African American United States Supreme Court justice? [Thurgood Marshall]
* Served, without a law degree, as a commissioner of the peace in Fairfax County, Virginia, and eventually opposed ratification of the U.S. Constitution that was being advocated by his neighbor George Washington? [George Mason]

* Was the first woman ever to serve as a United States District Court judge? [Burnita S. Matthews]
* Served as a criminal court judge in Birmingham, Alabama, and apparently killed himself after being accused of racketeering and extortion? [Jack Montgomery]
* Wrote a book in which she described herself as "America's Toughest Judge"? [Ellen Morphonious]
* Served as a justice in the peace in Wyoming, where she is believed to have been the first U.S. woman to have served as a judge? [Esther McQuigg Morris]
* Was a self-proclaimed "country judge" in Texas, where he was sworn in in 1949 as judge of the seventieth judicial district? [William P. Moss]
* Served in a variety of Indiana courts and helped initiate reforms of the state police courts? [John L. Niblack]
* Is a prominent scholar of Catholic canonical law who has continued to publish prolifically since his appointment to the Ninth United States Circuit Court of Appeals? [John T. Noonan Jr.]
* Served as an Arizona legislator before becoming the first woman ever appointed to the United States Supreme Court? [Sandra Day O'Connor]
* Served as a municipal judge in West Palm Beach and plotted to kill Florida circuit judge Curtis Chillingworth and his wife? [Joseph A. Peel]
* Recently reversed one of his earlier rulings in which he had questioned the scientific accuracy of fingerprint analysis? [Louis H. Pollack]
* Was a nineteenth-century Kentucky judge who was ferociously beaten by an attorney and apparently killed himself? [Richard Reid]
* Served as Hawaii's lieutenant governor before being installed as chief justice of the Hawaii Supreme Court? [William Shaw Richardson]
* Served as a Texas justice of the peace and became best known for issuing "peace bonds"? [W.E. "Bill" Richburg]
* Served as a law professor at Transylvania University (where he taught more than 1,200 lawyers) during part of the time that he served on the Kentucky Court of Appeals? [George Robertson]
* Was the first African American to graduate from the Harvard Law School and became a state district judge for the city of Charleston, Massachusetts? [George Lewis Ruffin]
* Was a diplomat before being elected as a judge in Cook County, Illinois? [Edith S. Sampson]
* Has written a book about his work as a Connecticut trial judge? [Robert Satter]

* Became the first U.S. citizen of Italian ancestry to be appointed to the United States Supreme Court and quickly established himself as one of the Court's most outspoken conservative members? [Antonin Scalia]
* Is best known as the star of the television show *Judge Judy?* [Judy Sheindlin]
* Once ordered a juvenile to attend the funeral of a pedestrian he had hit while driving a stolen car and later roamed the halls of her nursing home "sentencing" fellow patients? [Sadie L. Shulman]
* Was an Ohio judge born in Latvia and generally known simply as "Judge Sam"? [Samuel H. Silbert]
* Was born in Cuba to a Cuban father and an African American mother and became the first nonwhite judge to serve on the supreme court for the state of Washington? [Charles Z. Smith]
* Was gunned down by a federal marshal protecting United States Supreme Court justice Stephen Field? [David S. Terry]
* Is the second African American to serve on the United States Supreme Court and has established himself as a conservative who rarely questions attorneys during oral arguments? [Clarence Thomas]
* Was the chief judge of the New York Court of Appeals who was often suggested as a gubernatorial candidate before being convicted for threatening kidnapping and blackmail? [Sol Wachtler]
* Is best known as the onetime star of television's *The People's Court?* [Joseph A. Wapner]
* Served as a Pennsylvania congressman before being elected to the Court of Common Pleas in Pittsburgh and then, as during his service as a member of Congress, continued to officiate at college football games? [Samuel A. Weiss]
* Was denied reelection to the Tennessee Supreme Court when she became embroiled in controversy related to an opinion involving the death penalty? [Penny J. White]
* Served as the first female judge in the state of Washington? [Reah Mary Whitehead]
* Served as a United States district judge for Alaska and later served as a representative to the U.S. Congress from that state? [James Wickersham]
* Helped draft Oklahoma's constitution, served as a member of the state's judiciary and as a governor, and went on to serve as both a United States district judge and a judge on the Tenth United States Circuit Court of Appeals? [Robert L. Williams]
* Is an African American judge who was often called "Turn 'em Loose Bruce" for decisions that were regarded as being overly lenient toward criminals? [Bruce McMarion Wright]

Selected Bibliography

Abraham, Henry J. *The Judicial Process: An Introductory Analysis of the Courts of the United States, England, and France*. 7th ed. New York: Oxford University Press, 1988.

———. *Justices, Presidents, and Senators: A History of the U.S. Supreme Court Appointments from Washington to Clinton*. Lanham, Md.: Rowman and Littlefield Publishers, 1999.

Abrahamson, Shirley S. "All the World's a Courtroom: Judging in the New Millennium." *Hofstra University School of Law Law Review* 261 (Winter 1997): 273–292.

Abrahamson, Shirley S., Susan M. Fieber, and Gabrielle Lessard. "Judges on Judging: A Bibliography." *St. Mary's Law Journal* 24 (1993): 995.

Adams, Colleen L., et al. "A Life Well Lived: Remembrances of Judge A. Leon Higginbotham—His Days, His Jurisprudence, and His Legacy." *Loyola of Los Angeles Law Review* (April 2000): 33.

Adkinson, Janis Faye. "George Washington Stone and Alabama Criminal Law: A Battle against the Southern Legal Tradition." Master's thesis, University of Florida, 1991.

Adler, Renata. "A Court of No Appeal." *Harper's Magazine*, August 2000, 45–56.

Adrian, Erin. "Rose Elizabeth Bird: Choosing to Be Just." Stanford University Women's Legal History Project. Available at <http://www.stanford.edu/group/WLHP/profiles/BirdRose.shtml>. Accessed 1 January 2003.

Alexander, D. S. "Judge Blackford: A Sketch of His Life and Character." *Indianapolis News*, 21 February 1881, A1.

Alexander, James. *A Brief Narrative of the Case and Trial of John Peter Zenger*. 2d ed. Edited by Stanley N. Katz. Cambridge: Belknap Press of Harvard University Press, 1972.

Allen, Florence Ellinwood. *To Do Justly*. Cleveland, Ohio: The Press of Western Reserve University, 1965.

Allen, Francis A. "In Honor of Walter V. Schaefer." *Northwestern University Law Review* 74 (1979): 691–693. (Also see other honors in this same issue.)

———. "In Memoriam: Walter V. Schaefer." *Northwestern University Law Review* 80 (1986): 1149–1150. (Also see other memorials in this same issue.)

Allon, Gal. *Brandeis of Boston*. Cambridge: Harvard University Press, 1980.

Alschuler, Albert W. *Law without Values: The Life, Work and Legacy of Justice Holmes*. Chicago: University of Chicago Press, 2000.

Aman, Alfred C., Jr. "Elbert Parr Tuttle." *Cornell Law Review* 82 (November 1996): 1.

American Political Leaders, 1789–2000. Washington, D.C.: CQ Press, 2000.

Amidon, Charles F. "The Constitution and the Corporations." *The Outlook* 87 (1907): 19–26.

———. "The Quest for Error and the Doing of Justice." *American Law Review* 40 (1906): 681–686.

Appel, John W. "Gibson and a Progressive Jurisprudence." *Report of the Fifteenth Annual Meeting of the Pennsylvania Bar Association* (1909): 356–370. Philadelphia: The Association.

Appleton, John. *The Rules of Evidence: Stated and Discussed*. Philadelphia: T. and J. W. Johnson and Co., 1860.

Ashby, John B. "Reflections: Thomas M. Cooley—The Defendant's Rights Cases." *Cooley Law Review* 3 (1985): 524–545.

Ashman, Charles R. *The Finest Judges Money Can Buy: And Other Forms of Judicial Pollution*. Los Angeles: Nash Publishing, 1973.

Babcock, Barbara A. "Commentary." *New York University Law Review* 70 (June 1995): 707–713.

Bacon, Francis. *The Essays or Counsels, Civil and Moral of Francis Bacon*. Edited by Samuel Harvey Reynolds. Oxford: The Clarendon Press, 1890.

Baker, Liva. *Justice from Beacon Hill: The Life and Times of Oliver Wendell Holmes*. New York: HarperCollins, 1991.

———. *The Second Battle of New Orleans: The Hundred-Year Struggle to Integrate the Schools*. New York: HarperCollins, 1996.

Ball, Howard. *Hugo L. Black: Cold Steel Warrior*. New York: Oxford University Press, 1996.

Banks, Christopher P. *Judicial Politics in the D.C. Circuit Court*. Baltimore, Md.: The Johns Hopkins University Press, 1999.

Barnes, Bart. "John Sirica, Watergate Judge, Dies." *Washington Post*, 15 August 1992, A01.

Barrow, Deborah J., and Thomas G. Walker. *A Court Divided: The Fifth Circuit Court of Appeals and the Politics of Judicial Reform*. New Haven, Conn.: Yale University Press, 1998.

Bass, Jack. "Faces Turned to the Future." *Houston Law Review* 34 (Spring 1998): 1492.

———. "The Fifth Circuit in Southern History." *Georgia Law Review* 19 (1998): 473.

———. "John Minor Wisdom and the Impact of Law." *Mississippi Law Journal* 69 (Fall 1999): 25–37.

———. *Taming the Storm: The Life and Times of Frank M. Johnson, Jr., and the South's Fight over Civil Rights*. New York: Anchor Books, 1994.

———. *Unlikely Heroes: The Dramatic Story of the Southern Judges of the Fifth Circuit Who Translated the Supreme Court's Brown Decision into a Revolution for Equality*. New York: Simon and Schuster, 1981.

Bazelon, David L. *Questioning Authority: Justice and Criminal Law*. New York: Alfred A. Knopf, 1988.

Beal, Eric L. "Posner and Moral Hazard." *Connecticut Insurance Law Journal* 7 (2000/2001): 81–102.

Beitzinger, Alfons J. "Chief Justice Ryan and His Colleagues." *Wisconsin Law Review* (1955): 592.

———. *Edward G. Ryan: Lion of the Law*. Madison: The State Historical Society of Wisconsin, 1960.
Belknap, G. N. "The Printing of the Deady Code." *Oregon Law Review* 42 (1962): 25–34.
Belknap, Michal R. *Cold War Political Justice*. Westport, Conn.: Greenwood Press, 1977.
Bell, Griffin, and Ronald J. Ostrow. *Taking Care of the Law*. New York: William Morrow, 1982.
Beltran, Beatrice A. "Note and Commentary: Posner and Tort Law as Insurance." *Connecticut Insurance Law Journal* 7 (2000/2001): 153–193.
Benet, Stephen Vincent. *Selected Works of Stephen Vincent Benet*. Vol. 2: *Prose*. New York: Farrar and Rinehart, 1942.
Bent, Silas. *Justice Oliver Wendell Holmes: A Biography*. New York: Vanguard Press, 1932.
Berry, Dawn Bradley, ed. *The 50 Most Influential Women in American Law*. Los Angeles: Lowell House, 1997.
Beveridge, Albert J. *The Life of John Marshall*. 4 vols. Boston: Houghton Mifflin, 1916–1919.
Bicentennial Committee of the Judicial Conference of the United States. *Judges of the United States*. Washington, D.C.: The Committee, 1983.
Biddle, Francis. *Justice Holmes, Natural Law, and the Supreme Court*. New York: Macmillan, 1961.
Biddle, George W. *A Sketch of the Professional and Judicial Character of the Late George Sharswood*. Philadelphia: The Law Association of Philadelphia, 1883.
Billings, Warren M. "A Judicial Legacy: The Last Will and Testament of François-Xavier Martin." *Louisiana History* 25 (1984): 277–289.
Billings, Warren M., and Mark F. Fernandez, eds. *A Law unto Itself? Essays in the New Louisiana Legal History*. Baton Rouge: Louisiana State University Press, 2001.
Biography Resource Center. Available at <http://www.galenet.com>.
Bishop, Jim. *The Murder Trial of Judge Peel*. New York: Simon and Schuster, 1962.
Biskupic, Joan. "He Could Be the Next Supreme Court Justice." *USA Today*, 18 March 2002, 1–2.
Black, Hugo L. *A Constitutional Faith*. New York: Knopf, 1969.
Black, Hugo L., Jr. *My Father, A Remembrance*. New York: Random House, 1975.
Blackburn, Joyce. *George Wythe of Williamsburg*. New York: Harper and Row, 1975.
Blake, D. T. *An Historical Treatise on the Practice of the Court of Chancery of the State of New York*. New York: J. T. Murden, 1818.
Blasi, Vincent. *The Burger Court: The Counter-Revolution That Wasn't*. New Haven, Conn.: Yale University Press, 1983.
Bok, Curtis. *Backbone of the Herring*. New York: Alfred A. Knopf, 1941.
Boles, Donald E. *Mr. Justice Rehnquist, Judicial Activist: The Early Years*. Ames: University of Iowa Press, 1987.
Bontecou, Eleanor, ed. *Freedom in the Balance: Opinions of Judge Henry W. Edgerton Relating to Civil Liberties*. Ithaca, N.Y.: Cornell University Press, 1960.
Bork, Robert H. *The Antitrust Paradox: A Policy at War with Itself*. 2d ed. New York: Basic Books, 1993.
———. "Neutral Principles and Some First Amendment Problems." *Indiana Law Journal* 47 (Fall 1971): 1–35.

———. "Original Intent and the Constitution." *Humanities* 7 (February 1986): 22–26.
———. *Slouching towards Gomorrah: Modern Liberalism and American Decline*. New York: Regan Books, 1996.
———. *The Tempting of America: The Political Seduction of the Law*. New York: The Free Press, 1990.
Bowen, Catherine Drinker. *The Lion and the Throne: The Life and Times of Sir Edward Coke*. Boston: Little, Brown, 1957.
———. *Yankee from Olympus: Justice Holmes and His Family*. Boston: Little, Brown, 1945.
Bradley, Barbara. "Judge Jack Weinstein." National Public Radio, *Morning Edition*, 5 June 2000.
Brady, Patrick S. "Slavery, Race, and the Criminal Law in Antebellum North Carolina: A Reconsideration of the Thomas Ruffin Court." *North Carolina Central Law Journal* 10 (1978): 248–260.
Bragg, L. E. *More than Petticoats, Remarkable Washington Women*. Helena, Mont.: Falcon Publishing, 1998.
Brake, Patricia E. *Justice in the Valley: A Bicentennial Perspective of the United States District Court for the Eastern District of Tennessee*. Franklin, Tenn.: Hillsboro Press, 1998.
Brandt, Clare. *An American Aristocracy: The Livingstons*. Garden City, N.Y.: Doubleday, 1986.
Brantley, W. T. "Life and Character of Joseph Henry Lumpkin." An Oration Delivered in Athens, Ga., before the Phi Kappa Society, 5 August 1867.
Brenner, Marie. "Judge Motley's Verdict." *The New Yorker* 70, 16 May 1994, 65–71.
Breyer, Stephen. "In Memoriam: Charles E. Wyzanski, Jr." *Harvard Law Review* 100 (1987): 707.
Bright, Stephen B. "Judicial Review and Judicial Independence." *Georgia State University Law Review* 14 (July 1998): 817.
Brisbin, Richard A., Jr. *Justice Antonin Scalia and the Conservative Revival*. Baltimore, Md.: The Johns Hopkins University Press, 1997.
Brooks, Aubrey Lee. *Walter Clark: Fighting Judge*. Chapel Hill: University of North Carolina Press, 1944.
Brooks, Aubrey Lee, and Hugh Talmadge Leflar, eds. *The Papers of Walter Clark, 1857–1901*. Chapel Hill: University of North Carolina Press, 1950.
———. *The Papers of Walter Clark, 1902–1924*. Chapel Hill: University of North Carolina Press, 1950.
Brown, Imogene E. *American Aristides: A Biography of George Wythe*. Rutherford, N.J.: Farleigh Dickinson University Press, 1981.
Bruck, Connie. *The Predators' Ball: The Inside Story of Drexel Burnham and the Rise of the Junk Bond Raiders*. New York: Penguin Books U.S.A., 1989.
Buchanan, A. Russell. *David S. Terry of California: Dueling Judge*. San Marino, Calif.: The Huntington Library, 1956.
Buchsbaum, Peter. "The Courts: The 1947 'Revolution.'" *New Jersey Reporter* (November 1982): 33.
Burris, William C. *Duty and the Law: Judge John J. Parker and the Constitution*. Bessemer, Ala.: Colonial Press, 1987.
Burton, David H. *Political Ideas of Justice Holmes*. Cransbury, N.J.: Associated University Presses, 1992.

Burton, Jeffrey. *Indian Territory and the United States, 1866–1906: Courts, Government, and the Movement for Oklahoma Statehood.* Norman: University of Oklahoma Press, 1995.
Caldwell, Joshua W. *Sketches of the Bench and Bar of Tennessee.* Knoxville, Tenn.: Ogden Bros. and Co., 1898.
Campbell, Thomas P., Jr. "Chancellor Kent, Chief Justice Marshall and the Steamboat Cases." *Syracuse Law Review* 25 (1974): 497–534.
Capel, Wint. *Dethronement of Reason: The Travails of North Carolina's Murderous Dr. J. W. Peacock.* Chapel Hill, N.C.: Cape Corporation Press, 1998.
Cardozo, Benjamin N. *The Paradoxes of Legal Science.* New York: Columbia University Press, 1928.
Carosso, Vincent P. *Investment Banking in America.* Cambridge: Harvard University Press, 1970.
———. "The Wall Street Money Trust from Pugo through Medina." *Business History Review* 47 (1973): 421.
Carrington, Paul D. "'The Common Thoughts of Men': The Law-Teaching and Judging of Thomas McIntyre Cooley." *Stanford Law Review* 49 (1997): 495–546.
Carter, Dan T. *Scottsboro: A Tragedy of the American South.* Baton Rouge: Louisiana State University Press, 1979.
Carter, Stephen L. *The Confirmation Mess: Cleaning Up the Federal Appointment Process.* New York: Basic Books, 1994.
Cedarbaum, Miriam Goldman. "Women on the Federal Bench." *Boston University Law Review* 73 (1993): 39.
Chamberlain, N. H. *Samuel Sewall and the World He Lived In.* Boston: DeWolfe, Fiske and Company, 1897.
Chambers, Walter. *Samuel Seabury: A Challenge.* New York: The Century Company, 1932.
Chapman, Berlin Basil. *The Otoes and Missourias: A Study of Indian Removal and Its Legal Aftermath.* Oklahoma City, Okla.: Times Journal Publishing Company, 1965.
Chase, F. H. *Lemuel Shaw, Chief Justice of the Supreme Judicial Court of Massachusetts, 1830–1860.* Boston: Houghton Mifflin, 1918.
Chase, Harold, Samuel Krislov, Keith O. Boyum, and Jerry N. Clark. *Biographical Dictionary of the Federal Judiciary.* Detroit, Mich.: Gale Research Group, 1976.
Chin, Gabriel J. "The Plessy Myth: Justice Harlan on the Chinese Cases." *Iowa Law Review* 82 (October 1996): 151–182.
Clark, Charles. "John Minor Wisdom: A Brief Overview of His Epoch." *Mississippi Law Journal* 69 (Fall 1999): 39–42.
Clark, Charles E. "Augustus Noble Hand." *Harvard Law Review* 68 (May 1955): 1113.
Clark, Gilbert J. *Life Sketches of Eminent Lawyers.* 2 vols. Kansas City, Mo.: Lawyers International Publishing Co., 1895.
Clark, M., Jr., ed. *Pharisee among Philistines: The Diary of Judge Matthew P. Deady: 1871–1892.* Portland: Oregon Historical Society, 1975.
Clark, Walter. "Back to the Constitution." *Virginia Law Review* 3 (December 1915): 214–226.
———. "Some Defects in the Constitution of the United States." *American Law Register* 54 (May 1906): 263–288.

Clarkin, William. *Serene Patriot: A Life of George Wythe*. Albany, N.Y.: Alan Publications, 1970.

Cleary, Catherine B. "Lavinia Goodell, First Woman Lawyer in Wisconsin." *Wisconsin Magazine of History* 74 (1991): 243–271.

Clinton, Robert L. *Marbury v. Madison and Judicial Review*. Lawrence: University Press of Kansas, 1989.

Coffin, Frank M. *The Ways of a Judge: Reflections from the Federal Appellate Bench*. Boston: Houghton Mifflin, 1980.

Cohen, Jeremy. *Congress Shall Make No Law: Oliver Wendell Holmes, the First Amendment, and Judicial Decision Making*. Ames: Iowa State University Press, 1989.

Coleman, Mary Haldane. *St. George Tucker: Citizen of No Mean City*. Richmond, Va.: The Dietz Press, 1938.

Collins, Ronald K. L. "Hans Linde and His 1984 Judicial Election: The Primary." *Oregon Law Review* 70 (1991): 747–813.

Conley, Patrick T. *Neither Separate nor Equal: Legislature and Executive in Rhode Island Constitutional History*. East Providence: Rhode Island Publications Society, 1999.

Contemporary Authors Online. The Gale Group, 2001.

Conway, Moncure D. *A Discourse on the Life and Character of the Hon. William Cranch, L.L.D.* Washington, D.C.: Frank Taylor, 1855.

Cook, Beverly Blair. "Moral Authority and Gender Difference: Georgia Bullock and the Los Angeles Women's Court." *Judicature* 77 (November-December 1993): 144–155.

Cornyn, John. "The Roots of the Texas Constitution: Settlement to Statehood." *Texas Tech Law Review* 26 (1995): 1089.

"Court's Abrahamson to Discuss Women in the Law." Available at <http://www.uwrf.edu/news_bureau222992.html>.

Cover, Robert. *Justice Accused: Anti-Slavery and the Judicial Process*. New Haven, Conn.: Yale University Press, 1975.

Cox, Archibald. "Judge Learned Hand and the Interpretation of Statutes." *Harvard Law Review* 60 (1947): 370.

Cox, Patrick. *Ralph W. Yarborough, The People's Senator*. Austin: University of Texas Press, 2001.

Cranch, William. *Reports of Cases, Civil and Criminal, Argued and Adjudged in the Circuit Court of the District of Columbia for the County of Washington. 1801–1841*. 6 vols. Boston: Little, Brown; J. S. Vorhies, 1852–1853.

Cray, Ed. *Chief Justice: A Biography of Earl Warren*. New York: Simon and Schuster, 1997.

Creel, Von Russell, Bob Burke, and Kenny Franks. *American Jurist: The life of Alfred P. Murrah*. Oklahoma City, Okla.: Western Heritage Books, 1996.

Croy, Homer. *He Hanged Them High: An Authentic Account of the Fanatical Judge Who Hanged Eighty-eight Men*. New York: Duell, Sloan and Pearce, 1952.

Cullen, Charles T. *St. George Tucker and Law in Virginia, 1772–1804*. New York: Garland Publishing, 1987.

Culver, John. "The Transformation of the California Supreme Court: 1977–1997." *Albany Law Review* 61 (1998): 1461.

Cunningham, Lawrence A. "Cardozo and Posner: A Study in Contracts." *William and Mary Law Review* 36 (Spring 1995): 1379–1457.

Currie, David P. *The Constitution in the Supreme Court: The First Hundred Years, 1789–1888*. Chicago: University of Chicago Press, 1985.
Curtis, Rosalee Morris. *John Hemphill*. Austin, Tex.: Jenkins Publishing Co., 1971.
Cushman, Clare, ed. *The Supreme Court Justices: Illustrated Biographies, 1789–1995*. 2d ed. Washington, D.C.: Congressional Quarterly, 1995.
Dale, Edward Everett, and James D. Morrison. *Pioneer Judge: The Life of Robert Lee Williams*. Cedar Rapids, Iowa: The Torch Press, 1958.
Danforth, John C. *Resurrection: The Confirmation of Clarence Thomas*. New York: Viking, 1994.
Dangerfield, George. *Chancellor Robert R. Livingston of New York, 1746–1813*. New York: Harcourt, Brace, 1960.
Davis, Derek. *Original Intent: Chief Justice Rehnquist and the Course of American Church-State Relations*. Buffalo, N.Y.: Prometheus Books, 1991.
Davis, Richard. *Intellectual Life in Jefferson's Virginia*. Chapel Hill: University of North Carolina Press, 1964.
Davis, Sue. "The Chief Justice and Judicial Decision-Making: The Institutional Basis for Leadership on the Supreme Court." In *Supreme Court Decision-Making*, edited by Cornell W. Clayton and Howard Gillman. Chicago: The University of Chicago Press, 1999, 135–154.
———. *Justice Rehnquist and the Constitution*. Princeton, N.J.: Princeton University Press, 1989.
Davis, William Thomas. *Bench and Bar of the Commonwealth of Massachusetts*. 2 vols. Boston: Boston History Company, 1893.
Dennison, George M. *The Dorr War*. Lexington: The University Press of Kentucky, 1976.
Dill, Alonzo Thomas. *George Wythe, Teacher of Liberty*. Williamsburg: Virginia Independence Bicentennial Commission, 1979.
DiIulio, John J., Jr., ed. *Courts, Corrections, and the Constitution: The Impact of Judicial Intervention on Prisons and Jails*. New York: Oxford University Press, 1990.
Dodd, Carol S. *The Richardson Years: 1966–1982*. Honolulu: University of Hawaii Press, 1985.
Dorfman, Joseph. "Chancellor Kent and the Developing American Economy." *Columbia Law Review* 61 (1961): 1290–1317.
Dorsen, Norman. "The Second Mr. Justice Harlan: A Constitutional Conservative." *New York University Law Review* 44 (1969): 249–271.
———. *The Unpredictable Constitution*. New York: New York University Press, 2002.
Dunne, Gerald T. *Hugo Black and the Judicial Revolution*. New York: Simon and Schuster, 1972.
———. *Justice Joseph Story and the Rise of the Supreme Court*. New York: Simon and Schuster, 1970.
———. *The Missouri Supreme Court: From Dred Scott to Nancy Cruzan*. Columbia: University of Missouri Press, 1993.
Dworkin, Ronald. *Taking Rights Seriously*. Cambridge: Harvard University Press, 1977.
Easterbrook, Frank H. "Formalism, Functionalism, Ignorance, Judges." *Harvard Journal of Law and Public Policy* 22 (1998): 11–20.
———. "Forward: The Court and the Economic System." *Harvard Law Review* 98 (1984): 4–85.

———. "Method, Result and Authority: A Reply." *Harvard Law Review* 98 (1985): 622–629.

———. "Predatory Strategies and Counterstrategies." *The University of Chicago Law Review* 48 (1981): 263–337.

———. "Statute's Domain." *The University of Chicago Law Review* 50 (1984): 533–566.

Edgerton, Henry W. "The Incidence of Judicial Control over Congress." *Cornell Law Quarterly* 22 (April 1937): 299–348.

———. "A Liberal Judge: Cuthbert W. Pound." *Cornell Law Quarterly* 21 (December 1935): 7–45.

Edwards, George. "Why Justice Cooley Left the Bench: A Missing Page of Legal History." *Wayne Law Review* 33 (1987): 1563–1572.

Elder, Robert, Jr. "Disturbing the Peace: Remembering John R. Brown Who Spoke 'Against the Day.'" *Texas Lawyer*, 24 March 1997.

Ely, James W., Jr., ed. *The Chief Justiceship of Melville W. Fuller, 1888–1910*. Columbia: University of South Carolina Press, 1995.

———. *A History of the Tennessee Supreme Court*. Knoxville: The University of Tennessee Press, 2002.

Ely, John Hart. *Democracy and Distrust: A Theory of Judicial Review*. Cambridge: Harvard University Press, 1980.

Emanuel, Anne S. "Turning the Tide in the Civil Rights Revolution: Elbert Tuttle and the Desegregation of the University of Georgia." *Michigan Journal of Race and Law* 5 (Fall 1999): 1.

Enslen, Richard A. "ADR: Another Acronym or a Viable Alternative to the High Cost of Litigation and Crowded Court Dockets? The Debate Commences." *New Mexico Law Review* 18 (1988): 1–47.

Estreicher, Samuel. "Pragmatic Justice: The Contributions of Judge Harold Leventhal to Administrative Law." *Columbia Law Review* 80 (1980): 894.

Ewald, Alec C. "Getting Ready for Garza? Judge Emilio Garza, Civil Liberties and the Politics of Judicial Selection." *Law and Courts* 12 (Spring 2002): 11–21.

"Excerpts from Elbert Tuttle Portrait Ceremony and Eleventh Circuit Historical Society Ceremony." *Cornell Law Review* 68 (January 1983): 158.

Famesh, Ponnuru. "Speedy Gonzales: Bush's Fast-rising Counsel." *National Review* 53, 30 April 2001, 19–22.

Farrand, Max, ed. *The Records of the Federal Convention of 1787*. 4 vols. New Haven, Conn.: Yale University Press, 1966.

Faulkner, Robert K. *The Jurisprudence of John Marshall*. Princeton, N.J.: Princeton University Press, 1968.

Federal Cases: Comprising Cases Argued and Determined in the Circuit and District Courts of the United States from the Earliest Times to the Beginning of the Federal Reporter. 30 vols. St. Paul, Minn.: West Publishing Company, 1894–1897.

Feeley, Malcolm M., and Edward L. Rubin. *Judicial Policy Making and the Modern State: How the Courts Reformed America's Prisons*. Cambridge: Cambridge University Press, 1998.

Fernandez, Mark F. "From Chaos to Continuity: Early Reforms of the Supreme Court of Louisiana, 1845–1852." *Louisiana History* 28 (1987): 19–31.

———. *From Chaos to Continuity: The Evolution of Louisiana's Judicial System, 1712–1862*. Baton Rouge: Louisiana State University Press, 2001.

Field, Benjamin T. "Justice Roger Traynor and His Case for Judicial Activism." Ph.D. diss., University of California, 2000.
Field, Edward, ed. *State of Rhode Island and Providence Plantations at the end of the Century: A History*. 3 vols. Boston: Mason Publishing Company, 1902.
Field, Stephen J. *Personal Reminiscences of Early Days in California*. 1877. Reprint, New York: Da Capo Press, 1968.
Finkelman, John. "Politics, the Press, and the Law: The Trial of John Peter Zenger." In *American Political Trials*, edited by Michal R. Belknap. Westport, Conn.: Greenwood Press, 1994, 21–42.
Fish, Peter G. *Federal Justice in the Mid-Atlantic South: United States Courts from Maryland to the Carolinas, 1789–1835*. Washington, D.C.: Administrative Office of the United States Courts, 2002.
———. "Guarding the Judicial Ramparts: John J. Parker and the Administration of Federal Justice." *Justice System Journal* 3 (1977): 105–125.
———. "Judge Parker and the Public Service State." *Duke Law Magazine* 2 (1985): 37–44.
———. "A New Court Opens: The United States Court of Appeals for the Fourth Circuit." *Georgia Journal of Southern Legal History* 2 (1993): 171–182.
———. "Red Jacket Revisited: Saga of the Case that Unraveled John J. Parker's Appointment to the U.S. Supreme Court." *Law and History Review* 5 (1987): 51–104.
Fisher, George. "The Jury's Rise as Lie Detector." *Yale Law Journal* 107 (December 1997): 575–713.
Fisher, Linda E. "Content: Pragmatism Is as Pragmatism Does: Of Posner, Public Policy, and Empirical Reality." *New Mexico Law Review* 31 (Summer 2001): 455–492.
Fiss, Owen M. *Troubled Beginnings of the Modern State, 1888–1910*. New York: Macmillan, 1993.
Fiss, Owen M., and Charles Krauthammer. "A Return to the Antebellum Constitution: The Rehnquist Court." *New Republic* 185, 10 March 1982, 14.
Fitchett, E. Horace. "The Role of Claflin College in Negro Life in South Carolina." *Journal of Negro Education* 12 (Winter 1943): 42–68.
Ford, Paul Leicester, ed. *The Works of Thomas Jefferson*. 12 vols. New York: The Knickerbocker Press, 1904.
Forell, Caroline A. "Replacing Pragmatism and Policy with Analysis and Analogy: Justice Linde's Contribution to Oregon Tort Law." *Oregon Law Review* 70 (1991): 815–854.
Frank, Jerome. *Courts on Trial: Myth and Reality in American Justice*. Princeton, N.J.: Princeton University Press, 1949.
———. *Fate and Freedom: A Philosophy for Free Americans*. New York: Simon and Schuster, 1945.
———. *If Men Were Angels*. New York: Harper and Brothers, 1942.
———. *Law and the Modern Mind*. New York: Bretano's, 1930.
———. *Save America First*. New York: Harper and Brothers, 1938.
Frank, John P. *Clement Haynsworth, the Senate, and the Supreme Court*. Charlottesville: University Press of Virginia, 1991.
Frankfurter, Felix. "Learned Hand." *Harvard Law Review* 75 (1961): 3.
Franks, Kenny A., and Paul F. Lambert. *The Legacy of Dean Julien C. Monnet: Judge*

Luther Bohanon and the Desegregation of Oklahoma City's Public Schools. Moscogee, Okla.: Western Heritage Books, 1984.
Freund, Paul. "In Memoriam: Charles E. Wyzanski, Jr." *Harvard Law Review* 100 (1987): 710.
Freyer, Tony, and Timothy Dixon. *Democracy and Judicial Independence: Federal Courts in Alabama, 1820–1994*. Brooklyn, N.Y.: Carlson Press. 1995.
Friedman, Leon, and Fred L. Israel, eds. *The Justices of the United States Supreme Court, 1789–1969: Their Lives and Major Opinions*. 5 vols. New York: Chelsea House, 1965–1978.
Fritz, G. C. *Federal Justice in California: The Court of Ogden Hoffman, 1851–1891*. Lincoln: University of Nebraska Press, 1991.
Fritze, David. "His Courage Counts." *Oklahoma Monthly*, January 1978.
Fuke, Richard Paul. "Hugh Lennox Bond and Radical Republican Ideology." *Journal of Southern History* 44 (1979): 569–586.
Gannett, Ezra S. *A Good Old Age: A Sermon Occasioned by the Death of Hon. John Davis, LL.D., and Preached in the Federal Street Meetinghouse in Boston, January 24, 1847*. Boston: Wm. Crosby and H. P. Nichols, 1847.
Garraty, John A., and Mark C. Carnes, eds. *American National Biography*. 24 vols. New York: Oxford University Press, 1999.
Gaspard, Elizabeth. "The Rise of the Louisiana Bar: The Early Period, 1813–1839." *Louisiana History* 28 (1987): 183–197.
George, Robert. "The Supreme Court 2000: A Symposium." *First Things* 10, 6 October 2000, n.p.
Gerber, Scott. *Seriatim: The Supreme Court before John Marshall*. New York: New York University Press, 1998.
Gerhart, Eugene C. *Arthur T. Vanderbilt: The Compleat Counsellor*. Albany, N.Y.: Q Corporation, 1980.
Gillman, Howard. *The Votes That Counted: How the Court Decided the 2000 Presidential Election*. Chicago: The University of Chicago Press, 2001.
Ginsburg, Ruth Bader, and Laura W. Brill. "Women in the Federal Judiciary: Three Way Pavers and the Exhilarating Change President Carter Wrought." *Fordham Law Review* 64 (November 1995): 281–290.
Glennon, Robert J. *The Iconoclast as Reformer. Jerome Frank's Impact on American Law*. Ithaca, N.Y.: Cornell University Press, 1985.
Goebel, Julius, Jr. *The Law Practice of Alexander Hamilton: Documents and Commentary*. 2 vols. New York: Columbia University Press, 1964 and 1969.
Goings, Kenneth W. *"The NAACP Comes of Age": The Defeat of Judge John J. Parker*. Bloomington: Indiana University Press, 1990.
Gold, David M. "Chief Justice John Appleton." *Maine Historical Society Quarterly* 18 (Spring 1979): 193–216.
———. "Frustrated Glory: John Francis Appleton and Black Soldiers in the Civil War." *Maine Historical Society Quarterly* 31 (Summer 1991): 174–204.
———. *The Shaping of Nineteenth-Century Law: John Appleton and Responsible Individualism*. New York: Greenwood Press, 1990.
———. "The Tradition of Substantive Judicial Review: A Case Study of Continuity in Constitutional Jurisprudence." *Maine Law Review* 52 (2000): 356–378.
Goldberg, Irving L. "In Memoriam: Tribute to the Honorable John R. Brown." *Texas Law Review* 71 (April 1993): 907.

Goldberg, Louis P., and Eleanore Levenson. *Lawless Judges*. New York: Negro Universities Press, 1969.
Gollmar, Robert H. *Tales of a Country Judge*. Delavan, Wis.: Chas. Hallberg and Co., 1979.
Goodhard, Arthur L. *Five Jewish Lawyers of the Common Law*. New York: Oxford University Press, 1949.
Goodman, James. *Stories of Scottsboro*. New York: Pantheon Books, 1994.
Goodrich, Gillian White. "James Edwin Horton, Jr.: Scottsboro Judge." Master's thesis, University of Alabama–Birmingham, 1974.
Gordon, Philip L. "Judge Leads Fight for Workplace Privacy." *Denver Post*, 20 September 2001. Available at <www.privacyfoundation.org/pdf/judgeLeads/pdf>. Accessed 1 January 2003.
Gormley, Ken. *Archibald Cox: Conscience of a Nation*. Boston: Addison-Wesley, 1997.
Goulden, Joseph C. *The Benchwarmers: The Private World of the Powerful Federal Judges*. New York: Weybright and Talley, 1974.
Green, John W. *Lives of the Judges of the Supreme Court of Tennessee, 1796–1947*. Knoxville, Tenn.: Archer and Smith, 1947.
Greenhouse, Linda. "Beyond Original Intent: The Supreme Court's Majority Has Given Up on Strict Construction, a Judge Asserts." *New York Times*, 18 August 2002, 8.
———. "Burnita S. Matthews Dies at 93: First Woman on U.S. Trial Courts." *New York Times*, 28 April 1988, 27.
Gregg, Alexander. *Eulogy on the Hon. John Hemphill and Gen. Hugh C. McLeod*. Houston, Tex.: Telegraph Book and Job Establishment, 1862.
Griffith, Kathryn. *Judge Learned Hand and the Role of the Federal Judiciary*. Norman: University of Oklahoma Press, 1973.
Grodin. Joseph R. *In Pursuit of Justice: Reflections of a State Supreme Court Justice*. Berkeley: University of California Press, 1989.
Guice, John D. W. *The Rocky Mountain Bench: The Territorial Supreme Courts of Colorado, Montana, and Wyoming, 1861–1890*. New Haven: Yale University Press, 1972.
Gulati, Mitu, and Veronica Sanchez. "Giants in a World of Pygmies? Testing the Superstar Hypothesis with Judicial Opinions in Casebooks." *Iowa Law Review* 87 (May 2002): 1141–1212.
Guliuzza, Frank. "Protecting Judicial Leadership: Did Rehnquist Prefer to Switch than Fight?" *Willamette Law Review* 29 (1993): 151.
Gunther, Gerald. *Learned Hand: The Man and the Judge*. New York: Alfred A. Knopf, 1994.
Guthrie, Chris, Jeffrey J. Rachlinski, and Andrew J. Wistrich. "Inside the Judicial Mind." *Cornell Law Review* 86 (May 2001): 777.
Hall, Kermit L. *The Magic Mirror: Law in American History*. New York: Oxford University Press, 1989.
———. *The Oxford Companion to the Supreme Court of the United States*. New York: Oxford University Press, 1992.
———. "Political Power and Constitutional Legitimacy: The South Carolina Ku Klux Klan Trials, 1871–1872." *Emory Law Journal* 3 (1983): 921–951.
Hall, Margaret, ed. *Selected Writings of Benjamin Nathan Cardozo*. New York: Fallon Law Book Company, 1947.

Halpern, Stephen C., and Charles M. Lamb, eds. *Supreme Court Activism and Restraint*. Lexington, Mass.: Lexington Books, 1984.
Hamilton, Alexander, John Jay, and James Madison. *The Federalist*. Washington, D.C.: Robert B. Luce, 1976.
Hamilton, Virginia Van Der Veer. *Hugo Black: The Alabama Years*. Baton Rouge: Louisiana State University Press, 1972.
Hand, Learned. *The Spirit of Liberty: Papers and Addresses of Learned Hand*. 3d ed. Edited by Irving Dilliard. Chicago: University of Chicago Press, 1977.
Hand, Susan Train, ed. *Letters of the Hand Family*. New York: 1917.
Harlan, John M. *The Evolution of a Judicial Philosophy: Selected Opinions and Papers of Justice John M. Harlan*. Edited by David L. Shapiro. Cambridge: Harvard University Press, 1969.
Harlan, Malvina Shanklin. *Some Memories of a Long Life, 1854–1911*. Edited by Linda Przybyszewski. New York: Modern Library, 2001.
Harman, S. W. *Hell on the Border: He Hanged Eighty-Eight Men*. 1898. Reprint, Fort Washington, Pa.: Eastern National, 2001.
Harrington, Fred Harvey. *Hanging Judge*. Caldwell, Idaho: The Caxton Printers, 1951.
Hart, Charles Henry. *Memoir of George Sharswood*. Philadelphia: The Numismatic and Antiquarian Society of Philadelphia, 1884.
———. "State Celebrities—George Sharswood." *Philadelphia Press*, 30 March 1882.
Hart, James P. "John Hemphill—Chief Justice of Texas." *Southwestern Law Journal* 3 (1949): 395.
Hartz, Louis. "John Marshall Harlan in Kentucky, 1855–1877: The Story of His Pre-Court Political Career." *Filson Club Historical Quarterly* 14 (January 1940): 17–40.
Haskins, George L., and Herbert A. Johnson. *Foundations of Power, John Marshall, 1801–15*. Vol. 2 of *History of the Supreme Court of the United States*. New York: Macmillan, 1981.
Hawthorne, Daniel. *Judge Medina: A Biography*. New York: Wilfred Funk, 1952.
Hayman, John, and Clara Ruth Hayman. *A Judge in the Senate: Howell Heflin's Career of Politics and Principle*. Montgomery, Ala.: NewSouth Books, 2001.
Haynsworth, Clement F., Jr. "A New Court to Improve the Administration of Justice." *American Bar Association Journal* 59, no. 8 (1973): 841–845.
———. Papers. Manuscript Division, Library of Congress, Washington, D.C.
———. "Professionalism in Lawyering." *South Carolina Law Review* 27 (1976): 627–628.
Hellman, Arthur. *Restructuring Justice*. Ithaca, N.Y.: Cornell University Press, 1991.
Hellman, George S. *Benjamin N. Cardozo: American Judge*. New York: McGraw Hill Book Company, 1940.
Hickok, Eugene W., and Gary L. McDowell. *Justice vs. Law: Courts and Politics in American Society*. New York: The Free Press, 1993.
Hicks, Frederick C. *Men and Books Famous in the Law*. New York: Lawbook Exchange, 1992.
Hicks, Paul DeForest. *Joseph Henry Lumpkin, Georgia's First Chief Justice*. Athens: University of Georgia, 2002.

Higginbotham, A. Leon, Jr. *In the Matter of Color: Race and the American Legal Process: The Colonial Period*. New York: Oxford University Press, 1978.
———. "An Open Letter to Justice Clarence Thomas from a Federal Judicial Colleague." *University of Pennsylvania Law Review* 140 (1991): 1005.
———. *Shades of Freedom: Racial Politics and Presumptions of the American Legal Process*. New York: Oxford University Press, 1996.
Hilldrup, Robert Leroy. *The Life and Times of Edmund Pendleton*. Chapel Hill: University of North Carolina Press, 1939.
Hinton, John W. *Memorial Address on Edward G. Ryan, Late Chief Justice of Wisconsin, Delivered by John H. Hinton before the Moot Court of Milwaukee, November 4, 1880*. Milwaukee, Wis.: The Court, 1880.
Hirsch, H. N. *The Enigma of Felix Frankfurter*. New York: Basic Books, 1981.
Hobson, Charles F. *The Great Chief Justice: John Marshall and the Rule of Law*. Lawrence: University Press of Kansas, 1996.
Hocker, Cliff. "A. Leon Higginbotham: A Legal Giant." *National Bar Association Magazine*, March/June 1999, 16.
Hoffer, Peter C. *The Devil's Disciples: Makers of the Salem Witchcraft Trials*. Baltimore, Md.: Johns Hopkins University Press, 1996.
Holmes, Oliver Wendell, Jr. *The Common Law*. London: Macmillan, 1881.
Honeyman, A. Van Doren. "A Famous Western Jurist, Native of Somerset." *Somerset County Historical Quarterly* 5 (1916): 1–14.
Horsky, Charles A. "Augustus Noble Hand." *Harvard Law Review* 68 (May 1955): 1118.
Horsnell, Margaret. *Spencer Roane: Judicial Advocate of Jeffersonian Principles*. New York: Garland Publishing Co., 1986.
Horton, John T. *James Kent: A Study in Conservatism, 1763–1847*. New York: D. Appleton-Century Co., 1939. Reprint, New York: Da Capo Press, 1969.
Horwitz, Morton J. *The Transformation of American Law, 1780–1860*. New York: Oxford University Press, 1992.
Howard, J. Woodford, Jr. "The Amateurs Win: Harold R. Medina's Appointment as a Federal District Judge." *New York State Bar Journal* 61 (1989): 14–22.
———. "The *Cramer* Treason Case." *Journal of Supreme Court History* 1 (1966): 49–60.
Howington, Arthur F. "Not in the Condition of a Horse or an Ox." *Tennessee Historical Quarterly* 34 (1975): 249–263.
Hudson, David. "Federal Appellate Judge Speaks Out on the First Amendment." Available at <www.freedomforum.org>. Accessed 4 August 1998.
Huebner, Timothy S. "Encouraging Economic Development: Joseph Henry Lumpkin and the Law of Contract, 1846–1860." *Georgia Journal of Southern Legal History* 2 (Fall/Winter 1991): 357–375.
———. "Joseph Henry Lumpkin and Evangelical Reform in Georgia: Temperance, Education and Industrialization, 1830–1860." *Georgia Historical Quarterly* 75 (Summer 1992): 254–274.
———. *The Southern Judicial Tradition: State Judges and Sectional Distinctiveness, 1790–1890*. Athens: University of Georgia Press, 1999.
Hughes, Charles Evans. *The Autobiographical Notes of Charles Evans Hughes*. Edited by David J. Danelski and Joseph S. Tulchin. Cambridge: Harvard University Press, 1973.

Hughes, Sarah T. Oral history interviews. University of North Texas, Denton, 21 April 1969.

Hunt, Aurora. *Kirby Benedict: Frontier Federal Judge: An Account of Legal and Judicial Development in the Southwest, 1853–1874, with Special Reference to the Indian, Slavery, Social and Political Affairs, Journalism, and a Chapter on Circuit Riding with Abraham Lincoln in Illinois*. Glendale, Calif.: The Arthur H. Clark Company, 1961.

Hyde, H. Montgomery. *Judge Jeffreys*. London: Butterworth and Co., 1948.

"In Memoriam Honorable John Johnston Parker, 1885–1958: Proceedings in the United States Court of Appeals for the Fourth Circuit, April 22, 1958." *Federal Reporter* 253, 2d Ser. (1958): 3–55.

Irvine, Diana R., ed. *The American Bench: Judges of the Nation, 2001/2002*. 12th ed. 2002/2002. Sacramento, Calif.: Foster-Long, 2001.

Jackson, Donald Dale. *Judges*. New York: Atheneum, 1974.

Jacobs, Clyde E. *Law Writers and the Courts: The Influence of Thomas M. Cooley, Christopher G. Tiedeman, and John F. Dillon upon American Constitutional Law*. Berkeley: University of California Press, 1954.

Jacobstein, J. Myron, and Roy Mersky. *The Rejected: Sketches of the 26 Men Nominated for the Supreme Court but Not Confirmed by the Senate*. Milpitas, Calif.: Toucon Valley Publications, 1993.

Jenkins, John A. "The Partisan: A Talk with Justice Rehnquist." *New York Times Magazine*, 3 March 1985, 28–35, 88, 100–101.

Johnson, Frank M., Jr. "In Defense of Judicial Activism." *Emory Law Journal* 28 (1979): 901.

———. "Reflections on the Judicial Career of Robert S. Vance." *Alabama Law Review* 42 (1991): 964.

———. "The Role of the Federal Courts in Institutional Litigation." *Alabama Law Review* 32 (1981): 271.

———. "The Role of the Judiciary with Respect to the Other Branches of Government." *Georgia Law Review* 11 (1977): 455.

Johnson, Herbert A. *The Chief Justiceship of John Marshall, 1801–1835*. Columbia: University of South Carolina Press, 1988.

———. "*Gibbons v. Ogden* before John Marshall." In *Courts and Law in Early New York: Selected Essays*, edited by Leo Hershkowitz and Milton M. Klein. Port Washington, N.Y.: Kennikat Press, 1978.

Johnson, J. Edward, ed. *History of the Supreme Court Justices of California*. 2 vols. San Francisco: Bender-Mose Company, 1967.

Jones, Alan R. *The Constitutional Conservatism of Thomas McIntyre Cooley: A Study in the History of Ideas*. New York: Garland Publishing, 1987.

———. "Thomas M. Cooley and the Michigan Supreme Court: 1865–1885." *American Journal of Legal History* 10 (1966): 97–121.

Jones, Marnie. *Holy Toledo: Religion and Politics in the Life of "Golden Rule" Jones*. Lexington: The University Press of Kentucky, 1998.

Joynt, Steve. *Jack's Law: The Rise and Fall of Renegade Judge Jack Montgomery*. Birmingham, Ala.: Crane Hill Publishers, 1997.

"Judges of the United States Courts." Available at <http://air.fjc.gov/servlet/uGetInfo?jid=1301>.

Justice, William Wayne. "The New Awakening: Judicial Activism in a Conservative Age." *Southwestern Law Journal* 43 (October 1989): 657–676.

———. "The Two Faces of Judicial Activism." *George Washington Law Review* 61 (November 1992): 1–13.

Justices of the United States Supreme Court. New York: Macmillan Reference USA, 2001.

Kahn, Paul W. *The Reign of Law: Marbury v. Madison and the Construction of America*. New Haven, Conn.: Yale University Press, 1997.

Katcher, Leo. *Earl Warren: A Political Biography*. New York: McGraw Hill, 1967.

Katz, Stanley. *Newcastle's New York: Anglo-American Politics, 1732–1753*. Cambridge: Harvard University Press, 1968.

Kaufman, Andrew O. *Cardozo*. Cambridge: Harvard University Press, 1998.

Kaye, Judith S. "Things Judges Do: State Statutory Interpretation." *Touro Law Review* 13, no. 3 (Spring 1997): 56–72.

Kaysen, Carl. "In Memoriam: Charles E. Wyzanski, Jr." *Harvard Law Review* 100 (1987): 713.

Kazaks, Julia. "Architectural Archaeology: Women in the United States Courthouse for the District of Columbia." *Georgetown Law Journal* 83 (1994): 559.

Keller, Morton. *Affairs of State: Public Life in Nineteenth Century America*. Cambridge: Belknap Press of Harvard University Press, 1977.

Kelly, George E. *Sammy Blows His Whistle: A Biography of Judge Samuel A. Weiss*. Washington, D.C.: Progress Press, 1947.

Kelton, Elmer. *Hanging Judge*. New York: Forge, 1969.

Kemerer, Frank R. *William Wayne Justice: A Judicial Biography*. Austin: University of Texas Press, 1991.

Kennedy, Anthony. "Remarks of Justice Anthony Kennedy at the Presentation of the Devitt Award to the Honorable Milton Pollack." 909 F. Supp LXIX (1995).

Kennedy, Robert F., Jr. *Judge Frank M. Johnson, Jr.: A Biography*. New York: Putnam, 1978.

Kens, Paul. *Justice Stephen Field: Shaping Liberty from the Gold Rush to the Gilded Age*. Lawrence: University Press of Kansas, 1997.

Kent, James. *Commentaries on American Law*. 12th ed. Edited by Oliver W. Holmes Jr., 4 vols. Boston: Little, Brown, 1883–1884.

———. *Dissertations: Being the Preliminary Part of a Course of Law Lectures*. 1795. Reprint, Littleton, Colo.: Fred B. Rothman and Co., 1991.

Kiernan, Laura. "Mikva Could Shape U.S. Court's Future." *Washington Post*, 23 July 1979, C1.

Kierner, Cynthia A. *Traders and Gentlefolk: The Livingstons of New York, 1675–1790*. Ithaca, N.Y.: Cornell University Press, 1992.

Kilpatrick, James J. "7th Circuit Court Blessed with Two Very Skilled Writers." *Wisconsin State Journal*, 8 January 1996, 5A.

Kinch, Sam, and Ben Procter. *Texas under a Cloud*. Austin, Tex.: Jenkins Publishing Company, 1972.

Kirtland, Robert Bevier. "George Wythe: Lawyer, Revolutionary, Judge." Ph.D. diss., University of Michigan, 1983.

Klein, Philip Shriver. *Pennsylvania Politics 1817–1832: A Game without Rules*. Philadelphia: Historical Society of Pennsylvania, 1940.

Kleven, Thomas. "The Constitutional Philosophy of Justice William H. Rehnquist." *Vermont Law Review* 8 (Spring 1983): 3.

Knox, John C. *A Judge Comes of Age*. New York: Charles Scribner's Sons, 1940.

Konefsky, Samuel J. *Chief Justice Stone and the Supreme Court*. New York: Macmillan, 1946.

Kopel, David B. "The Self-Defense Cases: How the United States Supreme Court Confronted a Hanging Judge in the Nineteenth Century and Taught Some Lessons for Jurisprudence in the Twenty-first." *American Journal of Criminal Law* 27 (Summer 2000): 294–327.

Kotlowski, Dean. "Trial by Error: Nixon, the Senate, and the Haynsworth Nomination." *Presidential Studies Quarterly* 26 (Winter 1996): 71–91.

Kousser, J. Morgan. "Separate but Not Equal: The Supreme Court's First Decision on Racial Discrimination in Schools." *Journal of Southern History* 46 (1980): 17–44.

Kozinski, Alex. "The Anti-History and Pre-History of Commercial Speech." *Texas Law Review* 72 (1993): 747.

———. "A Penumbra Too Far." *Harvard Law Review* 106 (1993): 1639.

———. "Who's Afraid of Commercial Speech?" *Virginia Law Review* 76 (1990): 627.

Kramer, N. "Half a Century Past Midnight: The Life and Times of Judge William Cranch." Ph.D. diss., Claremont Graduate School, 1978.

Kramer, Victor H. "The Trial of the Investment Banking Case: United States v. Morgan." *Litigation* 14 (1988): 43–60.

Kravitch, Phillis A. "Women in the Legal Profession: The Past 100 Years." *Mississippi Law Journal* 69 (1999): 57.

Kristen, Barbara Frank, ed. *The Selected Writings of Jerome Frank: A Man's Reach*. New York: Macmillan, 1965.

Kritzer, Herbert M., ed. *Legal Systems of the World: A Political, Social, and Cultural Encyclopedia*. 4 vols. Santa Barbara, Calif.: ABC-CLIO, 2002.

Kutler, Stanley I. *The American Inquisition*. New York: Hill and Wang, 1982.

———. "John Bannister Gibson: Judicial Restraint and the 'Positive State.'" *Journal of Public Law* 14 (1965): 181–197.

———. "Pennsylvania Courts, the Abolition Act, and Negro Rights." *Pennsylvania History* 30 (1963): 14–27.

Kutler, Stanley I., ed. *The Supreme Court and the Constitution: Readings in American Constitutional History*. New York: W. W. Norton, 1977.

Lamb, Charles M., and Stephen C. Halpern. *The Burger Court: Political and Judicial Profiles*. Urbana: University of Illinois Press, 1991.

Landes, William M., Lawrence Lessig, and Michael E. Solimine. "Judicial Influence: A Citation Analysis of Federal Courts of Appeals Judges." *Journal of Legal Studies* 27 (June 1998): 271–332.

Landis, Kenesaw Mountain. "Presentation to the United States District Court of the Portrait of Judge Thomas Drummond (Proceedings in Judge Landis' Courtroom, February 1, 1913)." Chicago Historical Society Papers.

Larsen, Charles. *The Good Fight: The Life and Times of Ben B. Lindsey*. Chicago: Quadrangle Books, 1972.

Lash, Joseph P., ed. *From the Diaries of Felix Frankfurter*. New York: W. W. Norton, 1975.

Laville, Helen, and Scott Lucas. "The American Way: Edith Sampson, the NAACP, and African American Identity in the Cold War." *Diplomatic History* 20, no. 4 (Fall 1996): 565–591.

Lees, Edward. "William Mitchell." *Minnesota Law Review* 4 (1920): 377.

Lengel, James H. "Justice Jonathan Jasper Wright: An African American First." M.A. thesis, Vanderbilt University, 1997.
Leuchtenburg, William E. *The Supreme Court Reborn: The Constitutional Revolution in the Age of Roosevelt*. New York: Oxford University Press, 1995.
Leventhal, Harold. "Courts and Political Thickets." *Columbia Law Review* 77 (1977): 345.
———. "The Courts and the Labor Agencies." *University of Dayton Law Review* 3 (1978): 327.
———. "Cues and Compasses for Administrative Lawyers." *Administrative Law Review* 20 (1967): 237.
———. "Environmental Decisionmaking and the Role of the Courts." *University of Pennsylvania Law Review* 122 (1974): 509.
———. "Principled Fairness and Regulatory Urgency." *Case Western Reserve Law Review* 25 (1974): 66.
———. "The Role of the Price Lawyer." In *Problems in Price Control: Legal Phases*. 49 OPA Historical Reports on War Administration. Washington, D.C.: U.S. Government Printing Office, 1947.
Levin, H., ed. *The Lawyers and Lawmakers of Kentucky*. Easley, S.C.: Southern Historical Press, 1982.
Levy, Beryl H. *Cardozo and Frontiers of Legal Thinking with Selected Opinions*. Cleveland, Ohio: Case Western Reserve University, 1969.
Levy, Leonard W. *The Law of the Commonwealth and Chief Justice Shaw*. New York: Oxford University Press, 1957.
———. *Seasoned Judgments: The American Constitution, Rights, and History*. New Brunswick, N.J.: Transaction Publishers, 1995.
Lewis, Anthony. "A Talk with Warren on Crime, the Court, the Country." *New York Times Magazine*, 19 October 1969, 35.
Lewis, Neil A. "Presiding as Ideas Clash in Capital Appeals Court." *New York Times*, 1 February 1991, B4.
Lewis, Walker. *Without Fear or Favor: A Biography of Chief Justice Roger Brooke Taney*. Boston: Houghton Mifflin, 1965.
Lewis, William Draper. *Great American Lawyers*. 8 vols. Philadelphia: John C. Winston, 1907–1909.
Linde, Hans A. "Courts and Torts: 'Public Policy' without Public Politics?" *Valparaiso University Law Review* 28 (1994): 821–855.
———. "State Courts and Republican Government." *Santa Clara Law Review* 41 (2001): 951–971.
Linde, Hans A., and George Bunn. *Legislative and Administrative Processes*. Mineola, N.Y.: Foundation Press, 1976.
Linder, Douglas O. "Without Fear or Favor: Judge James Edwin Horton and the Trial of the 'Scottsboro Boys.'" *University of Missouri at Kansas City Law Review* 68 (Summer 2000): 549–583.
Lizza, Ryan. "Friend of the Court: Alberto Gonzales's High-wire Act." *The New Republic* 226, 27 May 2002, 16–18.
Llewellyn, Karl N. *The Common Law Tradition: Deciding Appeals*. Boston: Little, Brown, 1960.
Lloyd, Everett. *Law West of the Pecos: The Story of Roy Bean*. San Antonio, Tex.: The Naylor Company, 1967.

Locke, John. *Two Treatises of Government*. Edited by Peter Laslett. New York: New American Library, 1965.

Lockwood, Evelyn. *Index to Kentucky Legal History: References to Selected Sources of Information concerning the Eighteenth and Nineteenth Centuries*. Frankfort, Ky.: The State Law Library, 1983.

McClellan, James. *Joseph Story and the American Constitution*. Norman: University of Oklahoma Press, 1971.

McCloskey, Robert. *The American Supreme Court*. Chicago: University of Chicago Press, 1960.

McCombs, Rufe, with Karen Spears Zacharias. *Benched: The Memoirs of Judge Rufe McCombs*. Macon, Ga.: Mercer University Press, 1997.

McCoy, Samuel. "Indiana's First Lawyer and the Convivial Fraternity of the Early Days." *Indianapolis News*, 16 September 1911, A1.

McCurdy, Charles W. "Justice Field and the Jurisprudence of Government-Business Relations: Some Parameters of Laissez-Faire Constitutionalism." *Journal of American History* 61 (1975): 970.

———. "Stephen J. Field and the American Judicial Tradition." In *The Fields and the Law*. San Francisco: United States District Court for the Northern District of California Historical Society, 1986.

McDonald, Forrest. *Alexander Hamilton: A Biography*. New York: W. W. Norton, 1979.

MacFarquhar, Larissa. "The Bench Burner: How Did a Judge with Such Subversive Ideas Become a Leading Influence on American Legal Opinion?" *The New Yorker*, 10 December 2001, 78–86.

McGowan, Carl. "Congress and the Courts." *ABA Journal* 62 (1976): 1588–1591.

———. "Congress, Court, and Control of Delegated Power." *Columbia Law Review* 77 (December 1977): 1119–1174.

———. "Federal Jurisdiction: Legislative and Judicial Change." *Case Western Law Review* 28, no. 3 (Spring 1978): 517–555.

———. "Federalism—Old and New—and the Federal Courts." *The Georgetown Law Journal* 70 (1982): 1421–1432.

———. "The President's Veto Power: An Important Instrument of Conflict in Our Constitutional System." *San Diego Law Review* 23, no. 4 (July-August 1986): 791–821.

———. "Presidents and Their Papers." *Minnesota Law Review* 68 (1983): 409–437.

———. "A Reply to Judicialization." *Duke Law Review* (April 1986): 217–237.

———. "United States Courts of Appeal." In *Encyclopedia of the American Constitution*, edited by Leonard W. Levy, Kenneth Karst, and Dennis J. Mahoney. New York: Macmillan, 1986, 4:1939–1942.

———. "The View from an Inferior Court." *San Diego Law Review* 19 (1982): 659–674.

McGreevy, John T. "A Case of Doctrinal Development—John T. Noonan; Jurist, Historian, Author, Sage." *Commonweal* 127, 17 November 2002, 12.

McGuire, Phillip. *He, Too, Spoke for Democracy: Judge Hastie, World War II, and the Black Soldier*. Westport, Conn.: Greenwood Press, 1988.

McIntosh, Wayne V., and Cynthia L. Cates. *Judicial Entrepreneurship: The Role of the Judge in the Marketplace of Ideas*. Westport, Conn.: Greenwood Press, 1997.

McNeil, Gena Rae. *Groundwork: Charles Hamilton Houston and the Struggle for Civil Rights*. Philadelphia: University of Pennsylvania Press, 1983.

McWhirter, Darien A. *The Legal 100: A Ranking of the Individuals Who Have Most Influenced the Law*. Secaucus, N.J.: Carol Publishing Group, 1998.
Magee, James J. *Mr. Justice Black: Absolutist on the Court*. Charlottesville: University Press of Virginia, 1980.
Malone, Dumas. *Jefferson and His Times: The Sage of Monticello*. Boston: Little, Brown, 1981.
Malone, Dumas, ed. *Dictionary of American Biography*. 10 regular and 10 supplemental volumes. New York: Charles Scribner's Sons, 1963.
Maltese, John Anthony. *The Selling of Supreme Court Nominees*. Baltimore, Md.: Johns Hopkins University Press, 1995.
Maltz, Eric. "Only Partially Color-Blind: John Marshall Harlan's View of Race and the Constitution." *Georgia State Law Review* 12 (1996): 973–1016.
"Man of the Year. Judge John J. Sirica: Standing Firm for the Primacy of Law." *Time Magazine*, 7 January 1974, 8–15.
Manley, Walter W., II, E. Canton Brown Jr., and Eric W. Rise. *The Supreme Court of Florida and Its Predecessor Courts, 1821–1917*. Gainesville, Fla.: University Press of Florida, 1999.
Marshall, John. *The Papers of John Marshall*. 10 vols. to date. Edited by Charles F. Hobson et al. Chapel Hill: University of North Carolina Press, 1974– .
Mason, Alpheus Thomas. *Brandeis: A Free Man's Life*. New York: The Viking Press, 1946.
———. *Free Government in the Making: Readings in American Political Thought*. 4th ed. New York: Oxford University Press, 1985.
———. *Harlan Fiske Stone: Pillar of the Law*. New York: Viking, 1956.
Massaro, John. *Supremely Political: The Role of Ideology and Presidential Management in Unsuccessful Supreme Court Nominations*. Albany: State University of New York Press, 1990.
Mayer, David N. *The Constitutional Thought of Thomas Jefferson*. Charlottesville: University Press of Virginia, 1994.
Mays, David John. *Edmund Pendleton 1721–1803: A Biography*. 2 vols. Cambridge: Harvard University Press, 1952.
Mays, David John, ed. *The Letters and Papers of Edmund Pendleton 1734–1803*. 2 vols. Charlottesville: University Press of Virginia, 1967.
Medina, Harold R. *The Anatomy of Freedom*. New York: Henry Holt, 1959.
———. "John Johnston Parker, 1885–1958." *North Carolina Law Review* 38 (1960): 299.
———. *Judge Medina Speaks*. New York: Matthew Bender, 1954.
Medsger, Betty. *Framed: The New Right Attack on Chief Justice Rose Bird and the Courts*. New York: Pilgrim Press, 1983.
Menand, Louis. *The Metaphysical Club*. New York: Farrar, Straus and Giroux, 2001.
Merchant, Alice. "The Historical Background of the Procedural Reform Movement in Alabama." *Alabama Law Review* 9 (Spring 1957): 284–292.
Metzger, Stanley D. "Henry Edgerton, Law Teacher." *Cornell Alumni News* 73, November 1970, 37.
Mikva, Abner J. "Sturm und Drang at the D.C. Circuit." *George Washington Law Review* 57 (1989): 1063–1068.
———. "The Verdict on Judge Wapner." *TV Guide*, 22 April 1989, 12–14.
Miller, Arthur Selwyn. *A "Capacity for Outrage": The Judicial Odyssey of J. Skelly Wright*. Westport, Conn.: Greenwood Press, 1984.

Miller, Arthur Selwyn, ed. *On Courts and Democracy: Selected Nonjudicial Writings of J. Skelly Wright*. Westport, Conn.: Greenwood Press, 1984.
Minnow, Martha. "Tribute: The Legacy of David L. Bazelon: Questioning Our Policies: Judge David L. Bazelon's Legacy for Mental Health Law." *Georgetown Law Journal* 83 (1993): 7.
Mitford, John. *A Treatise on the Pleadings in Suits of the Court of Chancery, by English Bill*. New York: R. M. Dermut and D. D. Arden, 1816.
Mitgang, Herbert. *The Man Who Rode the Tiger: The Life and Times of Judge Samuel Seabury*. New York: Fordham University Press, 1963.
Mithoff, Richard Warren. "A Tribute to Justice." *Texas Law Review* 77 (November 1998): 9–12.
Moger, Allen W. "Railroad Practices and Policies in Virginia after the Civil War." *Virginia Historical Magazine* 59, 1951, 423–457.
Moglen, Eben. "Considering Zenger: Partisan Politics and the Legal Profession in Provincial New York." *Columbia Law Review* 94 (1994): 1495.
Monks, Leander J., ed. *Courts and Lawyers of Indiana*. Indianapolis: Federal Publishing Co., 1915.
Montesquieu, Baron de. *The Spirit of the Laws*. 2 vols. Translated by Thomas Nugent. New York: Hafner Press, 1949.
Mooney, R. J. "The Deady Years: 1859–1893." In *The First Duty: A History of the U.S. District Court for Oregon*, edited by Carolyn M. Buan. Portland: U.S. District Court of Oregon Historical Society, 1993, 63–125.
———. "Formalism and Fairness: Matthew Deady and Early Portland Land-title Disputes." *Oregon Benchmarks* 5 (1989): 1–4.
———. "Matthew Deady and the Federal Judicial Response to Racism in the Early West." *Oregon Law Review* 63 (1984): 561–637.
Moore, Lonnie W. *Gates of Hell: The Wrath of Judge Isaac Parker*. Kearney, Nebr.: Morris Publishing, 1998.
Morello, Karen Berger. *The Invisible Bar: The Woman Lawyer in America 1638 to the Present*. New York: Random House, 1986.
Morphonious, Ellen, with Mike Wilson. *Maximum Morphonious: The Life and Times of America's Toughest Judge*. New York: William Morrow, 1991.
Morris, Jeffrey B. *Calmly to Poise the Scales of Justice: A History of the Courts of the District of Columbia Circuit*. Durham, N.C.: Carolina Academic Press, 2001.
———. "The Second Most Important Court: The United States Court of Appeals for the District of Columbia Circuit." Ph.D. thesis, Columbia University, 1972.
Morris, Lewis. *The Opinion and Argument of the Chief Justice of the Province of New York concerning the Jurisdiction of the Supream Court of the Said Province, to Determine Causes in a Court of Equity*. New York: Sold by J. P. Zenger, 1733. Reprint, Boston: Massachusetts Historical Society, 1929.
Morris, Thomas Robbins. *The Virginia Supreme Court: An Institutional and Political Analysis*. Charlottesville: University Press of Virginia for the Institute of Government, 1975.
Moss, William Paul. *Rough and Tumble: The Autobiography of a West Texas Judge*. New York: Vantage Press, 1954.
Motley, Constance Baker. *Equal Justice under Law: An Autobiography*. New York: Farrar, Straus and Giroux, 1998.
"Mr. Justice Harlan: A Symposium." *Harvard Law Review* 85 (1971): 369–391.

Murphy, Bruce Allen. *The Brandeis/Frankfurter Connection: The Secret Political Activities of Two Supreme Court Justices*. New York: Oxford University Press, 1982.
Murphy, James Oakley. "The Work of Judge Parker in the United States District Court for the Western District of Arkansas—1875–1896." Master's thesis, University of Oklahoma, 1939.
Murphy, Reg. *Uncommon Sense: The Achievement of Griffin Bell*. Atlanta, Ga.: Longstreet, 1999.
Murphy, Walter F. *Elements of Judicial Strategy*. Chicago: University of Chicago Press, 1971.
———. *The Vicar of Christ*. New York: Macmillan, 1969.
Murphy, Walter F., James E. Fleming, and Sotirious A. Barber. *American Constitutional Interpretation*. 2d ed. Westbury, N.Y.: The Foundation Press, 1995.
Murray, Craig C. "Chief Justice Gibson of the Pennsylvania Supreme Court and Judicial Review." *University of Pittsburgh Law Review* 32 (1970): 127–166.
Nagel, Robert F., ed. *Intellect and Craft: The Contributions of Justice Hans Linde to American Constitutionalism*. Boulder, Colo.: Westview Press, 1995.
Nelson, Marcia, ed. *The Remarkable Hands: An Affectionate Portrait*. New York: Foundation of the Federal Bar Council, 1983.
Nelson, Margaret Virginia. *A Study of Judicial Review in Virginia: 1789–1928*. New York: Columbia University Press, 1947.
"New Kid on the Bench." *Time* 136, 19 November 1990, 46.
Newman, Helen. "William Cranch: Judge, Law School Professor, Reporter." *Law Library Journal* 26 (1933): 1–15.
Newman, Roger K. *Hugo Black: A Biography*. New York: Pantheon, 1994.
Newmyer, R. Kent. *John Marshall and the Heroic Age of the Supreme Court*. Baton Rouge: Louisiana State University Press, 2001.
———. *Supreme Court Justice Joseph Story: Statesman of the Old Republic*. Chapel Hill: University of North Carolina Press, 1985.
———. *The Supreme Court under Marshall and Taney*. Arlington Heights, Ill.: AHM Publishing Co., 1968.
Niblack, John Lewis. *The Life and Times of a Hoosier Judge*. 1973. N.p.
Noonan, John T. *Persons and Masks of the Law: Cardozo, Holmes, Jefferson, and Wythe as Makers of the Masks*. New York: Farrar, Straus, and Giroux, 1976.
Northup, William B., and John B. Northrup. *The Insolence of Office: The Story of the Seabury Investigations*. New York: G. P. Putnam's Sons, 1932.
Novick, Sheldon M. *Honorable Justice: The Life of Oliver Wendell Holmes*. Boston: Little, Brown, 1989.
O'Brien, David, ed. *Judges on Judging: Views from the Bench*. Chatham, N.J.: Chatham House Publishers, 1997.
Osgood, Russell K., ed. *The History of the Law in Massachusetts: The Supreme Judicial Court, 1692–1992*. Boston: Supreme Judicial Court Historical Society, 1992.
Overmeyer, P. H. "The Oregon Justinian: A Life of Matthew Paul Deady." Master's thesis, University of Oregon, 1935.
Parker, Isaac. "How to Arrest the Increase of Homicides in America." *North American Review*, June 1896, 667–674.
Parrish, Michael E. *Felix Frankfurter and His Times: The Reform Years*. New York: The Free Press, 1982.
Parsons, Theophilus, Jr. *Memoir of Theophilus Parsons*. 1859. Reprint, New York: De Capo Press, 1970.

Paul, Julius. *The Legal Realism of Jerome N. Frank: A Study of Fact-Skepticism and the Judicial Process*. The Hague: Martinas Nijhoff, 1957.
Paulsen, James W. "Community Property and Early American Women's Rights Movement: The Texas Connection." *Idaho Law Review* 32 (1996): 641.
———. "Introduction: The Texas Home Equity Controversy in Context." *St. Mary's Law Journal* 26 (1994): 307.
———. "A Short History of the Supreme Court of the Republic of Texas." *Texas Law Review* 65 (1986): 237.
Peltason, Jack W. *Fifty-eight Lonely Men: Southern Federal Judges and School Desegregation*. Urbana: University of Illinois Press, 1971.
Pencak, William, and Wythe W. Holt Jr. *The Law in America, 1607–1861*. New York: The New York Historical Society, 1989.
Pendleton, Edmund. *The Letters and Papers of Edmund Pendleton, 1734–1803*. 2 vols. Edited by David John Mays. Charlottesville: University Press of Virginia, 1967.
Perry, Barbara. *"The Supremes": Essays on the Current Justices of the Supreme Court of the United States*. New York: Peter Lang, 2001.
Peterson, William D., and Norman W. Provizer, eds. *Rating Game of the Greatest Supreme Court Justices: Polls and Case Studies*. In press.
Pfeffer, Leo. *This Honorable Court: A History of the United States Supreme Court*. Boston: Beacon Press, 1967.
Phillips, Harlan, ed. *Felix Frankfurter Reminisces: Recorded in Talks with Harlan B. Phillips*. New York: Reynal and Company, 1960.
Pietrusza, David. *Judge and Jury: The Life and Times of Judge Kenesaw Mountain Landis*. South Bend, Ind.: Diamond Communications, 1998.
Polenberg, Richard. *The World of Benjamin Cardozo: Personal Values and the Judicial Process*. Cambridge: Harvard University Press, 1997.
Pollack, Jack H. *Earl Warren: The Judge Who Changed America*. Englewood Cliffs, N.J.: Prentice Hall, 1979.
Porter, William A. *An Essay on the Life, Character and Writings of John G. Gibson, LL.D.* Philadelphia: T. and J. W. Johnson, 1855.
Posner, Richard A. *Cardozo: A Study in Reputation*. Chicago: University of Chicago Press, 1990.
———. "Diary: A Weeklong Electronic Journal." Slate.com. 14–18 January 2002.
———. "Exchange: The Concept of Unenumerated Rights; Legal Reasoning from the Top Down and from the Bottom Up: The Question of Unenumerated Constitutional Rights." *University of Chicago Law Review* 59 (Winter 1992): 433–450.
———. *The Federal Courts: Challenge and Reform*. 2d ed. Cambridge: Harvard University Press, 1996.
———. *Overcoming Law*. Cambridge: Harvard University Press, 1995.
———. *The Problematics of Moral and Legal Theory*. Cambridge: Harvard University Press, 1999.
Pound, Cuthbert W. "Constitutional Aspects of American Administrative Law." *American Bar Association Journal* 9 (July 1923): 409–416.
———. "Inquisitorial Confessions." *Cornell Law Quarterly* 1 (January 1916): 77–81.
Pound, Roscoe. *The Formative Era of America Law*. Boston: Little, Brown, 1938. Reprint, Gloucester, Mass.: Peter Smith, 1960.

Powell, H. Jefferson. "The Complete Jeffersonian: Justice Rehnquist and Federalism." *Yale Law Journal* 92 (1982): 1317–1370.
Powell, Lewis F., Jr., et al. "In Memoriam: Judge Carl McGowan." *The George Washington Law Review* 56, no. 4–5 (May-August 1988): 681–702.
Przybyszewski, Linda. *The Republic according to John Marshall Harlan*. Chapel Hill: University of North Carolina Press, 1999.
Purdum, Todd S. "Yale Law Dean Is Nominated to 2d Circuit Appeals Court." *New York Times*, 10 February 1994, B7.
Pusey, Merlo J. *Charles Evans Hughes*. 2 vols. New York: Columbia University Press, 1963.
Raack, David A. "'To Preserve the Best Fruits': The Legal Thought of Chancellor James Kent." *American Journal of Legal History* 33 (1989): 320–366.
Rabkin, Jeremy. *Judicial Compulsions: How Public Law Distorts Public Policy*. New York: Basic Books, 1989.
Ransom, William L. *Charles E. Hughes: The Statesman as Shown in the Opinions of the Jurist*. New York: Dutton, 1916.
Rasch, Jonathan J. "William H. Hastie and the Vindication of Civil Rights." *Howard Law Journal* 21 (1978): 749–820.
Ratliff, Beulah Amidon. "Charles Fremont Amidon." *North Dakota History* 7 (1941): 83–100.
Ratcliff, J. D. "Justice—Edith Sampson Style." *Reader's Digest*, November 1968, 167–174.
Read, Frank T., and Lucy S. McGough. *Let Them Be Judged: The Judicial Integration of the Deep South*. Metuchen, N.J.: The Scarecrow Press, 1978.
Rehnquist, William H. "The Notion of a Living Constitution." *Texas Law Review* 54 (May 1976): 693–706.
Reid, Elizabeth Jameson. *Judge Richard Reid: A Biography*. 2d ed. Cincinnati, Ohio: Standard Publishing Company, 1886.
Reid, John Phillip. "Biographies of Titans: Holmes, Brandeis, and Other Obsessions: Commentary beneath the Titans." *New York University Law Review* 70 (June 1995): 653–676.
———. *Chief Justice; The Judicial World of Charles Doe*. Cambridge: Harvard University Press, 1967.
———. "Lessons of Lumpkin: A Review of Recent Literature on Law, Comity and the Impending Crisis." *William and Mary Law Review* 23 (1982): 571–624.
Reid, Traciel V. "The Politicization of Retention Elections: Lessons from the Defeat of Justices Lanphier and White." *Judicature* 83 (September-October 1999): 68–77.
Remarks of Hon. Samuel Ames, Reporter of the Decisions of the Supreme Court, in Explanation of His Report of the Case, Robert H. Ives vs. Charles T. Hazard, et al. Providence, R.I.: Knowles, Anthony and Co., 1859.
Rhodes, Irwin S., ed. *The Papers of John Marshall: A Descriptive Calendar*. 2 vols. Norman: University of Oklahoma Press, 1969.
Richtel, Matt. "To One Judge, Cybermonitors Bring Uneasy Memories." *New York Times*, 18 August 2001, A8.
Riddlesperger, James W., Jr. "Sarah T. Hughes: Biography of a Federal District Judge." Master's thesis, North Texas State University, 1980.
Robarge, David. *A Chief Justice's Progress: John Marshall from Revolutionary Virginia to the Supreme Court*. Westport, Conn.: Greenwood Press, 2000.

Roberts, Thomas P. *Memoirs of John Bannister Gibson*. Pittsburgh, Pa.: Jos. Eichbaum, 1890.

Roper, Donald. "James Kent and the Emergence of New York's Libel Law." *American Journal of Legal History* 17 (1973): 221–231.

Rosen, Jeffrey. "Washington Diarist: Overqualified." *The New Republic*, 4 April 1994, 42.

Rosenberg, Gerald N. *The Hollow Hope: Can Courts Bring about Social Change?* Chicago: The University of Chicago Press, 1991.

Rosenberg, J. Mitchell. *Jerome Frank: Jurist and Philosopher*. New York: Philosophical Library, 1970.

Rosenthal, Lee H. "In Memoriam: Judge John R. Brown, Jr.: A Scrapbook." *Texas Law Review* 71 (April 1993): 909.

Ross, William G. "Walter Clark of North Carolina: Antagonist of the Federal Judiciary." *Journal of Southern Legal History* 3 (1994): 1–35.

Roth, Elizabeth. "The Two Voices of Roger Traynor." *American Journal of Legal History* 27, no. 3 (1983): 269–301.

Rowe, G. S. *Embattled Bench: The Pennsylvania Supreme Court and the Forging of a Democratic Society, 1684–1809*. Newark: University of Delaware Press, 1994.

Salley, Columus. *The Black 100: A Ranking of the Most Influential African-Americans, Past and Present*. New York: Carol Publishing Group, 1993.

Sams, Conway W., and Elihu S. Riley, eds. *Bench and Bar of Maryland*. Chicago: Lewis Publishing Co., 1901.

Satter, Robert. *Doing Justice: A Trial Judge at Work*. New York: Simon and Schuster, 1990.

Savage, David. *Turning Right*. New York: John Wiley and Sons, 1992.

Scalia, Antonin. *A Matter of Interpretation: Federal Courts and the Law*. Princeton, N.J.: Princeton University Press, 1997.

Schaefer, Walter V. "Chief Justice Traynor and the Judicial Process." *California Law Review* 53 (1965): 11–24.

———. "The Control of 'Sunbursts': Techniques of Prospective Overruling." *New York University Law Review* 42 (1967): 631–646.

———. "Federalism and State Criminal Procedure." *Harvard Law Review* 70 (1956): 1–26.

———. "The Fourteenth Amendment and the Sanctity of the Person." *Northwestern University Law Review* 64 (1969): 1–17.

———. "Police Interrogation and the Privilege against Self-Incrimination." *Northwestern University Law Review* 61 (1966): 506–521.

———. "Precedent and Policy." *University of Chicago Law Review* 34 (1966): 3–25.

———. "Prospective Rulings: Two Perspectives." *Supreme Court Review* (1982): 1–24.

———. "Unresolved Issues in the Law of Double Jeopardy: *Waller* and *Ashe*." *California Law Review* 58 (1970): 391–404.

Schafer, Judith Kelleher. "Roman Roots of the Louisiana Law of Slavery: Emancipation in American Louisiana, 1803–1857." *Louisiana Law Review* 56 (1995): 409–422.

Schafer, Judith Kelleher, and Warren M. Billings, eds. *An Uncommon Experience: Law and Judicial Institutions in Louisiana, 1803–2003*. The Louisiana Purchase Bicentennial Series in Louisiana History, vol. 13. Lafayette: The Center for Louisiana Studies, 1997.

Schick, Marvin. *Learned Hand's Court*. Baltimore, Md.: Johns Hopkins University Press, 1970.
Schmickle, Sharon, and Tom Hamburger. "Devitt Award Is Prestigious—and Unusual." *Minneapolis Star Tribune*, 5 March 1995.
Schuck, Peter H. *Agent Orange on Trial: Mass Toxic Disasters in the Courts*. Cambridge: Harvard University Press, 1986.
Schwartz, Bernard. *A Book of Legal Lists*. New York: Oxford University Press, 1997.
———. *The Burger Years*. New York: Viking, 1987.
———. *Main Currents in American Legal Thought*. Durham, N.C.: Carolina Academic Press, 1998.
The Scribner Encyclopedia of American Lives. New York: Charles Scribner's Sons, 1999. Reproduced in Biography Resource Center. Farmington Hills, Mich.: The Gale Group, 2001. Available at <http://www.galenet.com/servlet/BioRC>.
Seabury, Samuel. *Municipal Ownership and Operation of Public Utilities in New York City*. New York: Municipal Ownership Publishing Co., 1905.
———. *The New Federalism*. New York: E. P. Dutton, 1950.
———. *A Review of the Labor Laws Relative to the Rate of Wages and the Hours of Labor in the State of New York*. New York: E. R. Mantz, 1901.
Senese, Donald J., ed. *George Mason and the Legacy of Constitutional Liberty*. Fairfax, Va.: Fairfax County Historical Commission, 1989.
Sewall, Samuel. *The Diary of Samuel Sewall*. Edited by M. Halsey Thomas. New York: Farrar, Straus and Giroux, 1973.
———. *Slavery, the Civil Law, and the Supreme Court of Louisiana*. Baton Rouge: Louisiana State University Press, 1994.
Shanks, Hershel, ed. *The Art and Craft of Judging: The Decisions of Judge Learned Hand*. New York: Macmillan, 1968.
Shapiro, Fred R. "The Most Cited Legal Scholars." *Journal of Legal Studies* 29 (January 2000): 409–426.
Sheehy, Barbara A. "An Analysis of the Honorable Richard A. Posner's Social Security Law." *Connecticut Insurance Law Journal* 7 (2000/2001): 103–151.
Sheindlin, Judy, with Josh Getlin. *Don't Pee on My Leg and Tell Me It's Raining: America's Toughest Family Court Judge Speaks Out*. New York: HarperPerennial, 1997.
Sheldon, Charles H. *A Century of Judging: A Political History of the Washington Supreme Court*. Seattle, Wash.: 1998.
Sheridan, Eugene. *Lewis Morris, 1671–1746: A Study in Early American Politics*. Syracuse, N.Y.: Syracuse University Press, 1981.
Sheridan, Eugene, ed. *The Papers of Lewis Morris, Governor of the Province of New Jersey*. 4 vols. New Jersey Historical Society, 1991.
Shevory, Thomas C. *John Marshall's Law: Interpretation, Ideology, and Interest*. Greenwood, Conn.: Greenwood Press, 1994.
Shirley, Glenn. *Law West of Fort Smith: A History of Frontier Justice in the Indian Territory, 1834–1896*. Lincoln: University of Nebraska Press, 1988.
"Shirley S. Abrahamson." Available at <http://wwc.state.wi.us/static/bios/Shirley%20S.htm>. Accessed 2 January 2003.
Siegel, Martin. *The Taney Court, 1836–1864*. New York: Associated Faculty Press, 1987.
Sikora, Frank. *The Judge: The Life and Opinions of Alabama's Frank M. Johnson, Jr.* 1992. Montgomery, Ala.: Black Belt Press.

Silbert, Samuel H., with Eisenbert, Sidney A. *'Judge Sam.'* Manhasset, N.Y.: Channel Press, 1963.
Sirica, John J. *To Set the Record Straight: The Break-in, the Tapes, the Conspirators, the Pardon*. New York: W. W. Norton, 1979.
Slania, Laura J. "Dynamics Corp. of America v. CTS Corp.: Posner's Plan for Poison Pills." *Wisconsin Law Review* 1987 (July/August 1987): 711–735.
Smemo, Kenneth. *Against the Tide: The Life and Times of Federal Judge Charles F. Amidon, North Dakota Progressive*. New York: Garland Publishing, 1986.
Smith, Charles W., Jr. *Roger B. Taney: Jacksonian Jurist*. New York: Da Capo Press, 1973.
Smith, Christopher E. "Judicial Lobbying and Court Reform: U.S. Magistrate Judges and the Judicial Improvements Act of 1990." *University of Arkansas–Little Rock Law Journal* 14 (1992): 163–198.
———. *United States Magistrates in the Federal Courts: Subordinate Judges*. New York: Praeger, 1990.
Smith, J. Clay, Jr. "In Freedom's Birthplace: The Making of George Lewis Ruffin, the First Black Law Graduate of Harvard University." *Howard Law Journal* 39 (Fall 1995): 201–235.
Smith, Jean Edward. *John Marshall: Definer of a Nation*. New York: Henry Holt, 1996.
Smith, Jessie Carney, ed. *Black Firsts: 2,000 Years of Extraordinary Achievement*. Detroit, Mich.: Visible Ink Press, 1994.
———. *Notable Black American Women*. Detroit, Mich.: Gale, 1992.
Smith, Joseph A. "An Independent Judiciary: The Colonial Background." *University of Pennsylvania Law Review* 124 (1976): 1104.
Smith, O. H. *Early Indiana Trials and Sketches*. Cincinnati, Ohio: Moore, Wilstrach, Keys and Co., 1858.
Songer, Donald. *Continuity and Change on the United States Court of Appeals*. Ann Arbor: University of Michigan Press, 2000.
Sonnichsen, C. L. *Roy Bean: Law West of the Pecos*. New York: Macmillan, 1943.
Speech of Hon. Joseph M. Blake upon the Report of the Case Ives versus Hazard, Made by Chief Justice Samuel Ames, State Reporter. Providence, R.I.: Knowles, Anthony and Co., 1860–1869?
Spence, Vernon Gladden. *Judge Leggett of Abilene: A Texas Frontier Profile*. College Station: Texas A and M University Press, 1977.
Spink, J. G. Taylor. *Judge Landis and Twenty-five Years of Baseball*. New York: Thomas Y. Crowell Company, 1947.
Stein, David. *Judging the Judges: The Cause, Control and Cure of Judicial Jaundice*. Hicksville, N.Y.: Exposition Press, 1974.
Steinberg, Alfred. *Sam Rayburn: A Biography*. New York: Hawthorn Books, 1975.
Steiner, Bernard C. *Life of Roger Brooke Taney, Chief Justice of the United States Supreme Court*. Westport, Conn.: Greenwood Press, 1970.
Stempel, Jeffrey W. "An Inconsistently Sensitive Mind: Richard Posner's Celebration of Insurance and Continuing Blind Spots of Eco Nominalism." *Connecticut Insurance Law Journal* 7 (2000/2001): 7–79.
Stephenson, Mason D., and D. Grier Stephenson. "To Protect and Defend: Joseph Henry Lumpkin, the Supreme Court of Georgia and Slavery." *Emory Law Journal* 25 (1976): 579–608.

Steward, James B. *Den of Thieves*. New York: Simon and Schuster, 1991.
Stewart, Gail B. *What Happened to Judge Crater?* New York: Crestwood House, 1992.
Stolberg, Mary M. "The Evolution of Frontier Justice: The Case of Judge Isaac Parker." *Prologue* 20, Spring 1988, 7–23.
———. "Politician, Populist, Reformer: A Reexamination of 'Hanging Judge' Isaac C. Parker." *Arkansas Historical Quarterly* 47 (Spring 1988): 3–28.
Stone, George W. "Judicial Reform." *Proceedings of the Alabama State Bar Association* (1889): 108–121.
Stone, Harlan Fiske. *Law and Its Administration*. New York: AMS Press, 1967.
Story, Joseph. *Commentaries on the Constitution of the United States, with a Preliminary Review of the Constitutional History of the Colonies and States before the Adoption of the Constitution*. 3 vols. Boston: Hilliard, Gray, and Company, 1833.
Strandness, T. B. *Samuel Sewall: A Puritan Portrait*. Lansing: Michigan State University Press, 1967.
Strong, Theron G. *Landmarks of a Lawyer's Lifetime*. New York: Dodd, Mead and Company, 1914.
Strum, Philippa. *Louis D. Brandeis: Justice for the People*. Cambridge: Harvard University Press, 1984.
Stuntz, Jean. "Spanish Laws for Texas Women: The Development of Marital Property Law to 1850." *Southwestern Historical Quarterly* 104 (20 April 2001): 543–559.
Sturgis, Amy H. "Green, Nathan." In *The Tennessee Encyclopedia of History and Culture*, edited by Carroll Van West. Nashville, Tenn.: Rutledge Hill Press, 1998, 385.
Summers, Robert S. "Hans A. Linde as Seen by a Junior Colleague—A Personal Tribute." *Annual Survey of American Law* 1 (1984): xii–xv.
Sussman, Barry. *The Great Coverup: Nixon and the Scandal of Watergate*. New York: Crowell, 1974.
Swisher, Carl B. *History of the Supreme Court of the United States*. Vol. 5: *The Taney Period*. New York: Macmillan, 1974.
———. *Roger B. Taney*. Hamden, Conn.: Archon Books, 1961.
———. *Stephen J. Field: Craftsman of the Law*. Washington, D.C.: The Brookings Institution, 1930.
Tabor, Mary B. W. "Opportunities' Knocks Put Judge High on List." *New York Times*, 9 May 1994, 5.
Tamm, Edward, and Paul Reardon. "Warren E. Burger and the Administration of Justice." *Brigham Young University Law Review* 3 (1981): 447.
Tarr, G. Alan, and Mary Cornelia Aldis Porter. *State Supreme Courts in State and Nation*. New Haven, Conn.: Yale University Press, 1988.
Taylor, Charles W. *The Bench and Bar of Indiana*. Indianapolis: Bench and Bar Publishing, Co., 1895.
Taylor, Stuart, Jr. "Spokesman for Liberals Watched the Tide Flow Out." *New York Times*, 11 June 1985, A20.
Todd, Alden L. *Justice on Trial: The Case of Louis D. Brandeis*. New York: McGraw-Hill, 1964.
Toobin, Jeffrey. 1985. "Better Than Burger: States' Rights for Liberals." *The New Republic*, 4 March, 10–11.

Totenberg, Nina. "A Closing Argument on the Departing Attorney General, Who Chose to Leave a Legacy of Integrity, Patriotism and Nonpartisan Justice." *Washington Post*, 1 July 1979, 10.

Trafzer, Clifford Earl. *The Judge: The Life of Robert A. Hefner*. Norman: Oklahoma University Press, 1975.

Traynor, Roger J. *The Traynor Reader: Nous Verrons: A Collection of Essays*. San Francisco: O'Brien Center for Scholarly Publications, 1987.

Treanor, William Michael. "The Case of the Prisoners and the Origins of Judicial Review." *University of Pennsylvania Law Review* 143 (December 1994): 491–570.

"A Tribute to Chief Justice Warren E. Burger." *Harvard Law Review* 100 (1987): 969.

"Tribute to Judge J. Skelly Wright." *Hastings Constitutional Law Quarterly* 7 (1980): 857–999.

Tucker, St. George. "View of the Constitution of the United States." In *View of the Constitution of the United States with Selected Writings*, edited by Clyde Norman Wilson. Indianapolis, Ind.: Liberty Fund, 1999.

Tuller, Roger H. *"Let No Guilty Man Escape": A Judicial Biography of "Hanging Judge" Isaac C. Parker*. Norman: University of Oklahoma Press, 2001.

Tuma, Shawn E. "Law in Texas Literature: Texas Justice—Judge Roy Bean Style." *The Review of Litigation* 21 (Summer 2002): 551–592.

Tushnet, Mark. *Taking the Constitution Away from the Courts*. Princeton, N.J.: Princeton University Press, 1999.

———. *The Warren Court in Historical and Political Perspective*. Charlottesville: University Press of Virginia, 1996.

Tuttle, Elbert P. "In Memoriam: To My Dear Friend, John R. Brown." *Texas Law Review* 71 (April 1993): 903.

Tuve, Jeanette E. *First Lady of the Law*. Landham, Md.: University Press of America, 1984.

"Two Voices that Helped Shape the Law." *New York Times*, 21 February 1993, Sec. 1, p. 38.

Umbreit, Kenneth Bernard. *Our Eleven Chief Justices: A History of the Supreme Court in Terms of Their Personalities*. 3d ed. New York: Harper and Brothers Publishers, 1938.

Underwood, James Lowell, and W. Lewis Burke Jr. *At Freedom's Door: African American Founding Fathers and Lawyers in Reconstruction South Carolina*. Columbia: University of South Carolina Press, 2000.

Urofsky, Melvin I. *Division and Discord: The Supreme Court under Stone and Vinson*. Columbia: University of South Carolina Press, 1997.

———. *Felix Frankfurter: Judicial Restraint and Individual Liberties*. Boston: Twayne Publishers, 1991.

———. *A Mind of One Piece: Brandeis and American Reform*. New York: Scribner, 1971.

———. *The Supreme Court Justices: A Biographical Dictionary*. New York: Garland Publishing, 1994.

"U.S. Appeals Judge Denounces Reagan Crime-Fighting Ideas." *New York Times*, 14 February 1982, Sec. 1, p. 33.

Vanderbilt, Arthur T. *The Challenge of Law Reform*. Princeton, N.J.: Princeton University Press, 1955.

———. *The Doctrine of the Separation of Powers and Its Present-Day Significance*. Lincoln: University of Nebraska Press, 1963.

Vanderbilt, Arthur T., II. *Changing Law: A Biography of Arthur T. Vanderbilt.* New Brunswick, N.J.: Rutgers University Press, 1976.
Van Dervort, Thomas R. *American Law and the Legal System: Equal Justice under the Law.* 2d ed. Albany, N.Y.: West Legal Studies, 2000.
Viera, Norman, and Leonard Gross. *Supreme Court Appointments: Judge Bork and the Politicization of Senate Confirmations.* Carbondale: Southern Illinois University Press, 1998.
Vile, John R. *A Companion to the United States Constitution and Its Amendments.* 3d ed. Westport, Conn.: Praeger, 2001.
Vile, John R., ed. *Great American Lawyers: An Encyclopedia.* 2 vols. Santa Barbara, Calif.: ABC-CLIO, 2001.
Vile, John R., and Andrew W. Foshee. "Domestic Politics in the Book of Judges." *Journal of Political Science* 16 (Spring 1998): 33–42.
Vile, John R., and Mario Perez-Reilly. "The U.S. Constitution and Judicial Qualifications: A Curious Omission." *Judicature* 74 (December-January 1991): 198–202.
Wachtler, Sol. *After the Madness: A Judge's Own Prison Memoir.* New York: Random House, 1997.
Wald, Patricia M. "Hans Linde and the Elusive Art of Judging: Intellect and Craft Are Never Enough." *Texas Law Review* 75 (1996): 215–235.
Wald, Patricia M., et al. "In Memoriam: Carl McGowan, 1911–1987." *Northwestern University Law Review* 82, no. 2 (Winter 1988): 213–225.
———. "In Memoriam: Honorable Carl McGowan, 1911–1987." *Federal Reporter,* 852 F.2d (1988): 75–95.
Walker, David M. *The Oxford Companion to Law.* Oxford: Clarendon Press, 1980.
Wallman, Jeffrey. *The Western: Parables of the American Dream.* Lubbock: Texas Tech University Press, 1999.
Walsh, Walter J. "Introduction: Speaking Truth to Power: The Jurisprudence of Julia Cooper Mack." *Howard Law Journal* 40 (Winter 1977): 291.
Wapner, Joseph A. *A View from the Bench.* New York: Simon and Schuster, 1987.
Ware, Gilbert. *William Hastie: Grace under Pressure.* New York: Oxford University Press, 1984.
Warren, Earl. *The Memoirs of Earl Warren.* New York: Doubleday, 1977.
Wasby, Stephen L., and Joel B. Grossman. "Judge Clement F. Haynsworth, Jr.: New Perspective on His Nomination to the Supreme Court." *Duke Law Journal,* no. 1 (February 1990): 74–80.
Washburn, Emory. *Sketches of the Judicial History of Massachusetts.* Boston: C. C. Little and J. Brown, 1840.
Washington, Linn, ed. *Black Judges on Justice.* New York: The New Press, 1994.
Watson, Bruce. "Hang 'Em First, Try 'Em Later." *The Smithsonian* 19, June 1998, 96.
———. "The Judge Who Ruled Baseball." *Smithsonian Magazine* 31, no. 7, October 2000, 120.
Weaver, Jace. *Then to the Rock Let Me Fly: Luther Bohanon and Judicial Activism.* Norman: University of Oklahoma Press, 1993.
Weaver, John D. *Warren: The Man, the Court, the Era.* Boston: Little, Brown, 1967.
Weinstein, Jack B. "Death Penalty: The Torah and Today." *New York Law Journal* 224 (23 August 2000): 2.
———. *Individual Justice in Mass Tort Litigation: The Effect of Class Actions, Consolidations, and Other Multi-Party Devices.* Evanston, Ill.: Northwestern University Press, 1995.

———. "The War on Drugs Is Self-Defeating." *New York Times*, 8 July 1993, Op. ed. page.

Weinstein, Jack B., et al. *Evidence: Cases and Materials*. 9th ed. New York: Foundation Press, 1997.

Wells, William W., ed. "John Appleton: Through His Own Words." *Maine Historical Society Quarterly* 31 (Summer 1991): 205–220.

Westin, Alan F. "John Marshall Harlan and the Constitutional Rights of Negroes: The Transformation of a Southerner." *Yale Law Journal* 66 (April 1957): 637–710.

Whitaker, Lois Duke. *Women in Politics: Outsiders or Insiders*. 3d ed. Upper Saddle River, N.J.: Prentice Hall, 1999.

White, G. Edward. *The American Judicial Tradition: Profiles of Leading American Judges*. New York: Oxford University Press, 1976.

———. *Earl Warren: A Public Life*. New York: Oxford University Press, 1982.

———. *History of the Supreme Court of the United States*. Vols. 3 and 4: *The Marshall Court and Cultural Change, 1815–1835*. New York: Macmillan, 1988.

———. *Justice Oliver Wendell Holmes: Law and the Inner Self*. New York: Oxford University Press, 1993.

White, Penny J. "Judicial Independence: Judging Judges: Securing Judicial Independence by Use of Judicial Performance Evaluations." *Fordham Law Review* 29 (February 2000): 1053–1077.

Wickersham, James. *Old Yukon: Tales—Trails—and Trials*. Washington, D.C.: Washington Law Book Co., 1938.

Wilkinson, J. Harvie, III. "The Drawbacks of Growth in the Federal Judiciary." *Emory Law Journal* 43 (1994): 1147.

———. "Federalism and the Future." *Southern California Law Review* 74 (2001): 523.

———. *From Brown to Bakke: The Supreme Court and School Integration*. New York: Oxford University Press, 1979.

———. *One Nation Indivisible: How Ethnic Separatism Threatens America*. Old Tappan, N.J.: Addison-Wesley, 1997.

———. *Serving Justice: A Supreme Court Clerk's View*. New York: Charterhouse, 1974.

Williams, Lou Falkner. *The Great South Carolina Ku Klux Klan Trials 1871–1872*. Athens: University of Georgia Press, 1996.

Wilson, James G. "Constraints of Power: The Constitutional Opinions of Judges Scalia, Bork, Posner, Easterbrook and Winter." *University of Miami Law Review* 40 (September 1986): 1171–1266.

Winslow, John Bradley. *The Story of a Great Court*. Chicago: T. H. Flood and Company, 1912.

Winslow, Ola E. *Samuel Sewall of Boston*. New York: Macmillan, 1964.

"Wisconsin Supreme Court Chief Justice Shirley S. Abrahamson." Interview. Available at <http://www.watl.org/intrview.htm>.

Wise, Edward M. "The 'Ablest State Court': The Michigan Supreme Court before 1885." *Wayne Law Review* 33 (1987): 1509–1561.

Withered, Jerome. *Hoosier Justice: A History of the Supreme Court of Indiana*. Indianapolis: Indiana Supreme Court, 1998.

Witt, Elder. "Hans A. Linde: The Unassuming Architect of an Emerging Role for State Constitutions." *Governing Magazine*, July 1989, 56–60.

Wolfe, Christopher. *Judicial Activism: Bulwark of Freedom or Precarious Security?* Pacific Grove, Calif.: Brooks/Cole Publishing Company, 1991.
Wolfe, Linda. *Double Life: The Shattering Affair between Chief Judge Sol Wachtler and Socialite Joy Silverman.* New York: Pocket Books, 1994.
"Women on the Bench: A Different Voice?" *Judicature* 77 (November-December 1993).
Woody, R. H. "Jonathan Jasper Wright, Associate Justice of the Supreme Court of South Carolina, 1870–77." *Journal of Negro History* 18 (April 1933): 114–131.
Woollen, William W. *Biographical and Historical Sketches of Early Indiana.* Indianapolis: Hammond and Co., 1883.
Wren, John Thomas. "Republican Jurisprudence: Virginia Law and the New Order, 1776–1830." Ph.D. diss., College of William and Mary, 1988.
Wright, Bruce. *Black Justice in a White World: A Memoir.* New York: Barricade Books, 1996.
———. *Black Robes, White Justice.* New York: Carol Publishing Group, 1993.
Wythe, George. *Decisions of Cases in Virginia in the High Court of Chancery, with Remarks upon Decrees of the Court of Appeals, Reversing Some of Those Decisions.* Richmond, Va.: Thomas Nicolson, 1795.
Wyzanski, Charles E., Jr. "Augustus Noble Hand." *Harvard Law Review* 61 (April 1948): 573.
———. "Equal Justice through Law." *Tulane Law Review* 47 (1973): 951–960.
———. "Judge Learned Hand's Contributions to Public Law." *Harvard Law Review* 60 (1947).
———. "Nuremberg—A Fair Trial? Dangerous Precedent." *Atlantic Monthly* 177, no. 4, 1947, 66–70.
———. "Nuremberg in Retrospect." *Atlantic Monthly* 178, no. 6, 1946, 56–59.
———. "A Trial Judge's Freedom and Responsibility." *Harvard Law Review* 65 (1952): 1281.
———. *Whereas—A Judge's Premises, Essays in Judgment, Ethics, and the Law.* Boston: Little, Brown, 1965.
Yanuck, Julius. "Thomas Ruffin and North Carolina Slave Law." *The Journal of Southern History* 21 (November 1955): 456–475.
Yarbrough, Tinsley E. *John Marshall Harlan: Great Dissenter of the Warren Court.* New York: Oxford University Press, 1992.
———. *Mr. Justice Black and His Critics.* Durham, N.C.: Duke University Press, 1988.
———. *A Passion for Justice: J. Waties Waring and Civil Rights.* New York: Oxford University Press, 1987.

About the Editor & Contributors

Henry J. Abraham (Ph.D., University of Pennsylvania) is James Hart Professor of Government and Foreign Affairs Emeritus at the University of Virginia. His numerous books on the judiciary include *Justices, Presidents and Senators* (1999); *The Judicial Process*, 7th ed. (1988); *The Judiciary*, 10th ed. (1997); and, with Barbara A. Perry, *Freedom and the Court*, 7th ed. (1998).

Dean Alfange Jr. (Ph.D., Cornell University) is Professor of Political Science Emeritus at the University of Massachusetts, Amherst. He has published numerous essays in such legal periodicals as the *University of Pennsylvania Law Review* and the *George Washington Law Review* as well as many articles in volumes of essays on law and politics.

Brandi Snow Bozarth (B.S., Middle Tennessee State University) is a student at the University of Dayton School of Law who previously published an essay in *Great American Lawyers: An Encyclopedia* (2001).

Andrew G. Braniff (J.D., Pepperdine University) is a clerk for the Honorable Judge Daniel A. Manion of the United States Seventh Circuit Court of Appeals.

W. Hamilton Bryson (LL.B., Harvard University; LL.M, University of Virginia; Ph.D., Cambridge University) is the Blackstone Professor of Law at the University of Richmond in Virginia. His numerous books include *Interrogatories and Depositions in Virginia* (1969), *The Equity Side of the Exchequer* (1975), *Virginia Civil Procedure* (1997), *A Census of Law Books in Colonial Virginia* (1978), and *Legal Education in Virginia 1779–1979: A Biographical Approach* (1982).

Mark Byrnes (Ph.D., Vanderbilt University) is a professor of political science at Middle Tennessee State University. He is the author and editor of three books, the latest of which is *James K. Polk: A Biographical Companion* (2001).

Anthony Champagne (Ph.D., University of Illinois) is Professor of Government and Politics at the University of Texas at Dallas. His publications include *We the People* (Texas edition), *Sam Rayburn: A Bio-Bibliography* (1988), *Judicial Reform in the States* (editor) (1993), and *Texas Politics: A Reader* (editor) (1998).

Cornell Clayton (D. Phil., Oxford University) is Professor of Political Science at Washington State University. He is the author of *The Politics of Justice* (1992) and the editor or coeditor of *Government Lawyers* (1995), *Supreme Court* Politics (1991), and *Supreme Court Decision-Making* (1999).

Douglas Clouatre (Ph.D., University of Tennessee) is Assistant Professor of Political Science at Kennesaw State University. He contributed to *Great American Lawyers: An Encyclopedia*.

Susan Coleman (J.D., Texas Tech University) is an attorney at law and Director of Criminal Justice at West Texas A and M University. She has coedited *American Law and Legal Systems* (2000), *Texas Government* (1996), and *Cases in Constitutional Law: Summaries and Critiques* (1994).

Kevin Collins (B.A. and graduate work at Marquette University) has lectured at Marymount College in Salina, Kansas, and spent a year on the writing staff of *The Encyclopedia of Louisville* (2001). He is working on a history of Shelby County, Kentucky.

Derek H. Davis (J.D. and Ph.D., Baylor University; Ph.D., University of Texas at Dallas) is Professor of Political Science and Director of the J. M. Dawson Institute of Church-State Studies at Baylor University. He is the author of *Original Intent: Chief Justice Rehnquist and the Course of American Church-State Relations* (1991) and *Religion and the Continental Congress* (2000) and the editor of twelve other books.

Brannon P. Denning (J.D., University of Tennessee; LL.M., Yale University) is Associate Professor of Law at Cumberland School of Law at Samford University. He has written numerous law review articles and is coeditor of *Gun Control and Gun Rights* (2002).

Stephen Louis A. Dillard (J.D., Mississippi College) is a law clerk for the Honorable Judge Daniel A. Manion with the United States Seventh Circuit Court of Appeals and was a contributor to *Great American Lawyers: An Encyclopedia*.

James W. Ely Jr. (LL.B., Harvard University; Ph.D., University of Virginia) is the Milton R. Underwood Professor of Law and professor of history at Vanderbilt University. His publications include *The Guardian of Every Other Right: A Constitutional History of Property Rights* (1992), *The Chief Justiceship of Melville W. Fuller, 1888–1910* (1995), *Railroads and American Law* (2002), and *A History of the Tennessee Supreme Court* (2002). Ely has served as an editor of the *American Journal of Legal History* and as a coeditor of *The Oxford Companion to the Supreme Court of the United States*.

Norman B. Ferris (Ph.D., Emory University) is Professor of History Emeritus at Middle Tennessee State University. He is the author of *Desperate Diplomacy* (1976), *The Trent Affair* (1977), and a recent novel.

Peter G. Fish (Ph.D., Johns Hopkins University) is Professor of Political Science and Law at Duke University. He is the author of *The Politics of Federal Judicial Ad-*

ministration (1973), *The Office of Chief Justice* (1984), and *Federal Justice in the Mid-Atlantic South: United States Courts from Maryland to the Carolinas, 1789–1835* (2002).

Lorien Foote (Ph.D., University of Oklahoma) is Assistant Professor of History at the University of Central Arkansas and the author of *Seeking the One Great Remedy: Francis George Shaw and 19th Century Reform* (2003).

Mark A. Fulks (J.D., University of Memphis) is an assistant attorney general in Tennessee. Fulks's article represents the opinions of the author and not necessarily those of the Office of the Attorney General and Reporter.

Ellen Barrier Garrison (Ph.D., Stanford University) is Associate Professor of History at Middle Tennessee State University and has contributed to the *Dictionary of North Carolina Biography* (1996) and the *Dictionary of Georgia Biography* (1983).

Scott Douglas Gerber (J.D., Ph.D., University of Virginia) is a law professor at Ohio Northern University. He has published numerous articles and five books, including *To Secure These Rights* (1995), *Seriatim: The Supreme Court before John Marshall* (1998), *First Principles: The Jurisprudence of Clarence Thomas* (2002), *Founding Principles and Current Impact* (2002), and a novel.

Michael J. Gerhardt (J.D., University of Chicago) is the Arthur B. Hanson Professor of Law at the Marshall-Wythe Law School at the College of William and Mary. He is the author of *The Federal Impeachment Process: A Constitutional and Historical Analysis*, 2d ed. (2000), and *The Federal Appointment Process: A Constitutional and Historical Analysis* (2000).

Ken Gormley (J.D., Harvard University) is a professor at Duquesne University School of Law, where he specializes in constitutional law and related subjects. He is the author of *Archibald Cox: Conscience of a Nation* (1997), which received the 1999 Bruce K. Gould Book Award for best book relating to the law. Gormley recently served as mayor of Forest Hill, Pennsylvania, where he lives with his wife and four children.

Frank Guliuzza (Ph.D., University of Notre Dame) is Professor and Chair of the Department of Political Science at Weber State University. He is the author of *Over the Wall: Protecting Religious Expression in the Public Square* (2000).

Kermit L. Hall (Ph.D., University of Minnesota; M.S.L., Yale University) is president of Utah State University in Logan. He is the author and editor of numerous books, including *The Magic Mirror: Law in American History* (1989), *The Oxford Companion to the Supreme Court of the United States* (1992), *The Oxford Guide to United States Supreme Court Decisions* (1999), and *The Oxford Companion to American Law* (2002).

Jennifer Harrison (M.A., University of Richmond) is Instructor of History and Information Technology Specialist at the College of William and Mary. She has contributed to a number of other encyclopedias, including *Great American Lawyers*.

Judith A. Haydel (Ph.D., University of New Orleans) is Professor of Government at McNeese State University and a coeditor of *Judicial Reform in the States* (1995).

Paul DeForest Hicks (LL.B., Harvard University) is the author of *Joseph Henry Lumpkin, Georgia's First Chief Justice* (2002).

Kenneth M. Holland (Ph.D., University of Chicago) is Professor of Political Science at the University of Memphis. He is the editor of *Judicial Activism in Comparative Perspective* (1991) and *The Political Role of Law Courts in Modern Democracies* (1989).

J. Woodford Howard Jr. (Ph.D., Princeton University) is the Thomas P. Stran Professor Emeritus of Political Science at Johns Hopkins University. He is the author of *Mr. Justice Murphy: A Political Biography* (1968) and *Courts of Appeals in the Federal Judicial System: A Study of the Second, Fifth, and District of Columbia Circuits* (1981).

Geoffrey Hull (J.D., University of Virginia) is a professor in the Recording Industry Department at Middle Tennessee State University and the author of numerous articles and a book entitled *The Recording Industry* (1998).

Tim Hurley (Ph.D., University of Notre Dame) has taught in the Philosophy Department at Furman University and is currently working on a novel. He previously contributed to *Great American Lawyers*.

Herbert A. Johnson (LL.B., New York Law School; Ph.D., Columbia University) is the Distinguished Professor of Law Emeritus at the University of South Carolina. A past editor of *The Papers of John Marshall* (1974), he is coauthor of *Foundations of Power: John Marshall, 1801–1824* (1981) and author of *John Jay: Colonial Lawyer* (1989) and of *The Chief Justiceship of John Marshall, 1801–1835* (1988).

Ronald Kahn (Ph.D., University of Chicago) is James Monroe Professor of Politics at Oberlin College where he heads the Law and Society Program. He is also the author of *The Supreme Court and Constitutional Theory, 1953–1993* (1994) and numerous contributions to edited volumes, law reviews, and political science journals.

Tyson D. King-Meadows (Ph.D., University of North Carolina) teaches political science at the University of Maryland, Baltimore campus, and was a fellow with the W. E. B. DuBois Institute at Harvard University. He is now coauthoring a book.

Eric Leonard (M.L.S., University of Oklahoma) is a park ranger who has previously worked at Fort Smith, Arkansas, and is now working at the Arkansas Post National Memorial.

Carol Loar (Ph.D., Northwestern University) is Visiting Assistant Professor at the University of Central Arkansas.

Michael W. McConnell (J.D., University of Chicago) is a judge on the United States Court of Appeals for the Tenth Circuit. Formerly Presidential Professor of Law at the University of Utah, McConnell was a frequent contributor to law journals. He is the coeditor of *Christian Perspectives on Legal Thought* (2001).

Robb A. McDaniel (Ph.D., Vanderbilt University) is Associate Professor of Political Science at Middle Tennessee State University and has published articles in *Political Theory* and *Polity*.

Michael S. Martin (M.A., University of Southwestern Louisiana; completing a Ph.D. at the University of Arkansas) is a research assistant at the Albert Gore Sr. Research Center at Middle Tennessee State University and the author of *Chemical Engineering at the University of Arkansas: A Centennial History, 1902–2002* (2002).

Melanie K. Morris (Ph.D., University of Tennessee) teaches political science at Ball State University.

Bruce Allen Murphy (Ph.D., University of Virginia) is the Fred Morgan Kirby Professor of Civil Rights at Lafayette College in Easton, Pennsylvania. He is the author of *The Brandeis/Frankfurter Connection* (1982), *Fortas: The Rise and Ruin of a Supreme Court Justice* (1988), *Approaching Democracy* (with Larry Berman) (2001), and *Wild Bill: The Legend and Life of William O. Douglas, America's Most Controversial Supreme Court Justice* (2003). Murphy was assisted in the writing of his essay on Louis Brandeis by Maria A. Fekete, a graduate of Lafayette College, and of his essay on Felix Frankfurter by Arthur Owens, also a Lafayette College graduate who is attending law school at Seton Hall University.

Myra Norman (Ph.D., University of Missouri, Columbia) is Director of the Office of Sponsored Programs at Middle Tennessee State University.

William D. Pederson (Ph.D., University of Oregon) is the holder of the American Studies Endowed Chair and Head of the International Lincoln Center at Louisiana State University in Shreveport. He is coeditor of *The Rating Game in American Politics* (1987), *Grassroots Constitutionalism* (1988), *FDR and the Modern Presidency* (1997), *The New Deal and Public Policy* (1998), *Leaders of the Pack* (2002), and *Franklin D. Roosevelt and the Transformation of the Supreme Court* (2002).

Barbara A. Perry (Ph.D., University of Virginia) is Carter Glass Professor of Government at Sweet Briar College. Her publications include *The Priestly Tribe* (1999), *A "Representative" Supreme Court? The Impact of Race, Religion and Gender on Appointments* (1991), and, with Henry J. Abraham, *Freedom and the* Court, 7th ed. (1998).

J. Mitchell Pickerill (J.D., Indiana University–Bloomington; Ph.D., University of Wisconsin–Madison) is Assistant Professor of Political Science at Washington State University.

Lisa J. Pruitt (Ph.D., Vanderbilt University) is Assistant Professor of History and Director of the Albert Gore Sr. Research Center at Middle Tennessee State University.

Linda Przybyszewski (Ph.D., Stanford University) is Associate Professor of History at the University of Cincinnati. She is the author of *The Republic according to John Marshall Harlan* (1999) and the editor of *Some Memories of a Long Life, 1854–1911*, by Malvina S. Harlan (2002).

John David Rausch Jr. (Ph.D., University of Oklahoma) is Assistant Professor of Political Science at West Texas A and M University and is coeditor of *A Test of Time: Coping with Term Limits* (2002).

Peter G. Renstrom (Ph.D., Michigan State University) is Professor of Political Science at Western Michigan University. He is the author of a number of books, including *The Stone Court: Justices, Rulings and Legacy* (2001).

James W. Riddlesperger Jr. (Ph.D., University of Missouri) is Professor and Chair of the Department of Political Science at Texas Christian University. He has published widely and has written *Presidential Leadership and Civil Rights Policy* (1995). He is now completing a book dealing with presidential transitions.

William G. Ross (J.D., Harvard University) is Professor of Law at the Cumberland School of Law at Samford University who has published widely on legal ethics and the judicial appointment process. His publications include *A Muted Fury: Populists, Progressives and Labor Unions Confront the Courts, 1890–1937* (1994) and *Forging New Freedoms: Nativism, Education, and the Constitution, 1917–1927* (1994).

Douglas P. Sadler (B.S., Middle Tennessee State University) is a student at Stetson University Law School.

David Schultz (J.D., Ph.D., University of Minnesota) is Hamline University Professor of Public Administration with adjunct appointments at Hamline, the University of Minnesota, and the University of St. Thomas law schools. He has authored and edited sixteen books, more than forty articles, and numerous treatises on the law of eminent domain. His books include the *Encyclopedia of American Law* (2002).

Henry B. Sirgo (Ph.D., Florida State University) is Professor of Political Science at McNeese State University. He is completing a book entitled *Establishment of Environmentalism on the Nation's Political Agenda: The Brothers Udall.*

M. Keith Siskin (J.D., University of Georgia) served as editor in chief of the *Georgia Journal of International and Comparative Law* and contributed to *Great American Lawyers: An Encyclopedia.*

Christopher E. Smith (Ph.D., University of Connecticut; J.D., University of Tennessee) is Professor of Criminal Justice at Michigan State University. His books include *United States Magistrates in the Federal Courts* (1990); *Courts and the Poor* (1991); *Courts and Public Policy* (1993); *Courts, Politics and the Judicial Process*, 2d ed. (1997); and *Law and Contemporary Corrections* (2000).

Robert W. Smith (Ph.D., College of William and Mary) is an instructor in the Department of Politics and History at Curry College and an editorial contributor to volumes 9 and 10 of the *Papers of John Marshall.*

Mitch Sollenberger (M.A., Catholic University) is employed by the Congressional Research Service and is working on his Ph.D. in American Politics at Catholic University of America.

Otis H. Stephens (Ph.D., Johns Hopkins University; J.D., University of Tennessee) is the Distinguished Service Professor of Political Science and Resident Scholar of Constitutional Law at the University of Tennessee. His books include *The Supreme Court and Confessions of Guilt* (1973) and, with John M. Scheb, *American Constitutional Law*, 3d ed. (2002).

Donald Grier Stephenson Jr. (Ph.D., Princeton University) is the Charles A. Dana Professor of Government at Franklin and Marshall College. His books include *Campaigns and the Court: The U.S. Supreme Court in Presidential Elections* (1999) and, with Alpheus T. Mason, *American Constitutional Law*, 13th ed. (2002).

G. Alan Tarr (Ph.D., University of Chicago) is Distinguished Professor of Political Science and Director of the Center for State Constitutional Studies at Rutgers University–Camden. He is the author of numerous books and articles, including *Judicial Process and Judicial Policymaking*, 3d ed. (2002), *American Constitutional Law*, 5th ed. (1999), and *Understanding State Constitutions* (1998), and is coauthor of *State Supreme Courts in State and Nation* (1988).

Kathleen Uradnik (Ph.D., University of California, Berkeley; J.D., University of Virginia) is Associate Professor of Political Science at St. Cloud State University and the author of *A Student's Guide to Landmark Congressional Legislation on Youth* (2002).

John R. Vile (Ph.D., University of Virginia) is Professor and Chair of the Department of Political Science at Middle Tennessee State University. He is the author and editor of more than a dozen books, including *A Companion to the United States Constitution and Its Amendments*, 3d ed. (2001); *Great American Lawyers: An Encyclopedia* (2001); *Presidential Winners and Losers: Words of Victory and Concession* (2002); and *Encyclopedia of Constitutional Amendments, Proposed Amendments, and Amending Issues*, 2d ed. (2003).

Virginia L. Vile (B.A., Middle Tennessee State University) is attending the Marshall-Wythe Law School at the College of William and Mary.

James Wagoner (J.D., University of Louisville) is a partner in a law firm in Louisville and one of the coaches of Bellarmine University's mock trial teams.

Jace Weaver (J.D., Columbia University; Ph.D., Union Theological Seminary) is Associate Professor of Religion at the University of Georgia. He is the author or editor of seven books, including *Then to the Rock Let Me Fly: Luther Bohanon and Judicial Activism* (1993) and *Turtle Goes to War: Of Military Commissions, the Constitution, and American Indian Memory* (forthcoming).

Paul J. Weber (Ph.D., University of Chicago) is Professor of Political Science at the University of Louisville. Books that he has authored or coauthored include *Unfounded Fears: Myths and Realities of a Constitutional Convention* (1989), *Equal Separation: Understanding the Religion Clause* (1990), and *Private Churches and Public Money* (1981).

Christopher L. Whaley (J.D., University of Tennessee) is Director of Legal Studies at Roane State Community College. He contributed to *Great American Lawyers: An Encyclopedia*.

Angela N. White (B.S., Middle Tennessee State University) is attending law school at American University.

Clyde Willis (J.D., Ph.D., University of Tennessee) is a professor of political science at Middle Tennessee State University. He contributed to *Great American Lawyers: An Encyclopedia* (2001) and is the author of the *Student's Guide to Landmark Congressional Laws on the First Amendment* (2002).

Tinsley E. Yarbrough (Ph.D., University of Alabama) is University Research Professor of Political Science at East Carolina University. His books include *A Passion for Justice: J. Waties Waring and Civil Rights* (1987), *Mr. Justice Black and His Critics* (1988), *John Marshall Harlan: Great Dissenter of the Warren Court* (1992), and *The Burger Court: Justices, Rulings, and Legacy* (2000).

Sara L. Zeigler (Ph.D., University of California, Los Angeles) is Associate Professor of Political Science and Director of Women's Studies at Eastern Kentucky University. She is the coauthor of *What's Next for GI Jane? Women Warriors in the U.S. Military* (2003).

Index

5